IDEAS, INTERESTS, AND ISSUES

readings in introductory politics

second edition

EDITED BY

George A. MacLean
UNIVERSITY OF MANITOBA

Brenda O'Neill
UNIVERSITY OF CALGARY

PEARSON
Prentice
Hall

Toronto

Library and Archives Canada Cataloguing in Publication

Ideas, interests and issues : readings in introductory politics / edited
by George A. MacLean, Brenda O'Neill. —2nd ed.

ISBN 978-0-13-206896-3

1. Political science. I. MacLean, George A. (George Andrew), 1967–
II. O'Neill, Brenda, 1964–

JA66.I44 2009   320   C2007-906616-X

ISBN-13: 978-0-13-206896-3
ISBN-10: 0-13-206896-6

Vice President, Editorial Director: Gary Bennett
Senior Acquisitions Editor: Laura Paterson Forbes
Executive Marketing Manager: Judith Allen
Developmental Editor: Alexandra Dyer
Production Editor: Amanda Wesson
Copy Editor: Lenore Latta
Proofreader: Camille Isaacs
Production Manager: Peggy Brown
Composition: Laserwords
Art Director: Julia Hall
Cover Design: Miguel Angel Acevedo
Cover Image: Getty Images

1 2 3 4 5   12 11 10 09 08

Printed and bound in the United States of America.

TABLE OF CONTENTS

Preface

The second edition of *Ideas, Interests, and Issues* builds on the foundation of the first edition by pulling together a set of readings that provides a broad, yet balanced, review of some of the core themes addressed in the study of politics. Doing so, we hope, will allow students to develop not only their understanding of the discipline and its complexity, but also their understanding of the many different approaches that are employed by those who study it. The title of the reader remains *Ideas, Interests, and Issues* because we believe that it captures the essence of what it is that we study: politics is about the competition between ideas, the vocalization of interests, and the resolution of issues. Politics is a complex human activity, often with very high stakes; it is this complexity and importance that we believe makes the study of politics interesting and essential. Unfortunately, politics remains, for many people, something to be avoided at all costs. As authors, neither of us subscribes to this belief, and we both see this reader as one very small attempt to counter this perception.

The selection of readings in this new edition was guided by a number of goals: to cover as much as possible the various subfields in the discipline; to reflect the ever-changing focus within the discipline; to address key questions and issues in the practice of politics; to address the needs of instructors; and to develop the interest of students while at the same time challenging their beliefs and opinions. Balancing these sometimes competing goals can often be a challenge. This edition contains many pedagogical devices designed to assist students: a thematic directory, a list of important terminology and discussion questions at the end of each section, and a glossary of terminology at the end of the reader. New to the introduction in this edition is a *user's guide* designed to help students prepare for seminars, in which we believe most students will be discussing these readings.

Thanks are due to the many people we have worked with at Pearson Education Canada, but especially Alexandra Dyer, our developmental editor, who skilfully kept us focused on the publication schedule, and Christine Cozens and Duncan MacKinnon, who originally approached us with the idea of putting together a reader for introductory courses in Political Science. We are also thankful for the careful and helpful feedback that we received from Feyzi Baban (Trent University), Guy Gensey (Dalhousie University), Christopher Kukucha (University of Lethbridge), Mary Powell (Laurentian University), Madhura-Mitu Sengupta (Ryerson University), Jeffrey Steeves (University of Saskatchewan), and John von Heyking (University of Lethbridge). The strengths of this second edition are in no small measure due to their efforts. And again we are extremely grateful to all the authors who allowed their work to be included in this volume.

Finally, we thank our families for their love and laughter.

LIST OF CONTRIBUTORS

Warren Allmand was Minister of Indian Affairs and Northern Development under Prime Minister Pierre Trudeau. He is now a Montreal city councillor.

Louise Arbour, former Supreme Court of Canada Justice (1999–2004), is the United Nations High Commissioner for Human Rights.

Jennifer Baumgardner, a self-described "professional feminist," is a former editor at *Ms.* and writes for *The Nation*, *Jane*, *Nerve*, and *Out*.

Gerard W. Boychuk is Associate Professor and Associate Chair (Undergraduate Studies) in the Department of Political Science at the University of Waterloo.

David R. Boyd is an environmental lawyer, professor, writer, and activist.

J. Patrick Boyer was a Progressive Conservative Member of Parliament for Etobicoke (1984–1993), and in March 2007 was successfully nominated to stand as the Conservative Party of Canada candidate for the riding of Etobicoke-Lakeshore in the next federal election. He has taught law and politics at the University of Toronto, York University, University of Guelph, and Wilfrid Laurier University.

Stephen Clarkson is Professor of Political Science at the University of Toronto.

Larry Diamond is a senior fellow at the Hoover Institution, Stanford University, and founding co-editor of the *Journal of Democracy*.

Wayne Ellwood is an editor with *New Internationalist* magazine.

Francis Fukuyama is Bernard L. Schwartz Professor of International Political Economy at the Paul H. Nitze School of Advanced International Studies (SAIS) of Johns Hopkins University.

Carol C. Gould is Professor of Philosophy and Political Science and Director, Center for Global Ethics & Politics, Temple University.

David Herle is a principal of the Gandalf Group.

Janet L. Hiebert is Professor of Political Studies at Queen's University, Kingston.

Andrew F. Johnson is Dean of Social Science at Bishop's University, Lennoxville, Quebec.

Jarl K. Kampen is a senior researcher at the Centre for Political Science at the Vrije Universiteit Brussel.

Terry Lynn Karl is Professor of Political Science, Stanford University, California.

Russell Kirk (1918–1994) was a Guggenheim Fellow, a senior fellow of the American Council of Learned Societies, a Constitutional Fellow of the National Endowment for the Humanities, and a Fulbright Lecturer in Scotland.

Sarah Davidson Ladly practises law at Blake, Cassels & Graydon LLP in Toronto.

George A. MacLean is Associate Professor and Acting Head of Political Studies at the University of Manitoba, Winnipeg.

Beverley McLachlin is Chief Justice of the Supreme Court of Canada.

Walter Russell Mead is Henry A. Kissinger Senior Fellow for U.S. Foreign Policy at the Council on Foreign Relations.

Anne Milan is an analyst with Housing, Family and Social Statistics Division, Statistics Canada.

Kenneth Minogue is Emeritus Professor of Political Science at the London School of Economics and Political Science.

Kim Richard Nossal is Professor and Head of Political Studies at Queen's University, Kingston.

Rory O'Brien is Instructor of Political Science at Cabrillo College in Aptos, California.

Brenda O'Neill is Associate Professor of Political Science at the University of Calgary.

Amy Richards is a contributing editor at *Ms.* and co-founder of the Third Wave Foundation.

Gemma Rosenblatt is a Research Fellow on the Hansard Society's Parliament and Government Programme, London, England.

Philippe C. Schmitter is Professor of Political and Social Sciences at European University Institute of Florence, Italy.

Kris Snijkers is an academic researcher in the Public Management Institute at the Katholieke Universiteit Leuven.

Denis Stairs is Professor Emeritus of Political Science at Dalhousie University, Halifax.

Gerry Stoker is Professor of Politics at the University of Manchester.

Maurice Strong was Secretary-General of the 1992 UN Conference on Environment and Development in Rio de Janeiro, commonly described as the Earth Summit. He is ex officio President of the University for Peace and sits on the Management Committee of the Institute for Media, Peace, and Security.

Ramesh Thakur is Distinguished Fellow at the Centre for International Governance Innovation and Professor of Political Science at the University of Waterloo.

Stella Z. Theodoulou is Dean of the College of Social and Behavioral Sciences, California State University, Northridge.

Reg Whitaker is Distinguished Research Professor Emeritus at York University, Toronto, and Adjunct Professor of Political Science, University of Victoria.

Oliver H. Woshinsky is Emeritus Professor of Political Science at the University of Southern Maine.

THEMATIC DIRECTORY

Canadian politics: Boyer, ch. 11, p. 111; Boychuck, ch. 31, p. 343; CRIC, ch. 19, p. 198; Herle, ch. 12, p. 122; Hiebert, ch. 14, p. 141; McLachlin, ch. 29, p. 319; Milan, ch. 18, p. 190; Nossal, ch. 25, p. 277; Whitaker, ch. 15, p. 150

Civil society: Allmand, ch. 30, p. 332; Boyer, ch. 11, p. 111; CRIC, ch. 19, p. 198; Diamond, ch. 24, p. 265; Hiebert, ch. 14, p. 141; Johnson, ch. 17, p. 172; Mead, ch. 32, p. 349; Milan, ch. 18, p. 190; Minogue "The Experience of Politics," ch. 2, p. 19, and "The Classical Greeks," ch. 4, p. 39; Schmitter and Karl, ch. 16, p. 161; Stoker, ch. 1, p. 8; Whitaker, ch. 15, p. 150; Woshinsky, ch. 3, p. 24

Comparative politics: Diamond, ch. 24, p. 265; Clarkson et al., ch. 26, p. 283; Fukuyama, ch. 8, p. 73; Mead, ch. 32, p. 349; Rosenblatt, ch. 13, p. 130; Schmitter and Karl, ch. 16, p. 161; Stoker, ch. 1, p. 8; Woshinsky, ch. 3, p. 24

Democracy: Boyer, ch. 11, p. 111; CRIC, ch. 19, p. 198; Diamond, ch. 24, p. 265; Gould, ch. 9, p. 90; Herle, ch. 12, p. 122; Johnson, ch. 17, p. 172; Kampen and Snijkers, ch. 20, p. 227; Milan, ch. 18, p. 190; Rosenblatt, ch. 13, p. 130; Schmitter and Karl, ch. 16, p. 161; Stoker, ch. 1, p. 8; Whitaker, ch. 15, p. 150

Electoral systems: Boyer, ch. 11, p. 111; CRIC, ch. 19, p. 198; Johnson, ch. 17, p. 172; Minogue "The Classical Greeks," ch. 4, p. 39; Schmitter and Karl, ch. 16, p. 161; Whitaker, ch. 15, p. 150

Environment: Boyd, ch. 27, p. 295; Strong, ch. 28, p. 309

Globalization: Clarkson et al., ch. 26, p. 283; Ellwood, ch. 5, p. 44; Gould, ch. 9, p. 90; Johnson, ch. 17, p. 172; McLachlin, ch. 29, p. 319; Stairs, ch. 22, p. 252; Woshinsky, ch. 3, p. 24

Identity: Allmand, ch. 30, p. 332; Johnson, ch. 17, p. 172; McLachlin, ch. 29, p. 319; Minogue "The Classical Greeks," ch. 4, p. 39; Schmitter and Karl, ch. 16, p. 161; Woshinsky, ch. 3, p. 24

Ideology: Baumgardner and Richards, ch. 10, p. 101; Fukuyama, ch. 8, p. 73; Gould, ch. 9, p. 90; Kirk, ch. 7, p. 67; Mead, ch. 32, p. 349; Schmitter and Karl, ch. 16, p. 161; Stairs, ch. 22, p. 252 Stoker, ch. 1, p. 8; Woshinsky, ch. 3, p. 24

Institutions: Allmand, ch. 30, p. 332; Boychuck, ch. 31, p. 343; Boyer, ch. 11, p. 111; Clarkson et al., ch. 26, p. 283; Hiebert, ch. 14, p. 141; Kampen and Snijkers, ch. 20, p. 227; Rosenblatt, ch. 13, p. 130; Whitaker, ch. 15, p. 150

Interest groups: Baumgardner and Richards, ch. 10, p. 101; Herle, ch. 12, p. 122; Hiebert, ch. 14, p. 141; Minogue "The Experience of Politics," ch. 2, p. 19

International relations: Arbour, ch. 23, p. 258; Diamond, ch. 24, p. 265; Ellwood, ch. 5, p. 44; Fukuyama, ch. 8, p. 73; Gould, ch. 9, p. 90; Nossal, ch. 25, p. 277; Stairs, ch. 22, p. 252; Strong, ch. 28, p. 309; Thakur, ch. 21, p. 237

Justice: Allmand, ch. 30, p. 332; Arbour, ch. 23, p. 258; Baumgardner and Richards, ch. 10, p. 101; Boyd, ch. 27, p. 295; Boyer, ch. 11, p. 111; Hiebert, ch. 14, p. 141

Policy making: Allmand, ch. 30, p. 332; Boyd, ch. 27, p. 295; Herle, ch. 12, p. 122; Mead, ch. 32, p. 349

Political analysis: Kirk, ch. 7, p. 67; Minogue "The Experience of Politics," ch. 2, p. 19,

CREDITS

Page 150: Reg Whitaker, "Virtual Political Parties and the Decline of Democracy," *Policy Options* June 2001: 16–22. Reprinted by permission of the Institute for Research on Public Policy.

Page 161: Schmitter, Philippe C., and Terry Lynn Karl, What Democracy Is . . . and Is Not. *Journal of Democracy* 2: 3 (1991), 75–87. © National Endowment for Democracy and the Johns Hopkins University Press. Reprinted with permission of the Johns Hopkins University Press.

Page 172: Andrew F. Johnson, "Democracy, Prosperity, Citizens and the State," in *Canadian Foreign Policy*, 10 (Fall 2002).

Page 190: Anne Milan, "Willing to Participate: Political Engagement of Young Adults," Statistics Canada, *Canadian Social Trends*, Catalogue Number 11-008, Number 79, Winter 2005, pages 2–7.

Page 198: "Voter Participation in Canada: Is Canadian Democracy in Crisis?" *The CRIC Papers*, (Oct. 2001), abridged from the original available online at www.cric.ca/pdf/cahiers/cricpapers_nov2001.pdf.

Page 227: Kampen, Jarl K., and Kris Snijkers, "E-Democracy: A Critical Evaluation of the Ultimate E-Dream" in *Social Science Computer Review* (2003; Volume 21, No. 4, 491–496) This work is protected by copyright and it is being used with the permission of Access Copyright. Any alteration of its content or further copying in any form whatsoever is strictly prohibited.

Page 237: Ramesh Thakur, "Security in the New Millenium," *Canadian Foreign Policy*, 10 (Fall 2002). Reprinted by permission.

Page 252: Denis Stairs, "9/11 'Terrorism,' 'Root Causes' and All That: Political Implications of the Socio-Cultural Argument," in Policy Options, 23 (September 2002). Reprinted by permission of the Institute for Research on Public Policy.

Page 258: Louise Arbour, "The Responsibility to Protect and the Duty to Punish," *Behind the Headlines*, 59 (Autumn 2001). This article was first published by the Canadian Institute of International Affairs in *Behind the Headlines*, Vol. 59 No.1.

Page 265: Diamond, Larry, "Building Democracy after Conflict: Lessons from Iraq," in *Journal of Democracy* 16:1 (2005), 9–23 © National Endowment for Democracy and the Johns Hopkins University Press. Reprinted with permission of The Johns Hopkins University Press.

Page 277: Kim Richard Nossal, "Canada: Fading Power or Future Power?" *Behind the Headlines*, 59 (Spring 2002). This article was first published by the Canadian Institute of International Affairs in *Behind the Headlines*, Vol. 59 No. 3.

Page 283: Clarkson, Stephen, Sarah Davidson Ladly, Megan Merwart, and Carlton Thorne, "The Governance of North America: NAFTA's Stunted Institutions" in *McGill International Review* (Montreal: Fall 2005). Reproduced with permission.

Page 295: David R. Boyd, "Sustainability Law: Respecting the Laws of Nature," *in McGill International Review* (Montreal: Spring 2005). Reproduced with permission.

Page 309: Maurice Strong, "Report to the Shareholders," in *Where on Earth Are We Going?* by Maurice Strong. Copyright ©2000 by Maurice Strong. Reprinted by permission of Alfred A. Knopf Canada.

Page 319: "The Civilization of Difference" was presented by the Right Honourable Chief Justice of Canada, Beverley McLachlin, P.C., as part of the Dominion Institute's March 2003 LaFontaine-Baldwin Symposium (www.lafontaine-baldwin.com).

Page 332: Warren Allmand, "The International Recognition of Indigenous Rights" in *McGill International Review* (Montreal: Spring 2005). Adapted from an article originally published in *Rights and Democracy*.

Page 343: Gerard W. Boychuk, "The Illusion of Financial Unsustainability of Canadian Health Care," in *Policy Options*, 23 (November 2002). Reprinted by permission of the Institute for Research on Public Policy.

Page 349: Walter Russell Mead, "God's Country" in *Foreign Affairs* (New York: September/October 2006, Volume 75, Number 5). Reprinted by permission of FOREIGN AFFAIRS, Volume 85, Number 5, September/October 2006. Copyright © 2006 by the Council on Foreign Relations, Inc.

Introduction: How to Use This Book

There are many ways to introduce the subject of politics. Your first course in politics is the product of your instructor's ideas, the content of your textbook, and events taking place in daily life. Every year, thousands of students are presented with the study of politics in courses such as the one you are taking. And many of those courses are vastly different from yours. Your instructor will shape the material for your course in his or her own way, and the textbooks you read will influence the course as well. However, whether the course is entitled "Political Science," "Political Studies," or simply "Politics," certain topics and themes tend to appear regularly.

There is no single "customary" way to teach or to learn politics, but there are constants in most introductory courses in the subject. Politics is about ideas that communities have about governing themselves. Politics is an extension of the way that we deal with each other. Politics is about the many diverse interests that exist in our societies. Politics is about power, influence, control, and making our world a better place. Politics is often considered negative or pessimistic, but it is really a positive and optimistic discipline. Studying politics helps us to decide how to make our societies better and improve our world. In practice, of course, we often fail to achieve these goals.

Your first course in political science should be stimulating, timely, provocative, and thought-provoking. This reader hopes to provide a vehicle for bringing the "stuff" of politics alive for the first-time politics student, in a manner unlike introductory textbooks. Textbooks can be stimulating, to be sure, but often the objectives that need to be achieved can prevent the textbook from providing a consistent level of stimulating reading. Textbooks must span the breadth of the discipline, reviewing the key concepts, approaches, and methods employed in its study. A reader, on the other hand, does not need to provide a comprehensive review of the discipline, and so has the flexibility of offering a more limited set of issues and questions upon which to focus. This flexibility allows us to develop a package of readings that we hope will push you to challenge your ideas, to investigate new ways of thinking, and to develop an awareness of the challenges and rewards that come with the study of politics. We encourage you to engage with the material we have collected in this volume, both on your own and with your peers and instructors.

The title of this book is instructive. We believe that politics is about many things, but it is best understood and explained if we look at the ideas that underpin our societies, the interests that exist in our political systems, and the changing issues that affect all walks of political life. These are constants in politics, and thus in the study of politics as well.

Politics involves the various ideas that people have about the relationship that exists between citizens and government. Ideas are not just abstract theoretical notions. In fact, all political systems are based on ideas, which often change with the wishes of governments or their citizens. The many different ideas and ideologies push our communities to move in different directions, and they are often opposed to one another. Canada is a good example of a political system that is truly "pluralistic," which means that many different views exist, often competing with one another, but co-operating as well. Multiculturalism, religious diversity, economic disparity, and regional distinctions are just a few of the many forces that lead to an assortment of interests in any political system.

Politics is also about interests. No political system is made up of one point of view, or one ambition. People who study politics recognize the meaning of "interests" as preferences held for a given course of action or policy. The courts, legislatures, political parties, protest movements, election campaigns—even the very nature of democracy itself—are the product of numerous interests in society. And interests certainly shape how individuals and organizations act in the political system.

Politics is also about the issues that compete for a position on the political agenda. These issues may address questions that are domestic in nature or of a more international nature; often, however, issues are multidimensional in terms of the issues raised. Issues of identity, health care, the environment, Aboriginal rights, and religion are some of the issues addressed in this volume. This is but a very small sampling of the set of issues that politics addresses at any one given period of time.

At first, politics might seem fairly straightforward, since we all have our own opinions about the world around us. However, studying politics can be challenging for you as a first-time student because of the many contested concepts and multiple approaches, and the lack of established "standard" theories. Politics is not like biology or astronomy; we don't have a series of accepted concepts and theories that have been verified with scientific rigour. This is because politics is about human interaction, which is an interaction far more complicated than a simply physical or biological one. Subjecting human interaction to definitive statements about behaviour is impossible, since our impulses are so variable and complex. As a student of politics you will come to see this; in addition, you will experience the further challenge of discovering where your own beliefs lie.

One important distinction to understand, however, is that between the normative and positivist streams of political research. Normative research seeks to understand how the political system *ought* to be structured. To answer this question we need to establish a set of assumptions (e.g. What is the essential nature of men and women? Are they fundamentally nasty and brutish, or good-hearted?) and a set of values (e.g. What priorities should be kept in mind in thinking about the structures and processes of a political system? Liberty? Equality? Protection of minority interests?). Such questions form one key branch in the study of politics.

The second key branch, the positivist stream, asks how the political system and its processes *are* structured. As with the normative stream, however, understanding how the political system operates also requires the establishment of a set of assumptions about the key actors and processes at play (e.g. Is the key to understanding politics found in an investigation of institutions? Or is a true understanding to be found through studying the rationality of decision making, like the public choice approach suggests?). The distinction is an important one: while the positivist stream seeks to describe and explain, the normative stream is more focused on developing prescriptions for action. Developing an understanding of the degree to which our assumptions shape our conclusions might be difficult for you as a student of political science; developing an understanding of which set of assumptions we subscribe to can be even more difficult.

USER'S GUIDE

We hope that this reader helps to develop your knowledge and appreciation of politics. We have assembled a set of readings that we think will support what you learn in lecture and textbook readings. But this reader should do more than just help you out in your politics course. You should think of this reader as a tool for developing a number of the skills that you'll need as a post-secondary student.

The first is simply the ability to digest and understand material. To help you with this, each section of the reader provides a short summary of the key arguments in the set of readings, and a set of questions that stimulate you to think more deeply about the material covered from the perspective of a political scientist. A second skill you'll develop is the ability to apply the conceptual tools learned in a discipline-specific course to a particular reading. So the textbook you use contains definitions and explanations of key concepts. This book does as well; but it also gives you some insights into what these terms really mean for everyday use. The practical application of your education is always important. Third, you will see how these readings use very different writing styles and approaches; this shows the importance of diverse thinking. Fourth, these readings come from many sources: academic journals, periodicals, speeches, and books. What this indicates is that there is no single place to get your information. As these readings show, you should keep your mind open to potential sources for useful information for your course work.

This reader is likely to have been adopted in your course to guide seminar discussions. For many of you this may be one of your first experiences in a seminar setting. As such, we recommend adopting the following strategy to prepare for seminars.

- The key to preparing for seminars is to read the articles closely and more than once. Discussing an academic article requires carefully digesting its arguments, thoughtfully considering them, and commenting on or critiquing them.
- The first time that you read through an article, your purpose should be simply to identify the author's key argument(s). Don't worry too much at this point about the specific details; instead, concentrate on figuring out the main argument. Sometimes the title, the introduction, or the conclusion will provide a clear statement of the author's argument; others times you will have to work a little harder to determine what it is. When you've read it through once, write down the main argument in your notes *in your own words*. Using your own words, rather than copying down the author's words, will help you to remember the argument.
- The second time you read through the article, do so with the goal of identifying the support and/or evidence that the author provides for his or her argument. You will need to read more carefully this time, noting important passages or points in the article itself (try highlighting or underlining—but only if you own the book!) and taking notes for use in the seminar. Articles are often organized in a way that makes identifying the evidence/support relatively easy: paragraphs are normally developed around supporting arguments; subheadings can often provide hints to new directions in the articles; and introductions and conclusions will often summarize the main evidence and the support employed to defend the argument. You won't be expected to remember every point that an author makes, but you will be expected to remember the argument and how the author supported it.
- At this point you should try to provide some commentary on and/or critique of the argument, which is an important skill to develop in the social sciences. Start by asking yourself whether or not you agree with the author. Why do you or why do you not? Are there points that he/she neglected to consider? Are there alternative explanations that he/she failed to evaluate? Thinking about the concepts and theories that have been

reviewed in the lectures and in your textbook can help you to answer these questions. Preparing one or two critical points for the seminar ought to be your goal.

- Seminars provide an opportunity not only for commenting on the readings but also for obtaining answers to questions that you might have about them. As you read through the article, note any points, concepts, or passages that you don't understand and bring them up in the seminar. Although students often hate to admit in front of their peers that they don't understand something, more often than not several other students are struggling with exactly the same point. Higher learning is just that—learning—and to learn, one has to be prepared to say "I just don't get it."

- Finally, seminars are about dialogue: the quality of a seminar depends in part on the willingness of its participants to engage in a conversation. And often your participation grade will depend on the quality of the questions and comments that you bring to the seminar. If you hate the idea of speaking up in front of a group, the best way to overcome this fear is to be prepared. Rehearse one or two specific points or comments before you arrive at the seminar and make certain that you say them. And remember, you are likely not the only person in the seminar who is nervous about speaking up. Adequate preparation can help, however, to minimize your fears.

Simply put, these readings are meant to get you to think. Politics is all around us, and it is unavoidable in our daily lives. Politics affects us all, and it is crucial that we think about politics in an open and critical manner. We all have our own ideas, interests, and issues in political life. We hope the readings in this book will confirm or challenge yours.

Section 1

Political Science
and Political Action

SECTION SUMMARY

As is the case for many other fields in the social sciences, there are many ways to approach the discipline of political science. Politics, which is the basis of political science, involves the authority and power that surround organized social relations. Aside from this basic statement, however, one is much less likely to find agreement within the political science community. The lack of certainty in a "single approach" can be puzzling for those who expect some clarity of purpose. In fact, political science is often criticized for its diverse perspectives. However, as this set of readings shows, diversity is the strength of political science. Though ideas form the basis of our approaches, diversity allows us to see the complexity of politics without the barriers of ideas. Diversity is also one of the greatest assets we have in political science, because through diverse perspectives, we are more likely to develop a fuller understanding of politics and political systems. Ultimately, this raises our hopes of predicting, to the limited degree possible when dealing with human nature, political outcomes. This knowledge and predictability are fundamental to the development of "better" political systems.

Though the study of political science and the process of political action are inexorably connected, there are differences, as well. Political action can come in so many forms: protest, voting, debate, lawmaking, or even revolution. The study of political action—political science—gives us the tools we need to understand and explain the nature of politics: the "governance of social units, allocation of power and responsibility, and relationship among political actors in society."

What is the difference between political action and the study of political science? What makes these readings, or your lectures or textbook, different from— or even better than—simply reading a newspaper or watching television news? Why not simply read stories and commentary posted on the internet and come to your own conclusions about politics that way? Becoming informed about politics without having to attend class might seem appealing; and for most people, that is sufficient.

But studying political science is not the same as watching the news or reading the newspaper. It's not even the same as engaging in political debate with friends and colleagues, as useful and constructive as that may be. If we watch the news or read the paper, we might be able to explain events taking place around us: the action of politics. Studying politics, however, leads us to a greater understanding of these events—to peek behind the façade of daily political action to ask the deeper questions about why things happen, and what causes change.

Political science lets us question what we know and what we're told. Today we have more information at our disposal than ever before. But where does this information come from? Multinational media firms? Governments? Ideological zealots with some kind of an agenda? Moreover, is our information unfiltered? Strangely, while we have more information at our fingertips, we might wind up less informed.

This section offers some ideas about the current state of our political world. Gerry Stoker starts this discussion with a vigorous defence of democracy as our best alternative, but one with potential pitfalls. (Later, in Section 2, Francis Fukuyama comes at the democracy debate from another perspective.) Then Kenneth Minogue sounds a call to arms for the study of politics. His point about activism in politics is simply that nothing is more important in society than an interested electorate. The only way that we can effect change is to become involved. But being more aware does not necessarily make us more accepting. Indeed, the very act of creating a political community means that some groups are excluded. Oliver Woshinsky speaks of this in his contribution to this section.

Minogue's second contribution in this section provides insight into the earliest civilization to inform much of modern democratic politics and political science—Ancient Greece. Fundamental democratic tenets—the equality of citizens, the rationality of humans, and freedom of expression—grounded politics in this early civilization. Plato, Aristotle, and others were the first to attempt to describe existing political systems properly, but also the first to argue for the "ideal" regime, based on a particular set of evaluative criteria. Their arguments remain part of the core curriculum in political philosophy.

"Globalization" is a complex dynamic and encompasses much more than just the political world. Globalization also brings up questions of cultural difference. Today we travel more than we ever have, and more easily and inexpensively. Being more aware of events nationally and internationally means that we are also more aware of cultures other than our own. In his description of modern globalization, Wayne Ellwood gives us some insight into what may be the most important political concept in our contemporary world.

As a beginning student of political science, you should develop an understanding of the various approaches that are employed in the discipline, since the approach directly determines the questions that researchers ask, the focus of their gaze, and thus, to a certain extent, the answers and conclusions that are reached. Theodoulou and O'Brien's article summarizes key periods in the study of politics, including its more modern branches. As the authors make clear, the focus and central concerns of each period often originate in the perceived weaknesses of the approach adopted in the preceding period. Moreover, the authors make an important argument for ensuring that the study of politics remains relevant—that is, that the practices of government and politics are sufficiently important to warrant the attention of those who study them. This reading also serves as an excellent springboard for the following section in the book, which deals with political theories.

Politics is more alive today than it ever has been. Our ideas, our interests, and the issues that surround us are charged with politics. In an age of globalization, understanding politics as well as explaining it—in all its facets—makes us better citizens of our country, and of our world.

Chapter 1

The Triumph of Democracy?

GERRY STOKER*

* **Gerry Stoker** is Professor of Politics at the University of Manchester.

> In the summer of 1997, I was asked by a leading Japanese newspaper what I
> thought was the most important thing that had happened in the twentieth cen-
> tury. I found this to be an unusually thought-provoking question, since so many
> things of gravity have happened over the last hundred years. . . . I did not, ulti-
> mately, have any difficulty in choosing one as the preeminent development of
> the period: the rise of democracy. This is not to deny that other occurrences
> have been important, but I would argue that in the distant future, when people
> look back at what happened in this century, they will find it difficult not to
> accord primacy to the emergence of democracy as the preeminently acceptable
> form of governance.[1]

Amartya Sen, 1998 Nobel Laureate in Economics

Amartya Sen picks out democracy as the crowning achievement of the twentieth century.
It has to be admitted that it is possible to think of many other developments in the century worthy of praise, from widespread advances in economic welfare to space travel. But
I think the establishment of democracy deserves to be placed at the top of that century's
achievements. A powerful wave of democratization closed the twentieth century, and as a
result most politics now takes place in mass democracies whose citizens have been given
a voice in the processes and institutions that determine how power is exercised and how
decisions are made. This chapter shows how democratic governance has become a widely accepted and celebrated guide to how we should make decisions on a collective basis
in our societies. It explores the nature of this democratic governance, arguing that
democracy is a system worth defending and showing that it is not just a "western" idea
but also a universal value. The chapter continues by examining the spread of democratic
practice. It concludes by looking at the "dark side" of democracy in multiethnic nation
states where the arguments of democracy have been distorted to justify the "cleansing" of
one ethnic group by another. Nevertheless the overall message of this chapter is hooray
for democracy.

THE NATURE OF DEMOCRATIC GOVERNANCE

Large-scale democracy, based on voting rights for all adults, is a very new form of governance that got underway in the early decades of the twentieth century, although the concept

---

[1]   Amartya Sen, 'Democracy as a universal value', *Journal of Democracy*, 10(3) (1999), pp. 3–4.

of democracy has a longer history stretching back at least to the Greek states more than 2,000 years ago. In recent decades, it has become the world's preferred form of governance.

Let us define democratic governance as a political system that meets the following three criteria:

- Universal suffrage—that is, the right to vote in elections for all adults
- Governments chosen by regular, free and competitive election
- The presence of a set of political rights to free speech and freedom to organize in groups.

By these far-from-tough criteria, no nation state in 1900 could be called "democratic" because none had universal suffrage. By 1950, about a third of all nations could meet all three criteria to a reasonable extent; and in the last quarter of the century, a great wave of change saw democratic governance extended to about two-thirds of all countries.[2] Democracy now has pole position as the world's preferred form of governance.

The struggle to achieve democracy has often involved inspirational acts both by leaders and by populations at large. The experience of Nelson Mandela and South Africa in the 1990s stands out in our memories, but there have been countless other steps towards democracy taken in difficult and trying circumstances. In the 1980s, there were the long struggles of peoples in Poland and other eastern European countries to establish democracy. Further back, the early years of the twentieth century saw the continuation of a campaign to win votes for women, with the honour of first granting universal women's suffrage going to Finland in 1906.[3]

There have been a number of key influencing factors behind the spread of democracy in the last quarter of the twentieth century.[4] The most obvious is the break-up of the earlier colonial arrangements of western powers such as the UK, France and others. A second has been the fall of authoritarian regimes in some parts of western Europe including Spain, Portugal and Greece. A third is the collapse of the former Soviet Union (FSU) and the liberation of an associated group of satellite central and eastern European (CEE) states held under its influence. Fourth, there has been a resurgence of democracy in Latin America and Asia.

Economic development that in turn supports changes in the social structure—shifting the position of classes, ethnic groups and women—has been a key driver for democratization, as exemplified by the experience of South Korea, Taiwan, Brazil and Mexico. In some cases, the failure of authoritarian regimes to deliver economic performance has opened them to the challenge that democratic forces might do better. Crucially, in order for such a transition to occur a form of compromise between established elites and new political forces has had to emerge. The experience of some parts of Europe, Latin America and Africa can be seen as following this path.

But to an extent, the debate about democratization has changed. Traditional explanations focused on national structures or players to see if they were ready to provide the conditions and context for democracy, with the in-built assumption that democracy was an unusual form of governance and needed the right conditions to become established. More

---

[2] Larry Diamond, 'Universal democracy?', *Policy Review* (June–July 2003), p. 119.
[3] See Kenneth Newton and Jan W. van Deth, *Foundations of Comparative Politics* (Cambridge: Cambridge University Press, 2005).
[4] Diamond, 'Universal democracy?'.

recently, the emphasis has been on global and international factors. Since the end of the Cold War more international pressures have been brought to bear advocating the cause of democracy. Both the USA and the European Union (EU), although not always consistently, have promoted democratization as the right path to follow for other countries. Finally there has been more international pressure to support human rights and democracy as a basic right. Extending democracy is now the stated project of important and powerful global actors.[5]

DEMOCRACY AS A UNIVERSAL VALUE

What exactly is "democracy"? Our starting point should be a straightforward definition of democratic governance, identified above as a set of procedures and institutions through which decisions by societies are filtered. As a governance system—that is, as a way of making collective decisions in society—democracy requires free, fair and competitive elections, underwritten by universal suffrage in order to choose government leaders; it is also necessary that the results of those elections be respected. Democracy also entails respect for the freedoms and the basic rights of citizens, a capacity to deliver justice and respect for the rule of the law. It also demands a capacity for free exchange of views among citizens and an uncensored distribution of news and opinion. Democracy, even to achieve what might be regarded by many as these minimum conditions, asks a lot of a society.

Some argue that democracy is about much more than a set of arrangements for making decisions in society, as set out above. The starting concept of democracy that is used in [*Why Politics Matters: Making Democracy Work*] rests firmly in what can be described as the "realist camp," in that its focus is on an *operating system of decision making* rather than some far-off goal. The model is egalitarian, in its emphasis on equal rights to participation and protection, but it does not insist on a wider economic or social equality as a precursor to democracy. What I would say is that, ultimately, democracy must involve citizens in more than simply selecting leaders to govern them. It must be about the capacity of citizens to engage in and influence policy debates and outcomes. Democracy, rather than democratic governance, rests on the idea of those being affected by a decision having a right to a say in that decision.

For the present, it can simply be noted that there are other narratives of democracy, many of them emphasizing to a much greater degree than I do the need for direct participation and the need for egalitarian conditions to be established before democracy can flourish.[6] Indeed, in the processes that contribute to democratization in different countries there are likely to be different views about what democracy will bring and what it means, and these are in turn a source of inspiration, dispute—and, if undelivered, disappointment.[7] In some of the newer democracies, for example, the processes of democratization

---

[5]   Jean Grugel, *Democratization: A Critical Introduction* (Basingstoke and New York: Palgrave Macmillan, 2002), p. 241.

[6]   For a discussion of various concepts of democracy, see Michael Saward, *Democracy* (Cambridge: Polity, 2003).

[7]   Grugel, *Democratization*.

ran alongside other developments such as a shift to a market economy or (in the case of South Africa) the attempt to create a post-apartheid society. If democracy fails to support economic development or a more equal society, it may lose legitimacy and public support. Such matters will be considered later in the book, as will the possibility that more participation might help to revitalize politics in mass democracies.

Democracy, it is sometimes argued, is an exclusively western concept. While it is true that some politicians in the West tend to claim democracy as their own, such claims should be disputed. Some institutions dominated by powerful western countries—such as the World Bank—have pushed western-style democracy as part of a package of good governance from the 1980s onwards, but it would be a mistake to assume that democracy is just another export of the West.

Democracy is better understood as a universal value. As Nobel Prize winning academic Amartya Sen points out:

> *In any age and social climate, there are some sweeping beliefs that seem to command respect as a kind of general rule—like a "default" setting in a computer program; they are considered right unless their claim is somehow negated. While democracy is not yet universally practiced, nor indeed uniformly accepted, in the general climate of world opinion, democratic governance has now achieved the status of being taken as generally right.*[8]

Democracy is not a universal value because everyone agrees with it. Indeed, any value that achieved such general acclaim would be likely to fall into the "motherhood and apple pie" category of empty ideas that no one could object to. Democracy is a tougher concept than that. It has been hard fought over, and won respect. What makes it universal is that "people anywhere may have reason to see it as valuable."[9]

But there are still commentators who claim that particular sections of the world's population are culturally or practically incapable of democracy. Samuel Huntington[10] argues that the world has reached a historical period in which it is faced by a fundamental clash of civilizations, with the West versus the rest. The West's power and dominance is a source of antagonism, but fundamentally there is also a clash of *values*. Liberalism, democracy, the rule of law and a range of other "western" values have little resonance in Islamic, Confucian and other non-western cultures. According to this Harvard professor, the reality is that: "modern democratic government originated in the West. When it has developed in non-western societies it has usually been the product of western colonialism or imposition."[11] A less academic way of putting it would be to say that "Arabs or Africans just can't handle democracy."

Samuel Huntington may well be right to suggest that the West's use of its power to get its own way causes resentment elsewhere in the world, and a brash western commercial and political imperialism of ideas and products are sources of antagonism. Where he is mistaken is in suggesting that democracy is a western preserve. It is, to say the least, wide of the mark historically to suggest that, outside western democracies, democracy exists because of

---

[8] Sen, 'Democracy as a universal value', p. 5.
[9] Sen, 'Democracy as a universal value', p. 12.
[10] Samuel P. Huntington, 'A clash of civilizations?', *Foreign Affairs*, 72(3) (1993), pp. 22–49.
[11] Huntington, 'A clash of civilizations?', p. 41.

western colonialism or intervention. The people of India or South Africa could explain to him that democracy exists in their countries despite, not because of western input. Since his article about the clash of civilizations was published in 1993, democracy as a form of governance, as noted earlier, has become ever more widely established and present in Islamic, Confucian, African and Latin American regions, and by no means confined largely to the West.

There is a more fundamental reason for objecting to the "clash of civilizations" thesis: it places a false emphasis on a homogeneity of thought and practice in broad cultures or civilizations. As Amartya Sen points out, "diversity is a feature of most cultures in the world," so to suggest that western thought has shown "a historical commitment of the West—over the millennia—to democracy, and then to contrast it with non-Western traditions (treating each as monolithic) would be a great mistake."[12] Islamic and other traditions allow scope for democratic practice; western thought is not exclusively democratic. Authoritarianism—the major alternative to democracy—has been a core part of western thought and historical practice.

Democracy is attractive to a great many people for three fundamental reasons. Again following Amartya Sen, we can view democracy as having *intrinsic, instrumental* and *constructive* features that make it desirable. The intrinsic value of democracy is something much celebrated by political philosophers and rests on the idea that it is an integral part of being human to share decisions and choices with other humans. Participation in the political life of a community makes us more whole as people and gives us a chance to express ourselves as human beings.

Some may find the intrinsic value argument convincing, and others may not. It seems to rest on a rather romantic or even woolly view of politics, and I for one need some more practical arguments to support the case for democracy. How sustainable is the love of a procedure such as democracy unless it helps you achieve something? It is a better sell for democracy to claim that it will "help you achieve the outcomes which are the things closest to your heart."[13] This is the point where the *instrumental* argument for democracy kicks in. But in this case the marketing of what politics can do needs to be cautious. Democracy cannot guarantee you a happy life, but it can make some disasters of human life less likely to be imposed on you. One study suggests tentatively "there is a robust correlation between democratic institutions and health, resulting in greater life expectancy in democracies."[14] Amartya Sen, in part, won his Nobel Prize for showing that major famines generally do not occur in democracies; recent famines in Ethiopia and Somalia occurred under dictatorships, and great historical famines such as those in the Soviet Union in the 1930s or China in 1958–61 took place in authoritarian regimes. The evidence is clear and so, too, is the explanation:

> *Famines are easy to prevent if there is a serious effort to do so, and a democratic government facing elections and criticisms from opposition parties and independent newspapers, cannot help but make such an effort.*[15]

---

[12]   Sen, 'Democracy as a universal value', p. 15.

[13]   Saward, *Democracy*, p. 30.

[14]   See Timothy Besley and Masayuki Kudamatsu, 'Health and democracy', 10 January 2006 (unpublished paper, available at *http://econ.lse.ac.uk/staff/tbesley/index_own.html#pubs*).

[15]   Sen, 'Democracy as a universal value', p. 8.

When things are going fine, then the instrumental value of democracy may not be missed. It is when things go wrong, as they always will, that democracy is needed, because of the particular incentives it gives governments to behave in a way that takes the welfare of citizens into account. Democracy provides the mechanism to ensure that governments are only able to get away with so much.

Finally, democracy does positively help in the search for solutions to intractable problems and challenges. This is the *constructive* value of democracy. Open dialogue can be the key to resolving many of the most challenging issues we confront; it enables the sharing of ideas, learning and the thinking through of problems. It is that public airing of issues that can make all the difference. Sometimes, however, contrary to the view of some theorists of deliberative democracy, politics does its work through smoke and mirrors. By enabling people who fundamentally disagree to find a way forward by sometimes giving different meanings to the same words, politics does much valuable work. Democracy—more often than we often care to admit—relies on "weasel phrases," hidden compromises or delayed gratification and various other forms of ambiguous construction that enable all sides to claim victory, or at least emerge defeated but with their honour intact.

So democracy deserves its status as a universal value. It is not an exclusive western form of governance, but rather the preferred system of making decisions for people throughout the globe. It does its work in a variety of ways and with a considerable degree of messiness and compromise. It is constrained and limited. But in the last few decades it has become a living practice for the majority of countries on the planet, as the next section will show.

THE TRIUMPH OF DEMOCRACY

Here are five important facts about democracy:

- The most powerful nation in the world, by far, at the beginning of the twenty-first century—the USA—has a system of democratic governance.
- India—one of the world's most populated countries—has had a system of democratic governance for over fifty years and, despite enormous religious, social and ethnic divides, it has survived.
- The EU consists of a group of twenty-five countries, each operating a system of democratic governance, and constitutes a powerful bloc in economic, trading and foreign affairs.
- Most of the Latin American and Caribbean countries have some form of democratic governance, as do many African and Asian nations.
- Democratic governance and human rights are the largely unquestioned international standard for countries.

These facts do not command universal rejoicing. Some people think that the USA is powerful, but also an aggressive and dangerous actor on the global stage. Some citizens of Europe do not like the EU. The strength of the internal democracies of all nations—but particularly those in Africa, Asia and Latin America—are often questioned. Some fear that double standards and national self-interest cloud the rhetoric about international commitment to human rights and democracy: the West favours democracy when it suits

its interests and opposes, or at least fails to support, it when it does not; western countries stick up for human rights when trying to put other countries in the dock, but are willing to ignore human rights issues themselves. Democratic governance may be an international standard, but many express doubts about whether democracy can be imposed from the outside. Yet for the first time in human history it is possible to imagine a future in which authoritarian rule might be eliminated within two or three decades.[16] That should be a matter for universal rejoicing.

The rise of democracy is a story that stretches beyond the boundaries of [*Why Politics Matters: Making Democracy Work*]. At the beginning of the 1970s—when I first studied politics—writers about the constitutional arrangements of different nation states classified regimes under three headings. First, there was a relatively small group of democracies concentrated mostly in advanced industrial nations. Second, there was a larger group of communist states, and finally there were the developing countries, a few of which operated democratic forms of governance but most of which were prone to military or one-party dictatorships, or at least authoritarian rule. At the beginning of the 1970s, there had been no great surge in the growth of democratic governance and as a result the position was similar to that already noted in 1950. In total, around a third of the countries in the world could be classified as meeting the criteria of democratic governance of universal suffrage, regular elections to choose government leaders and basic political rights, in that period.

The great drive to democracy that dominated the last quarter of the twentieth century started with the collapse of the European dictatorships in Portugal, Spain and Greece in the 1970s.[17] Between 1979 and 1985 the military withdrew in favour of civilian governments in nine Latin American countries. In the 1980s and 1990s democratization began to spread to previously untouched parts of Asia. The Philippines saw the end of the Marcos dictatorship in 1986 and Taiwan, South Korea, Bangladesh, Nepal and Pakistan all strengthened their democracies or became democracies in this period, although in the last case, democracy did not survive. The fall of the Berlin Wall in 1989 and the collapse of the Soviet Union saw the start of a process that spread democracy throughout central and eastern Europe. In Africa, Benin led a move to democracy in 1990, followed by a process that led to democracy being established in South Africa in 1994. Other African states also established democratic rule during this period. As a result nearly three in five states had achieved some strong aspects of democratic governance by 1994, and the process has become firmly established, so that by the start of the twenty-first century nearly two-thirds of all countries met the basic criteria. Table 1.1 gives a breakdown by regions of the world.

Of course, the quality of democracy in all countries can be questioned. After all, it was in the "model" democracy of the USA that the presidential election of 2000 collapsed into an acrimonious dispute over whether George Bush or Al Gore had actually won because of irregularities or uncertainties in vote-counting. A detailed democratic audit of any country is unlikely to produce a clean bill of health.[18] All of the countries included in

---

[16]   Diamond, 'Universal democracy?'.
[17]   See Diamond, 'Universal democracy?'.
[18]   See David Beetham (ed.), *Defining and Measuring Democracy* (London: Sage, 1994).

TABLE 1.1	Democracies, by region, 2002	
Region	Number of countries	Number of democracies (per cent)
Western Europe and Anglophone states	28	28 (100)
Latin American and Caribbean	33	30 (91)
Eastern Europe and the FSU	27	18 (67)
East, South, South East Asia	25	12 (48)
Pacific Islands	12	11 (91)
Africa (sub-Sahara)	48	19 (40)
Middle East and North Africa	19	2 (11)
Total	192	120 (63)

Source: Data extracted from Table 5 in Larry Diamond, "Can the whole world become democratic? Democracy, development and international politics," Center for the Study of Democracy, paper 03.05, University of California, Irvine, 2003.

Table 1.1 meet the minimum requirement that they hold regular, free, fair and competitive elections to fill the positions in their governments. Citizens in these countries all have a secret ballot, fair access to a range of media and basic rights to organize, campaign and solicit votes. But many still suffer from significant human rights abuse, corruption and a weak rule of law.

As Table 1.1 shows, the democratic form of governance has a major foothold, if not a dominant position, in most regions of the world. Democratic governance exists in rich and poor countries and in countries with a range of cultures and traditions. It has been established in small and large countries, although more so in the former than the latter. Yet eight out of eleven countries with populations greater than 100 million have a form of democratic governance. Democratic governance is practised in countries with every major philosophical and religious tradition: Christian, Jewish, Buddhist, Confucian, Hindu and Muslim. All this suggests that comments about certain cultures not being suited to democracy are difficult to sustain. The region that is the missing link in the spread of democracy is the Middle East and North Africa, where in 2002 only two countries meeting the criteria of democratic governance could be found. But I think that this reflects the politics of the region and the negative impact of past western influences and interventions, rather than a cultural issue for the population.

Public opinion survey evidence backs up this judgement that the idea of democratic governance is popular in all parts of the globe. In particular, the survey research indicates that many Muslims prefer the idea of democracy to authoritarian rule, as do clear majorities of the population in all other parts of the world. The *World Values Survey*, a spectacular public opinion research effort covering over eighty nations, reveals the scale of the support for democratic governance. Table 1.2 provides detailed results: members of the public in many countries appear to agree with the direction of thought offered by Winston Churchill, that democracy may not be a perfect or all-wise form of government,

TABLE 1.2	Support for democracy	
Per cent agreeing that "Democracy may have problems but it's better than any other form of government"		
Region	**Highest (per cent agreeing)**	**Lowest (per cent agreeing)**
Western Europe and Anglophone states	Denmark (99)	Britain (78)
Latin America	Uruguay (96)	Mexico (79)
Eastern Europe and FSU	Croatia (96)	Russia (62)
East, South, South East Asia	Japan/India (92)	Indonesia (71)
Africa (sub-Sahara)	Uganda (93)	Nigeria (45)
Middle East and North Africa	Algeria (88)	Iran (69)

Note: No figures are available for Caribbean states and Pacific islands.

Source: Data from the *World Values Survey* (1999–2002) wave for most countries (drawn from a fuller analysis by Ronald Inglehart, "The worldviews of Islamic publics in global perspective," 2005, available at *www.worldvaluessurvey.org*).

but it is less bad than all the alternatives.[19] Specifically in relation to the issue of Islamic-populated states and democracy, Ronald Inglehart, a key mover behind the *World Values Survey*, concludes: "Islamic publics, including the Arab publics, overwhelmingly view democracy as the best form of government."[20]

Although a response to one survey question—the evidence provided in Table 1.2—is hardly likely to be the last word on the issue of world public opinion and democracy, it does provide support for the view that support is widespread and fairly strongly held in most countries. If you are British—as this author is—it is not too comforting to see the self-proclaimed "mother of democracy" as the lowest ranked of the "western" democracies when it comes to support for democracy. The response of citizens in many countries also suggests that they are able to distinguish between the *idea* of democratic governance and its, often less than perfect, *practice*. In short, people may well see failings in their own system of governance, but recognize that democracy is an ideal worth striving towards.

---

[19]   One of the anonymous reviewers of an ealier draft of [*Why Politics Matters*] kindly pointed out that Winston Churchill's exact words were: 'No one pretends that democracy is perfect or all-wise. Indeed, it has been said that democracy is the worst form of Government except all those other forms that have been tried from time to time.' As the reviewer went on to explain, the survey question offers a rather gentler judgement on democratic governance than that offered by Churchill. There are reasons to think that Churchill was not necessarily the greatest advocate of rule by the people, since another of his well-known quotations is: 'The best argument against democracy is a five minute conversation with the average voter.'

[20]   Ronald Inglehart, 'The worldviews of Islamic publics in global perspective' (2005) (available at *www.worldvaluessurvey.org*).

CONCLUSIONS: A "DARK SIDE" TO DEMOCRACY?

Broadly, we can be positive at this point. Democratic governance is widely supported in the public opinion expressed by the peoples of the world, regardless of culture, religion or other factors. If we had more time, we could probably identify some significant differences between the perceptions and value placed on democracy in different countries. People in many countries are not so sure that democracy is working for them, and there are substantial portions of many populations who it appears would not take much persuasion to consider a more authoritarian form of rule. In Latin America, East Asia and the post-communist countries of Eastern Europe and the Soviet Union there is much evidence of people being less than convinced by the development of democracy, as Table 1.2 makes clear. But it would be churlish not to recognize the degree to which the idea of democracy has become a dominant force in world public opinion. Moreover, two-thirds of the countries of the world are attempting to put democracy into practice in some form.

We know that if democracy is to work, it needs more than the establishment of a particular set of institutions. It has to be a lived practice, with at least two key elements.[21] The maintenance of democracy requires an effective state to regulate society, agree to compromises and organize the distribution of public goods. It also requires a civil society of non-state actors that is organized, active and engaged and capable at a minimum of holding the state to account and at a broader level offers the seed bed for the development of democratic ideas and practice.

It is because of these realities that even if the global order now in a formal sense favours democracy, the arrival of democratic practice in former authoritarian countries cannot be guaranteed. Certainly it is difficult to see how democracy can be imposed from the outside: the active engagement and commitment of key players within a nation state is an essential basis for the reform of the state and the strength of civil society, as exemplified by the struggles in Iraq following the US-led invasion that brought down Saddam Hussein. Establishing democracy in areas that have seen deep internal division is not an impossible task, as shown by the example of South Africa. But democracy is not easy to establish, and even in mature democracies it may not be easy to sustain commitment to it as a form of governance.

The assumption made in the discussion so far is that democracy is something that develops in nation states. We operate with a territorially bound idea of what a political community is, and the community of citizens granted universal suffrage and political rights are seen as delimited by the boundaries of different countries: democracy exists in India or Portugal; the right to have a say means the right to have a say in your own country. One challenge that can be raised to this assumption is the growing impact of global decision making and forces that are taking issues beyond the boundaries of our national political communities. For now, I want to note how democracy can be in trouble when the definition and status of the political community is based on the promotion of one group at the expense of another. Northern Ireland, Kosovo, Sri Lanka, Fiji and Rwanda—to pick

---

[21] Grugel, *Democratization*, pp. 238–47.

a range of cases from around the world—exemplify "a dark side" to democracy,[22] in the form of ethnic divisions and, most tragically, ethnic cleansing.

The trouble comes when, in ethically mixed nation states, the demos (the people) becomes defined as one ethnic group (the ethnos). Michael Mann explains:

> But if the people is to rule in its own nation-state, and if the people is defined in ethnic terms, then its ethnic unity may outweigh the kind of citizen diversity that is central to democracy. If such a people is to rule, what is to happen to those of different ethnicity? Answers have often been unpleasant. . . . Murderous ethnic cleansing is a hazard of the age of democracy since amid multiethnicity the ideal of rule by the people began to entwine the demos with the dominant ethnos, generating organic conceptions of the nation and the state that encouraged the cleansing of minorities.[23]

When rule by the people comes to mean rule by a particular ethnic group, then democracy can be a harbinger of brutal attacks on the minorities that fall foul of the majority. This is not to suggest that ethnic cleansing is justified by democratic ideals, but rather to recognize that the rhetoric of democracy can and has been used to justify barbaric acts. In modern colonies, settler democratic communities have in certain circumstances proved truly murderous. Mann describes in detail some of the activities of settlers in the USA and Australia. The break-up of former authoritarian regimes in Europe has created the conditions for ethnic conflict to flourish under democratic regimes: Mann examines the case of the former Yugoslavia (FYR). In democracy's defence, it can be said that by no means is ethnic cleansing a strategy that emerges from democratic states alone; authoritarian regimes are capable of such atrocities—think of Nazi Germany or Stalin's Soviet Union (both cases documented by Mann). Moreover, at the heart of the main practices of democratic governance is a commitment to formal political rights for all citizens and groups that make the case for the inclusion of all groups in decision making rather than the exclusion of some ethnic groups. Indeed, many democracies have developed quite elaborate mechanisms to enable different ethnic groups to share in decision making, as the cases of South Africa or Canada, in different ways, show.

Democratic governance as discussed in this chapter is about the protection of the rights of the minority, rather than the simple imposition of rule by the majority. So the "dark side" of democracy, that lends itself in some cases to ethnic cleansing, is a distortion of the democratic ideal, but it reflects a tension in democratic thought that cannot be wished away. Democratic governance, as advocated here, is committed to enshrining freedoms and constitutional protections into a system of collective decision making that opens access to decision making to include all social groups. That is the model of democratic governance that has gained a dominant grip on politics throughout the world, and is the model of democracy that we should be celebrating. Yet many citizens in democracies struggle to find much to celebrate about the practice of democratic politics in their countries.

---

[22]   Michael Mann, *The Dark Side of Democracy: Explaining Ethnic Cleansing* (Cambridge: Cambridge University Press, 2004).

[23]   Mann, *The Dark Side of Democracy*, p. 3.

Chapter 2

The Experience of Politics:
I. How to Be an Activist

*__Kenneth Minogue__ is Emeritus Professor of Political Science at the London School of Economics and Political Science.

Those who study politics are called political scientists, and we must presently consider politics as a science. First, however, we must look to what it is that scientists have to study: namely, the actual experience of engaging in politics.

This experience is sometimes compared to theatre. Politicians and actors certainly belong to related tribes. Much of the architecture of public life recalls the Classical inspiration of the Roman forum, especially that of Washington. In London, the Houses of Parliament, rebuilt in the middle of the nineteenth century, have been appropriately described as 'a basically classical structure with neo-Gothic detail'. The architecture of the Kremlin and its communist embellishments reflect the remoteness and grandiosity of despotism. French public architecture is imperial in its grandeur. That the British prime minister lives in a more or less ordinary house in a more or less ordinary street reveals something of the studied casualness of British public life.

These are the national theatres of politics, but most political drama, even in a televisual age, takes place in local and regional offices, in dusty halls and on windy street corners where electors can be harangued. Politics has its own logistics: it requires agents, premises, contacts with printers, a pool of supporters, money, and generally, as the condition of all these things, an established political party. The rich and famous are sometimes inclined to start a party from scratch, but it is a difficult option. The typical route taken by the ambitious politician is from the periphery to the centre, and each step of the way resembles a game of snakes and ladders.

The politician needs, for a start, the same kind of knowledge as the concerned citizen; just more of it. What American politician could move a step without a close knowledge of the Constitution, the Bill of Rights, and many of the decisions of the Supreme Court? Knowledge of history is indispensable, supplying a range of memories, references, and metaphors without which political talk is unintelligible. From the War of Independence, through the Civil War, to the very songs and slogans of the American past, the politician must be able to pick up the references, many of them highly local, which constitute the culture of those whom he seeks to represent. He must know how the Senate and Congress work in detail, not to mention the way in which the states relate to them. Much of this is low-level, slightly tedious, descriptive material, but without it the politician's understanding hardly rises above gossip.

Traditions of politics vary greatly. In beginning by contrasting politics with despotism, we have already suggested that there is an immense gulf dividing the possible ways of ordering a society. The very idea of what a human being is, and what is due to men, and especially to women, will in many countries be remote from what is believed by the average reader of this book. A tradition is something 'handed down' from one generation to another, and (perhaps re-described as 'political culture') must be the central object of understanding in any political system. It is composed of many strands, and what people say about the state may give very little sense of the reality of politics. A population long accustomed to being exploited by tax collectors, for example, has an attitude to the census, to governmental forms, and the rhetoric of leaders quite different from that which used to be found in European liberal democracies. In some traditions, people are sanguine about what can be changed, in others cynical and fatalistic. The very language in which the thoughts and sentiments pass down over the generations reveals a conceptual structure which affects political possibility. All languages have some analogue for 'justice', for example, but there are many variations on this broad theme—such as the idea of fairness—which can only be imported from other languages. Even European languages which are culturally similar to English do not yield a genuine translation of the subtitle—*Justice as Fairness*—of John Rawls's *A Theory of Justice*. Again, the Chinese character for 'freedom' connotes slipperiness and egoism rather than the courage and independence with which Europeans associate the term.

Most political knowledge generalizes experience. The politician cannot help but learn a great deal from the past, and especially from exemplary heroes and villains. Machiavelli recommended a close attention to the great deeds of ancient Rome, but modern history is not a whit less fertile in suggestive examples, and certainly much more revealing about our own political traditions. A British politician, for example, must know something of Magna Carta, Roundhead and Cavalier, Whig and Tory, the Reform Bills of the nineteenth century, the contrasting political styles of prime ministers such as Melbourne, Peel, Disraeli, Gladstone, Churchill, Attlee, and Wilson, not to mention the events of the twentieth century. Much of this will be legend, and what is heroic to some will be deplorable to others. A Labour politician might regard Ramsay MacDonald's formation of the National Government in 1931 as an act of treason to the party; a Conservative would treat the event quite differently, and would certainly see it as less important. Politicians train for the real world by endless talk about past landmarks and present possibilities, and they do so in a special language of their own. Thus 'appeasement' is no longer in politics the name of a type of response to someone's discontent, but refers to a dispute about foreign policy in the 1930s. For several decades after the Second World War it denoted an episode of shame and cowardice. Then came revision, an attack on the reputation of Churchill, the great critic of appeasement, and the argument that Britain's lone stand against Hitler in 1940 had merely delivered her into the hands of the rising empires of the USA and the USSR. It is very seldom that events stand still for long, and the paradox is that the past is nearly as opaque as the future.

For the aspiring politician in a country such as France, the past hangs more heavily than it commonly has in Anglo-Saxon countries. The French Revolution split France profoundly, largely along religious and secular lines, and the Nazi occupation left memories which determined political allegiances for the rest of the century. Irish politics has been similarly haunted by memory. The United States has, in general, been more fortunate, though the legacy of the Civil War has been bitter.

Since politics is talk, political skill requires wit, and politicians are remembered for their phrases. Winston Churchill is remembered both for the speeches which articulated 'the lion's roar' during the Second World War and for a string of witticisms, some of them malicious, like his description of Clement Attlee as 'a sheep in sheep's clothing'. Lincoln's political success came from his wisdom, but it is hard to imagine his political skill without his dazzling capacity for oratory. These men all belong, of course, to a vanished time when citizens attended like connoisseurs to long and complicated political speeches. Gladstone once took four hours to introduce his budget to the House of Commons—fortified, it is said, with raw eggs and sherry. That culture has been destroyed by the trivializing effect of radio and television, which provide such abundant distraction for the mind that politics must be fitted into a much smaller space: the 'sound-bite'. The sound-bite belongs to the simplified world of the slogan and the banner, but this does not diminish the need of the politician for the phrasemaker.

In modern democracies, a politician is a spokesman for some broadly based opinion, and what he or she hopes to become is the holder of an office. *Spokesmanship* and *office* are the polarities within which the men and women who go in for politics must live, and each reveals much about politics.

Spokesmanship is representation, and modern government must be conducted by representatives rather than by the citizens themselves because legislative enactments, often some hundreds of pages long, are too complicated to be mastered without unusual skill and attention. But the representative function of the politician begins long before policies emerge. It is the skill of constructing a position which will appeal to many people because it can harmonize conflicting desires. The superficial critic of politicians can see the vagueness and indeterminacy which are certainly often necessary for this, but generally fails to appreciate the trick of finding some essence of an issue that can unite different opinions. A skilful politician resembles a magician in his capacity to set an object before the mind of one audience, while keeping it invisible to others, sometimes in the same hall. Simple-minded rationalists sometimes stigmatize this characteristic of politicians as nothing but support-seeking duplicity, and journalists have taken to 'decoding' their speeches and disclosing the supposed 'message' behind the words. Better understood, this technique is the tact which allows people with very different judgments and preferences to live together in one society; where it fails—as, for example, in the difficulty Canadian politicians have had in projecting a 'Canada' that would accommodate Francophone and Anglophone opinion—then society moves to the brink of dissolution. American politicians finessed the division over slavery for as long as they could, for they suspected that the real alternative was civil war, and they were right.

Constrained by his representative function, the politician is further circumscribed by the responsibilities of his *office*. The raw brutalities of power are largely converted into the suavities of authority, and it is important to distinguish these two phenomena. The outsider is often impressed by the power of those who hold important positions in the state, but power, while attractive as a kind of melodrama, is mostly exaggerated. The office of a prime minister or president is constitutionally limited, and idealists quickly find that their capacity to improve the world requires whole streams of concessions they would prefer not to make. As Harry S. Truman remarked: 'About the biggest power the President has is the power to persuade people to do what they ought to do without having to be persuaded.' The power of an office is merely the skill by which a ruler can use his authority to get the right things done. Otherwise, when people talk of 'power' they merely mean the pleasure an office-holder may get from a purely personal exercise of will, which is basically a trivial thing. Most trivial of all is the pleasure in being the constant focus of attention in public places, and the capacity to please—but also to frustrate—the ambitious people by whom the politician is surrounded. It can no doubt be exploited for illicit purposes. President Kennedy notoriously used his prestige as president to induce large numbers of women to sleep with him, though since he was also handsome and rich, he hardly needed presidential prestige for that. It may be that, like the kinds of political groupie the Hungarian writer

Arthur Koestler talked about, some of them 'wanted to sleep with history'. Such power is not a thing possessed by the power-holder, but a moral relationship between the power-holder and the person over whom the power is supposedly exercised. Where it is a form of corruption, it involves the corruption of both parties.

The fact that persuasion lies at the heart of politics has one central implication: the reasons a politician decides upon a policy are categorically distinct from the reasons by which he publicly defends it. The two sets of reasons may overlap, or they may not, but in neither case need we conclude that politics is a cynical business. The reason lies in what we may call the *dimensions* of a political act. One such dimension concerns the practicality of the act in question. Will it have the desirable effects expected of it? What are its costs, and possible longer-term consequences? For the government to guarantee everyone an old age pension, for example, will certainly alleviate hardship, but it will also have economic consequences because the incentives to thrift and saving will diminish, and that will affect the economy. The real test is the long term. As the nineteenth-century journalist Walter Bagehot observed, one cannot judge the consequences of any reform until the generation in which it was passed has left the scene.

A second dimension: what is the consequence of pursuing this particular *type* of policy? It will infallibly become a precedent used in arguing for further policies of the same type. If it fails, there may be demands that the policy be pursued even further, rather than abandoned. When central direction of some economic activity produces anomalies, for example, the typical demand is that further central direction should be invoked to deal with the anomalies. Another dimension: what effect will this policy have on the short- and long-term prospects of its promoter? The promoter here is both the individual and the party legislating the policy. The Welfare State, for example, created in Britain after 1945, diffused benefits widely over the electorate, and its short-term effects might therefore have been to increase support for the Labour Party which carried it out. In the event, this did not happen—Labour lost the 1951 election. More seriously still, some welfare measures of the period have been thought to have 'gentrified' the working class and detached them from the Labour Party. As politicians sometimes say, nothing fails like success.

A typical form of cynicism revolves around concepts such as the 'public interest' or the 'common good'. It is easy to discredit such terms by pointing out that nearly every act of government will have both good and bad consequences for different sets of people. But it is to mistake the meaning of public interest to think it can be judged in terms of individual costs and benefits. Ideas of this kind are formal terms of political argument whose specific meaning can only emerge from the public debate itself. They are the necessary formal conditions of any political advocacy. It would be absurd for a politician to say: 'I want to do this because it is good for *me*.' Such a line would provide no reason why anyone else should do it. No doubt there is a vague sense in which everything any politician advocates is the best thing for him in the circumstances, but this does not at all mean that he is a hypocrite out for nothing else but personal benefit. There is plenty of self-serving conduct in politics, though it is reasonable to think that politicians are generally more rather than less public-spirited than the rest of us. That may not be much, of course, but it is something.

None of this is to deny the lowness of much of politics. A certain craftiness is essential. To know, for example, the rule whereby when votes are equal in a committee, the motion is lost, tells the crafty politician whether to frame a precarious motion in negative or in positive terms. For if, opposing the policy, he frames it in positive terms, and the vote is tied, then the motion is lost and he gets what he wants. In the 1994 Euro-elections in Britain, one candidate got thousands of votes from an unsophisticated electorate by calling himself the 'literal' (rather than liberal) democratic candidate. To have a name beginning with the early letters of the alphabet gives a candidate a slight but measurable advantage from the dimness of some citizens who simply fill in the ballot-paper from the top down. And no one called 'Kennedy' can fail to pick up extra votes in many American states. The main delinquencies of politicians, however, arise from highly prevalent human vices: cowardice in failing to challenge the fashionable opinion which the politician senses is wrong, fear of being thought stupid, desire to take up a virtuous-seeming posture, a preference for the comfortable option when the politician knows that the chickens will come home to roost some time after he has left the scene, and so on.

Politicians form a kind of club, sharing a culture in liberal democracies which cuts across party divisions. Friendships, for example, are often warmer *across* parties than within them. Certain ideas are always dominant in this culture, and some of these ideas may run counter to the opinions (known here as prejudices) of the people at large. In recent times, capital punishment, multiculturalism, and international idealism are examples of this class of idea, and politicians sometimes confuse them with the quite different thing called principle. The significance of this fact is that in certain respects politicians as a class constitute an oligarchy whose tendency is at odds with that of the population it rules. This oligarchic tendency is even more pronounced in countries whose electoral system requires voters to support party lists. When the gap between what politicians admire and what the people want widens, the general stock of politicians goes down, and they are recognized less as representing than as trying to hoodwink the people. The familiar ambiguities of politics become explicit sophistry. This is, of course, a dangerous situation in which opportunities for demagogues multiply.

The politician facing the question: how may my policy be commended to my audience? will think more of his audience than of his own introspections. Sometimes that audience will be colleagues, sometimes his own party, and sometimes the electorate as a whole. We may assume that he is persuaded of its wisdom, but the reasons which seem decisive to him may well not be decisive to others. The problem of persuasion is to find the reasons that will be decisive to the audience. In doing that, the politician must take off from whatever common ground he shares with them. The first act in persuasion is for the persuader to convince his audience of his fellow-feeling with their broad aims, and only then can he commend his own policy as something fitting in with those aims.

What this account of persuasion suggests is that the politician must be a special type of person, one capable of keeping his deepest convictions to himself. The rest of us can shoot off our mouths to our hearts' content, indulging in that massive new pleasure the modern world has invented, being opinionated about matters on which we are ignorant. The politician must generally consider the effect of his opinions on his likely future, and requires a special kind of personality structure. But it should not be concluded from this that a politician is simply a hypocrite. Such a person is engaged in a high-risk occupation in which he must always be looking to future developments. Opportunism is certainly part of the talent, but unless the politician has genuine convictions—both moral convictions, and convictions about how things are likely to move—he will lack the clear profile which is usually necessary for the greatest success. Statesmen—the highest grade of politician—are those who can balance inner conviction with the talent of turning every opportunity to advantage. Charles de Gaulle called for resistance to Germany from London in 1940, and withdrew from French politics in 1946, taking risks in both cases which could have doomed him to obloquy and insignificance. Churchill's stand against appeasement in the 1930s might have been a mere swansong to a moderately successful career. Barry Goldwater, who took disastrous risks in bidding for the presidency in 1964, turned out to be preparing the soil for the Reagan victory of 1980. The secret of politics is to care about success, but not too much.

Chapter 3

The Impact of Culture on Politics

OLIVER H. WOSHINSKY*

*Oliver H. Woshinsky is Emeritus Professor of Political Science at the University of Southern Maine.

People behave, from one place to another, in remarkably dissimilar ways. Brazilians bear hug when they meet friends. The French shake hands formally, and the Japanese bow. Transferring the behavior of one culture to another can produce dramatic misunderstandings. Bear hugging a Japanese businessman would hardly improve your chances for a contract. Fail to shake hands with a Frenchwoman each time you meet, and she will see you as a boor and a cad.[1]

Ian Robertson has written amusingly about the variety of human behavior.

> Americans eat oysters but not snails. The French each snails but not locusts. The Zulus eat locusts but not fish. The Jews eat fish but not pork. The Hindus eat pork but not beef. The Russians eat beef but not snakes. The Chinese eat snakes but not people. The Jalé of New Guinea find people delicious.[2]

Anecdotal accounts of human diversity can be fascinating, and they can also make a serious point. It pays to understand the variety of human mores, because every social pattern impinges in some way on politics. Candidates for office in Japan or France don't throw their arms around constituents while campaigning; in Brazil they do. Try it in Japan, or fail to do it in Brazil, and you will get nowhere in your bid for office.

In the same manner, what you eat (far-fetched though it may seem) will influence your political fortune. Imagine a politician in Israel known to dine on roast pig. Or an American politician who admits to loathing hot dogs and apple pie. George Bush [Sr.] had to claim that he loved pork rinds in order to win the trust of Texas voters, and Bill Clinton is known to enjoy that quintessential American food, the Big Mac. Had these men ever admitted, early in the political careers, that they preferred locusts and snakes to good old American food, they would never have had political careers, and none of us today would have heard of them.

P. J. O'Rourke, the flamboyant American journalist, once described some harrowing (though hilarious) adventures in Lebanon for his best-seller *Holidays in Hell*. One day he and his guide roamed the countryside looking for a farmer he was supposed to interview.

> It's hard to know what your driver is doing when he talks to the natives. He'll pull up somewhere and make a preliminary oration, which draws five or six people to

---

1. For an engaging account of the social significance of body language in different cultures, see Roger E. Axtell, *Gestures: The Do's and Taboos of Body Language around the World* (New York: John Wiley & Sons, Inc. 1991).
2. Ian Robertson, *Sociology* (New York: Worth Publishers, 1981) p. 63.

the car window. Then each of them speaks in turn. There will be a period of ges-
turing, some laughter, much arm clasping and handshaking, and a long speech by
the eldest or most prominent bystander. Then your driver will deliver an impas-
sioned soliloquy. This will be answered at length by each member of the audience
and anybody else who happens by. Another flurry of arm grabbing, shoulder slap-
ping and handshakes follows, then a series of protracted and emotional good-
byes. 'What did you ask them?' you'll say to your driver. 'Do they know your
friend.' 'What did they tell you?' 'No.[3]

Cultures vary. People differ radically from each other, depending on where they live and how they have been raised. People are emphatically *not* "just the same the world over," as the old cliché would have it. And as human behavior varies from one culture to anoth-er, so too does political behavior. The direct, straightforward American manner of asking questions would get nowhere in a Lebanese village. Just as obviously, a "straight-talking" American politician would fail miserably in a bid for office there. On the other hand, the bombastic, circuitous, and loquacious style of Lebanese interaction would produce career disaster for any American politician dim enough to adopt it in the United States.

POLITICS AND CULTURE

Politics everywhere reflects the culture of a time and place. This argument underpins the perspective of modern political science. To understand politics anywhere, you must first understand the culture within which political acts are embedded.

An intriguing item once appeared in my local newspaper: "In the Tonga Islands it is a compliment for a young man to say to your woman, 'Oh, fat liver full of oil, let us go and watch the moonrise.'"

Can you imagine using that line at a Saturday night fraternity party? It would prove a dismal failure in U.S. culture. The current American's ideal of beauty is often expressed in that famous cliché, "You can never be too rich or too thin." Studies show that the vast majority of American women consider themselves "too fat," when in fact most of them are not, by any reasonable standard, overweight.[4] But in a culture that glorifies slenderness, those who deviate even slightly from the reigning ideal of beauty see themselves (and indeed, are seen by others) as disadvantaged.

As it turns out, most cultures have fairly rigid notions of attractiveness, and those notions vary widely. Many societies prefer heftier body types than those admired in the West. A thin woman, attractive by American standards, once told me that growing up in West Africa in a missionary family, she was shunned by the young men of her village. Her plump sister, however, was considered stunning, and men came from miles around to offer her father many cows for the privilege of making her their bride.

---

[3]   P. J. O'Rourke, *Holidays in Hell* (London: Pan Books, Ltd., 1989), p. 36.
[4]   According to a recent survey, "three-quarters of American adults are not overweight." See "Losing Weight: What Works, What Doesn't," *Consumer Reports* 58 (June 1993): 347–52. See also Morton G. Harmatz., "The Misperception of Overweight in Normal and Underweight Women," *Journal of Obesity and Weight Regulation* 6 (1987): 38–54; and Marika Tiggemann and Esther D. Rothblum, "Gender Differences and Social Consequences of Perceived Overweight in the United States and Australia," *Sex Roles* 18 (1988): 75–86.

As this example suggests, attractiveness, however defined by a particular culture, is an asset. Study after study has shown that benefits accrue to "attractive" people—that is, to people deemed attractive by the standards of their specific culture. Compared to others, attractive people are better liked, believed to be more intelligent, and prove more likely to get and hold any given job.[5] They not only receive "undeserved" benefits from life, they avoid its worst punishments. For instance, these same studies show that attractive people are less likely than others to be arrested; if they are arrested, they are less likely than others to be convicted; and if they are convicted, they are less likely than others to serve time in jail. To cap this process of injustice, even when attractive people do go to jail, they spend less time there than other convicts.[6]

Continuing this examination of attractiveness, we know that Americans prefer tall to short and white to black. As we would expect, therefore, when a white or black person, equally qualified, apply for any given job, the white person is likely to be chosen.[7] Similarly, a tall person is more likely than a short person to be given a job, even when both hold the same credentials.[8] Indeed, this pattern is so powerful that in the entire history of American presidential elections, a candidate clearly shorter than the other has won office only four times.[9]

Deviation from a culture's norm of beauty is hardly fatal to our life chances. Still, it represents a modest hurdle. It subtly detracts from one's career potential. On an individual basis, it must be dealt with, compensated for. Consider famous people (the short Napoleon, the plain Eleanor Roosevelt, the handicapped Toulouse-Lautrec or Stephen Hawking) who have achieved brilliant success despite falling seriously short of their society's attractiveness norms. We can also think of individual examples, from among people we know, who are successful but not especially attractive, or—on the contrary—attractive but not particularly successful. "History" (and by implication, social science) "knows probabilities but not certainties," writes Stephen White,[10] reminding us that there are few rules of human behavior that don't allow for a number of exceptions.

Still, social science prefers generalization to exception, rule to deviant case; that is, attractiveness is an advantage. On the whole, those who come closest to their culture's ideal

---

[5] For a recent summary of these findings, see Robert B. Cialdini, *Influence: Science and Practice*, 3rd ed. (New York: Harper Collins College Publishers, 1993), pp. 140–42; see also David G. Myers, *Social Psychology*, 4th ed. (New York: McGraw-Hill, Inc., 1993), pp. 473–76.

[6] See the evidence cited in Myers, op. cit., pp. 354–55.

[7] See, for example, Richard Jenkins, *Racism and Recruitment: Managers, Organizations, and Equal Opportunity in the Labour Market* (Cambridge: Cambridge University Press, 1986), pp. 116–88. See also Andrew Hacker, *Two Nations: Black and White, Separate, Hostile, Unequal* (New York: Ballantine Books, 1992), especially his discussion of black–white differentials in income and employment in the U.S., pp. 93–133.

[8] For a summary and critique of the literature, see Wayne E. Hensley and Robin Cooper, "Height and Occupational Success: A Review and Critique," *Psychological Reports* 60 (1987): 843–49.

[9] The Clinton victory over Bush in 1992 may provide a fifth case. On paper, both candidates were listed as six feet, two inches tall, but most observers gave Bush a half-inch advantage over his challenger. This marginal difference does little to undermine the generalization that Americans like their leaders to be tall, since both men stood well above the height of the average middle-aged American male (around five feet, nine inches). Now if [Ross] Perot (five feet, four inches) had won the election, *that* would have represented a serious deviation from the pattern!

[10] Stephen White, *Political Culture and Soviet Politics* (London: Macmillan, 1979), p. x.

of beauty will, other things being equal, be better rewarded than others (with whatever that culture's idea of reward might happen to be—money, cows, penthouses, or poems written in their honor).

Those who doubt this point might ask themselves why one rarely sees an unattractive popular singer—especially in these days of MTV. Did nature really contrive to distribute musical potential only to those with pretty faces? From among the many talented singers available, generally we elevate to musical stardom only those people who also happen to meet our standards of beauty. The same point applies to a host of other social positions. Why are news anchors uniformly pleasant to look at? Is there really some correlation between looks and the ability to read from a teleprompter? Clearly, we can find thousands of excellent reporters in any country. Hundreds of these would be more than able to read aloud the day's news for us. From among this group, however, only the best-looking are chosen for this straightforward task.

You may be wondering: What on earth does this have to do with politics? The answer is simple. Politics is not some arcane ritual divorced from the life of society. It is inter-twined in the most integral way with all other social activity. *Political activity cannot be considered apart from society as a whole*, any more than blood can be considered apart from the body in which it circulates.

Political behavior reflects the culture in which it occurs. If a given society adulates strength, it will reward strong individuals. All social leaders of that culture, including polit-ical decisionmakers, will be aggressive. (Even those who aren't will strive to appear so, if they wish to achieve social status.) If a society prefers friendliness, it will choose amiable, cooperative types for all leadership posts, from president on down to head of the local ani-mal shelter. Pugnacious types in that culture will work at toning down their rough edges— or risk being ostracized.

Ruth Benedict found this precise pattern when she examined various North American indigenous peoples in the 1920s. The Pueblos, a peaceful and cooperative bunch, chose relatively weak, nonauthoritarian individuals to head their group. The Kwakiutl, on the other hand, an aggressive lot, chose their toughest and most assertive members for leader-ship positions.[11]

The simple *politics-reflects-culture* axiom explains a good deal about politics every-where. In a highly religious society, for example, political leaders will be emissaries of God on earth. Witness the doctrine of the divine rights of kings in the Middle Ages. Witness the political power of the Ayatollah Khomeini in the ardently religious Iran of the 1980s. By way of contrast, in a nonreligious (or antireligious) society (say, Russia under Marxist rule), political leaders too will be nonreligious or antireligious. In reverse, deeply religious people in a nonreligious society will rarely gain political power. They will most often be scorned and treated as outcasts, even persecuted as subversives.

In a moderately religious society like the United States, political leaders must be mod-erately religious—or at least believed to be. They must be seen going to church, invoking

---

[11]   See Ruth Benedict, *Patterns of Culture* (New York: The New American Library, 1934), esp. pp. 62–120 and 156–95. On the relation between cultural values and societal leadership patterns, see also Ruth Benedict, *Tales of the Indians* (Washington, D.C.: U.S. Government Printing Office, 1931), Margaret Mead, *Sex and Temperament in Three Primitive Societies* (New York: W. Morrow & Co., 1935), and David Riesman, *The Lonely Crowd: A Study of the Changing American Character* (Garden City, NY: Doubleday & Company, Inc., 1953), pp. 191–217.

God's will, praying publicly. Imagine the doleful fate awaiting the first presidential candidate bold enough (or foolish enough) to admit: I don't see much evidence of God's existence. In my humble opinion, prayer and churchgoing are a colossal waste of time, and I won't insult the intelligence of the American people by pretending otherwise. No such political leader exists in the United States today, nor should we expect one in the foreseeable future. On the other hand, excessive piety also works against someone seeking to rise in mainstream American politics. Many Americans feel uncomfortable around people who give voice regularly to intense religious fervor. Truly devout people rarely gain political power in the United States, thus joining atheists at the fringes of American politics.

Political activity, then, reflects cultural expectations. The proposition, used as a starting point, yields any number of useful predictions. We can confidently assert, for instance, that Americans will not soon elect any nonreligious person to the presidency. We also feel confident that they won't elect any clearly unattractive person to the Oval Office.

We must qualify and expand this last point. Remember the Tonga Islander's appreciation of fat? We can well imagine that the Tonga political leader is a large, burly fellow. (Indeed, I once came across a photograph of him and his wife, both towering over Great Britain's Queen Elizabeth, who was touring the island during a royal visit.) What one culture considers attractive, another may find distasteful. What, then, will an elected American president look like?

To begin, he will be a man—for reasons to be explained shortly. He will be tall—for reasons already explained. He will not be bald—Americans like men with a good head of hair. Indeed, in the history of this country (or at least since wigs went out of fashion), only two balding men have ever attained the presidential office. One was a national hero—General Dwight David Eisenhower. The other was something of a fluke: Gerald Ford. Through an odd chain of improbable events, Ford became president without ever facing the American electorate.[12] When he did try to win the voters' approval, in 1976, he lost a close race against Jimmy Carter, a man with a stylish head of hair. These two exceptions out of thirty-five presidents in the post-wig era do nothing but reinforce our conclusion: Men lacking in hirsute qualities will rarely make it to the top of the American political ladder.[13]

On another point of personal appearance, the president of the United States must be relatively thin. He certainly must not be overweight. Americans are so fanatical on this point that we can lay down the simple law: Anyone over ten percent heavier than average for his height and build will not be elected president. Think of all the significant presidential candidates we have seen in recent years: Jesse Jackson, Al Gore, Jerry Brown, Bob

---

[12]   Ford was the beneficiary—the only one so far—of the 25th Amendment to the U.S. Constitution, ratified only in 1967. This amendment set up a way to fill any vacancy that might occur in the vice-presidency. The amendment was put to use in 1973, when Spiro Agnew resigned from that office after corruption charges against him surfaced. President Richard Nixon then nominated Ford, minority leader in the House of Representatives, to replace Agnew, and Congress approved the appointment, making Ford vice-president. When Nixon himself resigned from the presidency a year later to avoid facing impeachment charges over the Watergate scandal, Ford acceded to the White House—having never faced the American electorate. Only residents of Michigan's Fifth Congressional District had ever voted for Ford before he gained the presidency.

[13]   Every ambitious politico is well aware of the phenomenon. More than one has addressed himself to the "misfortune" of hair loss. Within the last two decades, at least two senators who harbored hopes for the presidency undertook hair transplant treatment: William Proxmire and Joseph Biden.

Dole, Jack Kemp, Pat Robertson, Ross Perot. To a man, none is overweight. (When Ted Kennedy decided to run for president in 1980, he went on a diet and lost fifty pounds.) Among presidents themselves, none has been clearly obese since the days of William Howard Taft (1909–1913), who, at 300 pounds, stands out as an exceptional case. Exceptions can always occur, but we don't want to bet on them. Given the facts of American culture and the pattern of recent history, we can only conclude that it is advantageous to be thin if you harbor presidential ambitions.

Another matter of external appearance is crucial if you wish to become president. You must possess a friendly smile, one which gives you the appearance (at least) of being amiable and possessing a good sense of humor. Americans value these traits. Not all presidents have them, but most presidential contenders work at *appearing* to possess them— especially in recent years with the need to enhance one's television image uppermost in politicians' minds.[14]

Once into the spirit of this discussion, we can generate dozens of additional qualifications for candidates to the U.S. presidency. Among other requirements, for example, they must be (or at least seem to be) happily married and must have produced at least one healthy offspring. Nearly all our presidents fit this description. Only [James] Buchanan [1857–1861] was a bachelor. All other presidents were married, and most fathered several children.

American presidents, then, will be tall and well proportioned, possess a good head of hair, and show good teeth in a friendly smile, which they will display on all occasions. They will also have a supportive wife and at least one adoring child. To summarize: How many small, bald, overweight, scowling, single, childless men do you know with a serious chance at reaching the Oval Office?

What happens in politics, as these example illustrate, cannot be divorced from what happens in the rest of society. *A culture's deepest held values will be expressed in all its social institutions*. If society glorifies attractiveness, and if attractiveness is defined by height, hair, and smile, then those who are tall with nice hair and a cheerful grin will be advantaged in the struggle for political power.

WOMEN AND POLITICAL POWER

I have tried to use some amusing examples to get your attention. They may seem frivolous, but the principle they illustrate is profoundly important. Let us now apply it to a serious phenomenon. Our discussion of the attractiveness of U.S. presidential candidates focused entirely on men. The reason is obvious: We cannot generalize about the ideal features of a successful female presidential candidate. Not only have we never seen a successful woman candidate for president, but through the 1992 election we have not even seen a serious *potential* woman candidate for president!

---

[14] No one would quarrel with the assertion that television has stiffened the attractiveness requirement in all realms of American life, especially for those who must meet the public in their job—and that's one of the prime requirements for politicians. In short, the need for presidents to meet some kind of societal photogenic ideal has grown markedly in recent years, although I contend that it has never been absent from our history. The shrewd George Washington, for example, knew well the benefits of presenting an attractive image. He purposely made sure that he was always seen riding on a large white horse—to enhance his overall stature. (You will find no paintings of him on a steed of grey or brown.)

Some might argue this last point. Here's how I justify it. Let's define "a serious potential candidate" as anyone whom knowledgeable political observers would, one year before the next presidential election, place among the twenty people most likely to attain the Presidency. Under this admittedly loose definition, it is difficult to name *any* woman who might have *ever* qualified. Perhaps Pat Schroeder or Elizabeth Dole in 1987 would have made someone's list at number nineteen or twenty. Perhaps (though less likely) Shirley Chisholm might have made someone's list in 1971. But that's about it. The rule is clear. To be a serious candidate for president of the United States, even in this current era of feminism, you must be a man. (As I write these words in mid-1994, not one woman is being seriously suggested by anyone as a likely challenger to Bill Clinton in 1996.)

This absence of women at the very top of the political ladder is hardly a fluke. We don't find many women at the next rungs down either. No vice-president has ever been a woman. Only one vice-presidential *nominee* (out of roughly a hundred major party nominations) has ever been a woman—Geraldine Ferraro in 1984. We have never had more than four women in the Cabinet (out of ten to fourteen members, depending on the year), but the average number over the last twenty years has been two. (Before that, during the preceding 180 years, it was roughly zero.)

This pattern continues. No women can be found among the 101 justices named to the U.S. Supreme Court during its first 191 years. The first woman (Sandra Day O'Connor) reached the Court in 1981, and the second (Ruth Bader Ginsburg) twelve years later in 1993. (That makes two women currently on the nine-member Court—two out of the 108 Justices who have served since 1789.) The U.S. Senate has, over the past forty years, averaged two women members out of a hundred, although it had by mid-1993 reached its highest number ever: seven. The U.S. House of Representatives saw twenty to twenty-five female members (out of 435) from most of 1970 to 1990. (Before the 1994 elections, that number was approaching fifty—roughly, eleven percent of the total.) As late as 1994, the country had never had more than four women Governors in office at any given time (out of the fifty states). The total number of women in all state legislatures never attained the twenty percent level until 1993. The story continues in this vein; few women are in power, right down to school boards and town councils throughout the land.

Because women comprise the majority of the electorate, their drastic underrepresentation in nearly every political and governmental body is one of the most striking facts of American political life. To see this point more clearly, go back thirty years—or fifty. In those days, women were practically invisible in American politics.

They were, we must note in fairness, invisible in the political system of all other countries as well. Except for the occasional oddity of a powerful queen, women were missing from positions of power everywhere in the world until well into the twentieth century.

This absence of women from the structures of power is a vital political fact. After all, a number of studies suggest that when women do reach decision-making positions, they make different choices from those made by men.[15] For one thing, their energy is devoted to different issues. They work for day care funding, health services, and improvements to

---

[15]   For a good summary of this literature, see Rita Mae Kelly, Michelle A. Saint Germain, and Jody D. Horn, "Female Public Officials: A Different Voice?" *Annals of The American Academy of Political and Social Science* 515 (1991): 77–87. See also Debra Dodson and Susan Carroll, *Reshaping the Legislative Agenda: Women in State Legislatures* (New Brunswick, NJ: Center for the American

education rather than on tax policy, roadbuilding, and defense. They also vote differently from men. They show more support for social welfare programs and less for defense expenditures and business subsidies.

Whether you prefer these positions or not, the task of political analysis is to understand how politics works, and the point here is simple: *This dramatic absence of powerful women produces clear effects.* We as citizens get more conservative public policies than we would get if women were represented at something like their number in the population.

This phenomenon—the paucity of political women—is a central issue that touches us all. As students of politics, we must devote some time to understanding why it occurs. That means we must return to the concept of culture. It would be utterly impossible to explain the lack of women in power without reference to American norms, values, and social expectations. In other words, we must consider the broader culture within which U.S. politics take place.

Notice that if we try to understand this issue by examining narrower frameworks—the world of professional politics, for instance, or the realm of law—we get nowhere. Women aren't legally forbidden to run for political office. The political parties don't have rules preventing women from competing for nomination to public office. Voters don't even punish women who run for office by voting for their male competitors. When a man and a woman run against each other for any given office, studies show that (other things being equal) the man has no particular advantage.[16]

As far as law and politics go, then, women may freely compete for and win party nominations, go on to contest elections for office, and suffer no negative voter reaction when they do. Why, then, don't we find as many women *inside* politics as we do *outside* it, among the electorate?

Scholars have developed dozens of theories to explain this well-known phenomenon. We would need an entire book to account fully for it.[17] Yet one variable stands out as a central inhibitor of women's political activism. That is a simple but deepseated norm of American culture: Women, not men, have prime responsibility for the duties of homemaking and childrearing. Nowhere is this statement written down as law, but deeply implanted cultural beliefs have a stronger effect on human behavior than laws, which themselves are merely a reflection of those cultural beliefs. It will pay us to examine this norm and its many ramifications.

First, let's acknowledge it: Support for this norm is diminishing rapidly. We are all familiar with the changing relationship between men and women in our times, with the decline of traditional gender roles and norms. Still, the idea that women are homemakers and childrearers continues to maintain a significant hold on our society. But *even if it didn't,* I am going to argue, its near-universal acceptance in the recent past goes a long way toward explaining the small number of powerful women in the United States of the 1990s.

Woman and Politics, 1991); Susan Carroll, Debra Dodson, and Ruth Mandel, *The Impact of Women in Public Office* (New Brunswick, NJ: Center for the American Woman and Politics, 1991), esp. chap. 5; Sue Thomas, *How Women Legislate* (New York: Oxford University Press, 1994); and Joni Lovenduski and Pippa Norris, *Gender and Political Parties* (London: Sage, 1993).

[16]   See, for example, the evidence cited in R. Darcy, Susan Welch, and Janet Clark, *Women, Elections and Representation* (New York: Longman, 1987), pp. 51–57 and 75–77.

[17]   Many books already exist on the subject. Among the more useful, see Darcy Welch, and Clark, op. cit., and Vicky Randall, *Women and Politics* (New York: St. Martin's Press, 1982).

Why? Let us begin with a straightforward assertion: *power takes time to accumulate.* You have to work your way up the hierarchies of influence. Just as no one springs full-blown into the presidency of General Motors, so no one leaps from obscurity into the U.S. Senate.[18] Those who reach the upper levels of the American political system need first to attain education, status and wealth and then convert those assets into the skills that produce political clout.

Many skills are needed to become a political leader: speaking ability, self-confidence, and persuasiveness, to name a few. You also need a variety of resources. Wealth is perhaps the most obvious one. Having good connections is another.

But of all the resources needed to become influential in American politics, two are especially crucial for explaining the predominance of men over women at the upper levels of power. First, you need a good deal of *time* to develop those political skills, mentioned previously, that are crucial to political success. You also need time to convince a broad public segment that you actually have those skills and should be rewarded for having them.

In other words, you don't graduate from high school and get elected a senator. You have to study for and earn a college degree then work for and attain a graduate degree (typically the law), then win a seat on some local or regional body (city council, county board of commissioners), then spend some time in the state legislature, go on to win a statewide office (attorney general, lieutenant governor), then perhaps gain your state's governorship or a seat in the U.S. House of Representatives, and finally after several years in one of these latter posts, make your bid for a U.S. Senate seat.

Naturally, there are other ways up the ladder of power, but all of them have this in common: They take time, and they don't come easily.

The difficulty of attaining political success leads to the second key requirement for gaining that success: *motivation.* There are few accidental powerholders in this world. *Those who get power want it and want it badly.* Consider the enormous expenditure of effort it takes to follow the previous scenario for political success. To be willing to exert yourself doggedly onward for years in order to rise to some serious level of political influence you must be deeply motivated. That is to say, you must be career oriented, focused on making your way into the world, and willing to suffer those "slings and arrows of outrageous fortune," which are always associated with the bruising career path you have chosen. You must eat, sleep, and breathe politics—for years and years, from young adulthood to middle age—to have a reasonable chance of arriving at the upper-middle to upper levels of the political power hierarchy.[19]

Now who is likely to start out in young adulthood with that orientation? Consider the U.S. political hierarchy as it currently exists (the mid-1990s). Given the time it takes to

---

[18] Well, almost no one. Exceptions do occur, on occasion. One of the most dramatic was the election of Joseph Biden to the U.S. Senate from Delaware in 1972. At the time he was twenty-nine years old, and his entire political experience prior to that date consisted of two years on the Wilmington (Del.) City Council! In fact, Biden was so young that he did not turn thirty until two weeks *after* his election to the Senate and had to keep reassuring people during the campaign that he would be old enough to take his seat if elected. (The U.S. Constitution forbids anyone under thirty from serving as a U.S. senator, although it doesn't prohibit voters from *electing* someone under thirty to the Senate.)

[19] On the energy needed to move forward in politics, see James L. Payne and Oliver H. Woshinsky, "Incentives for Political Participation," *World Politics* 24 (1972): 518–46, esp. pp. 518–21.

reach a serious level of political power, we can see that few powerholders will be much under forty years of age.[20] Of course, there will be many exceptions, but let's focus on the norm. The median age of the average powerholder in the United States today is somewhere in the range of forty-five to sixty years.

We start, then, with this age factor. You are going to be middle-aged or older before reaching serious political power. And this power doesn't just come and tap you on the shoulder. You need to make an intense commitment of your energies and resources for years and years if you wish to gain power. You don't, in other words, spend twenty years as an accountant or an architect or an assembly-line worker and then suddenly decide to become governor or senator. Or to put it more accurately, if you do decide to make that kind of midlife career decisions, you have little hope of fulfilling it. If you haven't decided on a political career path by age thirty (or better still, by twenty or twenty-five), you aren't likely to rise far in politics.

I can think of one modest exception to this point. A person can occasionally trade power in some other line of work for political clout. A few people manage to make these lateral transfers from some other activity into political positions of real power; General Eisenhower, Ronald Reagan, and even Ross Perot are good examples. These people represent the world of the military, celebrityhood, and business. Going further back into the past, we can find similar examples: George Washington and Andrew Jackson from the military, for instance, celebrities like Horace Greeley or Will Rogers, and businessmen like William Randolph Hearst and Wendell Wilkie. All converted their fame from nonpolitical achievements into political influence of one kind or another *without* spending decades in the political process itself.

These seeming exceptions, on close examination, do little more than support the basic rule: You *still* must start early in life if you wish to attain political power. After all, these people who moved into politics from nonpolitical careers had first gained power for themselves in *another* key decision-making arena of society. All had clearly started early in life down the road toward power attainment. All had been obliged to struggle upward for years in their chosen profession. All needed decades of perseverance to reach a point at which they could trade the resource of power in their own career path for power in the world of politics.

These "exceptions" merely underline, then, the main proposition. *Political power is rarely attained without two or three decades of grueling effort,* beginning usually during the ages of twenty to thirty.

We must confront one additional fact before putting this argument together to explain why few women are currently found in positions of political power in the United States. A number of studies have shown that the average person's value system (his or her outlook on life) is shaped, roughly, during ages fifteen to twenty-five.[21] It will, of course, vary considerably from person to person. Furthermore, beliefs, once developed, aren't permanent;

---

[20] By "powerholder" in the United States, I am referring essentially to the president, vice-president, Cabinet and sub-Cabinet officers, House members, senators, Supreme Court justices, federal judges, governors, state legislative leaders, big-city mayors, top lobbyists, top political aides, and top media people.

[21] See, for example, Angus Campbell, Philip E. Converse, Warren E. Miller, and Donald Stokes, *The American Voter* (Chicago: University of Chicago Press, 1960), chap. 7; and M. Kent Jennings and Richard G. Niemi, *Generations and Politics: A Panel Study of Young Adults and Their Parents* (Princeton: Princeton University Press, 1981), chap. 4.

most people undergo modest changes in their thinking during the course of life. Still, the bulk of evidence suggests that after age thirty, at the latest, most of us will not deviate seriously from the central perspectives on life that we developed by that age.

By thirty, that means, most of us are pretty well set in our views on politics, religion, and society. We are liberal or conservative, feminist or traditionalist, religious or agnostic, rigid toward minorities or tolerant. For most of us, those perspectives developed early and often unconsciously, came to be understood and expressed between ages fifteen and twenty, then matured and hardened in the following decade. By thirty, we have a full-fledged world outlook and cling to it for the rest of life. With these facts in mind we conclude by simple mathematics that Americans aged about fifty today began to absorb their essential view of gender roles some time in the late 1950s.

Let us now put all of these points together. Average powerholders in the United States today are forty-five to sixty years old. These people must have *decided* to start seeking power in their twenties. There basic outlook on life started being shaped ten years before that—in their teens. The vast majority of people who currently hold power today, then, came of age between 1950 and 1970. Imprinted on their brain cells are the ideas that dominated that era. And what were those ideas? Whatever else we associate with that time, it was characterized by traditional norms about the division of labor between men and women. It was the era of suburbia and the baby boom. Men were to have careers, whereas women were to raise children and keep house. Public activities (like politics) were for men, whereas private activities (the home) was the proper sphere for women.

"The past is a foreign country," said L. P. Hartley. "They do things differently there."[22] It is always hard to enter the mind-set of another era, but we must try. Although it may seem incredible, women were *forbidden* to enter most law schools as late as the early 1970s. Women were legally *forced* to take their husband's name upon marriage. They could not get credit in their own names. Single women could not obtain mortgages to buy houses. These examples could continue for pages. The National Organization for Women (NOW), a crucial pressure group for women's rights in our time, was not even founded until 1966. No one noticed the event. NOW hardly entered national consciousness until the 1970s. *Ms. Magazine* published its first issue in 1972. The first woman elected governor in her own right (not as the spouse of some famous politician) was Ella Grasso of Connecticut in 1974.

People coming of age in the 1940s, 1950s, and 1960s—that is, those people most likely to be at the height of their political careers in the *1990s*—would have developed their political and social beliefs at a time when current feminist ideals stressing women's equality with men were hardly imagined by the average American citizen, male *or* female. Indeed, the precept that men have careers and women raise children was perhaps *at its height* when Americans who are currently middle-aged first came of political and social consciousness.

This cultural outlook, deeply ingrained in the children of the 1950s, gave a tremendous power advantage to the young men of that time over young women. A female baby boomer, by ages fifteen to twenty, would have accepted the norm that her social duty was to get married and start raising children. She might someday expect to "get a job," primarily to

---

[22]   L.P. Hartley, *The Go-Between* (London: H. Hamilton, 1953), Prologue, p. 9.

"help out" with family expenses, but she was rarely expected to *have a career*, especially not in any walk of life involving competition for power.

In only a few work areas was the 1950s woman actually allowed a career. We know those specialties are the "caring" or "nurturing" professions (teaching, nursing, secretarial help). They symbolized an extension of the "primary" female role and, as such, presented no threat to men. These jobs derived from activities centered on the home, from the women's role there as nurturer, caregiver, and helper. Most men didn't want these jobs, so women moved into them. Indeed, men encouraged them to do so.

Teenage males, by way of contrast, had been raised in the expectation of spending their entire lives building careers. At the least, they knew that they had to prepare for a life of continuous work outside the home, work in the paid labor force, in order to support a family (that is, wife and children).

Society taught these norms to most young people in the 1940s, 1950s, and 1960s. True, not everyone conformed. Some women raised in the 1950s sought careers and attained power. Some men of that era stayed home and raised children. They were the exceptions, however. The vast majority of people raised in that time behaved as the norms of that day dictated. Men finished school and went right to work. Many pursued careers associated with power—in the world of business, the military, law, or politics. Women raised children and shunned careers—except in a few traditional areas that never lead to societal power. (Quick! Name a famous librarian. Name a renowned nurse. Name a celebrated fourth-grade teacher. Get the point?)

These norms and work patterns devastated women's chances of ever reaching political power. First, they made women feel that the world of politics was for men only; hence, they simply stayed out of it. Furthermore, the skills that women developed from the activities they did engage in (childrearing) were not, in any obvious way, directly transferable to the world of politics. Knowing how to potty train a two-year-old does not help you learn to give a rousing political speech. Knowing how to teach a six-year-old to read doesn't help you become an expert on defense policy. Knowing how to cook macaroni-and-cheese doesn't help you learn the subtle art of winning party nominations.

Finally, the time and effort that women had to put into the years of childbearing, childrearing, and homemaking insured that they would be unable to devote much attention to the world of power gathering until it was essentially "too late." That is, if a woman in her early twenties started having children and had three or four (as was the norm for 1950s families), she would probably find herself in her early forties before her last child had entered the teen years and become reasonably independent. If she *then* decided to embark on a career that might lead to a power position, notice how greatly disadvantaged she became, in comparison to her male contemporaries (also in their early forties) who had been doggedly pursuing that very career path for the last twenty years.

Of course, the knowledge gained by women in those intervening years counts for something. Maturity and experience are assets that can be converted into skills that are useful in the struggle for power. But even with the best efforts and the best will in the world from well-wishers in society, any person, male or female, just starting out to achieve something at forty-two is at a severe disadvantage compared with another person of forty-two who has been pursuing that same objective since age sixteen (or twenty-three or twenty-eight).

This chain of reasoning suggests that by the time some woman, who doesn't decide until her forties to get into politics, starts to amass a serious amount of influence, she will be reaching, roughly, age sixty or older, a time when most people are more likely to be thinking of retirement than of continuing the difficult struggle for political power. Furthermore, voters and party activists (especially in youth-obsessed America) may start looking for a younger candidate to fill whatever job the sixty-year-old woman has her eye on.

In short, even if a middle-aged woman successfully gets past her early socialization into traditional gender roles, completes her decades of childrearing with some reasonable level of energy left to embark on her own career, and even if she does quite well at developing that career, she is *still* likely to arrive too late at the threshold of power to be able to make the leap over that threshold and into real power itself before deciding, or having the matter decided for her by a fickle electorate, that she is "too old" to be promoted any further up the rungs of the political ladder.

As if these facts weren't harsh enough, we must add yet another array of grim data. The older any population gets, the more likely it is that its members will fall by the wayside, succumbing to a variety of illnesses that either kill them or force them out of serious competition for power. These are statistical generalizations, but overall they hurt women badly in the struggle for upward political mobility. Let's say it takes twenty-five years on average to go from the day you receive your law degree to the U.S. Senate. If you get your degree at age twenty-seven, you will become senator at fifty-two. Few healthy Americans of age twenty-seven die before age fifty-two. Most don't even get seriously ill in that time frame.

But if you don't decide to start law school until age forty-two (when your children are grown), then you don't get your law degree until age forty-five, and you don't get to the Senate until you are seventy! Now many more Americans die, or become seriously ill, between forty-two and seventy than between twenty-two and fifty. Simply on the basis of these cruel facts of illness and mortality, we would expect that many fewer women than men would get to high levels of power, *if* women start their careers twenty years later. And we have already shown that they are likely to do exactly that, if they were born in the United States some time between 1945 and 1970.

Notice how far we have come. We have gained some serious insights into a key political pattern, by following a simple line of reasoning.

> *Cultures affect politics. Specifically, cultures affect politics by implanting deep-seated norms into people's heads, norms that affect how people behave in the social world. One deep-seated norm in American society of the 1940s and 1950s held that men and women were to play different roles in life, men seeking careers aimed at giving them wealth, power, fame, and status, and women staying at home to raise families. This gender-division norm from the 1950s explains why men dominated American politics in the 1980s and 1990s.*

This example illustrates the power of a social analysis that begins by focusing on culture.

WOMEN AND POLITICS: A NEW ERA

Incidentally, we can use this same approach to explain a dramatic new trend on the American political scene. The era of few women in American politics is coming to an end. Indeed, we are now witnessing the definite emergence of women onto the political scene and their rise to the upper level of American institutions. The 1990s appears to be the decade when women finally gained a serious share of political power.

Why have women gained their recent clout in politics? To answer that question, we must return to the same reasoning we used to explain why women were rarely found in politics in earlier years. If the norms young people absorb in their teenage years traditionally helped men and hurt women in the long-term struggle for political power, then changing those norms could make the playing field level. And changing norms is exactly what happened.

Even before the mid-1960s, some Americans had started questioning traditional gender roles.[23] Traditional attitudes began seriously eroding by 1970, and by the mid-1970s the modern feminist movement was in full swing. Indeed, by the 1980s it was taken for granted by the majority of Americans that women should have legal equality with men, that they had the right to pursue careers of their own, and that governments should work to obliterate the most egregious forms of gender discrimination.[24]

Given this development, we fully expect to find, as time goes by, an increasing number of women at the upper levels of all prestigious, power-wielding institutions of American life. Specifically, we can even predict that by the time women who were around fifteen in 1975 reach fifty, the number of women in serious positions of political power will look a great deal more like equality than it does now. That means keep a sharp eye out for the year 2010!

Just to be cautious, I'll predict numerical gender equality at all levels of American politics by the year 2020. I will also predict an increasing number of women in political power as each year passes between now and then.

We don't have to wait long to check on this prediction. Just in case it doesn't pan out, however, I have an explanation at the ready. Change is a law of life, but no trend is irreversible. The drive toward a redefinition of woman's traditional homemaker's role could peter out or reverse itself, depending on future social, economic, and cultural developments, which no one can foresee. Perhaps the Dan Quayle-Pat Robertson perspective on these matters will gather steam and overwhelm the forces of the Hillary Clintons and Donna Shalalas. I doubt it, but stranger developments have occurred in history. Who would have predicted the rise of fundamental Islam in the Middle East, setting back for decades the cause of women's rights in that region? I am personally betting on the advance of gender equality in the United States (and everywhere else, for that matter), but ultimately only time will tell.[25]

It is important to note that there exist few universal generalizations about human behavior. A given pattern today may or may not exist tomorrow. That depends on what

---

[23] The most famous and influential example of this questioning came in 1963 from Betty Friedan in her groundbreaking and eloquent plea for feminism, *The Feminine Mystique* (New York: Dell Publishing Company, 1963). For a survey of efforts on behalf of women's rights in this era, see Susan M. Hartmann, *From Margin to Mainstream: American Women and Politics since 1960* (New York: Alfred A. Knopf, 1989), esp. pp. 48–71.

[24] On recent American attitudes toward gender equality, see the data reported by Virginia Sapiro, "Feminism: A Generation Later," in *Annals of the American Academy of Political and Social Science* 515 (1991): 10–22.

[25] For a chilling vision of a different future from the one I imagine, a future in which American women lose all rights and become oppressed slaves, read Margaret Atwood's grim novel, *The Handmaid's Tale* (Boston: Houghton Mifflin, 1986).

caused the pattern and on whether or not those causes change. Change the cause of some human behavior, and you will change the behavior as well.[26]

These propositions apply specifically to the issue under discussion: gender equality. The cause of male political domination lies in the gender norms of our culture, which have been undergoing change. We should hardly be surprised to see these new norms produce a different set of effects. Our societal values once favored men; now they stress equality. They insured male domination of politics in the past. Now and into the foreseeable future they encourage a trend toward male-female sharing of political power.

Whether one hates or supports this development, it exists and it produces important political outcomes. Our job is to describe and explain. Powerful women were scarce in the past because of traditional cultural norms. Powerful women are more numerous now and will be much more numerous in the future because of modern cultural norms. If you wish to understand American politics—past, present, and future—you have to know these facts.

Now if you want to reverse or quicken the trend, that's another matter altogether. You must then get involved in politics and work to achieve your goals. The analyst's job is not to teach what your goals should be, but to help you understand the world as it is. What you wish the world to be is your own business. When you start trying to change the world to match your own desires, you become a political participant, an activist, and part of the very world that analysts like me work to explain. If you take that route, I wish you the very best of luck as you set off to realize your aims. In the meantime, I shall get back to the task at hand: explaining the world of politics as it currently works.

SUMMARY

Norms—deepseated beliefs about how people should behave—produce a powerful effect on society. When most people in any culture share a norm, they will act in a manner congruent with that norm. Norms, to put it simply, influence social behavior. It follows that any norm in any culture will influence political behavior, since all behavior is intertwined. We cannot separate social from economic from political activity.

This [text] has provided several examples of the way cultural norms affect politics. These examples merely scratch the surface. We could multiply them indefinitely. To understand the wellsprings of political action, we must learn the norms that underpin human thought. When we see any given pattern of political behavior, we must ask what cultural outlook has produced that particular way of dealing with political issues. This perspective, one that owes much to the insights of *cultural anthropology*,[27] will guide our thinking as we move forward to learn about the many, varied forms of political behavior.

---

[26]   Of course, change may be a long time in coming, especially if the original cause has existed for decades and has had time to create deeply imbedded attitudes and behavior patterns.

[27]   For the classic expression of this perspective, see Benedict, *Patterns of Culture*, op. cit. For a recent summary of the approach, see Michael C. Howard, *Contemporary Cultural Anthropology*, 2nd ed. (Boston: Little, Brown and Company, 1986).

Chapter 4

The Classical Greeks: How to be a Citizen

KENNETH MINOGUE*

__Kenneth Minogue__ is Emeritus Professor of Political Science at the London School of Economics and Political Science.

Politics among the ancient Greeks was a new way of thinking, feeling, and above all being related to one's fellows. Citizens varied in wealth, beauty, and intelligence, but as citizens they were equal. This was because citizens were rational, and the only appropriate relation between rational beings is that of persuasion. Persuasion differs from command in assuming equality between speaker and listener. Plato provides a noble vision of this form of political life in his dialogue the *Crito*. The philosopher Socrates, having been sentenced to death for corrupting the youth, refused the offer of help to escape Athens, arguing that to flee would be rationally inconsistent with the commitment to the city expressed in the way he had lived his whole life. Even the mode of his execution reflected this basic belief that violence was not an appropriate relation between citizens: he was given a cup of hemlock to drink. The Greek freely obeyed the law of his *polis* and was proud to do so. His very identity was bound up with his city. The worst of fates was exile, a form of civic death sometimes imposed by the convention of ostracism on Athenian statesmen whose power was thought to threaten the constitution.

Among the Greeks we find most of the conditions of freedom: a life lived among equals, subject only to law, and ruling and being ruled in turn. The Greeks were the first historical people to create societies having this form; certainly they were the first to create a literature exploring it as an experience. Politics was the activity specific to this new thing called a 'citizen'. It might take many forms, even the debased forms of tyranny and usurpation, but on one thing the later classical Greeks were adamant: oriental despotism was not politics.

Such is the formal position, and these were the forms which left so deep an imprint on our civilization. The reality was no doubt a great deal more complex. Democratic and oligarchic factions fought bitter battles within cities. Farmers lived on the edge of destitution, and bad harvests might impel them towards debt slavery. Equality within cities was not matched by equal relations *between* cities, and war was endemic. The Greeks were a talkative, passionate people, and their politics was often violent and sometimes corrupt. None of this qualifies, however, the fact that they were capable of brilliant exploits, such as their victory in repelling (and ultimately conquering) their Persian neighbours. In reading much of the literature of their time, we find it easy to think of them as our contemporaries: being rationalists, they speak across the millenniums to us, their cultural descendants, with a deceptive fluency. For all the common ground, however, they were immensely different from us, in their religion, their customs, and their conception of human life. It is this difference which makes studying their civilization so exhilarating.

The Greeks were humanists, but of a kind strikingly different from the humanism (transformed by Christianity) found in the modern world. Their basic proposition was that man is a rational animal, and that the meaning of human life is found in the exercise of rationality. When men succumbed to the passions, they were shamefully descending to a lower form of being. When pride, or hubris, led them to think they were gods, they lost sight of their human limitations and suffered nemesis, the destructive resentment of the gods. The secret of life was human self-knowledge, and a balanced expression of one's human capacities. In deliberating about law and public policy, man found his highest and purest form of self-expression. It could only be enjoyed in the political life of a city.

Humanists often look to the Greeks as ancestors, but their view of the world has one remarkable (and in modern terms, disturbing) implication. Since some are less rational than others, so also are they less human. Slaves in particular are defective in rationality when compared to masters. Those who explored this view, above all the philosopher Aristotle, were perfectly aware that some slaves are clever and some masters stupid; they were merely expounding what they took to be the rational foundation of the institution itself. Again, women were taken to be less rational than men, though Aristotle considered the barbarians to be quite wrong in thinking that they were indistinguishable from slaves. Citizenship was thus confined to free adult males, and in some cities not even to all of those. The activity of politics and that of waging war merged with each other, and it thus seemed natural that women should live domestic lives: they could hardly stand their ground in a phalanx. It might seem that, in taking this view, the Greeks were the prisoners of the prejudices of their time. Being immensely imaginative in their exploration of the world, however, they had no difficulty imagining women doing any number of things: becoming warriors in the form of Amazons; going on a sexual strike to enforce peace in the *Lysistrata* of Aristophanes: taking the role of philosopher-rulers in the Guardians of Plato's *Republic*; but these images were not the reality of everyday life.

The laws and policies of a Greek city emerged, then, not from the palace of a despot, but from discussion among notionally equal citizens in the *agora*, the market-place which also generally served as the arena of politics. Citizens enjoyed equality before the law (*isonomia*, a term sometimes used as a synonym for democracy) and an equal opportunity to speak in the assembly. In a large city such as Athens, thousands of people might turn up to such meetings, so that the speakers were predominantly aristocrats who had studied the art of speaking, or notable leaders who had managed to acquire a band of supporters. In democracies, many offices were filled by lot, but the main officers were elected and were commonly from powerful families. In Thucydides' history of the Peloponnesian War we can see the democratic process at work—for example in the Athenian debate, reported in Book III, as to how the people of Mitylene, who had rebelled against Athenian hegemony, should be punished. In this debate, the popular leader Cleon put the case for confirming the decision already taken to kill the men and sell the women and children into slavery. Cleon appealed to realism: if you want to have an empire, he argued, then you must be prepared to do the ruthless things necessary to keep it together. His opponent, Diodotus, argued for clemency on the ground that ruthlessness would merely turn every occasion of revolt among the clients of Athens into a life and death struggle. It was Diodotus who triumphed in this vivid intellectual contest.

The citizens who participated in the debates belonged in their private lives to households (*oikia*) which were the basic productive units of this ancient world. The *oikos* (from which our term 'economics' derives) was a system of orderly subordination described by Aristotle: subordination of female to male, of children to parents, and of slaves to masters. The household was the sphere in which the Greeks enjoyed family life and largely supplied their material needs: for food, warmth, shelter, procreation, and so on. Here was the world of nature in which everything had its season. In many civilizations, the distinction between artifice and nature is not developed, but it was the basis of the Greek understanding of the world. The idea that wisdom consisted in following the dictates of nature led to divergent philosophies, according to the way in which the concept of 'nature' developed. Greek political philosophy began in meditation upon the tension between recognizing that the *polis* was in one sense natural and in another sense a thing of artifice.

On becoming an adult, the young Greek male could step out of the household into the *agora,* where he found the freedom to transcend natural necessity and take responsibility, uttering words worth remembering and doing deeds that might give him a kind of immortality. The Greeks of the classical period were self-conscious enough to see themselves as a distinct culture, and it is in creating a historical understanding of themselves and their world that they were opening up quite new possibilities of human experience. Politics and history were thus born together, for they share the same conception of what a human being is, and what is worth remembering.

History was the memory of words and deeds, and words were the vehicles of memory. in political activity, men addressed each other in speech, which is a skill to be learned. It requires the marshalling of ideas, the construction of arguments, the capacity to understand an audience, a recognition of the dominant passions of human nature, and much else. For the first time in history, public decisions were made in the clear light of day and subject to open criticism. The skill of rhetoric was codified by teachers called 'sophists' for the benefit of ambitious young aristocrats whose power depended on swaying a popular audience. A speech was a performance to be remembered down the ages. Thucydides tells the story of the Peloponnesian War largely in terms of the arguments adduced in the speeches of the participants; taken together, these speeches amount to a comprehensive manual on political wisdom and political folly.

This approach to political thought and action was the product of one striking false belief, which remains influential to this day: the idea that everything in the world was the result of deliberate design. The Greeks believed their own cities to have been founded by semi-divine figures, such as Lycurgus in the case of Sparta, and Thekus in the case of Athens. Wise men were sometimes called on to restore some such design if it had fallen into disrepair. In politics, the most famous case of this was that of Solon at Athens in the early part of the sixth century BC. Two features of Solon's reforms illustrate essential features of Greek politics.

The first is that he was careful to base politics on territorial units which mixed up clan or tribal loyalties. The modern constituency, which lumps together all the heterogeneous people living in a given area, has the same effect of breaking down natural loyalties and encouraging people to act politically in terms of broad interests shared widely throughout a community.

The second is that, after establishing his reforms, Solon was careful to leave Athens for ten years so that the new constitution could be operated by others—an early version of the principle of the separation of powers. For the key to politics in the strict sense is that it is a nexus of abstract offices to which duties are attached, and in principle the work may be done by any competent office-holder. Whereas despotism depends on the personality (and often the caprice) of the individual despot, political rulers act in terms of the duties attaching to their offices.

The set of offices by which a *polis* was governed, and the laws specifying their relation, are the constitution. Government without a constitution would lack the specific kind of moral limitation which distinguishes politics. Constitutions function in two essential ways: they circumscribe the power of the office-holders, and as a result they create a predictable (though not rigid and fixed) world in which the citizens may conduct their lives. It is constitutions which give form to politics, and the study of them led to the emergence of political science.

A science of politics (as opposed to despotism) is possible because politics itself follows regular patterns, even though it is ultimately at the mercy of the human nature from which it arises. All that one can confidently say about despotism is that able rulers will sooner or later be followed by mad or feeble heirs. A despotism is thus subject to a fixed rhythm of rise and fall, like the seasons, and this confirmed the Greeks in their belief that despotisms, as associations of slaves, were unfree and belonged to the non-rational sphere of nature. But constitutions, because they belong to the sphere of rationality, can be studied in a more scientific way than despotisms, despite their ultimate fallibility.

For one thing, they can be classified according to certain characteristics which reveal dominant tendencies. In all constitutions, the ruler is either a monarch, or a small group of powerful leaders, or a popular assembly. There are no other possibilities than that rule must be by one, or a few, or by the many. During the classical period of Greek politics, the main division was between oligarchic states, which were thought to favour the rich and powerful, and democracies, which responded to the interests of the poor, and which were commonly thought violent and unstable.

Greek political science studied constitutions and generalized the relation between human nature and political associations. Perhaps its most powerful instrument was the theory of recurrent cycles. Monarchies tend to degenerate into tyranny, tyrannies are overthrown by aristocracies, which degenerate into oligarchies exploiting the population, which are overthrown by democracies, which in turn degenerate into the intolerable instability of mob rule, whereupon some powerful leader establishes himself as a monarch and the cycle begins all over again. This is the version of political science we find influentially expounded by a later Greek called Polybius whose main concern was to explain the character of Roman politics to his fellow Greeks; other versions of a political cycle are to be found in Plato and Aristotle.

Knowledge, as [Sir Francis] Bacon remarked, is power, and the knowledge of this cyclical rhythm in politics provoked the thought that institutions might be arranged in such a way as to break the cycle, allowing states to achieve, if not immortality, at least some long-term stability. The secret of breaking the cycle of decline lay in two propositions. The first was that government consists of a number of functions which may be parcelled out among different offices and assemblies. Executive decision requires a leader, deliberation about policy requires a small group of experienced citizens, while the acceptability of laws and the responsiveness of government depend upon effective ways of consulting the people. This is an argument for constructing a constitution in which power is distributed between the one, the few, and the many. The second proposition is that the very same distribution may also balance the interests of rich and poor, to prevent either from using political power for the purpose of economic exploitation. Such balance in politics was the equivalent of health in the body, and might keep corruption at bay for a very long time. Such is the theory of the balanced constitution which has played a central part in the politics of the West. It represents as a theory what practical politicians often evolve for themselves. The English constitution, for example, evolved into a balance between monarch, Commons, and Lords and is often cited as an example of this theory. Lawyers and statesmen were, indeed, aware of the theory, and sometimes it helped to guide them, but the actual institutions of British politics responded basically to the specific conditions of life in Britain.

It was Aristotle's view that some element of democracy was essential to the best kind of balanced constitution, which he called a 'polity'. He studied many constitutions, and was particularly interested in the mechanics of political change: revolutions, he thought, always arose out of some demand for equality. Concerning himself with both politics and ethics, he posed one question which has been found especially fascinating: can a good citizen be a good man? Rulers in some states may demand of their subjects actions which are wrong. Greek politics (like everything else in the Greek world) was powerfully theorized, to such an extent that it has often been thought that we rattle around within the limited set of possibilities revealed to us by Greek experience. Political judgement, to put the matter another way, is a choice between finite possibilities. This view assumes that human nature is fixed, and has been challenged, especially in modern times, by the view that human beings are always the creatures of their society. Very few possibilities that we discuss were not recognized in one form or another by the Greeks, who also left behind—indeed, it was their speciality—visions of the ideal: in philosophy, Plato's *Republic*, and in politics, the account of Athens put into the mouth of Pericles by Thucydides in his history of the Peloponnesian War.

Chapter 5

Globalization Then and Now

WAYNE ELLWOOD*

* **Wayne Ellwood** *is an editor with* New Internationalist *magazine.*

Globalization is a new word which describes an old process: the integration of the global economy that began in earnest with the launch of the European colonial era five centuries ago. But the process has accelerated over the past 30 years with the explosion of computer technology, the dismantling of barriers to the movement of goods and capital, and the expanding political and economic power of multinational corporations.

More than five centuries ago, in a world without electricity, cell phones, refrigeration, DVDs, the internet, automobiles, airplanes or nuclear weapons, one man had a foolish dream. Or so it seemed at the time. Cristóbal Colón, an ambitious young Genoese sailor and adventurer, was obsessed with Asia—a region about which he knew nothing, apart from unsubstantiated rumors of its colossal wealth. Such was the strength of his obsession (some say his greed) that he was able to convince the King and Queen of Spain to finance a voyage into the unknown across a dark, seemingly limitless expanse of water then known as the Ocean Sea. His goal: to find the Grand Khan of China and the gold that was reportedly there in profusion.

Centuries later Colón would become familiar to millions of school children across the West as Christopher Columbus, the famous 'discoverer' of the Americas. In fact, the 'discovery' was more of an accident. The intrepid Columbus never did reach Asia, not even close. Instead, after five weeks at sea, he found himself sailing under a tropical sun into the turquoise waters of the Caribbean, making his landfall somewhere in the Bahamas, which he promptly named San Salvador (the Savior). The place clearly delighted Columbus' weary crew. They loaded up with fresh water and unusual foodstuffs. And they were befriended by the island's indigenous population, the Taino.

'They are the best people in the world and above all the gentlest,' Columbus wrote in his journal. 'They very willingly showed my people where the water was, and they themselves carried the full barrels to the boat, and took great delight in pleasing us. They became so much our friends that it was a marvel.'[1]

Twenty years and several voyages later, most of the Taino were dead and the other indigenous peoples of the Caribbean were either enslaved or under attack. Globalization, even then, had moved quickly from an innocent process of cross-cultural exchange to a nasty scramble for wealth and power. As local populations died off from European diseases or were literally worked to death by their captors, thousands of European colonizers followed. Their desperate quest was for gold and silver. But the conversion of heathen souls to the Christian faith gave an added fillip to their plunder. Eventually European settlers colonized most of the new lands to the north and south of the Caribbean.

---

[1] *The Conquest of Paradise: Christopher Columbus and the Columbian Legacy*, Kirkpatrick Sale (Knopf, New York, 1990).

Columbus' adventure in the Americas was notable for many things, not least his focus on extracting as much wealth as possible from the land and the people. But more importantly his voyages opened the door to 450 years of European colonialism. And it was this centuries-long imperial era that laid the groundwork for today's global economy.

OLD GLOBALIZATION

Although globalization has become a commonplace term in recent years, many people would be hard-pressed to define what it actually means. The lens of history provides a useful beginning. Globalization is an age-old process and one firmly rooted in the experience of colonialism. One of Britain's most famous imperial spokesmen, Cecil Rhodes, put the case for colonialism succinctly in the 1890s. 'We must find new lands,' he said, 'from which we can easily obtain raw materials and at the same time exploit the cheap slave labor that is available from the natives of the colonies. The colonies [will] also provide a dumping ground for the surplus goods produced in our factories.'[2]

During the colonial era, European nations spread their rule across the globe. The British, French, Dutch, Spanish, Portuguese, Belgians, Germans, and later the Americans, took possession of most of what was later called the Third World. And of course they also expanded into Australia, New Zealand/Aotearoa and North America. In some places (the Americas, Australia, New Zealand and southern Africa) they did so with the intent of establishing new lands for European settlement. Elsewhere (Africa and Asia) their interest was more in the spirit of Rhodes' vision: markets and plunder. From 1600–1800 incalculable riches were siphoned out of Latin America to become the chief source of finance for Europe's industrial revolution.

Global trade expanded rapidly during the colonial period as European powers sucked in raw materials from their new dominions: furs, timber and fish from Canada; slaves and gold from Africa; sugar, rum and fruits from the Caribbean; coffee, sugar, meat, gold and silver from Latin America; opium, tea and spices from Asia. Ships crisscrossed the oceans. Heading towards the colonies their holds were filled with settlers and manufactured goods; returning home the stout galleons and streamlined clippers bulged with coffee, copra and cocoa. By the 1860s and the 1870s world trade was booming. It was a 'golden era' of international commerce—though the European powers pretty much stacked things in their favor. Wealth from their overseas colonies flooded into France, England, Holland and Spain but some of it also flowed back into the colonies as investment—into railways, roads, ports, dams and cities. Such was the range of global commerce in the 19th century that capital transfers from North to South were actually greater at the end of the 1890s than at the end of the 1990s. By 1913, exports (one of the hallmarks of increasing economic integration) accounted for a larger share of global production than they did in 1999.

When people talk about globalization today, they're still talking mostly about economics, about an expanding international trade in goods and services based on the concept of 'comparative advantage'. This theory was first developed in 1817 by the British economist David Ricardo in his *Principles of Political Economy and Taxation*. Ricardo wrote that nations should specialize in producing goods in which they have a natural advantage and thereby find their market niche. He believed this would benefit both buyer and seller but only if certain conditions were maintained, such as: 1) trade between partners must be balanced so that one

---

[2]   *The Ecologist*, Vol 29, No 3, May/June 1999.

FIGURE 1

Indian Population of the Americas: 1492 and 1992

Tyranny and poverty

Colonialism in the Americas separated Indians from their land, destroyed traditional economies and left native people among the poorest of the poor.

- The Spanish ran the Bolivian silver mines with a slave labor system known as the mita; nearly eight million Indians had died in the Potosi mines by 1650.
- Suicide and alcoholism are common responses to social dislocation. Suicide rates on Canadian Indian reserves are 10 to 20 times higher than the national average.
- In Guatemala life expectancy for non-natives is 61 years; for Indians it is 45. The infant mortality rate for Indian children is twice that of non-Indians (160 deaths per thousand versus 80).

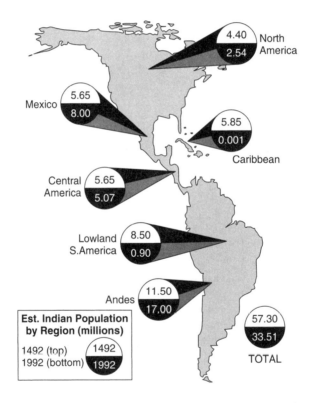

North America 4.40 / 2.54

Mexico 5.65 / 8.00

Caribbean 5.85 / 0.001

Central America 5.65 / 5.07

Lowland S.America 8.50 / 0.90

Andes 11.50 / 17.00

Est. Indian Population by Region (millions)
1492 (top)
1992 (bottom)
1492
1992

TOTAL 57.30 / 33.51

Source: SEDOS Bulletin, Rome. May 1990: The Dispossessed. Geoffrey York (Lester & Orpen Dennys, Toronto, 1989): Guatemala: False Hope, False Freedom, James Painter (CIIR, London, 1987): Ecuador Urgent Action Bulletin (Survival International, London, 1990): Native Population of the Americas in 1492, Ed. W. Denevan (University of Wisconsin Press, 1976) and GAIA Atlas of First Peoples, Julian Burger (Doubleday, New York, 1990).

country doesn't become indebted and dependent on another; and 2) investment capital must be anchored locally and not allowed to flow from a high-wage country to a low-wage country. Unfortunately, in today's high-tech world of instant communications, neither of these key conditions exists. The result: Ricardo's vision of local self-reliance mixed with balanced exports and imports is nowhere to be seen. Instead, export-led trade dominates the global economic agenda. Increasingly, the only route to growth is based on expanding exports to the rest of the world.

The rationale is that all countries and all peoples eventually benefit from the results of increased trade. And world trade has zoomed ahead in the last decade. It grew at an average 6.6 per cent during the 1990s and is set to grow at around 6 per cent a year over the next 10 years. Global trade is actually growing faster than total world output, which saw increases of 3.2 per cent during the 1990s and may reach 3 per cent annually over the next decade. This expansion of trade is expected to increase global income by up to $500 billion early in this new millennium. Unfortunately, most of this wealth will end up in the hands of the industrialized nations. They account for the lion's share of world trade and they mostly trade with each other. Indeed, the rich world accounts for almost two-thirds of global merchandise exports, a figure which has remained more or less steady since 1960. The share of Latin America, Central and Eastern Europe and Africa in total world exports was lower in 2002 than in 1960.[3]

Nonetheless, the world has changed in the last century in ways that have completely altered the character of the global economy and its impact on people and the natural world. Today's globalization is vastly different from both the colonial era and the immediate post-World War Two period. Even arch-capitalists like currency speculator George Soros have voiced doubts about the negative values that underlie the direction of the modern global economy.

'Insofar as there is a dominant belief in our society today,' he writes, 'it is a belief in the magic of the marketplace. The doctrine of laissez-faire capitalism holds that the common good is best served by the uninhibited pursuit of self-interest. . . . Unsure of what they stand for, people increasingly rely on money as the criterion of value. . . . The cult of success has replaced a belief in principles. Society has lost its anchor.'

MARKET MAGIC

The 'magic of the marketplace' is not a new concept. It's been around in one form or another since the father of modern economics, Adam Smith, first published his pioneering work *The Wealth of Nations* in 1776. Coincidentally, [that was] the same year Britain's 13 restless American colonies declared independence from the mother land. But Smith's concept of the market was a far cry from the one championed by today's globalization boosters. Smith was adamant that markets worked most efficiently when there was equality between buyer and seller, and when neither was large enough to influence the market price. This, he said, would ensure that all parties received a fair return and that society as a whole would benefit through the best use of its natural and human resources. Smith also believed that capital was best invested locally so that owners could see what was happening with their investment and could have hands-on management of its use. Author and activist David Korten sums up Smith's thinking as follows:

---

[3] *Development and Globalization: Facts and Figures 2004*, UNCTAD.

FIGURE 2	Growth in the volume of world merchandise trade and GDP, 1994-2004 (Annual percentage change)

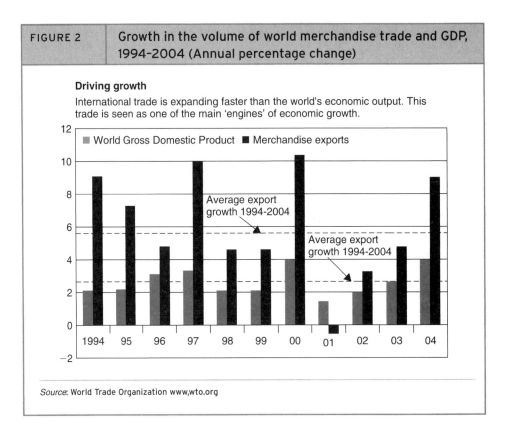

Driving growth

International trade is expanding faster than the world's economic output. This trade is seen as one of the main 'engines' of economic growth.

Source: World Trade Organization www,wto.org

'His vision of an efficient market was one composed of small owner-managed enterprises located in the communities where the owners resided. Such owners would share in the community's values and have a personal stake in its future. It is a market that has little in common with a globalized economy, dominated by massive corporations without local or national allegiance, managed by professionals who are removed from real owners by layers of investment institutions and holding companies.'[4]

As Korten hints, the world we live in today is vastly different from the one that Adam Smith inhabited. Take the communications technology revolution since 1980. In barely 25 years, computers, fiber-optics, satellites and microprocessors have radically altered the production, sales and distribution of goods and services as well as patterns of global investment. Coupled with improvements in air freight and ocean transport, companies can now move their plants and factories to wherever costs are lowest. Being close to the target market is no longer crucial. Improved technology and relatively inexpensive oil (for the moment anyway) has led to a massive increase in goods being transported by air and sea. World air traffic cargo tripled from 1985 to 1997 and is predicted to triple again by 2015. The Council of the International Civil Aviation Organization (ICAO) notes that about 2 billion passengers and 44 million tons of

---

[4]   *When Corporations Rule the World*, David Korten (Kumarian/Berrett-Koehler, West Hartford/San Francisco, 1995).

freight were carried by the world's airlines in 2005, a 44 and 74 per cent increase respectively over 10 years. The global shipping business which now consumes more than 140 million tons of fuel oil a year is expected to increase by 85 per cent in the next decade. And costs are falling too. According to the Washington-based World Shipping Council in 2004, 7,241 individual vessels made more than 72,000 US port calls. In the last 15 years, rates on the three major US trade shipping routes have fallen by between 23 and 46 per cent. In 2000, American exporters spent about $3 billion less than they did in 1985 to ship their goods to market—extraordinary considering inflation rose 65 per cent in that same period.

It's estimated that ocean freight unit costs have fallen 70 per cent since the 1980s while air freight costs have fallen three to four per cent a year on average over the last two decades.

These cheap transport rates in reality are 'cheap' only in a purely financial sense. They reflect 'internal' costs—the costs of packaging, marketing, labor, debt and profit. But they don't reflect the 'external' impact on the environment of this massive use of irreplaceable fossil fuels. Moving more goods around the planet increases pollution, contributes to ground-level ozone (i.e. smog) and boosts greenhouse gas emissions, a major source of global warming and climate change. These environmental costs are basically ignored in the profit and loss equation of business. This is one of the main reasons environmentalists object to the globalization of trade. Companies make the profits but society has to foot the bill.

The other key factor which makes globalization today so different has to do with structural changes to the world economy since the early 1970s. It was then that the system of rules set up at the end of World War Two to manage global trade collapsed. The fixed currency-exchange regime agreed [to] at Bretton Woods, New Hampshire, in 1944 gave the world 35 years of relatively steady economic growth.

But around 1980 things began to change with the emergence of fundamentalist free-market governments in Britain and the US; and the later disintegration of the state-run command economy in the former Soviet Union. The formula for economic progress adopted by the administrations of Margaret Thatcher in the UK and Ronald Reagan in the US called for a drastic reduction in the regulatory role of the state. According to their intellectual influences, Austrian economist Friedrich Hayek and University of Chicago academic Milton Friedman, meddlesome big government was the problem. Instead, government was to take its direction from the market. Companies must be free to move their operations anywhere in the world to minimize costs and maximize returns to investors. Free trade, unfettered investment, deregulation, balanced budgets, low inflation and privatization of publicly owned enterprises were trumpeted as the six-step plan to national prosperity.

The deregulation of world financial markets went hand-in-hand with an emphasis on free trade. Banks, insurance companies and investment dealers, whose operations had been mostly confined within national borders, were suddenly unleashed. Within a few years the big players from Europe, Japan and North America expanded into each other's markets as well as into the newly opened and fragile financial services markets in the Global South. Aided by sophisticated computer systems (which made it easy to transfer huge amounts of money instantly) and governments desperate for investment, the big banks and investment houses were quick to invest surplus cash anywhere they could turn a profit. In this new relaxed atmosphere, finance capital became a profoundly destabilizing influence on the global economy.

Instead of long-term investment in the production of real goods and services, speculators in the global casino make money from money—with little concern for the impact of their investments on local communities or national economies. Governments everywhere now fear the destabilizing impact of this 'hot money'. Recent United Nations (UN) studies show a direct correlation between the frequency of financial crises around the world and the huge increase in international capital flows during the 1990s.

The collapse of the East Asian currencies, which began in July 1997, was a catastrophic example of the damage caused by nervous short-term investors. Until then the 'Tiger

FIGURE 3	Percentage change in GDP before and after the Asian financial crisis

Pinball capital

Short-term speculative capital whizzes around the world leaving ravaged economies and human devastation in its wake. East Asia (Indonesia, South Korea, Thailand, Malaysia, the Philippines) suffered a destructive net reversal of private capital flows from 1996 to 1997 of $12 billion.

	Thailand	Indonesia	Malaysia	S. Korea
Average 1980–90	7.6	6.1	5.2	9.4
Average 1980–96	8.3	7.7	8.7	7.3
Average 1997	–7	–16	–6	–6

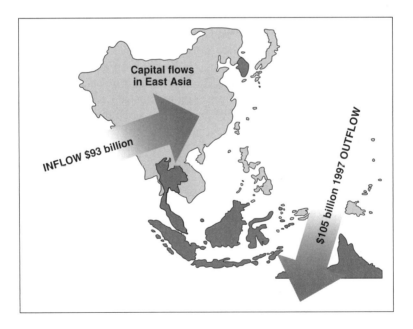

Capital flows in East Asia

INFLOW $93 billion

$105 billion 1997 OUTFLOW

Source: Human Development Report 1999, UN Development Progress / Oxford University Press financial crisis / libralization, speculation and Regulation, War on Want, London 1999.

THIRD WORLD

If there's a Third World. then there must be a First and Second World too. When the term was first coined in 1952 by the French demographer, Alfred Sauvy, there was a clear distinction, though the differences have become blurred over the past decade. Derived from the French phrase, *tiers monde*, the term was first used to suggest parallels between the *tiers monde* (the world of the poor countries) and the *tiers état* (the third estate or common people of the French revolutionary era). The First World was the North American/European 'Western bloc' while the Soviet-led 'Eastern bloc' was the Second World. These two groups had most of the economic and military power and faced off in a tense ideological confrontation commonly called the 'Cold War'. Third World countries in Africa, Latin America, Asia and the Pacific had just broken free of colonial rule and were attempting to make their own way rather than become entangled in the tug-of-war between East and West. Since the break-up of the Soviet Union in the early 1990s the term Third World has less meaning and its use is diminishing. Now many refer to the 'developing nations', the Majority World or just the South.

Economies' of Thailand, Taiwan, Singapore, Malaysia and South Korea had been the success stories of globalization. Advocates of open markets pointed to these countries as proof that classic capitalism would bring wealth and prosperity to millions in the developing world—though they conveniently ignored the fact that in all these countries the State took a strong and active role in shaping the economy. According to dissident ex-World Bank Chief Economist, Joseph Stiglitz: 'The combination of high savings rates, government investment in education and state-directed industrial policy all served to make the region an economic powerhouse. Growth rates were phenomenal for decades and the standard of living rose enormously for tens of millions of people.'[5]

Foreign investment was tightly controlled by national governments until the early 1990s, severely in South Korea and Taiwan, less so in Thailand and Malaysia. Then as a result of continued pressure from the International Monetary Fund (IMF) and others, the 'tigers' began to open up their capital accounts and private sector businesses began to borrow heavily.

Spectacular growth rates floated on a sea of foreign investment as offshore investors poured dollars into the region, eager to harvest double-digit returns. In 1996, capital was flowing into East Asia at almost $100 billion a year. But mostly the cash went into risky real estate ventures or onto the local stock market where it inflated share prices far beyond the value of their underlying assets.

In Thailand, where the Asian 'miracle' first began to sour, over-investment in real estate left the market glutted with $20 billion worth of new unsold properties. The house of cards collapsed when foreign investors began to realize that Thai financial institutions to which they had lent billions could not meet loan repayments. Spooked by the specter of falling profits and a stagnant real estate market, investors called in their loans and cashed in their investments—first slowly, then in a panic-stricken rush.

---

[5] *Globalization and its Discontents*, Joseph Stiglitz (WW Norton, New York/London, 2003).

More than $105 billion left the entire region in the next 12 months, equivalent to 11 per cent of the domestic output of the most seriously affected countries—Indonesia, the Philippines, South Korea, Thailand and Malaysia.[6] Having abandoned any kind of capital controls, Asian governments were powerless to stop the massive hemorrhage of funds. Ironically, the IMF's 1997 *Annual Report*, written just before the crisis, had singled out Thailand's 'remarkable economic performance' and 'consistent record of sound macro-economic policies'.

The IMF was to be proven wrong—disastrously so. Across the region economic output plummeted while unemployment soared, leaping by a factor of ten in Indonesia alone. The human costs of the East Asian economic crisis were immediate and devastating. As bank-ruptcies soared, firms shut their doors and millions of workers were laid off. More than 400 Malaysian companies declared bankruptcy between July 1997 and March 1998 while in Indonesia—the poorest country affected by the crisis—20 per cent of the population, nearly 40 million people, were pushed into poverty. The impact of the economic slowdown had the devastating effect of reducing both family income and government expenditures on social and health services for years afterwards. In Thailand, more than 100,000 children were yanked from school when parents could no longer afford tuition fees. The crash also had a knock-on effect outside Asia. Shock-waves rippled through Latin America, nearly tipping Brazil into recession while the Russian economy suffered worse damage. Growth rates slipped into reverse and the Russian ruble became nearly worthless as a medium of international exchange.

The East Asian crisis was a serious blow to the 'promise' of globalization—and a stiff challenge to the orthodox economic prescriptions of the IMF. Across the region, the Fund was reviled as the source of economic disaster. The citizens of East Asia saw their inter-ests ignored in favor of Western banks and investors. In the end, writes Stiglitz: 'It was the IMF policies which undermined the market as well as the long-run stability of the econo-my and society.' It was the first time that the 'global managers' and finance kingpins showed that the system wasn't all it was made out to be. The world economy was more fragile, and thus more explosive, than anybody had imagined. As the region slowly recov-ered, citizens around the world began to scratch their heads and wonder about the pros and cons of globalization, especially the wisdom of unregulated investment. The mass public protests against the WTO, the IMF/World Bank and the G8 were still to come—in Seattle, Prague, Genoa, Quebec City, Doha and elsewhere. But the East Asian crisis planted real seeds of doubt about the merits of corporate globalization.

[6] *Human Development Report 1999* (United Nations Development Program, New York/Oxford, 1999).

Chapter 6

Where We Stand Today: The State of Modern Political Science

STELLA Z. THEODOULOU AND RORY O'BRIEN*

*Stella Z. Theodoulou *is Dean of the College of Social and Behavioral Sciences, California State University, Northridge. **Rory O'Brien** is Professor of Political Science at Cabrillo College in Aptos, California.*

In this chapter, we will look at how political science developed as a discipline. Most people use the word *politics* without fully defining what it is they are interested in. However, it is easy to know when you are involved in a political discussion. In this sense, there seems to be a shared definition we all seem to work with in society to understand one another when we are talking about politics. The study of political phenomenon by applying scientific techniques involves multiple steps, including theory development, hypothesis building and testing, the drawing of conclusions that are based on the strengths or weaknesses of those hypotheses, and, ultimately, the proving of the theories themselves. In this way, political science operates in a circle, with empirical research being fueled by theory development, and theory, in turn, being the outcome of research findings.

We begin with an assessment of where our discipline is today and where it has come from. Political science, especially in terms of research methodology, has come into its own during the latter half of the twentieth century. As we step into the next millennium, we need to create a map for practitioners of our trade to follow. Before we can do that, we must first establish the groundwork in which the discipline finds its genesis.

TRACING THE DEVELOPMENT OF THE DISCIPLINE

Since the beginning of time, people have observed, thought about, evaluated, and analyzed politics. Thus, the study of politics is not a new phenomenon, and the broad questions and interests of political scientists remain in many ways the same over time. However, what has changed is the way in which political scientists have tried to find the answers to the questions. There is a growing body of literature that identifies and discusses the evolution of the discipline.[1] Within such a discussion, it is clear to see that political scientists over time

[1] See Gabriel Almond, *A Discipline Divided, Schools and Sects in Political Science* (Newbury Park: Sage Publishing, 1990); David Easton, *Political Science in the United States: Past and Present* (London & New York: Routledge, 1991); David Easton, John G. Gunnell, and Luigi Graziano (eds.), *The Development of Political Science: A Comparative Study* (London & New York: Routledge, 1991); James Parr and Raymond Seidelman, *Discipline & History: Political Science in the United States* (Ann Arbor: University of Michigan Press, 1993).

have taken different paths in their study of politics. Authors might disagree on whether to label these paths eras, approaches, orientations, models, or methods, but at least there is general consensus that at different times different directions have been taken and are still being taken by political scientists in their quest for political knowledge.

In the following discussion, we will identify four general paths that political scientists have taken over the years. Some may be surprised at the omission of what they consider to be other paths, such as feminism, discourse analysis, rational choice theory, and Marxism. However, it is our opinion that all of these are approaches that fall within our four general paths rather than being distinctive paths themselves.

Many would argue that we can trace the development of the discipline directly to the social disorder of the Athenian city-state and the response to it by Socrates, Plato, and Aristotle. These first political philosophers and those that follow them take a theoretical path in their study of politics.

THE THEORETICAL PATH (FROM 600 B.C.)

Perhaps the most audacious statement we can make from an epistemological point of view is embodied in our fundamental assumption that it is even possible for us to possess knowledge about human social interaction. Observation might easily lead us to conclude that human behavior is too erratic to ever be understood fully, and, if understood, is difficult to predict. And yet, these are the foundational aspects of how we go about studying society. Since the early nineteenth century, our study of society has been based on the positivism of [Auguste] Compte [1798–1857]. This French *philosophe* advanced the theory that the social order could be studied in a logical fashion. In contrast to the metaphysical reasoning of the Age of Enlightenment preceding him, and in a continued reaction to the earlier Christian era in Europe, Compte sought to ground a view of society in the sober logic of empirical investigation and analysis.

Thus, in the modern age, many have fallen victim to merely focusing on the empirical, and in the process an important aspect of what gives motivation to the research process itself has been missed. Research gives expression to theories, or ideas. Without those ideas, the research project would be meaningless. If we think of political ideas as a series of questions that are posed to humankind across a tradition, and political phenomena as the tangible (and testable) manifestations of possible answers to those questions, we see the relationship between theory and scientific research more clearly. Throughout our history cach age has presented us with both questions and answers. What we think of as *political theory* is a coherent body of work that has, in some sense, transcended time to provide us with enduring questions that continue to help us to evaluate current circumstances, as well as create solutions as we look towards the future.

Theory provides the context for the study of political science through the development of models and through the development of normative conclusions or prescriptions. Whereas empirical research yields empirical conclusions, normative pursuits involve questions about "what ought to be" or what "should be." Normative prescriptions are, thus, suggestions or recommendations concerning how society might best be configured.

Normative theory leads to empirical research in two ways. First, normative questions can drive empirical projects. In order to conduct research of any kind one must begin with a question, the answer to which may be elusive. The research questions that lead to fruitful hypotheses are grounded in a theoretical foundation. Moving in this way from theory to practice, scientific research gives practical application to the solely theoretical.

Second, theory can, and regularly does, arise from the practice of normal scientific enquiry. As social scientists realize how and in what ways their theoretical foundations differ from reality they are able to adjust their theories so as to better describe and predict the political world. Very few political theorists think like Plato did that the abstract forms of physical things are distinct from those things themselves. Instead, political theorists are involved in a journey of discovery that allows them to constantly update and refine theoretical perspectives so as to more effectively represent testable circumstances. Ultimately these adjustments to theory lead to further scientific investigation, beginning the process anew.

Finally, political theory creates models that political scientists can utilize to gain a broader understanding of their concepts and hypotheses. Models are artificial structures constructed by political scientists. They are human artifacts, made with the express purpose of developing ways in which students of society can more easily view the political order. Models are merely ways for us to get our minds around a concept as big as society itself. In essence, models provide the testing ground for hypotheses. But in a deeper context, the logical tests performed by our own intellects provide the most fertile ground for the creation of new political ideas and insights.

What Are We Looking For?

For the purpose of better understanding society in general and the political order in particular, political theorists have traditionally looked at various fundamental aspects of both social ideas and social organizations. Among these are our notions of what human nature is, what constitutes the "good life," and what terms such as *justice* and *equality* really mean to us. Additionally, the way we conceptualize freedom, democracy, power, and social cohesion all say something about our views of politics. Human society is dynamic and rarely, if ever, static. As the social and political order of societies change it is crucial to have some enduring ideas about how to assess that change. This is precisely what political theory provides in the form of a conceptual framework. Political philosophy is about developing ways and means for not only thinking about such things, but for using our ideas constructively to better understand society.

Human Nature

We'll begin by considering our motivations and activities in society based on who we are. This is what philosophers refer to as *human nature*. We often take for granted the composition of psychological elements that we refer to as our nature. Generally, we do not have to think about such things. But at the heart of any political theory is a conception of human nature. This is because society, which is made up of many individuals, is but a reflection of our nature, or our essential characteristics, on a large scale. When we view society as the reflection of many individuals, we can ask questions such as "Why are certain policies popular, or unpopular?" and "Why do some forms of government work better than others?"

Some political theorists take a dim view of human nature, pronouncing us to be wild beasts if not constrained by the forces of a strong and powerful government.[2] Other theorists

---

[2]   See David Easton, John G. Gunnell, and Luigi Graziano (eds.) *The Development of Political Science: A Comparative Study* (London & New York: Routledge, 1991).

speak to the human spirit, and seek ways to aid in its liberation and fulfillment.[3] Some thinkers find us to be hard-working and generous, while others see us as lazy and mean-spirited. But in every case, political theorists utilize their view of human nature to help them in the construction of their model of the social order.

The Good and the Just

In everyday language we talk about what is right and wrong, just or unjust, without taking the time to really formulate a position on these matters. In posing questions about what is *good* and what is *just*, the theorist develops ideas that help us to consider social successes (as well as failures) in order to further our general knowledge about the social world. At the same time we create categories through which we interpret our world.

When we talk about *the good* we are referring to our highest ideals. The best, finest, mostly highly valued are all captured by our notion of the good. When political theorists refer to the good they do not mean merely what we as individuals think is good. This *good* is not simply the opposite of *bad*. Humans often find that which is expedient to be the good. In other words, we may casually think of what we like as being good, or what is easiest as being the best. In many instances, modern society emphasizes that which is expedient over that which we know is truly good. Through the process of focusing on what is expedient we lose sight of any deeper value that the good may represent.

The notion of "the good life" makes reference to how each member of society might live so as to work toward developing his or her individual potential, and help to create a stronger community. The good life leads to happiness, in that excellence is its own reward.[4] When philosophers talk about happiness, they mean something that goes beyond material possessions.

By the same measure, *justice,* as well as our notions of the just, have at their roots the way we conceive of community. Every aspect of how a society is oriented tells us about that society's notions of justice. From distribution of wealth to welfare policy, from tax codes to educational requirements, all of these things refer us back to a concept of justice. And, if the members of society believe that in order to live together there must be a commonly agreed upon set of ideas about what is right and wrong (as every society does), the rules that are created on the basis of that contract will dictate the outlines of a theory of justice.[5]

Everything Put Together, Sooner or Later, Falls Apart

Politics is sometimes defined simply as power, and the ways in which power is distributed in society. All of the important structures and benefits of a society are arranged on the basis of the distribution of power. In most cases, the extent to which justice is dispersed in

---

[3] See St. Augustine; for instance, *City of God* (New York: Doubleday & Company, Inc.,1958); or Thomas Hobbes, *Leviathan* (New York: Penguin Books, 1968). See Karl Marx and Friedrich Engels, *The Communist Manifesto* (New York: Bantam Books, 1992).

[4] We refer here to the way Aristotle in the *Nicomachean Ethics* (Indianapolis: Bobbs-Merrill Educational Publishing, 1962), characterizes the good life.

[5] See chapter one of John Rawls, *A Theory of Justice* (Cambridge, Massachusetts: The Belknap Press, 1971).

society also has to do with the distribution of power. And the actual foundations of justice are often created as a form of compromise between competing interests. In fact, virtually all aspects of the political realm are influenced by how we construe power. But regardless of the ways in which power has been configured in various societies, across many cultures and throughout time (what we refer to as *transculturally* and *transhistorically*) power alone has never held a social group together. This leads us to ask, "Why do humans stay together in social groups?" And, it further begs the question, "Why do those groups sometimes disintegrate?" We'll take this up when we discuss *social contract* and *alienation.*

Social Contract

The *contractarian* view of society is based on the notion that in order to stay together, a group of people must have some common purposes.[6] Furthermore, the political order must be based on ideas that are agreeable to a sizable portion of the population. Contractarian perspective says that these political ideas form a *contract,* or agreement, between the people and the government. Here we are using the idea of a social contract to help us understand a larger concept, social cohesion. For instance, Aristotle thinks that part of what keeps human societies together is the fact that we are "social animals" in the sense that we only function well in the social milieu. Without others to live with in society, Aristotle notes, we would never be able to do our "civic duty," which, in part, involves our virtuously following common moral and ethical rules.

In his view, the pleasure derived from the experience of excellence as a social being far outstrips that enjoyed as a consequence of one of our generally hedonistic pursuits. Furthermore, according to Aristotle, we are in essence social animals. Much of Aristotle's view of the world is based on the notion that everything is made up of essential qualities that make particular things what they are.[7] Said differently, we can only reach our own individual potential if we exist in a social world.

Taking another political thinker, John Locke, we get a further elaboration of how a society is held together. In Locke's view, the power of government is controlled only through a formal procedural development like a constitution. In fact, we can view a constitution as the physical manifestation of a social contract. Although the contract itself goes far beyond the structure of any document, the reality is that the constitution (and the laws that are generated fromm it) are the embodiment of the broader contract. The point here is that citizens, in a sense, own the document itself. That they not only agree to its tenets, but, on a deeper level, are the source of the contents of the constitution. In this way, a temporal, material document has the ability to truly represent the wishes and finer aspirations of a social group.

People form together in social groups primarily because the alternative is relatively distasteful. In the main, human beings have found it far easier to agree to some set of rules, or compact, than they have found it to live together each with his or her own total license. Locke articulated this clearly, fully realizing that the better instincts in humankind would almost always prove to be subordinate to our baser motives. However, the point for those

---

[6]   This notion is fully discussed in the second of John Locke's *Two Treatises on Government* (New York: New American Library, 1963).

[7]   The best discussion of this idea is found in Section X of Aristotle, *Nicomachean Ethics.*

of us who are students of politics is that there appears to be a human striving for the safety and security of an organized social order. This observation alone may give us hope to move forward into the future armed with the sense that regardless of the countless examples of ruined societies, we may, in time, find ways to live with one another while reducing friction.

At the same time, Locke's entire project is held together on the basis of another tenet. According to Locke, the *legitimacy* of government rests in the consent of those who are governed. Said differently, the true power of government ought to lie in the fact that the people of a nation accept, or consent to that government, not merely in the government's ability to coerce the citizenry. A liberal government, founded on the consent of those governed, allows for the development of some of our most cherished political ideas. Equality, freedom, and democracy are nurtured in the Lockean-liberal schema, and representation in government is a natural outcome of legitimacy based on consent.

Alienation

Why don't societies stay together? A quick review of human history shows us that, in general, we seem to like changing social orders on a regular basis. There have been few governments throughout time that have been able to hold societies together for more than a few generations. Often governments are overthrown through revolutions. The revolutionary change of existing social orders has been a common thread around the world during the past three hundred years, and yet we have not learned much that helps us predict exactly where or when a revolution might next take place. Although we understand the larger social forces that *may* lead down the revolutionary road, when a revolution *will* take place is most often a function of how long the human spirit will endure before demanding liberating change.[8] In some societies (such as Europe during the Middle Ages), it has taken centuries to bring about change. In other situations (China during the twentieth century), change has come about quite rapidly.

We may be able to better understand more readily yet a different aspect of social cohesion, or the lack thereof. Social scientists use the term *alienation* to refer to a sense of being disconnected or separated from other people, things, experiences, and even ourselves. For instance, in the Marxist model of society, alienation is utilized to help explain why people feel a lack of connection with the work they are doing. In essence, when we are alienated from our work we are alienated from our own lives. If the level of this alienation is high enough, or if it goes on for too long a period of time, Marxist theory suggests that the social order may break down, leading to revolution.[9]

Although Marx's concern with alienation is focused in the economic sphere, this concept is also helpful in describing other ways in which people become disengaged from society. When a government is repressive, its citizens become alienated from the political order itself. The most effective way to overcome this disconnectedness between the people and the distribution of power in a society is through radical change. Whether one advocates

---

[8] See Barrington Moore, Jr., *Social Origins of Dictatorship and Democracy* (Boston: Beacon Press, 1967).

[9] See Isaac D. Balbus, *Marxism and Domination* (Princeton, New Jersey: Princeton University Press, 1982).

Lockean liberalism or Marxist economics makes little difference. The reality is that the lack of efficacy (or feeling of possessing political power), that groups of citizens, or entire populations often experience leads to a form of alienation which is remedied through the overthrow of an existent government.

In summary, political theory functions to provide a groundwork, or foundation for our continued research and observation of social phenomena. By probing some of our deeper questions about society and our own nature, theory gives us the ability to logically arrange our knowledge about the political order. By gaining a greater understanding of both those things that we can empirically measure and those that we only draw normative conclusions about, we learn about all aspects of the social world.

THE TRADITIONALIST PATH (FROM THE 1850s)

This is essentially a collection of different emphases brought together under the generic heading of *traditionalism*. However, within the tradition we can identify three dominant thrusts. The first is the *historical* thrust, which argues that the primary method of understanding politics is to draw lessons from history and apply them to politics. Much of the work undertaken in this area results in what we call *case studies.* Extensive use of generalizations are made in this type of research as the case study is used to test the assumptions of the researcher. The main problem with such research is that it is hard to apply findings beyond the case under study.

The second major thrust within traditionalism is the *legalistic* perspective, which views political science as mainly the study of laws, structures, institutions, and constitutions founded upon law. The last major thrust is the *institutional* view, which came about as a reaction to the historical and legalistic directions that the study of politics was undertaking. The emphasis is on the description of political institutions and structures. Thus, institutionalists would argue that political institutions should be researchers' primary focus, and that when we discuss them we should do so by looking at their powers, roles, and functions. The vast majority of introductory American government textbooks are written from this perspective. The weakness with the institutional emphasis is it goes little beyond description and thus there is little explanation as to the why or how of events or trends.

THE BEHAVIORALIST PATH (FROM THE 1950s)

Behavioralism came about as a protest to traditionalism, in particular to the institutionalist emphasis. The behavioralist path was advocated by a group of political scientists who claimed that traditionalism was not producing truly reliable political knowledge, and that rather than study structures and how they are supposed to function, we should be concerned with what is actually happening within the polity. The behavioralist path concentrates on the behavior of political actors and stresses the use of scientific method to study politics. Thus behavioralists argue that, although we cannot ignore institutions and their structural components, it is the activity within and the behavior around an institution that is of more concern. Yes, it is important to *know* the structure of the executive office, but it is more crucial to know why one president has more power than another, or why one bill gets passed by Congress and another does not. In their study of politics, behavioralists use scientific methodology and thus stress the empirical. They argue we should adopt natural science as a model for social inquiry. Thus, all political research should display scientific principles and characteristics [such] as determinism, observation, objectivity, verification, explanation, classification, and prediction. In their quest for scientific method and the need for rigorous and systematic research, behavioralists introduce statistical, mathematical, and other quantitative analyses of data to the discipline.

Behavioralism has by no means been universally accepted by political scientists. In fact, it has been criticized on many fronts. Critics are both political scientists who adhere to the traditionalist and theoretical paths as well as those who have attempted to push the boundaries of what we study and how we study politics into new applied settings. Such political scientists we will label as *neoeclectics*. They have most commonly been referred to as *postbehavioralists*.[10] The logic behind this is that they came just after behavioralism. However, this hides the diffuse and varied interests and activities of such political scientists. They have, in fact, formulated the latest path in studying politics. However, before we look at what they do we should consider two main criticisms of behavioralism, for that will explain neoeclecticism to a great degree.

The first criticism of behavioralism is that in their desire to follow the scientific method and their obsession with quantification, behavioralists have not always studied the most important political questions. A second criticism of behavioralists is that they have avoided normative issues and a discussion of values and thus there is no discussion of what should be. In short, the critique of behavioralism is that there is an obsession with methodology at the expense of what we study as political scientists.

THE NEOECLECTIC PATH (FROM THE 1970s)

The neoeclectic view has been taken by a group of political scientists who argue political science has to become relevant once again. They argue that attention should be focused beyond the empirical and that value judgements about government and politics must be considered. Neoeclectics are interested in describing both the goals of political activity as well as how to achieve those goals. Thus, there is an explicit place for normative considerations alongside empirical applications in the study of politics. Neoeclectics are not advocating an end to the scientific study of politics; rather, they argue such skills should be applied to the solution of crucial social and political problems. Neoeclectics use quantification to aid them in this quest and attempt to show the utility of quantification in the study of politics. Thus, we can term the neoeclectic path as the applied study of politics. Neoeclectics do not have a single method or focus; rather, they try to push the boundaries of how and what we study. They often consider problems that traditionalists and behavioralists would consider outside of the realm of political science. Many neoeclectics study public policy.

---

[10]   See David Easton, "Political Science in the United States: Past and Present," in *Discipline and History: Political Science in the U.S.: Part 4.* (ed.) James Farr and Raymond Seidelman (Ann Arbor: University of Michigan Press, 1993).

WHERE WE STAND TODAY AND WHAT
WE HAVE BECOME

In recent years, it seems as if we have gotten lost in *how* we study politics, rather than in *what* we study about the world of politics. Said differently, we have allowed our attention to focus on our methods instead of our actual areas of concern. We have become adept at the manipulation of empirical data while leaving behind the very reasons that we seek knowledge about politics in the first place. Through our interest in quantifiable bits of information we have taken the *politics* out of political science. This obsession with quantification, we will argue, has come at the expense of our understanding of society and the polity.

We have left behind the larger questions about social and political life in our rush towards neutrality. For decades, political scientists have struggled to be perceived as "value free" when in reality we have needed the opposite, to return what value sensitivity we have lost and develop an even greater ability to infuse value into our discussion of politics in the future. Political scientists need to be intersubjective rather than value free; that is, to acknowledge our values and how they frame our inquiry. To a great degree, we have learned that neutrality extinguishes debate. It is precisely to the degree that political science is capable of bringing a deeper level of value into our discourse on the political order that we will be successful in appropriately responding to a diversity of ideas.

As a discipline, the challenge to political science is to move forward in meaningful ways. It is not enough to trace where we have come from or merely to establish where we stand today. As previously discussed, the empirical is crucial in terms of our understanding of political and social phenomena. But, the key element here is to reintroduce the normative into our current discussion of the political world. Ultimately, the symbiotic relationship between empirical and normative theory construction allows the discipline to come full circle where scientific research is fueled by more profound considerations.

The important questions regarding politics have always been the same. In many ways, it seems as if political scientists are constantly trying to come up with a new list. Often, in our rush to find quantifiable answers we leave the dynamic qualities out of our study. Academics routinely write and lecture about the political realm as if it is some sort of fossil or specimen frozen in time. Those of us who have a passion for politics must return the zest to our pursuit of knowledge about the political world so that we can move together towards answering the enduring questions. The question before us concerns the nature of the discipline itself. Are we history, law, or philosophy? Or, are we the behaviorists and postbehaviorists, and all those "post-posts" who have come since? Indeed, political science is all of these disparate things, having its roots in the study of philosophy and its future in sophisticated, computerized statistical analysis. But the true science of politics is an *ideal* that combines all of these areas.

In other words, it is possible to construe political science as a sort of ideal type that integrates a diversity of intellectual categories, each of which has something to offer the other. If we view our discipline in this manner, it is possible to imagine political scientists creating the context for our continued study and greater understanding of the political world.

The context of our discipline is similar to a large jigsaw puzzle, and each subdiscipline is another piece of the puzzle. While we can understand separately the different elements of political science, the whole thing lacks a clarity of perspective until all of the pieces are in place. Essentially, the pieces themselves are no more, or less, than separate paradigms, in the sense that each subdivision of the discipline tends to see the world through its own lens. These paradigmatic lenses, or mental templates, that drive our study of the political world each reflect a different interpretation of reality. Collectively, the mosaic of these sub-disciplines in political science gives a richness to the whole that is not at all diminished by their number.

As the various component elements of political science represent different viewpoints we must have some sense of the entire discipline as a project in order to understand it. We need to know where the discipline is at today and indeed where it is headed in the future. By thinking about political science as a *project* (rather than as *merely* an academic area of interest, for instance), we remind ourselves that our discipline is constantly changing and evolving. It is also necessary to gain a general understanding of what the discipline is all about before it is truly possible to analyze the conclusions of political science appropriately. It is only by assessing the tapestry made up of the many sub-fields that we bring sharply into focus the *teleology*, or final cause, in Aristotle's words, of political science.

Our second question is, "Why do we want to know what it is we want to know?" As we have become sure of the hows and whats of the research process, we need to recapture our sense of *why* we pursue knowledge about politics and political life. What does it take for dedicated political scientists to return this intellectual curiosity to our pursuit? Finally, in order to return politics to the intersubjective study of the dynamic between people and institutions in society we must allow ourselves to consider the normative as well as the empirical. The question is, how can researchers accomplish this, thus allowing empirical investigation to be informed by normative considerations?

SECTION 1 TERMINOLOGY

Activist

Authoritarian

Autocratic

Capitalism

Central and Eastern
    European (CEE) states

Clash of civilizations

Comparative advantage

Conservative

Constitutionalism

Decision making

Democracy

Despotism

Developing world

Electorate

Ethnicity

European Union (EU)

Federalism

Former Soviet Union
    (FSU)

Group of 8 (G-8)

Globalization

Gold standard

Governance

Hierarchy

International Civil Aviation
    Organization (ICAO)

International Court of
    Justice (ICJ)

International Monetary
    Fund (IMF)

Laissez-faire

Liberal

Liberal democracy

Liberty

Macroeconomic
    policy

Nation-state

Norms

North American Free Trade
    Agreement (NAFTA)

Pinball capital

Polis

Political culture

Politics

Public interest

Regionalization

Security Council

Socialist

Sovereignty

Suffrage

Third World

Totalitarian

United Nations (UN)

World Bank

SECTION 1 DISCUSSION QUESTIONS

1. Winston Churchill said that "democracy is the worst form of government except all the others that have been tried." Is there a sound "alternative" to democracy? Is democracy a Western ideal, or universal in nature?

2. Can we be "political" and apathetic at the same time? What is it about politics that makes it so "activist"?

3. What makes this "era" of globalization different from those that came before it?

4. Is politics a "science"?

5. Ancient Greece is often held up as an example of the purest form of democracy. What limitations can you identify in attempting to adopt this system of government in today's modern world?

Section 2

Political Theories
and Perspectives

SECTION SUMMARY

The word "philosophy" is based on two ancient Greek words, *philos* (love) and *sophia* (wisdom), so the word loosely means "love of wisdom." All forms of philosophy involve the quest for understanding, and political philosophy (or political theory) examines the nature of politics. This branch of the discipline is more about theories and perspectives of politics than about the mechanics of political structures or institutions. Ultimately, the objective of political theory is to pose new and better ways to deal with the problems of human society.

In addition to dealing with perennial questions such as "what is the good life?" and issues such as equality or the relationship between governments and citizens, political theory is more important in our daily lives than we might think. What distinguishes the Conservative Party from the Liberals or New Democrats in Canada, or the Democrats from the Republicans in the United States? What makes "socialists" think the way they do, and why do people call themselves "fiscal conservatives"? The answers to these questions describe the ideas and philosophies about how our society ought to be organized. Societies have seen the development of many, many political philosophies. None of them can offer the "universal truth," but all aspire to bring about positive change in political systems.

The readings in this section of the book take a contemporary view of major political ideologies. Perhaps you have your own philosophy of political life. Will it change after you have finished these readings? Russell Kirk points out that conservatism means many different things, but that there are some central tenets (his "conservative principles") that define modern conservatives. Next, in one of the most famous (and infamous) contemporary political articles, Francis Fukuyama imagines the unimaginable: that humans have reached the "end point," as he calls it, of ideological evolution. Fukuyama argues we are left with "western liberal democracy," which he feels is the "final form" of human government. His article, first published in 1989, quickly became one of the most talked about points of view in political studies. Everyone, it seemed, had an opinion about his argument, including those who had never read it! Here you get to read the original, and form your own views on whether he was right in light of subsequent events over the past two decades.

Carol Gould brings socialism up to date by offering some non-polemical thoughts about the ideology. Gould suggests that we don't simply have to choose one perspective or another. She contends that modern democratic societies need socialist thought. And instead of just outlining the feminist movement, Jennifer Baumgardner and Amy Richards pose two scenarios: a day in an imaginary world in which feminist progress ceased in 1970, and the same day resulting from the continuation of feminist development since then. These two diametrically opposed scenarios are both the result of ideology.

Any field of study has its own "philosophies." In politics we study them because they tell us about our political lives, and they link our political ideas with real policies that get put into practice. These philosophies often lead to conflict, as anyone who has watched a political debate might agree, but this shows the relevance of philosophies. Rather than being in decline in modern life, political philosophies frame the way we see the world and directly determine the changes we would like to implement.

Chapter 7

Ten Conservative Principles

RUSSELL KIRK*

*__Russell Kirk__ (1918–1994) was a Guggenheim Fellow, a senior fellow of the American Council of Learned Societies, a Constitutional Fellow of the National Endowment for the Humanities, and a Fulbright Lecturer in Scotland. This extract is adapted from the author's The Politics of Prudence (ISI Books, 1993).

Being neither a religion nor an ideology, the body of opinion termed *conservatism* possesses no Holy Writ and no *Das Kapital* to provide dogmata. So far as it is possible to determine what conservatives believe, the first principles of the conservative persuasion are derived from what leading conservative writers and public men have professed during the past two centuries. After some introductory remarks on this general theme, I will proceed to list ten such conservative principles.

Perhaps it would be well, most of the time, to use this word "conservative" as an adjective chiefly. For there exists no Model Conservative, and conservatism is the negation of ideology: it is a state of mind, a type of character, a way of looking at the civil social order.

The attitude we call conservatism is sustained by a body of sentiments, rather than by a system of ideological dogmata. It is almost true that a conservative may be defined as a person who thinks himself such. The conservative movement or body of opinion can accommodate a considerable diversity of views on a good many subjects, there being no Test Act or Thirty-Nine Articles of the conservative creed.

In essence, the conservative person is simply one who finds the permanent things more pleasing than Chaos and Old Night. (Yet conservatives know, with Burke, that healthy "change is the means of our preservation.") A people's historic continuity of experience, says the conservative, offers a guide to policy far better than the abstract designs of coffee-house philosophers. But of course there is more to the conservative persuasion than this general attitude.

It is not possible to draw up a neat catalogue of conservatives' convictions; nevertheless, I offer you, summarily, ten general principles; it seems safe to say that most conservatives would subscribe to most of these maxims. In various editions of my book *The Conservative Mind* I have listed certain canons of conservative thought—the list differing somewhat from edition to edition; in my anthology *The Portable Conservative Reader* I offer variations upon this theme. Now I present to you a summary of conservative assumptions differing somewhat from my canons in those two books of mine. The diversity of ways in which conservative views may find expression is itself proof that conservatism is no fixed ideology. What particular principles conservatives emphasize during any given time will vary with the circumstances and necessities of that era. The following ten articles of belief reflect the emphases of conservatives in America nowadays.

1. AN ENDURING MORAL ORDER

First, the conservative believes that there exists an enduring moral order. That order is made for man, and man is made for it: human nature is a constant, and moral truths are permanent.

This word *order* signifies harmony. There are two aspects or types of order: the inner order of the soul, and the outer order of the commonwealth. Twenty-five centuries ago, Plato taught this doctrine, but even the educated nowadays find it difficult to understand. The problem of order has been a principal concern of conservatives ever since *conservative* became a term of politics.

Our twentieth-century world has experienced the hideous consequences of the collapse of belief in a moral order. Like the atrocities and disasters of Greece in the fifth century before Christ, the ruin of great nations in our century shows us the pit into which fall societies that mistake clever self-interest, or ingenious social controls, for pleasing alternatives to an oldfangled moral order.

It has been said by liberal intellectuals that the conservative believes all social questions, at heart, to be questions of private morality. Properly understood, this statement is quite true. A society in which men and women are governed by belief in an enduring moral order, by a strong sense of right and wrong, by personal convictions about justice and honor, will be a good society—whatever political machinery it may utilize; while a society in which men and women are morally adrift, ignorant of norms, and intent chiefly upon gratification of appetites, will be a bad society—no matter how many people vote and no matter how liberal its formal constitution may be.

2. CUSTOM, CONVENTION, AND CONTINUITY

Second, the conservative adheres to custom, convention, and continuity. It is old custom that enables people to live together peaceably; the destroyers of custom demolish more than they know or desire. It is through convention—a word much abused in our time—that we contrive to avoid perpetual disputes about rights and duties: law at base is a body of conventions. Continuity is the means of linking generation to generation; it matters as much for society as it does for the individual; without it, life is meaningless. When successful revolutionaries have effaced old customs, derided old conventions, and broken the continuity of social institutions—why, presently they discover the necessity of establishing fresh customs, conventions, and continuity; but that process is painful and slow; and the new social order that eventually emerges may be much inferior to the old order that radicals overthrew in their zeal for the Earthly Paradise.

Conservatives are champions of custom, convention, and continuity because they prefer the devil they know to the devil they don't know. Order and justice and freedom, they believe, are the artificial products of a long social experience, the result of centuries of trial and reflection and sacrifice. Thus the body social is a kind of spiritual corporation, comparable to the church; it may even be called a community of souls. Human society is no machine, to be treated mechanically. The continuity, the life-blood, of a society must not be interrupted. Burke's reminder of the necessity for prudent change is in the mind of the conservative. But necessary change, conservatives argue, ought to be gradual and discriminatory, never unfixing old interests at once.

3. STANDING ON THE SHOULDERS OF GIANTS

Third, conservatives believe in what may be called the principle of prescription. Conservatives sense that modern people are dwarfs on the shoulders of giants, able to see farther than their ancestors only because of the great stature of those who have preceded us in time. Therefore conservatives very often emphasize the importance of *prescription*—that is, of things established by immemorial usage, so that the mind of man runneth not to the contrary. There exist rights of which the chief sanction is their antiquity—including rights to property, often. Similarly, our morals are prescriptive in great part. Conservatives argue that we are unlikely, we moderns, to make any brave new discoveries in morals or politics or taste. It is perilous to weigh every passing issue on the basis of private judgment and private rationality. The individual is foolish, but the species is wise, Burke declared. In politics we do well to abide by precedent and precept and even prejudice, for the great mysterious incorporation of the human race has acquired a prescriptive wisdom far greater than any man's petty private rationality.

4. PRUDENCE IS CHIEF AMONG VIRTUES

Fourth, conservatives are guided by their principle of prudence. Burke agrees with Plato that in the statesman, prudence is chief among virtues. Any public measure ought to be judged by its probable long-run consequences, not merely by temporary advantage or popularity. Liberals and radicals, the conservative says, are imprudent: for they dash at their objectives without giving much heed to the risk of new abuses worse than the evils they hope to sweep away. As John Randolph of Roanoke put it, Providence moves slowly, but the devil always hurries. Human society being complex, remedies cannot be simple if they are to be efficacious. The conservative declares that he acts only after sufficient reflection, having weighed the consequences. Sudden and slashing reforms are as perilous as sudden and slashing surgery.

5. THE PRESERVATION OF DIFFERENCES

Fifth, conservatives pay attention to the principle of variety. They feel affection for the proliferating intricacy of long-established social institutions and modes of life, as distinguished from the narrowing uniformity and deadening egalitarianism of radical systems. For the preservation of a healthy diversity in any civilization, there must survive orders and classes, differences in material condition, and many sorts of inequality. The only true forms of equality are equality at the Last Judgment and equality before a just court of law; all other attempts at leveling must lead, at best, to social stagnation. Society requires honest and able leadership; and if natural and institutional differences are destroyed, presently some tyrant or host of squalid oligarchs will create new forms of inequality.

6. RESISTING THE UTOPIAN AND ANARCHIC IMPULSE

Human nature suffers irremediably from certain grave faults, the conservatives know. Man being imperfect, no perfect social order ever can be created. Because of human restlessness, mankind would grow rebellious under any utopian domination, and would break out once more in violent discontent—or else expire of boredom. To seek for utopia is to end in disaster, the conservative says: we are not made for perfect things. All that we reasonably can expect is a tolerably ordered, just, and free society, in which some evils, maladjustments, and suffering will continue to lurk. By proper attention to prudent reform, we may preserve and improve this tolerable order. But if the old institutional and moral safeguards of a nation are neglected, then the anarchic impulse in humankind breaks loose:

"the ceremony of innocence is drowned." The ideologues who promise the perfection of man and society have converted a great part of the twentieth-century world into a terrestrial hell.

7. FREEDOM AND PRIVATE PROPERTY ARE RELATED

Seventh, conservatives are persuaded that freedom and property are closely linked. Separate property from private possession, and Leviathan becomes master of all. Upon the foundation of private property, great civilizations are built. The more widespread is the possession of private property, the more stable and productive is a commonwealth. Economic leveling, conservatives maintain, is not economic progress. Getting and spending are not the chief aims of human existence; but a sound economic basis for the person, the family, and the commonwealth is much to be desired.

Sir Henry Maine, in his *Village Communities*, puts strongly the case for private property, as distinguished from communal property: "Nobody is at liberty to attack several property and to say at the same time that he values civilization. The history of the two cannot be disentangled." For the institution of several property—that is, private property—has been a powerful instrument for teaching men and women responsibility, for providing motives to integrity, for supporting general culture, for raising mankind above the level of mere drudgery, for affording leisure to think and freedom to act. To be able to retain the fruits of one's labor; to be able to see one's work made permanent; to be able to bequeath one's property to one's posterity; to be able to rise from the natural condition of grinding poverty to the security of enduring accomplishment; to have something that is really one's own—these are advantages difficult to deny. The conservative acknowledges that the possession of property fixes certain duties upon the possessor; he accepts those moral and legal obligations cheerfully.

8. VOLUNTARY COMMUNITY VS. INVOLUNTARY COLLECTIVISM

Eighth, conservatives uphold voluntary community, quite as they oppose involuntary collectivism. Although Americans have been attached strongly to privacy and private rights, they also have been a people conspicuous for a successful spirit of community. In a genuine community, the decisions most directly affecting the lives of citizens are made locally and voluntarily. Some of these functions are carried out by local political bodies, others by private associations: so long as they are kept local, and are marked by the general agreement of those affected, they constitute healthy community. But when these functions pass by default or usurpation to centralized authority, then community is in serious danger. Whatever is beneficent and prudent in modern democracy is made possible through cooperative volition. If, then, in the name of an abstract Democracy, the functions of community are transferred to distant political direction—why, real government by the consent of the governed gives way to a standardizing process hostile to freedom and human dignity.

For a nation is no stronger than the numerous little communities of which it is composed. A central administration, or a corps of select managers and civil servants, however well intentioned and well trained, cannot confer justice and prosperity and tranquility upon a mass of men and women deprived of their old responsibilities. That experiment has been made before; and it has been disastrous. It is the performance of our duties in community that teaches us prudence and efficiency and charity.

9. POWER AND PASSION REQUIRE RESTRAINT

Ninth, the conservative perceives the need for prudent restraints upon power and upon human passions. Politically speaking, power is the ability to do as one likes, regardless of the wills of one's fellows. A state in which an individual or a small group are able to dominate the wills of their fellows without check is a despotism, whether it is called monarchical or aristocratic or democratic. When every person claims to be a power unto himself, then society falls into anarchy. Anarchy never lasts long, being intolerable for everyone, and contrary to the ineluctable fact that some persons are more strong and more clever than their neighbors. To anarchy there succeeds tyranny or oligarchy, in which power is monopolized by a very few.

The conservative endeavors to so limit and balance political power that anarchy or tyranny may not arise. In every age, nevertheless, men and women are tempted to overthrow the limitations upon power, for the sake of some fancied temporary advantage. It is characteristic of the radical that he thinks of power as a force for good—so long as the power falls into his hands. In the name of liberty, the French and Russian revolutionaries abolished the old restraints upon power; but power cannot be abolished; it always finds its way into someone's hands. That power which the revolutionaries had thought oppressive in the hands of the old regime became many times as tyrannical in the hands of the radical new masters of the state.

Knowing human nature for a mixture of good and evil, the conservative does not put his trust in mere benevolence. Constitutional restrictions, political checks and balances, adequate enforcement of the laws, the old intricate web of restraints upon will and appetite— these the conservative approves as instruments of freedom and order. A just government maintains a healthy tension between the claims of authority and the claims of liberty.

10. PERMANENCE AND CHANGE MUST BE RECOGNIZED AND RECONCILED

Tenth, the thinking conservative understands that permanence and change must be recognized and reconciled in a vigorous society. The conservative is not opposed to social improvement, although he doubts whether there is any such force as a mystical Progress, with a Roman P, at work in the world. When a society is progressing in some respects, usually it is declining in other respects. The conservative knows that any healthy society is influenced by two forces, which Samuel Taylor Coleridge called its Permanence and its Progression. The Permanence of a society is formed by those enduring interests and convictions that gives us stability and continuity; without that Permanence, the fountains of the great deep are broken up, society slipping into anarchy. The Progression in a society is that spirit and that body of talents which urge us on to prudent reform and improvement; without that Progression, a people stagnate.

Therefore the intelligent conservative endeavors to reconcile the claims of Permanence and the claims of Progression. He thinks that the liberal and the radical, blind to the just claims of Permanence, would endanger the heritage bequeathed to us, in an endeavor to hurry us into some dubious Terrestrial Paradise. The conservative, in short, favors reasoned and temperate progress; he is opposed to the cult of Progress, whose votaries believe that everything new necessarily is superior to everything old.

Change is essential to the body social, the conservative reasons, just as it is essential to the human body. A body that has ceased to renew itself has begun to die. But if that body is to be vigorous, the change must occur in a regular manner, harmonizing with the form and nature of that body; otherwise change produces a monstrous growth, a cancer, which devours its host. The conservative takes care that nothing in a society should ever be wholly old, and that nothing should ever be wholly new. This is the means of the conservation of a nation, quite as it is the means of conservation of a living organism. Just how much change a society requires, and what sort of change, depend upon the circumstances of an age and a nation.

Such, then, are ten principles that have loomed large during the two centuries of modern conservative thought. Other principles of equal importance might have been discussed here: the conservative understanding of justice, for one, or the conservative view of education. But such subjects, time running on, I must leave to your private investigation.

The great line of demarcation in modern politics, Eric Voegelin used to point out, is not a division between liberals on one side and totalitarians on the other. No, on one side of that line are all those men and women who fancy that the temporal order is the only order, and that material needs are their only needs, and that they may do as they like with the human patrimony. On the other side of that line are all those people who recognize an enduring moral order in the universe, a constant human nature, and high duties toward the order spiritual and the order temporal.

Chapter 8

The End of History?

FRANCIS FUKUYAMA*

***Francis Fukuyama** is a Bernard L. Schwartz Professor of International Political Economy at the Paul H. Nitze School of Advanced International Studies (SAIS) of Johns Hopkins University, and the director of the SAIS International Development program. He is also chairman of the editorial board of a new magazine, The American Interest.

In watching the flow of events over the past decade or so, it is hard to avoid the feeling that something very fundamental has happened in world history. The past year has seen a flood of articles commemorating the end of the Cold War, and the fact that "peace" seems to be break-ing out in many regions of the world. Most of these analyses lack any larger conceptual frame-work for distinguishing between what is essential and what is contingent or accidental in world history, and are predictably superficial. If Mr. Gorbachev were ousted from the Kremlin or a new Ayatollah proclaimed the millennium for a desolate Middle Eastern capital, these same commentators would scramble to announce the rebirth of a new era of conflict.

And yet, all of these people sense dimly that there is some larger process at work, a process that gives coherence and order to the daily headlines. The twentieth century saw the developed world descend into a paroxysm of ideological violence, as liberalism con-tended first with the remnants of absolutism, then bolshevism and fascism, and finally an updated Marxism that threatened to lead to the ultimate apocalypse of nuclear war. But the century that began full of self-confidence in the ultimate triumph of Western liberal democracy seems at its close to be returning full circle to where it started: not to an "end of ideology" or a convergence between capitalism and socialism, as earlier predicted, but to an unabashed victory of economic and political liberalism.

The triumph of the West, of the Western *idea*, is evident first of all in the total exhaus-tion of viable systematic alternatives to Western liberalism. In the past decade, there have been unmistakable changes in the intellectual climate of the world's two largest commu-nist countries, and the beginnings of significant reform movements in both. But this phe-nomenon extends beyond high politics and it can be seen also in the ineluctable spread of consumerist Western culture in such diverse contexts as the peasants' markets and color television sets now omnipresent throughout China, the cooperative restaurants and cloth-ing stores opened in the past year in Moscow, the Beethoven piped into Japanese depart-ment stores, and the rock music enjoyed in Prague, Rangoon, and Tehran alike.

What we may be witnessing is not just the end of the Cold War, or the passing of a par-ticular period of postwar history, but the end of history as such: that is, the end point of mankind's ideological evolution and the universalization of Western liberal democracy as the final form of human government. This is not to say that there will no longer be events to fill the pages of *Foreign Affairs'* yearly summaries of international relations, for the victory of liberalism has occurred primarily in the realm of ideas or consciousness and is as yet incom-plete in the real or material world. But there are powerful reasons for believing that it is the ideal that will govern the material world *in the long run.* To understand how this is so, we must first consider some theoretical issues concerning the nature of historical change.

I

The notion of the end of history is not an original one. Its best known propagator was Karl Marx, who believed that the direction of historical development was a purposeful one determined by the interplay of material forces, and would come to an end only with the achievement of a communist utopia that would finally resolve all prior contradictions. But the concept of history as a dialectical process with a beginning, a middle, and an end was borrowed by Marx from his great German predecessor Georg Wilhelm Friedrich Hegel.

For better or worse, much of Hegel's historicism has become part of our contemporary intellectual baggage. The notion that mankind has progressed through a series of primitive stages of consciousness on his path to the present, and that these stages corresponded to concrete forms of social organization, such as tribal, slave owning, theocratic, and finally democratic-egalitarian societies, has become inseparable from the modern understanding of man. Hegel was the first philosopher to speak the language of modern social science, insofar as man for him was the product of his concrete historical and social environment and not, as earlier natural right[s] theorists would have it, a collection of more or less fixed "natural" attributes. The mastery and transformation of man's natural environment through the application of science and technology was originally not a Marxist concept, but a Hegelian one. Unlike later historicists whose historical relativism degenerated into relativism *tout court*, however, Hegel believed that history culminated in an absolute moment—a moment in which a final, rational form of society and state became victorious.

It is Hegel's misfortune to be known now primarily as Marx's precursor, and it is our misfortune that few of us are familiar with Hegel's work from direct study, but only as it has been filtered through the distorting lens of Marxism. In France, however, there has been an effort to save Hegel from his Marxist interpreters and to resurrect him as the philosopher who most correctly speaks to our time. Among those modern French interpreters of Hegel, the greatest was certainly Alexandre Kojève, a brilliant Russian émigré who taught a highly influential series of seminars in Paris in the 1930s at the *École Practique des Hautes Etudes,*[1] While largely unknown in the United States, Kojève had a major impact on the intellectual life of the continent. Among his students ranged such future luminaries as Jean-Paul Sartre on the Left and Raymond Aron on the Right; postwar existentialism borrowed many of its basic categories from Hegel via Kojève.

Kojève sought to resurrect the Hegel of the *Phenomenology of Mind*, the Hegel who proclaimed history to be at an end in 1806. For as early as this Hegel saw in Napoleon's defeat of the Prussian monarchy at the Battle of Jena the victory of the ideals of the French Revolution, and the imminent universalization of the state incorporating the principles of liberty and equality. Kojève, far from rejecting Hegel in light of the turbulent events of the next century and a half, insisted that the latter had been essentially correct.[2] The Battle of Jena marked the end of history because it was at that point that the *vanguard* of humanity

---

[1]   Kojève's best known work is his *Introduction à la lecture de Hegel* (Paris: Editions Gallimard, 1947), which is a transcript of the École Practique lectures from the 1930s. This book is available in English entitled *Introduction to the Reading of Hegel* arranged by Raymond Queneau, edited by Allan Bloom, and translated by James Nichols (New York: Basic Books, 1969).

[2]   In this respect Kojève stands in sharp contrast to contemporary German interpreters of Hegel like Herbert Marcuse who, being more sympathetic to Marx, regarded Hegel ultimately as an historically bound and incomplete philosopher.

(a term quite familiar to Marxists) actualized the principles of the French Revolution. While there was considerable work to be done after 1806—abolishing slavery and the slave trade, extending the franchise to workers, women, blacks, and other racial minorities, etc.—the basic *principles* of the liberal democratic state could not be improved upon. The two world wars in this century and their attendant revolutions and upheavals simply had the effect of extending those principles spatially, such that the various provinces of human civilization were brought up to the level of its most advanced outposts, and of forcing those societies in Europe and North America at the vanguard of civilization to implement their liberalism more fully.

The state that emerges at the end of history is liberal insofar as it recognizes and protects through a system of law man's universal right to freedom, and democratic insofar as it exists only with the consent of the governed. For Kojève, this so-called "universal homogenous state" found real-life embodiment in the countries of postwar Western Europe—precisely those flabby, prosperous, self-satisfied, inward-looking, weak-willed states whose grandest project was nothing more heroic than the creation of the Common Market.[3] But this was only to be expected. For human history and the conflict that characterized it was based on the existence of "contradictions": primitive man's quest for mutual recognition, the dialectic of the master and slave, the transformation and mastery of nature, the struggle for the universal recognition of rights, and the dichotomy between proletarian and capitalist. But in the universal homogenous state, all prior contradictions are resolved and all human needs are satisfied. There is no struggle or conflict over "large" issues, and consequently no need for generals or statesmen; what remains is primarily economic activity. And indeed, Kojève's life was consistent with his teaching. Believing that there was no more work for philosophers as well, since Hegel (correctly understood) had already achieved absolute knowledge, Kojève left teaching after the war and spent the remainder of his life working as a bureaucrat in the European Economic Community, until his death in 1968.

To his contemporaries at mid-century, Kojève's proclamation of the end of history must have seemed like the typical eccentric solipsism of a French intellectual, coming as it did on the heels of World War II and at the very height of the Cold War. To comprehend how Kojève could have been so audacious as to assert that history has ended, we must first of all understand the meaning of Hegelian idealism.

II

For Hegel, the contradictions that drive history exist first of all in the realm of human consciousness, i.e. on the level of ideas[4]—not the trivial election year proposals of American politicians, but ideas in the sense of large unifying world views that might best be understood under the rubric of ideology. Ideology in this sense is not restricted to the secular and explicit political doctrines we usually associate with the term, but can include religion, culture, and the complex of moral values underlying any society as well.

---

[3]   Kojève alternatively identified the end of history with the postwar "American way of life," toward which he thought the Soviet Union was moving as well.

[4]   This notion was expressed in the famous aphorism from the preface to the *Philosophy of History* to the effect that "everything that is rational is real, and everything that is real is rational."

Hegel's view of the relationship between the ideal and the real or material worlds was an extremely complicated one, beginning with the fact that for him the distinction between the two was apparent.[5] He did not believe that the real world conformed or could be made to conform to ideological preconceptions of philosophy professors in any simpleminded way, or that the "material" world could not impinge on the ideal. Indeed, Hegel the professor was temporarily thrown out of work as a result of a very material event, the Battle of Jena. But while Hegel's writing and thinking could be stopped by a bullet from the material world, the hand on the trigger of the gun was motivated in turn by the ideas of liberty and equality that had driven the French Revolution.

For Hegel, all human behavior in the material world, and hence all human history, is rooted in a prior state of consciousness—an idea similar to the one expressed by John Maynard Keynes when he said that the views of men of affairs were usually derived from defunct economists and academic scribblers of earlier generations. This consciousness may not be explicit and self-aware, as are modern political doctrines, but may rather take the form of religion or simple cultural or moral habits. And yet this realm of consciousness *in the long run* necessarily becomes manifest in the material world, indeed creates the material world in its own image. Consciousness is cause and not effect, and can develop autonomously from the material world, hence the real subtext underlying the apparent jumble of current events is the history of ideology.

Hegel's idealism has fared poorly at the hands of later thinkers. Marx revered the priority of the real and the ideal completely, relegating the entire realm of consciousness—religion, art, culture, philosophy itself—to a "superstructure" that was determined entirely by the prevailing material mode of production. Yet another unfortunate legacy of Marxism is our tendency to retreat into materialist or utilitarian explanations of political or historical phenomena, and our disinclination to believe in the autonomous power of ideas. A recent example of this is Paul Kennedy's hugely successful *The Rise and Fall of the Great Powers*, which ascribes the decline of great powers to simple economic overextension. Obviously, this is true on some level: an empire whose economy is barely above the level of subsistence cannot bankrupt its treasury indefinitely. But whether a highly productive modern industrial society chooses to spend 3 or 7 percent of its GNP on defense rather than consumption is entirely a matter of that society's political priorities, which are in turn determined in the realm of consciousness.

The materialist bias of modern thought is characteristic not only of people on the Left who may be sympathetic to Marxism, but of many passionate anti-Marxists as well. Indeed, there is on the right what one might label the *Wall Street Journal* school of deterministic materialism that discounts the importance of ideology and culture and sees man as essentially a rational, profit-maximizing individual. It is precisely this kind of individual and his pursuit of material incentives that is posited as the basis for economic life as such in economic textbooks.[6] One small example will illustrate the problematic character of such materialist views.

---

[5] Indeed, for Hegel the very dichotomy between the ideal and material worlds was itself only an apparent one that was ultimately overcome by the self-conscious subject; in his system, the material world is itself only an aspect of mind.

[6] In fact, modern economists, recognizing that man does not always behave as a *profit-* maximizer, posit a "utility" function, utility being either income or some other good that can be maximized: leisure, sexual satisfaction, or the pleasure of philosophizing. That profit must be replaced with a value like utility indicates the cogency of the idealist perspective.

Max Weber begins his famous book, *The Protestant Ethic and the Spirit of Capitalism*, by noting the different economic performance of Protestant and Catholic communities throughout Europe and America, summed up in the proverb that Protestants eat well while Catholics sleep well. Weber notes that according to any economic theory that posited man as a rational profit-maximizer, raising the piece-work rate should increase labor productivity. But in fact, in many traditional peasant communities, raising the piece-work rate actually had the opposite effect of *lowering* labor productivity: at the higher rate, a peasant accustomed to earning two and one-half marks per day found he could earn the same amount by working less, and did so because he valued leisure more than income. The choices of leisure over income, or of the militaristic life of the Spartan hoplite over the wealth of the Athenian trader, or even the ascetic life of the early capitalist entrepreneur over that of a traditional leisured aristocrat, cannot possibly be explained by the impersonal working of material forces, but come preeminently out of the sphere of consciousness— what we have labeled here broadly as ideology. And indeed, a central theme of Weber's work was to prove that contrary to Marx, the material mode of production, far from being the "base," was itself a "superstructure" with roots in religion and culture, and that to understand the emergence of modern capitalism and the profit motive one had to study their antecedents in the realm of the spirit.

As we look around the contemporary world, the poverty of materialist theories of economic development is all too apparent. The *Wall Street Journal* school of deterministic materialism habitually points to the stunning economic success of Asia in the past few decades as evidence of the viability of free market economics, with the implication that all societies would see similar development were they simply to allow their populations to pursue their material self-interest freely. Surely free markets and stable political systems are a necessary precondition to capitalist economic growth. But just as surely the cultural heritage of those Far Eastern societies, the ethic of work and saving and family, a religious heritage that does not, like Islam, place restrictions on certain forms of economic behavior, and other deeply ingrained moral qualities, are equally important in explaining their economic performance.[7] And yet the intellectual weight of materialism is such that not a single respectable contemporary theory of economic development addresses consciousness and culture seriously as the matrix within which economic behavior is formed.

Failure to understand that the roots of economic behavior lie in the realm of consciousness and culture leads to the common mistake of attributing material causes to phenomena that are essentially ideal in nature. For example, it is commonplace in the West to interpret the reform movements first in China and most recently in the Soviet Union as the victory of the material over the ideal—that is, a recognition that ideological incentives could not replace material ones in stimulating a highly productive modern economy, and that if one wanted to prosper one had to appeal to baser forms of self-interest. But the deep defects of socialist economies were evident thirty or forty years ago to anyone who chose to look. Why was it that these countries moved away from central planning in the 1980s?

[7] One need look no further than the recent performance of Vietnamese immigrants in the U.S. school system when compared to their black or Hispanic classmates to realize that culture and consciousness are absolutely crucial to explain not only economic behavior but virtually every other important aspect of life as well.

The answer must be found in the consciousness of the elites and leaders ruling them, who decided to opt for the "Protestant" life of wealth and risk over the "Catholic" path of poverty and security.[8] That change was in no way made inevitable by the material condition in which either country found itself on the eve of the reform, but instead came about as the result of the victory of one idea over another.[9]

For Kojève, as for all good Hegelians, understanding the underlying processes of history requires understanding developments in the realm of consciousness or ideas, since consciousness will ultimately remake the material world in its own image. To say that history ended in 1806 meant that mankind's ideological evolution ended in the ideals of the French or American Revolutions: while particular regimes in the real world might not implement these ideals fully, their theoretical truth is absolute and could not be improved upon. Hence it did not mater to Kojève that the consciousness of the postwar generation of Europeans had not been universalized throughout the world; if ideological development had in fact ended, the homogenous state would eventually become victorious throughout the material world.

I have neither the space nor, frankly, the ability to defend in depth Hegel's radical idealist perspective. The issue is not whether Hegel's system was right, but whether his perspective might uncover the problematic nature of many materialist explanations we often take for granted. This is not to deny the role of material factors as such. To a literal-minded idealist, human society can be built around any arbitrary set of principles regardless of their relationship to the material world. And in fact men have proven themselves able to endure the most extreme material hardships in the name of ideas that exist in the realm of the spirit alone, be it the divinity of cows or the nature of the Holy Trinity.[10]

But while man's very perception of the material world is shaped by his historical consciousness of it, the material world can clearly affect in return the viability of a particular state of consciousness. In particular, the spectacular abundance of advanced liberal economies and the infinitely diverse consumer culture made possible by them seem to both foster and preserve liberalism in the political sphere. I want to avoid the materialist determinism that says that liberal economics inevitably produces liberal politics, because I believe that both economics and politics presuppose an autonomous prior state of consciousness that makes them possible. But that state of consciousness that permits the growth of liberalism seems to stabilize in the way one would expect at the end of history

---

[8]   I understand that a full explanation of the origins of the reform movements in China and Russia is a good deal more complicated than this simple formula would suggest. The Soviet reform, for example, was motivated in good measure by Moscow's sense of *insecurity* in the technological-military realm. Nonetheless, neither country on the eve of its reforms was in such a state of *material* crisis that one could have predicted the surprising reform paths ultimately taken.

[9]   It is still not clear whether the Soviet people are as "Protestant" as Gorbachev and will follow him down that path.

[10]   The internal politics of the Byzantine Empire at the time of Justinian revolved around a conflict between the so-called monophysites and monothelites, who believed that the unity of the Holy Trinity was alternatively one of nature or of will. This conflict corresponded to some extent to one between proponents of different racing teams in the Hippodrome in Byzantium and led to a not insignificant level of political violence. Modern historians would tend to seek the roots of such conflicts in antagonisms between social classes or some other modern economic category, being unwilling to believe that men would kill each other over the nature of the Trinity.

if it is underwritten by the abundance of a modern free market economy. We might summarize the content of the universal homogenous state as liberal democracy in the political sphere combined with easy access to VCRs and stereos in the economic.

III

Have we in fact reached the end of history? Are there, in other words, any fundamental "contradictions" in human life that cannot be resolved in the context of modern liberalism, that would be resolvable by an alternative political-economic structure? If we accept the idealist premises laid out above, we must seek an answer to this question in the realm of ideology and consciousness. Our task is not to answer exhaustively the challenges to liberalism promoted by every crackpot messiah around the world, but only those that are embodied in important social or political forces and movements, and which are therefore part of world history. For our purposes, it matters very little what strange thoughts occur to people in Albania or Burkina Faso, for we are interested in what one could in some sense call the common ideological heritage of mankind.

In the past century, there have been two major challenges to liberalism, those of fascism and of communism. The former[11] saw the political weakness, materialism, anomie, and lack of community of the West as fundamental contradictions in liberal societies that could only be resolved by a strong state that forged a new "people" on the basis of national excessiveness. Fascism was destroyed as a living ideology by World War II. This was a defeat, of course, on a very material level, but it amounted to a defeat of the idea as well. What destroyed fascism as an idea was not universal moral revulsion against it, since plenty of people were willing to endorse the idea as long as it seemed the wave of the future, but its lack of success. After the war, it seemed to most people that German fascism as well as its other European and Asian variants were bound to self-destruct. There was no material reason why new fascist movements could not have sprung up again after the war in other locales, but for the fact that expansionist ultranationalism, with its promise of unending conflict leading to disastrous military defeat, had completely lost its appeal. The ruins of the Reich chancellory as well as the atomic bombs dropped on Hiroshima and Nagasaki killed this ideology on the level of consciousness as well as materially, and all of the proto-fascist movements spawned by the German and Japanese examples like the Peronist movement in Argentina or Subhas Chandra Bose's Indian National Army withered after the war.

The ideological challenge mounted by the other great alternative to liberalism, communism, was far more serious. Marx, speaking Hegel's language, asserted that liberal society contained a fundamental contradiction that could not be resolved within its context, that between capital and labor, and this contradiction has constituted the chief accusation

---

[11] I am not using the term "fascism" here in its most precise sense, fully aware of the frequent misuse of this term to denounce anyone to the right of the user. "Fascism" here denotes any organized ultranationalist movement with universalistic pretensions—not universalistic with regard to its nationalism, of course, since the latter is exclusive by definition, but with regard to the movement's belief in its right to rule other people. Hence Imperial Japan would qualify as fascist while former strongman Stoessner's Paraguay or Pinochet's Chile would not. Obviously fascist ideologies cannot be universalistic in the sense of Marxism or liberalism, but the structure of the doctrine can be transferred from country to country.

against liberalism ever since. But surely, the class issue has actually been successfully resolved in the West. As Kojève (among others) noted, the egalitarianism of modern America represents the essential achievement of the classless society envisioned by Marx. This is not to say that there are not rich people and poor people in the United States, or that the gap between them has not grown in recent years. But the root causes of economic inequality do not have to do with the underlying legal and social structure of our society, which remains fundamentally egalitarian and moderately redistributionist, so much as with the cultural and social characteristics of the groups that make it up, which are in turn the historical legacy of premodern conditions. Thus black poverty in the United States is not the inherent product of liberalism, but is rather the "legacy of slavery and racism" which persisted long after the formal abolition of slavery.

As a result of the receding of the class issue, the appeal of communism in the developed Western world, it is safe to say, is lower today than any time since the end of the First World War. This can be measured in any number of ways: in the declining membership and electoral pull of the major European communist parties, and their overtly revisionist programs; in the corresponding electoral success of conservative parties from Britain and Germany to the United States and Japan which are unabashedly pro-market and anti-statist; and in an intellectual climate whose most "advanced" members no longer believe that bourgeois society is something that ultimately needs to be overcome. This is to say that the opinions of progressive intellectuals in Western countries are not deeply pathological in any number of ways. But those who believe that the future must inevitably be socialist tend to be very old, or very marginal to the real political discourse of their societies.

One may argue that the socialist alternative was never terribly plausible for the North Atlantic world, and was sustained for the last several decades primarily by its success outside of this region. But it is precisely in the non-European world that one is most struck by the occurrence of major ideological transformations. Surely the most remarkable changes have occurred in Asia. Due to the strength and adaptability of the indigenous cultures there, Asia became a battleground for a variety of imported Western ideologies early in this century. Liberalism in Asia was a very weak reed in the period after World War I; it is easy today to forget how gloomy Asia's political future looked as recently as ten or fifteen years ago. It is easy to forget as well how momentous the outcome of Asian ideological struggles seemed for world political development as a whole.

The first Asian alternative to liberalism to be decisively defeated was the fascist one represented by Imperial Japan. Japanese fascism (like its German version) was defeated by the force of American arms in the Pacific war, and liberal democracy was imposed on Japan by a victorious United States. Western capitalism and political liberalism when transplanted to Japan were adapted and transformed by the Japanese in such a way as to be scarcely recognizable.[12] Many Americans are now aware that Japanese industrial organization is very different from that prevailing in the United States or Europe, and it is questionable what relationship the factional maneuvering that takes place with the governing

---

[12]   I use the example of Japan with some caution, since Kojève late in his life came to conclude that Japan, with its culture based on purely formal arts, proved that the universal homogenous state was not victorious and that history had perhaps not ended. See the long note at the end of the second edition of *Introduction à la Lecture de Hegel*, 462–3.

Liberal Democratic Party bears to democracy. Nonetheless, the very fact that the essential elements of economic and political liberalism have been so successfully grafted onto uniquely Japanese traditions and institutions guarantees their survival in the long run. More important is the contribution that Japan has made in turn to world history by following in the footsteps of the United States to create a truly universal consumer culture that has become both a symbol and an underpinning of the universal homogenous state. V.S. Naipaul traveling in Khomeini's Iran shortly after the revolution noted the omnipresent signs advertising the products of Sony, Hitachi, and JVC, whose appeal remained virtually irresistible and gave the lie to the regime's pretensions of restoring a state based on the rule of the *Shariah*. Desire for access to the consumer culture, created in large measure by Japan, has played a crucial role in fostering the spread of economic liberalism throughout Asia, and hence in promoting political liberalism as well.

The economic success of the other newly industrializing countries (NICs) in Asia following on the example of Japan is by now a familiar story. What is important from a Hegelian standpoint is that political liberalism has been following economic liberalism, more slowly than many had hoped but with seeming inevitability. Here again we see the victory of the idea of the universal homogenous state. South Korea had developed into a modern, urbanized society with an increasingly large and well-educated middle class that could not possibly be isolated from the larger democratic trends around them. Under these circumstances it seemed intolerable to a large part of this population that it should be ruled by an anachronistic military regime while Japan, only a decade or so ahead in economic terms, had parliamentary institutions for over forty years. Even the former socialist regime in Burma, which for so many decades existed in dismal isolation from the larger trends dominating Asia, was buffeted in the past year by pressures to liberalize both its economy and political system. It is said that unhappiness with strongman Ne Win began when a senior Burmese officer went to Singapore for medical treatment and broke down crying when he saw how far socialist Burma had been left behind by its ASEAN neighbors.

But the power of the liberal idea would seem much less impressive if it had not infected the largest and oldest culture in Asia, China. The simple existence of communist China created an alternative pole of ideological attraction, and as such constituted a threat to liberalism. But the past fifteen years have seen an almost total discrediting of Marxism-Leninism as an economic system. Beginning with the famous third plenum of the Tenth Central Committee in 1978, the Chinese Communist party set about decollectivizing agriculture for the 800 million Chinese who still lived in the countryside. The role of the state in agriculture was reduced to that of a tax collector, while production of consumer goods was sharply increased in order to give peasants a taste of the universal homogenous state and thereby an incentive to work. The reform doubled Chinese grain output in only five years, and in the process created for Deng Xiaoping a solid political base from which he was able to extend the reform to other parts of the economy. Economic statistics do not begin to describe the dynamism, initiative, and openness evident in China since the reform began.

China could not now be described in any way as a liberal democracy. At present, no more than 20 percent of its economy has been marketized, and most importantly it continues to be ruled by a self-appointed Communist party which has given no hint of wanting to devolve power. Deng has made none of Gorbachev's promises regarding democratization of the political system and there is no Chinese equivalent of *glasnost*. The Chinese leadership has in fact been much more circumspect in criticizing Mao and Maoism than Gorbachev with respect to Brezhnev and Stalin, and the regime continues to pay lip service to Marxism-Leninism as its ideological underpinning. But anyone familiar with the outlook and behavior of the new technocratic elite now governing China knows the Marxism and ideological principle have become virtually irrelevant as guides to policy, and that bourgeois consumerism has a real meaning in that country for the first time since the revolution. The various slowdowns in the pace of reform, the campaigns against "spiritual pollution" and crackdowns on political dissent are more properly seen as tactical adjustments made in the process of managing what is an extraordinarily difficult political transition. By ducking the question of political reform while putting the economy on a new footing, Deng has managed to avoid the breakdown of authority that has accompanied Gorbachev's *perestroika*. Yet the pull of the liberal idea continues to be very strong as economic power devolves and the economy becomes more open to the outside world. There are currently over 20,000 Chinese students studying in the U.S. and other Western countries, almost all of them the children of the Chinese elite. It is hard to believe that when they return home to run the country they will be content for China to be the only country in Asia unaffected by the larger democratizing trend. The student demonstrations in Beijing that broke out first in December 1986 and recurred recently on the occasion of Hu Yaobang's death were only the beginning of what will inevitably be mounting pressure for change in the political system as well.

What is important about China from the standpoint of world history is not the present state of the reform or even its future prospects. The central issue is the fact that the People's Republic of China can no longer act as a beacon for illiberal forces around the world, whether they be guerrillas in some Asian jungle or middle class students in Paris. Maoism, rather than being the pattern for Asia's future, became an anachronism, and it was the mainland Chinese who in fact were decisively influenced by the prosperity and dynamism of their overseas co-ethnics—the ironic ultimate victory of Taiwan.

Important as these changes in China have been, however, it is developments in the Soviet Union—the original "homeland of the world proletariat"—that have put the final nail in the coffin of the Marxist-Leninist alternative to liberal democracy. It should be clear that in terms of formal institutions, not much has changed in the four years since Gorbachev has come to power: free markets and the cooperative movement represent only a small part of the Soviet economy, which remains centrally planned; the political system is still dominated by the Communist party, which has only begun to democratize internally and to share power with other groups; the regime continues to assert that it is seeking only to modernize socialism and that its ideological basis remains Marxism-Leninism; and, finally, Gorbachev faces a potentially powerful conservative opposition that could undo many of the changes that have taken place to date. Moreover, it is hard to be too sanguine about the chances for success of Gorbachev's proposed reforms, either in the sphere of economics or politics. But my purpose here is not to analyze events in the short term, or to make predictions for policy purposes, but to look at underlying trends in the sphere of ideology and consciousness. And in that respect, it is clear that an astounding transformation has occurred.

Émigrés from the Soviet Union have been reporting for at least the last generation now that virtually nobody in that country truly believed in Marxism-Leninism any longer, and that this was nowhere more true than in the Soviet elite, which continued to mouth Marxist slogans out of sheer cynicism. The corruption and decadence of the late Brezhnev-era

Soviet state seemed to matter little, however, for as long as the state itself refused to throw into question any of the fundamental principles underlying Soviet society, the system was capable of functioning adequately out of sheer inertia and could even muster some dynamism in the realm of foreign and defense policy. Marxism-Leninism was like a magical incantation which, however absurd and devoid of meaning, was the only common basis on which the elite could agree to rule Soviet society.

What has happened in the four years since Gorbachev's coming to power is a revolutionary assault on the most fundamental institutions and principles of Stalinism, and their replacement by other principles which do not amount to liberalism *per se* but whose only connecting thread is liberalism. This is most evident in the economic sphere, where the reform economists around Gorbachev have become steadily more radical in their support for free markets, to the point where some like Nikolai Shmelev do not mind being compared in public to Milton Friedman. There is a virtual consensus among the currently dominant school of Soviet economists now that central planning and the command system of allocation are the root cause of economic inefficiency, and that if the Soviet system is ever to heal itself, it must permit free and decentralized decision-making with respect to investment, labor, and prices. After a couple of initial years of ideological confusion, these principles have finally been incorporated into policy with the promulgation of new laws on enterprise autonomy, cooperatives, and finally in 1988 on lease arrangements and family farming. There are, of course, a number of fatal flaws in the current implementation of the reform, most notably the absence of a thoroughgoing price reform. But the problem is no longer a *conceptual* one: Gorbachev and his lieutenants seem to understand the economic logic of marketization well enough, but like the leaders of a Third World country facing the IMF, are afraid of the social consequences of ending consumer subsidies and other forms of dependence on the state sector.

In the political sphere, the proposed changes to the Soviet constitution, legal system, and party rules amount to much less than the establishment of a liberal state. Gorbachev has spoken of democratization primarily in the sphere of internal party affairs, and has shown little intention of ending the Communist party's monopoly of power; indeed, the political reform seeks to legitimize and therefore strengthen the CPSU's rule.[13] Nonetheless, the general principles underlying many of the reforms—that the "people" should be truly responsible for their own affairs, that higher political bodies should be answerable to lower ones, and not vice versa, that the rule of law should prevail over arbitrary police actions, with separation of powers and an independent judiciary, that there should be legal protection for property rights, the need for open discussion of public issues and the right of public dissent, the empowering of the Soviets as a forum in which the whole Soviet people can participate, and of a political culture that is more tolerant and pluralistic—come from a source fundamentally alien to the USSR's Marxist-Leninist tradition, even if they are incompletely articulated and poorly implemented in practice.

Gorbachev's repeated assertions that he is doing no more than trying to restore the original meaning of Leninism are themselves a kind of Orwellian doublespeak. Gorbachev and his allies have consistently maintained that intraparty democracy was somehow the

[13] This is not true in Poland and Hungary, however, whose Communist parties have taken moves toward true power sharing and pluralism.

essence of Leninism, and that the various liberal practices of open debate, secret ballot elections, and rule of law were all part of the Leninist heritage, corrupted only later by Stalin. While almost anyone would look good compared to Stalin, drawing so sharp a line between Lenin and his successor is questionable. The essence of Lenin's democratic centralism was centralism, not democracy; that is, the absolutely rigid, monolithic, and disciplined dictatorship of a hierarchically organized vanguard Communist party, speaking in the name of the *demos*. All of Lenin's vicious polemics against Karl Kautsky, Rosa Luxemburg, and various other Menshevik and Social Democratic rivals, not to mention his contempt for "bourgeois legality" and freedoms, centered around his profound conviction that a revolution could not be successfully made by a democratically run organization.

Gorbachev's claim that he is seeking to return to the true Lenin is perfectly easy to understand: having fostered a thorough denunciation of Stalinism and Brezhnevism as the root of the USSR's present predicament, he needs some point in Soviet history on which to anchor the legitimacy of the CPSU's continued rule. But Gorbachev's tactical requirements should not blind us to the fact that the democratizing and decentralizing principles which he has enunciated in both the economic and political spheres are highly subversive of some of the most fundamental precepts of both Marxism and Leninism. Indeed, if the bulk of the present economic reform proposals were put into effect, it is hard to know how the Soviet economy would be more socialist than those of other Western countries with large public sectors.

The Soviet Union could in no way be described as a liberal or democratic country now, nor do I think that it is terribly likely that *perestroika* will succeed such that the label will be thinkable any time in the near future. But at the end of history it is not necessary that all societies become successful liberal societies, merely that they end their ideological pretensions of representing different and higher forms of human society. And in this respect I believe that something very important has happened in the Soviet Union in the past few years: the criticisms of the Soviet system sanctioned by Gorbachev have been so thorough and devastating that there is very little chance of going back to either Stalinism or Brezhnevism in any simple way. Gorbachev has finally permitted people to say what they had privately understood for many years, namely, that the magical incantations of Marxism-Leninism were nonsense, that Soviet socialism was not superior to the West in any respect but was in fact a monumental failure. The conservative opposition in the USSR, consisting both of simple workers afraid of unemployment and inflation and of party officials fearful of losing their jobs and privileges, is outspoken and may be strong enough to force Gorbachev's ouster in the next few years. But what both groups desire is tradition, order, and authority; they manifest no deep commitment to Marxism-Leninism, except insofar as they have invested much of their own lives in it.[14] For authority to be restored in the Soviet Union after Gorbachev's demolition work, it must be on the basis of some new and vigorous ideology which has not yet appeared on the horizon.

If we admit for the moment that the fascist and communist challenges to liberalism are dead, are there any other ideological competitors left? Or put another way, are there contradictions in liberal society beyond that of class that are not resolvable? Two possibilities suggest themselves, those of religion and nationalism.

---

[14]   This is particularly true of the leading Soviet conservative, former Second Secretary Yegor Ligachev, who has publicly recognized many of the deep defects of the Brezhnev period.

The rise of religious fundamentalism in recent years within the Christian, Jewish, and Muslim traditions has been widely noted. One is inclined to say that the revival of religion in some way attests to a broad unhappiness with the impersonality and spiritual vacuity of liberal consumerist societies. Yet while the emptiness at the core of liberalism is most certainly a defect in the ideology—indeed, a flaw that one does not need the perspective of religion to recognize[15]—it is not at all clear that it is remediable through politics. Modern liberalism itself was historically a consequence of the weakness of religiously based societies which, failing to agree on the nature of the good life, could not provide even the minimal preconditions of peace and stability. In the contemporary world only Islam has offered a theocratic state as a political alternative to both liberalism and communism. But the doctrine has little appeal for non-Muslims, and it is hard to believe that the movement will take on any universal significance. Other less organized religious impulses have been successfully satisfied within the sphere of personal life that is permitted in liberal societies.

The other major "contradiction" potentially unresolvable by liberalism is the one posed by nationalism and other forms of racial and ethnic consciousness. It is certainly true that a very large degree of conflict since the Battle of Jena has had its roots in nationalism. Two cataclysmic world wars in this century have been spawned by the nationalism of the developed world in various guises, and if those passions have been muted to a certain extent in postwar Europe, they are still extremely powerful in the Third World. Nationalism has been a threat to liberalism historically in Germany, and continues to be one in isolated parts of "post-historical" Europe like Northern Ireland.

But it is not clear that nationalism represents an irreconcilable contradiction in the heart of liberalism. In the first place, nationalism is not one single phenomenon but several, ranging from mild cultural nostalgia to the highly organized and elaborately articulated doctrine of National Socialism. Only systematic nationalisms of the latter sort can qualify as a formal ideology on the level of liberalism or communism. The vast majority of the world's nationalist movements do not have a political program beyond the negative desire of independence *from* some other group or people, and do not offer anything like a comprehensive agenda for socio-economic organization. As such, they are compatible with doctrines and ideologies that do offer such agendas. While they may constitute a source of conflict for liberal societies, this conflict does not arise from liberalism itself so much as from the fact that the liberalism in question is incomplete. Certainly a great deal of the world's ethnic and nationalist tension can be explained in terms of peoples who are forced to live in unrepresentative political systems that they have not chosen.

While it is impossible to rule out the sudden appearance of new ideologies or previously unrecognized contradictions in liberal societies, then, the present world seems to confirm that the fundamental principles of socio-political organization have not advanced terribly far since 1806. Many of the wars and revolutions fought since that time have been undertaken in the name of ideologies which claimed to be more advanced than liberalism, but whose pretensions were ultimately unmasked by history. In the meantime, they have helped to spread the universal homogenous state to the point where it could have a significant effect on the overall character of international relations.

---

[15] I am thinking particularly of Rousseau and the Western philosophical tradition that flows from him that was highly critical of Lockean or Hobbesian liberalism, though one could criticize liberalism from the standpoint of classical political philosophy as well.

IV

What are the implications of the end of history for international relations? Clearly, the vast bulk of the Third World remains very much mired in history, and will be a terrain of conflict for many years to come. But let us focus for the time being on the larger and more developed states of the world who after all account for the greater part of world politics. Russia and China are not likely to join the developed nations of the West as liberal societies any time in the foreseeable future, but suppose for a moment that Marxism-Leninism ceases to be a factor driving the foreign policies of these states—a prospect which, if not yet here, the last few years have made a real possibility. How will the overall characteristics of a de-ideologized world differ from those of the one with which we are familiar at such a hypothetical juncture?

The most common answer is—not very much. For there is a very widespread belief among many observers of international relations that underneath the skin of ideology is a hard core of great power national interest that guarantees a fairly high level of competition and conflict between nations. Indeed, according to one academically popular school of international relations theory, conflict inheres in the international system as such, and to understand the prospects for conflict one must look at the shape of the system—for example, whether it is bipolar or multipolar—rather than at the specific character of the nations and regimes that constitute it. This school in effect applies a Hobbesian view of politics to international relations, and assumes that aggression and insecurity are universal characteristics of human societies rather than the product of specific historical circumstances.

Believers in this line of thought take the relations that existed between the participants in the classical nineteenth-century European balance of power as a model for what a de-ideologized contemporary world would look like. Charles Krauthammer, for example, recently explained that if as a result of Gorbachev's reforms the USSR is shorn of Marxist-Leninist ideology, its behavior will revert to that of nineteenth-century imperial Russia.[16] While he finds this more reassuring than the threat posed by a communist Russia, he implies that there will still be a substantial degree of competition and conflict in the international system, just as there was say between Russia and Britain or Wilhelmine Germany in the last century. This is, of course, a convenient point of view for people who want to admit that something major is changing in the Soviet Union, but do not want to accept responsibility for recommending the radical policy redirection implicit in such a view. But is it true?

In fact, the notion that ideology is a superstructure imposed on a substratum of permanent great power interest is a highly questionable proposition. For the way in which any state defines its national interest is not universal but rests on some kind of prior ideological basis, just as we saw that economic behavior is determined by a prior state of consciousness. In this century, states have adopted highly articulated doctrines with explicit foreign policy agendas legitimizing expansionism, like Marxism-Leninism or National Socialism.

The expansionist and competitive behavior of nineteenth-century European states rested on no less ideal a basis; it just so happened that the ideology driving it was less explicit than the doctrines of the twentieth century. For one thing, most "liberal" European

---

[16] See his article, "Beyond the Cold War," *New Republic*, December 19, 1988.

societies were illiberal insofar as they believed in the legitimacy of imperialism, that is, the right of one nation to rule over other nations without regard for the wishes of the ruled. The justifications for imperialism varied from nation to nation, from a crude belief in the legitimacy of force, particularly when applied to non-Europeans, to the White Man's Burden and Europe's Christianizing mission, to the desire to give people of color access to the culture of Rabelais and Molière. But whatever the particular ideological basis, every "developed" country believed in the acceptability of higher civilizations ruling lower ones—including, incidentally, the United States with regard to the Philippines. This led to a drive for pure territorial aggrandizement in the latter half of the century and played no small role in causing the Great War.

The radical and deformed outgrowth of nineteenth-century imperialism was German fascism, an ideology which justified Germany's right not only to rule over non-European peoples, but over *all* non-German ones. But in retrospect it seems that Hitler represented a diseased bypath in the general course of European development, and since his fiery defeat, the legitimacy of any kind of territorial aggrandizement has been thoroughly discredited.[17] Since the Second World War, European nationalism has been defanged and shorn of any real relevance to foreign policy, with the consequence that the nineteenth-century model of great power behavior has become a serious anachronism. The most extreme form of nationalism that any Western European state has mustered since 1945 has been Gaullism, whose self-assertion has been confined largely to the realm of nuisance politics and culture. International life for the part of the world that has reached the end of history is far more preoccupied with economics than with politics or strategy.

The developed states of the West do maintain defense establishments and in the postwar period have competed vigorously for influence to meet a worldwide communist threat. This behavior has been driven, however, by an external threat from states that possess overtly expansionist ideologies, and would not exist in their absence. To take the "neorealist" theory seriously, one would have to believe that "natural" competitive behavior would reassert itself among the OECD states were Russia and China to disappear from the face of the earth. That is, West Germany and France would arm themselves against each other as they did in the 1930s, Australia and New Zealand would send military advisers to block each others' advances in Africa, and the U.S.–Canadian border would become fortified. Such a prospect is, of course, ludicrous: minus Marxist-Leninist ideology, we are far more likely to see the "Common Marketization" of world politics than the disintegration of the EEC into nineteenth-century competitiveness. Indeed, as our experience in dealing with Europe on matters such as terrorism or Libya prove, they are much further gone than we down the road that denies the legitimacy of the use of force in international politics, even in self-defense.

The automatic assumption that Russia shorn of its expansionist communist ideology should pick up where the czars left off just prior to the Bolshevik Revolution is therefore a curious one. It assumes that the evolution of human consciousness has stood still in the meantime, and that the Soviets, while picking up currently fashionable ideas in the realm of economics, will return to foreign policy views a century out of date in the rest of Europe.

[17] It took European colonial powers like France several years after the war to admit the illegitimacy of their empires, but decolonialization was an inevitable consequence of the Allied victory which had been based on the promise of a restoration of democratic freedoms.

This is certainly not what happened to China after it began its reform process. Chinese competitiveness and expansionism on the world scene have virtually disappeared: Beijing no longer sponsors Maoist insurgencies or tries to cultivate influence in distant Africa countries as it did in the 1960s. This is not to say that there are not troublesome aspects to contemporary Chinese foreign policy, such as the reckless sale of ballistic missile technology in the Middle East; and the [People's Republic of China] continues to manifest traditional great power behavior in its sponsorship of the Khmer Rouge against Vietnam. But the former is explained by commercial motives and the latter is a vestige of earlier ideologically based rivalries. The new China far more resembles Gaullist France than pre World War I Germany.

The real question for the future, however, is the degree to which Soviet elites have assimilated the consciousness of the universal homogenous state that is post-Hitler Europe. From their writings and from my own personal contacts with them, there is no question in my mind that the liberal Soviet intelligentsia rallying around Gorbachev has arrived at the end-of-history view in a remarkably short time, due in no small measure to the contacts they have had since the Brezhnev era with the larger European civilization around them. "New political thinking," the general rubric for their views, describes a world dominated by economic concerns, in which there are no ideological grounds for major conflict between nations, and in which, consequently, the use of military force becomes less legitimate. As Foreign Minister Shevardnadze put it in mid-1988:

> *The struggle between two opposing systems is no longer a determining tendency of the present-day era. At the modern stage, the ability to build up material wealth at an accelerated rate on the basis of front-ranking science and high level techniques and technology, and to distribute it fairly, and through joint efforts to restore and protect the resources necessary for mankind's survival acquires decisive importance.*[18]

The post-historical consciousness represented by "new thinking" is only one possible future for the Soviet Union, however. There has always been a very strong current of great Russian chauvinism in the Soviet Union, which has found freer expression since the advent of *glasnost*. It may be possible to return to traditional Marxism-Leninism for a while as a simple rallying point for those who want to restore the authority that Gorbachev has dissipated. But as in Poland, Marxism-Leninism is dead as a mobilizing ideology: under its banner people cannot be made to work harder, and its adherents have lost confidence in themselves. Unlike the propagators of traditional Marxism-Leninism, however, ultranationalists in the USSR believe in their Slavophile cause passionately, and one gets the sense that the fascist alternative is not one that has played itself out entirely there.

The Soviet Union, then, is at a fork in the road: it can start down the path that was staked out by Western Europe forty-five years ago, a path that most of Asia has followed, or it can realize its own uniqueness and remain stuck in history. The choice it makes will be highly important for us, given the Soviet Union's size and military strength, for that power will continue to preoccupy us and slow our realization that we have already emerged on the other side of history.

---

[18]   *Vestnik Ministerstva Inostrannikh Del SSSR* no. 15 (August 1988), 27–46. "New thinking" does of course serve a propagandistic purpose in persuading Western audiences of Soviet good intentions. But the fact that it is good propaganda does not mean that its formulators do not take many of its ideas seriously.

V

The passing of Marxism-Leninism first from China and then from the Soviet Union will mean its death as a living ideology of world historical significance. For while there may be some isolated true believers left in places like Managua, Pyongyang, or Cambridge, Massachusetts, the fact that there is not a single large state in which it is a going concern undermines completely its pretensions to being in the vanguard of human history. And the death of this ideology means the growing "Common Marketization" of international relations, and the diminution of the likelihood of large-scale conflict between states.

This docs not by any means imply the end of international conflict *per se*. For the world at that point would be divided between a part that was historical and a part that was post-historical. Conflict between states still in history, and between those states and those at the end of history, would still be possible. There would still be a high and perhaps rising level of ethnic and nationalist violence, since those are impulses incompletely played out, even in parts of the post-historical world. Palestinians and Kurds, Sikhs and Tamils, Irish Catholics and Walloons, Armenians and Azeris, will continue to have their unresolved grievances. This implies that terrorism and wars of national liberation will continue to be an important item on the international agenda. But large-scale conflict must involve large states still caught in the grip of history, and they are what appear to be passing from the scene.

The end of history will be a very sad time. The struggle for recognition, the willingness to risk one's life for a purely abstract goal, the worldwide ideological struggle that called forth daring, courage, imagination, and idealism, will be replaced by economic calculation, the endless solving of technical problems, environmental concerns, and the satisfaction of sophisticated consumer demands. In the post-historical period there will be neither art nor philosophy, just the perpetual care taking of the museum of human history. I can feel in myself, and see in others around me, a powerful nostalgia for the time when history existed. Such nostalgia, in fact, will continue to fuel competition and conflict even in the post-historical world for some time to come. Even though I recognize its inevitability, I have the most ambivalent feelings for the civilization that has been created in Europe since 1945, with its north Atlantic and Asian offshoots. Perhaps this very prospect of centuries of boredom at the end of history will serve to get history started once again.

Chapter 9

Socialism and Democracy

CAROL C. GOULD*

*Carol Gould is Professor of Philosophy and Political Science and Director, Center for Global Ethics and Politics, Temple University.

I. INTRODUCTION

Perhaps the leading problem for both political practice and political theory today [1981] is the relation between democracy and socialism. The problem in practice is that both Western democratic societies and contemporary socialist societies fail in different ways to provide the conditions for full individual freedom and meaningful social cooperation. Thus contemporary socialist societies, both in Eastern Europe and in the Third World, are undemocratic in that they fail to protect individual civil liberties, such as freedom of expression and association, and political rights, such as the right to choose one's political representatives freely and the equal right to stand for office. Furthermore, while such societies attempt to introduce cooperation as a principle of economic and social life, yet they exhibit serious domination in the form of extensive bureaucracy, state control, the repression of individual differences, and personal and psychological domination. On the other hand, Western democratic societies, while they protect individual civil liberties and political rights to a significant degree, nonetheless are not flatly democratic in that they do not permit effective political participation by the poor, disadvantaged minorities, and even by the working people who comprise the large majority of the population. This results from the distortion of the political process by the power of wealth and lobbying by special interest groups. Such societies are also not fully democratic in that social and economic life outside the political sphere are characterized by economic exploitation, special privilege, and forms of personal domination. Furthermore, Western democratic societies fail to take seriously the principle of social cooperation as a condition for full human freedom.

Correlative to these defects in practice are defects in the respective political theories of socialism and liberal democracy. Socialist theory, in its development, places emphasis on the social whole and on the state as the articulator of the needs of the whole and disregards the importance of individuality and of individual rights. Furthermore, in its stress on economic production, socialist theory fails to take into account the significance of the social and political dimensions as spheres of human cooperation and self-development. By contrast, liberal democratic theory places emphasis on individual freedom and individual rights and disregards the importance of social cooperation and community as a condition for the full development of this individual freedom. Moreover, liberal theory takes democracy as pertaining to political life alone and not also as applying to social and economic life.

Thus socialism and liberal democracy, both in practice and in theory, are faulty and stress one of the principles of social and political reality—namely, either individuality or social cooperation—at the expense of the other. In light of these defects in contemporary political theory, I would like to propose a new theoretical framework which brings the values of individual freedom and social cooperation to bear on each other in a coherent way. Such a theory would also suggest concrete forms in which these values could be realized in economic, social, and political life. In terms of this framework it will become clear that socialism and democracy, on a certain interpretation, are not only not incompatible with each other, but in fact entail each other.

Such an understanding that socialism and democracy are essentially related may be seen to gain support from an examination of the root meanings of the terms. In its original connotation, democracy meant self-rule by the people through a process of co-determination. Furthermore, at least in modern political theory, the concept of democracy was closely tied to that of individual freedom, in that political democracy was seen as the mode in which the equal individual liberty of the citizens could be preserved. Similarly, in its original connotation, socialism meant the control by the people over their own activities in economic, social and political life, through a process of social cooperation and co-determination. Here, too, the concept of socialism is closely connected to that of freedom, in the sense of freedom from domination and exploitation and in the sense that socialism is supposed to provide an equality of condition which would permit all individuals to develop themselves freely. Hence, both democracy and socialism in their root meanings involve the ideas of self-rule and co-determination as conditions for freedom. This connection between the concepts of democracy and socialism needs to be reclaimed. However, such a synthesis cannot remain at the abstract level of the original meanings of the terms. Rather, what is required is a new theoretical framework which would provide a philosophical foundation for the intimate relation between individuality and community or social cooperation, as well as the proposal of some concrete ways in which such a synthesis might occur. In this paper, I can only give a sketch of these philosophical ideas and a few concrete proposals as to how they could be realized.

II. PHILOSOPHICAL FOUNDATION FOR A RECONSTRUCTED DEMOCRATIC THEORY

If political theory is to satisfy the requirements which are set forth above, namely, to give an adequate account of individual freedom and social cooperation and of the relation between them, then the fundamental philosophical concepts and the normative grounds should be clarified at the outset. I would propose that the fundamental value which a system of social relations ought to serve is that of freedom, taken in the sense of the freedom of individuals to realize themselves. . . . This sense of freedom may be characterized as positive freedom or freedom *to* realize or develop oneself. Yet the realization of the purposes of an individual requires social interaction as its condition. That is, particular forms of social relations are necessary for the expression and development of human purposes and capacities. In addition, various material conditions also serve as necessary conditions for individual self-realization. Together, such social and material conditions may be characterized as the objective conditions for such self-development or human freedom. Thus, freedom requires access to these objective conditions. Such availability of conditions is part of what is connoted by the term "positive" in the idea of positive freedom. Thus on this view, freedom connotes more than free choice as a capacity; it involves the freedom to realize oneself through acting with others and by transforming the material means to suit one's purposes or ends. Yet this sense of freedom presupposes free choice as a universal feature of human activity. Such free choice is implicit in the structure of human activity as a process of fulfilling purposes. This feature of human activity constitutes the capacity for freedom as self-development. However, self-development or self-realization does not follow from this capacity alone, since it requires the availability of conditions in terms of which one's purposes can be fulfilled.

Since every human being equally possesses such a capacity for freedom inasmuch as they are human, no individual has more of a right to the exercise of this capacity than any other. That is to say, they have an equal right to self-development. But, as I have said, self-development requires access to objective conditions, both social and material. Therefore, the equal right to self-realization implies an equal right to access to such conditions.[1] Such an equal right to self-realization constitutes the value of equal positive freedom which is a cornerstone of the new democratic theory.

However, inasmuch as positive freedom presupposes that one exercise free choice, such positive freedom presupposes an absence of constraint on the free choice of agents. This means absence of constraint by other agents or by the state. Such absence of constraint, or "freedom from," has been characterized in classical liberal theory as negative freedom. Thus equal positive freedom has as its presupposition equal negative freedom. Such negative freedom includes the basic liberties, namely individual civil liberties and political rights. Thus on this theory too, each individual has a right to the full realization of these basic liberties compatible with a like right on the part of each of the others. Thus the liberal rights such as freedom of speech, press, association, etc., as well as the political rights of citizenship are seen to be crucial elements in the theory of positive freedom. It may be seen that such liberties and rights are among the social conditions for freedom as self-development. Beyond this, the theory of positive freedom implies that each individual has a right to the fullest self-realization compatible with a like right on the part of others. It therefore follows that no individual has a right to dominate or exploit any other. Each individual has the right to freedom from domination and exploitation. On this theory, therefore, the idea of negative freedom extends beyond the sphere of civil liberties and political rights and includes the right to absence of constraint in the domains of social and economic life.

. . . Since the concept of equal positive freedom entails that each individual has an equal right to such self-control, it follows from this concept that each individual has an equal right to participate in the co-determination of the social activities in which they are engaged. This may be called the *principle of democracy*, and it serves as a norm for the achievement of equal positive freedom. With respect to those social relations which are interpersonal and not institutional, the principle implies a mutual determination on the part of the individuals

---

[1]   C. B. Macpherson presents a similar view concerning the equal right of access to what he calls "the means of labor," and also stresses the value of positive freedom and self-development. See his *Democratic Theory: Essays in Retrieval* (Oxford, 1973), especially Chapters 1, 3, 5 and 6. However, there are important differences between the theory presented here and his. Among these are differences concerning the interpretation of self-development, the meaning of property, the importance given to social relations, and the scope and nature of participatory democracy. For a further discussion of these and other differences, see my "Contemporary Legal Conceptions of Property and their Implications for Democracy" *(Journal of Philosophy,* Vol. LXXVII, No. 11, November, 1980) and my "Freedom, Reciprocity and Democracy" (unpublished manuscript).

involved, so that none dominates or controls the activity of the others. In institutional social relations, e.g., in politics, the principle implies an equal right to democratically decide with others how such institutions are to be organized and how they are to function.

An important consequence of this view is that democratic decision-making must be extended beyond the political sphere to which classical political theory has assigned it. From the principle presented here, it follows that individuals have a right to co-determine all social decisions that affect them, whether these are in the domain of politics, culture, or social or community life more generally.

A second principle follows from the concept of equal positive freedom. It concerns the objective conditions of action, both material and social. It will be recalled that positive freedom requires the availability of conditions for the actions of an individual or a group of individuals, in order that their purposes may be achieved. We have also seen that equal positive freedom implies an equal right to the social and material conditions of action and further that freedom defined as self-development involves control over the conditions required for realizing one's purposes in activity. But I would argue that control over the conditions or means of activity is the meaning of property and this includes both social and material conditions. Therefore, there is an equal right to such property. This gives rise to what we may call the *principle of property right*. Namely, individuals have an equal right to means of subsistence and personal means for their self-realization, which belong to them as their personal or private property; and they have an equal right to control the material and social conditions or means of their common activity, which take the form of social property. The first aspect of this property right, namely the right to personal property, connotes that each has a right to means of subsistence and to the conditions of their own self-expression compatible with a like right on the part of the others. The second aspect, namely the right to social property, connotes that all those who engage in a common productive activity or joint project have an equal right to control of conditions, that is, to co-determine their use and function. It therefore excludes the possibility that only some of those engaged in the activity would control it to the exclusion of others or that any external agents not engaged in the activity would be in control of it. Thus this second aspect of the principle of property rules out denomination and exploitation in productive life and in social activity, just as the first aspect rules out domination in personal relations. Thus the principle excludes private ownership of social means of production, and it also excludes control by others over the means or conditions which individuals need for their individual or social activity.

From the analysis of the philosophical foundations thus far, it is clear that the concepts of democracy and socialism, on a certain interpretation, entail each other. For the principle of democracy states that each individual has an equal right to participate in the co-determination of all social activities in which he or she is engaged. As we have seen, this includes not only the sphere of political decision-making, but also decisions in economic, social and cultural life as well. But such co-determination or common control over social activity in these spheres, if it is to be meaningful, requires also co-determination or common control over the conditions for this activity. For if control over the conditions of such activity belongs to others, then the democracy involved in control over the activity would remain severely limited. But the common control over the conditions by those engaged in the activity is precisely what I designated as social property, which is one of the fundamental aspects of socialism. Conversely, the principle of social property was seen to involve common control over the social and material conditions of social production by means of democratic participation in decision-making concerning the use of such means. But this is a mode of democratic decision-making concerning the means which is closely related to the principle of democracy.

The equal right to participate in social decisions concerning both the activity and the means, as I have discussed it earlier, also has implications for the form and nature of the democratic process. Specifically, it implies that where feasible, the form of democratic decision-making should be participatory. For where such participation is feasible and an individual is excluded from such participation, then others are making decisions for that individual and violating the equal right which he or she has to co-determine these decisions. Furthermore, a participatory rather than a representative process is the most direct and surest way of taking into account each individual's choices. In addition, participation serves to develop the range of choices which an individual has, as well as the individual's capacities to deal with diverse situations. In this sense, also, it is a means for the fuller development of an individual's freedom. The realization of equal rights in social decision-making thus requires the extension and development of participatory processes. However, such processes of direct participation clearly cannot be instituted in all contexts, as for example in large-scale and centralized policy-making in government, industry, and cultural affairs. Here, what is required is an adequate system of representation founded on participation at the lower levels. Such participation and representation would not only characterize the political sphere but would also apply to decisions in economic, social and cultural life as well. In these various spheres, each would have an equal right to be represented and to serve as a representative. Furthermore, the representatives or delegates would be held accountable to those whom they represent by regular elections and regular consultations with those whom they represent, as well as by being subject to recall.

III. THE NEW DEMOCRACY—SOME CONCRETE PROPOSALS

The theoretical model of democracy and the value of equal positive freedom on which it is based need to be interpreted in terms of concrete social and institutional forms which would serve to realize them. The general political, economic and social forms which I will propose here seem to me to be required by the principles which I have discussed, although particular details of these forms may vary. In the formulation of these concrete proposals, I am concerned not only with the realization of these principles and values, but also with the feasibility of the institutional forms. In particular, it is important that they be suitable for large, complex societies and not serve simply as suggestions for small social experiments.

The first set of concrete proposals concerns the economic sphere. The four points I will deal with here are workers' self-management, the market, planning and regulatory functions, and the distribution of income. One of the most decisive features of the proposed social structure is the democratic management of economic activity by the workers themselves. This would be in the form of ownership, control and management of each firm by those who work there.[2] Such worker self-management means that the workers in a given

---

[2]   Similar proposals for workers' self-management have been made by a number of other authors, among them M. Marković's "New Legal Relations for New Social Institutions," in *Proceedings of the IVR World Congress,* 1975, and "Philosophical Foundations of the Idea of Self-Management," in B. Horvat *et al.* ed., *Self-Managing Socialism* (New York, 1975), pp. 327–350; C. Pateman, *Participation and Democratic Theory* (Cambridge, 1970); R. Selucký, *Marxism, Socialism, Freedom*

firm jointly determine the planning and production for the firm, and the work process (including allocation of work, rates of production, hours of work and work discipline). They also decide on the distribution of the firm's income, including reinvestment in production, depreciation costs and the division of wages to be paid among themselves. In addition, the workers control the sale of their firm's products. The capital of the firm is the workers' joint or social property, which is to say that they have the legal rights to possess, use, manage or alienate this property.

Such workers' self-management does not entail that all the workers decide on every feature of the production and sale of their products. They may well decide to appoint directors or managers of various aspects of the firm's activities. However, such delegation of powers and functions rests entirely upon the democratic decision of the workers. This democratic decision-making should involve the direct and immediate participation by the workers up through as many levels of the firm's activities as is feasible.

It may be seen that these forms of democratic and participatory control by the workers of their own economic activity are required by the principle of equal positive freedom. For, as will be recalled, such equal positive freedom implies each individual's right to control the conditions of his or her activity, and thus it implies the right to co-determine those common activities in which an individual is engaged, as well as the conditions for such activity. Therefore, the workers' activity as well as the objective conditions of this activity, namely the means of production, must be under their own control. This requirement is realized in workers' self-management, as I have described it.

The second major feature of the proposed economic structure is the market. Firms are free to buy and sell to other firms, institutions, or to individual consumers. The market therefore determines prices and serves as an instrument for adjusting supply and demand. Thus, the market functions as the locus for the exchange of commodities. However, unlike the capitalist market, what is excluded here is the market between capital and labor. Rather,

---

(New York, 1979); D. Schweickart, "Should Rawls be a Socialist? A Comparison of his Ideal Capitalism with Worker-Controlled Socialism," in *Social Theory and Practice,* vol. 5, no. 1 (Fall, 1978), pp. 1–27; J. Vanek, *The General Theory of Labor-Managed Market Economies* (Ithaca: N.Y., 1977); P. Rosanvallon, *l'Age de l'autogestion?* (Paris, 1978).

Although my proposal is similar in many respects to these, yet it differs from each of them in important ways. Thus, for example, although my proposal shares with Marković's an emphasis on participatory democracy in all spheres of social life, it differs from his in keeping the political and economic spheres separate from each other. Again, my proposal has in common with Selucký's an emphasis on the role of the market, on political democracy, and on the importance of the protection of individual rights. Yet my view, while holding that the market is important, does not regard it as the most decisive factor, as his does. Moreover, unlike him, I stress the need for the further democratization of the political sphere in addition to the economic sphere. Although my proposals are similar to Schweickart's in basic features of worker control, market and democracy, my differences with him concern his insufficient emphasis on democratizing the political sphere, and what seems to me an overextended planning function of the state, inasmuch as on his view it controls virtually all new investment, and dispenses it through a general plan. Furthermore, as will be seen, my proposal differs from several of those above in that it regards the social means of production as the common property of the workers in each firm rather than as belonging to society as a whole. However, some large-scale social means of production, e.g., utilities and railroads, and some natural resources should be owned by society as a whole.

the workers' incomes are determined by their own division of the net revenue or profits of the firm among themselves.

In terms of the values and principles discussed earlier, the virtues of such a market scheme are three: First, it preserves the freedom of workers to determine what to produce and the freedom of consumers to determine what, and from whom, to buy. In the market, the firms relate to each other and to individual consumers as free and equal exchangers. Second, the market is an efficient means of reflecting the needs and wants of consumers and of adjusting supply to meet the effective demand. Third, the market fosters variety in what is produced because it expresses the multiplicity of wants and it leaves producers free to satisfy them. In all these respects, the market is superior to a centralized planning scheme in which decisions are made from the top down, as they are in many contemporary socialist countries. Such centralized planning removes the autonomy of the workers in determining production, is often inefficient, and fails to provide variety because the planning bureaucracies tend to be insensitive to differentiated demands and cumbersome in adjusting supply to demand.[3] However, in claiming that the market is well-suited to realize the principles, I do not mean to imply that it is the only system that could satisfy these principles. But the market form is already available and well-developed and requires no third party to intervene between producers and consumers, or to validate their choices.

The third feature of the proposed economic structure is that there should be planning and market-regulatory commissions. The planning commissions would affect the direction of production in the economy indirectly, by making funds available for new investment to existing or prospective worker-managed firms. The commissions would derive these funds from taxation of the social capital of firms. They would operate regionally where possible, though some national planning would be necessary.

All of these commissions would be political bodies in the sense that they would be made up of elected representatives of the people. They would not be chosen as representatives of the workers in the firms, but rather by the workers in general, in their capacity as citizens, who would presumably be in a better position to make decisions in the interests of society as a whole. The unit to be represented on the planning commissions will, therefore, be a political unit at the most local levels possible, rather than an economic unit (e.g., a firm or an industry).

The market-regulatory commissions will function to see to it that the market is free of abuses, such as price-fixing, monopolistic practices, violations of contract, or deceptive advertising or merchandising practices. Thus, these commissions are not intended to control the market, but to permit it to operate fairly and effectively. Like the planning commissions, the market-regulatory commissions will also be democratically elected entities representing the public.

Both the planning commissions and the market-regulatory commissions are necessary to correct malfunctions of the economy and to help it to meet social needs. Thus, although worker self-managed firms together with the market are seen as the principal moving force and adjustment mechanism, respectively, of the economy, nonetheless, these cannot be expected to meet all needs optimally, or may sometimes meet them in a haphazard or

---

[3]   On the importance or usefulness of the market, cf. Selucký, *op. cit.,* esp. Chapter 5; and Schweickart, *op. cit.*

distorted way. The commissions, in representing the general social interest, are thus balancing the corrective mechanisms, and can also foster innovation to meet important social and economic needs.

The fourth feature of the proposed scheme concerns the principles and mode of distribution of income. It combines elements of the two well-known principles of distribution according to work and distribution according to needs. The scheme excludes deriving income from investment or from exploitation of the work of others.

Most generally, income will be distributed by the workers in each firm, by a process of participatory democratic decision in which they determine the allocation of the net revenue of that firm among themselves. Since this is an autonomous democratic procedure, the principle that they use for distributing income is up to them. However, since the amount of net revenue to be distributed among the workers in a firm depends in part on their work, the principle of distribution of income is to this degree a principle of distribution according to work.

In terms of the principle of equal positive freedom, the justification of such democratic allocation of income follows from the requirement for common control over the activity of production. I take such activity to include not only the conception and process of production, but also its product. Therefore, each worker has an equal right to control the common product of his or her work, and therefore also an equal right to co-determine the distribution of the income from that work.

This principle is complemented by the principle of distribution according to need in important areas of social and economic life. Thus, every individual is assured of free access to education and health-care according to their needs. In the case of education, this should be taken to include the provision of higher education to all those who want it. A principle of need should also be in effect with regard to subsistence needs which should be available to all regardless of their work. With respect to those unable to work because of age or illness, or those who are unemployed, this would mean that they should be provided with incomes approximating the average of those who work. With respect to those (hopefully few) who refuse to work, this principle would mean the provision of minimal subsistence needs. The principle of distribution according to need may also require that the state guarantee a minimum income for those who work, which would provide not merely means of subsistence but also means of self-development.

It may be seen that this combination of principles of distribution according to work and need is required by the value of equal positive freedom as discussed above, at least under the conditions of scarcity. This value was seen to imply not only the equal right to control over the work activity, but also the right of each individual to the means of subsistence and the conditions for self-realization, compatible with a like right on the part of each of the others. This latter aspect of the principle excludes exploitation of some by others, or some profiting from the work of others, in two senses: it excludes the accumulation and control of capital by those who have not produced it; and it also excludes parasitism, in the sense of those unwilling to work benefiting from the labor of others. Yet, because of the supreme value of human life, the principle of equal positive freedom implies that everyone has a right to the means of subsistence. These interpretations of the second part of the principle of equal positive freedom, combined with the first part which asserts the equal right of everyone to control their activity, seem to me to yield the principles of distribution sketched above.

Just as democracy is necessary in the economic sphere, so too is it necessary in the organization and relations of social and cultural life. I therefore turn to the question of how the social and cultural institutions and activities of society may be democratized. These institutions and activities include educational institutions such as schools and universities; cultural institutions such as museums and various arts organizations and activities; health services, including hospitals, community health organizations, etc.; welfare organizations; scientific institutions; sports; the media, e.g., newspapers, radio, T.V.; religious organizations; and charitable organizations. There would also be a wide variety of voluntary associations of individuals organized to pursue their various social and cultural interests. One may also include under the general heading of social and cultural life, the family and other child-raising and living arrangements.

With respect to the funding of these institutions, one would expect that some would operate wholly within the market, some would be publicly funded, some funded by firms, some privately funded, and many, perhaps most, would derive their funds from a mixture of these sources. It seems to me that in social and cultural affairs, such a proliferation of funding sources is important. Thus, for example, it would be good if the arts were funded from a multiplicity of sources, in order to preserve diversity and to prevent any control by the state, as well as to prevent the subservience of the arts to market fashions or requirements.

Here, as in the economic sphere, the institutions should be self-managing, and for the same reason: namely, to provide the conditions for the individuals' self-development by participating in the control of their own social activity. Thus, each such institution will have a managing board made up of those who work there or those who are involved in the range of that institution's activities. More specifically, where the social or cultural institutions operate in the market and are therefore subject directly to considerations of what consumers want, it is sufficient to have the board made up of the workers in the institution, who together decide upon the policy and activities of that institution. Where the institutions are partly or wholly exempt from market function, and depend largely on public funds, it would seem appropriate to include on the board not only those who work in the institution but also representatives of those who benefit from or use the institution, as well as representatives from the public at large, or the state.[4] In addition, there are those institutions which have to take into account the needs of consumers in a way which is more direct than a market permits, even though such institutions may function in the market. In such cases, the managing boards should have representatives of the users, in addition to those who work in the institution. Examples of this latter type of institution would be privately funded universities or hospitals which would operate in addition to those publicly funded ones that provide free education and health benefits.

In social and cultural institutions as in economic ones, self-management should be understood to operate in a participatory way. That is to say, the workers in such institutions, as well as representatives of those who use them or take part in their activities, have a right to participate in formulating policy and procedures. This is not to say that everyone should participate in deciding on all aspects of the institution's operation. Rather, all have a right to decide general matters of policy, as well as to make decisions concerning those areas directly related to their functions. Furthermore, decisions which require special expertise in order to make competent judgments should be reserved to those who are certifiably

---

[4]   A similar point is made by Selucký, *op. cit.,* p. 182.

competent to make such judgments. An example of this requirement of expertise would obviously be medical or surgical judgments.

The democratization of social and cultural institutions has to be understood as founded upon greater mutuality in interpersonal relations. That is, changes in the institutions can be fully effective only if people at the same time generally relate to each other as equals and with respect for each other's individuality. The reason for this is that the very process of participatory democratic decision-making which is required for the functioning of these institutions, if the principle of equal positive freedom is to be realized, entails that each participant treat the others as fully equal, and that they respect the differences among themselves. Such participation at the institutional level would very likely be undermined by lack of reciprocity in interpersonal relations, and would not endure for very long without such reciprocity. Conversely, the achievement of full mutuality in personal relations requires some changes in institutions, as well as the introduction of new institutions. Among the important interpersonal relations are male–female relations. Greater equality and mutuality here seem to me to require not only the elimination of domination, but also greater freedom to introduce new forms of child-raising, as well as new forms of living arrangements. In addition, in order to achieve women's equality at work, which would be one of the foundations of their equality more generally, extensive day-care facilities would be necessary. These proposals for the democratization of social and cultural life, together with economic democracy, bear upon the democratization of the political sphere to which I now turn.

The political sphere has traditionally been the domain in which democracy has been thought to apply. Democracy in this sphere has connoted forms of political representation, popular elections, and the protection of civil and political rights of individuals, among other features. Such features are also important in my proposed structure. Thus, a crucial aspect of democracy is the constitutional protection of equal civil liberties or basic freedoms (such as freedom of speech, press, association, etc.) as well as equal political rights (such as the right to vote, to be elected, etc.).

The principle of the separation and balance of powers is also of great importance, both among the various functions of government, as well as among the levels of government. Thus, the division of powers among the legislative, executive and judicial functions of government, together with a system of checks and balances, helps to prevent any one of these branches of government from dominating the others. A similar check on the over-centralization of power is provided by the division of political decision-making into various levels, e.g., local, state, regional, national. In addition, the separation of the political sphere itself from the economic sphere is also important in preventing the excessive concentration of power in either of these spheres. Furthermore, the universal right to vote, periodic free elections and a system of representation are important features of the proposed political democracy. As is clear, these are already features of modern political states. Yet, even with such features, these states are not fully democratic. This is in part because their political democracy is undermined by the lack of democracy in the economic and social spheres. Thus, the power of concentrated wealth can be used to influence the political process in its own interests. Or again, economic and social alienation may lead to feelings of political powerlessness and to voter apathy, leaving the process of governing without genuine popular support. The democratization of economic and social life in the structure proposed here should contribute to the elimination of alienation and of the distortion of the political process by the power of money. The proposed structure would therefore permit the fuller realization of these forms of political democracy.

These proposals concerning the concrete structures and practices of economic, social and political life are intended as realizations of the values and principles discussed earlier, namely, the value of equal positive freedom and the principles of democracy and of property right. My attempt was to synthesize the best features of liberal democracy on the one hand, and of socialism on the other, both in the theoretical system which I presented and in the specific proposals which I have discussed. However, I do not see this as a combination of presently existing forms of democracy and socialism, or of presently available theories. Rather, it seems to me that a start has to be made which, though it draws on both these traditions, introduces a decisively new foundation for social theory, namely, one which takes fully seriously both the values of individual freedom and of social cooperation.

Chapter 10

A Day Without Feminism

JENNIFER BAUMGARDNER AND AMY RICHARDS*

*Jennifer Baumgardner, a self-described "professional feminist," is a former editor at Ms. and writes for The Nation, Jane, Nerve, and Out. Amy Richards is a contributing editor at Ms. and co-founder of the Third Wave Foundation, an activist group for young feminists. This article is divided into two separate chapters, "Prologue: A Day Without Feminism" and "Epilogue: A Day With Feminism."

PROLOGUE: A DAY WITHOUT FEMINISM

We were both born in 1970, the baptismal moment of a decade that would change dramatically the lives of American Women. The two of us grew up thousands of miles apart, in entirely different kinds of families, yet we both came of age with the awareness that certain rights had been won by the women's movement. We've never doubted how important feminism is to people's lives—men's and women's. Both of our mothers went to consciousness-raising-type groups. Amy's mother raised Amy on her own, and Jennifer's mother, questioning the politics of housework, staged laundry strikes.

With the dawn of not just a new century but a new millennium, people are looking back and taking stock of feminism. Do we need new strategies? Is feminism dead? Has society changed so much that the idea of a feminist movement is obsolete? For us, the only way to answer these questions is to imagine what our lives would have been if the women's movement had never happened and the conditions for women had remained as they were in the year of our births.

Imagine that for a day it's still 1970, and women have only the rights they had then. Sly and the Family Stone and Dionne Warwick are on the radio, the kitchen appliances are Harvest Gold, and the name of your Whirlpool gas stove is Mrs. America. What is it like to be female?

Babies born on this day are automatically given their father's name. If no father is listed, "illegitimate" is likely to be typed on the birth certificate. There are virtually no child-care centers, so all preschool children are in the hands of their mothers, a baby-sitter, or an expensive nursery school. In elementary school, girls can't play in Little League and almost all of the teachers are female. (The latter is still true.) In a few states, it may be against the law for a male to teach grades lower than the sixth, on the basis that it's unnatural, or that men can't be trusted with young children.

In junior high, girls probably take home ec; boys take shop or small-engine repair. Boys who want to learn how to cook or sew on a button are out of luck, as are girls who want to learn how to fix a car. *Seventeen* magazine doesn't run feminist-influenced current columns like "Sex + Body" and "Traumarama." Instead the magazine encourages girls not to have sex; pleasure isn't part of its vocabulary. Judy Blume's books are just beginning to be published, and *Free to Be . . . You and Me* does not exist. No one reads much about masturbation as a natural activity; nor do they learn that sex is for anything other than procreation. Girls do read mystery stories about Nancy Drew, for whom there is no sex, only her blue roadster and having "luncheon." (The real mystery is how Nancy gets along without a purse and manages to meet only white people.) Boys read about the Hardy Boys, for whom there are no girls.

In high school, the principal is a man. Girls have physical-education class and play half-court basketball, but not soccer, track, or cross country; nor do they have any varsity sports teams. The only prestigious physical activity for girls is cheerleading, or being a drum majorette. Most girls don't take calculus or physics; they plan the dances and decorate the gym. Even when girls get better grades than their male counterparts, they are half as likely to qualify for a National Merit Scholarship because many of the test questions favor boys. Standardized tests refer to males and male experiences much more than to females and their experiences. If a girl "gets herself pregnant," she loses her membership in the National Honor Society (which is still true today) and is expelled.

Girls and young women might have sex while they're unmarried, but they may be ruining their chances of landing a guy full-time, and they're probably getting a bad reputation. If a pregnancy happens, an enterprising gal can get a legal abortion only if she lives in New York or is rich enough to fly there, or to Cuba, London, or Scandinavia. There's also the Chicago-based Jane Collective, an underground abortion-referral service, which can hook you up with an illegal or legal termination. (Any of these options are going to cost you. Illegal abortions average $300 to $500, sometimes as much as $2,000.) To prevent pregnancy, a sexually active woman might go to a doctor to be fitted for a diaphragm, or take the high-dose birth-control pill, but her doctor isn't likely to inform her of the possibility of deadly blood clots. Those who do take the Pill also may have to endure this contraceptive's crappy side effects: migraine headaches, severe weight gain, irregular bleeding, and hair loss (or gain), plus the possibility of an increased risk of breast cancer in the long run. It is unlikely that women or their male partners know much about the clitoris and its role in orgasm unless someone happens to fumble upon it. Instead, the myth that vaginal orgasms from penile penetration are the only "mature" (according to Freud) climaxes prevails.

Lesbians are rarely "out," except in certain bars owned by organized crime (the only businessmen who recognize this untapped market), and if lesbians don't know about the bars, they're less likely to know whether there are any other women like them. Radclyffe Hall's depressing early-twentieth-century novel *The Well of Loneliness* pretty much indicates their fate.

The Miss America Pageant is the biggest source of scholarship money for women. Women can't be students at Dartmouth, Columbia, Harvard, West Point, Boston College, or the Citadel, among other all-male institutions. Women's colleges are referred to as "girls' schools." There are no Take Back the Night marches to protest women's lack of safety after dark, but that's okay because college girls aren't allowed out much after dark anyway. Curfew is likely to be midnight on Saturday and 9 or 10 p.m. the rest of the week. Guys get to stay out as late as they want. Women tend to major in teaching, home economics, English, or maybe a language—a good skill for translating someone else's words. The women's studies major does not exist, although you can take a women's studies course at six universities, including Cornell and San Diego State College. The absence of women's history, black history, Chicano studies, Asian-American history, queer studies, and Native American history from college curricula implies that they are not worth studying. A student is lucky if he or she learns that women were "given" the vote in 1920, just as Columbus "discovered" America in 1492. They might also learn that Sojourner Truth, Mary Church Terrell, and Fannie Lou Hamer were black abolitionists or civil-rights leaders, but not that they were feminists. There are practically no tenured female professors at any school, and campuses are not racially diverse. Women of color are either not there or they're lonely as hell. There is no nationally recognized Women's History Month or Black

History Month. Only 14 percent of doctorates are awarded to women. Only 3.5 percent of MBAs are female.

Only 2 percent of everybody in the military is female, and these women are mostly nurses. There are no female generals in the U.S. Air Force, no female naval pilots, and no Marine brigadier generals. On the religious front, there are no female cantors or rabbis, Episcopal canons, or Catholic priests. (This is still true of Catholic priests.)

Only 44 percent of women are employed outside the home. And those women make, on average, fifty-two cents to the dollar earned by males. Want ads are segregated into "Help Wanted Male" and "Help Wanted Female." The female side is preponderantly for secretaries, domestic workers, and other low-wage service jobs, so if you're a female lawyer you must look under "Help Wanted Male." There are female doctors, but twenty states have only five female gynecologists or fewer. Women workers can be fired or demoted for being pregnant, especially if they are teachers, since the kids they teach aren't supposed to think that women have sex. If a boss demands sex, refers to his female employee exclusively as "Baby," or says he won't pay her unless she gives him a blow job, she either has to quit or succumb—no pun intended. Women can't be airline pilots. Flight attendants are "stewardesses"—waitresses in the sky—and necessarily female. Sex appeal is a job requirement, wearing makeup is a rule, and women are fired if they exceed the age or weight deemed sexy. Stewardesses can get married without getting canned, but this is a new development. (In 1968 the Equal Employment Opportunity Commission—EEOC— made it illegal to forcibly retire stewardesses for getting hitched.) Less than 2 percent of dentists are women; 100 percent of dental assistants are women. The "glass ceiling" that keeps women from moving naturally up the ranks, as well as the sticky floor that keeps them unnaturally down in low-wage work, has not been named, much less challenged.

When a woman gets married, she vows to love, honor, and obey her husband, though he gets off doing just the first two to uphold his end of the bargain. A married woman can't obtain credit without her husband's signature. She doesn't have her own credit rating, legal domicile, or even her own name unless she goes to court to get it back. If she gets a loan with her husband—and she has a job—she may have to sign a "baby letter" swearing that she won't have one and have to leave her job.

Women have been voting for up to fifty years, but their turnout rate is lower than that for men, and they tend to vote right along with their husbands, not with their own interests in mind. The divorce rate is about the same as it is in 2000, contrary to popular fiction's blaming the women's movement for divorce. However, divorce required that one person be at fault, therefore if you just want out of your marriage, you have to lie or blame your spouse. Property division and settlements, too, are based on fault. (And at a time when domestic violence isn't a term, much less a crime, women are legally encouraged to remain in abusive marriages.) If fathers ask for custody of the children, they get it in 60 to 80 percent of the cases. (This is still true.) If a husband or a lover hits his partner, she has no shelter to go to unless she happens to live near the one in northern California or the other in upper Michigan. If a woman is downsized from her role as a housewife (a.k.a. left by her husband), there is no word for being a displaced homemaker. As a divorcée, she may be regarded as a family disgrace or as easy sexual prey. After all, she had sex with one guy, so why not all guys?

If a woman is not a Mrs., she's a Miss. A woman without makeup and a hairdo is as suspect as a man with them. Without a male escort she may be refused service in a restaurant or a bar, and a woman alone is hard-pressed to find a landlord who will rent her an apartment.

After all, she'll probably be leaving to get married soon, and, if she isn't, the landlord doesn't want to deal with a potential brothel.

Except among the very poor or in very rural areas, babies are born in hospitals. There are no certified midwives, and women are knocked out during birth. Most likely, they are also strapped down and lying down, made to have the baby against gravity for the doctor's convenience. If he has a schedule to keep, the likelihood of a cesarean is also very high. *Our Bodies, Ourselves* doesn't exist, nor does the women's health movement. Women aren't taught how to look at their cervixes, and their bodies are nothing to worry their pretty little heads about; however, they are supposed to worry about keeping their little heads pretty. If a woman goes under the knife to see if she has breast cancer, the surgeon won't wake her up to consult about her options before performing a Halsted mastectomy (a disfiguring radical procedure, in which the breast, the muscle wall, and the nodes under the arm, right down to the bone, are removed). She'll just wake up and find that the choice has been made for her.

Husbands are likely to die eight years earlier than their same-age wives due to the stress of having to support a family and repress an emotional life, and a lot earlier than that if women have followed the custom of marrying older, authoritative, paternal men. The stress of raising kids, managing a household, and being undervalued by society doesn't seem to kill off women at the same rate. Upon a man's death, his beloved gets a portion of his Social Security. Even if she has worked outside the home for her entire adult life, she is probably better off with that portion than with hers in its entirety, because she has earned less and is likely to have taken time out for such unproductive acts as having kids.

Has feminism changed our lives? Was it necessary? After thirty years of feminism, the world we inhabit barely resembles the world we were born into. And there's still a lot left to do.

EPILOGUE: A DAY WITH FEMINISM

Women and men are paid equal wages for work of comparable value, as is every race and ethnic group, co-parenting is a given, men lengthen their lives by crying and otherwise expressing emotion, and women say "I'm sorry" only when they truly should be. To the extent that we can imagine this even now, this is the equality feminists have been working for since that day in Seneca Falls in 1848. With each generation, the picture will get bigger and at the same time more finely detailed.

When Elizabeth Cady Stanton and her crew wrote the Declaration of Sentiments, they knew that this nation's Declaration of Independence would have no justice or power unless it included the female half of the country. For these women, equality was being full citizens who were able to own and inherit property, just as men were, to have the right to their own children, and the ability to vote. In 1923, Alice Paul had the vision to write the Equal Rights Amendment so that laws could not be made based on sex, any more than they could be made based on race, religion, or national origin. By the 1970s, Betty Friedan, Audre Lorde, Gloria Steinem, and Shirley Chisholm could imagine women's equality in the paid workforce, a new vision of family and sexuality, and legislative bodies that truly reflected the country. They could not have foreseen a twenty-three-year-old White House intern who owned her own libido and sexual prowess the way Monica Lewinsky did. (They certainly wouldn't have imagined that a woman with that much access to power would just want to blow it.)

Now, at the beginning of a new millennium, we have witnessed a woman running for President who has a chance of winning, a first lady who translates that unparalleled Washington experience into her own high-flying political ambitions, easily reversible male birth control, gay parenting, a women's soccer team that surpasses the popular appeal of men's, and parental leave for both parents. And we can imagine more: federally subsidized child-care centers for every child and legalized gay marriage in all fifty states. A number of leaps are still needed to bring us to a day of equality, but at least we can begin to picture what such a future might hold.

Whether children are born to a single mother, a single father, two mothers, two fathers, or a mother and a father, a family is defined by love, commitment, and support. A child who has two parents is just as likely to have a hyphenated last name, or choose a whole new name, as she or he is to have a father's or birth mother's name. Carrying on a lineage is an individual choice, not the province of the father or the state.

Men work in child-care centers and are paid at least as well as plumbers, sanitation workers, or firefighters. When kids sit down to their breakfast Wheaties, they are as likely to confront a tennis star like Venus Williams as a golf pro like Tiger Woods. On TV, the male and female newscasters are about the same age and, whether black or white, are as likely to report foreign policy as sports. In general, people on camera come in all shapes and sizes. If you are watching drama, women are just as likely to be the rescuers as the rescued, and men are just as likely to ask for help as to give it. Women are as valued for their sense of humor as men are for their sex appeal. On Monday-night television, women's soccer or basketball is just as popular as men's basketball or football. Barbie no longer has feet too tiny to stand on or finds math hard; nor do girls. G.I. Joe, now a member of a peacekeeping force, likes to shop at the mall. In grade school, boys and girls decorate their bedrooms with posters of female athletes.

By the time girls hit junior high, they have already had the opportunity to play sports, from soccer to Little League, hockey to wrestling, and they share gymnastics and ballet classes with boys. Boys think ballet and gymnastics are cool. Kids hit puberty fully aware of how their bodies work: erections, nocturnal emissions, periods, cramps, masturbation, body hair—the works. These topics still cause giggling, curiosity, and excitement, but paralyzing shame and utter ignorance are things of the past. In fact, sweet-sixteen birthdays have given way to coming-of-age rituals for both genders, and don't assume that the birthday kid has never been kissed. Around the time that girls and boys are learning how to drive, both have mastered manual stimulation for their own sexual pleasure.

In high school, many varsity teams have coed cheerleaders, athletes all, but mostly cheering is left to the fans. Differences in girls' and boys' academic performance are as indistinguishable as differences in their athletic performance though they are very different as unique individuals. Some girls ask other girls to the prom, some boys ask boys, and that is as okay as going in as a mixed couple. Some go alone or not at all, and that's okay, too. Athletic scholarships have no more prestige or funding than arts scholarships.

Students take field trips to local museums where women are the creators of the art as often as they are its subjects. In preparation for this trip, students study art history from Artemisia Gentileschi to Mark Rothko, from Ndebele wall paintings to Yayoi Kusama. The museums themselves were designed by architects who may have been among the 11 percent of architects who were female in the 1990s. Military school is open to everyone and teaches peacekeeping as much as defense. Women's colleges no longer exist, because women no longer need a compensatory environment, and women's history, African-American history, and all those remedial areas have become people's and world history.

Women achieved parity long ago, so the idea of bean counting is irrelevant. At Harvard, 75 percent of the tenured professors are women, and at nearby Boston College, 30 percent of the tenured faculty is female. History courses cover the relevance of a movement that ended sexual violence against women. Though there is still a throwback incident now and then, men are even more outraged by it than women are. Once a year, there is a party in the quad to commemorate what was once called Take Back the Night.

Women walking through a park at night can feel just as safe as they do during the day, when kids play while white male nannies watch over them, right along with women and men of every group. In fact, it's as common to see a white man taking care of a black or a brown baby as it is to see a woman of color taking care of a white baby.

Sex is separate from procreation. Because there is now a national system of health insurance, birth control and abortions are covered right along with births, and the Hyde Amendment's ban of federal funding for abortions is regarded as a shameful moment in history, much like the time of Jim Crow laws. A judicial decision known as *Doe* v. *Hyde* effectively affirmed a woman's right to bodily integrity, and went way past the right to privacy guaranteed by *Roe* v. *Wade*. Abortion isn't morally contested territory because citizens don't interfere with one another's life choices, and women have the right to determine when and whether to have no children, a single child, or five children.

Environmentally sound menstrual products are government subsidized and cost the same as a month's worth of shaving supplies. After all, women's childbearing capacity is a national asset, and young, sexually active men often opt for freezing their sperm or undergoing a simple vasectomy to control their paternity. Many men choose vasectomies, given that it's the least dangerous and most foolproof form of birth control—as well as the easiest to reverse. Men are screened for chlamydia, human papilloma virus, herpes, and other sexually transmitted diseases during their annual trip to the andrologist. Doctors learn how to detect and treat all of the above, in both men and women. Although the old number of three million or so new cases of STDs each year has dropped to half that amount, STDs are still as common (and about as shameful) as the common cold and are finally acknowledged as such.

The Equal Rights Amendment has put females in the U.S. Constitution. There are many women of all races in fields or institutions formerly considered to be the province of men, from the Virginia Military Institute and the Citadel to fire departments and airline cockpits. Women are not only free to be as exceptional as men but also as mediocre. Men are as critiqued or praised as women are. Women's salaries have jumped up 26 to 40 percent from pre-equality days to match men's. There are no economic divisions based on race, and the salary categories have been equalized. This categorization is the result of legislation that requires the private sector—even companies that employ fewer than 50 people—to report employees' wages. Many older women are averaging half a million dollars in back pay as a result of the years in which they were unjustly underpaid. Women and men in the NBA make an average of $100,000 per year. Haircuts, dry cleaning, and clothes for women cost the same as they do for men.

The media are accountable to their constituency. Magazines cover stories about congressional hearings on how to help transition men on welfare back into the workforce. Many of these men are single fathers—by choice. Welfare is viewed as a subsidy, just as corporate tax breaks used to be, and receiving government assistance to help rear one's own child is as destigmatized as it is to be paid to rear a foster child. Howard Stern, who gave up his declining radio show to become a stay-at-home granddad, has been replaced on radio by Janeane Garofalo, who no longer jokes primarily about her "back fat" and other perceived imperfections. (Primary caregiving has humanized Stern so that people no longer have to fear for his influence on his offspring.) Leading ladies and leading men are all around the same age. There is always fanfare around *Time* magazine's Person of the Year and *Sports Illustrated*'s coed swimsuit issue. *Rolling Stone* covers female pop stars and music groups in equal numbers with male stars, and women are often photographed for the cover with their shirts on. Classic-rock stations play Janis Joplin as often as they play Led Zeppelin.

Women who choose to have babies give birth in a birthing center with a midwife, a hospital with a doctor, or at home with a medicine woman. Paid child-care leave is for four months, and it is required of both parents (if there is more than one). Child rearing is subsidized by a trust not unlike Social Security, a concept pioneered by the welfare-rights activist Theresa Funiciello and based on Gloria Steinem's earlier mandate that every child have a minimum income. The attributed economic value of housework is figured into the gross national product (which increases the United States' GNP by almost 30 percent), and primary caregivers are paid. Whether you work in or out of the home, you are taxed only on your income; married couples and people in domestic partnerships are taxed as individuals, too. When women retire, they get as much Social Security as men do, and all people receive a base amount on which they can live.

The amount of philanthropic dollars going to programs that address or specifically include women and girls is now pushing 60 percent, to make up for all the time it was about 5 percent. More important, these female-centered programs no longer have to provide basic services, because the government does that. All school meals, vaccinations, public libraries, and museums are government-funded and thus available to everybody. Taxpayers have made their wishes clear because more than 90 percent of the electorate actually votes.

"Postmenopausal zest" is as well documented and as anticipated as puberty. Women in their fifties—free from pregnancy, menstruation, and birth control—are regarded as sexpots and envied for their wild and free libidos. "Wine and women," as the saying goes, "get better with age."

Every man and woman remembers exactly where they were the moment they heard that the Equal Rights Amendment passed. The President addressed the nation on the night of that victory and said, "Americans didn't know what we were missing before today . . . until we could truly say that all people are created equal." The first man stood at her side with a tear running down his face.

The social-justice movement, formerly known as feminism, is now just *life*.

SECTION 2 TERMINOLOGY

Anarchy

Bureaucracy

Checks and balances

Civil liberties

Civil servants

Cold War

Command economy

Communism

Communist Party of the
   Soviet Union (CPSU)

Conservatism

Democracy

Democratization

Econometrics

Fascism

Feminism

Free market

Game theory

Gross Domestic Product
   (GDP)

Gross National Product
   (GNP)

Glass ceiling

Ideology

Invisible Hand

Laissez-faire

Liberal democracy

Liberalism

Liberty

Market economy

Marxism

Marxism-Leninism

Morality

Nationalism

National socialism

Norms

Organization for Economic
   Co-operation and
   Development (OECD)

Prescription

Prudence

Rights

Socialism

Society

Suffrage

Third World

Union of Soviet Socialist
   Republics (USSR)

Utopia

SECTION 2 DISCUSSION QUESTIONS

1. Is it simplistic to think that political theories can contribute to a better life?

2. It is quite easy to get conservatism and liberalism confused, in spite of the fact that they are quite different. But they both have changed over time. In what way?

3. Some say that we need socialism for a fair society. Why?

4. Can ideology be constructive, or does it just cause conflict?

5. Is it possible to speak of the "end" of ideological development? Is it fair to depict the "victory of economic and political liberalism"?

6. Is feminism a theory of its own, or is it the product of other ideologies?

Section 3

Structures and Processes

SECTION SUMMARY

It is often said that the act of governing has become far more complex given the increased pace at which decisions must be made, the tangle of domestic and international regulations that has to be navigated to protect legislation and policies from challenge, and the increasing number of actors claiming a legitimate place at the decision-making table. Developing an understanding of modern politics and governing necessarily requires an understanding of the many actors, institutions, and processes involved, but the lack of transparency that often accompanies political decision-making can make this a difficult endeavour. Yet such an understanding is critical, for with this understanding comes an ability to identify not only the various forces and actors that shape and influence political decision-making, but also when and how these forces and actors come into play.

The set of readings in this section identifies several key issues facing governments within modern democracies. The first reading by J. Patrick Boyer provides a critical evaluation of the principle of responsible government as it is practised in Canada's parliamentary system. Boyer's key concern, the lack of government accountability, is especially important in modern systems that claim to respond to the "will of the people" and that are often rocked by scandals. His premise, that the myths and fictions shrouding modern government in Canada provide the executive branch with a level of power that goes largely unchecked, speaks to the root causes of much of the political dissatisfaction currently felt among citizens.

Similar concepts—government accountability, responsiveness, and transparency—are taken up by David Herle in the next reading. Having worked as a pollster for both the Department of Finance and the Liberal Party of Canada, he argues that polling enhances democracy by providing a mechanism for assessing public opinion on issues, for deciding between policy options, and for guiding governmental communications. This view is contrary to that which often links its use to weak and unprincipled governments and to the worst form of "partisan" politics. He offers a balanced view, however, for he outlines how the use of polling can undermine consensus building in Canadian politics.

Shifting the lens to the legislative branch of government, Gemma Rosenblatt provides a detailed picture of the multiple roles occupied by members of parliament (MPs) in the United Kingdom. Based on surveys of and interviews with MPs elected in 2005, this one chapter from her longer report clearly identifies the long hours, multiple demands, and cross-pressures experienced by individuals who act as public representatives. Contrary to much conventional wisdom, theirs is not an easy profession, and dispelling this myth is an important first step in rendering a judgment on the quality of the work that they perform.

The relationship between the government and the courts is the focus of Janet Hiebert's article on equality rights within the Charter of Rights and Freedoms. The key debate—the right of a democratically elected legislature to legislate the "will of the people" versus the Supreme Court's right and, some might argue, duty to uphold the rights and freedoms outlined in the Charter—represents a very real example of the difficulties of bringing into practice the separation of powers. Reg Whitaker, on the other hand, addresses the changes that have taken place in one of the core institutions in democratic systems—political parties. Likening party strategy to the marketing of a product, Whitaker sees a "democratic deficit" resulting from a hollowing out of parties' ideological cores, in turn caused by the single-minded pursuit of electoral victory focused on the party brand and leader. He argues that political parties are an essential link between civil society and the state—because they perform functions that interest groups and social movements cannot—and that reforming the current political system is unlikely to be successful if political parties are not included in the process.

The political system is just that—a *system*, made up of various parts that must work together to function efficiently. And like any system of parts, a malfunction in one area is felt throughout. As important, however, is the degree to which the various parts of that system work together to perform the task at hand, which in a political system is to make decisions about the allocation of both goods and values—that is, decisions about what we can access and, more importantly, who has that access.

Chapter 11

Responsible Government Won and Lost: Parliamentarians Play-Act Their Accountability Roles

J. PATRICK BOYER*

*J. Patrick Boyer, Progressive Conservative Member of Parliament for Etobicoke (1984–1993), is Adjunct Professor at the University of Guelph.

Getting to Parliament, newly elected MPs are often shocked to find that on a functional level we do not have responsible government. Before I was first elected in 1984 I'd spent years training and preparing to participate in an accountable parliamentary process as the representative of the 100,000 citizens in my district, but I discovered there simply were no effective means by which to do so. My experience was no aberration. For most MPs, getting to Parliament Hill is like going to play hockey in an arena but finding no ice to skate on. In recent decades many MPs on both sides of the House have given vent, often in acute frustration and occasionally with considerable eloquence, to this sense of futility. It's even a bit ominous because the historical conditions that first gave rise to responsible government in Canada seem so familiar in our present circumstances. You start to wonder if history doesn't repeat itself.

Consider, for example, that in the early 1800s government was run by a small group of the powerful and privileged, or what is called an oligarchy. As confident in their own plans as they were arrogant in their use of power, these colonial leaders paid little heed to elected representatives in the legislature, and didn't really need to. By about 1815 demands for reform began to build. By the 1830s our expanding Loyalist colonies of British North America, increasingly outgrowing the forms of overseas government laid down at the close of the American Revolution, were growing less content to be ruled from above by a local oligarchy. As grievances piled up, reform movements developed. More people began expressing an impatient desire to gain local control over local affairs.

The British government in London neglected this pressure. The oligarchy gave only token attention to petitions, resolutions, practical grievances and real problems. (Is the picture looking familiar?) For its part the government seemed focused instead on its international trade agenda. The economy was globalizing. Britain's rise as an industrial power meant the world wanted its manufactured products, not just access to its colonial markets controlled under the older mercantilist trading system. After the American Revolution the remnant British North American colonies were being marginalized, losing their relative importance in the new patterns of world trade. In matters of governance the creaking colonial system continued to operate almost as a matter of habit, and Britain was largely content to keep things as they were, which meant supporting an increasingly unpopular political system. (Does this not seem to be echoing across the years too?)

The parallels don't end there. Back then the colonial assemblies represented the people but did not fully control either law making or public finances, and reformers felt these important roles should be taken up more rigorously and responsibly; they even wrote about the absence of accountability in publications of the day. Some main sources of government revenue were not under the control of elected representatives. Their enacted laws were often revised by the Cabinet ministers, vetoed by the governor or set aside for consideration by the overseas mperial authorities. Government was not responsible—or accountable—to the elected assemblies, and the constituency representatives complained, then as today, about being as impotent as the people they represented.

Real power lay in the hands of the small governing executive, an oligarchy in each colonial province called, for example, the "Council of Twelve" in Nova Scotia, the "Chateau Clique" in Quebec and the "Family Compact" in Ontario. The situation was not dissimilar in other British North American colonies such as Newfoundland, Prince Edward Island, Vancouver Island and British Columbia. Each colony faced particular issues and unique grievances, but sooner or later all roads led back to the same central problem of the unaccountable exercise of power by those in positions of privilege. Elected members in the legislative assemblies, weak against the inertia of a solidly planted establishment, expressed frustration over being ineffectual and sought to expose the hollowness of these nominal institutions of representative democracy. As decades passed it grew clearer that little could be achieved to respond to people's needs until these self-reinforcing oligarchies had been dislodged, or at least made to govern in some accountable fashion. The battle to gain responsible government was under way.

In Nova Scotia, Quebec (Canada East) and Ontario (Canada West) moderate reform parties emerged under strong leaders such as Joseph Howe, Louis Lafontaine and Robert Baldwin pushing politically for responsible government. Others, such as Louis-Joseph Papineau and William Lyon Mackenzie, sought swifter changes to the shortcomings and abuses of the existing system, leading armed rebellions in 1837 to overthrow the oligarchy by force. After British soldiers suppressed this Canadian revolution-in-the-making, Lord Durham was quickly dispatched from the Home Office in London to figure out what the devil was wrong in the colonies.

Given that ministers in government were not paying much attention to the people's elected representatives in the legislature, Durham recommended making them live together under one roof. Then they'd be forced to talk together, listen, debate, answer, argue and explain. There were to be other benefits to Durham's forced marriage of Cabinet and legislature. Elected representatives could no longer just give fiery speeches atop a country stump or in a village hall, or to one another in the echoing legislative chamber, but would now have to address their sharp complaints directly to those wielding power. Ministers of the Crown, by the same token, could no longer make decisions or set policies without facing directly those who might criticize and even improve them. Moreover, by imposing a new rule that ministers themselves had to be chosen from among the members of the legislature, ministers and members would now share a common footing; they would moderate one another, a process that institutionalized accountability and ensured more focused responsibility in providing peace, order and good government.

By 1848, with Durham's proposal implemented in a new Constitution enacted by Britain's Parliament, responsible government was in full swing in Canada East, Canada West and

Nova Scotia. Within the decade it had also been gained by Britain's other eastern colonies: Prince Edward Island, New Brunswick and Newfoundland. This plan for responsible government was carried forward into the new Canadian Constitution in 1867. Other provinces that subsequently joined Confederation operated on the same plan.

The theory of responsible government is one thing; the present-day operation of government in Canada, quite another. It would be overly dramatic to say that responsible government in Canada has collapsed, but there is very little remaining to actually support it. To come to grips with the absence of accountability in the way Parliament works, not in theory but in practice, it is instructive to begin with some of the myths, fictions and misconceptions pertaining to governing doctrines. Perhaps four of the greatest myths are the following:

Myth #1: Accountability is enhanced because power is divided between different levels of government.

Myth #2: The re-election of a government shows that people endorse it.

Myth #3: MPs go to Ottawa to run the country.

Myth #4: General elections give the winning party a mandate to govern.

Let's consider each in turn to see how our actual government system has become shrouded behind these misconceptions and myths.

Myth #1: Accountability is enhanced because power is divided between different levels of government.

Jurisdictional clarity, which is a precondition for accountability, and which is represented in our Constitution by the division of powers between the national and provincial governments, no longer exists in Canada today.

. . . In the case of the Canada Infrastructure Works Program—not to mention in the more challenging areas of health, transportation, security, environment, trade, labour and social services—when it comes to figuring out who is responsible for government spending, the buck stops nowhere; the result is that *accountability is impossible*. Over time, combining a parliamentary system with our federal system, which formally has two levels of government (national and provincial) and operationally has three (national, provincial and local), actually fragmented jurisdictional accountability, to the point where it has been lost completely. Seldom in all my years around government did I find anyone who said, "I did that, I'm the one responsible." Instead it was invariably, "I'll have to consult my advisors on this." When it comes to the way our government works today, no one really knows who is doing what, or who is responsible.

Myth #2: The re-election of a government shows that people endorse it.

The Canadian electoral system does not accurately measure voter support. Winning an election does not mean that a party is supported by a majority of the population; nor can the victory be cited as evidence that the public approves of the party's style of governing.

Our electoral system is dysfunctional in terms of its ability to translate levels of popular support for different parties across the country into a comparable ratio of seats in Parliament. Because the system was designed to determine elections fought between only two parties, it has been out of date since the 1920s when the country moved from a two-party to a multiparty system. Yet privilege and inertia have kept this defective system in place, which is just one more reason why many Canadians are increasingly disowning the electoral process and the distorted results it generates.

Our country does not speak with one voice, but is divided into some 300 constituencies. Within these constituencies, or ridings, those who are elected often assume office with only a plurality, not a majority, of the votes cast by people living there. A plurality just means getting more votes than any other candidate, which is all it takes to win. Typically, four, five or even six candidates run in each riding. The result is that many MPs go to Ottawa with only a minority of voters having cast ballots for them. For example, when I was elected to Parliament in 1984, it was with 44 percent of the popular vote; when I was re-elected in 1988, it was again with 44 percent of the popular vote; when I was defeated in 1993, it was still with a mid-40s mark of popular vote. Whether I won—or lost—depended not on the accuracy of a representative electoral system, but on the relative fates and fortunes of the numerous other candidates also in the field. Although the majority of voters in my riding of Etobicoke-Lakeshore did not vote for me, there I was in Parliament, voting for the GST, for borrowing bills, for free trade, for Meech Lake. When I looked around the Commons at the 294 other elected "representatives," I saw a number of MPs from all parties who won with considerably narrower victories and even lower pluralities than mine.

The second Chrétien Liberal government, with its "huge majority" of seats in the Commons, took office having won only 38 percent of the popular vote. In 2000 Jean Chrétien and the Liberals won their third majority in a row, with the support of a minority of the electorate—42 percent of the popular vote. Nevertheless, the Liberals secured 172 of the 301 seats in the Commons, or 57 percent of the seats. Holding a majority of seats gives the appearance of a majority government because of the distorting hall-of-mirrors effect of our antiquated (though much tinkered with) electoral system. The reality, however, is that the levels of representation in our national legislative assembly are not an accurate reflection of the levels of voter support, of citizens' considered electoral conclusions.

So once again we discover that we do not have "representative government" in Canada and that our political superstructure, along with the laws and institutions it brings into being, rests upon shaky supports.

Myth #3: MPs go to Ottawa to run the country.

It is *not* Parliament's role to run the country. That's what the government does.

In the overall structure of Canadian government, the primary role of Parliament is to provide accountability in the way government is being run. If people (including MPs) don't know what government is really doing, it is a measure of how greatly Parliament has failed to shed light on the proper object of its attention.

Unfortunately there is confusion here because many people *think* that Parliament is the government. Even many MPs think and act this way with embarrassing frequency. The bleak truth about the role of MPs in Canada is that—and I'm speaking as someone who once was one—their main task ends the very night they are elected. That's when their aggregated numbers determine which party, and which small group within that party, will form the government. Having then served their leadership-selection function, MPs are kept busy and generally out of trouble for several years with highly public make-work projects until it's time for the party's leaders to again work MPs up into a state of partisan fervour sufficient, the leaders hope, to win another election.

Perhaps the distinction between the government and Parliament can best be illustrated by comparing Cabinet ministers in Parliament to a hand in a glove. The fact that one fits inside the other, so that they move as one and even function together, does not mean they are the same thing. Because our MPs and government leaders (the prime minister and Cabinet ministers) are combined institutionally within the legislative assembly, the hand is in the glove. This reality, and the appearance of it, contributes to the confusion of roles. It is the government that runs the country, and it is the job of Parliament to hold that government to account. Today, however, Parliament is failing to perform its primary role. Parliament, in fact, is no longer an institution of representative democracy, but has instead become a *government institution*. The elected representatives of the people do not hold the government to account, but rather function as extensions of the government itself, and generally are satisfied and proud to do so. Canadian legislatures do perform important roles in recruitment and education, for it is through the legislative chamber that new people are constantly drawn into government service, and it is also from MPs that a stream of publications, speeches and public-service advertisements flows to the public. Yet neither of these functions has much to do with holding government accountable. They are, if anything, just the opposite: a measure of how far and in how many ways our national legislature has devolved into little more than an operating extension of government—its recruitment office and public relations bureau.

Some political scientists add that Parliament performs a legitimizing role. By this they mean that when the government has decided to do something, it may appear more acceptable to the country or to the international community if Parliament enacts a law or passes a resolution endorsing it. Legitimacy is extremely important for a government because if the people (and the governments of other countries) believe someone is legitimately in power, or is acting with the endorsement of the country's principal democratic institution, they will obey even if they don't agree. Again, however, according legitimacy to a government is in many important respects the very antithesis of holding it accountable.

Myth #4: General elections give the winning party a mandate to govern.

The "mandate theory," even in the best of circumstances, was never more than a convenient constitutional fiction.

Powerful governments have long promoted a doctrine of parliamentary democracy which holds that once elected by virtue of winning the most seats in a general election, regardless of the size of the party's popular vote, the government has a mandate to deal with any issue that comes up during the life of that Parliament. Most political scientists and media commentators also operate within this accepted view and have, along with many compliant politicians, reinforced its popularity by their teachings, commentaries and behaviour. This doctrine makes sense as a practical approach to the many details and issues that can never be aired and debated, let alone anticipated, in an election campaign. It nevertheless enshrines a very bold fiction in a country that operates with the theory of being a representative parliamentary democracy: it is one of the major reasons why Canadian governments have lost credibility and Canadian legislatures are generally viewed with disrespect, even by many who are members of them.

To assert that a government can go to war, amend the country's constitution or reverse a whole pattern of trade policies or immigration programs without ever talking about such courses of action in its election campaign is to stretch the mandate doctrine further than is reasonable in a parliamentary democracy. Yet each of these has happened in Canada. To brazenly reverse aspects of the mandate—clear promises made by the political party that won voters' endorsement during the campaign—such as freezing prices and wages (as Prime

Minister Trudeau did, although he'd pledged he wouldn't) or cancelling the acquisition of nuclear-powered submarines (as Prime Minister Mulroney did, even though he'd said his government would buy them) or continuing the GST and the free trade treaty (as Prime Minister Chrétien has, despite ardently campaigning against both) stretches the doctrine to the point of meaninglessness, and, not surprisingly, the government loses its authority and legitimacy. If prime ministers shrug with indifference, so will citizens.

People reasonably understand that some issues not addressed in an election campaign may later emerge and influence the stated positions of the party in office. Most Canadians also accept that the government basically governs as it must, and even as it chooses, provided it can maintain majority support in the Commons. The mandate doctrine itself, however, is increasingly untenable. Many Canadians are now prepared to challenge it by declaring that a mandate does not empower a government to deal with any and all issues or crises that arise over its term in office, especially if those issues were never discussed in the previous election campaign. All political parties campaign on the basis of some program; the party that forms the government may even try to implement part of it! Yet many Canadians have grown increasingly skeptical about the election promises of parties right across the political spectrum, based on practice and performance. Part of the reason for this shift is that we understand an election is no longer principally an accountability session. Elements of renewal and accountability assuredly remain part of an election, but only a part.

To reveal the different ways a majority government mandate can cover vastly different practices and policies, just contrast the two Liberal majority governments, both headed by Pierre Trudeau, elected in 1974 and 1980. When the Liberals won a convincing majority in the 1974 general election, we saw how the parliamentary theories about an electoral mandate camouflaged the actual practices of the government that had received the public's "blank cheque" to govern. Prime Minister Trudeau, suggests Richard Gwyn in his biography of him, "interpreted a majority victory as a mandate to goof off." When the Conservatives, led by Joe Clark, defeated the Liberals in May 1979, Marc Lalonde, a principal minister in the Trudeau Cabinet, looked back bleakly and saw no significant achievement of his government in many portfolios, especially the economic ones. "It was quite clear in our minds that if we came back, it would have to mean something," Lalonde later explained in a 1982 interview.

Back in power following the 1980 election, the Liberals displayed a newfound conviction, according to authors Robert Sheppard and Michael Valpy, that Ottawa "must reassert itself in a number of key fields—energy, regional economic development, fiscal transfers and constitutional reform." The revived Trudeau government soon "embarked on a new age of confrontational politics—competitive rather than co-operative federalism." In the spring of 1980, the same writers said, Pierre Trudeau was "probably wielding more raw prime ministerial power than any of his predecessors. He had a majority government and was facing a dispirited opposition ... his caucus and party were beholden to him for leading them out of the wilderness; and ... his few promises in the winter campaign effectively gave him a free hand to pursue the national interest in his own fashion."

This gap between what leaders say during campaigns and then do in office is not a uniquely Liberal phenomenon. After the Progressive Conservatives won a huge majority government in 1984, Prime Minister Mulroney used his "licence to govern" to initiate a free trade treaty with the United States, thereby reversing the historic position of the Conservative Party and his own position during his successful PC leadership campaign, when he had made specific statements opposing "continentalism." His government soon began to get into real trouble on this issue, "not because they had promised more than they had delivered," observed pollster and author Michael Adams, "but because they had delivered more than they had promised, namely the free trade agreement with the United States." Free trade, which had not been mentioned during the 1984 election campaign and thus could not in any sense be considered part of the people's mandate given to the Mulroney Conservatives, consequently became the central issue of the 1988 election campaign.

These important policy reversals by Liberal and Progressive Conservative governments show how, at a theoretical and policy level, the ballot box is not necessarily an effective mechanism for ensuring accountability—at least not if one examines the correlation between election campaign promises and subsequent government actions. This flip-flop approach has become endemic in recent decades—on such matters as new military helicopters, repeal of the GST and renegotiation of the free trade treaty—a discrepancy between promise and performance that cannot be ignored as a factor contributing to the decline in the credibility of our political leaders and a growing embarrassment about our governmental processes.

These four political myths or constitutional fictions are no longer believable in the face of the reality of Parliament's structural operations and performance record. Parliament has lost credibility and relevance not only among most Canadians, but also with senior civil servants and many highly frustrated MPs. Parliament has turned into a scene of bittersweet theatre, sadly incapable of being accountable even unto itself. Does this have consequences for Canadians? Unfortunately, and sometimes tragically, the answer is yes. Nowhere is the increasing irrelevance of Parliament, as well as the government's tendency to ignore or overstep its mandate, more evident than in the realm of military and defence policy. The same accountability issues relevant to any area of government apply to the Canadian military too, except that the consequences of incompetence and unaccountability are more serious because "mistakes" may risk the lives of Canadians in uniform and the lives of others. Accordingly, in a system of responsible government decisions regarding the Canadian Armed Forces should call for the very highest standards of accountability.

When I was parliamentary secretary for the Department of National Defence in 1992, in Washington one morning driving with Defence Minister Marcel Masse to a meeting at the Pentagon, we learned that External Affairs Minister Barbara McDougall had announced Canada would send a further 1,200 soldiers overseas for the UN peacekeeping mission in the former Yugoslavia. We were reading faxed copies of a newspaper report. There had been no consultation, not even an inquiry to ascertain the availability of military personnel for this mission—at least none that either of us knew anything about. Certainly there had been no debate about it in Parliament, let alone a vote by Parliament to authorize and support the deployment. Similarly, during the summer of 1990 when the Iraqi forces of Saddam Hussein invaded Kuwait, Prime Minister Mulroney announced, not before the House of Commons but into a television camera, that Canadian ships, aircraft and military personnel were being dispatched to the Persian Gulf. Canadians learned the news of this major commitment as a fait accompli, a military mission overseas, undebated and unauthorized by Parliament.

The ascendancy of prime ministerial power at the expense of parliamentary accountability has transformed the country in profound ways, as these matters concerning the deployment of the Canadian Forces overseas demonstrate. Colonel (Ret) John English explained to researchers for the *underground royal commission*, "Over the years we got in this business of deploying peacekeeping forces by order-in-council or by Cabinet decision—that they will go over and there will be no parliamentary debate called. There will be no debate within the Canadian public at large." A succession of Canadian prime ministers—William Lyon Mackenzie King, John Diefenbaker, Lester Pearson, Pierre Trudeau, Brian Mulroney, Jean Chrétien—has sought to play a major role on the international stage; these leaders have appropriated for themselves through the Privy Council Office a significant role in relation to foreign policy and defence matters. "No minister likes to mess with the food on a prime minister's plate," observed John Dixon, who served as Kim Campbell's senior advisor when she was defence minister, "so he stands back to let the prime minister run foreign policy and defence. Meanwhile, the prime minister rightly thinks his minister is running the Defence Department. So there is a deep confusion that has been institutionalized in our structure of government."

This confusion has only been increased by the absence of Parliament from any decision-making or review process with respect to foreign policy and defence matters. While it is not Parliament's role to run the government, it is Parliament's job to air issues, debate different considerations, approve the annual budgets of the Defence and Foreign Affairs ministries, vote to ratify treaties and authorize military involvement overseas. So why doesn't it? The rise of "partyism" in Parliament means that our national legislature now functions more as an arena for team sport than as a centre for contending issues and serious debate on legitimate differences of policy. Party solidarity, considered a prime virtue in this setting at all times, is especially valued and enforced in times of crisis and international confrontation. The government's instinct to show solidarity with our allies in collective security arrangements when a global crisis hits is then refracted back into its control over Parliament. Why give hostility and dissent a chance to display itself on the floor of the House of Commons when we want to show unanimity and solidarity of purpose?

With respect to these fundamental military matters, Parliament no longer plays its historic and proper role, is no longer an instrument for accountability on the national political scene or touching the affairs of state. Our country's original policy was that no Canadian in uniform could ever be sent beyond our borders without parliamentary authorization. The prime minister and ministers of defence and foreign affairs would have to justify such life-and-death policies to the people's elected representatives. For some even that seemed inadequate. When debating Canadian participation in the Boer War in 1899, for example, Sir Wilfrid Laurier suggested holding a national referendum on the question. At a minimum Parliament was always fully involved in authorizing war activity. In August 1914 Prime Minister Robert Borden interrupted his Muskoka vacation to summon Parliament, which debated and voted to declare war on Germany. The Borden government had, moreover, also been on the brink of holding a national referendum on going to war, but pulled back at the last moment—a hesitation in taking the matter directly to the people that Arthur Meighen, attorney general of Canada at the time and later Conservative Party leader and prime minister, came to openly regret. In 1939 Parliament, now under the leadership of Prime Minister Mackenzie King, again voted, following debate, upon a resolution for a declaration of war. However, when Canadian forces sailed in 1950 for Korea, they did so without the approval of Parliament; the Cabinet of Prime Minister St. Laurent, dispensing with the required parliamentary debate, merely issued an order-in-council as authorization. The limp excuse that Korea was a so-called "police action" by the United Nations, not a war, was already enough to persuade some folks that Parliament didn't have to be involved. Although it was not a "war," 27,000 Canadians served overseas under arms and over 800 died in the "action." From Wilfrid Laurier to Louis St. Laurent, the country had turned 180 degrees and a new pattern was set. Our prime ministers in the modern era came to think that Canadians should just trust them to do the right thing.

Thus it was Cabinet, not Parliament, that approved the decision to intervene in Somalia in October 1992. The mission was presented in the Commons during Question Period and to the media in press briefings as traditional peacekeeping, but it was not in any fashion like other United Nations military missions with which Canadians were familiar. The nature and purpose of the military's role, having been neither clarified nor endorsed by Parliament, was ambiguous and uncertain to those in the field, a situation that recurred in late 2001 and 2002 when Canadian troops were sent to Afghanistan in an cloud of uncertainty about their overall mission, and even about such matters as taking prisoners.

Our soldiers' experiences in Bosnia in the early 1990s highlight the problems encountered when accountability is avoided for long periods. Ambush greeted the Canadian soldiers who thought they had been sent on a peacekeeping mission. Hatred between different ethnic groups created deep and mean responses, and Canadians found themselves right in the middle. Even the seasoning gained from Canada's decades' long role in keeping peace between Turks and Greeks in Cyprus was no preparation for what the soldiers faced in Bosnia. Furthermore, silence on the home front covered this operation with a mask of unreality. Canadian soldiers, on the ground in a hot war, discovered no one in Ottawa was seriously accountable for what was unfolding. This examination of Parliament's role (or lack thereof) in military matters shows that the consequences of inaction, or action based on inaccurate or incomplete information, can be extremely serious. While the stakes are higher and the results of decisions more dramatic, the lack of accountability evident in both Parliament's and the government's attitude toward the Canadian Armed Forces is indicative of the way in which contemporary Canadian government operates in general.

In theory government is subject to a number of constraints. It must be accountable to an official Opposition in the House of Commons. It must enact new laws through Parliament. It is constitutionally obligated to meet Parliament every year, submit a budget and all spending estimates to Parliament annually and call a general election at least every five years. The government's laws and actions can be challenged in court and scrutinized by an independent judiciary. Provincial governments can balance Ottawa's broad power. All the while a competitive and often critical news media continually examines the government's exercise of power. Yet in reality, for every minute of reckoning achieved by Parliament, there are hours of non-accountability. For every law passed openly in Parliament, a dozen more are enacted inconspicuously by orders-in-council. For every budget items scrutinized, a thousand others are deemed approved unexamined. For every election held when the government's back is to the wall or its constitutional time limit of five years has run out, three more are self-servingly called at the moment most propitious to those who already hold power. Parliament, once central to expressing peoples' views on issues facing Canadians, has become an anachronism ever since this role was scooped out by government-hired public opinion pollsters, leaving the House of Commons a hollow chamber rather than a connector between Canadians and our government's policies and programs. Parliament's role in controlling government spending has been eviscerated, procedurally and behaviourally, step by step over the past 30 years, to the point where MPs no longer control the public purse strings either.

As citizens we no doubt conclude, the more we watch television or read newspaper accounts about the increasing role of lobbyists and interest groups and the ineffectiveness of our elected representatives, that our own chance to individually influence public decisions grows slimmer and more remote with each passing day. We do not have representative government so much as a system of government where representations are made behind closed doors and away from any mechanisms of accountability. So it's hardly a surprise that, as reported by Leger Marketing in April 2002, 69 percent of Canadians think that the federal government is corrupt. Some citizens have expressed their growing dissatisfaction with the decision making of elected and appointed officials by suggesting that government should hold community forums and town hall meetings as a regular part of the ongoing governing process. People do not advance such alternatives unless they feel dissatisfied with the existing arrangements. Those who make these suggestions are trying to improve a system evidently in need of an overhaul. Others just boycott it altogether, staying away from polling stations on election day.

The power of Parliament to monitor the government's activities and provide accountability to the Canadian people once came about through the mechanism of approving the government's spending program, voting for taxes, approving of borrowing, questioning Cabinet ministers and enacting or amending the laws that the government introduced in Parliament. Along the way there was debate, sometimes humour, and invariably deep differences of opinion. Today these parliamentary powers are exercised formally but seldom substantively. However, in considering the ephemeral nature of governmental accountability in our Canadian context, it would he wrong to focus on Parliament alone; Parliament was once our most important national political institution, but not the only one. It functions within a matrix of institutions that connect and interact. One's role picks up where another's leaves off. If Parliament no longer exercises much effective power, it is not because power has evaporated, but because it has flowed and been taken elsewhere. Each governmental institution in our capital and across the country is part of a larger picture we need to see more clearly for accurate perception of our functioning realities.

Most Canadians believe, and are in fact encouraged to think, that the MP is our connector. We believe that MPs, individually and collectively, make the system work, especially in terms of accountability. Isn't that also what we teach our children? Don't we say the meaning of responsible government—the executive held to account—is all about answering to the people's elected representatives in Parliament? The truth is, the Parliament of Canada is no longer a seriously functioning part of the accountability equation. As an MP I was no connector. I was a pushed and battered shock absorber between the needs of the people I represented and the predetermined plans of a tightly controlled top-down government. In my case it was the Mulroney government because I was elected as a Tory; had I run and been elected as a Grit, I'd have experienced the same phenomenon under the Trudeau or Chrétien governments. This is not a partisan issue; it is a parliamentary issue. Until you've been there to experience this, you cannot hope to know with just how much excruciating humiliation parliamentarians are forced to absorb and internalize our governing system's deepest contradictions—while seeking to salvage a measure of human dignity with a broken smile toward constituents and into the cameras.

During its cross-country interviews the *underground royal commission* encountered many MPs and former MPs who had similar views about their experiences in Parliament. Reg Alcock, Liberal MP for Winnipeg-South, was both perceptive and clear:

The House actually has enormous authority, but at certain key points, who exercises that authority is controlled by one person—the prime minister. We need to separate that to allow the House to function as a body to demand accountability from the government. That's what it has to be.

In a similar way George Baker, a Newfoundland Liberal MP for some 30 years before being appointed to the Senate in 2002, pointed out that once MPs are elected to the House they face "a situation where a member has to be in good standing with the party even to get on Question Period. A member has to be in good standing with the party leader and the whip in order to even speak in the House of Commons. Where does this leave members of Parliament?" Former Conservative Cabinet minister John Crosbie was candid too. He said an MP can be "a good representative of their area but as members of a party influencing policy, what a government actually does, rather than settling up this man's unemployment claim or this woman's rent problem, they basically don't have much influence. They are a very frustrated group."

Having been in Parliament, I share the contradictory feelings of Canadians who are disenchanted with the way our country's system of government works, but are also aware of so much that is good and of permanent value in it. The problem? Our democratic theory is premised on citizens and citizens' elected representatives playing an active and informed role in the political system, but theory is not matched by opportunity. Instead, MPs and the people they represent are relegated to the periphery of political life by government officials who prefer to say, in effect, "Just trust us." In this atmosphere it's most beneficial for members to portray themselves as ombudsmen for their constituents and lean heavily toward service and problem solving and speaking up for local concerns, all helpful for getting re-elected. That's how Canadians evidently perceive them too.

For instance, a 1999 Environics poll asked respondents to rank the most important functions of MPs from a list provided. "Representing local concerns to Parliament" was chosen by 42 percent; 24 percent said it was "solving constituents' problems"; 22 percent picked "providing their constituents with information on government?" Only nine percent said the fourth role, "supporting the objectives of their political party," should rank as most important. Even more revealing is that none of the "most important" roles identified in the question had anything to do with holding government accountable or scrutinizing spending. The pollsters, being realists, didn't even bother to ask. They, too, know that what we teach the children about responsible government is not the way it really works. On good days the most that happens is that MPs play-act at accountability.

With this evaluation of the institutional and behavioural problems facing those who represent the people of Canada in mind, it makes sense to now step back a little further, or rise above the parliamentary fray a little higher, and see the nature of just who we are, the Canadian citizens that our MPs endeavour to represent.

Chapter 12

Poll-Driven Politics—The Role of Public Opinion in Canada

DAVID HERLE*

* **David Herle** is a principal of the Gandalf Group, which is a leading polling and market research firm.

> *"The role public opinion research plays in guiding governmental communications is often dismissed as partisan and not necessarily in the public interest," writes David Herle, who begs to differ. As the former pollster to the federal finance ministry in the 1990s, Herle's polls and focus groups shaped support for balancing the budget and creating the fiscal dividend. Other policies, he writes, "can be sacrificed because (Ottawa) couldn't talk about them to Canadians in a way that made sense to them." He also identifies five rules of current Canadian public opinion: Canadian social values, transparent governance, activism rather than retrenchment in government, and the enduring regionalism and evolving views of the Canadian federation.*

I have been in the public opinion research business for the past 14 years. My firm was the official pollster of the Liberal Party of Canada from 2003 to 2007. And from 1993 to 2003, I had the great opportunity to work closely with a number of government departments and ministers at the federal and provincial levels.

Let me first deal with the role of polling in government. Essentially, governments use research for the following unique reasons:

- to assess the acceptability of support levels for various policy options
- to learn how to best communicate a policy idea
- to understand the policy priorities of the population
- to determine which of their policies to accentuate, and which to hide under a bushel

There are implications for each of these, all of which have been the subjects of many academic studies. All I can usefully add is the perspective that my personal experiences have given me.

The idea that polling is influential in government decisions is almost universally derided as a negative. It is said to be the sign of an unprincipled government, like a weather vane reflecting the impulses of the masses. Sometimes the money spent on it becomes a news item, and it is always characterized as a waste. It is the antithesis of strong leadership that does what it knows to be right, no matter what pressures come from the public.

I can't agree with any of that, and I find it anti-democratic.

First, governments rarely decide fundamental policy directions on the basis of polling. Those decisions are made by the prime minister and his or her cabinet, in my experience, based on what they believe are the necessary issues to address and advice from civil servants.

However, once the policy direction is set, there is a myriad of choices that need to be made in the implementation of that policy. I see nothing wrong with the public's preferences being reflected in that decision making. If it is not clear which option would be more effective at meeting the policy goal, why shouldn't the government know which option the public would prefer? Canadians regularly say they want more, not less input into these kinds of decisions.

On the occasions where polling forces the government to change direction on a major policy issue, it is generally the result of such a strong consensus of opinion that it would be anti-democratic, not to mention politically suicidal, not to address it.

For example, Prime Minister Harper's recent conversion on the subject of global warming is certainly the result of strong pressure from Canadians, as reflected in government polling. So the Prime Minister was poll-driven. Is anybody suggesting that he should have ignored those polls? Would that have been a better result for Canadians?

For many years, ministers in the Chrétien and Martin governments gritted their teeth about increasing health transfers to the provinces. They hated cutting cheques to the provinces. They did it because the public's concern about health care dwarfed every other issue. Again, should those governments have ignored public opinion and refused to provide provincial governments with more money for health care? When that level of consensus exists, under most circumstances, I would argue that the government should pay attention.

There are cases where governments do disregard dire warnings from the pollsters. And those tend to be on the core priorities of the government or the Prime Minister.

I am told that when the Mulroney cabinet approved the GST they knew the government would almost certainly be defeated over it. However, the government knew that Canadian business could not compete under free trade unless they replaced the manufacturer's sales tax with a value-added tax. It has been reported that Mr. Trudeau ignored the pleas of his pollster Martin Goldfarb and his advisers as he spent the last weeks of the losing 1979 election campaigning on the need to patriate the Constitution—an issue nobody cared about. But Mr. Trudeau did.

And when I first talked politics with Paul Martin, he spoke passionately about the need to improve the situation of First Nations people. I told him then and I told him when he was prime minister, a sad truth of our country is that there are no votes to be had by helping the First Nations. In fact, it's a vote-loser. And yet, in the dying days of his government he was hosting a First Minister's Conference in Kelowna on a new deal for First Nations people to conclude the work that took up a substantial amount of his time as Prime Minister. And he campaigned passionately on it in the election that followed.

One of the lessons of these anecdotes is that if you are going to do something really unpopular on a point of principle, you had better be prepared to be defeated and lose office over it.

The best use of public opinion research in my experience was by the Department of Finance. First of all, there was an extremely collegial and collaborative relationship between the minister's office and the department. Therefore, there were none of the tensions that often emerge when a minister's office and a department have different agendas, and [this fact] played out in the research.

In the critical years of 1994–97, David Dodge and the other senior officials at Finance believed that they could only successfully eliminate the deficit—which they considered to be the most urgent and important public policy challenge of the day—if they had broad buy-in from the Canadian people.

Important principles for deficit reduction were derived from public opinion research: more spending cuts than tax increases, but a mixture of the two; the federal government infrastructure itself should bear the greatest share of spending cuts; and every sector of the economy and walk of life should feel the cuts equally. Sometimes a dubious bauble—the special tax on banks—would be added in order to make the package seem fairer.

The research itself was a kind of public consultative exercise, in which respondents were asked to make the very trade-offs and choices that the government was facing. A different media environment allowed the government time to build a consensus through a broad public consultation.

It is important to recall that, at the time, eliminating the deficit was considered to be impossible. In the 1993 election only the Progressive Conservatives and the Reform Party even promised to try to do it. And nobody thought their promise was credible.

It is not that policy people couldn't figure out how to make the math work. The reason why deficit elimination was considered an intractable problem was because it was impossible politically. No government could possibly survive what eliminating the deficit would take. Jean Chrétien, Paul Martin, David Dodge and the Department of Finance turned that on its ear by not only eliminating the deficit but doing so with enormous public approval and support. Most Canadians felt something important had been accomplished, and it had been done in a fair and equitable way.

The role public opinion research plays in guiding governmental communications is often dismissed as partisan and not necessarily in the public interest.

Again, I can't agree. I think it is an integral part of the policy process.

Many departments in Ottawa have a bias against doing polling, or they just don't have a culture that knows how to use it. In any event, they try to communicate complex initiatives to the public without a realistic sense of the public's knowledge base, how interested Canadians will be, how much attention they will pay to your communication, or how to make it relevant for the average person's life. They tend to think Canadians have the same information, use the same vocabulary, care about the same things and see everything in the same way as those who work in these departments.

As a consequence, policies that are the result of years of work, that might make a real change for the better, may end up being sacrificed because their creators couldn't talk about them to Canadians in a way that made sense to them, and as a result Canadians opposed the policies. If we get those things wrong we erode confidence in public service.

Since the elimination of the deficit, the Department of Finance and the Department of Industry have been convinced that the major challenge facing the economy is productivity. But they have been unwilling to invest the same time and effort into understanding how Canadians think about productivity and adapting to it. Canadians find the concept threatening and insulting, because it seems as if the government or business community is telling them that they don't work hard enough or they aren't smart enough. Policy discussions about productivity generally centre around corporate tax cuts and loosening regulations. Neither of these is high on the public agenda. In fact, most people do not see how those policy items or the productivity agenda in general will have a positive impact on their lives. For Canadians, a true productivity/competitiveness agenda would have education and training at the heart of it.

One factor that really inhibits the effective use of public opinion research in government is the way media covers research that is publicized under the *Access to Information Act*. Because the results of any poll must be made public within a relatively short period of time, government departments do not want to ask questions that might possibly yield answers that would be embarrassing to the government.

It also means that you can rarely test the actual policy propositions that are under consideration since it is quite possible that the poll would have to be released before the policy had even been to cabinet, in which case the government would be reeling on the defensive. I'm not suggesting that polling shouldn't be subject to access to information, just pointing out that it has an impact on the quality of the information that the government has. Perhaps a longer time frame before release is mandated would strike a better balance.

Modern polling emerged in Canada in the 1960s, when Keith Davey brought Lou Harris, John F. Kennedy's pollster, to Ottawa. Before that governments had to assume they understood public priorities and managed public opinion through their MPs.

One criticism of the use of polling in government comes from those who say it has diminished the role of the member of Parliament. I think it is a fair comment, but I think it has also been a positive thing.

First, no person could possibly replicate through personal consultations the reliable information polling provides. Second, my experience has been that many MPs either have no idea what people in their riding think or want, or they know but have no interest in reflecting it, which makes taking their advice on public opinion a dubious proposition.

I actually feel less positive about the role of polling in politics than I do about its use in government. I believe in brokerage government. I think the job of government is to find a way to accomplish its objectives in a way that makes as many Canadians as possible comfortable with what it is doing.

I don't believe in "wedge government"—where governments cater exclusively to their support base. I don't see consensus-building or compromise as signs of weakness. Neither do the many women who choose not to follow politics, much less run for elected office, because they see it as a male exercise based on conflict and aggression rather than consensus and collegiality.

However, political campaigns are supposed to be the forum where competing visions and different ideas and objectives are played out. Political parties are made up of people who have very different perspectives and ambitions for Canada. There is a substantial amount of opinion research on members of political parties that allows us to know that there are stark differences between, for instance, the views of the average Liberal delegate to a convention and a Conservative delegate to a convention.

Parties don't run on what their members think, and can't if they want to be successful. They run on what will get them the most votes. It is a strategic marketing exercise rather than a genuine contest of ideas. It drives everybody to blunt their definitions, to shave off the rough edges of their ideas.

The result is that Stéphane Dion wants you to think he's tough on crime. But he doesn't really care that much about that and neither do most Liberal activists. The concept of the Conservative five priorities in the last election was almost certainly derived from research, as were each of the five priorities themselves. Does anybody think that Stephen Harper got into politics to find a way to preserve the public health care system and reduce wait times within it?

And let's not forget the NDP's unwavering commitment to balanced budgets and fiscal responsibility.

It makes people cynical because it is not genuine enough, and people sense that. Canadians know it is not a reflection of what the leader or party is truly about or interested in. And therefore they know it won't have that much to do with what that party does in government.

It has had a devastating effect on the role of political parties, and they have lost virtually all of their policy function.

Parties can still dig in their heels and get their way on an issue—as the Liberal Party did on missile defence a couple of years ago—but it rarely happens. Most of what happens in party policy conventions is of little consequence to party election planners. As a result, people who are committed to getting policy action are more likely to work locally or join NGOs, rather than becoming active in a national political party.

The problem is that the professional polling work is so effective, now that it is done this way, it is impossible to imagine it not being done this way. I know, as a campaign chair in two elections who had to decide what kind of advertising to put on the air, where the leader's tour should go and where we should expend resources, that polling information is invaluable.

Every once in a while you can see the spark that politics can generate when it breaks out of that managed, predictable mode. One such moment occurred with the selection of Stéphane Dion as Liberal leader. The Liberal post-convention bubble in support was a product of interest and enthusiasm about the notion of a seemingly very genuine and unpackaged guy overcoming the odds and the party establishment to win. For a while it seemed that maybe politics had changed and things could be different. Turns out that might not be true, but it was a glimpse of the power that something genuine in politics can have.

The professionals in politics are using polling to make the best tactical and strategic decisions at every turn. But in the process, we are managing an ever-declining voter base. Federal politics has never been less relevant to people than it is now. The voter turnout numbers speak for themselves.

In 1988, 75 percent of Canadians cast ballots. By 2004 that percentage had dropped to 61 percent, before rebounding slightly in 2006 to 65 percent. There is great excitement in the media and among pundits whenever support for one or another party moves three or four points in one direction or another.

Yet the candidate or party that can motivate the 10 to 15 percent of Canadians who have stopped voting probably holds the key to breaking this political deadlock where no party can build a majority coalition.

As the parties all attempt to position themselves, if they are using public opinion as I suspect they are, they will all be paying attention to the following rules of public opinion. These are the tectonic plates that lie beneath the day-to-day tactics of politics.

Rule 1—There is a Canadian consensus on social values.

Although there remain cleavages on "values" issues and, in particular, rural Canada is different from urban Canada on these issues, Canada is primarily a socially progressive nation and becoming more so.

Concepts like tolerance, diversity, and legal equality are core values that are now central to most people's idea of being Canadian.

In fact, the recent prominence in the US of social conservatism has prompted Canadians to re-examine their belief systems. This has reinforced and driven the evolution toward greater social progressiveness on values.

This is a development that has many causes, not least the essential diversity of the country, but it is primarily driven by the young people and the women of this country.

In 25 years the Charter of Rights and Freedoms has become a central and defining document for the country. Politicians who do not accept this fact are hitching their wagon to a minority and declining opinion base.

Rule 2—There is a new attitude about ethics, patronage and transparency in government.

Canadians are increasingly demanding of their governments and their politicians in this area.

The old "nudge nudge—that's politics" attitude is gone: what was once acceptable is now unacceptable.

The reaction to the Auditor-General's Report on the sponsorship program should have been a shot across everybody's bow. It was far more dramatic than reactions would have been to a similar thing years ago, and it may have brought us close to a "tipping point." We are moving into a new era of ethics in government that will affect many of the ways governments do business. Those politicians who understand that will have a future, and those who do not understand it are not likely to.

This will not only affect politicians, it will also affect business in spades. Business is going to have to find ways to meet these tests consistently as well, and to ensure that there is transparency and accountability in decision making and in the operation of business. Investors and the general public will demand it.

Less and less deferential all the time, Canadians want to open up the entire system and let some air in.

Rule 3—The years of anti-government retrenchment are over—Canadians want an activist government.

By the early 1990s, Canadians had lost much of their faith in governments as a force for positive change. There was a complete "crisis of competence" in Canadian politics. In that era, one had a difficult time even getting people in focus groups to talk about what the federal government should do. Now, people have moved from doubting that governments could solve anything and therefore it was better not to try, to demanding that governments act as agents of change.

The first step toward breaking the back of that attitude was, ironically, the elimination of the federal deficit and balancing the budget for the first time in a generation. A whole generation of Canadians grew up with governments having failed to do what people themselves do every day—manage their money responsibly.

It re-established that governments could be competent. The deficit was a problem that Canadians had come to believe was utterly intractable.

It was also accomplished through a process that met the tests of openness and accountability I referred to earlier. Consultations were extensive. Targets were set openly and with no wiggle room, and they were consistently met or bettered.

Now that fiscal pressures are less problematic and there has been some tax relief, Canadians want governments to start trying to solve problems again. In many instances, people want government to fix problems that are seen to have been created by the fiscal cuts that led to balanced budgets.

Indeed, there is a confidence that problems can and should be solved, and Canadians want their governments to do more than just get out of their faces. They want them to aspire to make the country better. This lack of an aspirational vision is a major factor in the Conservatives' inability to capture a really substantial amount of public support.

An essential caveat is the importance that people place on economic management and fiscal responsibility. Deficits at the federal level are a nonstarter. Canadians are proud of balanced budgets and think they are an essential part of our economic success.

Rule 4—Regionalism remains a strong factor in Canadian politics.

Regional identity continues to be one of the most important prisms through which people see government policy and political behaviour.

This may seem like an obvious thing to say, because it has been the case for so long. However, there are many other major cleavages—urban/rural, French/English, gender, age, income—that cross regional lines.

Nonetheless, it is important to understand how people in different regions view the same things differently.

The gun registry is good case in point. The most obvious differences in opinion on this subject were between rural and urban Canada. However, there was also [a] wide difference in the perceptions of the program between urban areas in different regions.

Residents of the major western cities share most values and attitudes with residents of major central Canadian cities, yet they saw this program very differently because their perceptions were shaped by their region, rather than by their status as urbanites.

In the 2004 and 2006 election campaigns the Liberal Party was competing in at least five different campaigns across the country, with different primary opponents and different issues in each. We ran specially tailored advertising in almost every province. It is still the case that outside Ontario, the federal government is often seen as an outside force that does not have that region's best interests at heart. It means that everything the government does has to pass through a barrier of cynicism.

This puts a special onus on the government to find ways to communicate what it is doing, and to do so in a way and a language that makes sense to people in that region.

For public servants, there will be an increasing demand for more consultation and to adopt policy solutions that take into account regional differences in the country.

This leads directly into my next rule.

Rule 5—Views of the federation are evolving.

The fight between "a strong central government," on one side, and "a community of communities," on the other side, is over, and both sides won.

Most Canadians have settled on a division of labour between levels of government that is based on what they see as the appropriate roles and competencies.

Program delivery is seen as being best done by provincial or even local governments. They are seen as being better able to manage programs and are thought to have a better sense of what the actual needs are, province by province, community by community.

The cities agenda is coming up into the national agenda for a reason. However, that does not mean that people want or will accept a balkanized Canada. They see it as completely appropriate for the federal government to fund programs in areas of provincial jurisdiction—in fact, most of the things people really care about, such as health care, education, early childhood education and the environment, are outside federal jurisdiction. They would not stand for a federal government that refused to help in those areas. In addition, they want the federal government to demand national principles and consistent approaches and applications.

Politics in Canada is indeed poll-driven. I have defended the use of polling in government, because I believe that governments should be responsive to public priorities and I believe that government should seek to build consensus among Canadians for their policies. I have lamented the use of polls in politics, despite having utterly relied on them when I was a campaign chair. It works, but it is having a corrosive effect on political parties and on public interest in our politics.

Canadians have shed the defeatist attitude about the possibilities of government they held 15 years ago, but they are becoming increasingly disengaged from our politics.

While most Canadians see an opportunity for public policy that reflects the full spectrum of opinion and ideas that exist in the country, they are getting disengaged from a political world that offers too much political management, too much false confrontation, and not enough real discussion of problems and ideas.

Chapter 13

How They Operate

GEMMA ROSENBLATT*

Gemma Rosenblatt is a Research Fellow on the Hansard Society's Parliament and Government Programme.

INTRODUCTION

> *I don't know how other MPs organise their work and their life. I think they are slightly secretive!– Anne Milton*

Members of Parliament are expected to hold the government of the day to account and scrutinise legislation as it makes its way though the House of Commons. They are elected to represent their constituencies in Parliament but also operate as community leaders in their local area and act, as one participant described it, as the local 'Queen Mother' figure. Most MPs are elected on a party ticket and so therefore feel a responsibility to work on its behalf.

There is a general understanding that each individual needs to find an acceptable approach to balancing these roles in order to be adequately fulfilling the job he or she was elected to do. In reality, however, the absence of a job description gives Members considerable scope to interpret the role of MP as they choose. There is no prescribed list of responsibilities, only conventions, customs and the desire to be re-elected.

Participants explained how they approached the job and how they divided their time between constituency work, time in the Chamber, committee work and other areas. Alongside this, MPs told us the extent to which they allowed the advice of party leadership, personal opinion, constituency opinion and interest or pressure groups to influence how they act and vote in Parliament. This chapter sets out what additional factors shaped the work of new MPs, from family and personal circumstances to the size of their electoral majority.

DAY-TO-DAY ACTIVITY

The judgement as to whether parliamentarians are effective in their roles is for others to make, but there is no doubt that they 'put in the hours'. In 1982, MPs reported working, on average, just over 62 hours a week; this rose to 69 hours a week when the House was sitting, and fell to 42 hours over the recess.[1] By the end of their first year, the 2005 intake reported working an average of 71 hours per week. This ranged between Members from a low of 50 hours a week to a high of 100 hours a week. In terms of how this time was allocated, MPs

---

[1] Review Body on Top Salaries (1983), Report No. 2: *Review of Parliamentary Pay and Allowances*, Chair Rt. Hon Lord Plowden, Vol. 1 Report (HMSO: London).

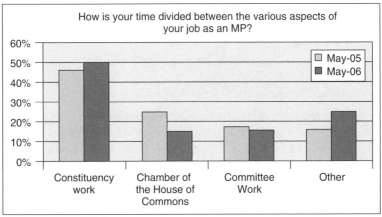

How is your time divided between the various aspects of your job as an MP?

* In May 2005, the new Members were asked; 'How do you expect to divide your time between the various aspects of your job as an MP?'

were asked in surveys to differentiate between constituency work, the Chamber of the House of Commons, committee work, and other work.

Constituency work: MPs are now easily accessible to their constituents and longer-serving Members have noted the change in culture this has produced. Working practices have evolved to adapt to new technologies. The use of computers and then the internet and email have changed the way in which most of us work and MPs have not been immune to this phenomenon. Emails arrive 24 hours a day, with the expectation that a response will be immediate. It is not surprising that compromises were sometimes made in terms of the parliamentary nature of the role:

> *We [MPs] have become the extended family, the social support, the information centre.–Dari Taylor, first elected in 1997*

> *The biggest chunk of time and biggest role in terms of importance is the constituency MP bit. I would be surprised if that takes up less than 90 per cent of my time.–Tim Farron*

> *The calls on your time from the constituency are immense. It takes quite an effort of will to start to turn down opportunities in the constituency and concentrate on Parliament.– Ed Vaizey*

> *I now get several hundred letters and emails a day.–Susan Kramer*

At the outset, new MPs had anticipated spending 46 per cent of their time on constituency work. When asked about this a year later, in May 2006, they reported spending 49 per cent of their time on constituency work. The amount of time allocated varied significantly between MPs, with one reporting spending 15 per cent of his or her time on this, compared to the 97 per cent reported by another respondent. The samples are small when broken down by party and cannot therefore be regarded as conclusive. However, it is worth noting that Labour Party respondents reported that 40 per cent of their time was allocated to constituency work, compared to 59 per cent by Conservative MPs. The greatest proportion of time spent on constituency work was reported by the Liberal Democrats (62 per cent).

Underlying this focus on the constituency was the notion of a permanent campaign. Taking on casework and attending events in the local area is one way to build a network of supporters in the years between elections:

> *Most MPs will do what they think helps them get re-elected. . . . Is going to open a local school going to help you get elected more or less than standing up and arguing a clause on the Climate Change Bill?– Philip Davies*

A handful shared their frustration with the constituency aspect of the role. One MP protested at the end of the project that her role was not to be a social worker. The framework by which she viewed her responsibilities had shifted during the year. She came to see her objectives in light of her national duties, with her profile in the constituency placed second. The MP in question admitted that she barely ever read constituency casework, leaving it in the hands of her staff. She was very unusual in this respect.

In the Chamber: Immediately after their election to the Commons, new MPs anticipated spending 24 per cent of their time in the Chamber. **Over the course of the year, the amount of time MPs actually devoted to the Chamber declined.** The MPs were now spending 14 per cent of their time on the green benches. The greatest proportion of time reported to be spent by an MP in the Chamber was 40 per cent. In contrast, one respondent admitted to spending only two per cent of his or her time there.

There are a range of explanations for a drop in the amount of time new MPs spent in the Chamber, not least their frustration with its proceedings. The reduction of time in the Chamber could also indicate that they were beginning to adopt the working patterns of their longer-serving colleagues. Surveys conducted during the 1997–2001 Parliament found that almost 90 per cent of MPs spent fewer than 10 hours a week in the Chamber.[2]

The Westminster week

A close look at the weekly comings-and-goings of participants found that many did not stay in the Commons for the whole parliamentary week; the constituency often encroached on their Monday to Thursday routine:

> *I do four days in Westminster and one day in the constituency. Although I squeeze that to three days up here and two days in the constituency if I possibly can, because actually there is a lot of pressure on me to visit local organisations and to see people in the constituency and I don't have enough diary time currently to do that quickly enough. Then I obviously do some weekend work as well.– Anne Milton*

> *Normally come down on Monday and get the very last train on Wednesday if I possibly can.– Tim Farron*

> *Monday to Thursday in the first few months, I was exclusively in Parliament. I needed to do that to get myself established. I'm now blurring the lines a little.– James Duddridge*

---

[2]   Hansard Society Commission on Parliamentary Scrutiny (2001), *The Challenge for Parliament: Making Government Accountable.* Chaired by Rt Hon Lord Newton of Braintree (Hansard Society: London).

Committee work and 'other': After their election to Parliament, the new Members anticipated allocating16 per cent of their time to committee work. Twelve months on, they were
spending 14 per cent of their time on this. Some MPs spent no time at all in committees,
possibly because they had not been allocated to one, whilst others believed it took up to 70
per cent of their time.

New MPs often developed a niche that related to their membership of a particular
select committee. Appointments to a select committee (or two select committees, as happened in some instances) could not only shape an MP's approach to the role, it could, in
some instances, dominate the diary. For one participant, Linda Riordan, her appointment
to the Crossrail Committee has meant that half her time in Parliament is spent listening to
legal petitions on this matter.

There was an increase in time allocated to 'other' responsibilities, which included
responsibilities relating to a spokesperson position, commitments with All Party Groups
or writing a column in the local newspaper. The new MPs had anticipated spending 14 per
cent of their time on 'other' work. By the end of the year, they were in fact spending 22
per cent of their time on this category.

> *I am still learning how to balance the responsibilities of the frontbench with
> constituency duties discharged here and being a proper constituency Member.
> I don't think it is possible for anyone to feel after their first year that they have
> the balance quite right.–Michael Gove*

> *When I was first elected, I concentrated so much on the constituency stuff. I was
> really wanting to do that, and make sure that people knew I was around, and how
> to get hold of me ... now I am probably starting to use the opportunities up here
> a little bit more.– Dan Rogerson*

Enjoying the role

Participants were asked midway through the year if they were enjoying the role. The
response was unambiguous:

> Sometimes you will be sitting on the benches and get this complete wave of
> happiness that I can't describe. And it only comes in little shots, like drinking a
> strong whiskey—'wow, I am here, I made it'.– Charles Walker

> About 95 per cent of the time I love it to pieces, the other five per cent, when I
> have done something wrong, I love it less!– Lynne Featherstone

> I'm enjoying it very, very much. More than I thought I would.– David Anderson

WHAT INFLUENCES THEIR ACTIONS?

The majority of those in the Commons are members of one of the three main political parties. Yet to a great extent, all MPs operate as individuals and the Commons is often said to
contain 646 separate businesses:

There is a great sense of being on your own, to get on with it. As a councillor, there was a bigger sense of team ethos; there is less of that up here.– Dan Rogerson

This place does not encourage you to build networks, partly because you are very isolated in your offices.– Susan Kramer

Very few MPs appreciate, and I think it is true of all generations, how much you work by yourself here. In a better organised, more rational world, the MPs of each party in each generation would act much more corporately and collectively and we would make intelligent use of each other's time and skills.– Mark Fisher, first elected in 1983

A range of factors shaped how individuals operated, including the particular political party which they were elected to represent, the location of their constituency, the size of their majority and family responsibilities.

***Political party*:** The experience of new MPs depended on which political party they were elected to represent. There were clear differences between those who arrived as a member of the governing party, those who belonged to the main opposition party and those elected for the third party. All MPs, new and longer-serving, are affected by the fortunes of their party and the performance of its leadership.

In 2005, the Labour Party won a third term of office and its newest Members arrived into a parliamentary party that was settled into the business of government. The Conservatives had just lost a third election but nevertheless had an influx of new and younger members. The Liberal Democrats saw a steady gain in the size of their parliamentary party. Like the Conservatives, their intake was young and ambitious.

Arriving as a member of the governing party meant that Labour MPs tended to have better access to ministers. However, the Conservative and Liberal Democrat Members felt that they had more opportunities to influence their party's policy. As one Liberal Democrat MP explained:

As a backbench Liberal Democrat, your immediate grasp on the levers of power is a bit limited! So it's about influence and raising issues, moving debate forward, checking government on particular items of policy and trying to get your agenda across.– New MP

***Location of constituency*:** The location of an MP's constituency was a talking point amongst participants. **The distinction between MPs representing an area a commutable distance to Westminster and those who would travel back to the constituency only at the end of the parliamentary week was noted frequently.** The London MPs emphasised the mid-week pressure to attend to the needs of the constituency; the rest raised concerns about being unable to attend to the needs of the constituency whilst at the Commons:

Not being able to attend things in the constituency during the week is something that worries me about being in London. The constituents know I'm an MP but don't twig that I'm in London.– Kitty Ussher

***Size of majority*:** Becoming embedded in the local area is more urgent for some than for others. Those elected with a small majority or on a big swing were ever-conscious of the need to nurture the constituency. Some commented wistfully (or resentfully) about colleagues representing 'safe' seats.

Those MPs in target seats undoubtedly worked hard on constituency matters and many spoke of the need to consolidate their position in their local area. The first term of Parliament was seen as the time to become established in the constituency, so even those with significant majorities would highlight the importance they placed on constituency work.

Family responsibilities: The year appeared to be dominated by work and the desire to establish oneself as a respected politician. Yet MPs, like everybody else, have personal lives outside of work. Balancing family time with their work could be difficult, and the pressures on MPs varied according to their individual circumstances:

> *You are here as an MP, but you have other life experiences. I got married two years ago and we just had our first child. That's had a profound effect over the last few weeks on how I view things and how I handle the job. And I am sure as I experience other things in family life and external life, it will change the way I interact with Parliament.– James Duddridge*

> *From a personal point of view, I am also making a judgement about what I am capable of doing at this point in my life. I am 26 and I don't have children. If there is a time when I can do everything possible in the constituency and go to every-thing and be there, then that is now.– Jo Swinson*

Work tended to encroach on the time that MPs spent with their partners when they returned to the constituency. Weekends became overrun by events and visits and many participants worked seven days a week:

> *If you have a partner who is not supportive, then you are finished—either finished as a partnership or as an MP. It's one or the other, but something would have to give.–Andrew Gwynne*

> *You give up a lot. You give up a lot of family time. In some cases you give up money. Some people come here and really don't like it and go away because they can't deal with it. . . . It is very make or break. People don't realise that it can be a very destructive system.– Gwyneth Dunwoody, first elected in 1966*

WHAT INFLUENCES THEIR VOTE?

This project sought to find out not only how MPs approached their role, but what factors shaped how they act and vote in Parliament. Our surveys to new Members asked them to rate the influence of party leadership, personal opinion, constituency opinion and representations from interest and pressure groups.

The findings illustrated that at the beginning of the year the new MPs anticipated that the advice of party leadership and personal opinion would be the two most important factors in influencing their vote.

Advice of party leadership: After their election to the Commons, 43 per cent of new MPs expected 'nearly always' to be strongly influenced by the advice of party leadership when deciding how to act and vote in Parliament, with 48 per cent expecting that this would 'usually' be the case. Ten per cent anticipated that they would 'sometimes' be strongly influenced by the advice of party leadership and no respondents thought that this would 'never' be the case.

One MP later explained that at the start of the week they are provided with a list of Bills and the Whips tell them how to vote. Admitting that the public would probably be horrified if they knew how little MPs often know about the things on which they vote, he said that:

> *In under four days, you couldn't possibly have the first chance of sitting in the Chamber all the time and listening to all the debates, you couldn't possibly read all the legislation before the House of Commons to be an expert on what you're voting on.–New MP*

From this perspective, the influence of party on the voting behaviour of MPs is essential in ensuring an efficient and workable legislative body. Moreover, MPs were indebted to their political party; they were not under the illusion that they would have been elected without the words 'Conservative', 'Labour' or 'Liberal Democrat' after their names. This imbued them with a responsibility to promote the party line in Parliament:

> *On big issues, issues where the party is very strong and takes a principled stand, then rightly you are expected to vote with current party policy. But I wouldn't necessarily need the party to tell me that. I've been elected by the hard work of hundreds of Liberal Democrat activists and you would really feel like you were letting people down if you didn't.–Jo Swinson*

> *18,600 people voted for me and I would guess 18,500 voted not for Philip Davies, but because I had the word Conservative after my name. And so you have got a responsibility to promote the Conservative line in Parliament, because that on the whole is what most people who voted for me want me to do.– Philip Davies*

By May 2006, the balance between those expecting to be 'nearly always' influenced by the advice of their party leadership and those 'usually' influenced had swung marginally in favour of the former. Fifty per cent of the new MPs now expected to be 'nearly always' influenced by this, with 44 per cent 'usually' influenced. Only six per cent said they would 'sometimes' be strongly influenced by the advice of their party leadership and once again, nobody said this was 'never' the case.

Yet some did indeed vote against the party line and we were told of the difficulties faced when this happened. They did not enjoy voting against their party, but did so when they felt compelled by the circumstances. By the end of their first 12 months, 36 new Members had voted against their party.[3]

Personal opinion: At the outset of the year, 45 per cent reported that they would 'nearly always' be strongly influenced by personal opinion and the same proportion said they would 'usually' be influenced by this. Nobody said that personal opinion would 'never' be a strong influence.

Andrew Gwynne explained that while a combination of factors influenced how he approached the role, ultimately, 'it is your own personal choice, so long as you can defend what you have done'. For Michael Gove, the starting point was, 'the set of principles,

---

[3]   The party breakdown for this was seven Labour MPs, 26 Conservative MPs and three Liberal Democrats. Data provided by Philip Cowley and Mark Stuart. More information on rebellions can be found at www.revolts.co.uk.

beliefs, prejudices or values which I have'. While personal opinion is brought to bear on most issues, this was particularly the case for free votes.

However, at the end of the year there was a slight move away from personal opinion as the key determining factor in deciding how to act and vote in Parliament. The number reporting to be 'nearly always' strongly influenced by personal opinion dropped from 45 per cent to 39 per cent. Forty-eight per cent now reported themselves to be usually' influenced by this and 14 per cent to be 'sometimes' influenced.

Constituency opinion: The constituency featured heavily in the priorities of new MPs, but only 17 per cent of respondents said they expected to 'nearly always' be strongly influenced by constituency opinion following their election to the Commons. Over 80 per cent believed they would 'usually' or 'sometimes' be strongly influenced by constituency opinion (48 per cent and 36 per cent respectively).

Their most important role
Survey results

The new MPs were asked to rank the most important aspects of their job. They were asked to distinguish between:

- supporting the party
- holding the government to account
- scrutinising legislation
- dealing with constituents' problems
- informing/consulting constituents about government activity
- protecting/promoting the interests of the constituency

At both the beginning and the end of their first year, MPs ranked 'protecting/promoting the interests of the constituency' and 'dealing with constituents' problems' as more important than 'holding the government to account' and 'scrutinising legislation'.

The most common first choice at the beginning of the year was 'protecting/promoting the interests of the constituency'. Twelve months later it had been overtaken by 'dealing with constituents' problems'. At the other end of the scale, 'informing/consulting constituents about government activity' was the factor most commonly ranked as their least important role. 'Supporting the party' was also regarded as one of the least important aspects of the job.

Constituency opinion may incorporate the views of the local party, as well as all individuals who live in the local area. There was a general awareness that the views of those who are active in the local party do not always correlate with the views of constituents as a whole. However, MPs may be aware of the views of only a relatively small proportion of the constituency's residents. People who have made the effort to contact their MP do not necessarily hold views that are representative of those in the constituency as a whole:

If it is a constituency problem, then my view is that anyone who has a legitimate complaint has a right to some of my time and energy to try and solve it ... when it comes to the constituency party, they have an absolute right to time, to access, to consideration. But MPs recognise that the constituency party is only ever a portion of those whom they represent.– New MP

If it is a contentious issue, I will ask the opinion of one or two key people in the constituency. . . . I need to keep my colleagues and friends on board. I'm only here because of the support they have given me in the first place.– John Leech

There was a small increase during the year in the number who reported themselves to be strongly influenced by constituency opinion. Twenty-one per cent reported that they were 'nearly always' influenced by constituency opinion; 46 per cent reported themselves to be 'usually' influenced; and 33 per cent said they were 'sometimes' influenced.

Representations from interest or pressure groups: Over four-fifths (81 per cent) of the respondents believed they would 'sometimes' be strongly influenced by representations from interest or pressure groups. Only two per cent said they would 'nearly always' be strongly influenced by such representations, and 10 per cent said they would 'sometimes' be influenced. Seven per cent of respondents thought this would 'never' be the case.

During the year, several new MPs expressed their surprise at the level of lobbying activity that takes place within the House of Commons. Others were disdainful at the quality of this lobbying, describing it as 'extremely low grade'. Postcard lobbying in particular was very unpopular. However, most believed that pressure groups did make a positive contribution overall to the decision-making process.

There was a willingness to meet with charitable organisations, but sometimes a wariness about business interests. Greg Mulholland explained that he had 'relationships with pressure groups that I want to, and pretty much ignore the rest'. Local constituents were prioritised over the lobbying of interest groups, as Jo Swinson explained: 'Being lobbied by a pressure group does not have a huge impact; being lobbied by a constituent on behalf of a pressure group has more of an impact.'

The proportion reporting that they were strongly influenced by representations from interest or pressure groups remained fairly consistent over the course of the year. There

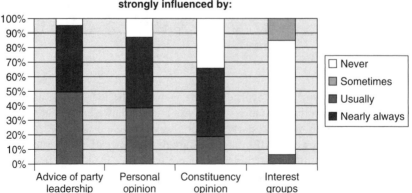

May 2006: In deciding how to act and vote in Parliament are you strongly influenced by:

was a small swing towards those who said they were 'never' influenced by such groups (14 per cent). Two per cent reported that they were 'nearly always' strongly influenced by such groups, six per cent reported that they were 'usually' influenced and 77 per cent said 'sometimes'.

A YEAR TO THE DAY–THEIR PROMOTIONS

A year to the day of the general election, a Labour Party reshuffle placed first-timers into more senior government roles. For those appointed to such positions, changes to their way of operating were inevitable.

By this time, a third of the intake had some form of party spokesperson position. This was more common among Liberal Democrat Members, as smaller parliamentary parties give positions more readily to newcomers. However, about a fifth of the Labour and Conservative intake also held positions. During the year, our participants expressed pleasure at their appointment to such roles and described the impact that this had on their workload and their approach to the job:

> *It alters the way you approach the job—you feel more directly involved in shaping the outward perceptions of the party. Before, as a backbencher, your primary concerns would have been servicing your constituency and then carving out a niche particular to yourself. Now you have to concentrate a little less on pursuing those things that interest you and much more on fitting in with the rest of the team.– New MP*

> *I love the police spokesperson position that I was given. I have had a baptism of fire in terms of having to handle things that you might not expect to have to handle in your first few months as an MP ... to be on the frontbench during the terror debate and see the Government defeated over something I feel passionate about. It feels as if you are taking part in history.– Lynne Featherstone*

CONCLUSION

The absence of a job description by which independent evaluation can be conducted means that MPs are free to decide their own priorities. Yet the approach that MPs take to their role does not only define their effectiveness as individual representatives; collectively, their approaches ensure the success or otherwise of our central legislature and therefore our democratic system.

At the outset, new MPs rated the advice of party leadership and personal opinion as having comparable importance in determining how they vote and act in Parliament. **By the end of the year, the advice of party leadership had risen in importance and personal opinion had declined somewhat.** However, whilst the participants recognised that political parties are a guiding hand, ultimately all believed that party came second to other priorities. The MPs operated as individuals within Parliament.

We found that MPs were working over 70 hours a week on average. Some of the participants looked sufficiently tired to ensure this was believable! They arrived at Parliament with a firm focus on the constituency, but also a desire to learn how to be effective in the Commons. **They did not want to pigeon hole themselves into being either a 'constituency MP' or a 'parliamentarian'.** They wanted to tick both boxes.

Participants were not always certain how their colleagues organised their time. Over the year, our surveys found a small rise in the amount of time the new MPs allocated to constituency work. Yet several participants acknowledged that as they became more comfortable with the workings of Parliament they began to devote more attention to Westminster. This gave a mixed message.

The new MPs hoped to improve legislation that affects their constituents on the ground but were also aware that it is through their parliamentary work that they could raise their profile in Parliament. Speaking in the Chamber could impress colleagues; attending standing committees could please the Whips; and networking in the division lobbies could improve their chances of promotion. The first step of the junior ministerial ladder was within their grasp.

Chapter 14

From Equality Rights to Same-Sex Marriage: Parliament and the Courts in the Age of the Charter

JANET L. HIEBERT*

***Janet L. Hiebert** is Professor of Political Studies at Queen's University.

Should the definition of marriage change to include same-sex unions? This issue has prompted more controversy than any other area of social policy affected by Canada's decision in 1982 to adopt the Canadian Charter of Rights and Freedoms. Lesbians and gay men argue that no principled reason exists to deny them the opportunity to marry, and they are confident that the Supreme Court of Canada will soon rule that a legal prohibition on same-sex marriage is unconstitutional. Yet a sizeable and increasingly vocal segment of the Canadian population remains staunchly opposed to the idea of gay marriage. Many believe that the moral and social norms for Canadian society are, and should remain, the heterosexual family and repudiate claims that equality under the Charter must embrace the legal recognition of same-sex relationships. Other critics accept that same-sex partners should be permitted to legally register their relationships if they so wish, but oppose same-sex marriage, preferring instead the idea of a civil union.

Not only does the prospect of same-sex marriage represent what many critics consider to be a moral crisis of deep proportions, it also raises important questions about the respective roles of, and relationship between, Parliament and the courts. Should Parliament lead or follow judicial pronouncements when the Charter affects important matters of social policy? If the Supreme Court of Canada declares that the prohibition on same-sex marriage is unconstitutional, can Parliament establish civil unions as an alternative to marriage? How should the federal government proceed if it encounters, as it well might, a conflict between judicial judgment and the will of a majority of Parliament? Is use of the notwithstanding clause an acceptable means to resolve this disagreement?

At the time the Charter was included in the Canadian Constitution, few could have anticipated that within a period of scarcely more than 20 years, courts would outlaw social policy distinctions that deny same-sex partners benefits given to heterosexual couples and would determine whether the definition of marriage must change to embrace same-sex unions. In the lead-up to the Charter, lesbian and gay activists in Canada had little reason to look either to Parliament or to the judiciary as allies in their quest for social reforms. At the time the pattern of political behaviour was steadfast refusal to acknowledge or redress claims that discrimination occurs not only from blatant prejudicial treatment of lesbians and gay men, but also from an exclusive reliance on heterosexuality as the basis for determining the legal recognition of spouses and families, benefits and responsibilities. Legislation was not the only source of discrimination. Employers and landlords could discriminate against lesbians and gay men with relative impunity. Judicial relief was rarely forthcoming. Courts and tribunals regularly ruled that since legislation did not conceive of lesbians and gay men as constituting families or spouses, and since human rights codes did not identify sexual orientation as a prohibited ground of discrimination, they had no reason to conclude that differential treatment based on sexual orientation was discriminatory.

When the Charter was first drafted it was extremely difficult to anticipate whether and how it would offer lesbians and gay men protection from discrimination. The equality rights in the Charter do not specifically mention sexual orientation as a prohibited ground of discrimination, because the Charter's political drafters were not prepared to include it. Jean Chrétien, who was justice minister at the time, made it clear that although the federal Liberal government was not willing to include sexual orientation as a prohibited ground for discrimination, it was aware that courts might one day interpret equality as if the Charter did preclude this form of discrimination. The equality rights in section 15 (1) of the Charter stipulate:

> *Every individual is equal before and under the law and has the right to the equal protection and equal benefit of the law without discrimination and, in particular, without discrimination based on race, national or ethnic origin, colour, religion, sex, age, or mental or physical disability.*

Lesbian and gay activists did not initially see the Charter as a likely tool for their liberation from social, political and legal discrimination. It is hardly surprising that many at the time doubted the prudence of relying on a legal rights tradition that previously had not questioned the legitimacy of discriminatory treatment of lesbians and gay men. Moreover, many lesbians and gay men had, and continue to have, misgivings about reliance on the Charter's paradigm of liberal rights, particularly those who have no desire to construe their relationships in terms that are analogous to heterosexual families. Nevertheless, many lesbian and gay activists are relying on Charter equality claims as an important component in their strategies for legislative and social reforms.

Within a few years of equality rights coming into force (this was delayed three years to give governments an opportunity to review and redress existing discrimination in legislation), a steady stream of lower court and tribunal decisions revealed sympathy for the position that section 15 of the Charter should be interpreted to protect against discrimination on the basis of sexual orientation. In 1993 the Supreme Court of Canada indicated for the first time that it might also be receptive to this idea. Two years later the Supreme Court unanimously declared in *Egan and Nesbit v. Canada* that section 15 prohibits discrimination on the basis of sexual orientation, despite the absence of any explicit reference to sexual orientation in the Charter. In the Court's view, sexual orientation is analogous to the prohibited forms of discrimination that the equality rights in the Charter address. At issue in *Egan* was the legitimacy of the federal *Old Age Security Act,* which provided an allowance for the spouse of a pensioner who was already receiving a guaranteed income supplement. Both entitlements were based on need. Spouse was defined and interpreted by administrators as meaning persons of the opposite sex. Consequently when James Egan applied for the monthly spousal allowance on behalf of his same-sex partner, his application was denied because his partner did not satisfy the definition of spouse.

Although the Court ruled that in principle the Charter's equality rights prohibit discrimination on the basis of sexual orientation, not all judges believed that the denial of benefits in this case constituted discrimination. Four judges ruled that the denial did not violate equality, arguing that the policy distinction between heterosexual and same-sex partners is "firmly anchored in the biological and social realities that heterosexual couples have the unique ability to procreate." Five judges disagreed, ruling that the "opposite-sex" restriction in the definition of spouse in the *Old Age Security Act* violates equality, emphasizing the importance of protecting human dignity by according equal concern, respect and consideration to all. But one of the five concluded that this infringement should be upheld under section 1 of the Charter as a reasonable limit on equality, suggesting that parliament should be given time to determine how to extend social benefits within the context of newly recognized social relationships. This view, when combined with the four judges who did not think equality had been violated, constituted a narrow majority that upheld the constitutional validity of the legislation.

Thus the decision conveyed mixed messages about whether and when governments must extend social policy benefits to same-sex partners. On the one hand, it confirmed that discrimination on the basis of sexual orientation violates equality rights in the Charter. Yet, on the other hand, it held out the possibility that some judges were willing to accept the denial of benefits to same-sex partners, either because they did not believe this denial constituted discrimination, or because parliament should be given more time to redress the problem. The *Egan* decision was interpreted by federal and provincial departments and ministers as removing the immediacy for legislative reforms and therefore reinforcing the status quo.

The turning points for compelling governments to change legislation so as not to deny lesbians or gay men protection or benefits given to heterosexual spouses were the back-to-back decisions of *Vriend v. Alberta* in 1998 and *M v. H* in 1999. These decisions made it clear that a majority of the Supreme Court was not willing to countenance continued legislative inaction. At issue in *Vriend* was the termination of employment of a laboratory assistant in an Alberta college after the college learned that he was gay. After his termination, Mr. Vriend attempted to file a complaint with the Alberta Human Rights Commission but was advised that this was not possible because the province's human rights legislation, the *Individual's Rights Protection Act* (IRPA), did not include sexual orientation as a prohibited ground for discrimination. The Supreme Court unanimously ruled that his equality rights were violated, suggesting that the Alberta government's decision not to include sexual orientation in the IRPA was tantamount to "condoning or even encouraging discrimination against lesbians and gay men," and that it conveyed a "sinister message" that lesbians and gay men are less worthy than others. The Court interpreted the IRPA so that it would henceforth include this protection, a remedy many found controversial because it is tantamount to the judiciary acting as if it were the legislature.

The next and most significant Supreme Court ruling in terms of putting pressure on governments to introduce broad legislative reforms was *M v. H*. At issue was the failure of Ontario's *Family Law Act* to recognize same-sex relationships in its processes for resolving property and other issues arising from the dissolution of family relationships. The act utilized a heterosexual definition of spouse. The Supreme Court ruled 8–1 that this definition of spouse violated equality in a manner that could not be justified as a reasonable limit on equality.

The importance of *M v. H* for prompting significant and far-reaching legislative reforms stemmed from the Court's unambiguous statement that same-sex partners must be treated with the same degree of respect and recognition given to heterosexual spouses. The majority emphasized that the purpose of equality rights in the Charter is to "prevent the violation of essential human dignity and freedom through the imposition of disadvantage, stereotyping, or political or social prejudice" and to promote a society where all persons are recognized as "equally capable and equally deserving of concern, respect and consideration." Although the decision applied specifically to Ontario, Justice Iacobucci provided a warning, applicable to all governments, that the Court's ruling "may well affect numerous other statutes that rely upon a similar definition of the term 'spouse'." At the time of this decision, more than 360 federal and substantial numbers of provincial legislative provisions recognized relationships or conferred benefits where eligibility was based on a heterosexual definition of spouse.

Ottawa and a majority of the provinces have now passed legislation that extends most of the social policy benefits given to heterosexual couples to same-sex partners. In most jurisdictions, changes have come about only after courts have ruled that existing legislation is unconstitutional, and often have been attended by substantial controversy. Consider, for example, the federal government's response to the *M v. H* ruling, which was the *Modernization of Benefits and Obligations Act* (Bill C-23), introduced in February 2000. This omnibus legislation amended 68 statutes and covered 20 federal departments and agencies. The federal Liberal government tried to side-step a previous controversy that had emerged: should the term "spouse" be used to depict same-sex relationships? It did so by introducing a new term—"common-law partner"—that would include same-sex partners. The government also argued that it could respect the Charter by eliminating discrimination against same-sex partners and yet still preserve marriage as the privileged and exclusive domain of heterosexual spouses. Some critics argued that the legislation was deficient because it did not redefine marriage to include same-sex partners. But others, including many in Parliament, had the opposite reaction and argued that the legislation would alter the definition of marriage, a claim repeatedly denied by then justice minister Anne McLellan. The government eventually bowed to political pressure from the Canadian Alliance party and also from some Liberal members by agreeing to include a legislative preamble indicating that the legislative changes did not affect the traditional definition of marriage. This was not the first time the government has given into pressure to identify marriage as an exclusively heterosexual relationship. In 1999 the government supported a Reform Party motion that stated that marriage would remain the lawful union of one man and one woman to the exclusion of all others. That motion easily passed by a vote of 216–55. The overwhelming majority of Liberal MPs, including Jean Chrétien and Paul Martin, voted in favour.

When Parliament reconvened in September 2003, the Alliance Party tried unsuccessfully to obtain parliamentary approval for a motion that not only reaffirmed the traditional heterosexual understanding of marriage but also committed parliament to take "all necessary steps" to preserve this definition, which implied use of the unpopular notwithstanding clause. At the time of the motion, the federal government had promised to redefine marriage so as to include same-sex partners. This time the vote was extremely close, 137–132. It came moments after an earlier, failed attempt to amend the motion by removing the reference to "all necessary steps." The intent of this proposed amendment was to make it easier for more MPs to vote in favour of the reaffirmation of traditional marriage by removing the threat of having to use the notwithstanding clause to support this definition. Prime Minister Chrétien, who voted against the motion to retain a traditional, heterosexual definition of marriage, attributed his reversal on this issue to recognition that "society has evolved."

The question of whether the law on marriage must change remains the most significant issue yet to be resolved in terms of legislative treatment of lesbians and gay men. Under the constitutional division of powers, the federal parliament has authority over the legal capacity to marry while the provincial and territorial legislatures have authority over solemnization, which includes issuing licences. But the federal parliament has never enacted legislation that defines eligibility for marriage. Its only statements on this issue have come in the form of agreements to the motions discussed above. Thus, what has prevented same-sex partners from marrying has been a common law definition of marriage that is more than one century old and utilizes a heterosexual criterion for eligibility.

But as of the summer 2003, lesbians and gay men have been able to marry in two provinces—Ontario and British Columbia. This ability has arisen because the courts of appeal in these two provinces have ruled that the current prohibition on same-sex marriage is unconstitutional. A Quebec court agrees, and at the time of writing the case was before the province's Court of Appeal. The B.C. case, *Barbeau v. British Columbia (Attorney General),* did not immediately allow for same-sex marriages because the court suspended the effects of its judgment until July 2004 so that Parliament could legislate on this issue. But in June 2003 the Ontario Court of Appeal in *Halpern v. Canada (Attorney General)* declared a new definition of marriage, to take effect immediately in the province, which allows same-sex partners to marry. The B.C. court subsequently lifted its suspension, allowing same-sex partners in B.C. to also marry. In the remaining provinces, the earlier common law rule prevails, which prohibits same-sex marriage.

The Ontario ruling is controversial, both for its conclusion and its remedy. At the time of the judgment a parliamentary committee (Standing Committee on Justice and Human Rights) was about to embark on its report on whether and how the government should address the recognition of same-sex unions, after holding hearings across the country and listening to 467 witnesses. The majority of these, 59 percent (274), favoured extending equal marriage rights to same-sex couples, while 35.5 percent (166) opposed. Although the committee has garnered negative headlines that raise questions about whether some members' critical views on same-sex marriage are too entrenched to be influenced by testimony, the judicial decision to change the law before Parliament had completed its deliberations demonstrates contempt for Parliament. What further undermined Parliament was the federal government's attempt to secure a positive committee vote on NDP member Svend Robinson's motion to urge the government to accept the Ontario court ruling. As the vote was about to occur, the government suddenly altered the composition of its government members of the committee, replacing two members (one of whom was Derek Lee, who has expressed disagreement with the idea of same-sex marriage) with two new members who voted in favour of the motion. The vote resulted in a tie, which was resolved by the Liberal chair in favour of the motion.

The Chrétien government has now changed its position on same-sex marriage. It has decided not to appeal the Ontario ruling and has drafted legislation to change the definition of marriage so as to read: "Marriage, for civil purposes, is the lawful union of two persons to the exclusion of all others." The government has asked the Supreme Court to review its draft legislation. The Court is being asked to address three questions:

- Is the government's draft bill defining marriage within the exclusive legislative authority of the Parliament of Canada?
- If the answer to the above question is yes, is the capacity to marry to persons of the same sex consistent with the *Canadian Charter of Rights and Freedoms*?

- Does the freedom of religion guaranteed by the Charter protect religious officials from being compelled to perform a marriage between two persons of the same sex that is contrary to their religious beliefs?

What is most interesting about the reference questions is what the Court is not being asked to address. The Court is being asked whether the government's intention to change marriage to allow for same-sex unions is consistent with the Charter. It is hard to envisage any reason why the Court wouldn't affirm that parliament has the capacity to define marriage in these terms, since the constitutional division of powers gives the federal parliament authority over marriage. The real issue is whether a prohibition on same-sex marriage violates the Charter's equality rights. Although not asked to address this question, the Court in all likelihood will address it, since three courts have already declared that the prohibition on same-sex marriage violates the Charter and because the B.C. and Ontario courts of appeal have already changed the law in their provinces. What is also significant about the questions is that the Supreme Court is not being asked whether a civil union is an acceptable alternative to same-sex marriage. Many members of parliament and a substantial portion of the public prefer the concept of same-sex civil union to same-sex marriage.

In addition to the Charter dimension of the reference questions, there is also an important federalism aspect. By asking the Court if the federal government has exclusive authority over marriage, the government is in effect asking the Court to address whether the provinces can do anything that would interfere with the federal government's power to define who can marry. Three provincial governments (Alberta, Quebec and B.C.) have filed notices of intent to intervene in this reference case. Quebec has indicated it is not opposed to same-sex marriages but wants to preserve the concept of civil unions in Quebec. Alberta Premier Ralph Klein has stated publicly that his government would invoke the notwithstanding clause if necessary to prevent same-sex marriages in Alberta. This power gives Parliament and the provincial legislatures the ability to have legislation prevail for five-year renewable periods despite an inconsistency with a judicial interpretation of the Charter. But the notwithstanding clause would not give Klein power to prevent same-sex marriages in Alberta if the Supreme Court affirms that Ottawa has exclusive jurisdiction to define who can marry. This is because the notwithstanding clause does not apply to disagreements about the constitutional division of powers, it applies only to the Charter. What remains unclear is whether a province can exercise its authority for the solemnization of marriage so as to negate or frustrate the effect of how the federal parliament has defined marriage. Patrick Monahan, a noted constitutional scholar, states emphatically that a province's constitutional power to issue marriage licences cannot be used to frustrate federal law.

Both the government's decision not to appeal the *Halpern* ruling and its intent to pass legislation that recognizes same-sex marriages have been extremely controversial. The government faces deep and vocal divisions on this issue, unattended by the declining authority Jean Chrétien wields in the dwindling days of his leadership and the ambivalence expressed on this issue by his successor, Paul Martin. As of late August [2003], 50 of 171 Liberal MPs had indicated their intention to vote against the legislation as currently proposed. A newspaper poll conducted that month suggested that 126 of 301 MPs intended to vote against the same-sex marriage legislation. The vote on the September Alliance motion, which drew the support of more than 50 Liberal MPs, underscored just how seriously the governing party is divided on this issue. The government has indicated that it will wait for the Supreme Court's answer to its questions before introducing legislation in the House of Commons, which will be subject to a free vote. But since the Supreme Court will not hear the case until next spring [2004], and its ruling won't be known for some time after that, many within the Liberal party worry that the issue of same-sex marriage will become a serious political liability for Liberal MPs when they seek re-election, likely in spring 2004.

This opposition to same-sex marriage raises two important questions. One is, what will be the law on marriage if Parliament defeats the government's legislation and the Supreme Court indicates that a prohibition on same-sex marriage violates the Charter? If both events occur, Canada would temporarily have two different laws on marriage in play. Two provinces (Ontario and B.C.) would permit same-sex marriages, because courts have changed the common law definition. When Quebec's Court of Appeal rules on this issue, Quebec might become the third province to permit same-sex marriage. Lesbian and gay couples in other provinces will likely initiate Charter litigation, seeking a declaration from other provincial courts that the common law prohibition on marriage is unconstitutional. If the Supreme Court of Canada confirms that the prohibition on same-sex marriage is unconstitutional, provincial courts that have not yet ruled on this issue will likely take their lead from its opinion and the common law prohibition on same-sex marriage will gradually disappear throughout the country. This means that if Parliament is intent on preventing same-sex marriages from occurring, federal legislation will be required to define marriage as an exclusively heterosexual union. But this would likely require use of the notwithstanding clause, which is unpopular and considered by many to be an inappropriate way to resolve parliamentary/judicial disagreements.

The second question that arises in light of the conflict about same-sex marriage is, what, if anything, is a constitutionally valid alternative? Some who favour a traditional heterosexual definition of marriage believe that if Parliament were to establish civil unions for same-sex partners, it would not need to invoke the notwithstanding clause to retain a heterosexual definition of marriage. Their assumption is that the judiciary will accept a traditional definition of marriage under the Charter, as long as lesbians or gay men are permitted to register their relationship as a civil union. Although the reference decision may not shed light on this issue, it is important to remember that the Supreme Court has interpreted equality as requiring not only the equal benefit and effect of law, but also has stated that the law must confer equal dignity and respect. Although many have expressed profound differences on whether equality is violated by denying same-sex partners the opportunity to marry as long as they can enter into civil unions, the Supreme Court will be skeptical of any arrangement that has separate but equal implications, particularly in light of historical injustices perpetrated on minorities and sustained by this doctrinal approach. Thus, it seems unlikely that the Supreme Court will accept the constitutional validity of a two-tier structure that recognizes marriage for heterosexual spouses and civil-unions for same-sex partners (and also those heterosexual spouses who prefer this to marriage).

Another alternative that has been floated in this debate is the idea that Parliament should abandon authority for marriage altogether, and instead establish a national registry for civil unions. Under this model, marriage would only be conducted by religious organizations according to their beliefs and criteria, and would occur in addition to a civil union. But a large percentage of the Canadian population is not deeply religious. Many who are not religious might be offended by the idea that Parliament would no longer recognize secular marriage (even if existing marriages are protected or "grandparented"), particularly if they interpret this as diminishing the importance and legitimacy of their nonreligious marriages. This option received little support from those appearing before the parliamentary committee studying the issue of same-sex marriage. Moreover, the provinces may contest the idea that the federal Parliament has jurisdiction over civil unions. During the parliamentary committee hearings, a representative from the Canadian Bar Association advised the committee that the federal Parliament does not have jurisdiction to create a national registry of civil unions. If the provinces are recognized as having jurisdiction over civil unions, some provinces might oppose civil unions that apply to same-sex partners and, if challenged under the Charter, could invoke the notwithstanding clause.

Critics of same-sex marriage might take comfort from Paul Martin's indication that not only is he interested in alternatives to same-sex marriage, such as civil unions, but that once installed as leader he intends to revise the same-sex marriage legislation. Yet it is not obvious there are alternatives to same-sex marriage that will either be considered publicly acceptable or are considered constitutionally viable by Martin himself. As suggested above, the idea that marriage is delegated entirely to religious organizations will offend many who value and desire marriage but who are not deeply religious. As for the possibility of establishing civil unions for same-sex partners (while retaining a traditional definition of marriage for heterosexual spouses), this approach would likely require use of the notwithstanding clause if the Supreme Court continues to relate equality to human dignity and interprets equality as imposing an obligation that governments treat all persons as equally deserving of concern, respect and consideration. Martin has stated publicly that he is not prepared to proceed with an option that is inconsistent with the Supreme Court's interpretation of the Charter, and he therefore will not use the notwithstanding clause.

In the event that Parliament defeats the government's same-sex marriage legislation and the Supreme Court makes it clear that a prohibition on same-sex marriage is unconstitutional, it may be some time before Canadians know whether the Supreme Court considers a civil union to be a constitutionally valid alternative to marriage. That is, unless the Court is willing to be subject to accusations for being too activist by answering a question the government has not asked of it.

Many worry that the Charter provides a convenient refuge for politicians to avoid controversial issues, claiming a need to wait for courts to resolve the issue and then blaming judges for forcing them to pass controversial legislative changes. This hypothesis may explain prolonged government inaction to redress many other forms of legislative discrimination against lesbians and gay men. But it does not explain why the Chrétien government has now decided to legislate to allow for same-sex marriage. Had the Chrétien government genuinely wished to minimize or avoid unnecessary controversy, at least until after the next federal election, a more plausible strategy would have been to delay any new policy initiative involving marriage until after the 2004 election. This could have been accomplished by either appealing the *Halpern* ruling or by asking the Supreme Court the question "Does the Charter prohibit a ban on same-sex marriage and, if so, is the concept of a civil union instead of same-sex marriage a valid constitutional alternative?" Either of these options would have carried the government through until the next federal election without obliging it to publicly contemplate such controversial and divisive legislation. At a later date, if the Supreme Court ruled that a civil union was not an acceptable alternative to same-sex marriage, federal politicians could then have tried to deflect responsibility and "blame" the need to redefine marriage on the courts. In short, this author can only conclude that Jean Chrétien accepts, either on his own or because of pressure by others within his Cabinet, including his justice minister Martin Cauchon, that the prohibition of same-sex marriage constitutes such a serious and unjust form of discrimination that the government must now redefine marriage, despite the inevitable controversy and internal divisions this initiative precipitates. Whether or not one approves of the government's new commitment to same-sex marriage, an unfortunate consequence is that controversy on this issue will shroud political debate until and through the next election. This risks transforming the election into a single-issue event that overshadows or ignores important and pressing issues about which Canadians need to understand the parties' positions. These include health care reforms, redressing poverty, Canada's relations with the United States, foreign aid, the appropriate relationship between security and civil rights, parliamentary reforms, and electoral reform, to name but a few.

Chapter 15

Virtual Political Parties and the Decline of Democracy

REG WHITAKER*

Reg Whitaker is Distinguished Research Professor Emeritus at York University, Toronto, and Adjunct Professor of Political Science, University of Victoria.

A quick quiz on the major events of the political year 2000 might elicit the following list: the emergence out of the old Reform party of the new Canadian Alliance under Stockwell Day; the re-election of Jean Chrétien's Liberals to a third successive majority; the apparent stagnation of the Bloc Québécois; the continued marginalization of the federal Progressive Conservative and New Democratic parties.

Appearances can sometimes be misleading, however. Surface events and personalities mask deeper, structural changes taking place beneath the veneer. Distracted by the rise and fall of party labels and leaders, it has been easy to miss the subterranean transformation of political parties into different sorts of creatures than in the past. In an age of relentless change imposed by markets and technology, political parties have had to adapt to the challenges of globalization, the information revolution and the new media, or fade into irrelevance.

The flavour of these changes can be caught in the language used by party insiders to describe their business. Alister Campbell, one of the leading architects of Ontario premier Mike Harris' Common Sense Revolution, and a former federal Progressive Conservative official, early in 2000 wrote an open letter to PC supporters urging them to abandon their federal party for the Canadian Alliance. He complained about his own "wasted investment" in this "brand": "It was time to invest elsewhere." He went on: "If the federal PC party in which you have invested so much was a mutual fund you would have dumped it years ago."

Two of Campbell's words are particularly significant: investment and brand. Parties are no longer about commitment in the sense of principles, loyalty and tradition. Long ago, partisans rallied to Sir John A. Macdonald's Tories under the slogan "the Old Man, the Old Flag, the Old Policy." No more. A party is not a collective project. It is a "mutual fund." Commitment has become investment, and investment demands appropriate returns. If "wasted," it should be pulled out and put "elsewhere." The party's name and symbols are no longer marks of allegiance, but are merely a "brand." Brands are corporate marketing devices for products. Brand identification is intended to promote sales. If sales falter, re-branding may be required. In Campbell's worst-case scenario, the wise investor pulls out altogether and invests in a new product line with a more marketable brand. Hence, like a good investment analyst, Campbell is advising his clients to sell PC and buy CA.

According to political scientists, political parties are crucial linkages between civil society and the state: a noble calling. But in capitalist democracies, parties are poor cousins to their private sector counterparts, the corporations. Corporations sell goods and services and make profits. Parties sell promises of policy and patronage. At best, they offer insurance that profits in the private sector will not be impeded by policies pursued in the public sector, a kind of respectable protection racket. But in a competitive political market, few parties can bank promises contingent upon victory at the polls. Not surprisingly, it is the corporate sector where research and innovation in the technology of marketing and communications take place. Parties have to catch up with trends in the private sector, and struggle to cope with new techniques and tools of marketing as best they can, with limited resources.

One of the organizational forms pioneered in the new economy is the "virtual corporation," a form adapted to the flexibility required of a networked world. Old corporations were heavy, stand-alone entities, with high fixed investment in plant and product, centralized and hierarchical in structure, slow to react to changes in their environment, commanding market share by sheer weight and inertia. Exemplars of old corporate culture were the big three North American automakers before the challenge of Japanese and European competition hit home. New corporations are somewhat less hierarchical, more decentralized, more flexible and adaptive, with less fixed investment. New corporations are leaner, which does not mean that they necessarily employ fewer people. Rather, they employ fewer people directly, but many more indirectly, through outsourcing. Here is where the idea of the virtual corporation comes in. For specific purposes or projects, networks are formed that flow around and over the old organizational boundaries. They may involve temporary partnerships or alliances with other corporations, or at least components of other corporations. These networks are functionalist in design, strictly goal-oriented, and evanescent, forming and reforming around particular projects, and disappearing when the goals are achieved. These commando units may be considered, during their transitory lives, as "virtual" corporations.

Like "virtual" corporations in the networked information economy, virtual parties form and reform for specific purposes. With more tasks "outsourced" and less done in-house, the virtual party networks across traditional organizational boundaries, drawing in specialists who perform specific functions to meet specific, market-driven needs. Virtual parties form around politicians seeking the leadership of parties, as relatively small entourages or coteries of political strategists, marketing and communications experts, "spin doctors," PR flacks and policy "wonks." If successful, the same coterie then in effect colonizes the party and runs its subsequent election campaign. The party, as such, serves as little more than a convenient franchise with brand recognition, marketing "location," and ready sources of campaign funding. Sometimes, it is more convenient to "re-brand" the old party for better location. The real campaign dynamic derives from the virtual party within the shell of the traditional party. If the electoral campaign is successful, the virtual party then colonizes the strategic heights of government, around the office of the prime minister or premier, setting policy priorities, interfacing with the permanent bureaucracy and managing the government's image and media presentation. Many of the real high flyers in the team, however, will choose to return to the more lucrative private sector, only coming out again for a brief burst of activity during a re-election campaign. All this is dependent upon the leader, and the policy package he or she represents. These are the products being marketed.

There are some spectacular examples of the virtual party in operation. One of the most remarkable is the transformation of the British Labour party under Tony Blair. Blair's communications and publicity entourage, led by Peter Mandelson, the former Northern Ireland secretary, remade the party from the top down. They even re-branded it as New Labour, to distinguish it from the electorally unsuccessful and media-unfriendly "Old" Labour. Helped by a decaying Tory *ancien régime,* New Labour swept to office in 1997. Millbank, the permanent party headquarters where its publicity directors and spin doctors reside, has become a kind of rival power centre to Whitehall. In office, Blair and company have been assailed by both critics and supporters as lacking in any clear or distinctive policy direction, yet at the same time as control freaks obsessed with spin doctoring their image at the expense of substance. This is a trap that virtual parties can fall into, given that they are constructed in the first instance for the immediate purpose of getting elected, rather than for governing. Yet some Canadian experience suggests that virtual parties may be quite well prepared not only to get elected, but also to govern programmatically with distinctive policy agendas.

A remarkable case study of a programmatic, even ideological, "virtual" party is the "Mike Harris party," as the Progressive Conservative party of Ontario was re-branded in 1995, the year of its return to power from the wilderness. In the years following its trau-matic defeat in 1985, after 42 years of uninterrupted rule, the Ontario Tory party was "hol-lowed out, broke, leaderless," as journalist and author John Ibbitson put it. The Ontario Tories had been known and feared for the "Big Blue Machine," the Conservative party organization that raised lavish funds from Bay Street, ran one successful electoral cam-paign after another, and then discreetly and efficiently managed the patronage that came with seemingly perpetual political power. It had over the years governed resolutely from the centre, mixing policy pragmatism with a kind of Red Tory sense of the importance of the public sector.

The Big Blue Machine was now defunct and the party a shell that could be taken over. This represented an opportunity for ideologically committed young right-wingers to seize the party franchise. A small group of young activists formed up in 1990 to back the lead-ership candidacy of the Tory MPP from North Bay, Mike Harris, an affable yet ambitious politician with few ties to the crumbling party establishment. With Harris as leader the moderate policy orientation of the past could be discarded, and replaced with a hard-right neo-liberalism. Although initially unsuccessful in the 1990 provincial election, the Mike Harris virtual Tory party took brilliant advantage of the conjuncture in the early 1990s of an NDP government and a severe economic recession to lay the groundwork for a surprise victory in 1995 on a rigorously right-wing ideological party program, the Common Sense Revolution. Moreover, throughout their first term, the Harrisites were committed to enacting their program with unusual zeal and exactitude. Returning to the electorate in 1999, they could truthfully assert something few Canadian parties in office could claim: They had leveled with the voters about what they intended to do, and then carried out their promises.

The Harris party has been successful because it has tightly integrated marketing with policy. It was re-branded the "Harris" party not because Mike Harris is the product, but because it is a useful way of distinguishing its new policy orientation front the soft, cen-trist conservatism that characterized the old Tory party. The real product is the Common Sense Revolution, an ideological program that reflects the goals and preferences of its architects, the core of the virtual party. But right-wing ideological purity in itself is no guarantee of electoral success. Prior to the 1995 campaign, the Harris people had carefully identified their potential core supporters and what specifically they wanted from govern-ment. This is in line with the dramatic shift in recent years in the private sector from mass to niche, or "micro" marketing. New media and new information technologies have com-bined to provide tools that can profile and target ever more finely honed markets. The Harris Tories have never looked for the illusory grail of the "public." Instead they have concentrated on very specific "publics"—all those elements in the Ontario population angry and resentful over the results of previous NDP and Liberal governments—and turned to these refined marketing tools to identity specific policies that would sell to these potential buyers. As it turned out, a fortuitous synergy developed between the hard-right policy orientation of the Harris team and the policy preference profile of a critical mass of voters in the conjuncture of mid-1990s Ontario. The Common Sense Revolution was a product whose time, and market niche, had come. The virtual Ontario Tory party was the marketing vehicle that delivered the product. Following their re-election [in 1999], the Tories have seemed directionless. They await a further re-branding, this time as a party of government, no longer a party of angry outsiders, a marketing task that may present diffi-culties for a virtual party designed to appear as outsiders.

The federal Liberals under Jean Chrétien have been a highly successful political enter-prise, winning three successive majority governments. The Liberal party too has become a virtual party, distinct from its roots, although it chooses not to re-brand itself, but rather to link its pitch with a long history of positive brand identification (since 1896, the Liberal Party has been in national office 70 per cent of the time). Yet the party of Chrétien is a different creature than its predecessors. It is neither the elite-run "ministerialist" party of the King-St. Laurent era, nor the "participatory" party of the Pearson-Trudeau era. It remains a formidable patronage machine, and an engine for organizing Parliament to pass the agendas set by the prime minister. But neither cabinet ministers nor the grass roots matter as much as they once did. National campaigns are poll and media-driven as never before, and the virtual party at the heart of the shell that is called the "Liberal Party" forms the real dynamic.

But there is one oddity about the virtual Liberal Party—its two-headedness—that sets it apart from other virtual parties, and has lent the Chrétien years a distinctive coloration. Virtual parties form up around particular leaders, in the first instance at the time they chal-lenge for control of the party at a leadership contest. Winners then usually take all, and los-ers typically are isolated, neutralized and quite often blown right out of the party and/or the government. In the case of Ralph Klein when he gained the leadership of the Alberta Progressive Conservative Party, his chief competitor was blown all the way into the lead-ership of the Alberta Liberal Party, where she opposed him as the official opposition leader in the 2001 election, before resigning after another crushing Klein majority. More often, losers simply drop out to the private sector and are heard of no more, or at least until the leadership reopens.

When Jean Chrétien was himself defeated by John Turner for the Liberal leadership in 1984, he had felt humiliated by the winner. When he in turn won the leadership over Paul Martin, Jr. in 1990, he behaved differently toward his rival. The Chrétien virtual Liberal Party has in office controlled most of the patronage, and the prime minister runs a notoriously centralized and very tight ship. Yet Mr. Chrétien came to the top with no policy agenda whatever, other than becoming prime minister. The *Red Book* of policy promises, a crucial element in the 1993 campaign, was constructed by a team led by Martin as co-chair of the platform committee. And early on in the Liberals' first term, Martin was permitted to set the major agenda of the government: deficit elimination. The success of this priority became the defining mark of the Chrétien government, and Martin has consequently grown in stature, to the point of becoming a putative rival to the prime minister, certainly in the eyes of his own entourage (the nascent Martin virtual Liberal Party) and of the media, always alert to a saleable personality conflict narrative. Thus the Liberal Party has appeared as a strange, two-headed beast. The Chrétien loyalists argue that while the PM controls the patronage, the finance minister controls the policy agenda, a functional division of labour of sorts. It is an unusual form for the virtual party, but in the Liberals' case, who can argue with success?

The Liberals also lay claim, with some justification, to being the only genuinely national party in a system now characterized by opposition parties locked, either willingly in the case of the Bloc Québécois, or unwillingly in the case of the Alliance and the PCs, into regional ghettoes. Yet the Liberals are relatively weak in the West. The regional fragmentation of our present party system is a manifestation of an underlying feature of the virtual party system. As mass marketing gives way to niche or micro marketing, the "public" becomes fragmented into many publics, each targeted for votes by parties that tailor and hone their appeals to particular niches. In the most comprehensive examination yet published of the emerging party system (*Rebuilding Canadian Party Politics,* UBC Press, 2000), Professors R. Kenneth Carty, William Cross and Lisa Young argue that the national discussion of politics in an election campaign will "increasingly be replaced by a series of highly focused, private conversations. When coupled with the regional dynamics of campaigns, this trend is contributing to the end of pan-Canadian politics." They go on to suggest that "despite calls for further democratization of political parties, these new communication patterns ensure that pollsters, advertising and marketing specialists, and those skilled in the management and manipulation of data sets will retain a central role within campaign organizations. Fragmented and private political communication requires the skills and technology of these professionals, reinforcing their place within the party structure."

The most striking example of how the virtual party is superseding the real party can be found in the transformation of the Reform Party into the Canadian Alliance. Ostensibly designed to break Reform out of its Western ghetto and challenge the Liberals in Canada's biggest electoral battleground, Ontario, the "United Alternative" project was actually about transforming the structure of the party. When Preston Manning urged the Reform Party faithful to abandon their short-lived party attachment for a new and more efficacious vehicle (which soon showed its disdain for loyalty by ditching Manning himself), he exhorted them to "Think Big." The subtext of this message was that Reform had been thinking small, not only in terms of its regional base, but also in terms of its conception of itself as a party. For those who would like to see our parties strive to become more democratic vehicles, there is considerable irony in this message.

The rapid rise of the Reform Party from nowhere to Official Opposition was a remarkable example of innovation in the party system. Along with the Bloc Québécois, Reform brought to Ottawa a more programmatic, ideological and principled politics than the cynical old brokerage parties had offered. Above all, Reform brought an insistence upon concrete democratic accountability, and provided elaborate institutional mechanisms to ensure that accountability: referenda, initiatives, recall, free votes in Parliament, fixed terms for governments and so on. To a public jaded by such undemocratic exercises as Meech Lake, free trade, and the GST, Reform's democratization agenda seems a breath of fresh air, and indeed Reform was able to steal ownership of the democracy issue away from the NDP, which had monopolized the concept for decades. To be sure, populism of this kind is always open to a kind of plebiscitarian manipulation by the leadership. But the early Reform Party did demonstrate signs of genuine grassroots participation, in organizing and financing the party, and in asserting real influence over the party's policy directions. A populist network sprang up in western Canada that did something very unusual in this country by successfully launching and sustaining a new party from below. This could only go so far, however. It stalled in Ontario and failed to evict its Conservative rivals from the political map. Hence the Alliance, a re-branding of the Reform product designed to appeal more to the potential Ontario market.

Although the Alliance did hold a founding convention much like traditional party conventions, it made one major decision about process that moved the new party away from Reform's structure. The Alliance's first leadership contest was to be a national primary, not a convention. The rationalization for this was that new members would be brought into the party structure as they were mobilized by competing candidates—most specifically, Ontarians mobilized by the candidacy of Tom Long, one of the architects of the Harris Common Sense Revolution, and a key catch for the Alliance's Ontario strategy. But voters mobilized by candidates in a primary-type contest are not socialized into the party in the way that those who join local constituencies and attend regional and national meetings are socialized into the solidarity and camaraderie of shared endeavour. They simply pay for a membership and cast a vote for their candidate in much the same isolation that characterizes voting in general elections. They miss the social matrix of the party, and miss learning its norms and practices, its sense of collective memory and shared identity. The Progressive Conservatives had adopted the same procedure for their earlier national leadership contest: It produced the bizarre result of the David Orchard candidacy, and a singular lack of a sense of organized purpose at the centre of the national party. The Joe Clark virtual Tory party was, and is, a large head with a tiny body or, to shift metaphors, a racing driver with a track record but a toy car to drive.

In the case of the Canadian Alliance, the Long candidacy failed to ignite an influx of new recruits from the Ontario Tory party. This failure was foreshadowed by the curious "poison pill" adherence of Ernie Eves, provincial treasurer and No. 2 man in the Harris government (since retired), and long the most prominent supporter of the federal Tories within the Harris cabinet. Eves declared that he would support the Alliance, but only if it adopted the Ontario candidate as its leader. When Long finished last, Eves was as good as his word, brusquely taking his leave of the Alliance. Although the Alliance under Day did do better with Ontario voters than Reform under Manning, clearly outdistancing the PCs in the popular vote, they were able to elect only two MPs. There was certainly no sense of gaining a durable new mass federal base to match that of the Harris Tories. The 905 suburban belt around Toronto, the very heartland of the Common Sense Revolution where Long had symbolically chosen to launch his leadership campaign, actually threw its support so monolithically to the Liberals as to run ahead of the 51 per cent the Chrétien party garnered province-wide.

The failure to mobilize lasting grassroots support in Ontario partially masked one very important contribution to the new party by Tom Long, although this only strengthened the party's virtual status. Long was able to open up financial support from Bay Street that was unprecedented in the previous short history of the Reform Party. Although Manning had the financial support of certain Western regional economic interests, especially oil money, and had gained a few supporters here and there on Bay Street, Reform had never been able to match the corporate fundraising prowess of the Mulroney Tories or the Chrétien Liberals, and had had to rely to a degree on grassroots donations. Manning and his Western supporters had appeared a bit too rough-edged and *outré* for Bay Street's liking. Long was one of their own, and, urged on by the *National Post*, they opened up their coffers for him. Unlike Long's vanishing voting support, Bay Street money stuck to the Day-led Alliance.

In the 2000 election, the Alliance was able to rival the Liberals in corporate campaign funding. However important in establishing a financial base for the Alliance's future stability, this shift in funding from small, grassroots donations to big corporate giving completes a cycle within the Reform/Alliance from a grassroots populist movement to a political marketing tool for Bay Street. The Alliance as a virtual Ontario party had the money, and a vociferous mouthpiece of Bay Street in the form of the *National Post* to push it forward. All that was missing were the voters.

Stockwell Day's campaign in 2000 was of course ambushed by a far more sophisticated and ruthless marketing machine centred on the prime minister's office, and the Chrétien virtual party's pollsters and spin doctors. But the scale of the disaster should not obscure the effects of campaign exigencies on the Alliance as a party in its first, formative national campaign. Distinctive policies that set the Alliance apart from its competitors, including the Progressive Conservatives, were quickly dropped on the advice of Alliance advertising advisers. Delegates to the party's founding convention had enthusiastically adopted a flat tax. Moreover, as Alberta Treasurer, Day had already begun implementation of a flat (or at least flatter) provincial income tax, so the idea was clearly in the realm of the possible and practical. No matter: Focus groups showed there were perception problems with a flat tax, and it was unceremoniously dumped from the party platform.

Another distinctive feature of Day's ascent to the leadership had been the adhesion of pro-lifers and the Christian Right, who had flocked into the Alliance to elect a candidate who forthrightly defended their moral positions on sensitive public issues like abortion and homosexuality. Once the national campaign was launched, however, all mention of anti-abortion and anti-gay rights positions was dropped. When the Liberals cleverly ambushed Day by raising the spectre of an Alliance government encouraging referenda on abortion and gay rights, there was furtive backpedaling even on the Alliance's commitment to direct democracy. Finally, one might cite the Alliance's frantic efforts to deny any distinctive conservative position on health care, despite the Klein government's trail-blazing efforts to open up private clinics as a component of health care delivery. Their flight from principle was embodied in the rather forlorn spectacle of Day holding up his hand-lettered sign, "No two-tier health care," during the leaders' TV debate.

The 2000 election results produced very small gains for the Alliance outside the West, along with further deepening of support in the West. Whether the party can ever break out of Reform's Western ghetto, or even force a merger with the PCs, remains to be seen. But even if it does succeed, the Alliance, as a structure that has moved further along the continuum away from "party" toward "virtual party," will represent one more step in the decline of deliberative, negotiated democracy and its replacement by unmediated telemarketing.

Referring to the emergence of the modern social welfare state in Canada in the 1960s, former Ontario premier Bob Rae writes (in *The Three Questions: Prosperity and the Public Good*) that "these achievements were brought about because political parties, the little platoons of loyalty bound together by common affection and common conviction, advocated, persuaded, compromised, and negotiated their way to achieving tangible, real, practical progress. That's what politics is."

Rae draws the phrase "little platoons" from Burke, who meant all the institutions of civil society that mediate between the individual and the state. Parties were, for the political system, the pre-eminent mediating institutions. Whether they ever quite fulfilled the role Rae has lovingly ascribed to them is open to question. Ambition, patronage and venality were often enough in as much evidence as "loyalty ... common affection and common conviction" as motives for partisanship. Yet Rae's emphasis on how parties "advocated, persuaded, compromised, and negotiated" surely gets the hang of what these peculiar institutions were supposed to do. States must arrive at authoritative resolutions of conflicts in the society. Parties were there to articulate demands, focus debates, negotiate workable solutions and then build broad support for the compromises thus arrived at. This was referred to as the "brokerage model" of parties, usually in recent years with disdain. Brokerage politics, it has been said repeatedly, were mundane, uninspiring, conservative, often corrupt and ineffective.

At one time or another, no doubt, they were all of these things. Like all other established institutions they have suffered over recent decades a decline in the trust and deference accorded them by the democratic citizenry, most spectacularly in the case of the state itself, but followed by corporations, unions, churches and so on. The reasons for this decline are many and complex, and still perhaps obscure to contemporary observers too close in time and place to fully decipher the clues. But take away the capacity of parties to link and mediate between society and the state, take away their capacity to fulfill the functions accorded them in theory, and we have a serious problem with our politics. Parties have been largely denuded of their old legitimacy, incapacitated in filling their traditional roles, and held up to public ridicule and scorn. But no new and better institutions have been invented to replace them. Interest groups act directly upon the legislative and administrative processes, without the mediation of parties, and with the result that the more powerful get their way, while leaving the losers bitter, angry and paranoiac about what is done behind closed doors and in the dark corridors of power. Social movements and public interest groups try to influence governments directly from the outside by raising their voices and making threatening gestures, but they are largely ignored, leaving their supporters further alienated. Everywhere the "democratic deficit" is identified and decried, yet the traditional instruments for making government accountable to the people—political parties—tend to be seen as part of the problem rather than part of the solution.

Neither corporatism nor populism, neither technocracy from above nor electronic direct democracy from below, have actually succeeded so far in replacing parties. In the 21st century, parties remain as crucial to the workings of liberal democratic politics as they have always been. A democratic political system without parties is like an automobile without a transmission: It might look good, but it won't take you anywhere. But this does not mean that under their old labels, "parties" are in continuity with their past. Here is where virtual parties step in. Like the body snatchers of the Hollywood horror-movie, they take over the old shells, but fill them with something quite different. Virtual parties in opposition are not so much participants in ongoing debate and deliberation as marketing tools for selling their product—themselves. Virtual parties in power do not preside over and organize the parliamentary process, as such; rather they are devices for establishing unmediated producer–consumer relations between the leader and the population, while bypassing or end-running Parliament and press and any other institutions that get in the way. Not much room is left for the "little platoons of loyalty bound together by common affection and common conviction."

Structural reforms of the electoral process and enhancing the role of Parliament are worthy objectives in themselves, but unlikely to get far under the present circumstances of Liberal self-satisfaction. Yet even such reforms might do little to dislodge the virtual party, which has sunk roots in economic and technological changes that lie deeper than political institutions. Perhaps more radical changes in forms of representation are required to address a growing democratic deficit.

SECTION 3 TERMINOLOGY

Accountability
Auditor-General
Brokerage party
Cabinet minister
Canadian Charter of Rights and Freedoms
Casework
Civil society
Common law
Constituency/riding
Convention
Direct democracy
Elected assembly
Electoral system
Executive
Federalism
Free vote
Globalization
Governing party

Judiciary
Legislative Assembly/Legislature (House)
Legitimacy
Lobbying
Majority (majority government)
Mandate
Ministers of the Crown
MPs (Members of Parliament)
Notwithstanding clause
Oligarchy
Opposition party
Orders-in-council
Parliament
Patronage
Plurality

Pollster
Populism
Primary
Privy Council Office (PCO)
Programmatic party
Public interest group
Public service
Question Period
Reference Question
Referenda
Regionalism
Representative democracy
Responsible government
Social movement
Spin doctors
Whip

SECTION 3 DISCUSSION QUESTIONS

1. Increasing the executive branch's accountability would bring with it not only benefits but also certain negative consequences. List and discuss the likely results, both positive and negative, of requiring the executive branch to be more accountable to the legislature.

2. Survey evidence reveals that the Canadian public is likely to support the courts over Parliament in cases where legislation challenges the Charter. Can you think of a situation in which Parliament should be able to overrule the courts?

3. Political parties play an important role in the smooth functioning of the political system. What roles do parties play that interest groups and social movements cannot?

4. MPs appear to work tremendously long hours yet the public perceives their job to be a relatively easy one. Why do think the public has such a distorted view of the work undertaken by elected representatives?

5. Are you convinced that public opinion polling plays an important and vital role in modern representative democracies? Why or why not?

6. Thinking of the political arena as a system made up of various parts, what evidence would you need to argue that it was functioning efficiently? Effectively?

Section 4

Citizenship and Participation

SECTION SUMMARY

The readings in this section of the book bring us back to some of the questions raised in Section 1: How do we become "active" in the political process? What are the best means of facilitating this action? What does it mean to be a citizen? Most of us today live in political systems that are democratic. Certainly, most students of political science will have heard the term "democracy" prior to their first class. The term is commonly employed in the West to identify the "ideal" or "best" political system—a normative evaluation. So why, then, did Winston Churchill refer to it as "the worst form of government, except all those other forms that have been tried from time to time" (Hansard, 11 November 1947)—in other words, as merely the "least bad" system? This paradox is best understood by distinguishing between the theory that lies behind the concept and its practice. While democratic systems are the best designed to uphold the set of political values deemed central within Western civilizations, in practice they often fall short of the mark. Studying democracy necessitates understanding both what it ought to be as well as the reality of what it is, and gives us greater insight into what it means to be a citizen.

The set of readings in this section provides a foundation for understanding democracy in its many guises and, importantly, addresses the current preoccupation with the "democratic deficit." Characterized by a lack of civic engagement in such acts as voting and party membership, and by low levels of political satisfaction and contentment, much attention has been directed, first, to understanding the nature of the phenomenon; second, to explaining its underlying causes; and third, to addressing it. Given that the success of democracies is often gauged by the levels of participation and satisfaction exhibited by citizens, governments in the West have been occupied with establishing policies and programs designed to stem the tide of unhappiness and withdrawal.

The first article, by Philippe C. Schmitter and Terry Lynn Karl, establishes the key concepts, principles, and procedures underlying the democratic ideal. As they make clear, the practice of democracy can take many different forms and entails more than simply the holding of elections. Additionally, their identification of the many unrealistic expectations made of democratic systems stands as an important reminder of the need for a clear understanding of the limited ability of single institutions to solve the many troubles within modern political systems.

The next two readings tackle the question of the "democratic deficit." First, Andrew F. Johnson suggests that the root cause of this political discontent is the changed relationship between governments and citizens in Western democracies. The opening up of markets in an age of globalization can be deemed an economic success, but governments have to yield a certain level of autonomy, and citizens have been redefined as consumers. In this new world, Johnson argues, governments cannot meet the demands of all citizens. But politics should not be about satisfying the desires of each and every citizen; rather, it is about generating "the greatest good for the greatest number."

Next, using data from the 2003 General Social Survey, Anne Milan focuses on the political behaviour of younger Canadians. Milan examines their political engagement—both traditional and alternative forms of political participation—with the goal of determining whether their decreased turnout levels are offset by increased engagement in other forms of participation. The question is an important one, for a withdrawal from politics altogether suggests different sources of discontent and, therefore, different policy prescriptions than would a purposeful shift away from electoral politics toward more direct forms of political activity. The paper by the Centre for Research and Information on Canada provides a comprehensive review of the evidence suggesting that Canadians are no longer as politically engaged, at least in elections, as they were in the past. Evaluating several possible explanations for the decline, as well as a number of possible solutions, the piece illustrates the complexity of attempting to adopt institutional reform as a remedy when faced with less-than-perfect information about the problem being confronted.

The final reading in this section, by Jarl K. Kampen and Kris Snijkers, provides a critical evaluation of what is sometimes advocated as a remedy for the crisis in modern representative democracies. E-democracy, which involves the adoption of information communication technology (ICT) to increase citizen participation in democratic decision making, is the focus of this reading. Kampen and Snijkers provide a cautious review of the ability of technology to overcome problems that they see as inherent to representative government. As a band-aid solution, e-democracy has the potential to create many, if not more, problems than it solves.

Chapter 16

What Democracy Is . . . and Is Not

PHILIPPE C. SCHMITTER AND TERRY LYNN KARL*

***Philippe C. Schmitter** is Professor of Political and Social Sciences at the European University Institute of Florence, Italy. **Terry Lynn Karl** is Professor of Political Science, Stanford University, California.

For some time, the word democracy has been circulating as a debased currency in the political marketplace. Politicians with a wide range of convictions and practices strove to appropriate the label and attach it to their actions. Scholars, conversely, hesitated to use it—without adding qualifying adjectives—because of the ambiguity that surrounds it. The distinguished American political theorist Robert Dahl even tried to introduce a new term, "polyarchy," in its stead in the (vain) hope of gaining a greater measure of conceptual precision. But for better or worse, we are "stuck" with democracy as the catchword of contemporary political discourse. It is the word that resonates in people's minds and springs from their lips as they struggle for freedom and a better way of life; it is the word whose meaning we must discern if it is to be of any use in guiding political analysis and practice.

The wave of transitions away from autocratic rule that began with Portugal's "Revolution of the Carnations" in 1974 and seems to have crested with the collapse of communist regimes across Eastern Europe in 1989 has produced a welcome convergence toward [a] common definition of democracy.[1] Everywhere there has been a silent abandonment of dubious adjectives like "popular," "guided," "bourgeois," and "formal" to modify "democracy." At the same time, a remarkable consensus has emerged concerning the minimal conditions that polities must meet in order to merit the prestigious appellation of "democratic." Moreover, a number of international organizations now monitor how well these standards are met; indeed, some countries even consider them when formulating foreign policy.[2]

---

[1] For a comparative analysis of the recent regime changes in southern Europe and Latin America, see Guillermo O'Donnell, Philippe C. Schmitter, and Laurence Whitehead, eds., *Transitions from Authoritarian Rule,* 4 vols. (Baltimore: Johns Hopkins University Press, 1986). For another compilation that adopts a more structural approach see Larry Diamond, Juan Linz, and Seymour Martin Lipset, eds., *Democracy in Developing Countries,* vols. 2, 3, and 4 (Boulder, CO: Lynne Rienner, 1989).

[2] Numerous attempts have been made to codify and quantify the existence of democracy across political systems. The best known is probably Freedom House's *Freedom in the World: Political Rights and Civil Liberties,* published since 1973 by Greenwood Press and since 1988 by University Press of America. Also see Charles Humana, *World Human Rights Guide* (New York: Facts on File, 1986).

WHAT DEMOCRACY IS

Let us begin by broadly defining democracy and the generic *concepts* that distinguish it as a unique system for organizing relations between rulers and the ruled. We will then briefly review *procedures,* the rules and arrangements that are needed if democracy is to endure. Finally, we will discuss two operative *principles* that make democracy work. They are not expressly included among the generic concepts or formal procedures, but the prospect for democracy is grim if their underlying conditioning effects are not present.

One of the major themes of this essay is that democracy does not consist of a single unique set of institutions. There are many types of democracy, and their diverse practices produce a similarly varied set of effects. The specific form democracy takes is contingent upon a country's socioeconomic conditions as well as its entrenched state structures and policy practices.

Modern political democracy is a system of governance in which rulers are held accountable for their actions in the public realm by citizens, acting indirectly through the competition and cooperation of their elected representatives.[3]

A *regime or system of governance* is an ensemble of patterns that determines the methods of access to the principal public offices; the characteristics of the actors admitted to or excluded from such access; the strategies that actors may use to gain access; and the rules that are followed in the making of publicly binding decisions. To work properly, the ensemble must be institutionalized—that is to say, the various patterns must be habitually known, practiced, and accepted by most, if not all, actors. Increasingly, the preferred mechanism of institutionalization is a written body of laws undergirded by a written constitution, though many enduring political norms can have an informal, prudential, or traditional basis.[4]

For the sake of economy and comparison, these forms, characteristics, and rules are usually bundled together and given a generic label. Democratic is one; others are autocratic, authoritarian, despotic, dictatorial, tyrannical, totalitarian, absolutist, traditional, monarchic, oligarchic, plutocratic, aristocratic, and sultanistic.[5] Each of these regime forms may in turn be broken down into subtypes.

Like all regimes, democracies depend upon the presence of *rulers,* persons who occupy specialized authority roles and can give legitimate commands to others. What distinguishes

---

[3]   The definition most commonly used by American social scientists is that of Joseph Schumpeter: "that institutional arrangement for arriving at political decisions in which individuals acquire the power to decide by means of a competitive struggle for the people's vote." *Capitalism, Socialism, and Democracy* (London: George Allen and Unwin, 1943), 269. We accept certain aspects of the classical procedural approach to modern democracy, but differ primarily in our emphasis on the accountability of rulers to citizens and the relevance of mechanisms of competition other than elections.

[4]   Not only do some countries practice a stable form of democracy without a formal constitution (e.g. Great Britain and Israel), but even more countries have constitutions and legal codes that offer no guarantee of reliable practice. On paper, Stalin's 1936 constitution for the USSR was a virtual model of democratic rights and entitlements.

[5]   For the most valiant attempt to make some sense out of this thicket of distinctions, see Juan Linz, "Totalitarian and Authoritarian Regimes" in *Handbook of Political Science,* eds. Fred I. Greenstein and Nelson W. Polsby (Reading, MA: Addison Wesley, 1975), 175–411.

democratic rulers from nondemocratic ones are the norms that condition how the former come to power and the practices that hold them accountable for their actions.

The *public realm* encompasses the making of collective norms and choices that are binding on the society and backed by state coercion. Its content can vary a great deal across democracies, depending upon preexisting distinctions between the public and the private, state and society, legitimate coercion and voluntary exchange, and collective needs and individual preferences. The liberal conception of democracy advocates circumscribing the public realm as narrowly as possible, while the socialist or social-democratic approach would extend that realm through regulation, subsidization, and, in some cases, collective ownership of property. Neither is intrinsically more democratic than the other—just *differently* democratic. This implies that measures aimed at "developing the private sector" are no more democratic than those aimed at "developing the public sector." Both, if carried to extremes, could undermine the practice of democracy, the former by destroying the basis for satisfying collective needs and exercising legitimate authority; the latter by destroying the basis for satisfying individual preferences and controlling illegitimate government actions. Differences of opinion over the optimal mix of the two provide much of the substantive content of political conflict within established democracies.

Citizens are the most distinctive element in democracies. All regimes have rulers and a public realm, but only to the extent that they are democratic do they have citizens. Historically, severe restrictions on citizenship were imposed in most emerging or partial democracies according to criteria of age, gender, class, race, literacy, property ownership, tax-paying status, and so on. Only a small part of the total population was eligible to vote or run for office. Only restricted social categories were allowed to form, join, or support political associations. After protracted struggle—in some cases involving violent domestic upheaval or international war—most of these restrictions were lifted. Today, the criteria for inclusion are fairly standard. All native-born adults are eligible, although somewhat higher age limits may still be imposed upon candidates for certain offices. Unlike the early American and European democracies of the nineteenth century, none of the recent democracies in southern Europe, Latin America, Asia, or Eastern Europe has even attempted to impose formal restrictions on the franchise or eligibility to office. When it comes to informal restrictions on the effective exercise of citizenship rights, however, the story can be quite different. This explains the central importance (discussed below) of procedures.

Competition has not always been considered an essential defining condition of democracy. "Classic" democracies presumed decision making based on direct participation leading to consensus. The assembled citizenry was expected to agree on a common course of action after listening to the alternatives and weighing their respective merits and demerits. A tradition of hostility to "faction," and "particular interests" persists in democratic thought, but at least since *The Federalist Papers* it has become widely accepted that competition among factions is a necessary evil in democracies that operate on a more-than-local scale. Since, as James Madison argued, "the latent causes of faction are sown into the nature of man," and the possible remedies for "the mischief of faction" are worse than the disease, the best course is to recognize them and to attempt to control their effects.[6] Yet

---

[6]   "Publius" (Alexander Hamilton, John Jay, and James Madison), *The Federalist Papers* (New York: Anchor Books, 1961). The quote is from Number 10.

while democrats may agree on the inevitability of factions, they tend to disagree about the best forms and rules for governing factional competition. Indeed, differences over the preferred modes and boundaries of competition contribute most to distinguishing one subtype of democracy from another.

The most popular definition of democracy equates it with regular *elections,* fairly conducted and honestly counted. Some even consider the mere fact of elections—even ones from which specific parties or candidates are excluded, or in which substantial portions of the population cannot freely participate—as a sufficient condition for the existence of democracy. This fallacy has been called "electoralism" or "the faith that merely holding elections will channel political action into peaceful contests among elites and accord public legitimacy to the winners"—no matter how they are conducted or what else constrains those who win them.[7] However central to democracy, elections occur intermittently and only allow citizens to choose between the highly aggregated alternatives offered by political parties, which can, especially in the early stages of a democratic transition, proliferate in a bewildering variety. During the intervals between elections, citizens can seek to influence public policy through a wide variety of other intermediaries: interest associations, social movements, locality groupings, clientelistic arrangements, and so forth. *Modern democracy, in other words, offers a variety of competitive processes and channels for the expression of interests and values—associational as well as partisan, functional as well as territorial, collective as well as individual. All are integral to its practice.*

Another commonly accepted image of democracy identifies it with *majority rule.* Any governing body that makes decisions by combining the votes of more than half of those eligible and present is said to be democratic, whether that majority emerges within an electorate, a parliament, a committee, a city council, or a party caucus. For exceptional purposes (e.g., amending the constitution or expelling a member), "qualified majorities" of more than 50 percent may be required, but few would deny that democracy must involve some means of aggregating the equal preferences of individuals.

A problem arises, however, when *numbers* meet *intensities.* What happens when a properly assembled majority (especially a stable, self-perpetuating one) regularly makes decisions that harm some minority (especially a threatened cultural or ethnic group)? In these circumstances, successful democracies tend to qualify the central principle of majority rule in order to protect minority rights. Such qualifications can take the form of constitutional provisions that place certain matters beyond the reach of majorities (bills of rights); requirements for concurrent majorities in several different constituencies (confederalism); guarantees securing the autonomy of local or regional governments against the demands of the central authority (federalism); grand coalition governments that incorporate all parties (consociationalism); or the negotiation of social pacts between major social groups like business and labor (neocorporatism). The most common and effective way of protecting minorities, however, lies in the everyday operation of interest associations and social movements. These reflect (some would say, amplify) the different intensities of preference that exist in the population and bring them to bear on democratically elected decision

---

[7]   See Terry Karl, "Imposing Consent? Electoralism versus Democratization in El Salvador," in *Elections and Democratization in Latin America, 1980–1985,* eds. Paul Drake and Eduardo Silva (San Diego: Center for Iberian and Latin American Studies, Center for US/Mexican Studies, University of California, San Diego, 1986), 9–36.

makers. Another way of putting this intrinsic tension between numbers and intensities would be to say that "in modern democracies, votes may be counted, but influences alone are weighted."

Cooperation has always been a central feature of democracy. Actors must voluntarily make collective decisions binding on the polity as a whole. They must cooperate in order to compete. They must be capable of acting collectively through parties, associations, and movements in order to select candidates, articulate preferences, petition authorities, and influence policies.

But democracy's freedoms should also encourage citizens to deliberate among themselves, to discover their common needs, and to resolve their differences without relying on some supreme central authority. Classical democracy emphasized these qualities, and they are by no means extinct, despite repeated efforts by contemporary theorists to stress the analogy with behavior in the economic marketplace and to reduce all of democracy's operations to competitive interest maximization. Alexis de Tocqueville best described the importance of independent groups for democracy in his *Democracy in America,* a work which remains a major source of inspiration for all those who persist in viewing democracy as something more than a struggle for election and re-election among competing candidates.[8]

In contemporary political discourse, this phenomenon of cooperation and deliberation via autonomous group activity goes under the rubric of "civil society." The diverse units of social identity and interest, by remaining independent of the state (and perhaps even of parties), not only can restrain the arbitrary actions of rulers, but can also contribute to forming better citizens who are more aware of the preferences of others, more self-confident in their actions, and more civic-minded in their willingness to sacrifice for the common good. At its best, civil society provides an intermediate layer of governance between the individual and the state that is capable of resolving conflicts and controlling the behavior of members without public coercion. Rather than overloading decision makers with increased demands and making the system ungovernable,[9] a viable civil society can mitigate conflicts and improve the quality of citizenship—without relying exclusively on the privatism of the marketplace.

Representatives—whether directly or indirectly elected—do most of the real work in modern democracies. Most are professional politicians who orient their careers around the desire to fill key offices. It is doubtful that any democracy could survive without such people. The central question, therefore, is not whether or not there will be a political elite or even a professional political class, but how these representatives are chosen and then held accountable for their actions.

As noted above, there are many channels of representation in modern democracy. The electoral one, based on territorial constituencies, is the most visible and public. It culminates in a parliament or a presidency that is periodically accountable to the citizenry as a whole.

---

[8] Alexis de Tocqueville, *Democracy in America,* 2 vols. (New York: Vintage Books, 1945).

[9] This fear of overloaded government and the imminent collapse of democracy is well reflected in the work of Samuel P. Huntington during the 1970s. See especially Michel Crozier, Samuel P. Huntington, and Joji Watanuki, *The Crisis of Democracy* (New York: New York University Press, 1975). For Huntington's (revised) thoughts about the prospects for democracy, see his "Will More Countries Become Democratic?," *Political Science Quarterly* 99 (Summer 1984): 193–218.

Yet the sheer growth of government (in large part as a byproduct of popular demand) has increased the number, variety, and power of agencies charged with making public decisions and not subject to elections. Around these agencies there has developed a vast apparatus of specialized representation based largely on functional interests, not territorial constituencies. These interest associations, and not political parties, have become the primary expression of civil society in most stable democracies, supplemented by the more sporadic interventions of social movements.

The new and fragile democracies that have sprung up since 1974 must live in "compressed time." They will not resemble the European democracies of the nineteenth and early twentieth centuries, and they cannot expect to acquire the multiple channels of representation in gradual historical progression as did most of their predecessors. A bewildering array of parties, interests, and movements will all simultaneously seek political influence in them, creating challenges to the polity that did not exist in earlier processes of democratization.

PROCEDURES THAT MAKE DEMOCRACY POSSIBLE

The defining components of democracy are necessarily abstract, and may give rise to a considerable variety of institutions and subtypes of democracy. For democracy to thrive, however, specific procedural norms must be followed and civic rights must be respected. Any polity that fails to impose such restrictions upon itself, that fails to follow the "rule of law" with regard to its own procedures, should not be considered democratic. These procedures alone do not define democracy, but their presence is indispensable to its persistence. In essence, they are necessary but not sufficient conditions for its existence.

Robert Dahl has offered the most generally accepted listing of what he terms the "procedural minimal" conditions that must be present for modern political democracy (or as he puts it, "polyarchy") to exist:

1. Control over government decisions about policy is constitutionally vested in elected officials.
2. Elected officials are chosen in frequent and fairly conducted elections in which coercion is comparatively uncommon.
3. Practically all adults have the right to vote in the election of officials.
4. Practically all adults have the right to run for elective offices.
5. Citizens have a right to express themselves without the danger of severe punishment on political matters broadly defined. . . .
6. Citizens have a right to seek out alternative sources of information. Moreover, alternative sources of information exist and are protected by law.
7. ... Citizens also have the right to form relatively independent associations or organizations, including independent political parties and interest groups.[10]

---

[10]   Robert Dahl, *Dilemmas of Pluralist Democracy* (New Haven: Yale University Press, 1982), 11.

These seven conditions seem to capture the essence of procedural democracy for many theorists, but we propose to add two others. The first might be thought of as a further refinement of item (1), while the second might be called an implicit prior condition to all seven of the above.

1. Popularly elected officials must be able to exercise their constitutional powers without being subjected to overriding (albeit informal) opposition from unelected officials. Democracy is in jeopardy if military officers, entrenched civil servants, or state managers retain the capacity to act independently of elected civilians or even veto decisions made by the people's representatives. Without this additional caveat, the militarized polities of contemporary Central America, where civilian control over the military does not exist, might be classified by many scholars as democracies, just as they have been (with the exception of Sandinista Nicaragua) by U.S. policy makers. The caveat thus guards against what we earlier called "electoralism"—the tendency to focus on the holding of elections while ignoring other political realities.

2. The polity must be self-governing; it must be able to act independently of constraints imposed by some other overarching political system. DahI and other contemporary democratic theorists probably took this condition for granted since they referred to formally sovereign nation-states. However, with the development of blocs, alliances, spheres of influence, and a variety of "neocolonial" arrangements, the question of autonomy has been a salient one. Is a system really democratic if its elected officials are unable to make binding decisions without the approval of actors outside their territorial domain? This is significant even if the outsiders are relatively free to alter or even end the encompassing arrangement (as in Puerto Rico), but it becomes especially critical if neither condition obtains (as in the Baltic states).

PRINCIPLES THAT MAKE DEMOCRACY FEASIBLE

Lists of component processes and procedural norms help us to specify what democracy is, but they do not tell us much about how it actually functions. The simplest answer is "by the consent of the people"; the more complex one is "by the contingent consent of politicians acting under conditions of bounded uncertainty."

In a democracy, representatives must at least informally agree that those who win greater electoral support or influence over policy will not use their temporary superiority to bar the losers from taking office or exerting influence in the future, and that in exchange for this opportunity to keep competing for power and place, momentary losers will respect the winners' right to make binding decisions. Citizens are expected to obey the decisions ensuing from such a process of competition, provided its outcome remains contingent upon their collective preferences as expressed through fair and regular elections or open and repeated negotiations.

The challenge is not so much to find a set of goals that command widespread consensus as to find a set of rules that embody contingent consent. The precise shape of this "democratic bargain," to use Dahl's expression,[11] can vary a good deal from society to society. It depends on social cleavages and such subjective factors as mutual trust, the standard of fairness, and

---

[11] Robert Dahl, *After the Revolution: Authority in a Good Society* (New Haven: Yale University Press, 1970).

the willingness to compromise. It may even be compatible with a great deal of dissensus on substantive policy issues.

All democracies involve a degree of uncertainty about who will be elected and what policies they will pursue. Even in those polities where one party persists in winning elections or one policy is consistently implemented, the possibility of change through independent collective action still exists, as in Italy, Japan, and the Scandinavian social democracies. If it does not, the system is not democratic, as in Mexico, Senegal, or Indonesia.

But the uncertainty embedded in the core of all democracies is bounded. Not just any actor can get into the competition and raise any issue he or she pleases—there are previously established rules that must be respected. Not just any policy can be adopted—there are conditions that must be met. Democracy institutionalizes "normal," limited political uncertainty. These boundaries vary from country to country. Constitutional guarantees of property, privacy, expression, and other rights are a part of this, but the most effective boundaries are generated by competition among interest groups and cooperation within civil society. Whatever the rhetoric (and some polities appear to offer their citizens more dramatic alternatives than others), once the rules of contingent consent have been agreed upon, the actual variation is likely to stay within a predictable and generally accepted range.

This emphasis on operative guidelines contrasts with a highly persistent, but misleading theme in recent literature on democracy—namely, the emphasis upon "civic culture." The principles we have suggested here rest on rules of prudence, not on deeply ingrained habits of tolerance, moderation, mutual respect, fair play, readiness to compromise, or trust in public authorities. Waiting for such habits to sink deep and lasting roots implies a very slow process of regime consolidation—one that takes generations—and it would probably condemn most contemporary experiences *ex hypothesi* to failure. Our assertion is that contingent consent and bounded uncertainty can emerge from the interaction between antagonistic and mutually suspicious actors and that the far more benevolent and ingrained norms of a civic culture are better thought of as a *product* and not a producer of democracy.

HOW DEMOCRACIES DIFFER

Several concepts have been deliberately excluded from our generic definition of democracy, despite the fact that they have been frequently associated with it in both everyday practice and scholarly work. They are, nevertheless, especially important when it comes to distinguishing subtypes of democracy. Since no single set of actual institutions, practices, or values embodies democracy, polities moving away from authoritarian rule can mix different components to produce different democracies. It is important to recognize that these do not define points along a single continuum of improving performance, but a matrix of potential combinations that are *differently* democratic.

1. *Consensus:* All citizens may not agree on the substantive goals of political action or on the role of the state (although if they did, it would certainly make governing democracies much easier).

2. *Participation:* All citizens may not take an active and equal part in politics, although it must be legally possible for them to do so.

3. *Access:* Rulers may not weigh equally the preferences of all who come before them, although citizenship implies that individuals and groups should have an equal opportunity to express their preferences if they choose to do so.

4. *Responsiveness:* Rulers may not always follow the course of action preferred by the citizenry. But when they deviate from such a policy, say on grounds of "reason of state" or "overriding national interest," they must ultimately be held accountable for their actions through regular and fair processes.

5. *Majority rule:* Positions may not be allocated or rules may not be decided solely on the basis of assembling the most votes, although deviations from this principle usually must be explicitly defended and previously approved.

6. *Parliamentary sovereignty:* The legislature may not be the only body that can make rules or even the one with final authority in deciding which laws are binding, although where executive, judicial, or other public bodies make that ultimate choice, they too must be accountable for their actions.

7. *Party government:* Rulers may not be nominated, promoted, and disciplined in their activities by well-organized and programmatically coherent political parties, although where they are not, it may prove more difficult to form an effective government.

8. *Pluralism:* The political process may not be based on a multiplicity of overlapping, voluntaristic, and autonomous private groups. However, where there are monopolies of representation, hierarchies of association, and obligatory memberships, it is likely that the interests involved will be more closely linked to the state and the separation between the public and private spheres of action will be much less distinct.

9. *Federalism:* The territorial division of authority may not involve multiple levels and local autonomies, least of all ones enshrined in a constitutional document, although some dispersal of power across territorial and/or functional units is characteristic of all democracies.

10. *Presidentialism:* The chief executive officer may not be a single person and he or she may not be directly elected by the citizenry as a whole, although some concentration of authority is present in all democracies, even if it is exercised collectively and only held indirectly accountable to the electorate.

11. *Checks and Balances:* It is not necessary that the different branches of government be systematically pitted against one another, although governments by assembly, by executive concentrations, by judicial command, or even by dictatorial fiat (as in time of war) must be ultimately accountable to the citizenry as a whole.

While each of the above has been named as an essential component of democracy, they should instead be seen either as indicators of this or that type of democracy, or else as useful standards for evaluating the performance of particular regimes. To include them as part of the generic definition of democracy itself would be to mistake the American polity for the universal model of democratic governance. Indeed, the parliamentary, consociational, unitary, corporatist, and concentrated arrangements of continental Europe may have some unique virtues for guiding polities through the uncertain transition from autocratic to democratic rule.[12]

---

[12] See Juan Linz, "The Perils of Presidentialism," *Journal of Democracy* 1 (Winter 1990): 51–69, and the ensuing discussion by Donald Horowitz, Seymour Martin Lipset, and Juan Linz in *Journal of Democracy* 1 (Fall 1990): 73–91.

WHAT DEMOCRACY IS NOT

We have attempted to convey the general meaning of modern democracy without identi-fying it with some particular set of rules and institutions or restricting it to some specific culture or level of development. We have also argued that it cannot be reduced to the reg-ular holding of elections or equated with a particular notion of the role of the state, but we have not said much more about what democracy is not or about what democracy may not be capable of producing.

There is an understandable temptation to load too many expectations on this concept and to imagine that by attaining democracy, a society will have resolved all of its political, social, economic, administrative, and cultural problems. Unfortunately, "all good things do not necessarily go together."

First, democracies are not necessarily more efficient economically than other forms of government. Their rates of aggregate growth, savings, and investment may be no better than those of nondemocracies. This is especially likely during the transition, when proper-tied groups and administrative elites may respond to real or imagined threats to the "rights" they enjoyed under authoritarian rule by initiating capital flight, disinvestment, or sabo-tage. In time, depending upon the type of democracy, benevolent long-term effects upon income distribution, aggregate demand, education, productivity, and creativity may even-tually combine to improve economic and social performance, but it is certainly too much to expect that these improvements will occur immediately—much less that they will be defining characteristics of democratization.

Second, democracies are not necessarily more efficient administratively. Their capaci-ty to make decisions may even be slower than that of the regimes they replace, if only because more actors must be consulted. The costs of getting things done may be higher, if only because "payoffs" have to be made to a wider and more resourceful set of clients (although one should never underestimate the degree of corruption to be found within autocracies). Popular satisfaction with the new democratic government's performance may not even seem greater, if only because necessary compromises often please no one com-pletely, and because the losers are free to complain.

Third, democracies are not likely to appear more orderly, consensual, stable, or gov-ernable than the autocracies they replace. This is partly a byproduct of democratic freedom of expression, but it is also a reflection of the likelihood of continuing disagreement over new rules and institutions. These products of imposition or compromise are often initially quite ambiguous in nature and uncertain in effect until actors have learned how to use them. What is more, they come in the aftermath of serious struggles motivated by high ideals. Groups and individuals with recently acquired autonomy will test certain rules, protest against the actions of certain institutions, and insist on renegotiating their part of the bargain. Thus the presence of antisystem parties should be neither surprising nor seen as a failure of democratic consolidation. What counts is whether such parties are willing, however reluctantly, to play by the general rules of bounded uncertainty and contingent consent.

Governability is a challenge for all regimes, not just democratic ones. Given the polit-ical exhaustion and loss of legitimacy that have befallen autocracies from sultanistic Paraguay to totalitarian Albania, it may seem that only democracies can now be expected to govern effectively and legitimately. Experience has shown, however, that democracies too can lose the ability to govern. Mass publics can become disenchanted with their performance. Even more threatening is the temptation for leaders to fiddle with procedures and ultimately undermine the principles of contingent consent and bounded uncertainty. Perhaps the most critical moment comes once the politicians begin to settle into the more predictable roles and relations of a consolidated democracy. Many will find their expectations frustrated; some will discover that the new rules of competition put them at a disadvantage, a few may even feel that their vital interests are threatened by popular majorities.

Finally, democracies will have more open societies and polities than the autocracies they replace, but not necessarily more open economies. Many of today's most successful and well-established democracies have historically resorted to protectionism and closed borders, and have relied extensively upon public institutions to promote economic development. While the long-term compatibility between democracy and capitalism does not seem to be in doubt, despite their continuous tension, it is not clear whether the promotion of such liberal economic goals as the right of individuals to own property and retain profits, the clearing function of markets, the private settlement of disputes, the freedom to produce within government regulation, or the privatization of state-owned enterprises necessarily furthers the consolidation of democracy. After all, democracies do need to levy taxes and regulate certain transactions, especially where private monopolies and oligopolies exist. Citizens or their representatives may decide that it is desirable to protect the rights of collectivities from encroachment by individuals, especial propertied ones, and they may choose to set aside certain forms of property for public or cooperative ownership. In short, notions of economic liberty that are currently put forward in neoliberal economic models are not synonymous with political freedom—and may even impede it.

Democratization will not necessarily bring in its wake economic growth, social peace, administrative efficiency, political harmony, free markets, or "the end of ideology." Least of all will it bring about "the end of history." No doubt some of these qualities could make the consolidation of democracy easier, but they are neither prerequisites for it nor immediate products of it. Instead, what we should be hoping for is the emergence of political institutions that can peacefully compete to form governments and influence public policy, that can channel social and economic conflicts through regular procedures, and that have sufficient linkages to civil society to represent their constituencies and commit them to collective courses of action. Some types of democracies, especially in developing countries, have been unable to fulfill this promise, perhaps due to the circumstances of their transition from authoritarian rule.[13] The democratic wager is that such a regime, once established, will not only persist by reproducing itself within its initial confining conditions, but will eventually expand beyond them.[14] Unlike authoritarian regimes, democracies have the capacity to modify their rules and institutions consensually in response to changing circumstances. They may not immediately produce all the goods mentioned above, but they stand a better chance of eventually doing so than do autocracies.

---

[13] Terry Lynn Karl, "Dilemmas of Democratization in Latin America," *Comparative Politics* 23 (October 1990): 1–23.
[14] Otto Kirchheimer, "Confining Conditions and Revolutionary Breakthroughs," *American Political Science Review* 59 (1965): 964–74.

Chapter 17

Democracy, Prosperity, Citizens and the State

ANDREW F. JOHNSON*

*_Andrew Johnson_ is Dean of Social Science at Bishop's University, Lennoxville, Québec. This paper was
prepared for the Canadian Centre for Foreign Policy Development's Thinkers' Retreat: Clash of Civilizations?,
Ottawa, May 2–4, 2002.

_The survival of the West depends on Americans reaffirming their Western identity
and Westerners accepting their civilization as unique, not universal and uniting
to renew and preserve it against the challenges from non-Western societies._

(Huntington 1996: 20)

_The central issue for the West is whether, quite apart from any external challenges,
it is capable of stopping and reversing the internal process of decay._

(Huntington 1996: 303)

Democracy may be a universal value but the longevity of functioning democratic institutions has become the quintessence of Western identity. Its components—direct and representative decision-making, citizen participation as a means to good governance, and
respect for individual freedom (Lenihan _et al._ 2000: 26)—are deeply ingrained in Western
political institutions, laws and values.

Prosperity is another defining characteristic of Western civilization. There are myriad
factors identified to explain the West's prosperity, not the least of which is democracy
itself. Yet prosperity, as an independent variable, seems to have sown an inverse relationship with democracy. While prosperity has increased for nearly three decades, confidence
in democratic institutions has decreased.

Prosperity is not directly linked to the political discontent that has steadily grown in
Western democracies. Rather, it is the relationship that has evolved between governments
and citizens, concomitant to prosperity, which has cumulated in overall political discontent. At least, such is the central thesis of this paper that describes, compares, and explains
long-term political discontent in the United States and Canada. The responses of the
American and Canadian governments to the erosion of confidence in government are also
delineated and assessed comparatively. Finally, the concluding section relates the tensions
between market relations and democratic relations, identified as a fundamental source of
discontent in the U.S. and Canada, to the alleged clash of civilizations and to the supposed
"decay" of Western civilization.

The decay of contentment in democratic political institutions may well be an integral
part of the decay of Western civilization to which [Samuel] Huntington enjoins the West to

redress by considering its values to be unique and not universal. However, Huntington also asserts "political principles are a fickle base on which to build a lasting community". (Huntington 1996: 306) It is difficult to fathom how his assertion applies to the United States. It is also exceedingly difficult to determine whether Huntington's assertion applies to Canada, a state that is not exactly embedded in lofty democratic principles such as those that preceded the founding of the U.S.

Indeed, one should be wary of the curse of ideas—the principles of ideologies and nationalism—that plagued the Twentieth Century. (Conquest 1999) However, one should also be aware that "life, liberty and the pursuit of happiness"—not tribalism, ethnicity, race, religion, or doctrinaire economic formulae—are the very principles upon which America has built a lasting community. To be an American is to be a liberal. Seymour Martin Lipset puts it this way:

> ... in Europe and Canada, nationality is related to community; one cannot become un-English, or un-Swedish. Being an American, however, is an ideological commitment. It is not a matter of birth. Those who reject American [liberal] values are un-American.
>
> *(Lipset 1990: 19)*

Accordingly, adherence to liberal principles is a prerequisite to membership in the American community.

To illustrate, political principles hardly seemed fickle as a bond for America in the aftermath of 9/11. The entire nation displayed the Star Spangled Banner as the symbol of commitment to certain principles encapsulated by one word: "freedom". Freedom is emblematic of "lasting community". For Canadians, the principle of having no emotive attachment to principles, symbolized like American ones in simple emotive words, is, ironically, very much demonstrative of an attachment to principles—an attachment to the principles of diversity, tolerance, and pragmatism which define Canada's lasting community.

Additionally, the lasting community is not exclusive in the sense that it is normally reinvigorated—not hermetically sealed—in the face of challenges from non-Western influences. In the Anglo-democracies, political arrangements are much like the English language, which continuously renews itself through its absorptive capacities and tolerance of diversity. Accordingly, America is identified as a "melting pot" while Canada defines itself as a "multi-cultural society". That is precisely what makes America and Canada capable of facing, moderating and assimilating internal and external challenges. Moreover, each state's respective political principles, as expressed in their respective political institutions, may well have served to engender prosperity.

Why should democratic political institutions in America and Canada (as well as in all of the trilateral democracies) be objects of political discontent from their citizens, those who have flourished from the most accelerated and prolonged period—the post-war period—of economic growth and prosperity in the history of mankind? One is not required to look too hard for answers. The subject of political discontent in Western democracies has become a growth industry in terms of both unique and general explanations. However, one has to look hard for satisfying structural explanations. Accordingly, an overview of the former will be presented in Section II while a structural explanation will be proffered in Section III. These explanations, however, will be preceded by a description of the problem (in Section I) to which we now turn.

POLITICAL DISCONTENT: A DESCRIPTIVE OVERVIEW OF THE UNITED STATES AND CANADA

Recently, there has been a startling reversal of three decades of uninterrupted and cumulating political discontent that has plagued America. A *Los Angeles Times* poll of almost 2,000 American adults in late November 2001 indicated that 25 percent felt that 9/11 had transformed their lives for the better—they had better relations with neighbours and family and a new appreciation of their nation's values and of their own values. Moreover, now it is being reported there are strong indications that young Americans—previously harbouring very little confidence in politics—are embracing government as a highly respected career path. (*The Globe and Mail* 2002: A6) Accordingly, at university job fairs this year, the longest queues have been at government booths, including those for the CIA and FBI.

Such observations are supported by survey research. Robert Putnam and his colleagues conducted a nationwide survey of civic attitudes and behaviours in the summer and fall of 2000 and returned to "many of the same people and posed the same questions" in a survey conducted from mid-October to mid-November 2001. (Putnam 2002) Using a standard question to measure political confidence,[1] they found that 51 percent of respondents expressed greater confidence in the federal government than they had a year earlier while seven percent expressed less, for a net increase of 44 percent. Furthermore, political confidence increased more sharply among younger respondents than among older respondents, as did their interest in public affairs. Almost as a bonus, there were notable increases in trust of each other as well as in civic and political communities.

The Canadian opinion poll data is less comprehensive and considerably more parochial than America data, but to put it as diplomatically and as ineloquently as do Putnam and his colleague Susan Pharr, the Canadian data, "if less abundant and dramatic" at least "conforms to the general picture". (Putnam, Pharr and Dalton 2000: 10) The "general picture", as it were and according to an Ekos Poll, indicates that the Liberal government's support has increased from the election held in 2000 by almost 15 percent, that is, from 40.9 percent of the electorate to about 55 percent by the fall of 2001. (Ekos 2001) Additionally, 52 percent considered that the government was moving in the right direction in its fight against terrorism (29 percent indicated "neither" while 17 percent responded with "wrong"). As if to underscore and bolster renewed Canadian confidence in politics, President Bush, who, prior to 9/11 was not exactly a popular world figure among Canadians, received an excellent and dramatic approval rating of 68 percent among Canadians.

So does all of this conform to a "general picture" of renewed trust in government as suggested by the American data? Probably not. A Canadian Press/Leger Marketing Poll (January 2002) reveals that Canadians possess a great deal of trust in those in the safety professions (e.g., 98 percent for firefighters and 96 percent for nurses) but very little trust in politicians. In fact the lowest level of trust of all professions listed is accorded to politicians—18 percent, a rate that reaches as low as eight percent in British Columbia—substantially below car salespeople who earn the trust of 23 percent of Canadians.

---

[1]   The question was the following: "How much can you trust the government in Washington to do what is right—all of the time, most of the time, some of the time, or none of the time?"

Yet, pre-9/11 Canadian polling data may be instructive, however politically confident the American and Canadian publics may be in the recent performance of their governments. Short-term and immediate trust in politicians, political institutions, and public policy initiatives may mask long-term or structural trends of political discontent or distrust, as hard as it is to imagine in prosperous nations—nations that have delivered the goods, so to speak, for their citizens.

The long-term structural patterns of political discontent in prosperous European nations, North American nations and, potentially, Japan were identified by Huntington and others just over a quarter of a century ago. The "crisis of democracy" faced by these nations was understood to be largely a consequence of "excessive" democracy. A surge of democracy had culminated in a superabundance of demands being placed on governments, a condition of "demand overload". (Crosier, Huntington and Wantanuki 1975) They forecasted a bleak future for democratic political institutions.

A "crisis" did not occur but subsequent evidence demonstrates that general unhappiness with government continued to accrue. According to the World Values Surveys, as interpreted by Nevitte (1996: 56), the overall decline of public confidence in political institutions was "consistent and substantial" in ten of twelve nations, including the U.S. and Canada, during the decade of the 1980s. As Nevitte notes, confidence in political institutions at the beginning of the decade was higher in America than in Canada but in their descent, confidence levels converged by 1991.

The erosion of political confidence continued unabated throughout the decade of the 1990s in the U.S. and in Canada, as it did in all of the other nations of the trilateral democracies. However, the U.S. endures the dubious distinction, according to Putnam and Pharr, of being the nation in which "the down trend is longest and clearest . . . where polling has produced the most abundant and systematic evidence". (Putnam *et al* 2000: 8) Polling data related to questions posed on fundamental abstract (rather than ever changing concrete) associations with government declined precipitously by 1998. Thus they reported that only 39 percent of Americans felt that they could count on government to "do what is right" by that year. *Washington Post* data shows that the proportion slipped again in 1999 and in 2000, to less than one-third of respondents but then increased in one fell swoop to slightly over 50 percent of respondents in the immediate aftermath of 9/11.

Putnam and Pharr (2000: 9) also presented the *Harris Poll* on political alienation as proof positive that political discontent was in a free fall. The poll measures political alienation by presenting five statements to national samples of Americans:

- The people running the country don't really care what is happening to you.
- Most people in power try to take advantage of people like you.
- You're left out of things going on around you.
- The rich get richer and the poor get poorer.
- What you think doesn't count much anymore.

Putnam and Pharr reported that the index had won increasing assent since it was established in 1966. The tendency to feel alienated from politics continued to increase until 1995 but fell by about ten percent in the five year period between 1995 and 2000 and then plummeted by another ten percent in just one year (to 47 percent of respondents) after 9/11. Nevertheless, political alienation still remains at a rather high level.

However and despite the high levels registered on the "Harris Alienation Index", Americans continue to score high values on the "Harris Feel Good Index". Approximately three-fourths of Americans continue to feel good since 1998, according to a 16-question composite index on the quality of life. The lowest scores of approval on average, including the May 2001 poll, tend to be on "the state of the nation"—58 percent—and "the morals and values of Americans in general"—39 percent. Questions relating to economic well-being receive higher ratings.

To date, there is no evidence to suggest that the institutions of democracy are in imminent danger of collapse. However, the *Harris Poll* perceptions of "the state of the nation" and for "the morals and values of Americans in general" suggest that, whatever the case may be in the immediate wake of 9/11, democratic institutions should not be taken for granted. After all, the Council for Excellence in Government reports that, as recently as 1999, Americans feeling "disconnected" from government at all levels outweighed those feeling "very connected" or "fairly connected".

Canadians, for their part, are not normally asked to respond to questions on such an authentically American concept as the "state of the nation". They were, however, asked to register their feelings towards democracy in a poll carried out by York University's Institute for Social Research in 2000. (Howe and Northrup 2000: 6) A total of 71 percent of respondents were "very satisfied" and "fairly satisfied" with democracy. The researchers recognized, however, that respondents could have been responding positively to the notion of a democratic ethos. Thus, they were asked to register their satisfaction with concrete political structures—"government" and "politics". Satisfaction dropped markedly to a total of 58 percent and 53 percent, respectively, for the "very" and "fairly" satisfied respondents. The drop is not huge but sufficient to suggest that the 71 percent figure may overstate the general level of democratic contentment, as the researchers are quick to emphasize. (Howe and Northrup 2000: 7–8)

In addition to polling data, there are other signs of a decline in political contentment. Voluntary civic engagement, civic literacy and political participation are also falling. Significantly, they are dropping among younger citizens; this does not bode well for the future of democracy. The dip in voluntary activity is a case in point.

"Social capital", in which voluntary activity is central, refers "to connections among individuals—social networks and the norms of reciprocity and trustworthiness that arise from them", according to Robert D. Putnam, who coined the term. (2000: 19) By participating in voluntary organizations, people learn the skills of citizenship—and the values of a civic culture—by building bonds of mutual trust, tolerance and cooperation, ideally prerequisites for participation in democratic institutions. Accordingly, a nation that is rich in social capital is also likely to be endowed with a high level of political contentment.

In Canada, a national survey indicated that the number of volunteers dropped by almost one million or by 13 percent between 1997 and 2000. (*Independent Sector* 1999, 2001) Put otherwise, the number of Canadian volunteers dropped from 31 percent to 27 percent in the three-year period. In the U.S., however, the percentage decrease in adult volunteers in an even shorter time period, from 1998 to 2000, was more than double Canada's—from 56 percent to 44 percent.

It is encouraging that there are more volunteers in the U.S. as a proportion of population than in Canada but the drop in formal voluntary activity is equally discouraging. Of course, the everyday generosity of Americans cannot be overlooked. In fact, the percentage of household income (from contributing households) given to charitable organizations

has increased from 1.9 percent in 1987 to 3.2 percent in 2000, that is, to a substantial dona-
tion of US $1,620 per household. Despite the outpouring of trust and giving—from giving
to charities to giving blood—in the weeks following the September tragedy, the American
reservoir of social capital has not necessarily expanded. Paul C. Light of The Brookings
Institution succinctly summarizes the notion that it is easier to give than to become
involved even since 9/11:

> *Unfortunately, little of this civic enthusiasm has spilled over into volunteering. We
> spent more time last fall renting videos and ordering take-out food than volun-
> teering. Although Americans are venturing out more these days, the level of vol-
> unteering has not grown substantially. Americans have the will to volunteer but
> they do not have the time.*

(Light 2002)

Whatever the time constraints of Americans, Light's comment that they lack the will to
volunteer is a matter of fact. This can be concluded from a survey of young adults, conducted in January 2002. (Centre for Democracy and Citizenship 2002) Young adults,
according to the survey, show remarkable levels of trust in government in the wake of the
terrorist attacks. However, just under half of young adults (47 percent) and 18 to 24 year-
olds (48 percent) volunteer in their communities once a year compared to 54 percent of the
18 to 24 group in a survey conducted in 2000, despite a seemingly broad definition of volunteerism, which includes involvement as well as donations. More to the point, the data
also indicate that whatever the value of the social capital accumulated by young
Americans, "noticeably strong pluralities to majorities of young adults are certain that they
will not engage in political activism". (Centre for Democracy and Citizenship 2002) Thus
the data about those in whom the future of democracy resides are not comforting, but then
neither are other rough indicators for the future of democracy. Consider, for example, the
store of civic literacy in Canada and in the U.S., which, Henry Milner argues is more
important to the sustenance of democratic institutions than social capital *per se*.

Civic literacy, "the knowledge to become effective citizens", from Henry Milner's perspective, is the key ingredient in the stock of social capital required to bolster democracy.
His argument makes good sense. (Milner 2001: 7) Informed individuals are likely to be able
to assess policy options more effectively than the ill-informed, and thus be inclined to participate in politics. Milner cites a reliable study, which asserts "the political ignorance of the
American voter is one of the best documented [findings] in political science". (Barrels cited
in Milner 2001: 8) He also identifies data from the 1984 and 1997 Canadian Election
Studies and other data to demonstrate that basic knowledge of civics is highly deficient. For
instance, a majority of respondents were unable to identify ostensibly popular political participants. Sadly, the data shows that the least knowledgeable are young people.

Milner's findings conform to an "exam" survey conducted by Angus Reid on behalf of
the Dominion Institute in late 1997. (Dominion Institute 1997) Forty-five percent of
Canadians failed a mock citizenship exam similar to the one immigrants take to become
Canadian citizens. Participants in the middle age bracket (35 to 54 years old) performed
better (61 percent passed) than those in the older and younger age groups, each of which
had a mere 52 percent pass rate. At least it was comforting to learn that respondents recognized their shortcomings as citizens: 74 percent agreed with the statement, "not enough
history and civics are being taught in schools".

However one might weigh civic literacy relative to social capital, as catalysts for political participation, it is clear that political participation has declined significantly in all Western democracies if we take the most basic measure, voting, as a rough indicator. Voter turnout in all elections throughout the OECD has decidedly declined since 1970. While voter turnout has remained below the OECD average in the U.S. and in Canada, the drop has been most precipitous in Canada. However, voter turnout in the OECD remains lowest in the U.S., where less than half of eligible American voters vote.

Additionally, throughout Europe, as well as in America, participation as measured by political party membership has withered. (*The Economist* 1999: 51) Membership figures for Canadian political parties are somewhat unreliable. However, the York University survey data suggest that membership diminished from 18 percent to 16 percent among those who "had ever been" members of political parties—a statistically insignificant drop. (Howe and Northrup 2000: 31) But previous surveys indicate that only two to three percent of samples respond affirmatively if asked if they are currently members of political parties. The point is that the proportion of Canadians participating in political party activity is low. Moreover, participation rates are not increasing and past members are neglecting to renew party memberships.

Perhaps most discomforting is that participation, even at these most basic and relatively effortless levels, is lowest among young people. The trend holds for Americans (Conway 2000: 19–24) as well as for Canadians. Accordingly, Brenda O'Neill concludes that:

> . . . *today's young Canadians are participating in the political system at lower levels than previous generations did at the same age, suggesting that recent declines in voting turnout and other measures of political participation will not be reversed in future years.*

> *(O'Neill 2001: 3)*

In explaining the declining membership in European political parties, *The Economist* (1999: 51) asserts "people's behaviour is becoming more private" and asks rhetorically "why join a political party when you can go fly fishing or surf the web?" The same may be legitimately asked of American and Canadian citizens, that is, if one assumes a private contractual relationship—a market relationship—between citizen and government. In such a relationship, it makes perfect sense to enjoy the leisurely self-indulgent benefits of prosperity while neglecting the civic obligations of democracy—to be politically knowledgeable, to contribute to civil society and to participate in the political process. But heretofore, the contractual nature of the relationship between citizen and government has not been fully explored as an explanation for the political malaise that infects the West, particularly in the U.S. and Canada. Instead, unique circumstances and general factors affecting specific nations, and Western nations in general, have been proffered to account for growing discontent. These factors are evaluated next and the new contractual relationship between citizen and government, as a fundamental explanation for ongoing and growing political discontent, will be discussed subsequently.

POLITICAL DISCONTENT: FROM UNIQUE TO GENERAL EXPLANATIONS FOR THE U.S. AND CANADA

In his comparative analysis of the causes of continuing political discontent in the U.S. and Canada, Richard Simeon (1995: 25) refers metaphorically to government as "a circus performer riding two horses". The performer exists perilously "precisely at the point where . . . two sets of forces intersect or collide". Democracy and globalization are identified as "the two sets of forces". And political discontent lies in a government's ability or lack thereof to balance and "accommodate" these forces.

To be sure, federal systems tend to reinforce regional and provincial or state claims on the polity. Such cleavages might be expected to add to the plethora of demands, stemming from democracy and resulting from the ever increasing complexity of government, however determined successive governments in the U.S. and Canada have been in reducing their respective functions. However, in Canada, political discontent is alleged to come from "democracy itself". (Clarke *et al.* 2000: 24) It is not just a matter of an operational "performance deficit" on the part of government—a widespread perception that it is unable to effectively deliver programs and services. It is a matter of a fundamental performance deficit on the part of the federal government—a prevalent and profound belief that it is unable and/or unwilling to resolve longstanding constitutional as well as socio-political issues.

Thus, Canada's political disaffection, its current existence as a "polity on the edge, is the end result of a ten-year accumulation of five inter-connected but unique events: two failed constitutional proposals—the 1992 Charlottetown Accord and the 1995 Quebec Referendum—combined with three elections, two of which (1988 and 1993) were on major economic issues and the last of which (1997) is characterized as "a collective frustration" which appeared to change nothing and resolve nothing". (Clarke *et al* 2000: 20) And to this we could add the 2001 election, which was very much a replay of the 1997 election.

There are events stemming from democracy, and unique to the U.S., which may also be identified as accounting for the decline in political contentment. One major factor is the alleged historical and unique mistrust of government in the USA. (Wills 1999) Mistrust is then customarily propped up by a considerable inventory of supplementary, but similarly unique circumstances. Thus, for example, Anthony King, (2000: 74–98) who is no stranger to the subject of political discontent, identifies two long-term factors—mistrust of government and "limited constituency" or limited bonds with citizens—and several short-term factors, from unmet expectations, to Vietnam, Watergate and flawed leaders, to the "incomprehensibility of government" to, finally, the "decline of comity".

Just as success of democracy has generated political discontent, so has the economic success of the state. The state has enlarged its scope and functions during the last five decades by managing demand within a Keynesian perspective and by promoting trade liberalization, international monetary stability, the mobility of capital and of labour and by stimulating and nurturing rapid technological change. In doing so, the state has unleashed internal and external forces that are alleged to have eroded the state's autonomy and sovereignty. (Horseman and Marshal 1994 and Barber 1995) The external forces, particularly multi-national enterprises, are thought to be most threatening to the authority of the modern state. (Leys 2001: 8–19) Indeed the ostensible threat posed by the primary agents of globalization, transnational corporations and international financial capital, have spawned a growth industry in publications which at worst predicts the death of the nation state and at best describes its current comatose condition. (Johnson and Stritch 1997: 9–14)

However, if the authority of the state is measured rather crudely by expenditures and revenues as ratios of GDP, then the proportions indicate that in both the U.S. and Canada sovereignty is not "at bay" as *The Economist* so aptly puts it. (1997: 8) And whatever the extent of the threat posed by globalization to the authority of the state, a World Economic Forum (WEF) survey, conducted among 25,000 respondents in 18 states during 2000 and 2001, clearly indicates that economic globalization is viewed positively in the U.S. and Canada in absolute and in relative terms. Moreover, people tend to have high expectations of economic globalization. Majorities anticipate improvements on eight of 15 factors surveyed, most notably greater access to world markets, cheaper goods, improved cultural life, a better quality of life, strengthened human rights, a more robust national economy, and a higher personal income. Significantly, respondents in a national survey voiced support for those who wish to express political discontent on a global scale. Almost half of the citizens overall, and majorities in half of the states surveyed, "support people who take part in peaceful demonstrations against globalization because they are supporting my interests". However, such support in the U.S. only stood at 40 percent after September 11.

Thus, citizens in the U.S. and Canada apparently support the prosperity that has accompanied globalization (and also express concern for those who have not profited from economic globalization). Nevertheless political discontent in both states has risen steadily despite the growth of prosperity. There appears to be a negligible relationship (McAllister 1999) or, at most a tenuous relationship (Lawrence 1997) between economic performance and political confidence, a conclusion that can be deduced from the WEF survey above. In other words, strong evidence does not exist to support the notion that political discontent, however defined, fluctuates with the ups and downs of the business cycle.

Yet, a reasonably sound case can be made—and has been made—that the very success of the state in engendering prosperity has led to a shift in values—from modern to postmodern—because economic growth has lessened concerns about economic and physical security and has stimulated absorption in self-expression and self-realization which, in turn, challenges democratic institutions. (Inglehart 1997: 211) This thesis is consistent with the empirically substantiated signs that political discontent is especially rife among young adults who, as a group, are the repository of post-modern values. (Inglehart 1997: 213)

Curiously, by the middle of the 1990s the Western world had come to a stark realization that economic prosperity was not continuous and, more particularly, that a crisis in unemployment among the G-7 countries had interrupted the economic and physical security of the previous decade, especially among young people. Was there a concomitant shift from post-modern values back to modern values or in another direction to some other set of values? In the absence of suitable polling data, we do not know. We do know, however, that the erosion of political contentment has steadily persisted and is especially marked among young adults, whatever the impact of dramatically altered circumstances on post-modern values as they relate to politics. This suggests that there may be widespread and fundamental patterns of attitudinal change, which are not necessarily discerned by polling data. Put otherwise, the very success of the state in generating prosperity may have shifted modern values of participatory democracy into the self-indulgent realm of the postmodern. But let us take Inglehart's thesis one step further: the long-term economic success of the American and Canadian states may have basically modified the relationship between state and citizen in a manner which has inevitably bred structural political discontent.

POLITICAL DISCONTENT: PROSPERITY IN THE U.S. AND CANADA AS A STRUCTURAL EXPLANATION

In the last half of the last century, government fashioned a role for itself in the image of Keynesian economic theory as the harbinger, manager, and distributor of prosperity. In so doing, government relinquished its role as leader and repository of principles advancing civic virtue. Government became at once the master and servant of economic forces, inasmuch as its assumed role was to manage macroeconomic policy by way of fiscal and monetary policy in the service of its shareholders, the electorate. In other words, government's preoccupation with making the market work has eclipsed its role of making politics work.

Hence, a main role of North American governments in the 1960s was to create and distribute social policy largesse. In the following decade, they were primarily absorbed with manipulating their fiscal and monetary levers to offset the effects of a new economic phenomenon in which recession existed side-by-side with inflation. During the 1980s President Reagan and Prime Minister Mulroney advanced a new Trinity: expenditure cutbacks, deregulation, and privatization. Their governments held a common objective, which was to free the market from public sector entanglements so that the invisible hand would presumably become more effective than government in creating, sustaining and distributing the benefits of prosperity. At the same time, their governments worked, as had their successors, to "liberalize" the international market from the putative fetters of governments and to expedite the process of disentangling their own polities from the North American market by creating a free trade agreement.

Thus, by the end of the 1980s the U.S. and Canadian governments had surrendered much of their control of the market to the market. The market now eclipsed the polity, for better or for worse. This simply completed a process that began 40 years earlier when governments adopted a Keynesian path to prosperity while pretty much ignoring the need to sustain the polity. Governments had begun the last half of the Twentieth Century as agents for the market, and ended up by the 1990s as agents of the market.

Governments, much like business corporations, now define their primary role and responsibility as delivering services to "customers" or "clients", not "citizens". By the 1990s governments were re-designing themselves in accordance with business principles or with "managerialism", such as Japanese production principles embedded in Total Quality Management (TQM). Indeed, TQM, which essentially involves maintaining high quality to serve the needs of the "customer", lies at the core of the New Public Management (NPM) philosophy.

NPM has been fully embraced during the last decade by governments in the U.S. and in Canada. More to the point of our thesis, the full-scale adoption of market culture in government indicates that government essentially sees itself as just another business engaged in a commercial or contractual relation with "customers"; it does not necessarily see itself as involved in social cum communal relationship with citizens. And that, according to Jeremy Rifkin (2000: 241), is the "Achilles heel" of the new age. Commercial obligations are no substitute for social obligations. More importantly, the commercial relationship that governments have developed with their citizens may well be the structural source of political discontent in the U.S. and Canada as well as elsewhere.

Social relations originate from kinship, ethnicity, geography, religion or adherence to a political ideal, i.e., from a communitarian ideal. They are long-term and sustained by notions of "reciprocal obligations and visions of common destinies". They are nurtured by communities "whose mission it is to reproduce and continually secure the shared meanings that make up the common culture". (Rifkin 2000: 241) Commercial relations, by contrast, typically involve short-term and individual—rather than group—commitment; they are explicit, generally delineated in legal or contractual terms, and are quantifiable. In short, social relationships are embedded in custom and obligation to community; commercial relationships stem from delivering the goods and commitment between individuals. Rifkin eloquently elucidates the distinctive nature of commercial relationships:

> *[They] are designed to maintain a distance between parties. It is understood at the outset that the relationship is based on nothing deeper than the exchange of money. Whatever shared experience occurs between the parties in the course of their relationship is meant to be superficial, expedient and short-lived.*
>
> *(2000: 242)*

That is precisely the nature of the relationship that governments in the U.S., Canada, and elsewhere in the OECD have cultivated with their citizens in the last half of the 20th Century.

Governments and citizens alike have traded individual freedom to participate in the decisions about their collective destiny for freedom to choose our values and ends for ourselves, as Sandel puts it. (1996: 275) Values and ends are located in the market, that is, in the commercial plenitude of prosperity.

However, commercial relationships are fleeting and shallow. They last as long as the customer gets a deal. In the world of business, Robert Reich contends that in this "age of the terrific deal" commercial relationships are not expected to last and everyone will switch to a better alternative if one becomes available. Accordingly, "disloyalty is 'normalized' and loyalty itself comes under suspicion". (2001: 83) Why should it be any different with government? It is not different, except for the discontent that accrues because government activities are comprehensive and its services are monopolistic. Government cannot possibly please all of the people all of the time in their commercial wants and needs. Yet, one cannot switch to a better deal. What better recipe for discontentment with politics, especially for young people who have only known government in its commercial role as architect and dispenser of goods and services?

In short, political discontent is an outcome of a clash between social and commercial relationships, or between the institutions of democracy and the market. At least in this day and age, governments seem to recognize the deficiencies inherent in maintaining a one-sided relationship with citizens—a predominantly commercial relationship. At the same time, they seem hard pressed to devise ways of restoring a social relationship or, at the very least, creating balance between the two.

REDRESS: GOVERNMENT AND CITIZEN ENGAGEMENT

Since 9/11, there has been a sea change in U.S. civic attitudes which has been reinforced by powerful television ads and images, promoting and fostering American unity and political community. Nevertheless, Thomas H. Sander and Robert D. Putnam (2002) of Harvard's Saguaro Seminar on Civic Engagement assert that "attitudes are outrunning our actions". Americans have not reported joining more community organizations or attending more organizational meetings despite the "historical window of opportunity for civic renewal" afforded by the tragic events of September which left Americans more united than in recent memory. Accordingly, Sander and Putnam recommend that institutional changes be made to spur and assimilate civic mindedness and that civic literacy be promoted to enhance political contentment. To date, the American response has been focussed relative to Canada's response. Social capital has been designated by President Bush, in his January 2002 State of the Union Address, as the means to rouse and foster civic engagement and, presumably, political contentment. To this end, $560 million in new funds alone in fiscal 2003 are to be allocated to the U.S. Freedom Corps, an umbrella program to reinvigorate old volunteer programs and to sustain new ones so that Americans are encouraged to devote two years—4000 hours—over a lifetime to community service.

Will stockpiling social capital, combined with a renewed determination to revitalize America's civic culture as advocated by Sander and Putnam, be sufficient to transform the commercial relationship with government to a social or genuinely civic relationship? The question must be considered against the backdrop of other broad government initiatives for the reform of government. The 2003 budget contains three such broad initiatives. (The White House 2002) First, the federal government is to be transformed into "citizen-centred" government from a "bureaucracy-centred" one. This is to be accomplished by flattening the federal hierarchy and, mainly, by improving e-government facilities. Second, government is to be made "results-oriented—not process oriented", largely by inaugurating more effective financial controls and performance indicators than are currently in place, and by applying private sector reforms to the public service. Finally, government is to be "market-based" which entails opening up government programs and activities to competition from the private sector.

The three initiatives will undoubtedly make government a better business, so to speak, and concomitantly strengthen the efficiency of its commercial relationship with American taxpayers. And overall, they may (or may not) make good sense, depending on the nature of operational designs. Yet against this backdrop of government reform, the Freedom Corps initiative seems almost futile. After all, the ultimate goal of strengthening social capital is to foster political participation and involvement. If there are few institutional means to absorb social capital into the political process and to convert it into a non-commercial relationship between citizens and government, then the structural cause of political discontent will largely remain.

The OECD's Public Management Service (PUMA) Working Group on Strengthening Government-Citizen Connections suitably frames the problem of redress by devising three separate analytic categories: information, consultation, and active participation. (OECD 2001: 23) Information, consultation, and active participation are identified as sequential but, also, intertwined, as a means to alleviate political discontentment.

Information, a one-way relationship, is expected to be enhanced by access to information laws and by the Internet. Both the U.S. and Canadian governments have long since succeeded in this category, especially in the realm of e-government services. A recent report of the Accenture consulting group ranks the Internet services of the Canadian and American governments as first and third, respectively, in the world. Accordingly, Accenture characterizes both governments as "innovative leaders" but cautions that they "still have a long way to go to providing fully mature online government". (Accenture web site) Both governments recognize as much, having committed substantial sums to further developing e-government. However, these expenditures are not necessarily designed to establish closer non-commercial ties between citizen and government as is expected in the realms of consultation and active participation.

Consultation, a two-way relationship in which citizens can provide feedback to government by way of public opinion polls and comments on draft legislation, has long since been elevated to a fine art, and provides input into policy-making on governance in Canada and, especially, in the U.S.. Indeed, experimentation has already begun in the U.S. (but not in Canada) with "deliberative polling" in which randomly selected respondents are provided with an opportunity to become informed and engaged. (Averill 2001: 11) Briefing materials are given to respondents and, subsequently, they are invited to discuss issues with each other, experts, and politicians. Then their opinions are polled. Deliberative polling may well appeal to Canadians, according to Averill, who cites a Canadian opinion poll, conducted in 2000 to verify her claim. (2001: 11) It is a reasonable step towards connecting with government but it, like polling in general, seems limited to random samples or very small groups and inclined to forge close relationships with pollsters more so than with government. However, sophisticated polling may serve as a prerequisite to forming institutions of active participation, a category which has been somewhat neglected by the U.S., in contrast to its neighbour to the north.

Active participation, "relations based on partnership with government, in which citizens actively engage in defining the policy process and content of policy-making" is expected to transpire by way of consensus conferences and citizen juries, according to the OECD. (2001: 23) Moreover, civil society organizations (CSOs) are expected to serve as intermediaries between citizen and governments. CSOs now function under a new aura of legitimacy in the U.S. and in Canada. However, third party democracy is no substitute for political party democracy in which the elector has input if one chooses to exercise it. Nevertheless, CSO activity may help to restore the stock of social capital in the U.S. and in Canada.

In the meantime, the process of generating participation seems to be far more advanced in Canada than in the U.S. Against the backdrop of Privy Council Office directives that promote better service, departmental co-operation and financial economies (PCO web site)—much like the directives in the U.S. budget—the federal government has begun to consider new ways in which to forge closer relationships with citizens. The PCO is setting guidelines for initiatives in consultation but individual departments and agencies have also devised new ways of bringing citizens back into politics.

Participation initiatives are characterized by recent attempts to re-define the nature of citizenship and citizen engagement in government. They range from heuristic devices such as the Reformcraft Project, which has sought to define and measure good governance by way of engaging 160 citizens "in all walks of life" in a series of 15 conferences (Hubbard 2000), to Heritage Canada's innovative CanadaPlace, a part of which would include a "digital commons". (Lenihan 2002: 12) The proposed digital commons would be designed to provide citizen and community interaction, including interaction with government by way of the Internet, audio, and video conferencing, all supported by full information and consultation.

Indeed, it maybe useful to re-think the nature of citizenship and citizenship engagement with government. However, the advent of new and breathtaking communications technologies should not seduce one into thinking that there may be a quick techno-bureaucratic fix for the problem of political discontent in prosperous nations. Technology is form, not substance. Technology cannot redress the unique causes, cited above, as sources of political discontent in the U.S. and Canada. Political will and determination can only resolve those issues.

More importantly, the technologies available to enhance the information, consultation and participation elements of citizenship engagement cannot redress the structural source of political discontent, as alluring as these devices may be to young people. Governments will never fully neutralize the commercial relationship that they have developed with their citizens. Politicians—especially politicians—and public servants must make a determined and concerted effort to explain to citizens the importance of what they do, and the importance of citizen involvement to guide them in doing what they do. Moreover, politicians and public servants must continuously inform citizens that public policies are truly social policies, policies that are an outcome of a covenant that requires trust and participation. Above all, governments must abandon the current vogue of applying the lexicon of the market to their own operations. After all, the public and private sectors have different goals, which are, at the most basic level, to foster social as distinct from commercial gain.

Governments using the quixotic institutional jargon, evocative of a romanticized bygone era of simple communitarian democracy—"fireside chats", "town hall meetings", "national forums" and "global villages"—will not restore citizen engagement and contentment. Quaint images may comfort older citizens but younger people, whose current convictions must be redressed, have a great deal more savvy about images than previous generations. More importantly, the younger generation—the least politically contented— have grown up in prosperity and have been gradually indoctrinated with the notion that the market is above politics, that is, as Harvey Cox puts it: the Market is God. (1999) Thus, Western governments, notably the governments of the U.S. and Canada, must de-theologize government of the Market if governments of Western civilization are to nurture political contentment and sustain democratic institutions, not only as a bulwark from attacks from other civilizations, but also as a sop and a positive channel for discontent originating elsewhere. In other words, governments of the West must continue to address political discontent from external sources in order to peacefully secure their own identities. This includes being open to new ideas from the outside as a precondition to maintaining their own security and prosperity.

CONCLUSION: ABSORBING THE CLASH OF CIVILIZATIONS?

The Market as God has eclipsed the perhaps idealistic principle of government as warden and progenitor of community values, and has transformed governments into disciples of the Market. Governments, especially the U.S. and Canadian governments, have accepted their subordinate role willingly by adopting and applying the logic and lexicon of the market to themselves. They have become agents of the market—mere instruments of prosperity. In doing so, governments have abandoned their somewhat idealized role as arbiter and repository of community values and have formed pedestrian contractual relationships with citizens. Governments and citizens are connected to each other only by the ephemeral quest for prosperity; a relationship that is bound to lead to discontent once prosperity is, as it has been, realized.

The ideal of citizens as participants in their own collective destiny has been replaced by the metaphysics of the market. The metaphysics of the market—its invisible hand—is, much like theology, accepted and sustained by faith. Accordingly, faith posits that the Market as God is omnipotent, omniscient, and omnipresent and that economic success or failure can be explained by its manifestation, the Invisible Hand. (Cox 1999)

However, Western governments must demystify the Invisible Hand by way of making a concerted effort to explain to citizens the importance of what they do and the significance of the impact of public policies on social and community relationships. Above all, governments must make it clear that they are not inert pawns at the mercy of the Invisible Hand, particularly in the guise of globalization. Nowadays, governments simply make policies differently—in concert with other nations through multilateral forums (Kapstein 1994)—than they did decades ago. In other words, governments must correct the imbalance between contractual and social relationships—the clash between the market and democracy—in order to restore political contentment and to stem the decay of democratic political institutions.

There is nothing new about tensions between these types of relationships. The conflicts between social and contractual types of relationships were pondered systematically over a hundred years ago by [Émile] Durkheim, who drew the distinction between mechanical solidarity—characterized by "social resemblances"—and organic solidarity, while [Ferdinand] Tönnies theorized about the distinctions between *Gemeinschaft* and *Gesellschaft*—a temporary and artificial mechanism of social cohesion. (Lukes 1975: 140) Similar tensions are even reported in the Old Testament wherein, unlike and diametrically opposed to the present, social covenant takes total precedence over contractual behaviour.[2] In a sense, civilizations have been confronting the same issue for more than two thousand years.

Islamic civilization seems to be no exception, although the imbalance in relationships is just the opposite of that in the West. Many Islamic governments identify themselves in terms of true faith by cloaking their activities in the tenets of Islam. However, governments clouded by theological legitimization will not likely cure Muslim nations of economic problems or propel them towards prosperity. Instead, de-theologized politics may attenuate the religious tendency to accept what exists; it may also create a political will to mend structural defects in domestic political economies that cultivate poverty. A new balance between social and contractual relationships, marked by progress towards the secularization of politics in Islamic civilizations and matched by a secularization of the market in the West, might help defuse the apparent clash between Islam and the West. In other words, a new balance might moderate the apparent prevalent Islamic view that the West is characterized by crass commercialism

---

2   See Numbers 15: 32–36 in which the Lord commands Moses to put to death, by stoning, a man caught gathering wood, a contractual act, on the Sabbath and in violation of laws which sustain the social cohesion of the Israelites.

in most of its relations; it might also vitiate the Western perception that the Islamic world is rife with blind religious intolerance in most of its internal and external relations.

In the meantime and to reiterate, Western governments must re-establish themselves as entities separate from the market and ennobled by social purpose as well as social covenant in order to prevent further deterioration in political contentment. Accordingly, governments must go beyond just providing better information to citizens. They must progress beyond mere consultation that has also become highly sophisticated by virtue of the rapid development of advanced communications technology. They must build political institutions that effectively require citizen engagement and effectively integrate citizen input—a formidable challenge in an age in which democracy has long since been commodified, and in which commercial relationships seem to have become infinitely more preferable to social relationships.

Governments in the U.S. and Canada have no choice but to do so. Prosperity—and their significant role in generating prosperity—in and of itself is not sufficient to meet internal challenges, let alone external challenges. Political contentment can only sustain the institutions of democracy which, to date, have proven resilient to attacks from others, not just by virtue of military capability, but by virtue of absorptive capacity. Stable, vigorous, and well-supported democratic institutions have a prodigious capacity to absorb challenges from within and from without and to assimilate those challenges into new directions in policy, to the benefit of citizens of Western nations as well as to the benefit of people from nations based on other civilizations.

REFERENCES

Accenture, *Governments Closing the Gap Between Political Rhetoric and eGovernment Reality.* www.accenture.ca

Averill, Nancy (2001). "Doing Democracy: How Deliberative Polling Works." *Canadian Government Executive,* 1.

Barber, Benjamin (1995). *Jihad vs. McWorld* (New York: Times Books).

Bartels, Larry (1996). "Uninformed Votes: Informational Effects in Presidential Elections." *American Journal of Political Science 40*:1. February.

Canadian Press/Leger Marketing (2002). *The Perception of Canadians with Regard to Various Professions,* January.

Centre for Democracy and Citizenship, et al. (2002). *Short Term Impacts, Long Term Opportunities: The Political and Civic Engagements of Young Adults in America,* March 2002. www.youngcitizensurvey.org.

Clarke, Harold D., Allan Kornberg and Peter Wearing (2000). *A Polity on the Edge: Canada and the Politics of Fragmentation* (Peterborough, Ontario: The Broadview Press).

Conquest, Robert (1999). *Reflections on a Ravaged Century* (NY: W.W. Norton & Co.)

Conway, M. Margaret (2000). *Political Participation in the United States,* 3rd ed. (Washington DC: Congressional Quarterly Press).

Cox, Harvey (1999). "The Market as God." *The Atlantic Monthly,* March.

Crozier, Michel, Samuel P. Huntington, and J. Wantanuki (1975). *The Crisis of Democracy: Report on the Governability of Democracies to the Trilateral Commission* (New York: New York University Press).

Dominion Institute/National Angus Reid Group Poll (1997). *The Dominion National Citizenship Exam Survey of 1997,* November 10.

Ekos Research Associates (2001). *Security, Sovereignty, and Continentalism: Canadian Perspectives on September 11,* September 27.

Horsman, Mathew and Andrew Marshal (1994). *After the Nation State: Citizens, Tribalism and the New World Order* (London: HarperCollins, 1994).

Howe, Paul and David Northrup (2000). "Strengthening Canadian Democracy: The Views of Canadians." *Policy Matters* (July) *11*:5.

Hubbard, Ruth (Senior Advisor to the PCO) (2000). *Good Governance: Reformcraft Final Report,* June 5. www.pco-bcp.gc.ca.

Huntington, Samuel P. (1996). *The Clash of Civilizations and the Remaking of the World Order* (New York: Simon and Schuster).

Independent Sector (1999). *Giving and Volunteering in the United States, (Executive Summary).* www.independentsector.org/.

Independent Sector (2001). *Giving and Volunteering in the United States (Executive Summary)* www.independentsector.org/.

Inglehart, Ronald (1997). *Modernization and Postmodernization: Cultural, Economic, and Political Change in 43 Societies* (Princeton: Princeton University Press).

Johnson, Andrew F. and Andrew Stritch eds. (1997). *Canadian Public Policy: Globalization and Political Parties* (Toronto: Copp Clark).

Kapstein, Ethan B. (1994). *Governing the Global Economy: International Finance and the State* (Cambridge: Harvard University Press).

King, Anthony (2000). "Distrust of Government: Explaining American Exceptionalism" in Susan J. Pharr and Robert D. Putnam, eds. *Disaffected Democracies: What's Troubling the Trilateral Countries?* (Princeton: Princeton University Press).

Lawrence, Robert Z. (1997). "Is It Really the Economy, Stupid?" in Joseph S. Nye, Jr. et al. eds. *Why People Don't Trust Government* (Cambridge, MA: Harvard University Press).

Lenihan, Donald G. (2002). Post-Industrial Governance: *Designing a Canadian Cultural Institution for the Global Village* (Ottawa: Centre for Collaborative Government), January.

Lenihan, Donald G. et al. (2000). *Collaborative Government in the Post-Industrial Age: Five Discussion Pieces* (Ottawa: Centre for Collaborative Government), May.

Leys, Colin (2001). *Market-Driven Politics: Neoliberal Democracy and the Public Interest* (New York: Verso).

Light, Paul C. (2001). An interview with Paul C. Light, Vice-President and Director of Governmental Studies, The Brookings Institution, on National Public Radio's Morning Edition, February 7. www.brook.edu/views/op-edAight/20020207.htm.

Lipset, Seymour Martin (1990). *Continental Divide: The Values and Institutions of the United States and Canada* (New York: Routledge).

Lukes, Steven (1975). *Emile Durkheim: His Life and Work* (Markham: Penguin Books).

McAllister, Ian (1999). "The Economic Performance of Governments" in Pippa Norris ed. *Critical Citizens: Global Support for Democratic Government* (New York: Oxford University Press).

Milner, Henry (2001). "Civic Literacy in Comparative Context: Why Canadians Should Be Concerned." *Policy Matters* (July) 2:2.

Nevitte, Neil (1996). *The Decline of Deference: Canadian Value Change in Cross-National Perspective* (Peterborough, Ontario: Broadview Press).

O'Neill, Brenda (2001). "Generational Patterns in the Political Opinions and Behaviour of Canadians: Separating the Wheat From the Chaff." *Policy Matters* 2:5.

OECD (2001). *Citizens as Partners: Information, Consultation and Public Participation in Policy-Making* (Paris: OECD publications).

Privy Council Office *Executive and Deputy Minister Performance Agreements—Strategic Directions for the Public Service of Canada: Priorities for 2001–2002.* www.pco-bcp.gc.ca.

Putnam, Robert D. (2002). "Bowling Together." *The American Prospect* (February 11) *13*:3.

Putnam, Robert D. (2000). *Bowling Alone: The Collapse and Revival of American Community* (NY: Simon and Schuster).

Putnam, Robert D., Susan J. Pharr, and Russell J. Dalton (2000). "Introduction: What's Troubling the Trilateral Democracies?" in Susan J. Pharr and Robert D. Putnam eds. *Disaffected Democracies: What's Troubling the Trilateral Countries?* (Princeton: Princeton University Press).

Reich, Robert B. (2001). *The Future of Success* (New York: Alfred A. Knopf).

Rifkin, Jeremy (2000). *The Age of Access* (NY: Tarcher/Putnam).

Sandel, Michael J. (1996). *Democracy's Discontent: America in Search of a Public Philosophy* (Cambridge: The Belknap Press).

Sander, Thomas H. and Robert D. Putnam (2002). "Walking the Civic Talk After Sept.11." *The Christian Science Monitor,* February 19.

Simeon, Richard (1995). "Globalization, Domestic Societies, and Governance" in C.E.S. Franks, J.E. Flodgetts, *et al.* eds. *Canada's Century: Governance in a Maturing Society* (Montreal: McGill-Queen's Press).

The Economist (1999). "Empty Vessels?" July 24:51.

The Economist (1997). "The Future of the State." September 20:8.

The Globe and Mail (2002). March 8:A6.

The White House (2002). *A Blueprint for New Beginnings—IX. Government Reform.* www.whitehouse.gov/news/usbudget/blueprint/budix.html.

Wills, Garry (1999). *A Necessary Evil: A History of American Distrust of Government* (New York: Simon and Schuster).

Chapter 18

Willing to Participate: Political Engagement of Young Adults

ANNE MILAN*

*__Anne Milan__ *is a senior analyst at Statistics Canada.*

Young adults are often viewed as uninterested in political activity. Is it true that they are more disillusioned by traditional methods of participation than other age groups, as shown by the proportion who cast ballots in the municipal, provincial or federal elections? Do young adults engage in politics through activities outside of the ballot box? Or do those who vote also engage in non-voting political behaviour?

Using the 2003 General Social Survey (GSS), this article outlines the extent of political engagement among young adults aged 22 to 29,[1] as measured by traditional (voting) and alternative (non-voting) political participation. It then examines some of the links between young adults' selected characteristics and their political behaviours such as voting, signing petitions, boycotting certain products, attending public meetings or participating in demonstrations.

YOUNG ADULTS LESS LIKELY TO VOTE THAN OLDER ADULTS

In a democracy, electoral voting is generally seen as the classic or traditional type of participation in the political process. Indeed, many adults do exercise their right to vote, although voter turnout at federal elections has decreased over the last 20 years.[2] Despite the fact that 77% of the voting-age population voted in at least one of the last elections prior to the survey in 2003, there were large differences in voting participation by age. According to GSS data, only 59% of those in their twenties voted, compared with 71% of 30- to 44-year-olds and 85% or more of individuals aged 45 and over. As with the older age groups, young adults were less likely to vote in local than in federal and provincial elections.

WHY DON'T YOUNG PEOPLE VOTE?

There are several possible reasons why young adults are not as likely to go to the polls as their older counterparts. According to some researchers, compared to previous

---

[1]   This particular age group is examined in order to include those who were aged 18 in 2000, the date of the most recent federal election prior to the 2003 GSS.

[2]   Elections Canada website. Voter turnout at federal elections and referendums, 1867–2000. www.elections.ca (accessed May 25, 2005).

CST **What you should know about this study**

This study draws from the 2003 General Social Survey, (GSS), which interviewed nearly 25,000 Individuals aged 15 and over living in the 10 provides in private households. It focuses on Individuals aged 22 to 29, resulting in a sample of roughly 3,000 people representing about 3.4 million Canadians in this age group. This particular age group was chosen in order to include those Individuals who were aged 18 or over in 2000, the year of the most recent federal election prior to the survey date.

To conduct its analysis, the study developed a non-voting or alternative political Involvement scale ranging from 0 to 8, based on whether the respondent had, in the past 12 months, searched for information on a political issue; volunteered for a political party, expressed his/her views on an issue by conducting a newspaper or a politician; signed a petition; boycotted a product or chosen a product for ethical reasons; attended a public meeting; spoken out at a public meeting; participated in a demonstration or march.

A score of 0 indicates no non-voting political participation, while a score of 8 reflects participation on all possible indicators.

Two statistical models were developed to examine the impact of specific characteristics on young people's political engagement. The first model identifies selected factors associated with non-voting alternative political participation; the second model determines the influence of the same factors on voting behaviour. These factors include age, youth involvement in community activities, group affiliation, sex, place of birth, religious attendance, volunteering, sense of belonging to community, region, educational level, main activity, household income, and (for the first model on non-voting political engagement) voting behaviour.

generations, young adults are simply tuned out of the political process,[3] lacking the ability, the motivation or both to get involved. In some ways, the sheer volume of available information coming from the Internet and television, as well as other media, can be overwhelming when trying to find a starting point for becoming informed.[4] Consequently,

---

[3]   O'Neill, B. December 2004. "Youth participation—What we know, and what we don't know." *Canadian Democracy: Bringing Youth back into the Political Process.* Centre for Research and Information on Canada. p. 2–5; Centre for Research and Information on Canada. 2001. *Voter Participation in Canada: Is Canadian Democracy in Crisis?* Montréal: Centre for Research and Information on Canada; Gidengil, E., A. Blais, J. Everitt, P. Fournier and P. Nevitte. January 2005. "Missing the message: Young adults and the election issues." *Electoral Insight*: 2004 *General Election* 7, 1: 6–11.

[4]   See, for example, O'Neill. 2004.

	Young adults under 30 were involved in political activity differently than older adults

	Political participation (%)					
		Age group				
	Total	15 to 21	22 to 29	30 to 44	45 to 64	65 or older
Follow news and current affairs daily	68*	35*	51	66*	81*	89*
Voting behaviour						
Voted in at least one election	77*	.....	59	71*	85*	89*
Last federal	74*	.....	52	68*	83*	89*
Last provincial	73*	.....	50	66*	82*	88*
Last municipal or local	60*	.....	35	52*	70*	79*
Non-voting political behaviour						
At least one non-voting political behaviour	54*	59	58	57	56	39*
Searched for information on a political issue	26*	36	32	26*	25*	17*
Signed a petition	28*	27*	31	31	29	16*
Boycotted a product or chose a product for ethical reasons	20*	16*	25	25	21*	8*
Attended a public meeting	22*	17	16	23*	25*	20*
Expressed his/her views on an issue by contacting a newspaper a politician	13*	8	9	13*	16*	12*
Participated in a demonstration or march	6*	12*	8	6	6*	2*
Spoke out at a public meeting	8*	4	5	9*	10*	7*
Volunteered for a political party	3	2	3	2	4*	4

..... Not applicable

* Statistically significant difference from 22- to 29-year-olds ($p<0.05$).

Note: Voting rates will differ from those of Elections Canada, which calculates voter participation rates based on number of eligible voters.

Source: Statistics Canada, General Social Survey, 2003.

young adults may be less aware of the relevance of elections, and feel removed from the idea that decisions made by politicians affect them directly.[5]

One Canadian researcher has argued that young adults today feel marginalized from mainstream political discourse.[6] She contends that youth account for a declining share of the voting-age population, a situation that limits their political clout. At the same time, government has reduced or limited its support for issues that interest young adults, such as postsecondary education, equality and human rights.

---

[5] Bishop, G. and R. Low. December 2004. "Exploring young Canadians' attitudes towards government, politics and community." *Canadian Democracy: Bringing Youth back into the Political Process.* Centre for Research and Information on Canada, p. 6–8.

[6] Adsett, M. 2003. "Changes in political era and demographic weight as explanations of youth "disenfranchisement" in federal elections in Canada, 1965–2000." *Journal of Youth Studies* 6, 3: 247–264.

Yet it seems that young adults share at least some of the same political interests as older Canadians. A 2005 study found that, following the last election, 18- to 29-year-olds ranked health care as the issue that was most important to them personally.[7] In fact, all respondents, regardless of age, rated health care as the primary concern, although proportionally more older Canadians did so. Furthermore, the study found that levels of political alienation were similar for younger and older adults.

Some researchers have referred to young people as "engaged sceptics"—interested in political issues, but wary of politicians.[8] In other words, they are committed to the tenets of democracy, but tend to be more interested in participative political behaviour and issues which are immediately pertinent to their lives. Young people's feeling of disconnect from conventional political parties may partially account for their negative view of traditional politics and for their interest in alternative forms of political behaviour.[9]

MOST ADULTS UNDER 65 ENGAGE IN AT LEAST ONE NON-VOTING POLITICAL ACTIVITY

While young adults are less likely to vote than those over 30, this is not true of their political behaviour on other fronts. In the year preceding the survey, nearly three in five (58%) 22- to 29-year-olds engaged in at least one non-voting political activity, virtually the same proportion as that of 30- to 64-year-olds (56%). In contrast, only two in five (39%) Canadians aged 65 or over took part in any alternative political behaviour, although this age group was the most likely to vote.

Because participating in a non-voting or alternative activity "can be a valuable source of political education, [which develops] politically relevant knowledge, awareness, understanding and skills,"[10] young people's involvement in alternative political behaviour is central to assessing their level of political interest.

According to the 2003 GSS, the most common non-voting political behaviours young adults engaged in during the year were searching for information on a political issue (32%) and signing a petition (31%). One-quarter of young adults boycotted—or chose—a product for ethical reasons, while over one-sixth attended a public meeting. About 1 in 10 expressed their views on an issue by contacting a newspaper or a politician, or participating in a demonstration or protest march. A very small proportion (3%) had worked as a volunteer for a political party.

Overall, young adults in their twenties were much more likely than seniors to seek to inform themselves about a political issue, to sign a petition, to boycott (or purchase) products for ethical reasons or to participate in demonstrations or marches. However,

---

[7]   Gidengil et al. 2005.

[8]   Henn, M., M. Weinstein and D. Wring. 2002. "A generation apart? Youth and political participation in Britain." *British Journal of Politics and Intergenerational Relations 4*, 2: 167–192.

[9]   Ibid.

[10] Roker, D., K. Player and J. Coleman. 1999. "Young people's voluntary and campaigning activities as sources of political education." *Oxford Review of Education 25*, 1 and 2: 195.

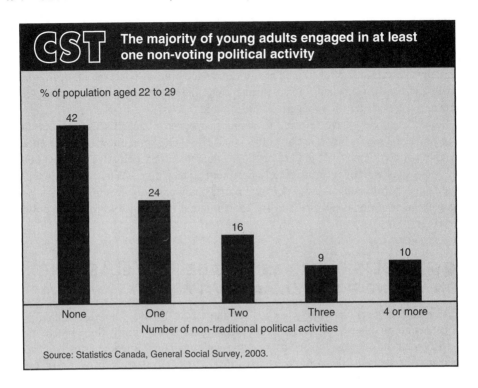

they were significantly less likely than older adults to attend and speak up in public meetings and to express their views to the media or politicians.

COMMUNITY INVOLVEMENT CONNECTED TO POLITICAL ENGAGEMENT

It appears that individuals' level of involvement in various community-oriented activities may contribute to greater civic-mindedness. Whether it's belonging to a sports team, book club, volunteer group or religious association, groups can meet the personal needs of participants as well as connect them to the wider society. Indeed, the proportion of young adults engaged in non-voting political activity was nearly twice as high among those involved with three or more organizations as among their peers with no group affiliation (81% versus 43%). Similarly, individuals who, as children or young adults, took part in a number of community activities were considerably more likely than others to be engaged in alternative political behaviour as adults.

Perhaps because volunteering also reflects a sense of civic responsibility and a desire to help others, young adults who volunteered in the year prior to the survey were much more likely to be involved in at least one political activity (voting or non-voting) than those who did not volunteer (71% compared with 52%).

Statistical regression models were developed to identify the factors that influence a person's level of political engagement.[11] The results of these models show that, even after

---

[11]   It should be noted that the correlates for engaging in either voting or non-voting behaviour were similar across age groups.

CST 22-to 29-year-olds with a very strong sense of community have higher odds of voting than those with a weaker sense of belonging

	Odds ratio		Odds ratio
Age[1]	1.03	**Region**	
Youth Involvement[2]	1.03	*Quebec*	*1.00*
Number of groups of which a member	1.11[3]	Atlantic	0.38*
		Ontario	0.30*
Sex		*Prairies*	*0.3v2*
Female	*1.00*	British Columbia	0.36*
Male	1.08	**Educational level**	
Place of birth		*University degree*	*1.00*
Foreign born	*1.00*	Less than high school	0.25*
Canadian-born	4.27*	High school graduate	0.48*
Religious observance		Some post secondary	0.74
Rarely/never	*1.00*	Diploma or certificate	0.68*
Weekly	0.86	**Main activity**	
Sometimes	1.40*	*Other**	*1.00*
Volunteer in past year		Labour force	1.10
No	*1.00*	Student	0.81
Yes	1.42	**Household Income**	
Sense of belonging to community		*$60,000 or more*	*1.00*
Very weak	*1.00*	Less than $20,000	0.51*
Very strong	*1.74**	$20,000 to $29,999	0.74
Somewhat strong	1.30	$30,000 to $39,999	0.75
Somewhat weak	1.26	$40,000 to $49,999	1.00
		$50,000 to $59,999	0.66*

Note: This table presents the odds that a respondent voted in the last election prior to the survey, relative to the odds of a benchmark group when all other variables in the analysis are held constant. Benchmark group is shown in italics.
* Statistically significant difference from benchmark group ($p<0.05$).
1. For each additional year, the odds of voting increase by 3%.
2. For each additional activity during youth, the odds of voting increase by 3%.
3. For each additional group, the odds of voting increase by 11%, which is statistically significant ($p<0.05$).
4. "Other" includes activities such as homemaking, retirement, volunteer work or illness.
Source: Statistics Canada, General Social Survey, 2003.

controlling for all other variables, volunteering or being affiliated with a group were both strongly associated with non-voting political participation. Furthermore, the more groups a person belonged to, the more non-voting activities they took part in. Similarly, if people were volunteers or involved with multiple groups, the odds that they voted increased substantially.

Interestingly, engaging in community-oriented activities as a child or teenager was positively associated with non-voting political behaviour, but not with voting. On the other hand, a strong sense of belonging to the community as a young adult resulted in higher odds of voting, but did not influence non-voting political participation.

NEARLY 7 IN 10 UNIVERSITY-EDUCATED YOUNG ADULTS PARTICIPATE IN NON-VOTING POLITICAL BEHAVIOUR

The models reveal a positive relationship between educational level and political engagement, even when controlling for other factors. Some 32% of young adults with less than a high school education engaged in at least one non-voting activity, compared with 69% of those with a university degree. Higher levels of education were also associated with higher odds of voting.

The effect of household income on political participation is mixed: 22- to 29-year-olds with household incomes under $20,000 engaged in more non-voting behaviours than did those with household incomes of $60,000 or more. On the other hand, young adults in low-income households had almost 50% lower odds of voting than those in high-income households, even when other factors (including student status) were taken into account.

YOUNG ADULTS MOST LIKELY TO VOTE IN QUEBEC

Across the country, there are differences in the extent of political engagement. The share of young people who turned out to vote was highest in Quebec (74%), followed by the Atlantic provinces (64%), the Prairies (56%), Ontario (53%), and British Columbia (49%), a relationship which continued after controlling for other factors.

A 2003 review of youth participation in Quebec suggests that activities beyond voting, such as pressure groups and demonstrations on issues ranging from education to anti-globalization, are also an important component of their political involvement.[12] According to the GSS, young adults in the Atlantic provinces engaged in fewer alternative political activities than their Quebec counterparts. However, the differences between other regions and Quebec were not statistically significant.

CANADIAN-BORN MORE POLITICALLY ENGAGED THAN IMMIGRANTS

Some 66% of young Canadian-born adults cast a ballot in the last election prior to the survey, compared with only 29% of foreign-born youth. Of course, because Canadian citizenship is a prerequisite for voting, it is possible that not all of the foreign-born respondents to the GSS were eligible to vote. However, there would be no such restrictions on the ability to engage in non-voting political behaviour. Yet the Canadian-born were still more likely to engage in at least one non-voting form of political behaviour: 61% compared with 44% of foreign-born. The strong relationship between place of birth and political engagement remained even when other factors, such as education, income, and province of residence, were taken into account.

VOTING AND NON-VOTING BEHAVIOUR GO HAND IN HAND

Although voting is a more traditional method of political behaviour than activities such as boycotting a product or signing a petition, there is a connection between these political activities. Two-thirds (66%) of young adults who voted had also engaged in at least one form of non-voting behaviour, compared to less than half (46%) of those who had not voted. This relationship held in the statistical model, even when other factors were taken into account.

In other words, young adults who went to the polls were also more apt to be politically engaged in other ways. However, it is also important to note that many individuals who did not cast a ballot still acted in a political manner, even when they themselves might not have

---

[12] Gauthier, M. 2003. "The inadequacy of concepts: The rise of youth interest in civic participation in Quebec." *Journal of Youth Studies* 6, 3: 265–276.

CST **Frequency of following news and current affairs**

Patterns of following news and current affairs tend to reflect other types of political participation. According to the 2003 General Social Survey, 51% of young adults in their twenties followed news and current affairs on a daily basis. An additional 31% apprised themselves several times a week, and 8% did so several times a month. This is far lower than the rates for other adults, particularly seniors, 89% of whom follow news and current affairs daily (perhaps reflecting their greater interest, more free time, or both).

The results also showed that young men were more likely to follow current affairs daily than were young women (56% compared to 46%). Voting in any type of election—municipal, provincial, or federal—was also associated with a greater likelihood of following current affairs. For example, 56% of those who had cast a ballot followed current affairs on a daily basis, compared to 45% of those who had not voted. Similarly, 57% of young adults who had engaged in a non-voting political activity followed news every day, compared to 44% of those with no such behaviour. Residents of Quebec followed the news most closely of all regions (59% did so daily), particularly compared to the Atlantic provinces (42%). Young adults who had less than a high school education were less inclined to follow the news daily (45% compared to 57% of those with university degree).

necessarily recognized that they were behaving politically. For example, a 2004 study of 20- to 29-year-olds found that they were fairly active in their communities, although they did not always identify their behaviour as volunteering.[13] Many people express interest in issues and activities that could be seen as political, such as the environment or the community, but they do not always view their involvement as political engagement.

SUMMARY

The political engagement of adults in their twenties is a complex issue. Young adults are politically involved, but in a different manner than older Canadians. Specifically, adults in their twenties voted less than any other age group; however, their rate of participation in non-voting political activities was comparable to that of adults aged 30 to 64, and exceeded that of seniors, who have the highest voter participation rates of all age groups. Results of statistical models developed to isolate significant factors associated with engagement in the political process identified the following factors to be strongly associated with both voting and non-voting political behaviour: educational level, group involvement, and activities which promote civic-mindedness and public service, such as volunteering. Finally, young adults who voted were more likely to engage in non-voting political behaviour, but not casting a ballot did not preclude them from participating in non-voting activities.

---

[13]   Bishop and Low. December 2004. p. 7.

Chapter 19

Voter Participation in Canada: Is Canadian Democracy in Crisis?

CENTRE FOR RESEARCH AND INFORMATION ON CANADA (CRIC)

INTRODUCTION

The November 2000 general election in Canada saw Jean Chrétien's Liberal Party win its third consecutive parliamentary majority. It also saw the third straight decline in voter participation—that is, in the number of registered voters who cast a ballot. And while some 12.86 million Canadians cast ballots, some 8.25 million registered voters (or 39 percent of the total) did not vote at all.[1] Never before have so many voters abstained.

The decline in voter participation, or turnout, is worrying. The defining characteristic of a representative democracy is that those who govern are chosen by the people. A democracy without willing voters is a sham. It is important to ask what the decline in turnout says about the health of Canadian democracy, and what can be done to reverse the trend.

There are countless reasons why people do not vote, and not every instance of non-voting should be interpreted as an indictment of the existing political system. Many do not vote because they are travelling, sick, or have difficulty getting to a polling station. Others are not sure whether they are eligible to vote, or about how to get their names on the voters list. Still others may be inclined to vote, but nonetheless decide that they can sit this one out because the result in their own constituency or across the country as a whole is a foregone conclusion. Few of these people can be described as overly cynical about Canadian democracy or genuinely disaffected with politics.

But as the number of non-voters grows, the situation becomes more worrisome. What is keeping more and more voters away from the polls? Is declining voter turnout a symptom of growing dissatisfaction with parliament, political parties and politicians? Is non-voting more pronounced among certain groups within the population, such as young people? Does it really matter if fewer people are voting than in the past? Is Canadian democracy really in crisis?

These are the questions that this paper will address.

---

[1] All figures related to turnout and voting results in Canada are from Elections Canada (see *www.elections.ca*). Figures for 1997 and 2000 are taken from the official voting results published by the Chief Electoral Officer. Figures for elections prior to 1997 are taken from Elections Canada, *A History of the Vote in Canada* (Ottawa: Public Works and Government Services Canada), 1997.

VOTER PARTICIPATION IN CANADA

Federal Elections

Voter participation in Canada is declining. Consider these facts:

- Turnout has declined in three straight federal elections, falling from 75 percent in 1988 to 61 percent in 2000—a 14-point drop over the course of 12 years (see Figure 1).[2]
- Turnout at the last federal election was the lowest ever recorded in Canada.
- The average turnout at federal elections in the 1990s was much lower than it was in the decades that immediately preceded it (see Figure 2), and the lowest of any decade in Canadian history.

    Turnout at federal elections has fallen in each province, but the decline has been more pronounced in some than in others.

- Average turnout in the 1990s was at least 10 percentage points lower than it was in the previous decade in six provinces: Newfoundland, PEI, Ontario, Saskatchewan, Alberta and British Columbia. The largest drop in average turnout between the 1980s and the 1990s was in Saskatchewan and BC—almost 13 percentage points in each case.
- In Nova Scotia, Ontario, and Saskatchewan, turnout for the 2000 federal election was about over 20 percentage points lower than it was in the 1960s.
- The province where the drop in turnout has been the most moderate is Quebec. Average turnout in the 1990s was only 4 percentage points lower than it was in the 1980s.

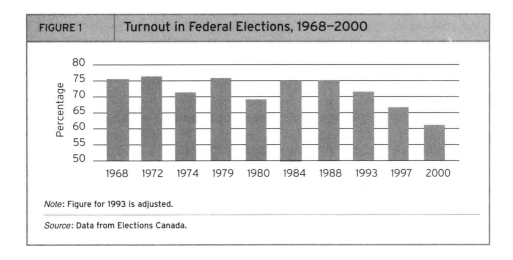

FIGURE 1 | **Turnout in Federal Elections, 1968–2000**

Note: Figure for 1993 is adjusted.

Source: Data from Elections Canada.

---

[2]   In most democracies, including Canada, turnout is calculated by dividing the number of ballots cast by the number of voters who were registered to vote. In the US, where the system of voter registration fails to reach large numbers of potential voters, turnout is calculated differently, by dividing the number of ballots cast by an estimate of the voting age population.

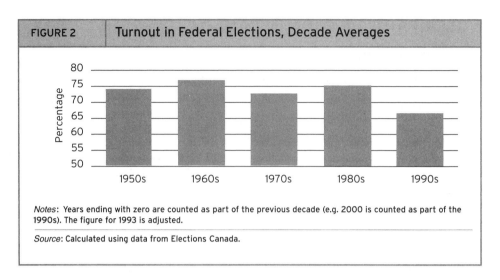

FIGURE 2 | Turnout in Federal Elections, Decade Averages

Notes: Years ending with zero are counted as part of the previous decade (e.g. 2000 is counted as part of the 1990s). The figure for 1993 is adjusted.

Source: Calculated using data from Elections Canada.

Provincial Elections

Voter participation has also been falling in provincial elections, though not as uniformly or a dramatically.

- A comparison of the average turnout within each province for elections from 1980 to 1989 with the average since 1990 gives the following results: turnout has declined in 5 provinces, risen in three provinces, and remained unchanged in two (see Appendix, Table 1A). Where turnout has increased, the size of the increase has been relatively small.[3]
- Saskatchewan experiences the most dramatic change. Turnout at the last two elections (1995 and 1999) was 17 points lower than it was at the previous three elections (1982, 1986 and 1991).
- Turnout has also declined by several points in recent elections in Nova Scotia, New Brunswick, Manitoba and BC.
- Average turnout has not changed significantly in Ontario or Alberta, but the level of participation in those provinces (respectively, 58 percent and 53 percent at the most recent elections) nonetheless is very low.

An International Trend?

Canada is not unique. Researchers have noted a decline in voter participation in other democratic countries. In fact, speaking of this decline, US political scientist Martin Wattenberg

---

[3]   The largest increase (+ 2.3 percentage points) was in Quebec, where the return of sovereignty to the agenda of party politics after 1990 heightened the stakes of electoral contests.

writes: "it is rare in comparative politics to find a trend that is so widely generalizable."[4] In a range of democracies, including the United Kingdom, Ireland, the Netherlands, Portugal, Italy, Finland, Austria and Japan, turnout at the most recent election was the lowest recorded in the post-war period.[5] In the case of the UK, voter turnout in the 2001 election fell by a dramatic 12 points to 59 percent, a level lower than that at the most recent election in Canada.

There are exceptions. For instance, there has been no downward trend in Australia—like Canada, a parliamentary democracy with a federal system—because voting there is compulsory. In the United States, voter turnout has not changed much over the last 30 years, but it was already very low to begin with. In many other west European countries, turnout has fallen slightly in recent years, but remains high by Canadian standards.

Despite some possible exceptions, it remains the case that voter turnout is falling in many countries, and not just in Canada. This has implications for how the causes of the problem, and the possible solutions, should be understood. At the same time, it should also be noted that few western democracies have experienced as steady and as significant a drop in turnout over the last 15 years as has Canada.[6]

EXPLAINING THE DECLINE IN VOTER PARTICIPATION

Political scientists and commentators have identified a number of factors that may be responsible for lower voter participation. But they do not agree on which is the most important. More specifically, they do not agree as to whether the decline in voter turnout in Canada is a cause for alarm. While some argue that lower turnout simply reflects the uninteresting or uncompetitive nature of recent election campaigns, others see it as a more worrying product of deteriorating public perceptions of parliament, parties and politicians.

What follows is a review of the four main explanations for low turnout in Canada, and a discussion of their strengths and weaknesses.

Liberal Hegemony

People are more likely to vote when they think their vote counts. And they are more likely to think their vote counts when the election is hotly contested, or when there are major

---

[4]   Martin P. Wattenberg, "Turnout Decline in the U.S. and other Advanced Industrial Democracies," Centre for the Study of Democracy Research Paper Series in Empirical Democracy Theory (University of California, Irvine: Center for the Study of Democracy, 1998), p. 14 (available on the website of the Center for the Study of Democracy at: *www.democ.uci.edu/democ/papers/marty.html*). See also: André Blais, *To Vote or Not to Vote: The Merits and Limits of Rational Choice Theory* (Pittsburgh: University of Pittsburgh Press, 2001): 33–36; Mark Franklin and Michael Marsh, "The Tally of Turnout: Understanding Cross-National Turnout Decline Since 1945," paper prepared for delivery at the annual meeting of the American Political Association, Washington D.C., August–September 2000, 2–3.

[5]   See the figures for turnout posted on the website of International IDEA, at *http://www.idea.int/voter_turnout/index.html*.

[6]   One exception is Japan, where turnout has fallen sharply.

issues at stake.[7] In the 1995 Quebec referendum, for instance, turnout was an unprecedented 93.5 percent. This figure is astoundingly high, yet understandable, given what was at stake and the small margin separating the two sides in the campaign.

In contrast, many observers argue that the federal election of 1997 and 2000, when turnout fell below 70 percent, were singularly uninteresting. In both cases, the Liberal Party faced a divided opposition and won by a large margin over its nearest rival. In neither case did the election appear to be fought over an issue of great importance to the future of the country, such as national unity or free trade. By and large, there was no widespread anger with the current government that could be counted on to drive Canadians to the polls to vote for change.

The decline in turnout, therefore, reflects the relatively uncompetitive period of national politics. There is no reason not to expect voters to participate in greater numbers once elections become more competitive and more meaningful.

The following points support this theory:

- The number of people who said that there were no important election issues at stake was much higher in 1997 and 2000 than in previous elections (see Figure 3).[8] And research has shown that those who say there are no important election issues are much less likely to vote.[9]
- At the last election, the margin of victory for winning candidates was generally much smaller in constituencies with high voter turnout than it was in those with low voter turnout. In the 10 constituencies where turnout was highest, the average margin of victory was 17 percent. In the ten constituencies where turnout was lowest, the average margin of victory was 42 percent.[10] This suggests that there is a relation between voter

---

[7] Political scientists who have studied political participation in a large number of democratic countries have concluded one of the factors affecting turnout is the voters' own sense of whether the election is either close (in terms of the winning party's margin of victory), or important (in terms of its political consequences, or how much the outcome is deemed to matter). See Blais, *To Vote or Not to Vote*, p. 43; see 17–44; Franklin and Marsh, "The Tally of Turnout," p. 29. See also Mark N. Franklin, "The Dynamics of Electoral Participation," in *Comparing Democracies 2: Elections and Voting in Global Perspective*, edited by Lawrence LeDuc, Richard G. Niemi and Pippa Norris (Thousand Oaks: Sage Publications, 2002).

[8] Jon H. Pammett, "The People's Verdict," in *The Canadian General Election of 2000*, edited by Jon H. Pammett and Christopher Dornan (Toronto: Dundurn, 2001), p. 300; Jon H. Pammett, "The Voters Decide," in *The Canadian General Election of 1997*, edited by Alan Frizzell and Jon H. Pammett (Toronto: Dundurn, 1997), p. 235.

[9] Tony Coulson, "Voter Turnout in Canada: Findings from the 1997 Canadian Elections Survey," *Electoral Insight* Vol. 1, No. 2 (November 1999): 19. Available on the website of Elections Canada at *www.elections.ca*.

[10] The margin of victory is the difference between the number of votes won by the winning candidate and his or her nearest rival, expressed as a percent of the total votes cast for all candidates in the constituency. On this point, see the analysis of the 2000 federal election results in the province of Quebec, offered by Louis Massicotte and Édith Brochu. They note that turnout in that province declined most notably in Liberal strongholds on the island of Montreal. (Louis Massicotte et Édith Brochu, "Élections fédérales de novembre: coup de loupe sur un scrutin." *Le Devoir* 26 février 2001, page A7. Available on the website of *Le Devoir* at *www.ledevoir.com/public/client-css/news-webview.jsp?newsid=165.*)

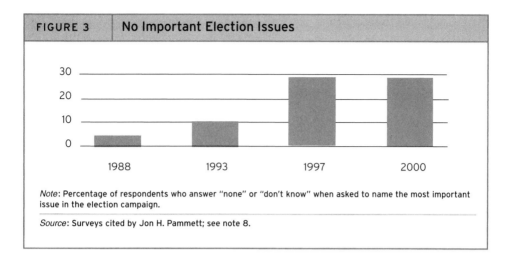

FIGURE 3 | No Important Election Issues

Note: Percentage of respondents who answer "none" or "don't know" when asked to name the most important issue in the election campaign.

Source: Surveys cited by Jon H. Pammett; see note 8.

turnout and the closeness of the election result, and implies that turnout might be higher in future elections, should they be more competitive.

However, there are several weaknesses in the argument that turnout has fallen because recent elections were not all that interesting.

First, there have been previous elections in Canada where the results were predictable, or at least not very close, but where turnout remained high. For instance, turnout was as high at the time of the 1958 Diefenbaker landslide as it was for the much more closely contested elections that ensued.

Second, citizens are called upon to vote, not only because their vote might decide a close election, or because the central issue in the campaign is also their own top priority, but because it is a civic duty to participate in selecting the government. Research conducted by André Blais has shown that most people agree that it is their duty to vote. He writes: "the feeling that voting is a moral obligation and that not voting implies a failure to fulfill one's civic duty is widespread and strongly ingrained in the population."[11] This raises a question: is the decline in turnout related not so much to the peculiarities of any one election campaign, but to more worrying changes in how people perceive and act on their sense of their obligations as citizens?

Third, the lack of an election issue or of competitiveness among parties is an explanation that begs more questions than it answers. There is simply no objective reason why this past election campaign should have been so devoid of debate about the country's priorities and the best means to achieve them. At the time of the election, the government was wrestling with a number of acute challenges—the reform of the health care system, the need to manage globalization and negotiate new trade agreements, the rapidly deteriorating environment, and the plight of Canada's disadvantaged Aboriginal communities, to name a few. Moreover, with five official parties spanning a wide range on the ideological spectrum, Canadian voters were offered a variety of choices at the ballot box. And yet the

[11]   Blais, *To Vote or Not to Vote*, p. 99.

parties were collectively unable to initiate a debate about these issues, one capable of capturing the voters' imaginations and of spurring them to cast a ballot. We need to ask why this was the case.

The Permanent Voters List

The November 2000 election was the first one conducted on the basis of the new method for registering voters that Canada adopted in 1996.[12] In previous elections, a new voters list was compiled during each election campaign by enumerators, who visited every household in the country to obtain the names of those eligible to vote. Enumeration "was repeatedly hailed as a highly effective method of registration, one that produce an up-to-date and accurate list of electors" at relatively low cost.[13] Since a person needs to be correctly registered in order to vote, the accuracy of the list is very important. If the list is very complete and accurate, few people will be discouraged from voting because they are not registered, do not know how to register, or do not have the time or inclination to do what is necessary in order to register.

The decision was made to do away with door-to-door enumeration in favour of what is known as the permanent voters list. It is so named because rather than being produced from scratch at the start of each election, it is maintained from year to year and continuously updated. Unless voters otherwise object, their names remain on the list. Revisions to the list—changes of address, deletions of those deceased and addition of new citizens—are made automatically through electronic information sharing among Elections Canada and different federal and provincial government departments and agencies. Those who become eligible to vote on their 18th birthday automatically receive a card from Elections Canada, asking them to agree to have their names added to the list.[14] Because it is a permanent list, the new voters list is in place at the time an election is called, although voters whose names are not on the list can register throughout the election campaign, up to and including voting day itself.[15]

---

[12]   As in 2000, there was no door-to-door enumeration of voters during the June 1997 electoral campaign. But the voters' list used in 1997 was the product of a final door-to-door enumeration carried out in April of that year, in preparation of the new permanent voters' list. Therefore that election cannot be said to be the first one to have been conducted without the benefit of door-to-door enumeration.

[13]   Jerome H. Black, "The National Registry of Electors: Raising Questions About the New Approach to Voter Registration in Canada," *Policy Matters* Vol. 1, No. 10 (December 2000), p. 8. Available on the website of the Institute for Research on Public Policy at *www.irpp.org*.

[14]   Except in Quebec, where the names of 18 year olds are automatically added to the provincial list of electors, and then added to the federal list.

[15]   In 2000, there were 959,774 net additions of names to the voters list prior to election day, and a further 872,552 voters registered on election day itself. This means that 8.6 percent of all voters who were finally registered added their names to the list during the campaign or on election day. Many more had to revise their registration, for example, by recording a change of address. See the Chief Electoral Officer's report on the 37th General Election, available on the website of Elections Canada at *www.elections.ca*.

Two points have been made about the impact of the new list on voter participation:

- The old system was better at *encouraging* people to vote, because door-to-door enumeration reminded votes that an election had been called and that they were eligible to vote.
- The new system *discourages* more people from voting. All observers agree that, because it does not rely on door-to-door enumeration, the permanent voters list is less accurate. By the time an election comes around, more voters are likely to find that they are not registered correctly or at all. At this point, the onus is on the voter to add his or her name to the list. While many find this easy, others do not.

Is there evidence to support these claims?

- On the one hand, difficulties with voter registration were not the main reasons why non-voters did not vote in the last election (see Figure 4). According to a post-election survey conducted for Elections Canada,[16] only 16 percent of non-voters said that they did not vote because of a reason associated with the system of voter registration, namely: (a) they didn't have enough information about where and when to vote; (b) they weren't registered or on the voters list in their riding; or (c) they didn't receive their voter's card.[17]
- On the other hand, the number of non-voters in 2000 who did not vote because they were not on the voters list appears to have been higher than in previous elections.[18]

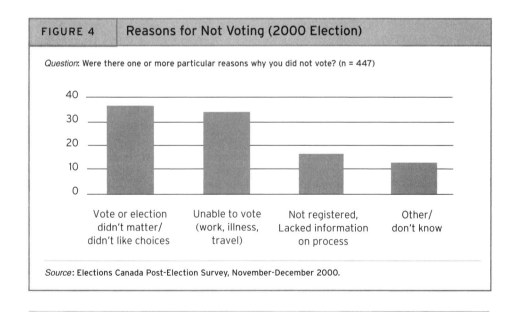

FIGURE 4 | Reasons for Not Voting (2000 Election)

Question: Were there one or more particular reasons why you did not vote? (n = 447)

Source: Elections Canada Post-Election Survey, November-December 2000.

---

[16] The survey was conducted between November 28 and December 11, 2000 by Ipsos-Reid. A total of 2,500 Canadians were surveyed, including 1,400 persons between 18 and 34 years of age.

[17] The voter's card indicates that a person is registered to vote, and states where and when votes can be cast.

[18] Pammett, "The People's Verdict," p. 310.

Thus, it could be that some people did not vote in 2000 because of the switch from enumeration to a permanent voters list. *But this was clearly not the main reason why people did not vote*. Moreover, it cannot account for the general downward trend in turnout, which began before the switch to the permanent voters list.

Yet it is important to note that the reduced accuracy of the permanent voters list, and the greater onus it placed on individual voters to ensure they are registered, likely discourages participation among *particular groups* within the population. As Jerome Black notes, "the impact of the registration system is not neutral across social categories. More demanding regimes will generally lead to under-registration and lower levels of voter turnout on the part of those who are less well-off or who are less favoured (e.g., in terms of income, occupation and education).[19] Those who already feel shut out by the political system are more likely to be put off by the need to register. And because of their mobility, students, young people and tenants are least likely to be correctly registered in the constituencies where they reside. Only about one in four 18-year-olds return the card sent to them by Elections Canada, asking them to agree to have their names added to the list. While Elections Canada tries to address these problems by various means, the fact remains that, for some people at least, the new system of voter registration places a new obstacle in the path of voting.

Changing Times, Changing Values

Canadian society has changed considerably over the past 25 years. Canadians are much better educated, and receive much more information through the media. They are less religious, more morally permissive, more likely to have grown up within a "non-traditional" family structure, and more likely to change jobs several times throughout their working life. They are more egalitarian and open to cultural and other forms of social diversity. They are less accepting of hierarchies and more interested in participating directly in decision-making at work and within society. These changes are not unique to Canada.[20] Researchers argue that many of these trends help to explain why citizens have become less likely to vote.

Religion

The declining importance of religion is especially significant. Only 34 percent of adult Canadians attended church at least once a month in 1998, down from 41 percent a decade earlier.[21] But research shows that "people who regularly attend religious services and who

---

[19]   Black, "The National Registry of Electors," p. 13.

[20]   See: Neil Nevitte, *The Decline of Deference: Canadian Value Change in Cross-National Perspective* (Peterborough: Broadview Press, 1996); Neil Nevitte and Mebs Kanji, "Canadian Political Culture and Value Change," in *Citizen Politics: Research and Theory in Canadian Political Behaviour*, edited by Joanna Everitt and Brenda O'Neill (Toronto: Oxford University Press, 2001), esp. p. 71.

[21]   Statistics Canada, *The Daily*, 12 December 2000. See: *http://www.statcan.ca/Daily/ English/001212/d001212b.htm*. For other evidence on the declining importance of religion in the lives of Canadians, see Nevitte, *Decline of Deference*, Chapter 7.

say they are very religious are more likely to vote."[22] It can be argued people who are more religious are likely to feel their obligation to vote more acutely.[23] And church groups and leaders often encourage their members to vote, especially when issues that are important to the church are at stake. But religion is also important because church attendance helps to foster people's sense of attachment to and involvement in their community.[24] In other words, participation in religious services integrates people into community life in general, and this has a positive effect on non-religious activities like voting.

Political Parties

People's changing values have also made them less likely to identify strongly with any one political party.[25] As citizens become better educated and more informed, they also become more independent in their thinking and less likely to accept the lead of any given political party over the long term. The increasing unease with rigid hierarchies also makes citizens less comfortable with traditional party organizations. Some also argue that with the rise of television as the main medium of political communication, parties have increasingly crafted their election campaigns around the party leader, focusing more on his or her image, and less on the party as a whole.[26] TV elections ads now regularly emphasize the leader's qualities (or attack the qualities of other leaders) and all but fail to mention the name of the leader's party. These trends weaken loyalty to particular parties. This, in turn, has an effect on turnout, because those who are strongly attached to a party will be more likely to vote.

Attitudes Toward Authority

Another factor underlined by political scientists is people's growing sense of personal autonomy and their changing attitudes toward authority. It is argued that citizens today tend to be more assertive and less deferential towards authority.[27] They are also more inclined

---

[22]   Blais, *To Vote or Not to Vote*, p. 52.

[23]   This hypothesis has been put forward tentatively by André Blais. He notes that "the process of secularization . . . has nourished a sense of moral relativism that makes it more difficult for people to be certain that voting is a good and not voting is wrong." See Blais, *To Vote or Not to Vote*, p. 114.

[24]   Blais, *To Vote or Not to Vote*, p. 52.

[25]   Again, this is a gradual but unmistakable trend that is visible throughout the industrialized world. See, for instance, Nevitte, *Decline of Deference*, p. 49; Russell J. Dalton, "Political Support in Advanced Industrial Democracies," in *Critical Citizens: Global Support for Democratic Government*, edited by Pippa Norris (Oxford: Oxford University Press, 1999) pp. 65–66. Dalton reports that "the empirical evidence now presents a clear and striking picture of the erosion of partisan attachments among contemporary publics."

[26]   Wattenberg, "Turnout Declines in the U.S. and other Advanced Industrial Democracies," p. 18.

[27]   The most well-known statement of this thesis in Canada is Nevitte, *Decline of Deference*. See also Dalton, "Political Support in Advanced Industrial Democracies," pp. 67–68 and 74. Dalton concludes that "citizens have grown more distant from political parties, more critical of political elites and political institutions, and less positive toward government. . . . The deference to authority that once was common in many Western democracies has partially been replaced by public scepticism of elites."

to look within themselves for moral guidance. Pollster Michael Adams thinks that Canadians over time have moved away from traditional values (including respect for hierarchy and authority) and have become less "socially inclined or other-directed" and more "inner-directed"—a gradual shift that represents a "significant evolution of values current in our society and culture."[28] For these reasons, contemporary citizens are somewhat less likely to vote out of a sense of civic obligation, or respect for political institutions or authorities. This does not mean necessarily that citizens have an overly negative view of politics (a point that will be covered below), but simply that they are more individualist and less willing to be guided by tradition and moral absolutes.

To sum up, researchers have confirmed that Canadian values are changing. Some will see these changes as positive, while others will not. But none of these changes is *necessarily* a sign that the Canadian political system is in crisis. Rather, they are developments that have taken shape over the longer term and across most industrialized societies. They reflect a variety of profound and likely irreversible changes such as rising education levels, innovations in information technology, the changing nature of work and shifts in family structure.

Political Disaffection

Many observers argue that the decline in voter turnout is a result of citizens losing confidence in their political leaders and becoming cynical about the political process. They see voter apathy as driven by a growing disaffection with politics that, in turn, is fueled by the perception that politicians and political parties are self-interested, dishonest and out-of-touch.

Evidence of cynicism—that is, contempt for the political system—and of a growing lack of confidence in politicians and political institutions in Canada is plentiful:

- According to a recent CRIC survey, 86 percent of Canadians agree that politicians often lie to get elected. And more than 7 out of 10 of those surveyed agree with the statement: "I don't think governments care very much about what people like me think."[29] And there is evidence that these negative views are much more pronounced than they were 20 or 30 years ago (see Figure 5).[30]
- Over the past 25 years, the percentage of Canadians who say they have a great deal of confidence in the House of Commons or in political parties has declined significantly, while the percentage saying they have very little confidence has increased (see Figures 6 and 7).

---

[28] Michael Adams, *Better Happy than Rich: Canadians, Money and the Meaning of Life* (Toronto: Viking, 2000), pp. 19–23.

[29] CRIC survey on Trade, Globalization and Canadian Values, 2001, February–March 2000. See: CRIC, *Opinion Canada*, Vol. 3, No. 23 (June 21, 2000); available online at *http://www.ccu-cuc.ca/en/op/archives/opv3n23.htm#file*.

[30] See for instance: Lawrence LeDuc, "The Canadian Voter," in *Introductory Readings in Canadian Government and Politics*, second edition, edited by Robert M. Krause and R.H. Wagenberg (Toronto: Copp Clark, 1995), p. 371.

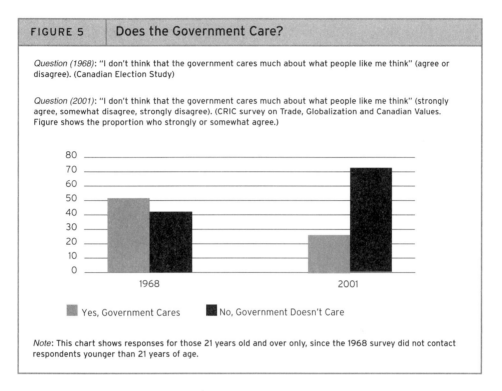

FIGURE 5 | Does the Government Care?

Question (1968): "I don't think that the government cares much about what people like me think" (agree or disagree). (Canadian Election Study)

Question (2001): "I don't think that the government cares much about what people like me think" (strongly agree, somewhat disagree, strongly disagree). (CRIC survey on Trade, Globalization and Canadian Values. Figure shows the proportion who strongly or somewhat agree.)

Yes, Government Cares   No, Government Doesn't Care

Note: This chart shows responses for those 21 years old and over only, since the 1968 survey did not contact respondents younger than 21 years of age.

- Similarly, surveys conducted by Environics show that the percentage of Canadians saying they have little or no confidence in governments rose from about 40 percent in the early 1980s to over 60 percent in the early 1990s.[31]
- Over 50 percent of Canadians surveyed in the 1960s said that they could trust the government in Ottawa to do what is right "just about always" or "most of the time." By the 1990s, only about one-third took this position.[32]
- A 1997 CRIC survey of Canadians between the ages of 18 and 34 found that respondents had less confidence in political leaders than in any of the other eight groups that they were asked about. Almost two-thirds of respondents said that they had "not much confidence" or "no confidence" in political leaders (see Figure 8).

Unlike the previous explanation, which focused on changing values, this explanation clearly implies that the problem lies with the way the political system is working. The point here is not that citizens have changed, but that the political system is perceived to be less and less responsive to people's concerns.

---

[31] Data from Environics Research Group, cited in George Perlin and Andrew Parkin, "Regime Legitimacy," in George Perlin, *Canadian Politics, Volume 2: Canadian Democracy in Critical Perspective* (Kingston and Toronto: Queen's University and CBC Newsworld, 2000).

[32] Data from Canadian Elections Studies, cited in Perlin and Parkin, "Regime Legitimacy."

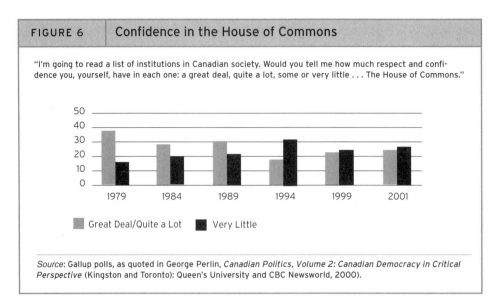

FIGURE 6 | **Confidence in the House of Commons**

"I'm going to read a list of institutions in Canadian society. Would you tell me how much respect and confidence you, yourself, have in each one: a great deal, quite a lot, some or very little . . . The House of Commons."

■ Great Deal/Quite a Lot   ■ Very Little

Source: Gallup polls, as quoted in George Perlin, *Canadian Politics, Volume 2: Canadian Democracy in Critical Perspective* (Kingston and Toronto): Queen's University and CBC Newsworld, 2000).

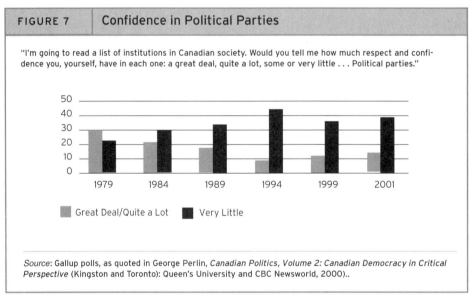

FIGURE 7 | **Confidence in Political Parties**

"I'm going to read a list of institutions in Canadian society. Would you tell me how much respect and confidence you, yourself, have in each one: a great deal, quite a lot, some or very little . . . Political parties."

■ Great Deal/Quite a Lot   ■ Very Little

Source: Gallup polls, as quoted in George Perlin, *Canadian Politics, Volume 2: Canadian Democracy in Critical Perspective* (Kingston and Toronto): Queen's University and CBC Newsworld, 2000)..

Political scientists in Canada have varied views on which factors are to blame for heightening voter cynicism.[33] Some point to the way in which the news media cover politics. Television news emphasizes style over substance and portrays election campaigns as strategic contests among party leaders. This reinforces the sense that there are few major issues at stake and accentuates the negative tone of the campaign—a tone that some

---

[33]   See Perlin and Parkin, "Regime Legitimacy."

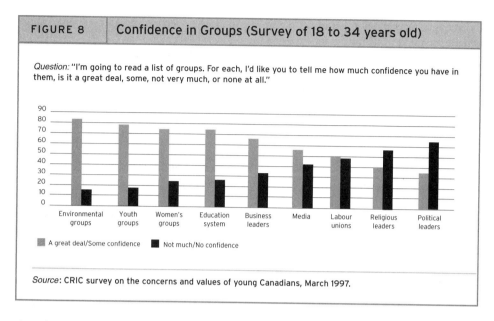

FIGURE 8 | Confidence in Groups (Survey of 18 to 34 years old)

Question: "I'm going to read a list of groups. For each, I'd like you to tell me how much confidence you have in them, is it a great deal, some, not very much, or none at all."

A great deal/Some confidence ■ Not much/No confidence

Source: CRIC survey on the concerns and values of young Canadians, March 1997.

American researchers have shown to "contribute to the general antipathy toward politicians and parties."[34]

Others point to the limited role played in decision-making by the majority of members of Parliament. As power has become increasingly concentrated in the hands of the inner circle surrounding the Prime Minister and his or her key ministers,[35] parliament, as a whole, becomes less relevant as a forum for political deliberation. Backbench and opposition MPs, in particular, are seen as having no power to shape the political agenda and no input into legislation. Citizens are left to wonder if their votes really matter, since in almost every case the MPs they select will be far removed from the centre of political power.

Furthermore, without a meaningful role to play, MPs are reduced to trying to score partisan political points through cajoling and heckling—precisely the activity that increases the public's negative view of politicians.

Discussion

There is much about political turnout that political scientists do not know. One problem that researchers face is that many non-voters simply refuse to be interviewed in telephone surveys about politics. This limits our understanding of why some people don't vote.

Even if we cannot be sure which of the various factors in the single most important one, we can still draw the following conclusion: both the relative lack of competitiveness of the last two elections, and the problems associated with the switch to a permanent voters list,

---

[34] Stephen Ansolabehere and Shanto Iyengar, *Going Negative, How Political Advertisements Shrink and Polarize the Electorate* (New York: The Free Press 1995), p. 112.

[35] See: Donald J. Savoie, *Governing from the Centre: The Concentration of Power in Canadian Politics* (Toronto: University of Toronto Press, 1999), e.g. pages 108, 362.

discouraged a certain number of people from voting. But even taken together, these factors cannot account in full for the longer-term trend toward lower turnout.

This means that the gradual shift in values, along with the increasing political cynicism or disaffection, have to be taken into account. The key point of disagreement is over how much weight to give to each of these two explanations. Those who argue that voter turnout is declining because Canadians, like most citizens in the Western world, are becoming more "inner-focused," more secular and less deferential to authority, are less likely to see cause for alarm. That is because these changes can be linked to developments, common to all industrialized countries, that have little to do with the performance of the political system.

But those who stress the coincidence of lower turnout and greater cynicism about politics are more apt to worry, since the implication is that declining turnout is a symptom of a deeper malaise. Given the apparent extent of political disaffection among citizens, there is little room for complacency. It should be stressed that while the above-noted changed values have been recorded in most Western democracies, the decline in voter turnout in Canada in the past decade has been especially acute. Moreover, the most common type of reason for not voting given by those surveyed in 2000 by Elections Canada was that they didn't think the election or their vote mattered, or that they didn't like the choices they were offered (see Figure 4). This again prompts us to take seriously the idea that the Canadian political system may be performing particularly poorly in the eyes of its citizens.

A consideration of the case of young Canadians, which follows below, further reinforces the sense that all is not well with Canada's political system.

YOUNG CANADIANS: ACTIVIST OR APATHETIC?

Voting and Non-Voting

Younger people are less interested in politics (see Figures 9 and 10) and are less likely to vote than their elders.[36] This is not surprising. On the whole, voters who only recently have become adults will be less familiar with politics. They are at a relatively "care free" stage of life, and have had less opportunity to see how elections could affect their interests.

Many young adults are highly mobile, and so less rooted in their communities and less aware of community needs and issues. For these reasons, they are likely to be less interested in elections. But as they grow older, it is generally assumed that they will become more likely to vote.

The decline in voter turnout raises questions about this assumption. Contrary to expectations, are more and more young people continuing to abstain from voting as they grow older? And are young people today even less likely to vote than they were a generation ago?

---

[36] Blais, *To Vote or Not to Vote*, 52; Neil Nevitte, André Blais, Elisabeth Gidengil and Richard Nadeau, *Unsteady State: The 1997 Canadian Federal Election* (Don Mills: Oxford University Press, 2000), 61; Jon H. Pammett and John Myles, "Lowering the Voting Age to 16," in *Youth in Canadian Politics: Participation and Involvement*, edited by Kathy Megyery, Volume 8 of the Research Studies prepared for the Royal Commission on Electoral Reform and Party Financing (Toronto: Dundurn Press, 1991), 99–101.

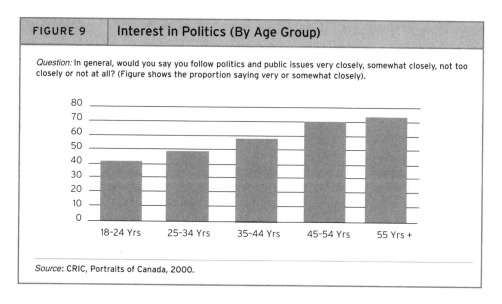

FIGURE 9 | Interest in Politics (By Age Group)

Question: In general, would you say you follow politics and public issues very closely, somewhat closely, not too closely or not at all? (Figure shows the proportion saying very or somewhat closely).

Source: CRIC, Portraits of Canada, 2000.

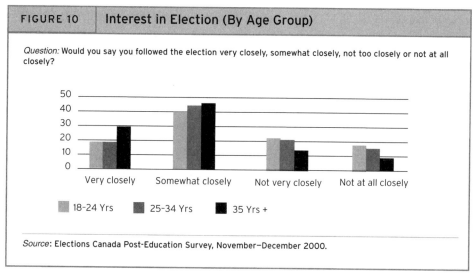

FIGURE 10 | Interest in Election (By Age Group)

Question: Would you say you followed the election very closely, somewhat closely, not too closely or not at all closely?

Source: Elections Canada Post-Education Survey, November–December 2000.

The answer is "yes."[37] The team or researchers leading the 2000 Canadian Election Study have found that, at the same age, turnout among those born in the 1960s is 10 points lower than it was for earlier generations, and it is a further 10 points lower among those born in the 1970s. In other words, turnout for younger Canadians (those born after 1970) is 20 points lower than it was at the same age for those born before the 1960s.[38] This

---

[37] Nevitte, Blais, Gidengil and Nadeau, *Unsteady State*, 62.

[38] André Blais, Elisabeth Gidengil, Neil Nevitte and Richard Nadeau, "The Evolving Nature of Non Voting: Evidence from Canada," paper prepared for delivery at the Annual Meeting of the American Political Science Association, San Francisco, August 30–September 2, 2001, p. 3.

research confirms that it is less and less the case that voters who abstain when they are young are opting to vote as they get older. And this in turn accounts for much of the decline in turnout experienced in Canada; that is, turnout is declining because, as time passes, newer generations of Canadians, who are less inclined to vote, are coming to represent a larger share of the electorate.[39]

Neither Cynicism Nor Apathy

It might be assumed that young people are voting less because they have become especially cynical about politics. But this is not the case.

Elections Canada's recent post-election survey found 18 to 24 year olds are more likely to agree that their vote doesn't really matter, and less likely to agree that it is important to vote. But the difference in the responses given by older and younger people is relatively small (see Figure 11). As expected, the same survey found a very large difference in the proportion within each age group who said they had voted in the election. Clearly, the much lower voter turnout among 18 to 24 year olds cannot be attributed to the fact that they were only slightly less likely to think that voting matters.

In addition, consider the following:

- The same survey asked those who had not voted to say why they had abstained. Non-voters, 18 to 24, were *less* likely than older non-voters to say that they had abstained

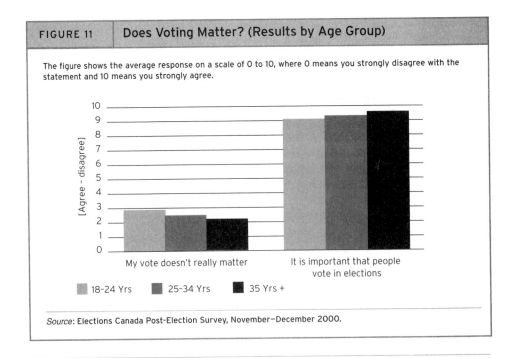

| FIGURE 11 | Does Voting Matter? (Results by Age Group) |

The figure shows the average response on a scale of 0 to 10, where 0 means you strongly disagree with the statement and 10 means you strongly agree.

Source: Elections Canada Post-Election Survey, November–December 2000.

---

[39]   Blais, Nevitte and Nadeau, "The Evolving Nature of Non Voting," pp. 4–5. The authors note, however, that "it also remains to be explained *why* younger generations are less prone to vote than their predecessors" (p. 7). See also: Nevitte, Blais, Gidengil and Nadeau, *Unsteady State*, 63.

because they didn't think their vote made a difference, because the election didn't matter to them, or because they didn't like any of the candidates or the political parties.

• As noted above, a majority of Canadians agree that governments don't care very much about what they think, and that politicians often lie to get elected. But younger people are no more likely to agree with these statements than are older people.[40]

• Data from Environics' *Focus Canada* surveys show that the percentage of those saying they had confidence in governments fell by a dramatic 28 points between 1988 and 1992. However, the decline was less pronounced among younger Canadians: among 18 to 29 year olds it fell by 23 points, whereas it fell by 28 points among those aged 30 to 44, and by 33 points among those aged 45 to 59.

• CRIC's *Portraits of Canada 2000* survey found that young people are slightly less likely to say that the main parties running in that year's federal election are basically the same, and about as likely to say that there are real differences between some of them.[41]

These latest findings confirm previous studies' findings that "young people are less cynical about politics and have higher feelings of political efficacy than do older people."[42] Or, in the words of another group of researchers, "there is no relationship between age and cynicism. It is *not* because they are more cynical that the generation born after 1970 is less prone to vote."[43]

Some commentators also claim that the evidence that young people today are less interested in politics is misleading. While they may be less interested in federal elections, they are more attracted than ever to other political activities at the local and international levels. As is often noted, the cultural, economic and political horizons of young people have become much more global. And where conventional political institutions appear remote, hierarchical and ineffective, community politics is "hands-on," co-operative and promises to deliver concrete results in the short term. In short, many socially and politically engaged young people "do not feel that voting is an empowering form of change. They would rather put their energies into other forms of political engagement."[44]

This argument is compelling. At the same time, it is interesting to note that recent surveys have shown that the views of young adults in Canada are not all that different from those of our parents.

---

[40] CRIC survey on Trade, Globalization and Canadian Values, 2001, February–March 2001. See: CRIC, *Opinion Canada*, Vol. 3, No. 23 (June 21, 2001); available online at *http://www.ccu-cuc.ca/en/op/archives/opv3n23.htm#file*.

[41] Similarly, the IRPP found that young people are less likely to agree with the statement that "all federal parties are basically the same; there isn't really a choice." See: Paul Howe and David Northrup, "Strengthening Canadian Democracy: The Views of Canadians," *Policy Matters* Vol. 1, No. 5 (July 2000), 88. Available from the website of the Institute of Research on Public Policy at *www.irpp.org*. There is one exception to the statement made above: in the CRIC survey, 18 to 24 year olds were less likely than every other age group, *except those over 55 years of age*, to say that all parties were the same.

[42] Pammett and Myles, "Lowering the Voting Age to 16," 101.

[43] Nevitte, Blais, Gidengil and Nadeau, *Unsteady State*, 63.

[44] D-Code Inc., *Social Vision Report: Young Adult Perspectives on Social and Civic Responsibility* (Toronto: D-Code, Inc., 2001), p. 21.

- An Institute for Research for Public Policy survey asked "what do you think is a more effective way to work for change nowadays: joining a political party or an interest group?" Only 21 percent of 18 to 29 year olds said that it is more effective to join a political party, but the proportion of 46 to 60 year olds who preferred this option was exactly the same.[45]
- Similarly, a CRIC survey found that young Canadians essentially are no more likely than their parents to approve of acts of civil disobedience. Seventy-two percent of 18 to 29 year olds said they would never engage in acts of civil disobedience, such as occupying a building or blockading a road—a figure only slightly lower than the 76 percent of 46 to 60 year olds who said the same.[46]

In each case, the real difference of opinion was between those under 60 years of age, and those over that age. In other words, it is the oldest generation of Canadians that has distinctive views about the efficacy of political parties or the legitimacy of political protest, not the youngest.

These limited findings do not invalidate the argument that, increasingly, young people are ill at ease with the country's political institutions. But they do suggest that other factors need to be considered in order to explain the growing reluctance of young Canadians to participate in elections.

Civic Education

One example is the decline in "civic education" in schools—classes that focus on the country and its political system, and encourage discussion of current affairs. Some argue that the education system is not doing as much as it once did to familiarize young people with the political system and its underlying values. This may help to explain the fact that Canadian citizens appear to be less knowledgeable about politics than they once were. As Paul Howe reports, "a sizeable and growing section of the population is woefully ill-informed about political matters. . . . Nor are things likely to improve down the road. Young Canadians are the least politically knowledgeable group in the country, and by a wider margin today than ten years ago . . . . What's more, this relative decline in levels of political knowledge also holds true of young Canadians who have received post-secondary education."[47] Howe adds that those who are less knowledgeable about politics are also less likely to vote.

Perceptions about Government

A second factor is changes in perceptions about government and its role in society. The current generation of young voters came of age during the 1990s, at a time when political debate focused on the deficit and debt problem, wasteful spending and excessive levels of

---

[45]   Howe and Northrup, "Strengthening Canadian Democracy," p. 95.

[46]   CRIC survey on Trade, Globalization and Canadian Values, February–March 2001. See: CRIC, *Opinion Canada*, Vol. 3, No. 23 (June 21, 2001): available online at *http://www.ccu-cuc.ca/en/op/archives/opv3n23.htm#file.*

[47]   Paul Howe, "The Sources of Campaign Intemperance," *Policy Options/Options Politiques* Vol. 22, No. 1 (January–February 2001), p. 22.

taxation. Governments were frequently portrayed as the source of Canada's problems, not the solution. Government program spending was dramatically curtailed, sending young people the message that citizens should become more self-reliant and seek more opportunities outside the public sector. Thus, it is no surprise that young Canadians question the effectiveness and relevance of government and the value of political participation.[48]

Furthermore, for young adults full of creative energy and ideals, the world of politics is arguably less inviting than it once was. Until recently, post-war governments in Canada had been preoccupied with managing economic expansion, creating the welfare state, "nation-building" through constitutional renewal, and promoting peace and justice abroad. But government's role has been curtailed, both as a result of the need to cut spending and in response to the constraints of economic globalization. Once again, it is perhaps no surprise that young Canadians with more ambitious goals are by-passing traditional political institutions.

A Fragmented Community

A third factor is the gradual fragmentation of public communication and debate. Much has been said about the Internet's impact on Canadian society. Some argue that it is a means through which young people can become socially engaged. Via the Internet, citizens with similar interests can form "virtual" communities. But virtual communities are still diffused communities. There is little that connects them to one another or to a larger, all-encompassing community. With the proliferation of virtual communities, the common community becomes less and less visible.

Similarly, developments in other forms of electronic media—including the expansion of cable, satellite and digital television—mean that there are many more channels of public communication to choose from. Fred Fletcher has argued that, among other things, the proliferation of TV channels may bring about a fragmentation of the Canadian public—turning it into numerous micro-audiences.[49] Again, common community is partially eclipsed.

Each of these three developments is important, since research has shown that voter participation is linked to the degree to which citizens are connected with the larger community. Voting is, in part, an expression of one's sense of community. As the visibility or salience of the shared community is eroded for the reasons mentioned above, then one of the most important forces that once encouraged young people to participate in the country's political life is weakened. The problem is not that more and more young people feel hostility towards the political system, but that more and more are indifferent to it.

---

[48] I am grateful to Lisa Young and Phillip Haid for bringing this point to my attention. As one indication of how the effort to contain government spending has affected the lives of young Canadians, consider that average university tuition for an undergraduate arts program doubled over the course of the 1990s. See Statistics Canada, *The Daily*, 27 August 2001, available online at: *http://www.statcan.ca/Daily/English/010827/d019827b.htm*.

[49] Frederick J. Fletcher, "Media, Education, and Democracy," *Canadian Journal of Communication* Vol. 19, No. 1 (1994), pp. 143–44.

DOES TURNOUT MATTER?

Does it really matter if 40 percent of the electorate chooses not to vote?

No

Low turnout could be a sign of what pollster Michael Adams calls a "new consensus" about the need for smaller governments and the reduced importance of national politics in our day-to-day lives. Elections matter less than they did before, he argues, but not because there is a crisis in Canadian democracy. They matter less because governments are doing less, because globalization places more policy issues beyond Ottawa's control, and because citizens are more self-reliant and less willing to be led by traditional figures of authority. According to Adams, "there is life after electoral politics"—by which he presumably means that the health of a society must be measured by more than the tally of those willing to trudge to the polls every four years to cast a vote.[50]

It can also be noted that turnout is not necessarily the best measure of the health of a democratic society. For various reasons, Switzerland has very low turnout at national elections, yet in many ways constitutes a model democracy. Conversely, some countries whose democratic institutions rest on very shaky foundations can nonetheless boast high levels of voter participation.

Yes

There are at least three good reasons why turnout does matter.

Equality of Influence First, it matters because declining turnout sows the seeds of increasing inequality among social groups in terms of political participation and political influence.

As political scientist Jerome Black reminds us, it is important to look at who is voting, and who is not. The decline in voter participation is particularly acute among certain groups within society—young people and those who are less well-off economically. This means that, as overall turnout declines, the active electorate becomes less and less representative of society as a whole; "low voter turnout means unequal and socioeconomically biased turnout."[51] Voters no longer appear to speak with the voice of "the people"—they speak more and more with the voice of those who are relatively privileged.

This reality in turn shapes the behaviour of political parties. As noted American political scientist Arend Lijphart argues, "unequal participation spells unequal influence," a fact that he calls "a major dilemma for representative democracy."[52] Political parties craft their platforms in order to gain the votes they need to win power. There is little incentive for them to aim their appeal at those groups that are the least likely to vote. As non-voting

---

[50] Michael Adams, "The Revolt of the Voting Classes" (30 November, 2000). Available on the website of Environics Research Group at *http://erg.environics.net/news/default.asp?aID=424*. Published in *The Globe and Mail* under the title "Death of Politics."

[51] Arend Lijphart, "Unequal Participation: Democracy's Unresolved Dilemma," *American Political Science Review* Vol. 91, No. 1 (March 1997), p. 2.

[52] Lijphart, "Unequal Participation: Democracy's Unresolved Dilemma," p. 1.

increases among the less affluent, political parties and, ultimately, governments will tailor their messages and policies to an increasingly narrow segment of the population. The result: the political system will seem even less relevant to the less affluent than before— reinforcing their sense that there is little point in voting.

Legitimacy Second, turnout matters because the government's moral authority to govern rests on its claim that it won the support of the largest share of the electorate. Many people may oppose the current party in government, but they recognize that it has legitimacy because it won a mandate from the people.

As more voters abstain, however, the total votes won by the winning party, measured as a share of the number of eligible voters, decreases. For example, the last two Liberal majorities were elected by only 25 percent of eligible voters, whereas at least 30 percent supported the majority governments elected in 1968, 1974, 1984 and 1988. Indeed, minority governments elected in 1972 and 1979 were supported by a greater share of the electorate than were the two most recent majority governments.

What is more striking is that the proportion of the electorate who vote for the winning party is now smaller than the proportion who do not vote at all (see Figure 12). In 1988 for instance, the Conservative party attracted the support of 32 percent of the electorate, while 25 percent did not vote at all. In 2000, as mentioned, only 25 percent voted Liberal, compared to the 39 percent who abstained.

Therefore, as turnout decreases, the ability of the winning party in an election to claim that it has won the support of the public is brought into question. As the American political scientist Ruy Teixeira writes, "as fewer and fewer citizens participate in elections, the extent to which government truly rests on the consent of the governed may be called into question. As a result elites may feel they do not have sufficient legitimacy among citizens to pursue desired policy objectives, and citizens may feel the government is not legitimate enough for them to support these elites and their policy objectives."[53]

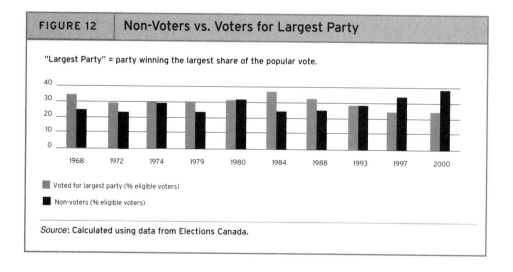

| FIGURE 12 | Non-Voters vs. Voters for Largest Party |

"Largest Party" = party winning the largest share of the popular vote.

■ Voted for largest party (% eligible voters)

■ Non-voters (% eligible voters)

Source: Calculated using data from Elections Canada.

---

[53] Ruy Teixeira, *The Disappearing American Voter* (Washington: Brookings Institute, 1992), p. 101.

Political Community Third, turnout matters because of what it tells us about the health of our political community. It is arguable that the decline in voter turnout can be seen as but one symptom of a growing disconnect between Canadians and their community, a growing distrust of public officials and institutions, and a weakening sense of civic duty or obligation. It is notable that volunteerism is also on the decline, with 1 million fewer Canadians giving their time in 2000 as compared to 1997.[54] Statistics Canada reports the proportion of Canadians who were members of a political organization also fell during that period, from 4 to 3 percent.[55] The problem, therefore, may not be simply that fewer people vote, but that fewer are engaged, as citizens, in the public life of the common community.

This does not place Canada in a very good position to meet the challenges that will likely befall it in the years to come. It is foreseeable that in the next five to ten years the country will have to respond to developments as varied as the completion of the Free Trade Area of the Americas, the need to reinvent medicare, a third referendum on sovereignty in Quebec, the coming-of-age of a young and more assertive Aboriginal population, and the moral issues raised by new medical and biological technologies. The finding of effective policy responses must be rooted in citizen participation, for at least two reasons: first, those advancing creative policy ideas must seek public support in order for these ideas to find a place on the political agenda; and second, governments that cannot connect with citizens are unlikely to be able to build the support to ensure that their policies are accepted and effectively implemented.

It is even possible to suggest that Canada's future depends at least in part on the ability of its population to cohere as a community. Many commentators have stressed how the shifting flow of trade, from an east-west axis to a north-south one, weakens the economic bonds that once tied Canada's regions together.[56] More than ever, Canadian unity must be forged through an appeal, not to economic self-interest, but to a sense of shared values and common purpose. The more citizens become non-participants in key political events, such as elections, and lose respect for political institutions, the greater the likelihood that appeals to shared values and common purpose will fall on deaf ears.

LOOKING FORWARD

If turnout does matter, can anything be done to encourage more citizens to go to the polls? A number of suggestions have been put forward. But at the outset, it should be noted that some of the principal causes of declining voter participation—notably shifting values and rising political disaffection—are not "problems" to which easy solutions readily can be found.

---

[54]   Statistics Canada, *The Daily*, 17 August 2001, available online at: *http://www.statcan.ca/Daily/English/010817/d010817c.htm*.

[55]   Michael Hall, Larry McKeown and Karen Roberts, *Caring Canadians, Involved Canadians: Highlights from the 2000 National Survey of Giving, Volunteering and Participating*, Statistics Canada Cat. No. 71-542 (August 2001), p. 50; supplemented by communication with Statistics Canada.

[56]   See, for instance, John Ibbitson, *Loyal No More: Ontario's Struggle for a Separate Destiny* (Toronto: HarperCollins Publishers, 2001).

Internet Voting

Some argue that new communications technology offers a possible solution. Voters might be more inclined to vote if they could do so online or by telephone. In the wake of the low turnout in the recent UK election, that country's Electoral Commission proposed a review of both these methods of voting.[57] Elections Canada has also studied the implication of information technology for the voting process.[58]

Canadians are currently divided on the question of whether such innovations are advisable. The Elections Canada post-election survey found that 47 percent said they would like to vote online in future elections, if technology allowed, while 52 percent said they would not. Similarly, 38 percent agreed with the proposition that "to make it easier for people to vote, Internet voting should be allowed for a general election," but the same proportion disagreed.[59] (In the case of telephone voting, only 28 percent agreed that it should be allowed, compared to 47 percent who disagreed). Furthermore, 48 percent agreed that "there is too much potential for fraud and mistakes to ever have Internet voting for a general election," and 30 percent remained opposed to Internet voting even in the event that "systems are proven safe and secure." Those most likely to be familiar with computers and the Internet—that is, younger, better-educated and wealthier Canadians—were more supportive of voting online.

Concerns have been expressed about the potential for fraud, should voting online be allowed. For instance, hackers could disrupt the system, cause it to misallocate votes, obtain voters' passwords, or reveal whom individual voters supported.

The biggest problem with voting online, however, has nothing to do with the technology. It has to do with the potential for abuse simply because more and more voters would be voting outside of a polling station, where nothing prevents someone from looking over voters' shoulders to make sure they support the "right" candidate. If families gather to vote around the household terminal, it will be harder for spouses or children to secretly defy the political wishes of their partners or parents. More serious abuses could follow from the actions of unscrupulous political activists. In tightly fought constituencies, one can readily imagine activists armed with portable, wireless computers seeking out otherwise apathetic voters and buying their online votes.

Finally, it can be argued that the visit to a polling station has a positive influence on citizens in a democracy. It is perhaps one of the most important exercises in civic education that voters are likely to experience. The traditional voting process can be seen as a ritual that, like many other rituals in human life, heightens the sense of importance of the act in question. These intangible effects of voting would be lost in the transition to voting online.

---

[57] Kevin Ward, "Britain Looks at Internet Voting, Ballot Redesign to Overcome Voter Apathy," Canadian Press article posted on CBC News website on July 24, 2001.

[58] See "The Feasibility of Electronic Voting in Canada," in *Electoral Insight* Vol. 2, No. 1 (June 2000): 2–5. Available on the website of Election Canada at *www.elections.ca*.

[59] Respondents were asked to use a scale of 0 to 10, where 0 means strong disagreement and 10 means strong agreement. For the purpose of the results cited above, answers from 0 to 2 were coded as "disagree" and answers from 8 to 10 were coded as "agree." The remaining responses were coded as "neutral."

For all these reasons, new communications technology is not the best solution to the problem of low voter turnout.

Compulsory Voting

The simplest way for Canada to boost turnout at elections would be to adopt compulsory voting. As Arend Lijphart argues, "compulsory voting is the only institutional mechanism . . . that can assure high turnout virtually by itself."[60] Countries such as Australia, Belgium and Greece each make voting mandatory, and as a direct result, turnout in these countries is very high.

Compulsory voting does more than increase the number of ballots cast. It can have a "spillover effect," acting as a "form of civic education and political stimulation" that encourages citizens to become more interested and involved in politics.[61] And it can enhance democracy by counteracting the tendency, noted above, for certain groups within the population—notably those who are better-off—to vote in greater numbers than others.

There are two compelling arguments against compulsory voting. The first is that it likely would be opposed by a majority of the public, who would see it as an unwarranted restriction on the freedom of the individual. In a survey conduced last year by the IRPP, only 24 percent supported compulsory voting, while 73 percent opposed it.[62] Compelling citizens to vote might therefore *contribute* to their sense of anger toward the political system, even if a greater number of them turned out to vote.

Second, compulsory voting does little to address the underlying causes of low voter turnout, and might only mask the problem. It turnout were artificially high through mandatory voting, we would not have the evidence of declining turnout to alert us that something is wrong with the political system, with the level of civic education, or the sense of civic duty in Canada.

For these reasons, compulsory voting is not the best solution for Canada.

Proportional Representation

In recent years, Canada's electoral system has been increasingly criticized. Under the existing "first-past-the-post" system, the candidate who wins the most votes in an individual constituency is elected. While this seems fair, it produces results that on the aggregate are peculiar. Examples are familiar and plentiful: in 1993, the party with the fourth highest popular vote (the Bloc Québécois) won the second highest number of seats and formed the official opposition; in 1997, the Progressive Conservative Party won almost as many votes as the Reform Party, but one-third as many seats; in 2000, the Tories won more votes than the Bloc but less than one-third as many seats. And parties regularly form majority governments on the basis of the support of only 2 in 5 votes.

---

[60] Lijphart, "Unequal Participation," p. 10.

[61] Lijphart, "Unequal Participation," p. 10.

[62] Howe and Northrup, "Strengthening Canadian Democracy," p. 86. The question was: "In Australia and a number of other countries, people must vote or pay a small fine. Do you think Canada should have a law like this?"

In response, many argue that Canada should adopt a system of proportional representation (PR). Under PR, parties would be allocated a share of the seats in the House of Commons that more closely reflected their level of popular support. Advocates of PR argue that it is fairer to voters and to parties. In Canada, PR would also alleviate regionalism, as it would make it possible for each of the major parties to win seats in all regions of the country.

But it can also be argued that a switch to PR would give voters added incentives to cast their ballots, and thereby enhance turnout. There are several reasons why this might be the case:

a. PR would do away with "wasted" votes. At present, many voters know that their preferred candidate has no chance of winning in their constituency. Under PR, each vote is weighed in the calculations used to allocate seats in the House of Commons. Therefore every vote counts in a way that it does not under the existing system.

b. PR would make elections more interesting and competitive. Easy majority victories would be unlikely, and election outcomes less predictable. The electoral monopolies that certain parties exercise over specific areas of the country would be disrupted. Smaller parties would emerge as potential coalition partners, giving their supporters an added incentive to turn out to vote.

c. Since the relative standing of the parties in the House of Commons would more closely reflect their level of popular support, the political system would appear more responsive. It would no longer be the case that some parties could lose official party status despite winning a significant portion of the vote, or that others could win large majority despite being supported by less than half the electorate. The more direct relation between votes cast and seats won would contribute to the sense that voting matters.

In general, then, advocates of PR argue that it is more responsive to voters' intentions and therefore removes the disincentives to vote that characterise the electoral system as it now stands. As Mark Franklin writes, "voters are not fools, and an unresponsive system will motivate many fewer of them to vote."[63] From this standpoint, it is perhaps not surprising that researchers have found that, other things being equal, countries that use a form of PR tend to have higher turnout (although there is some disagreement as to how much of a difference PR makes).[64]

Since the lack of competitiveness in recent elections, combined with some citizens' view that voting or elections don't matter, are among factors contributing to low turnout in Canada, the need to examine PR is evident. The government could give Elections Canada a mandate to engage Canadians in a serious debate about changing the electoral system, establish a commission of enquiry to recommend alternatives, and ultimately put the question of PR to the people in a referendum on electoral reform.[65]

---

[63] Franklin, "The Dynamics of Electoral Participation."

[64] See, for instance: Franklin, "The Dynamics of Electoral Participation"; André Blais and Agnieska Dobrynska, "Turnout in Electoral Democracies," *European Journal of Political Research* Vol. 33 (March 1998), pp. 247–248; André Blais and Ken Carty, "Does Proportional Representation Foster Voter Turnout?" *European Journal of Political Research* Vol. 18 (1990), pp. 174 ff.

[65] For some thoughts on how the process of electoral reform in Canada might proceed, see Matthew Mendelsohn and Andrew Parkin, with Alex Van Kralinger, "Getting from Here to There: A Process for Electoral Reform in Canada," *Policy Options/Options Politiques* Vol. 22, No. 6 (July–August 2001): 55–60.

Institutional Reform

A change in the electoral system is only one of a number of possible reforms that could reinvigorate Canada's political system. Others include:

- Enhancing the role of individual members of parliament by relaxing party discipline and allowing more free votes in the House of Commons. (Note that, in CRIC's March 2001 survey of the four western provinces, 55 percent of respondents said that "changing the rules of the House of Commons so that members of parliament can vote more freely, rather than having to vote the same way as their party" was a high priority for making the country work better.[66])
- Further expanding the influence of MPs by strengthening parliamentary committees (Canadian parliamentary committees are much weaker than those of similar countries[67]).
- Subjecting leadership campaigns within political parties to public regulation, in order to make fund-raising and spending, as well as the voting process, more transparent and worthy of public confidence.
- Hold more referendums on key public policy issues (as was done recently in New Brunswick, on the question of video lottery terminals), or allow citizens to initiate referendums on issues of their choice.[68]

Each of these changes could be debated at length. Some may be found to be more appropriate than others. But the need to embrace at least some of these proposals is clear. The challenge is to convince citizens that elections matter, either because their own votes make a difference, or because their elected representatives do. And citizens are sufficiently cynical about politics, and sufficiently savvy, that they cannot be won over by public relations campaigns that offer nothing more than slogans. In order to rekindle their interest in politics, the political system must become more responsive. Only reforms designed to further these objectives can raise public confidence in the system. Without such changes, citizens committed to improving their communities and country will be drawn away increasingly from an ossified parliamentary system.

Thus, declining turnout can be seen as a challenge that calls for a bold, innovative and far-sighted response from Canada's political leaders. They need not look elsewhere, since they themselves have the power to reinvigorate the institutions over which they preside.

---

[66] A report in this survey is available on the website of the Council for Canadian Unity at: *http://www.ccu-cuc.ca/en/polls/data/cric.html*.

[67] See for instance, Peter Dobell, "Reforming Parliamentary Practice: The Views of MPs," *Policy Matters* Volume 1, No. 9, p. 11. Available from the website of the Institute for Research on Public Policy at *www.irpp.org*. In this paper, Dobell outlines several ways in which the role of committees could be expanded.

[68] This idea was widely dismissed during the 2000 election campaign, but did not receive the serious consideration it deserves. See Matthew Mendelsohn and Andrew Parkin, "Introducing Direct Democracy in Canada," *Choices* Vol. 7, No. 5 (June 2001). Available from the website of the Institute for Research on Public Policy at *www.irpp.org*.

More Questions Than Answers

Electoral reform and changes to other political institutions are measures that are intended to make elections more competitive, make parliament more responsive and more relevant, and ultimately raise citizen's interest and confidence in the political process as a whole. In so doing, they clearly address some of the causes of declining voter turnout that were discussed earlier in this paper. But several notes of caution are in order.

First, there is no solid evidence from other countries that measures such as a loosening of party discipline or a revitalization of parliamentary committees will boost turnout. It could be that such measures will only impress those who are already interested and active in politics, yet fail to inspire non-voters.

Second, changes to the political institutions may not have the desired effect unless there is also a commitment among politicians, their advisors and the media to improve the tone and depth of political debate. In the US, for instance, referendums on policy issues are often manipulated by narrow interest groups with ample money to spend on negative TV advertising, and hardly serve to instill greater public confidence in government.

Third, none of these reforms directly address the issue of the long-term change in values, such as decreasing deference to authority or the declining importance of religion. Indeed, as noted above, many observers see such value change as irreversible.

For these reasons, many political scientists in Canada seem uncertain whether anything can be done to reverse the trend toward declining turnout over the long term. This uncertainty may serve to keep our expectations in check, but does not stand as a valid reason to avoid undertaking the modest reforms suggested above.

CONCLUSION: IS CANADIAN DEMOCRACY IN CRISIS?

Does the decline in voter turnout constitute a crisis for Canadian democracy? It is tempting to adopt a "wait and see" attitude—turnout might rise again at the next election, especially in the event that a stronger opposition emerges to challenge the governing party. But this is too complacent an approach. As we have seen, the problem goes well beyond the issue of the lack of excitement generated by the last two election campaigns. For this reason, the trend toward lower turnout may prove difficult to reverse. Even if turnout rises somewhat at the next election, in the coming decade we are unlikely to see, on a consistent basis, a return to the level of voter participation that we experienced in the 1960s or even the 1980s.

Whether or not this amounts to a crisis depends on the extent to which one values citizen participation in politics as a good thing in and of itself. It is true that parliament currently works equally well, whether it is elected on the basis of high voter turnout or on the basis of low voter turnout. In this sense, turnout does not really matter. But if citizen participation in politics is taken to be a fundamental characteristic of democracy, then the situation appears more grave. What is especially worrying is that the younger generations of Canadians—those who are now beginning to move into positions of leadership—are voting in lesser number than ever before. Those who must be relied upon to give the country its future direction and vision presently are much less engaged in the political process than were their parents or grandparents. It remains to be seen what implications this will have for the ability of the country's political leadership, political parties, and civil service to renew themselves and respond to Canada's needs in the years to come.

APPENDIX TABLES

TABLE 1A	Turnout at Provincial Elections

Percentages of registered voters actually voting in provincial elections since 1980 (year of election precedes turnout figure):

Province	1980–1989			1990–2001			Average: 1980–1989	Average: 1990–2001	Change
NF	1982: 70	1985: 77	1989: 81	1993: 84	1996: 74	1999: 70	76.0	76.0	0.0
PEI	1982: 78	1986: 88	1989: 81	1993: 81	1996: 85	2000: 85	82.3	83.7	1.3
NS	1981: 74	1984: 68	1988: 76	1993: 75	1998: 69	1999: 68	72.7	70.7	-2.0
NB		1982: 82	1987: 82	1991: 80	1996: 75	1999: 76	82.0	77.0	-5.0
QUE	1981: 82	1985: 76	1989: 75	1994: 82	1998: 78		77.7	80.0	2.3
ONT	1981: 58	1985: 62	1987: 63	1990: 64	1995: 63	1999: 58	61.0	61.7	0.7
MA	1981: 72	1986: 68	1988: 74	1990: 69	1995: 69	1999: 68	71.3	68.7	-2.7
SA		1982: 84	1986: 82	1991: 83	1995: 65	1999: 66	83.0	71.3	-11.7
AB	1982: 66	1986: 47	1989: 54	1993: 60	1997: 54	2001: 53	55.7	55.7	0.0
BC		1983: 78	1986: 77	1991: 75	1996: 72	2001: 71	77.5	72.7	-4.8

Sources: websites of the provincial elections agencies supplemented by communications with these agencies.

TABLE 2A	Margin of Victory for the Ten Constituencies With the Highest Turnout (2000 Election)

Constituency	Province	Winning Party	Turnout	Margin of Victory[69]
Saanich–Gulf Islands	BC	Alliance	70.6	10.9
Louis-Hébert	Quebec	Liberal	70.8	4.3
Beauséjour–Petitcodiac	NB	Liberal	71.3	15
Miramichi	NB	Liberal	71.4	26.3
Lac-Saint-Louis	Quebec	Liberal	71.7	66.6
Saint-Maurice	Quebec	Liberal	72.5	15.1
Egmont	PEI	Liberal	72.8	11.5
Malpeque	PEI	Liberal	73.2	9.7
Acadie–Bathurst	NB	N.D.P.	75.4	6.3
Cardigan	PEI	Liberal	79.2	1.6
Average			**72.9**	**16.7**

[69]   See note 10.

Chapter 20

E-Democracy: A Critical Evaluation of the Ultimate E-Dream

JARL K. KAMPEN AND KRIS SNIJKERS

Jarl K. Kampen *is a senior researcher at the Centre for Political Science at the Vrije Universiteit Brussel.* **Kris Snijkers** *is an academic researcher in the Public Management Institute at the Katholieke Universiteit Leuven.*

INTRODUCTION

For more than two decades now, modernization of the public sector with the aim of increasing service quality and productivity has been on the political agenda (Pollitt & Bouckaert, 2000). The modernization ideology broke through in the early 1980s and was advocated and spread out in particular by the big consultancy firms and the Organization for Economic Co-operation and Development (van Gunsteren, 2002). The French motto *au plus près des besoins* means almost exactly the same as the American slogan *bringing government closer to the people*. In many government modernization programs, for instance the United Kingdom Action Plan, information communication technology (ICT) plays a central role, a role that it had begun to play since the 1990s. The effect of ICT on modernization processes within public administrations is partly passive and partly active. Or, as the French government put it:

> *Organizational and managerial changes within enterprises have been very numerous during the last twenty years. Not all of these were caused by the introduction of new technologies. However, a good part of them had not been possible if information management systems and infrastructures for communication were not gradually introduced throughout the period. (Ministère de la fonction publique et de la réforme de l'Etat, 2002, author's translation)*

The development of e-government is usually thought to consist of a sequence of distinct steps. A number of models exist next to each other, but all agree that the first two steps consist of presence of government or governmental institutions on the web followed by the possibility of transactions with government by citizens and businesses, whereas the third (and further) step(s) involve(s) interactive government. For instance, Kakabadse, Kakabadse, and Kouzmin (2003) spoke of the electronic bureaucracy model, the information model, the populist model, and the civil society model as e-government applications with increasing complexity. Another useful scheme speaks of the retooling, restructuring, and reframing of government (Paquet & Roy, 2000). On the level of a single administration, retooling means the introduction of ICT, mainly personal computers, in the working process. Restructuring involves the reorganization of the hierarchical (vertical) relationships within the administration. Reframing, finally, implies the reorganization of horizontal relationships among different but related administrations. On the level of government, retooling consists of the introduction of e-voting and of e-services and e-administrations in terms of organization of the front office; restructuring implies the reorganization of services and administrations in terms of their back office; and reframing could mean the introduction of e-democracy and a revision of the governmental system altogether.

In most schemes, it is the final stage (i.e., transformation or reframing) that presumes the largest reforms of government but that is also the least worked out in its concrete contents. In the final stage, e-government in general and e-democracy in particular serve as melting pots for all feasible governmental reforms, ranging from the introduction of referenda and direct democracy to proactive government (the evolution of one-stop shopping to no-stop shopping). In this article, we make a critical evaluation of the ideas and myths that contribute to the ultimate e-dream: that ICT can solve the problems that are inherent to modern representative democracies.

THE DEMOCRATIC POWER OF TECHNOLOGY

It seems unlikely that Alan Turing, the founding father of the computer, imagined that the Turing machine would in the future play a role in the democratic process. It seems equally unlikely that John von Neumann, who developed the synergism between computer capabilities and the need for computational solutions (simulations) to nuclear problems related to the hydrogen bomb, would have thought of such a peaceful application of the computer.

Yet, in the 21st century, there is vested interest in the idea of e-democracy that, in short, [is comprised] of the thesis that accelerated communication of citizens and politicians through the means of ICT will lead to increased participation of citizens in the making of policy in democratic nations. True, Internet has greatly enhanced the possibilities of long-distance written and verbal communication by the "information super highway." Access to information and ability to communicate are indeed crucial factors in a (representative) democracy. E-mail to politicians, chat rooms, forums for discussion, e-reporting, and so on and so forth open unprecedented opportunities for interactions between citizens and politicians.

However, when taking the view that Internet is in fact no more and no less than an upgrading of both the telephone and the telegraph, the question of whether ICT in general and Internet in particular can improve the democratic process boils down to the question of whether in the past Albert James Myer's telegraph and Alexander Graham Bell's telephone have contributed to citizen participation in policy making. Or, to that effect, whether steam engines or any other technical invention have had impact on governmental decision making. Of course, society changes in pace with the progress of sciences and technology (e.g., Lenihan & Kaufman, 2001). But as stated by Ann McIntosh (2001), there is nothing democratic about technology.

Still, as it is well known that modern Western democracies suffer from a decline of trust by its citizens (e.g., Kampen & Molenberghs, 2002; Nye, Zelikow, & King, 1997), it is worthwhile to make an effort to investigate to what extent ICT can help in rebuilding trust. Many of the old problems that exist in Western democracies can in the information age simply be reformulated and need only be preceded by *e*. For instance, the distrust of government of Flemish citizens can be attributed to a great extent to feelings of political alienation in the Flemish population (Kampen & Van de Walle, 2003). Translating this problem to the e-era reduces to equating *digital divide* with *e-alienation*. And so on. If information and communication technology are to improve the democratic process, which is the venture of e-democracy, we must first give an account of the known problems of our political system and then access if, how, and to what extent ICT can contribute to a solution [to] these problems.

PROBLEMS INHERENT TO REPRESENTATIVE DEMOCRACY

There are a number of well-documented problems inherent to representative government, none of which seem to be solvable by the introduction of ICT. According to Weimer and Vining (1989), two factors greatly influence the way that representatives actually behave. First, representatives have their own private interest, in particular job security, and tend to be responsive to their constituencies to maximize the percentage of votes they will receive rather than to be concerned for the broader welfare. ICT cannot play a role in the solution to this problem. Second, given financial and time constraints, those who monitor legislators have typically strong ideological and/or financial interests, leading to the enjoyment of a disproportional amount of influence of these interest groups. That is, in the real world, most people pay little attention to their representatives, and the politically active few tend to obtain influence disproportionate to their number. Lack of interest in decision making shows by decreasing voting activity in the whole of Europe, low interest in confidential posts, and the concentration of decision-making power (Matilla, 2003).

Without doubt, ICT enhances the availability of information and provides means of monitoring representatives. Many web sites of parliaments already offer the possibility to search in (legislative) databases. This gives the citizen the opportunity to monitor the activities of his or her member of parliament. An example of such a database is the Parolis database of the Flemish Parliament. In this database, every citizen can control the activities of the members of parliament, follow the legislative processes, and read full-text transcripts of the debates. However, the information and the means for monitoring are available only to those who own and master the necessary infrastructure, the e-lite say, and representatives are again susceptible to the tyranny of a minority.

Another problem in a representative democracy is the relation between the parliament on the one hand and the public administration on the other. The representatives are elected to control the actions of the administration. ICT offers the administration a lot of strong tools to control the citizens, for example by the development of all sorts of databases and the possibility to connect these with each other (e.g., Van Duivenboden, 1999). Also, other applications such as management information systems and decision-supporting systems are increasingly applied to create a more efficient and effective public administration. Besides the necessity of developing the capacities and rights of the parliament to control these systems, ICT also poses questions on the way data are stored by the public administration. What if an ombudsman wants to reconstruct the behavior of a certain department in a case where the administration and the citizen communicated via e-mail? Are all the messages stored? [And if they are filed digitally, can they be recovered quickly and easily?] Meijer (2002) argued that the implementation of ICT in the public administration offers both threats and opportunities to the controlling branch. The durability and authenticity of data that are stored in a digital way poses some problems: Software changes over time, causing problems of compatibility in that data become inaccessible; furthermore, there are no guarantees that the digital data have not been manipulated or were stored at all. The challenges that are posed by the use of ICT in public administration will demand serious investments if a digital divide between the public administration and its controllers is to be avoided.

PROBLEMS INHERENT TO DIRECT DEMOCRACY

The fact that the logistics of massive referenda can potentially be solved by means of ICT is sometimes used as an argument to introduce direct democracy. Proposals for the introduction of binding referenda, however, were withdrawn by both the Belgian and the Dutch governments in 2002. In both cases, motivation of these withdrawals was based on one of the two documented drawbacks of direct democracy (see Weimer & Vining, 1989), [which is] the risk that minorities will have to bear the cost of inefficient social choices.

Hardly any country has expressed so much skepticism about the concept of e-democracy as Germany. In the aftermath of World War II and because of the bad experiences during the Weimar republic and National Socialism, making the concept of representative democracy an unalienable and unflinchable part of the German constitution has been tried (Hagen, 1997). The expressed fear is that direct democracy or even weaker forms of e-democracy could enhance populism (Holznagel & Hanssmann, 2001). Technocracy, in particular social Darwinism, is thought to be partly responsible for the ideas expressed in Nazism, leading to a widespread aversion [to] technical metaphoric visions in present-day Germany. In fact, Kleinsteuber (2001) stated that the German tradition of tying up the state with technique has been exaggerated in the past to the extent that democracy was lost.

Besides the fear for minorities and populism, a direct democracy poses other inherent problems. How many decisions will be made by a referendum? According to McLean (1989), the amount of time citizens are prepared to spend on referenda is limited. When the frequency of the referenda increases, there is a severe risk that the motivation of the citizens to participate in the decision-making process decreases. Another problem in the view of McLean lies in the risk that citizens can [m]ake inconsistent decisions in a direct democracy. Snellen (1995) called this the problem of a "single issue approach." This means that in a direct democracy a certain problem will be treated as an isolated case. This is, however, not a realistic approach [to] political problems. A lot of policy matters are connected in a complex way and cannot be handled as isolated problems. What if, for instance, citizens vote for a tax reduction on the one hand and an increase of retirement fees on the other? Think about tax or budgetary policies or other issues about which a minority in a certain society has very different opinions. Indeed, there are a lot of subjects [on] which it seems difficult to decide by means of direct democracy: A lot of political issues need some form of negotiation, bargaining, and compromise. The mere fact that ICT helps us to bridge some practical problems of a direct democracy (e.g., the problem of scale) is no justification to actually install a direct democracy. There still is a large difference between a technical possibility and a democratic feasibility.

THE MYTH OF E-DEMOCRACY

The myth of e-democracy was said by Levine (2002) to be based on four premises: the idea that convenience will lead to participation, that the public needs more information, that the Internet is a "massive town meeting," and that in the absence of so-called power brokers democracy will flourish. None of these premises seems to be ultimately defensible. Empirical studies suggest that of all possible reasons to use the Internet, e-democracy is the least impressive (Thomas, 2003). The Internet seems to be a source for information and routine transactions and not for political actions. The key assumption of advocates of the introduction of e-democracy seems to be the theorem that more information is better information. This foregoes the fact that there is such a thing as information overload and also that there is tremendous variability in the quality of information. Undoubtedly, better information can lead to better decisions, provided that policy makers resist the temptation to follow their own agendas, but there is certainly no guarantee that more information will lead to better decisions. Of course, there are also merits to the introduction of ICT in government. In Ireland, for instance, clientilism (casework) has been greatly reduced by the improving of communication channels with the public administration (Janssen, in press; Komito, 1999). But the presumption that ICT will make intensive communications between politicians and citizens possible is not feasible unless the number of representatives is significantly enlarged, which by itself seems to be a defensible idea as a single member of parliament in the 21st century represents quadruple [the] number of citizens that he would have represented in the beginning of the 20th century. To be sure: A single representative can handle only so much information. Democracy by its nature converges to a tyranny so long as its population grows and the number of representatives is kept constant, simply because the ratio of the representatives and the represented tends to zero. Either way, the e-era requires more representatives to handle more information and represent more citizens.

REFERENCES

Hagen, M. (1997). *Computernetzwerke und politische Theorie in den USA* (Computer networks and political theory in the USA). Hamburg, Germany: LIT-Verlag.

Holznagel, B., & Hanssmann, A. (2001). Möglichkeiten von wahlen und Bürgerbeteiligung per Internet (Possibilities of voting and participation of the citizens through the Internet). In B. Holznagel, A. Grünwald, & A. Hanssmann (Eds.), *Elektronische Demokratie* (pp. 55–72). München, Germany: C. H. Beck.

Janssen, D. (in press). Ierland (Ireland). In J. K. Kampen, D. Janssen, S. Rotthier, & K. Snijkers (Eds.), *De praktijk van e-Government in zeven landen van de OECD*. Brugge, Belgium: Die Keure.

Kakabadse, A., Kakabadse, N. K., & Kouzmin, A. (2003). Reinventing the democratic governance project through information technology? A growing agenda for debate. *Public Administration Review*, 1, 44–60.

Kampen, J. K., & Molenberghs, G. (2002). Vertrouwen in De Regering En Tevredenheid Met Het Gevoerde Beleid (Trust in government and satisfaction with pursued policies). In M. Swyngedouw & J. Billiet (Eds.), *De Kiezer Heeft Zijn Redenen: 13 Juni 1999 En De Politieke Opvattingen Van Vlamingen* (pp. 179–191). Leuven, Belgium: Acco.

Kampen, J. K., & Van de Walle, S. (2003). Het vertrouwen van de Vlaming opgesplitst in dimensies en indicatoren (Trust of the Fleming split up into dimensions and indicators). In *Vlaanderen Gepeild* (pp. 175–197). Brussels, Belgium: Ministerie van de Vlaamse Gemeenschap.

Kleinsteuber, H. J. (2001). Das Internet in der Demokratie (The Internet in a democracy). In B. Holznagel, A. Grünwald, & A. Hanssmann (Eds.), *Elektronische Demokratie* (pp. 7–27). München, Germany: C. H. Beck.

Komito, L. (1999). Political transformations: Clientelism and technological change. In J. Armintage & J. Roberts (Eds.), *Exploring Cyber Society conference proceedings Volume II.* Retrieved July 2003, from http://www.ucd.ie/lis/staff/komito.

Lenihan, D. G., & Kaufman, J. (2001). Leveraging our diversity: Canada as a learning society. Ottawa, Canada: Centre for Collaborative Government.

Levine, P. (2002). Can the Internet save democracy? Toward an on-line commons. In R. Hayduk & K. Mattson (Eds.), *Democracy's moment: Reforming the American political systems* (pp. 121–137). New York: Rowman & Littlefield.

Matilla, J. (2003). Participatory e-governance—A new solution to an old problem? In A. Salminan (Ed.), *Governing networks* (pp. 161–170). Amsterdam: IOS Press.

McIntosh, A. (2001). E-democracy: The European experience. *Public Policy Forum, 3,* 1–2.

McLean, I. (1989). *Democracy and new technology.* Cambridge, UK: Polity.

Meijer, A. (2002). *De doorzichtige overheid: Parlementaire en juridische controle in het informatietijdperk* (The transparent government: Parliamentary and juridical control in the information age). Delft, the Netherlands: Eburon.

Ministère de la fonction publique et de la réforme de l'Etat. (2002). *Nouvelles technologies et organisation travail et des services dans l'administration* (New technologies and the organization of work and services in the administration). Information retrieved July 2003, from http://www.fonction-publique.gouv.fr/reforme/admelec/dossiers/travail.htm.

Nye, J. S., Zelikow, P. D., & King, D. C. (1997). *Why people don't trust government.* Cambridge, MA: Harvard University Press.

Paquet, G., & Roy, J. (2000). *Information technology, public policy and Canadian governance: Partnerships and predicaments.* Ottawa, Canada: Centre on Governance, University of Ottawa.

Pollitt, C., & Bouckaert, G. (2000). *Public management reform. A comparative analysis.* Oxford, UK: Oxford University Press.

Snellen, I. T. M. (1995). Informatie-communicatietechnologie en democratie (Information and communication technology and democracy). *Wijsgerig Perspectief op Maatschappij en Wetenschap, 1,* 6–13.

Thomas, J. C. (2003, March). *E-democracy, e-commerce, and e-research: Examining the electronic ties between citizens and governments.* Paper prepared for ASPA's 64th National conference: The Power of Public Service, Washington, DC.

Van Duivenboden, H. P. M. (1999). *Koppeling in uitvoering: Een verkennende studie naar de betekenis van het koppelen van persoonsgegevens door uitvoerende overheidsorganisaties voor de positie van de burger als cliënt van de overheid* (Linking in practice: An explorative study to the effect of the linking of personal data by executive governmental organizations for the position of the citizen as a client of government). Delft, the Netherlands: Eburon.

Van Gunsteren, H. (2002). Voor democratie maar tegen politiek (Pro-democracy but anti-politics). In J. Van Holsteyn & C. Mudde (Eds.), *Democratie in verval?* (pp. 17–32). Amsterdam: Boom.

Weimer, D. L., & Vining, A. R. (1989). *Policy analysis: Concepts and practice.* Englewood Cliffs, NJ: Prentice Hall.

SECTION 4 TERMINOLOGY

Autocratic

Charlottetown Accord
  (1992)

Checks and balances

Citizen

Civic literacy

Civic responsibility

Civil society

Civil Society Organizations
  (CSOs)

Compulsory voting

Concurrent majority (dou-
  ble majority)

Democracy

Digital divide

Direct democracy

E-democracy

E-government

Elections

Electoralism

Enumeration

Factions

Federalism

General Social Survey
  (GSS)

Globalization

Information communica-
  tion technology (ICT)

Interest group (public
  interest group)

Invisible Hand

Keynesianism

Majority rule

Mandate

Melting pot

Multicultural society

New public management

OECD

Parliamentary sovereignty

Party discipline

Permanent voters list

Pluralism

Political cynicism

Political efficacy

Political participation (traditional and alternative)

Post-modern values

Presidentialism

Privy Council Office
  (PCO)

Proportional representation
  (PR)

Public realm

Qualified majority

Quebec Referendum
  (1995)

Referendum

Regime

Representatives

Rule of law

Single-member plurality
  system (first-past-the-
  post)

Social capital

Social movement

Trilateral democracies

Turnout rate

Western civilization

SECTION 4 DISCUSSION QUESTIONS

1. Does Schmitter and Karl's definition of democracy differ from what you have normally understood it to mean? If so, in what way? Why do you think it is so important to come up with a clear definition of concepts such as "democracy" in the study of politics?

2. How would you characterize the relationship that exists between the government and yourself? Do you think that government does more than "simply meet your demands"? Are you a customer or citizen?

3. Given the data assembled by the Centre for Research and Information on Canada, do you think that Canadian democracy is in crisis?

4. If you are eligible, do you vote? Why—or why not? If you are not eligible, would you vote if you could? Why—or why not? Does it matter whether people vote?

5. Kampen and Snijkers argue that ICTs, while increasing the potential for communication between citizens and government, provide limited mechanisms for engaging citizens in discussion, debate, bargaining, and compromise, key requirements for effective democratic decision-making. Are you convinced?

Section 5

Going Global

SECTION SUMMARY

In this section of the reader, we introduce global politics, a field also referred to as International Relations (IR). IR is one of the most prominent subfields of Political Studies, and is similar to domestic politics in that a number of actors are competing for limited resources. But unlike domestic politics, IR is about the distribution of resources at the global level. That means that the "actors" in IR include the nation-state, non-governmental organizations (NGOs), international institutions, and corporations. In a domestic environment, the various participants provide checks on each other's powers. For instance, legislatures offset the powers of the courts or the executive. But in IR, there is no set order to the hierarchy of powers. This leads to the eventual question: who has ultimate authority?

Global politics differs drastically from domestic politics when we consider the matter of authority. All nations have levels of authority, and governments theoretically have the ultimate say concerning policies for their citizens. But IR has no "world government," meaning that states themselves are their own highest authority. This creates all manner of disagreements about who, or what, has the right to decide proper conduct on the world stage. Since we are more connected than we ever have been in the past, some have taken to referring to the global environment today as a "global village." This may be true in part, but it is perhaps also true that we are still as divided as we were in the past. Sometimes, learning more about each other shows us things we don't like about each other.

Many, but not all, of the readings in this section have topics in common with those in the final section, which concerns issues in politics. These interrelated readings show how international events have more and more consequences for domestic affairs. Global politics covers many different aspects of affairs at the international level. The mixed set of readings contained in this section of the book illustrates this.

In the first reading in this section, Ramesh Thakur considers how international security has changed since the end of the Cold War. He suggests that security is just as important now as it was then, although it is more complicated and multifaceted than ever. He cautions that our old definitions do not address the range of security issues we face today. Next, Denis Stairs examines a subject that is not new, but has more meaning than ever: terrorism. Anyone with a passing interest in modern global politics is conscious of the threat that terrorism poses to nation-states. Moving beyond the threat and reaction surrounding terrorism, Stairs asks deeper questions about understanding the phenomenon. He concludes that better knowledge about the causes of terrorism will not necessarily lead us to a solution to the problem. Looking more widely, Louise Arbour takes on an issue that at one time may not have received much attention at all. Humanitarian intervention is more than a "trend," and its growing importance shows the implications of greater connection in the international system. If globalization is occurring (and most agree it is, even if they can't agree what it looks like), then the issues presented by Arbour will require more attention in the future.

Larry Diamond shows how political ideas mesh with current affairs. In his analysis of a very controversial American foreign policy decision—the invasion of Iraq in 2003—Diamond takes up the debate over democracy that we first encountered in Sections 1 and 2: can it be a "universal" form of government? Helpfully, he provides lessons learned and prescriptions for making political change work in Iraq. Staying with foreign policy, Kim Richard Nossal's critique of Canadian foreign relations considers Canada's place in the world. In Nossal's line of reasoning, Canada's loss of much of its former influence in international affairs and the challenges ahead will require a fundamental reconsideration of alliances and objectives. Free trade, always controversial in international relations, gets a careful look in the article on NAFTA by Stephen Clarkson, Sarah Davidson Ladly, Megan Merwart, and Carlton Thorne. Rather than taking a normative or ideological perspective, these authors critique the lack of a clear and workable institutional framework under the NAFTA agreement, creating both threats and obstacles to effective free trade in the region. Finally, on a related topic, David R. Boyd looks at the institutional failures of environmental law, and suggests that we need to move beyond simply moderating the damage created by humans to actually transforming the very relationship we have with nature.

Global politics is a many-sided field. The readings in this section may leave you with more questions than you had before you started, but perhaps with some different answers as well.

Chapter 21

Security in the New Millennium

RAMESH THAKUR*

*Ramesh Thakur is Distinguished Fellow at the Centre for International Governance Innovation and Professor of Political Science at the University of Waterloo.

The business of the world has changed almost beyond recognition over the course of the last 100 years. There are many more actors today, and their patterns of interaction are far more complex. The locus of power and influence is shifting. The demands and expectations made on governments and international organizations by the people of the world can no longer be satisfied through isolated and self-contained efforts. The international policy-making stage is increasingly congested as private and public non-state actors jostle alongside national governments in setting and implementing the agenda of the new century. The multitude of new actors adds depth and texture to the increasingly rich tapestry of international civil society.

In today's seamless world, political frontiers have become less salient both for national governments whose responsibilities within borders can be held up to international scrutiny, and for international organizations whose rights and duties can extend beyond borders. The gradual erosion of the once sacrosanct principle of national sovereignty is rooted today in the reality of global interdependence: no country is an island unto itself any more. Ours is a world of major cities and agglomerations, with nodes of financial and economic power and their globally wired transport and communications networks. Cumulatively, they span an increasingly interconnected and interactive world characterized more by technology-driven exchange and communication than by territorial borders and political separation.

The meaning and scope of security have become much broader. The number and types of security providers have grown enormously, and the relationship between them has become more dense and complex. As well as armed terrorism, for example, states have to contend with eco-terrorism and cyber-terrorism, e.g., the "I love you" bug. All three are cross-border phenomena of global scope and ramifications requiring active collaboration among the defence and constabulary forces, law enforcement authorities and non-government groups and organizations.

In this period of transition, the UN is the focus of the hopes and aspirations for a future where men and women live at peace with themselves and in harmony with nature. Over a billion people living in abject poverty have had neither the spirit nor the means to cheer the arrival of the new millennium. The reality of human insecurity cannot simply be wished away. Yet the idea of a universal organization dedicated to protecting peace and promoting welfare—of achieving a better life in a safer world for all—survived the death, destruction, and disillusionment of armed conflicts, genocide, persistent poverty, environmental degradation, and the many assaults on human dignity of the Twentieth Century.

The UN has the responsibility to protect international peace and promote human development. The UN Charter codifies best practice in state behaviour. Universities are the market place of ideas. Scientists have a duty to make their knowledge available for the betterment of humanity. The United Nations University has the mandate to link the two normally isolated worlds of scholarship and policy-making. It lies at the interface of ideas, international organizations, and international public policy. In an information society and world, the comparative advantage of the UNU lies in its identity as the custodian and manager of knowledge-based networks and coalitions that give it a global mandate and reach.

One recurring refrain in our projects in recent times has been the tension between the twin processes of globalization and localization; a second is the need for partnerships between different actors, including individuals, at all levels of social organization; and a third is the comprehensive and interconnected nature of many of today's major problems that require urgent policy measures. Solutions must be individual-centred, within a framework of human security that puts people first; they must be integrated and coordinated; and they must be holistic, tackling the roots of the problems even while ameliorating the symptoms of stress and distress.

Globalization refers both to process and outcome. National frontiers are becoming less relevant in determining the flow of ideas, information, goods, services, capital, labour, and technology. The speed of modern communications makes borders increasingly permeable, while the volume of cross-border flows threatens to overwhelm the capacity of states to manage them. Globalization releases many productive forces that, if properly harnessed, can help to uplift millions from poverty, deprivation, and degradation. But it can also unleash destructive forces—uncivil society—such as flows of arms, terrorism, disease, prostitution, drug and people smuggling, etc., that are neither controllable nor solvable by individual governments. At the same time, and indeed partly in reaction to globalization, communities are beginning to re-identify with local levels of group identity.

Recommended solutions to the dilemma include decentralization and subsidiarity, on the principle that the locus of action and solution should be where the problems are. There must be active participation of the local government, non-government organizations, and private actors in all phases of planning and implementation. Thus, international democracy promotion should be directed at building local capacity—supporting, financially and technically, the various pillars of democratization processes, the rule of law and the judicial system, and the legislatures, in addition to assisting the conducting of elections.

The combined effect of globalization—both the process and the outcome—and localization is to erode the legitimacy and effectiveness of national governments and intergovernmental organizations. There has been a corresponding decline in levels of resources and support for international organizations, including the UN. In the meantime, a host of new actors from civil society—NGOs, labour unions, churches—have become progressively more assertive in demanding a voice at all top decision-making tables. Sometimes developing countries attach their concerns to NGOs, while at other times NGOs attack the state of affairs in developing countries (slave labour, child labour, environmental laxness).

The solution to many of these challenges lies in global governance. The goal of global governance is not the creation of world government, but of an additional layer of international decision-making between governments and international organizations which is comprehensive—not merely piecemeal social engineering—multisectoral, democratically accountable, and inclusive of civil society actors in the shared management of the troubled and fragile world order.

Partnerships are called for between governments, international organizations, NGOs, other civil society organizations, and individuals. Some countries are beginning to involve citizens more substantially in the political decision-making process through well-designed public choice mechanisms like referenda. We are likely to witness increasing issue-specific networks and coalitions. The UN has the moral legitimacy, political credibility, and administrative impartiality to mediate, moderate, and reconcile the competing pulls and tensions associated with both the process and outcomes of globalization. Human security can provide the conceptual umbrella that brings together the main themes of the Millennium Summit—security, development, environment, and governance—within one coherent framework. This would help to give practical content to the opening words of the UN Charter, We the peoples. . . .

TRADITIONAL SECURITY PARADIGM: TOWARDS A WORLD FREE OF WARS

War lies at the heart of traditional security paradigms, and military force is the sharp edge of the realist school of international relations. The incidence of war is as pervasive as the wish for peace is universal. At any given time, most countries are at peace and long to keep it so. Yet most are also ready to go to war if necessary. Some of the most charismatic and influential personalities in human history—from Gautama Buddha and Jesus Christ to Mahatma Gandhi—have dwelt on the renunciation of force and the possibility of eliminating it from human relationships.

The Twentieth Century captured the paradox only too well. On the one hand, we tried to emplace increasing normative, legislative, and operational fetters on the right of states to go to war. Yet the century turned out to be the most murderous in human history, with over 250 wars, including two world wars and the Cold War, twice as many dead than in all previous wars of the past 2,000 years. Another six million more have died since the Cold War ended.

Confronted with a world that cannot be changed, reasonable people adapt and accommodate. The turning points of history and progress in human civilization have come from those who set out to change the world. This section is a story about a group of unreasonable people who met recently for the first steering committee of "GlobalAction to Prevent War: An International Coalition to Abolish Armed Conflict and Genocide".

The causes of war are many and complex. Our call to end it is single-minded and simple. Cynics insist that war is an inherent part of human society. To end war would indeed be to end history. Maybe. But, so too have crime and poverty always been part of human history. Any political leader who admitted to giving up on the fight to end crime or poverty would quickly be returned to private life by voters. Paradoxically, in the case of war it is those who seek to abolish it who are considered to be soft in the head.

The deadly situation does not have to continue into the new century. We already have resources and knowledge that can drastically cut the level of armed violence in the world and make war increasingly rare. What has been missing is a programme for the worldwide, systematic, and continuing application of these resources and knowledge. GlobalAction offers such a programme, and it is building a worldwide coalition of interested individuals, civil society organizations, and governments to carry it out (www.globalactionpw.org).

For internal conflicts, GlobalAction proposes a broad array of conflict prevention measures to be applied by the UN, regional security organizations, and international courts. For conflicts between neighbouring states, it recommends force reductions, defensively oriented changes in force structure, confidence-building measures, and constraints on force activities tailored to each situation. The possibility of conflict among the major powers can be reduced by fostering their cooperation in preventing smaller wars and through step-by-step cuts in their conventional and nuclear forces, eliminating their capacity to attack each other with any chance of success.

GlobalAction's conflict prevention and conventional disarmament measures will promote nuclear disarmament. Nuclear cuts, in turn, will facilitate conflict prevention and conventional disarmament. Achievement of nuclear disarmament will very probably require both reduced levels of conflict worldwide and some effective and acceptable way to cut back the conventional forces of the major powers, especially their force projection capability with naval and air forces. Countries like China, Russia, and India are not likely to relinquish their nuclear weapons if the main effect of doing so is to enhance the already large conventional superiority of the U.S. Other governments are unlikely to be prepared to reduce their conventional armed forces drastically unless there is evidence that nuclear weapons are on the one-way road to elimination.

GlobalAction's deliberate focus is on violent armed conflict. The world also faces fundamental crises of poverty, human rights violations, environmental degradation, and discrimination based on race, gender, ethnicity, and religion. All of these challenges must be met before human security and a just peace can be fully achieved. To meet these challenges, many efforts must be pursued; no single campaign can deal with all of them. But efforts to address these global problems can and should complement and support one another. The abolition of war will make it possible to focus all remaining energy and efforts on resolving the fundamental structural problems.

One analogy is with domestic violence. Faced with incidents of violence within the family, the first and most urgent order of business is to stop the violence. Only then can we look at probable causes and possible solutions, including if necessary separation and divorce.

FROM NATIONAL SECURITY TO HUMAN SECURITY

The shift from the national security to the human security paradigm is of historic importance. The object of security changes from the state to the individual; the focus changes from security through armaments to security through human development; from territorial security to food, employment, and environmental security. The fundamental components of human security—the security of people against threats to life, health, livelihood, personal safety, and human dignity—can be put at risk by external aggression, but also by factors within a country, including security forces. Over the course of the Twentieth Century, 30 million people were killed in international wars, seven million in civil wars, and an additional 170 million by their own governments. *(The Economist* 1999)

In his Millennium Report, (Annan 2000) Secretary-General Kofi Annan writes of the quest for freedom from fear, freedom from want, and securing a sustainable future. A recurring theme in his report is the importance of making the transition from the culture of reaction to the culture of prevention. This is even more fundamental for the attainment of human security than for national security, as even a cursory glance at threats to human security will show.

Mankind—including the rich countries—will not be able to live free of fear, will not be able to secure a sustainable future, so long as over a billion people live in servitude to want. That is, freedom from want is a precondition of the other two elements in the trinity. The safest and most peaceful communities are composed of individuals who have their basic needs and aspirations met.

The multidimensional approach to security sacrifices precision for inclusiveness. In order to rescue it from being diluted into nothingness, we need to focus on security policy in relation to crisis. Short of that it is more accurate to assess welfare gains and losses rather than increased security and insecurity. Security policy can then be posited as crisis prevention and crisis management, with regard to both institutional capacity and material capability.

Even if we limit security to anything which threatens the core integrity of our units of analysis (namely, human lives), many non-traditional concerns merit the gravity of the security label and require exceptional policy measures in response: environmental threats of total inundation or desertification; political threats of the complete collapse of state structures; population flows so large as to destroy the basic identity of host societies and cultures; structural coercion so severe as to turn human beings into de facto chattels; and suchlike. The annual mortality correlates of Afro-Asiatic poverty—low levels of life expectancy, high levels of maternal and infant mortality—run into several million. Annual deaths—preventable killings—even on this scale cannot be accommodated within the analytical framework of national security, but they can in human security.

The traditional, narrow concept of security leaves out the most elementary and legitimate concerns of ordinary people regarding security in their daily lives. It also diverts enormous amounts of national wealth and human resources into armaments and armed forces, while countries fail to protect their citizens from chronic insecurities of hunger, disease, inadequate shelter, crime, unemployment, social conflict, and environmental hazards: *Na roti, na kapara, na makan—par Bharat mera mahan.*[1]

When rape is used as an instrument of war and ethnic 'impurification', when thousands are killed by floods resulting from a ravaged countryside, and when citizens are killed by their own security forces, then the concept of national security is immaterial and of zero utility. By contrast, human security can embrace such diverse phenomena. To insist on national security at the expense of human security is to trivialize the concept of security in many real-world circumstances to the point of sterility, bereft of any practical meaning.[2]

A recent report on health as a global security challenge concluded that health and security converge at three intersections. (CSIS 2000) First, faced with domestic economic crises and shrinking foreign assistance, many developing countries have had to make difficult budgetary choices to reduce the level of public services. But the failure of governments to provide the

---

[1]   The first part is a popular saying in India; the second is a patriotic boast. The two have been combined for ironic effect: *Neither food, nor clothing, nor shelter—but my India is great.*

[2]   For an attempt to apply the human security concept to the Asia Pacific region, see Tow, Thakur, and Hyun 2000.

basic public health services, including garbage removal, water treatment, and sewage disposal, has two further consequences. It erodes governmental legitimacy, and encourages the spirit of self-help and 'beggar thy neighbour' among citizens at the expense of the public interest. Often the competition degenerates into violence. Thus, the withdrawal of the state from the public health domain can be both a symptom and a cause of failing states. Second, there has been an increasing trend in recent internal armed conflicts to manipulate the supplies of food and medicine. Indeed, the struggle to control food and medicine can define the war strategies of some of the conflict parties. And third, the use of biological weapons represents the deliberate spread of disease against an adversary.

The narrow definition of security also presents a falsified image of the policy process. The military is only one of several competing interest groups vying for a larger share of the collective goods being allocated authoritatively by the government. Environmental and social groups also compete for the allocation of scarce resources. There is, therefore, competition, tension, and conflict among major value clusters. The concept of military security as a subset of the national interest serves to disguise the reality of inter-value competition. By contrast, the multidimensional concept of security highlights the need for integrative strategies that resolve or transcend value conflicts. If they are rational, policy-makers will allocate resources to security only so long as the marginal return is greater for security than for other uses of the resources.

Once security is defined as human security, security policy embraces the totality of state responsibilities for the welfare of citizens from the cradle to the grave. The mark of a civilization is not the deference and respect paid to the glamorous and the powerful, but the care and attention devoted to the least privileged and the most vulnerable. Children, in particular, need and should have the most protection in any society. Regrettably, the many hazards to children's survival, healthy growth, and normal development, in rich as well as poor countries, constitute a pervasive threat to human security at present and in the foreseeable future.

UN calculations[3] show that in the last decade alone, two million children have been killed, one million orphaned, six million disabled or otherwise seriously injured, 12 million made homeless, and ten million left with serious psychological scars. Large numbers of them, especially young women, are the targets of rape and other forms of sexual violence as deliberate instruments of war. The steps taken in defence of the rights of children remain small, hesitant, and limited. The biggest danger is compassion fatigue: we will get so used to the statistics that they will cease to shock us, and we will learn to live with the unacceptable.

Being wedded still to national security may be one reason why half the world's governments spend more to protect their citizens against undefined external military attack than to guard them against the omnipresent enemies of good health. Human dignity is at stake here. How can one experience the joys and the meaning attached to human life, how can one experience a life of human dignity, when survival from day to day is under threat?

---

[3]   For details, see Annan 2001. For the latest annual publication of the most authoritative compilation on the state of the world's children, see UN 2002.

FROM ARMS CONTROL TO INTERNATIONAL HUMANITARIAN LAW

Human security gives us a template for international action. Canada and Japan are two countries that have taken the lead in attempting to incorporate human security into their foreign policies. A practical expression of this was the Ottawa Treaty proscribing the production, stockpiling, use, and export of anti-personnel land mines. The first to impose a ban on an entire class of weapons already in widespread use, the convention was a triumph for an unusual coalition of governments, international organizations, and NGOs. Such 'new diplomacy'[4] has been impelled by a growing intensity of public impatience with the slow pace of traditional diplomacy. Many people have grown tired of years of negotiations leading to a final product that may be accepted or rejected by countries. They look instead for a sense of urgency and timely action that will prevent human insecurity, not just react to outbreaks of conflict.

It would be as big a mistake to interpret the Ottawa Treaty from the analytic lens of national security, instead of human security; as to judge it by criteria devised for the evaluation of arms control regimes. Instead, it falls into the stream of measures that make up international humanitarian law.[5] Such measures derive from motives different from those which prompt the negotiation of arms control regimes, are concerned with different subject matters, involve radically different compliance mechanisms, and ultimately have different political functions. The basic purpose of international humanitarian law is not the exacting one of securing the absolute disappearance of particular forms of conduct, but rather the more realistic one of producing some amelioration of the circumstances which combatants and non-combatants will confront should war break out. While its rules are cast in the language of prohibition, it operates through the process of anathematization.

Sceptical observers of the Ottawa process have focused on such important non-signatories as the U.S., Russia, China, and India; the allegedly perilous simplicity of the treaty, which creates scope for disagreement as to its exact meaning; and the relative ease with which a perfidious state party could move to violate its provisions. These criticisms are, for the most part, misconceived, and arise from a misunderstanding of the functions that the Ottawa Treaty can appropriately be expected to perform. In principle, every country whose participation is vital to the credibility and integrity of an arms control regime must be party to the Treaty. A humanitarian treaty seeks to make progress through stigmatization and the construction of normative barriers to use and deployment. While major power endorsements of the convention would have added significantly to its political weight, amending the Treaty provisions to accommodate their preferences would have greatly diluted the humanitarian content of the regime. The integrity of the convention, as a humanitarian treaty, was held to be more important than the inclusion even of the U.S. The humanitarian impulse proved stronger than the arms control caution. Even those key states that have not signed the Treaty have voiced sympathy for its objectives. To that extent, it has changed the parameters of discussion of anti-personnel mines from a strictly military framework to one that is strongly shaped by humanitarian concerns.

---

[4] Matthews 1989: 176. Matthews was writing in the context of environmental negotiations.
[5] This section summarizes Thakur and Maley 1999: 273–302.

NON-GOVERNMENTAL ORGANIZATIONS

In recent major diplomatic landmarks, like the Ottawa Treaty banning of anti-personnel land mines, the Rome Treaty establishing the International Criminal Court, and human-itarian interventions in Kosovo and East Timor, the impact of NGOs on international public policy has been very evident. The consequence of the rise of NGOs as significant policy-influencing actors is to tilt the balance away from hard to soft security.

There are four broad reasons for the rise of NGO influence. Political space for them opened up with the end of the Cold War. New issues like human rights, environmental degradation, and gender equality came to the forefront of public consciousness. These are issues on which NGOs enjoy many comparative advantages over governments in terms of experience, expertise, and often, let it be noted, public credibility. These are also issues on which it is more difficult to marginalize and exclude NGOs than was the case with the hard security issues during the Cold War.

Second, the global scope and multi-layered complexity of the new issues increased the need for partnerships between the established state actors and proliferating NGOs. They are partners in policy formation, information dissemination, standard-setting advocacy, monitoring, and implementation.

Third, the opportunities provided to NGOs have expanded enormously as a result of modern communications technology that enables people to forge real-time cyberspace communities on shared interests, values, and goals. The Internet and the fax machine have expanded the range, volume, and quality of networking activity. Globally networked NGOs can serve as focal points for mobilizing interests shared by people living in different countries.

Fourth, and finally, people with special skills and expertise have increasingly been drawn to work for and with NGOs, thereby muting some of their earlier amateurishness. The more effective and credible NGOs are increasingly professional in personnel and oper-ations, including research, lobbying, fundraising, advocacy, and networking.

The expanding worldwide networks of NGOs embrace virtually every level of organi-zation, from the village community to global summits, and almost every sector of public life, from the provision of microcredit and the delivery of paramedical assistance to envi-ronmental and human rights activism. Much of the UN's work in the field involves inti-mate partnerships with dedicated NGOs. They can complement UN efforts in several ways.

1. The presence of NGOs in the field can be a vital link in providing early warning for dealing with humanitarian crises.
2. Their specialized knowledge and contacts can be important components of the post-crisis peace-building process.
3. They can mediate between the peace and security functions of intergovernmental organizations and the needs and wants of local civilian populations.
4. They can exert a positive influence on the restoration of a climate of confidence for rehabilitation and reconstruction to take place.

This is not to imply that states are being replaced by NGOs and international organi-zations—far from it. Nor does it mean that all NGOs are 'good' ones, always on the side of angels. Instead we must confront, address, and redress the problem of unelected, unac-countable, unrepresentative, and self-aggrandizing NGOs. They can be just as undemocra-tic as the governments and organizations they criticize, and represent single-issue vested interests such as the gun lobby. By contrast, most industrialized country governments are multipurpose organizations trying to represent the public interest by the choice of the voters. In many developing countries, societies are busy building sound national governments as the prerequisite to effective governance: good governance is not possible without effective government. However, it does imply that national governments and international organizations will have to learn to live with the rise of NGOs. Indeed, those who learn to exploit the new opportunities for partnership between the different actors will be among the more effective new-age diplomats.

HUMAN RIGHTS

NGOs have been especially active, often intrusive, and sometimes even obtrusive on human rights. Fifty years ago, conscious of the atrocities committed by the Nazis while the world looked silently away, the UN adopted the Universal Declaration of Human Rights. It is the embodiment and the proclamation of the human rights norm. Covenants in 1966 add force and specificity, affirming both civil-political and social-economic-cultural rights, without privileging either. Together with the Declaration, they map out the international human rights agenda, establish the benchmark for state conduct, inspire provisions in many national laws and international conventions, and provide a beacon of hope to many whose rights are snuffed out by brutal regimes.

A right is a claim, an entitlement that may be neither conferred nor denied. A human right, owed to every person simply as a human being, is inherently universal. Held only by human beings, but equally by all, it does not flow from any office, rank, or relationship.

The idea of universal rights is denied by some who insist that moral standards are always culture-specific. If value relativism were to be accepted literally, then no tyrant—Hitler, Stalin, Idi Amin, Pol Pot—could be criticized by outsiders for any action. Relativism is often the first refuge of repressive governments. The false dichotomy between development and human rights is often a smoke-screen for corruption and cronyism. Relativism requires an acknowledgement that each culture has its own moral system. Government behaviour is still open to evaluation by the moral code of its own society. Internal moral standards can comply with international conventions; the two do not always have to diverge. The fact that moral precepts vary from culture to culture does not mean that different peoples do not hold some values in common.

Few, if any, moral systems proscribe the act of killing absolutely under all circumstances. At different times, in different societies, war, capital punishment, or abortion may or may not be morally permissible. Yet, for every society, murder is always wrong. All societies require retribution to be proportionate to the wrong done. All prize children, the link between succeeding generations of human civilization; every culture abhors their abuse.

The doctrine of national security has been especially corrosive of human rights. It is used frequently by governments, charged with the responsibility to protect citizens, to assault them instead. Under military rule, the instrument of protection from without becomes the means of attack from within.

The UN—an organization of, by, and for member states—has been impartial and successful in a standard-setting role, selectively successful in monitoring abuses, and almost feeble in enforcement. Governments usually subordinate considerations of UN effectiveness to the principle of non-interference.

The modesty of UN achievement should not blind us to its reality. The Universal Declaration embodies the moral code, political consensus, and legal synthesis of human rights. The world has grown vastly more complex in the 50 years since. But the simplicity of the declaration's language belies the passion of conviction underpinning it. Its elegance has been the font of inspiration down the decades; its provisions comprise the vocabulary of complaint.

Activists and NGOs use the declaration as the concrete point of reference against which to judge state conduct. The covenants require the submission of periodic reports by signatory countries, and so entail the creation of long-term national infrastructures for the protection and promotion of human rights. UN efforts are greatly helped by NGOs and other elements of civil society. NGOs work to protect victims, and contribute to the development and promotion of social commitment and the enactment of laws reflecting the more enlightened human rights culture.

Between them, the UN and NGOs have achieved many successes. National laws and international instruments have been improved, many political prisoners have been freed, and some victims of abuse have been compensated. The most recent advances on international human rights are the progressive incorporation of wartime behaviour and policy within the prohibitionary provisions of humanitarian law, e.g., the Ottawa Treaty, which subordinated military calculations to humanitarian concerns about a weapon that cannot distinguish a soldier from a child. In 1998 the world community established the first International Criminal Court. The U.S. absence from both shows the extent to which human rights have moved ahead of their strongest advocate in the past.

HUMANITARIAN INTERVENTION

The refusal to accept the discipline of universal norms of international humanitarian law is especially difficult to fathom in the case of a country that insists on the right to humanitarian intervention. We cannot accept the doctrine that any one state or coalition can decide when to intervene with force in the internal affairs of other countries, for down that path lies total chaos. Nevertheless, the doctrine of national sovereignty in its absolute and unqualified form, which gave the most brutal tyrant protection against attack from without while engaged in oppression within, has gone with the wind. On the other hand, war is itself a major humanitarian tragedy that can be justified under only the most compelling circumstances regarding the provocation, the likelihood of success—bearing in mind that goals are metamorphosed in the crucible of war once started—and the consequences that may reasonably be predicted. And the burden of proof rests on the proponents of force, not on dissenters.

If the Gulf War marked the birth of the new world order after the Cold War, Somalia was the slide into the new world disorder and Rwanda marked the loss of innocence after the end of the Cold War. Worse was to follow in the 'safe area' of Srebrenica in July 1995 in a tragedy that, in the words of the official UN report, 'will haunt our history forever'. (UN 1998: 503)

While Rwanda stands as the symbol of inaction in the face of genocide, Kosovo raised many questions about the consequences of action when the international community is divided in the face of a humanitarian tragedy. (Schnabel and Thakur 2000) It confronts us with an abiding series of challenges regarding humanitarian intervention: is it morally just, legally permissible, militarily feasible, and politically possible? What happens when the different lessons of the Twentieth Century, encapsulated in such slogans as 'no more wars' and 'no more Auschwitzes', come into collision? Who decides, following what rules of procedure and evidence, that mass atrocities have been committed, by which party, and what the appropriate response should be?

To supporters, NATO cured Europe of the Milosevic-borne disease of ethnic cleansing. The spectre of racial genocide had come back to haunt Europe from the dark days of the Second World War. Military action outside the UN framework was not NATO's preferred option of choice, Rather, its resort to force was a critical comment on the institutional hurdles to effective and timely action by the UN. To critics, however, the NATO cure greatly worsened the Milosevic disease. The trickle of refugees before the war turned into a flood during it, and afterwards the Serbs were ethnically cleansed by vengeful Albanians.

The sense of moral outrage provoked by humanitarian atrocities must be tempered by an appreciation of the limits of power, a concern for international institution-building, and a sensitivity to the law of unintended consequences. In today's unstable world full of complex conflicts, we face the painful dilemma of being 'damned if we do and damned if we don't'.

- To respect sovereignty all the time is to be complicit in human rights violations sometimes.
- To argue that the UN Security Council must give its consent to humanitarian war is to risk policy paralysis by handing over the agenda to the most egregious and obstreperous.
- To use force unilaterally is to violate international law and undermine world order.

The bottom-line question is this: faced with another Holocaust or Rwanda-type genocide on the one hand and a Security Council veto on the other, what should we do? Because there is no clear answer to this poignant question within the existing consensus as embodied in the UN Charter, a new consensus on humanitarian intervention is urgently needed.

The UN Charter contains an inherent tension between the principles of state sovereignty with the corollary of non-intervention, and the principles of human rights. In the first four decades of the Charter's existence, state sovereignty was privileged almost absolutely over human rights, with the one significant exception of apartheid in South Africa. The balance tilted a little in the 1990s, and is more delicately poised between the two competing principles at the start of the new millennium. The indictment of President Slobodan Milosevic as a war criminal, as well as the arresting saga of former Chilean President Augusto Pinochet, shows the inexorable shift from the culture of impunity of yesteryears to a culture of accountability at the dawn of the Twenty-first Century.

The UN Security Council lies at the heart of the international law enforcement system. The justification for bypassing it to launch an offensive war remains problematic, and the precedent that was set remains deeply troubling. By fighting and defeating Serbia, NATO became the tool for the KLA policy of inciting Serb reprisals through terrorist attacks in order to provoke NATO intervention. Communities, bitterly divided for centuries, cannot be forced by outsiders to live together peacefully. Another lesson that has been reinforced is that it is easier to bomb than to build. The willingness of the strong to fund a campaign of destruction stands in marked contrast to the reluctance of the rich—who happen to be almost the same group of countries—to find far less money for reconstruction. In turn, this seriously, if retrospectively, undermines the humanitarian claims for having gone to war.

Many of today's wars are nasty, brutish, anything but short, and mainly internal. The world community cannot help all victims, but must step in where it can make a difference. However, unless the member states of the UN agree on some broad principles to guide interventions in similar circumstances, the Kosovo precedent will have dangerously undermined world order. Not being able to act everywhere can never be a reason for not acting where effective intervention is both possible and urgently needed. Selective indignation is inevitable, for we simply cannot intervene everywhere, every time. However, community support for selective intervention will quickly dissipate if the only criterion of selection is friends (where the norm of non-intervention has primacy) versus adversaries (when the right to intervene is privileged).

In addition, we must still pursue policies of effective indignation. Humanitarian intervention must be collective, not unilateral. And it must be legitimate, not in violation of the agreed upon rules that comprise the foundations of world order. Being the indispensable power can temper one into being indisposed to accept the constraints of multilateral diplomacy. However, being indispensable does not confer the authority to dispense with the legitimacy of the UN as the only entity that can speak in the name of the international community. The reason for much disquiet around the world with the precedent of NATO action in Kosovo was not because their abhorrence of ethnic cleansing was any less. Rather, it was because of their dissent from a world order that permits or tolerates unilateral behaviour by the strong, and their preference for an order in which principles and values are embedded in universally applicable norms with the rough edges of power softened by institutionalized multilateralism.

THE UNITED NATIONS

It used to be said during the Cold War that the purpose of NATO was to keep the Americans in, the Germans down, and the Russians out. Does Kosovo mark a turning point, changing NATO into a tool for keeping the Americans in, the Russians down, and the UN out?

International organizations are an essential means of conducting world affairs more satisfactorily than would be possible under conditions of international anarchy or total self-help. The UN lies at their legislative and normative centre. If it did not exist, we would surely have to invent it. Yet its founding vision of a world community equal in rights and united in action is still to be realized.

For the cynics, the UN can do nothing right and is the source of many ills. For the romantics, the UN can do no wrong and is the solution to all the world's problems. Its failures reflect the weakness of member states, prevented only by a lack of political will from fulfilling its destiny as the global commons, the custodian of the international interest, and the conscience of all humanity.

The UN Charter was a triumph of hope and idealism over the experience of two world wars. The flame flickered in the chill winds of the Cold War, but has not yet died out. In the midst of the swirling tides of change, the UN must strive for a balance between the desirable and the possible. The global public goods of peace, prosperity, sustainable development, and good governance cannot be achieved by any country acting on its own. The UN is still the symbol of our dreams for a better world, where weakness can be compensated by justice and fairness, and the law of the jungle replaced by the rule of law.

The innovation of peacekeeping notwithstanding, the UN has not fully lived up to expectations in securing a disarmed and peaceful world. As with sustainable development, which seeks to strike a balance between growth and conservation, the UN must be at the centre of efforts to achieve sustainable disarmament, i.e., the reduction of armaments to the lowest level where the security needs of any one country at a given time, or any one generation over time, are met without compromising the security and welfare needs of other countries or future generations.

The UN system can take justified pride in mapping the demographic details of the human family, and also in the stupendous improvements to human welfare that have been achieved. The advances in health, life expectancy, and satisfaction of basic needs and other desires were truly phenomenal over the course of the Twentieth Century. The symbolic six billionth child was born just recently.

At the same time, as the sun rises on the new century and illumines some of the darker legacies of the last one, we should engage in sober reflection and sombre introspection. It is simply not acceptable that:

- at a time of unprecedented economic prosperity and stock market booms in some parts of the world, millions of people should continue to be condemned to a life of poverty, illiteracy, and ill-health;
- the combined GDP of the 48 least developed countries should be less than the assets of the world's three richest people;
- the annual income of 2.5 billion—47 per cent—of the world's poorest people should be less than that of the richest 225.

The need for international assistance in many continents is an unhappy reminder of man's inhumanity against fellow man and his rapaciousness against nature. Secretary-General Kofi Annan has noted that there were three times as many major natural disasters in the 1990s as in the 1960s. (Annan 2000: 58, fig. 11) Moreover, most disaster victims live in developing countries. Poverty and the pressures of population force growing numbers of people to live in harm's way at the same time that unsound development and environmental practices place more of nature at risk. The rich reap the benefits, the poor pay the price.

Success that is sustained requires us all to make a greater commitment to the vision and values of the UN, and to make systematic use of the UN forum and modalities for managing and ending conflicts. People continue to look to the UN to guide them and protect them when the tasks are too big and complex for nations and regions to handle by themselves. The comparative advantages of the UN are its universal membership, political legitimacy, administrative impartiality, technical expertise, convening and mobilizing power, and the dedication of its staff. Its comparative disadvantages are excessive politicization, ponderous pace of decision-making, impossible mandate, high cost structure, insufficient resources, rigid bureaucracy, and institutional timidity. Many of the disadvantages are the products of demands and intrusions by the 188 member states that own and control the organization, but some key members disown responsibility for giving it the requisite support and resources. For the UN to succeed, the world community must match the demands made on the organization with the means given to it.

The UN represents the idea that unbridled nationalism and the raw interplay of power must be mediated and moderated in an international framework. It is the centre for harmonizing national interests and forging the international interest. Only the UN can legitimately authorize military action on behalf of the entire international community, instead of a select few. However, the UN does not have its own military and police forces, and a multinational coalition of allies can offer a more credible and efficient military force when robust action is needed and warranted. What will be increasingly needed in the future are partnerships of the able, the willing, and the high-minded, with the duly authorized. What we should most fear are partnerships of the able, the willing, and the low-minded, in violation of due process. What if the UN Security Council itself acts in violation of the Charter of the UN? Unlike domestic systems, there is no independent judicial check on the constitutionality of Security Council decisions. No liberal democracy would tolerate such a situation domestically; why should liberal democrats, who generally lead the charge for humanitarian intervention, find it acceptable internationally?

The UN has to strike a balance between realism and idealism. Its decisions must reflect current realities of military and economic power. It will be incapacitated if it alienates its most important members, but it will also lose credibility if it compromises core values. The UN is the repository of international idealism, and utopia is fundamental to its identity. Even the sense of disenchantment and disillusionment on the part of some cannot be understood other than against this background.

The learning curve of human history shows that the UN ideal can be neither fully attained nor abandoned. Like most organizations, the UN is condemned to an eternal credibility gap between aspiration and performance. The real challenge is to ensure that the gap does not widen, but stays within a narrow band. Sustained, coordinated efforts can turn killing fields into playing fields and rice fields. Success comes from having the courage to fail. If you have never failed, then you have not tried enough: you have not pushed yourself hard enough, not tested the limits of your potential.

REFERENCES

Annan, Kofi A. (2000). *We the Peoples: The Role of the United Nations in the 21st Century* (New York: UN Department of Public Information).

Annan, Kofi A. (2001). *We the Children: End-decade review of the follow-up to the World Summit for Children,* Report of the Secretary-General: A/S-27/3 (New York: United Nations) May 4.

CSIS (2000). "Contagion and Conflict: Health as a Global Security Challenge. A report of the Chemical and Biological Arms Control Institute and the CSIS International Security Programme," (Washington DC: Centre for Strategic and International Studies) January.

GlobalAction website address: www.globalactionpw.org.

Mathews, Jessica Tuchman (1989). "Redefining Security," *Foreign Affairs* (Spring):68.

Schnabel, Albrecht and Ramesh Thakur (2000) eds. *Kosovo and the Challenge of Humanitarian Intervention: International Citizenship, Selective Indignation, and Collective Action* (Tokyo: United Nations University Press).

Thakur, Ramesh and William Maley (1999). "The Ottawa Convention on Landmines: A Landmark Humanitarian Treaty in Arms Control?" *Global Governance* 5.3 (July–September):273–302.

The Economist (1999). "Freedom's Journey," survey. September 11.

Tow, William T., Ramesh Thakur, and In-taek Hyun, eds, (2000). *Asia's Emerging Regional Order: Reconciling Traditional and Human Security* (Tokyo: United Nations University Press).

UN (1999). "Report of the Secretary-General Pursuant to General Assembly," Resolution 53/35 1998 (New York: UN Secretariat) November.

UN (2002). *The State of the World's Children 2002* (New York: United Nations Children Fund).

Chapter 22

9/11 "Terrorism," "Root Causes" and All That: Policy Implications of the Socio-Cultural Argument

DENIS STAIRS*

Denis Stairs is Professor Emeritus of Political Science at Dalhousie University, Halifax.

The attacks on New York and Washington a year ago were ghastly phenomena. They killed (most Westerners would argue) the innocent. They also killed by surprise. They killed, too, in large numbers. And they killed to extraordinarily symbolic effect. Of the two primary targets, one—the Pentagon—was the official home of the most powerful and sophisticated military machine ever devised by humankind, and the other—the World Trade Center— manifested the capitalist enterprise not only of the United States, but of the entire OECD world. If the Great Republic presides over a hegemonic empire, this was a frontal assault on the two core components of its imperial being.

It was an unfamiliar experience, and stunningly exotic. Continental Americans had not been so directly attacked by forces emanating from an overseas politics since the War of 1812. That the explosive projectiles used against them should be contrived of their own civilian airliners compounded the horror, deepened the disbelief. Hasty conclusions were drawn. Things would never be the same. A new kind of vigilance was required, and a new kind of "war" had to be fought. For the instrument of the enemy was "terrorism," and terrorism is "special."

As understandable as this last conclusion may be, it warrants a closer look. *Why* do we think of terrorism as "special"? Why, indeed, do we think of it as "terrorism" at all? For the term itself is politically loaded. One observer's "terrorism" may be another's legitimate act of resistance to oppression. Such arguments over terminology, the contrarious often assert, reflect nothing more than a difference of perspective—a difference very reminiscent of a similar phenomenon in the disarmament trade. As the old saw has it, whether you think a weapon is "defensive" or "offensive" depends on whether you're standing behind the trigger or in front of it.

But there may be a difference. We think of terrorism as both "special" and objectively identifiable not just because our security personnel have trouble dealing with it, but also because it seems *aberrational*. In effect, we regard it as a pathology—a pathology that is particularly awful (a) because it's violent, (b) because the violence is often (although not always) directed to the random slaughter of the innocent, and (c) because it sometimes (again, not always) requires for its successful execution the certain death of the terrorist— a characteristic that seems to connote the presence of an alarming dose of wantonly fanatical "irrationality." And since it *is* "special" in these ways, the phenomenon appears also to require a special kind of explanation, and possibly a special kind of policy response.

From the political scientist's point of view, on the other hand, terrorism is not a manifestation of pathological behaviour at all. Quite the contrary. It is simply an *instrument of politics,* a technique for getting one's way, a means of changing the prevailing pattern of who gets what, when and how.

Moreover, it is not in the least bit unusual in being violent. All sorts of instruments of politics involve death and destruction, and most political authorities are quite good at mounting "just cause" reasons for their deployment.

Nor is terrorism unique in its targeting of the innocent. We could ask the ghost of Hermann Goering. Or the bombers of Dresden. Or the architects of the cataclysms of Hiroshima and Nagasaki. Or the inventors of the doctrine of Mutual Assured Destruction. Or any of a multitude of others, great and small.

Nor, finally, is it singular in demanding the death of its perpetrators. In this respect (although perhaps not in other respects), *everyone* compares it with the performance of *kamikaze* pilots in World War II. But it could be compared in modern times also with the behaviour of self-immolating Buddhist priests in Vietnam. It could even be compared with the extraordinary courage exhibited by many of those who have received, posthumously, the Victoria Cross (Canadians among them).

"Terrorist" behaviour, in short, is not "psychotic" behaviour, even if we were to find on close examination that some individual terrorists (like many of the clandestine members of the Communist Party in the United States in the 1950s and 1960s) give evidence of having social or psychological problems of one sort or another.

It may therefore be more instructive to think of terrorism as a political activity akin to guerrilla warfare—a phenomenon upon which there is a massive literature, much of it linked in the 20th century to the politics of decolonization, and informed by the writings and practices of Mao Tse-tung, Che Guevara, General (Vo Nguyen) Giap and others of that ilk. Among other things, this has the advantage of reminding us that terrorism, like other forms of guerrilla warfare, is a very *unpleasant* activity, entailing enormous—and often the ultimate—sacrifice. As an instrument of politics, therefore, it is not the instrument of first choice but the instrument of last resort. It is used only where other instruments are unavailable, or, if available, are unequal to the political task—that is, in situations where the tactics of conventional politics are denied to the political actors involved, or have no prospect of being effective, and where the advantage in terms of the more conventional instruments of force (armies and police) is very clearly held by the other side.

Cognoscenti will regard these as commonplace observations, but they help to open up the question of "root causes" and thereby lead us directly to a consideration of the sociocultural factor as a source of terrorist behaviour. This is because playing politics with the intensity of motivation that recourse to terrorism entails requires a deep attachment to a *cause*—a cause for which the terrorist is actually prepared to die, and to die, moreover, not by accident but wilfully, by his or her own hand.

Usually, attachment to the cause has to be shared (although perhaps not so intensely) by others as well, since such sharing of purposes is essential to the creation of a wider base of support. Hence Mao Tse-tung's famous dictum that guerrilla fighters have to be like "fish in the sea"—a view which has been echoed by almost all modern authorities on the subject, irrespective of which side of the battle they have been on.

In the 9/11 context, of course, the guerrillas, or the terrorists (like the corporate and other agents of the secular world of modern liberalism and Western capitalism that they appear to so profoundly hate), have gone "transnational," so that the areas in which they are operating are geographically distant from the sea that ultimately provides their sustenance. Their local target communities don't even know they're there—until it's too late. But that is simply a new wrinkle on an ancient political phenomenon, a wrinkle introduced (like so much else in the modern world) with the help of technology.

For the purpose of the present discussion, however, the focus needs to be on the "cause" itself, because this, presumably, is where the socio-cultural factor (like other potential candidates for "root cause" status) comes into play. Culturally bound assumptions, after all, help human beings everywhere to define themselves, and what they want. They also help them to define their enemies, and what they think their enemies want. Above all, they help them to determine how much they *care*—how much they think the contested issues really matter.

The prevailing societal culture, along with the processes by which it is either spontaneously learned or systematically inculcated, helps, in short, to give definition to the politics. (It does this, incidentally, as much for the forces of the establishment—and in the present situation that means for *us*—as it does for the forces of those who see themselves as gravely dishonoured, or gravely dispossessed.)

But this analysis leads to a problem. Certainly it leads to a problem when we focus on terrorism as organized political behaviour, as opposed to concentrating on the motivations of particular individuals who may happen to engage in terrorist acts. Simply put, this is because the cultural variables—the cultural drivers—affect a much larger proportion of the population than the one we associate with the relatively small community of terrorists and their immediate supporters. That being so, it appears that other things have to be going on—that the cleavages of identity and culture have to be reinforced by cleavages of another kind—before the terrorist behaviour is triggered.

While the socio-cultural environment may be a permissive, or even facilitating, factor in the emergence of certain kinds of terrorist activity, therefore, it cannot be sufficient in itself as a cause of the behaviour (although conceivably it could be sufficient as a foundation upon which to build the indoctrination of individual terrorist "warriors"). The cultural element, in other words, does not appear to have enough causal power to account for the phenomenon as a whole, even if it can account for why certain individuals are prepared to commit extraordinarily self-sacrificial political acts.

The problem of weighting the cultural factor relative to other variables is compounded by the fact that the leaders of any terrorist campaign are unlikely to be as simply motivated as those who follow them. Their political thinking is likely to be far more calculating, far more complex, and probably far more pragmatic and "instrumentalist" in orientation. For them, the cultural factor may be more pertinent as a vehicle for the mobilization and indoctrination of others than as a recipe from which they seek guidance for their own behaviour. On the other hand, it may well affect the "lens," or the "intellectual prism," through which they interpret the world around them—influencing, as it were, their "intelligence assessment."

This relatively modest interpretation of the importance and role of the cultural variable as a stimulus for terrorist activity (relative to the role played by variables of other kinds) could easily be wrong-headed. Reaching conclusions on such issues is ultimately, after all, a matter of judgment. But whether the judgment offered here is wrong-headed or not, there can be no doubt that the weights we assign respectively to the various causal factors that may be driving the behaviour involved have profoundly significant implications for our views of the appropriate policy response.

To illustrate this point, it may be useful to consider three commonly suggested propositions about what may have been going on in the minds of Osama bin Laden and his senior colleagues over the past decade or so.

One account has it that he was profoundly offended—and ultimately radicalized—by the presence of the American military on the soil of Saudi Arabia.

Now, if that were truly the driver of al-Qaeda behaviour, the long-term solution might seem relatively simple—although certainly not strategically or politically "cost-free" from the Washington vantage point. On such an interpretation, to de-escalate the problem it is necessary only to remove the American armed forces contingent from Saudi Arabian territory (obviously not the stratagem that the Americans have adopted thus far, and probably not one they are likely to pursue in the immediately foreseeable future).

A second account of the problem holds that the core source of the radicalism of the terrorists is the presence of Israel in a land that Palestinians and their supporters elsewhere in the Islamic world regard as properly Palestinian, and not Israeli.

Here again, the solution is technically straightforward, but from the political point of view it may be even more difficult to achieve. Israel has to give up some of its land (or the land it currently controls). On some accounts, it has to give up *all* of its land. The former might conceivably happen in the context of a negotiated settlement. The latter won't.

But a third account has it that the current round of terrorist radicalism has roots that are deeply imbedded in the Islamic culture, or at least in one or more versions of it. They are imbedded specifically in that part of the culture that leads to the perception that the "West" represents a way of living that is so fundamentally a violation of the will of God that it creates for true believers an obligation to try to bring it down.

This is not very difficult to understand. For a start, the West has insisted (after a centuries-long struggle in Europe) on separating Church from State, or the world of God from the world of Caesar. This, clearly, is a position that makes for a more civilized politics in largely secular societies, but it also has the effect of demoting the salience of "God" to the conduct of an important and pervasive part of our lives. The West has concluded, in effect, that our relations with our respective gods are private matters entirely, and that theological considerations have no place in the way we do our community politics—which is a quite extraordinary idea when one thinks of it from the vantage point of those of deeply committed faith.

Moreover, if one's view of the will of God incorporates an attachment both to family and to what Westerners describe as "puritan" values, the offensiveness of the West assumes truly monumental proportions. It requires only a moment's reflection on how an evening of North American television would look to someone holding such beliefs to grasp the implication. The experience would seem like an odyssey in corruption and decadence—an almost unbroken display of violence and greed, along with illicit (and alarmingly public) sexual activity, an overwhelming fascination with the pampering trivia of personal hygiene, a voyeuristic portrayal of the responses of the police to the degraded vulgarities of the gutter, and so on. What, after all, would John Milton have made of Jerry Springer? What must a committed Muslim make of him in our own time?

On this account of the problem, however, there is no policy "cure" at all—not, at least, a policy cure short of the conversion of a dedicated and militant Islam to what we may have to acknowledge is a world-view akin to the libertarian.

This list of potential "root causes" could easily be expanded. Some would be inclined to argue that the disaffection of the terrorists is ultimately the product of economic deprivation, or perhaps more accurately, in the present context, of gross disparities in the distribution of wealth. Their leaders may be wealthy and be guided by other considerations—considerations typical of authoritarian elites everywhere, in every time—but their capacity to recruit their foot-soldiers is nurtured by the poverty of the many, and it would go away if the pertinent populations were appropriately enriched. Alternatively, it can be held that the true source of the alienation lies with political regimes that are transparently corrupt, oppressive and undemocratic, so that the solution must ultimately rest on the advance of democratization. It can also be suggested that the difficulty really lies with the structural integration of *both* these conditions—the underlying poverty and the disparities in the distribution of wealth being themselves the inevitable consequence of an oligarchical politics.

Here, too, the implications of the argument—even if the analysis itself is well-founded—are such as to leave little hope of effective remedy in the short term, since the necessary reforms are unlikely to occur in the absence of invasive interventions of the imperial sort—interventions that would be no more acceptable to the indigenous populations than they would be to the constituencies of the intervening powers.

In practice, these various interpretations (and others like them) of bin Laden's behaviour, and perhaps even more of the behaviour of those who follow him, may *all* be right—in the sense that they are all "in the picture" and actually serve to reinforce one another. Israel, in such an account of the bin Laden view, is not just the stealer of Palestinian land; it is also the purveyor in the Middle East of Western corruption—a corruption that among other things has turned the leadership of Saudi Arabia into a comprador elite, willing to lend part of its territory to the armed might of the United States in a way that helps the Saudi leadership to sustain its own position of political, economic and social privilege.

If there is any merit in this assessment of the "root causes" analysis of the current terrorist problem, the practical implication from the Western point of view is both clear and depressing, since it effectively denies the viability of remedies based on root-cause engineering. Attempting, for example, to change the substance of a given socio-political culture, much less the institutions and processes by which the socialization of the culture occurs, is not an easy or reliable undertaking. Certainly it is not a *short-term* undertaking. That being so, the security problem that terrorist "guerrilla warfare" represents has to be regarded as just that—a *security* problem. The liberal world that Canadians and others in the West inhabit has enemies—and some of them are understandably determined. We can fiddle at the margins in attempting to dissuade them of their views, and here and there we can even make policy changes in the hope that this will make us appear less offensive to them. But in the final analysis, we will need to defend ourselves against their belligerence.

The defensive strategy required is obviously multi-faceted, and there can be no surprise in the fact that almost every major agency and department of the federal government (and many at other levels of government, too) have been involved in both the Canadian and the American responses.

But one particular requirement may warrant special emphasis. For to do the job as effectively as possible we need to understand not only the "terrorists" and their "culture," along with the ways in which they are "socialized," but also the reality of the circumstances they face, and the various cleavages of wealth, power and status that help to sustain their alienation. In effect, we need first-class "intelligence." Even more, we need first-class intelligence *analysts.*

For the reasons already indicated, this is not a matter of finding a "cure." It is a matter of knowing one's adversaries, and of being able to think like them. This, in turn, is not just a question of being able to understand their culture, but of being able to understand their world in *all* of its dimensions, so as to be better equipped to predict their behaviour and make the most of their vulnerabilities.

For such a purpose, research is required. So is higher education. And the two go together. We cannot properly staff CSIS, or the DND, or the RCMP, or DFAIT, or the PCO, or the folks in Customs, or in Immigration, without both. Canada is a trifle short of educational and research personnel with these sorts of capacities in most of the fields in which we now seem to need them. We need them, moreover, with "critical mass." And to get them, we need to fund their training and make it financially possible for them to do their research— not only here, but in the field.

To fill the gap in the short term, of course, we can rely in some measure on our capacity to borrow enlightenment and instruction from our friends—not just our friends in the United States, but those elsewhere, too. This cannot be a substitute, however, for having effective analytical capacities of our own. For there is a strong case for maintaining a certain distance from the assumptions and perspectives that guide the assessments, in particular, of our neighbours. Information liberates. Informational dependency imprisons.

That said, it should be noted that the cultivating of our own analytical capacities can be as useful to our neighbours as to ourselves. This is partly because there are things that researchers from a small power can do that researchers from a hegemonic superpower cannot. Canadian social scientists asking questions in the Middle East may be tolerated. American social scientists trying to do the same may not. More importantly, however, there are perspectives on "reality" that flourish in smaller powers but are quick to die in the more muscular world of the great powers.

In this arena, as in others, there is value in diversity. It inhibits myopia, and inhibiting myopia is helpful to the making of sound policy.

Chapter 23

The Responsibility to Protect and the Duty to Punish: Politics and Justice in a Safer World

LOUISE ARBOUR*

*Louise Arbour, *former Supreme Court of Canada Justice (1999–2004) is the United Nations High Commissioner for Human Rights.*

Prior to her appointment to the Supreme Court of Canada, Arbour was Chief Prosecutor, International War Crimes Tribunals for the Former Yugoslavia and for Rwanda. This is a slightly amended version of the first H.R. MacMillan Lecture, held by the CIIA in Vancouver in February 2002.

On 17 April 2002, Canadians celebrated the 20th anniversary of the coming into force of the Canadian Charter of Rights and Freedoms. Much was said on that happy occasion about the immeasurable impact of that constitutional document on our lives and on our aspirations, not only for ourselves, but also for others because this is indeed the genius of the charter. Inasmuch as it is truly a document asserting individual freedoms, liberties, and rights, its implementation invariably brings to the forefront of public awareness the existence of the rights and aspirations of others, usually those who claim to be ill-served by a democratic process reduced to a self-serving majority rule. One does not think of the charter as having any particular international significance. It has, of course, had implications for immigration and refugee law, and in that sense its impact is felt outside our immediate boundaries. It has also brought us closer to those, like the European Union, who are engaged in similar human rights litigation. And there is no question that Canadian charter jurisprudence is having an important influence on the thinking of constitutional courts in many jurisdictions confronting the difficult issues we have so recently tackled.

Beyond this, I believe that the contribution that Canada has made on the international scene, particularly in the last decade, reflects our new identity, born of charter awareness, about the universality of rights and the imperative of enforcing those rights. Michael Ignatieff addressed this issue in *The Rights Revolution*.[1] But in a sense he spoke even more forcefully about the idea of rights in *Virtual War,* his book about the war in Kosovo,[2] in which he documents the dilemma, very overtly expressed in particular in the United Kingdom, about the morality, the legitimacy, and the legality of waging war in defence of someone else's

---

[1] Michael Ignatieff, *The Rights Revolution* (Toronto: Anansi 2000).

[2] Michael Ignatieff, *Virtual War: Kosovo and Beyond* (Toronto: Penguin 2001).

rights. His book precipitated a vigorous public debate about state sovereignty and military intervention. That debate led the secretary-general of the United Nations to question whether we had entered a new era of internationalism, one essentially dominated by concerns over the protection of fundamental individual rights.

The probing of these issues could not have been more timely for Canadians, who had themselves examined the outer limits of the state's obligations to support human rights and fundamental freedoms in two decades of charter litigation. We heard and understood the implications of the question raised by the secretary-general, and in particular I suggest that we understood that there had to be a legal framework, not just a political one, within which to search for answers. This led to the Canadian initiative of convening the International Commission of Intervention and State Sovereignty, which published its report in December 2001. The report, *The Responsibility to Protect,* is concerned primarily with establishing guidelines for triggering military intervention in the face of human catastrophes fed by either the collusion or the impotence of national states.[3]

To be fair, the report is not narrowly preoccupied with militarism. It argues that the international community has a responsibility to prevent, to react, and to rebuild: not surprisingly, it stresses prevention as the most important aspect of the responsibility to protect. But the most striking aspect of the conclusions reached by this international body of experts is the recognition that the concept of state sovereignty is not just a question of state prerogative, representing the always superior interest of the state, but that it is a voucher for human security. The rationale for the international order deferring to the will of individual states in the management of their own affairs is that the vindication of state sovereignty will best serve peace and, therefore, safety and security. In other words, sovereign states have a responsibility to protect their citizens, and if they forfeit that responsibility they surrender part of their sovereignty accordingly. In that sense, international intervention for human protection purposes is justified if and when a state no longer lives up to the obligations imposed upon it by its sovereign status.

There is little doubt that these ideas are rooted in part in the growth of international legalism. Since the Second World War, we have witnessed a proliferation of legal instruments, particularly in the human rights field, which have led to a similar growth of domestic legislation and, although at a much slower pace, a growth in enforcement of these international norms that are now universally accepted, if not universally implemented. We have witnessed, particularly since the end of the cold war, a gradual consensus that the rule of law can and should override the pragmatism of the rule of necessity, the rule of convenience, and the rule of force.

The events of 11 September 2001, which now dominate so many concerns in international relations, in a sense have temporarily obscured the common trends on security issues that had prevailed since at least the end of the cold war, in particular the proliferation of deadly armed conflicts within states or, as in the former Yugoslavia, between states emerging from the disintegration of previously sovereign states. What 11 September has not obscured, in fact what it has highlighted in the most tragic fashion, is the pernicious vulnerability of civilians, who are indeed often deliberately targeted by those who claim, explicitly or otherwise, to be waging war.

---

[3]   International Development Research Centre, *The Responsibility to Protect: Report of the International Committee on Intervention and State Sovereignty* (Ottawa: IDRC 2001).

The report of the Commission on intervention and State Sovereignty stresses the need for a framework for anticipating and then responding to acute crises in human security. It is not surprising that its existence was essentially a by-product of the multinational military intervention in Kosovo, the culmination of more than a decade of attempts at conflict management in that region. Indeed, the level, the diversity, and the intensity of international attention devoted to the Balkans will probably provide one of the most complex case studies in international diplomacy, NGO monitoring and pressure, and sustained media attention, all within the oversight of sophisticated organizations such as the United Nations (UN), the North Atlantic Treaty Organization (NATO), the European Union, and the Organization for Security and Co-operation in Europe (OSCE).

It is interesting, from my point of view, that the insertion, for the first time ever, of an operational international judicial institution both complicated matters and provided a fresh and promising outlook for the management of that unmanageable conflict. The original perception that international criminal justice was very much a misfit within this array of political interveners became acute with the Dayton Peace Agreement. There was to be an inevitable operational interaction between the theoretical and the practical international law enforcers in Bosnia and Herzegovina. Leading the former was the International Criminal Tribunal for the former Yugoslavia (ICTY), created two years earlier by the Security Council under its chapter VII powers. The tribunal, as a judicial organ of the Security Council, was mandated to investigate and prosecute serious violations of international humanitarian law on the territory of the former Yugoslavia from 1991 onwards. It was specifically directed to apply the law of command responsibility, and no immunities from prosecutions were given to anyone, including heads of state. The tribunal's jurisdiction encompasses genocide, war crimes, and crimes against humanity—crimes that continued to be perpetrated during the existence of the tribunal—and it had jurisdiction, some of it very theoretical indeed, to conduct on-site investigations. Under article 29 of the tribunal's constituting statute, all states were required to co-operate with it, and all states were compelled to obey its orders.

The more practical law enforcers in the field were, of course IFOR, subsequently SFOR, and then, in Kosovo, KFOR. IFOR, the Dayton implementation force, was a NATO-led, Security Council mandated military force in which more than two-dozen countries were represented, including Russia and other eastern European countries. At its peak, it deployed over 50,000 troops. It took over from UNPROFOR, the long-serving UN peacekeeping mission, first in Croatia then in Bosnia-Herzegovina. UNPROFOR had struggled with its ever-expanding mandate of providing humanitarian assistance as well as managing safe areas. Both the political and the military command of IFOR were firmly in NATO (the North Atlantic Council and the Supreme Allied Commander Europe). Its rules of engagement provided for the robust use of force both for force protection and to ensure the discharge of its mandate.

In annex 1-A of the peace agreement, the parties agreed to authorize and assist IFOR in the discharge of its mandate, including the use of necessary force. The Dayton agreement also dealt with the ICTY. Under article IX of annex 4 on the Constitution of Bosnia and Herzegovina the agreement said: 'No person who is serving a sentence imposed by the International Tribunal for the Former Yugoslavia, and no person who is under indictment by the Tribunal and who has failed to comply with an order to appear before the Tribunal, may stand as a candidate or hold any appointive, elective or other public office in the territory of Bosnia and Herzegovina.'

Referring to the role of IFOR vis-à-vis ICTY, the Dutch commentator, Dick A. Leurdijk, had this to say: 'The role of the IFOR troops when it comes to apprehending war criminals has been an extremely sensitive issue both for the military and diplomats. The position of the international community was, as so often before, ambiguous.' He added, with reference to the paragraph in the Dayton agreement quoted above: 'This paragraph would become one of the most contentious provisions of the Dayton implementation process. It was also directly related to another Dayton provision, which obliged all parties "to cooperate in the investigation and prosecution of war crimes and other violations of international humanitarian law." Similarly, Security Council Resolution 1031, which authorised the deployment of IFOR, recognised that the "parties shall cooperate fully with all entities involved in implementation of the peace settlement, as described in the Peace Agreement, or which are otherwise authorised by the Security Council, including the international Tribunal for the Former Yugoslavia."' At NATO'S headquarters, the consensus was that this paragraph did not provide a 'clear mandate for IFOR to arrest indicted war criminals, suggesting that it was up to the UN Security Council to take a decision.'

I will spare you the detailed account of the efforts deployed by tribunal officials at persuading IFOR and then SFOR to take a more robust stance on the issue of arresting persons indicted by The Hague tribunal. Much of it was widely reported in the international press at the time. NATO's position was clearly expressed in a press release of 14 February 1996, which stated that the North Atlantic Council strongly supported the tribunal and that IFOR would provide logistical assistance, within its means, to ICTY and concentrate on providing a safe environment in which organizations like ICTY could best operate. As for apprehension of indictees, ICTY would provide detailed information about them to IFOR, and IFOR would apprehend them if and when 'they come into contact with such persons in carrying out their duties.' This was the 'no manhunt' policy that captured so well NATO's lack of enthusiasm for another chapter VII institution, one that it preferred to view as another NGO, intent on doing good, but frankly just standing in the way of getting things done. That lack of enthusiasm, I must add, was not exclusive to NATO but was endemic even among some members of the Security Council, such as Russia, who just three years earlier had launched this unprecedented initiative.

This was the first of many interactions between international criminal justice and what it thought were its partners in the peace implementation process. Nowhere more than on this thorny issue of arrest was the latent conflict between peace and justice brought to the surface—a conflict, in my view, that has no rational foundation but that served to express the profound ambivalence of those who, unlike Canadians under their Charter of Rights and Freedoms, had difficulty embracing an international rights revolution.

Although the Report on Intervention and State Sovereignty does not address explicitly international criminal law enforcement, it is clear that the framework that it proposes will be relevant to the decision-making process of the Office of the Prosecutor of the imminent International Criminal Court (ICC). The report envisages a responsibility to punish as integral to the responsibility to protect. As I indicated earlier, the responsibility to protect is broken down into three elements: the responsibility to prevent, to react, and to rebuild. The duty to react encompasses the use of coercive measures such as sanctions and international prosecutions, with military intervention reserved for the most extreme cases. In the duty to rebuild, the report expresses the need not only for reconstruction but also for reconciliation—a task often linked to justice, particularly criminal justice. This endorsement of the continuing role that international accountability through criminal justice is likely to play in serious conflict management comes at a critical moment in the rapidly moving history of the enforcement of the laws of war.

Under the Rome Statute that created the ICC, signed in the summer of 1998, 60 ratifications are necessary to bring the court into existence. This number was reached in April 2002. The consensus is that the court will be in existence before the end of the year [2002]. Despite the considerable assistance that he or she will derive from the work of the existing ad hoc tribunals, the work of the ICC prosecutor will be truly unprecedented.

The prosecutor will be dependent on the co-operation of many states, and that co-operation will not always be nudged along by the threat of Security Council intervention, if only in the form of an expressed concern or disapproval. The prosecutor will also have to exercise discretion over whether or not to launch an investigation, in an environment that is likely to be much more political than that which surrounded most of the decisions of the prosecutor for the Yugoslav and Rwanda tribunals. The work of the ICC prosecutor will be prospective only. It will therefore inevitably deal with ongoing conflicts, where the prosecutor's initiative will be intermingled with other forms of international attention and intervention. In short, it will have all the features that were so conducive to the SFOR-ICC clashes that marked the early years of the tribunal's attempt to impose itself as a genuine law enforcement institution in the Balkans.

On the eve of the launch of the ICC, it is more important then ever to recall the basic imperatives of any functioning and trustworthy criminal justice system. I can do no better here than to refer to a short speech that I delivered in The Hague on 13 May 1999. The occasion was the launch of a global ratification campaign for the ICC, organized by the Coalition for International Justice, during the height of the NATO bombing campaign in Kosovo. In my remarks, 'Despair and Hope: Kosovo and the ICC,' I added my voice to the call for an immediate, universal, and effective repression of the most serious violations of the most fundamental international human rights, perpetrated against civilian populations rendered particularly vulnerable by the collusion, the impotence, or the indifference of governments. We did not then have a language within which to cast that obligation. It can now be referred to as the responsibility to protect, in the terminology of the Commission on Intervention and State Sovereignty. The three arguments I advanced in support of the speedy ratification of the ICC stature—authority, universality, and urgency—are as cogent today as they were then.

My first point is that any international criminal jurisdiction has to be authoritative, both in theory and in reality. The existing ad hoc tribunals are powerful judicial institutions. The prosecutor of the tribunals is explicitly empowered by the Security Council of the United Nations, through resolutions that all member states have agreed will bind them, to conduct investigations and prosecutions, acting independently and on her own initiative, and, in the exercise of that power, to question witnesses and to conduct on-site investigations. Furthermore, all states are required, by the same binding Security Council resolutions to comply with requests for assistance and court orders issued by the tribunal.

It was in that empowering environment that I affirmed publicly in March 1998 the jurisdiction of the tribunal over alleged war crimes and crimes against humanity being committed in Kosovo. It was in that same empowering environment that the Security Council in three separate resolutions throughout 1998 supported that position and reaffirmed the obligations of all states to assist our efforts to investigate. And it was also in that empowering environment that the tribunal's investigators and I were systematically denied visas for Kosovo and that I was turned back at the border of the Federal Republic of Yugoslavia, two days after the Racak massacre, on my way to conduct an on-site investigation, as I was mandated to do by the Security Council.

That experience has persuaded me that when it comes to the exercise of lawful authoritative powers, empty threats are a grave folly. The political spirit of accommodation and compromise, which is so crucial for the peaceful resolution of many types of conflicts, is entirely inappropriate when it comes to compliance with the law. It is an affront to those who obey the law and a betrayal of those who rely on it for protection.

What was activated in Rome in the summer of 1998 was the promise that something greater than force will govern, something that does not get traded away, something worthy of trust.

My second point deals with the need to expand the reach of accountability. Irrationally selective prosecutions undermine the perception of justice as fair and even-handed and therefore serve as the basis for defiance and contempt. The ad hoc nature of the existing tribunals is indeed a severe fault line in the aspirations towards a universally applicable system of criminal accountability. There is no answer to the complaint of those who have been called to account for their actions that others, even more culpable, were never subjected to scrutiny. Why Yugoslavia? Why Rwanda? Not that the impunity of some makes others less culpable, but it makes it less just to single them out. It therefore runs the risk of giving credence to their claim of victimization, and, even if it does not cast doubt on the legitimacy of their punishment, it taints the process that turns a blind eye to the culpability of others.

The broader the reach of the International Criminal Court, the better it will overcome the shortcomings of ad hoc justice. That is why the ratification of the Rome Treaty by 60 states should be only the beginning. A broad-based and ongoing ratification drive should deploy all efforts to ensure that its reach is truly universal.

My last point is to stress the continued urgency of establishing this indispensable institution. The willingness to submit to impartial, unbiased scrutiny is not only the hallmark of law-abiding persons and institutions; it is, in my view, a prerequisite of their moral entitlement to calling others to account. The 120 countries that signed the text of the Rome treaty recognized that we live in a world where warfare inflicts unspeakable harm to many, often in the most unexpected ways, ranging from hand combat with agricultural implements and cheap landmines to high-tech precision instruments that still sometimes fail in catastrophic ways.

Justice Robert Jackson, the United States Supreme Court judge who was one of the four prosecutors at Nuremberg before the International Military Tribunal set up by the victorious allies to try the leaders of the Nazi regime for war crimes and crimes against humanity, made a powerful and often quoted opening statement at that extraordinary trial. Referring to the unprecedented nature of the international tribunal, he said: 'That four great nations, flushed with victory and stung with injury, stay the hand of vengeance and voluntarily submit their captive enemies to the judgement of the law is one of the most significant tributes that Power has ever paid to Reason.'

This statement lays the foundation of the morally superior choice of justice over brutal revenge. it also lays very explicitly the foundation for victor's justice. The choice that faces the international community today is of the same nature but of a different order.

Justice Jackson might well have put it this way, referring to the countries who have and will ratify the Rome treaty creating the ICC: That these great nations willingly submit themselves to the judgment of the law is not only another vindication of Reason over Power, but is a most significant step towards equality, justice, and peace.

The legitimacy of the ICC cannot simply be asserted. It will have to be established, day by day, as is the case for all institutions in a democracy, under the scrutiny of the press and the public. Much has been said in Canada on the theme of the legalization, and indeed the judiciarization, of politics. There is no doubt that since the advent of the Canadian Charter of Rights and Freedoms, the courts have indeed become for many Canadians the forum of choice for the vindication of claims based essentially on an idea, or an ideal, of justice. That was certainly the situation with the early cases dealing with procedural fairness in the criminal context, and it has become even more acute in the litigation dealing with fundamental freedoms and with equality. I am not so naive as to suggest that we are on the eve of experiencing a primacy of the juridical over the political on the international scene. But I do think that legalism is the by-product of globalization of rights.

It is fair to say that in liberal democracies, not everyone views the legalization of politics as a positive development, just as the emergence of a juridical international regime of accountability for gross human rights violations is encountering everything from scepticism to outright hostility. Yet international criminal justice has become an inseparable component of the international efforts to make and to keep peace and security. Our ruling generation holds in trust the enforcement of the rules of governance. If we are to embark on wars of values, I think it is worth fighting for international justice. Authoritative, universal justice.

Chapter 24

Building Democracy after Conflict: Lessons from Iraq

LARRY DIAMOND*

* ***Larry Diamond*** *is a senior fellow at the Hoover Institution, Stanford University, and founding co-editor of the* Journal of Democracy.

Among the growing number of recent cases where international actors have become engaged in trying to rebuild a shattered state and construct democracy after conflict, Iraq is somewhat unique. The state collapsed not as a result of a civil war or internal conflict, but as a result of external military action to overthrow it. As in Afghanistan, the military action that deposed an extremely repressive, brutal, and irresponsible regime was waged by an international military coalition in which one country, the United States, was overwhelmingly dominant. Unlike in Afghanistan, however, the United States enjoyed very little support for the invasion of Iraq from regional or international public opinion, and its military campaign was not assisted by indigenous rebel forces. These factors had distinctive implications for postwar political reconstruction in Iraq, and therefore should caution us against drawing too many generalizations from Iraq's recent postwar experience.

Nevertheless, the political challenges in Iraq from around 9 April 2003—when Saddam's regime fell in Baghdad and a U.S.-led postwar administration began to assert itself—resembled many of the other recent postconflict-reconstruction or nation-building efforts. Once the Ba'athists were ousted from power, the vacuum of political authority had somehow to be filled, and order on the streets had to be reestablished. The state as an institution had to be restructured and revived. Basic services had to be restored, infrastructure repaired, and jobs created. Fighting between disparate ethnic, regional, and religious groups—many of them with well-armed militias—had to be prevented or preempted. The political culture of fear, distrust, brutal dominance, and blind submission had to be transformed. Political parties and civil society organizations working to represent citizen interests, rebuild communities, and educate for democracy had to be assisted, trained, and protected. A plan needed to be developed to produce a broadly representative and legitimate new government, and to write a new constitution for the future political order. And sooner or later, democratic elections would need to be held.

The first weeks of America's postwar engagement in Iraq were chaotic and ineffectual, as most of the infrastructure of the country was systematically looted, sabotaged, and destroyed while American troops stood by. Having failed to meet the first and most basic imperative after conflict—to restore order—and having failed to establish, through its Office of Reconstruction and Humanitarian Assistance (ORHA), effective political authority as well, the United States quickly created, in mid-May 2003, a new instrument for political and economic reconstruction in Iraq. This was the Coalition Provisional Authority

(CPA)—in essence, an occupation administration—led by a highly regarded former American diplomat, L. Paul Bremer III. Like the occupying military forces, the CPA had extensive British participation, and involved officials and troops from many other nations (including Poland, Spain, Italy, and Ukraine), but both the political and military aspects of the occupation were overwhelmingly American, and Iraqis quickly came to see the international presence in Iraq essentially as an American occupation.

An extended occupation had not been part of the Pentagon's plan to administer postwar Iraq. Rather, when the United States invaded Iraq in March 2003, the Pentagon's expectation was that U.S. forces would be welcomed as liberators by a relieved and jubilant Iraqi people, and that it would be possible to hand over power fairly quickly to an Iraqi interim government led by Ahmed Chalabi and other prodemocratic Iraqi exiles. In the face of the postwar chaos, however, the Bush administration was forced to abandon this strategy. So when Bremer landed in Baghdad on May 13, it was with a set of bold new initiatives: to dissolve the Iraqi army, thoroughly "de-Ba'athify" Iraqi government and society, and reshape Iraq's politics and economy through a full-scale occupation that might last two years or longer.

Although hastily assembled, Bremer's plan for the postwar reconstruction and transformation of Iraq was ambitious and comprehensive. But it underwent repeated and dramatic changes in the face of the realities on the ground. The United States' own chosen partners among the exiled forces (including the two political parties that had ruled the autonomous Kurdish region during the 12 years since the previous Gulf war) pressed continually for a rapid transfer of authority to an Iraqi interim government that they would lead. Some concessions had to be made to these demands, and the result was the 25-member Iraqi Governing Council (IGC), which was appointed in July 2003. The IGC was neither fish nor fowl: It was not really a "governing" council, as Bremer made it clear that he would continue to exercise supreme power, including the power to veto any IGC decisions. But it was given some ability to advise the American viceroy and to nominate Iraqi ministers (who would themselves have limited power), as well as to propose a timetable and formula for drafting and ratifying the new constitution and then conducting elections for a new government.

The IGC was never able to agree on a formula for political transition, partly because of its own deep internal divisions along philosophical, ethnic, and sectarian lines; and partly because its members resented not having real power. Over the months after its establishment, it kept insisting that a prolonged U.S. occupation was wrong for Iraq, and that an Iraqi interim government needed to be appointed. At the same time, many other Iraqis, particularly from the majority Shi'ite section of the country, were demanding national elections as soon as possible to choose a new Iraqi government. As the Governing Council dithered and the December 15 deadline (established by the UN Security Council for the IGC to deliver a plan and timetable for constitutional transition) drew nearer, the United States became frustrated and developed its own plan for transition, which was quickly pressed upon the IGC and then announced as the "November 15 Agreement."

That plan was significant in several respects. For the first time, the United States outlined a comprehensive timetable for Iraq's political transition and set a specific date for an end to the political occupation—30 June 2004. Well before then, by February 28, the IGC would draft and adopt a "Transitional Administrative Law"—in essence an interim constitution that would structure and limit power for the roughly 18 months between the end of the occupation and the seating of an elected government under the permanent constitution (by 31 December 2005). The November 15 Agreement also stipulated that by 31 May 2004 a 15-member Organizing Committee in each of Iraq's 18 provinces would select members of a provincial caucus. Each caucus would then elect representatives to the Transitional National Assembly (TNA), which would appoint a prime minister, cabinet, and three-member presidency council. After months of ignoring the *fatwa* of Grand Ayatollah Ali al-Sistani insisting that any constitution-making body for Iraq had to be elected rather than appointed, the United States conceded that point and called for direct elections to a constitutional assembly by 15 March 2005. This elected constitutional assembly would draft a constitution by August 2005, a national referendum to approve it would be held by October, and then national elections would be held for a new government by the end of the year.

A FLAWED PLAN

The November 15 Agreement was a step forward in many respects, but it failed to address a few key problems of the political transition. Many Iraqis viewed the arcane process for electing the TNA from different tiers of caucuses to be unduly subject to CPA control, as the organizing committees would be selected by three actors—the provincial council, the local councils of the five largest municipalities, and the national Governing Council—all of which the CPA itself had largely appointed. Ayatollah Sistani quickly condemned the proposal for its plan to install an unelected transitional government. Many Iraqis, while welcoming the establishment of a timetable for an end to the political occupation, remained suspicious of U.S. motives and wanted a timetable for ending the military occupation as well. Beyond this, there was also widespread resentment over the extensive insecurity in the country—a result of rising insurgent, terrorist, and criminal violence—and frustration with the slow pace of economic reconstruction.

Because of the speed with which the November 15 plan was developed by the Bush administration and then "negotiated" with the IGC, it was never vetted with a broad cross-section of Iraqi society, and thus there was no sense among Iraqis of ownership of the new transition plan. While some adjustments were grudgingly made to this and other transition plans, they were always late and inadequate as a result of the lack of popular consultation. This only served to reinforce the imperial, centralized, and top-down character of the U.S. postwar engagement in Iraq.

By January 2004, it was becoming apparent that the November 15 Agreement was in serious political trouble because of its intention to constitute the transitional government through indirect caucuses rather than direct elections. This led the Bush administration to welcome the mediation of UN special envoy Lakhdar Brahimi. In persuading Ayatollah Sistani that "reasonably credible" elections could not possibly be organized by the end of the political occupation on 30 June 2004, Brahimi managed to work out a compromise: An appointed interim government would take office for a brief period on June 30, and then elections for a transitional government would be held at the earliest possible date thereafter—but no later than 31 January 2005.

Ambassador Brahimi's artful, imaginative, and just mediation rescued the political transition in Iraq and made possible a transfer of power on June 28 to an Iraqi interim government, which he had constructed by balancing the interests and inputs of the United States, the IGC, and other key Iraqi constituencies. With the transfer of sovereignty and the termination of the Coalition Provisional Authority, it was hoped that a corner had been turned and that a significant reduction in violence and a smooth path to elections some time in January would follow. In June, the UN electoral-assistance mission appointed a seven-member Iraqi Independent Electoral Commission composed of fresh faces without ties to any of the political parties. The head of the UN electoral team in Iraq, Carlos Valenzuela, joined that body as well.

Iraqi political parties flocked to training and information programs, and a wide range of civil society organizations took part in programs preparing them to serve as election monitors. Clearly, Iraqis were hungry for elections. But in the months after the political handover, the continuing terrorist and insurgent violence obstructed economic reconstruction, eroded Iraqi confidence in the appointed Interim Government, and raised serious doubts about the country's capacity to stage elections by the January 31 deadline that would be sufficiently inclusive, transparent, fair, and free of violence and intimidation to be considered "reasonably credible." As this article went to press in mid-December 2004, it was not clear that the deadline would be met, or what kind of elections would result if it were met.

LESSONS (NOT) LEARNED

We are still very much in the middle of an internationally assisted political-reconstruction process in Iraq. Even in an initial sense, we will not know for another year or two—maybe even five or ten—the outcome of the postwar effort to rebuild the Iraqi state. Nevertheless, from the period of the U.S. political occupation and the first few months of the Interim Government, some rather important lessons can be identified, most of which underscore key themes in the emerging literature on postconflict reconstruction.

1) *Prepare for a major commitment.*

Rebuilding a failed state is an extremely expensive and difficult task under any circumstance, and even more so in the wake of violent conflict. A recent RAND Corporation study on the United States' post–World War II nation-building experiences found that "among controllable factors, the most important determinant [of success] is the level of effort—measured in time, manpower, and money."[1] Indeed, success requires a very substantial commitment of human and financial resources, delivered in timely and effective fashion, and sustained over an extended period of time, lasting (not necessarily through occupation or trusteeship, but at least through intensive international engagement) for a minimum of five to ten years. While the scope of any such endeavor is daunting, it grows larger with the size of the failed state. In absolute terms, it is obviously much easier to bring to bear the adequate financial and human resources in a small state, such as Bosnia, Kosovo, or East Timor, than in a state like Iraq, which has a population of 25 million and a territory the size of California.

2) *Commit enough troops, with the proper rules of engagement, to secure the postwar order.*

One of the major problems with the U.S. engagement in Iraq was that there were not enough international troops on the ground in the wake of state collapse to secure the immediate postwar order. As a result, Iraq descended into lawless chaos once Saddam's regime fell. Save for the oil ministry—protected by U.S. troops—virtually every significant public building was methodically looted and gutted in the days and weeks following the fall of Baghdad. The power and water supply, along with other public infrastructure, was

---

[1]   James Dobbins et al., *America's Role in Nation-Building: From Germany to Iraq* (Santa Monica, Calif.: RAND, 2003), 165.

impaired. As U.S. troops held back or stood by, spontaneous acts of destruction and theft turned into systematic looting and orchestrated sabotage. The results were devastating: huge economic losses; further disruption and devastation of the state's capacity to function; a stunning loss of Iraqi confidence in the occupiers; and a climate of lawlessness that emboldened surviving regime loyalists, other Iraqi nationalists, religious extremists, and organized-crime rings to launch an even broader campaign of terror, murder, and mayhem.

Senior U.S. military leaders wanted a large force—something like 400,000 troops—on the ground in order to secure the postwar order. Yet the total stabilization force never amounted to half that number. The Army's initial request was much more in line with the ratio of foreign troops to domestic population in the international interventions in Bosnia and Kosovo, which if replicated in Iraq would have meant an initial international force of 460,000 to 500,000 troops.[2] Pentagon planners probably worried about the capacity of the United States to mobilize such a large force, and about the resulting casualties. But the RAND study, led by James Dobbins—who had served in the previous decade as U.S. special envoy for the postconflict missions in Bosnia, Kosovo, Haiti, Somalia, and Afghanistan—concluded: "There appears to be an inverse correlation between the size of the stabilization force and the level of risk. The higher the proportion of stabilizing troops, the lower the number of casualties suffered and inflicted."[3]

Of course, the need is not simply for *enough* troops, but for the right kind of troops, equipped with the proper rules of engagement. It does no good to have troops on the ground if they simply stand by and watch what is left of the state being stolen and burned. One lesson from Iraq is that international postconflict stabilization missions need to be able to deploy not just a conventional army but a muscular peace-implementation force that is somewhere between a war-making army and a crime-fighting police—a rapid-reaction or riot-control force on the order of the French *gendarmerie*. In the end, however, such a force must come from or be led by the military, as only the military can fill the public-order void that often appears in the immediate aftermath of state collapse. As Simon Chesterman notes in his powerful study of UN experiences with postconflict intervention and state-building: "The military is rightly reluctant to embrace law and order duties that are outside its expertise, but in many situations only the military is in a position to exercise comparable functions in the first weeks and months of an operation."[4] Moreover, just as more troops usually mean fewer casualties, more robust rules of engagement, clearly projected from the start, generally mean less violence. Chesterman concludes: "A key finding from surveying past operations is that, very often, the more willing and able an operation is to use force, the less likely it is to have to do so."[5]

3) *Mobilize international legitimacy and cooperation.*

In the contemporary era, a successful effort at postconflict reconstruction requires broad international legitimacy and cooperation for at least two key reasons. First, the scope and duration of engagement is typically more than any one country—and public—is willing to bear on its own. The broader the international coalition, the greater the human and financial resources that can be mobilized, and the more likely it is that the engagement of

[2]   James Dobbins et al., *America's Role in Nation-Building*, 198.
[3]   James Dobbins et al., *America's Role in Nation-Building*, 165–66.
[4]   Simon Chesterman, *You the People: The United Nations, Transitional Administration, and State-Building* (Oxford: Oxford University Press, 2004), 123.
[5]   Simon Chesterman, *You the People*, 125.

any participating country can be sustained, as its public sees a sense of shared international commitment and sacrifice. Second, when there is broad international engagement and legitimacy, people within the postconflict country are less likely to see it as the imperial project of one country or set of countries. All else being equal, international legitimacy tends to generate greater domestic legitimacy, or at least acceptance, for the intervention. Accordingly, the abovementioned RAND study concludes: "Multilateral nation-building can produce more thoroughgoing transformations and greater regional reconciliation than can unilateral efforts."[6]

The coalition that came together to invade Iraq and topple Saddam's regime comprised mainly the United States and Britain. In the post-9/11 climate of national threat, such a thin coalition was enough to sustain the support of the American public. Subsequently, the Bush administration could claim that more than thirty other countries were involved on the ground in the postwar coalition effort to rebuild Iraq. What the Iraqis saw, however, was not a broad international coalition but rather the United States and Britain—the most powerful country in the world, paired with Iraq's former colonial ruler.

4) *Generate legitimacy and trust within the postconflict country.*

No international reconstruction effort can succeed without some degree of acceptance and cooperation—and eventually support and positive engagement—from the country's population. If the local population has no trust in the initial international administration and its intentions, the intervention can become the target of popular wrath, and will then need to spend most of its military (and administrative) energies defending *itself* rather than rebuilding the country and its political and social order.

In the final page of an impressively wise and learned book on postconflict state-building, Simon Chesterman writes: "Modern trusteeships demand, above all, trust on the part of local actors. Earning and keeping that trust requires a level of understanding, sensitivity, and respect for local traditions and political aspirations that has often been lacking in international administration."[7] Unfortunately, the occupation of Iraq lacked these qualities, and the Iraqi people knew it. From the very beginning, the U.S. occupation failed to earn the trust and respect of the Iraqis: First, as noted above, it failed in its most important obligation as an occupying power—establishing order and public safety—and then it failed to convey early on any clear plan for postconflict transition. The suspicion of U.S. intentions was further exacerbated by its excessive reliance on Iraqi exiles, some of whom were themselves widely distrusted by the Iraqi public.

All international postconflict interventions to reconstruct a failed state on democratic foundations confront a fundamental contradiction. Their goal is, in large measure, democracy—popular, representative, and accountable government in which "the people" are sovereign. Yet their means are undemocratic—in essence, some form of imperial domination, however temporary and transitional. How can the circle be squared? Chesterman advises that when the United Nations and other international actors come "to exercise state-like functions, they must not lose sight of their limited mandate to hold that sovereign power in trust for the population that will ultimately claim it."[8] This requires a balancing of international trusteeship or

---

6   James Dobbins et al., *America's Role in Nation-Building*, 164.
7   Simon Chesterman, *You the People*, 257.
8   Simon Chesterman, *You the People*, 257.

imperial functions with a distinctly nonimperial attitude and a clear and early specification of an acceptable timetable for the restoration of full sovereignty. The humiliating features of an extended, all-out occupation should be avoided as much as possible.

In recent years, a few bold thinkers have called for a new era of "liberal empire," in which the United States, as the world's "indispensable nation," and perhaps Europe as well, would use their power to impose on the world's failed and failing states the institutions and norms of political and economic freedom—even if in some cases this requires direct and extended colonial administration. Perhaps the most audacious advocate of this approach is British historian Niall Ferguson, who recently suggested that "Liberia would benefit immeasurably from something like an American colonial administration," and that, even if formal sovereignty were to be transferred soon in Iraq (as it was in June 2004) the United States should retain effective control over "military, fiscal, and monetary policies" through a "viceroy in all but name for decades."[9] Reviewing some of the history of the British colonial empire, Ferguson concludes that the United States should resist the pressure for an early end to effective domination of Iraq: "[I]t is possible to occupy a country for decades, while consistently denying that you have any intention of doing so. This is known as hypocrisy, and it is something to which liberal empires must sometimes resort."[10]

I draw a radically different lesson from the American experience in Iraq. We are not in the late nineteenth century, when the question Gladstone put in his diary—"how to plant solidly western & beneficent institutions in the soil of a Mohamedan community?"—can begin to be answered with Ferguson's observation, "not … overnight."[11] The answer today must be, "not by a nineteenth-century style occupation." In their norms, perceptions, expectations, and capacities for mobilization, the peoples of the twenty-first century are very different from those of earlier eras—and as Ferguson notes, and as the British painfully encountered in Iraq after World War I, there was already plenty of capacity for violent resistance back then. In today's world, the principles and impulses of nationalism and anti-colonialism run very deep, and gratitude for international protection or liberation can very quickly turn into anger against the intervening force.

It was the failure to comprehend these dynamics—and indeed to ponder seriously the lessons of the British experience as colonizers in Iraq—that was perhaps the single greatest mistake of the U.S. intervention. From this flowed everything else: the glib confidence that the occupiers would be welcomed as liberators, the expectation that only a relatively light force would be required for the postwar era, and the decision to embark on a formal, extended occupation when U.S. plans for a rapid handover and exit collapsed amidst the mounting disorder. That latter decision, embodied in the sweeping legal authority and comprehensive architecture of the CPA and the formal recognition of the occupation by UN Resolution 1483 on May 22, gave rise to a ferocious indigenous resistance. The occupying forces constantly underestimated the scope of that resistance, allowing considerable assistance and encouragement to be provided to Iraqi insurgents by external terrorist organizations and neighboring countries like Iran and Syria.

---

[9] Niall Ferguson, *Colossus: The Price of America's Empire* (New York: Penguin, 2004), 198, 223, 225.

[10] Niall Ferguson, *Colossus*, 222.

[11] Gladstone quote in Ferguson; the response is Ferguson's. Niall Ferguson, *Colossus*, 220, 222.

The question today is whether there is a formula for international intervention to democratize failed states that stops short of full-scale imperial rule—whether by one nation or many. There is real promise in the various formulas of "shared sovereignty" that Stephen D. Krasner advances in this issue of the *Journal*. Yet these formulas are viable precisely because they build not only on the de jure sovereignty of a state, but also on that state's retention of de facto sovereignty over most conventional aspects of policy. Such formal abridgements of sovereignty are likely to be more palatable if they are negotiated with international institutions or multilateral actors rather than a single powerful state.

Shared sovereignty is for the longer run, when failed states have begun to revive. In the nearer term, only military occupation in some form can fill the vacuum left behind when a state has collapsed and a country is in or at the edge of chaos and civil war. Force must be used, or at least effectively deployed and exhibited, to restore order. Military occupation does not legitimate itself, however, but needs to be paired with a clear indication, from the very beginning, "as to how a temporary military occupation is to begin the process of transferring political control to local hands."[12] Such a framework should limit the political occupation not only in time, but in scope as well, allowing for the occupier to be held accountable. Chesterman writes:

> *[O]nce the political trajectory towards normalization of the political environment has begun, creating mechanisms by which the international presence may be held accountable can both encourage the emergence of an indigenous human rights and rule of law culture as well as improve the day-to-day governance of the territory. The failure to do so—or an actual or apprehended reversal of the political trajectory towards self-governance—will lead to frustration and suspicion on the part of local actors.*[13]

In light of this latter calculus, the United States made two additional critical miscalculations in Iraq. First, when Bremer entered in May 2003, he did so with an open-ended mandate in terms of the scope and duration of his authority. Although he spoke of transferring power through elections by mid or late 2004, there were other reports of a two-year occupation, and the broad scope of his apparent mandate (including radical de-Ba'athification and sweeping free-market reforms) suggested to many Iraqis a prolonged imperial presence. In fact, Bremer's first six months—until the announcement of the November 15 plan—were consumed with the search for some kind of timetable and formula for the restoration of sovereignty, a search that was shrouded in the largely closed dealings between the CPA and the Iraqi Governing Council.

In a second miscalculation, the CPA never allowed for the U.S. occupation itself to be held accountable, though it moved quickly to revive and cleanse the Iraqi court system, construct a new framework of transitional justice, and investigate the brutal crimes of the past (unearthing some 300 mass graves). With increasing bitterness and anger over what they regarded as blatant hypocrisy and suffocating arrogance, Iraqis complained about corruption and abuse in the awarding of reconstruction contracts by the

---

12   Simon Chesterman, *You the People*, 153.
13   Simon Chesterman, *You the People*, 153.

CPA, the lack of information on Iraqi detainees, and serious abuses of Iraqi prisoners held by the Americans. The inability or unwillingness of U.S. occupation forces to respond to these concerns early on made possible the scale of prisoner abuse at Abu Ghraib, a disaster for U.S. credibility in Iraq and the world.

5) *Hold local elections first.*

No issue is tougher than the timing of elections. Ill-timed and ill-prepared elections do not produce democracy, or even political stability, after conflict. Instead, they may only enhance the power of actors who mobilize coercion, fear, and prejudice, thereby reviving autocracy and even precipitating large-scale violent strife. In Angola in 1992, in Bosnia in 1996, and in Liberia in 1997, rushed elections set back the prospects for democracy and, in Angola and Liberia, paved the way for renewed civil war.[14] There are compelling reasons, based on logic and recent historical experience, for deferring national elections until militias have been demobilized, new moderate parties trained and assisted, electoral infrastructure created, and democratic media and ideas generated. If one takes these cautions too literally and inflexibly, however, it can mean deferring national elections for a decade or more, and the dilemma then becomes how to constitute authority that will have any degree of legitimacy in the interim.

As suggested above, international interventions that seek to construct democracy after conflict must balance the tension between domination for the sake of implanting democracy and withdrawal in the name of democracy: The two competing temptations are 1) to transform the country's institutions and values through an extended and penetrating occupation (*à la* British colonial rule); and 2) to hold elections and get out as soon as possible. A key question is always how long international rule can be viable. In the case of Iraq, the answer—readily apparent from history and from the profound and widespread suspicion among Iraqis of U.S. motives—was "not long."

As discussed above, the failure to establish early on a date for national elections to choose a constitutional assembly became a major bone of contention between the U.S.-led occupation and the most revered religious and moral leader in Iraq, Ayatollah Sistani. If soon after taking control of Baghdad, the United States had invited the United Nations to do in the spring of 2003 what it did one year later—consult widely among Iraqi constituencies in order to assemble an interim government to receive sovereignty—and if it had then transferred sovereignty to a broad-based Iraqi interim government during the summer of 2003, the bulk of Iraqis might have accepted the deferral of national elections until the following year.

With the occupation settling in and elections postponed, many Iraqis came to suspect that the United States did not want early elections because it feared the outcome. There was partial truth in this. Yes, it would have been impossible administratively to organize elections within just a few months of the occupation, because there were no reliable voter rolls, no electoral laws, and no institutions for independent and credible management of the electoral process. At the same time, however, the U.S. authorities did fear that premature national elections would favor radical Islamist forces that had organized effectively and built up strong militias in the underground or in exile (in Iran), while more moderate, secular, and independent political forces needed more time to build up their organizations and spread their messages. For this reason, but even more so out of fear that holding early local elections would undermine the CPA's

---

[14] Stephen John Stedman, Donald Rothchild, and Elizabeth M. Cousens, eds., *Ending Civil Wars: The Implementation of Peace Agreements* (Boulder, Colo.: Lynne Rienner, 2002). See in particular in this collection Terrence Lyons, "The Role of Postsettlement Elections," 215–36.

insistence that national elections were impossible to organize any time soon, Bremer vetoed or reversed plans by many local CPA officials to hold direct elections (using such rough-and-ready means as the food ration-card system) for municipal and town councils.

With the help of civic teams organized by an independent contractor (Research Triangle International), the CPA did constitute provincial and local councils throughout the country on the basis of various processes of consultation and indirect selection. In many instances, these were a step forward and a foundation for the potential reconstruction of the political order. But it was a foundation undermined by the CPA's failure to give these councils meaningful resources and authority, and by the failure to hold direct elections to these bodies wherever possible. This violated Chesterman's general guideline that executive authority should be devolved to local actors as soon as practical, and that "once power is transferred to local hands, whether at the municipal or national level, local actors should be able to exercise that power meaningfully, constrained only by the rule of law."[15]

If it generally makes sense to defer national elections as long as possible, there is also a strong logic to holding local elections earlier, and in any case before national ones. Dobbins and his RAND coauthors find that holding local elections first "provides an opportunity for new local leaders to emerge and gain experience and for political parties to build a support base."[16] That could well have happened in Iraq if local elections had been allowed to proceed during 2003, and if some meaningful scope of authority and resources had been devolved to the newly elected bodies. Then the United States would have faced a broader, more diverse, and more legitimate array of Iraqi interlocutors, and the elected local bodies could have provided one basis for selecting an interim government.

6) *Disperse economic reconstruction funds and democratic assistance as widely as possible.*

Both for the effectiveness and speed of economic revival and for the building of local trust and acceptance, there is a compelling need to decentralize relief and reconstruction efforts as well as democratic civic assistance. The more the international administration and private donors work with and through local partners, the more likely that relief and reconstruction efforts will be directed toward the most urgent needs, and the better the prospect for the accumulation of political trust and cooperation with the overall transition project. In Iraq there was a particularly compelling need for the creation of jobs, a need that could have been met more rapidly if the repair and reconstruction contracts had been channeled more extensively through a wide range of local Iraqi contractors, instead of through the big U.S. corporations. The high degree of centralization in the contracting process for reconstruction, combined with the widespread terrorism and violence, meant that most of the $18.4 billion appropriated by the U.S. Congress in November of 2003 for Iraqi reconstruction was not spent within the first year, adding to Iraqi frustrations.

7) *Proceed with some humility and a decent respect for the opinions of the people in whose interest the intervention is supposedly staged.*

It is hard to imagine a bolder, more assertive, and self-confident act than a nation, or a set of nations, or "the international community" intervening to seize effectively the sovereignty of another nation. There is nothing the least bit humble about it. But ultimately the

---

[15]   Simon Chesterman, *You the People*, 243.

[16]   James Dobbins et al., *America's Role in Nation-Building*, 154.

intervention cannot succeed—and the institutions it establishes cannot be viable—unless there is some sense of participation and ownership on the part of the people in the state being reconstructed. This is why holding local elections as early as possible is so important. It is why it is so vital to engage local partners, as extensively as possible, in postconflict relief and economic reconstruction. And it is why the process of constitution-making must be democratic and broadly participatory, not merely through the election of a constituent assembly or a constitutional referendum (or ideally, both), but through the involvement of the widest possible range of stakeholders in the substantive discussions and procedural planning, and through the organization of an extensive national dialogue on constitutional issues and principles. As Jamal Benomar observes, "Constitutions produced without transparency and adequate public participation will lack legitimacy."[17] And illegitimate constitutions augur poorly for future stability.

Ultimately, the CPA did concede to the demand for an elected Iraqi constituent assembly, whose draft constitution is to be approved in a national referendum. The interim constitution also requires broad public consultation and debate in the making of the permanent constitution. But the interim constitution, while impressively liberal in many respects, was itself produced under great pressure of time through a process that was not transparent. As a result, many Iraqis were deeply aggrieved that major constitutional principles such as federalism, extensive minority vetoes, and a very limited role for religion in public life were being foisted upon them without debate. Through an extensive and expensive public-relations campaign, the CPA attempted to explain and "sell" the interim constitution to the Iraqi people after it was signed on 8 March 2004. But there was never a true dialogue, and the numerous objections that were raised received no response or consideration.

As a result, the status of the interim constitution, so crucial to defining the rules of the political game during what could be a two-year transitional period, and to protecting the rights of long-suffering and deeply anxious minorities, is now uncertain. The bargains struck by the Governing Council in the interim constitution do not yet have broad public understanding and support, and the newly elected Transitional National Assembly could attempt to declare some of its provisions null and void, ignoring the formidable requirements for amendment of the document. In short, when decisions are made by occupation powers and by their chosen interlocutors, without adequate national consultation and consensus, problems are kicked down the road and new ones are created that could undermine the prospects for democracy and tolerance.

Postconflict situations vary significantly in the degree to which the occupying authority can exercise sovereignty and effect or mediate institutional change. In cases where the state is truly shattered, conflict has been endemic, and the population is exhausted and disorganized, a longer and more ambitious reconstruction project may be possible. In other instances, national patience and consent will be quite limited. As a general rule, the less multilateral the intervention, the less thoroughly discredited and destroyed the old state structures, and the stronger and more nationalistic the preexisting state, the more difficult it will be for an external authority to stage a prolonged and far-reaching project to rebuild

---

[17] Jamal Benomar, "Constitution-Making After Conflict: Lessons for Iraq," *Journal of Democracy* 15 (April 2004): 89.

the state. Among recent postconflict situations, Iraq was at the more difficult, impatient end of the spectrum in terms of tolerance for prolonged occupation.

THE ROAD AHEAD

These "lessons" from the U.S. experience in postwar Iraq are derived while the postwar history of that country is still being forged. Even with all the mistakes made by the United States—in failing to plan and prepare adequately for the postwar reconstruction of Iraq and in imposing a political occupation upon a proud and nationalistic people, suspicious of the West—it is still possible that Iraq could become a democracy if a political agreement can be reached that enables the elections to go forward with the broad participation of all major ethnic, religious, political, and regional groups. But every mistake has its consequences, not only in lives lost and resources wasted, but also in lowering the odds for future progress. In the near term, Iraq would be fortunate to witness the emergence of a semi-democracy through elections that were viewed by most Iraqis as flawed but still "reasonably credible."

Even such an incremental and partial success, however, will require rapid progress on two important fronts. First, the political arena must be widened so that all major Iraqi groups—including Sunni nationalists, Islamists, and Ba'athists not charged with a specific crime—participate in the electoral process. A stable and even partially democratic Iraq will not be possible unless all major groups decide that they have more to gain from the arena of peaceful politics than they do from violent insurgency and terrorism. Second, for violence to become a less plausible and less attractive political option, it must be met with a vigorous and vigilant response by a reconstructed Iraqi state. The most fundamental requirement of any state is a relative monopoly on the use of force. Until the army, national guard, police force, and other elements of the new security sector are sufficiently numerous, trained, armed, equipped, organized, and mobilized to establish law and order in the country, no political stability—democratic or otherwise—will be possible. Until the Iraqi state achieves that level of coherence and capacity, international (primarily U.S.) forces will need to provide the principal bulwark against a total breakdown of order and a possible descent into civil war. While fending off total chaos, however, the presence of these forces is also a constant stimulus to insurgency. Until foreign forces are fully withdrawn from its soil, Iraq will never truly be at peace. Such are the dilemmas and contradictions at the heart of the intrinsically difficult task of building democracy after conflict.

Chapter 25

Canada: Fading Power or Future Power?

KIM RICHARD NOSSAL*

*__Kim Richard Nossal__ is Professor and Head of Political Studies at Queen's University, Kingston.

While by some measures Canada might be described as a principal power—its membership in the G-8 and the Quad, for example—by many other measures it is simply no longer as prominent in world politics as it used to be. Canadian spending on international affairs, on security and defence, on development assistance, has declined over the past decade. The government is no longer as active in international affairs as it used to be. Its capacity to be involved has shrunk. And when it seeks to be active, Canadian influence on key international events and issues appears limited.

Needless to say, debates about the kind of power Canada is in world politics are by no means new. How to measure Canadian power and influence in world politics has been the subject of a running academic—and political—debate for at least two generations. Nor is the idea that Canadian diplomacy is in decline new. In 1993, Arthur Andrew, a seasoned Canadian diplomat, argued in *The Rise and Fall of a Middle Power: Canadian Diplomacy from King to Mulroney* that the foreign policy of the Progressive Conservative government of Brian Mulroney finished the process of decline.

However, the 'fading power' theme became more pronounced after 11 September 2001, when the international system changed so dramatically. There was perhaps nothing more emblematic of the supposed growing 'invisibility' of the government of Jean Chrétien on the international stage than the treatment accorded Canada in the speech delivered by President George W. Bush to the United States after 11 September. Bush's speech was framed by the Manichean assertion that all countries had a stark choice: 'If you are not with us, you are with the terrorists.' The president made a point of mentioning a number of friends and allies by name, but did not mention Canada, despite the various Canadian contributions on 11 September, notably the emergency care of some 30,000 stranded air travellers barred from US air space. The absence of any mention of Canada might not have been intentional, but it caused a great deal of angst in Canada because it was so highly symbolic and reflected the growing distance between Ottawa and Washington.

The fading power thesis was given a particular boost by the sub-title chosen for the 2002 volume of *Canada Among Nations*. The editors of the collection, Maureen Appel Molot and Norman Hillmer, used the 'fading power' motif to explore the degree to which Canadian foreign policy in 2002 was a mere shadow of the robust presence in global politics that Ottawa had enjoyed in the 1950s.[1]

---

[1]   Maureen Appel Molot and Norman Hillmer, eds., *Canada Among Nations 2002: A Fading Power* (Toronto: Oxford University Press 2002).

The motif was picked up by numerous commentators in the months before the American-led attack on Iraq loomed and the distance between Canada and the US widened. For example, Richard Gwyn noted in the *Toronto Star* that Chrétien's major foreign policy address to the Chicago Council on Foreign Relations in February 2003 was not mentioned in any of the major papers in the United States and got only passing reference in the Chicago media.

Andrew Coyne of the *National Post* went further: in a column under the headline 'Canada on the sidelines,' Coyne asserted that the prime minister's Chicago speech demonstrated how irrelevant Canada had become. No one listens to us any more, he wrote, not least because nothing we say is worth listening to. 'If a Canadian speaks in Chicago and no one gives a damn,' Coyne concluded, 'does he make a sound?'

And indeed it would appear: the so-called Canadian proposal at the Security Council, which sought a middling way between the two polar positions on the Security Council, was dismissed by all sides. Christopher Sands, of the Center for Strategic and International Studies in Washington—one of the few American Canada-watchers—put it succinctly: Canada is simply not thought about in Washington. 'That is where Canada is. Not at the margins. Not whispering in the ear of the global power. But outside the game.' And in the spring of 2003, Andrew Cohen published *While Canada Slept: How We Lost Our Place in the World*, an argument that detailed the nature and extent of Canada's decline in world politics.

To what extent is Canada the fading power that the pundits suggest? Looking at the evolution of Canadian foreign policy in the spring of 2003, one might go further than the pundits and suggest that in the months before the attack on Iraq in March 2003, the Chrétien government transformed Canada from a fading power to an utterly irrelevant power in Washington. The deterioration was the result of a combination of both substantive policy decisions and symbolic rhetorical attacks on the United States.

For many months, the Chrétien government refused to rule anything in—or anything out—as a conscious policy. Canada might go to war if the United Nations Security Council gave its approval; but Canada might go to war if the UN didn't approve. Perhaps the best measure of the success of the government's efforts to make its policy as ambiguous as possible were the entirely contradictory headlines in the English-language press on 24 January 2003 reporting Chrétien's comments on Canada's approach to a possible war in Iraq: in the *Globe and Mail*, the headline was 'PM to Bush: Hold off on war—Canada will break with U.S. if it hits Hussein without mandate from UN.' By contrast, the *National Post* headline claimed that 'Chrétien opens door to possibility of Canada joining U.S.-led attack on Iraq.' (Given Ottawa's purposeful ambiguity, it is perhaps not surprising that the British ambassador to the United Nations would publicly admonish the Canadian government to make up its mind.) Eventually, of course, the Chrétien government did make up its mind: refusing to lend either concrete or even symbolic legitimacy to the attack on Iraq.

In the process, the government in Ottawa made a couple of decisions that ensured its marginality as war grew closer. First, it arranged things so that Canada could not contribute forces even if it had wanted to. In February the prime minister dispatched fully 3000 troops for stabilization force work in Kabul, Afghanistan. Since the Canadian Forces found it impossible to sustain 750 troops in Kandahar for more than six months, the 3000 troops committed to Kabul are sure to stretch capabilities to the breaking point. But there was method in this: with such a large force in Kabul, there simply were no Canadian troops left for any coalition of the willing, even if the Chrétien government had been willing.

Second, even though it was not ruling anything in or anything out, the longer it played its hide-and-seek game, the more it distanced itself from Washington and London. With each passing week, the Canadian government sharpened its opposition to the unilateral option the closer the war got. Eventually the prime minister openly criticized the regime change agenda of the Bush administration, noting that if we embraced regime change for the regime in Iraq, who might be next? By that time, while it was still possible for Canada to join the coalition at the last minute, Chrétien no longer had any entrée in Washington.

Third, Ottawa also made little effort to engage in traditional Canadian diplomatic behaviour—by working alongside the United States but behind the scenes trying to use quiet persuasion to constrain American behaviour. It is useful to contrast the Chrétien government's diplomacy on Iraq with the diplomacy of the government of Louis St. Laurent over the Korean conflict. In Korea, the Canadian government worked hard to constrain the impulses of the Democratic administration of Harry S. Truman and its expanding war aims. There was a real concern in Ottawa about the implications of widening the war to include the on-going civil war between the Chinese Nationalists on Taiwan and the newly established communist Peoples Republic of China. And Canadians tried on a number of occasions to change the course of American policy. For Lester Pearson, the foreign minister, the key assumption was 'that the possibilities for containing the behaviour of great power decision-makers are increased if they can be induced to operate within a multilateral arena. In such a context they are subject to the demands and pressures of smaller states, whose representatives can sometimes be mobilized in concert. At the same time, however, it is vital to recall that the essence of great power status . . . is the capacity in the final analysis to treat lesser powers as incidental. This being the case, the leverage of small power statesmen is always limited by the degree to which their views are regarded as important . . . Hence, in the Korean case, Washington could be constrained, but only to a point.'[2]

Pearson's assumptions remain as relevant today as they were in Korea in the early 1950s. However, there was an essential necessary condition: for the Canadian government to be able to exercise influence in Washington on matters of global policy, the government in Washington had to be willing to listen to what Canadians had to say on such matters.

But over the last six months prior to the start of the war against Iraq, the Chrétien government made itself progressively more irrelevant in Washington. Thus when Ottawa did float an eleventh-hour compromise proposal, it came far too late—by then the Canadian government was completely irrelevant in the eyes of the major players, including the United States. By that time, no one cared. And indeed, when the Canadian government finally abandoned its ambiguity and announced that it was not participating, no one was really surprised.

It can be argued that the concrete decision not to join the 'coalition of the willing' was made worse by the parade of insulting, rude, insensitive, short-sighted behaviour on the part of the Chrétien government. The list is long: Chrétien wondering on the first anniversary of 11 September whether the inattentiveness of Americans to global poverty might have brought the terrorist attacks on themselves: Chrétien's communication director, Françoise Ducros, calling the president a moron, not being disciplined by Chrétien, and

---

[2] Denis Stairs, *The Diplomacy of Constraint: Canada, the Korean War, and the United States* (Toronto: University of Toronto Press 1974), 311.

only falling on her sword when American commentators refused to let the comment go; Liberal members of parliament such as Carolyn Parrish claiming that she 'hated' Americans, terming them 'bastards,' or Karen Kraft Sloan sniggering at Bush's religious beliefs; cabinet ministers such as Herb Dhaliwal slagging Bush for his lack of statesmanship, or Bill Graham, the minister of foreign affairs, not bothering to call the US ambassador prior to the prime minister's announcement to inform him of Canada's decision, and then saying that Paul Cellucci was quite capable of watching Canadian TV; or the video clip of the entire Liberal caucus jumping up in joyful applause when Chrétien finally announced to the House of Commons that Canada was not going to support the US.

What are the likely consequences of Canada's stand on Iraq? First, it is likely that until there is 'regime change' in either Ottawa or Washington, the Canadian government will cease to have any meaningful voice in Washington on matters of global policy. This means that at the very time that the United States government is embarking on what is a radically different kind of foreign policy, Canadians will have no means of even trying to influence the direction and nature of that revised course. Canadians will be reduced to kvetching from the sidelines, and we can be fairly sure that whatever advice comes from Ottawa will be ignored with great pleasure by anyone who matters in Washington.

Second, the decision on Iraq is likely to have an adverse effect on the well-being of Canadians. This is not the tired old argument that Canadians will face overt retaliation from the US government for having diverged from American policy on this issue. That is not how politics in North America works. Rather, it is the argument, most commonly associated with John W. Holmes, that Canadians have an enduring interest in maintaining a certain kind of relationship with the United States. Holmes used to make this point on many occasions. For example, in *Life With Uncle*, a book written in 1981 when the administration of Ronald Reagan had just arrived in Washington, and Canadian-American relations were heading into one of their cyclical downturns, he put it this way: 'It is of very great importance to Canada to maintain amicable relations with whatever administration the Americans elect. That does not mean supine agreement, but it suggests caution in picking a quarrel. The danger [of not picking one's quarrels carefully] is that we forfeit not only our vested interests but also the disposition in Washington to listen to our arguments on world affairs.'[3]

Twelve years later, in an era when even more of Canada's wealth depends on cross-border trade, Denis Stairs would restate the Holmesian prescription when he wrote that there is 'only one imperative in Canadian foreign policy. That imperative is the maintenance of a politically amicable, and hence economically effective working relationship with the United States.'[4]

In other words, it is not that the United States government—or ordinary Americans—will lash out at Canada in retaliation. Rather, the consequences of cocking a snook at the US on such an important issue as the war against Iraq will be far more subtle, and thus far more damaging to Canadian interests. The real danger is to the smooth management of the

3   John W. Holmes *Life with Uncle: Canadian–American Relationship* (Toronto: University of Toronto Press 1981), 91.
4   Denis Stairs, 'Canada in the New International Environment,' Inaugural Meeting, Canadian Consortium on Asia Pacific Security, York University, Toronto 3–4 December 1993.

vast complexity that is the Canadian–American relationship. To be sure, this will probably only be manifest in a number of small ways, but the very size of the Canadian–American relationship tends to take small things and magnify them. For example, if a mere fifteen seconds of processing time were added for every border visitor, the impact would be profound if that were multiplied by 550,000—the number of people who cross the border each day. Likewise, if Canada is unable to secure extensive exceptions to the Draconian provision of the US Patriot Act of 2002, just-in-time production arrangements in North America will be seriously affected. In the long term, it is likely that investment decisions in the next five years will be affected by the degree to which the border starts to become a real impediment to the flow of goods and people, since rational investors are unlikely to invest in Canada when getting goods to market is impeded by a border that slows flows down to a crawl.

The argument here is not that the Canadian government should have joined the Bush coalition of the willing simply in an effort to keep the border open. Rather, the argument is that there are clever ways to deal with the US and not-so-clever ways. And while it may be very satisfying to stick one's finger in the American eye and give it a little wiggle, such satisfaction is not only juvenile but could be highly damaging to the interests of those who do not have fat parliamentary pensions to cushion them from the effects of recession or unemployment that may be one of the consequences of puerile approaches to global politics.

This leads to a second argument, which has a more positive aspect: we have been here before, and there is an interesting historical dynamic that appears to play out in Canadian politics. Canadians, it would appear from their voting behaviour, tend to understand, however inchoately, the wisdom of the argument advanced by policy-makers like Holmes and academics like Stairs. They appear to understand, again however inchoately, that Canada's aggregate wealth—and the wealth of those in the Quebec-Windsor corridor in particular—is heavily dependent on amicable political relations between Canada and the United States. Canadians get uncomfortable when the relationship sours. By the same token, however, Canadians appear not to like it when relations between Ottawa and Washington get too close or chummy.

When the relationship between the two governments veers into the outer zones of overly friendly or overly antagonistic, an interesting phenomenon appears to occur in Canadian politics: a strong counter-reaction emerges that provides fertile soil for a political force to bubble up to argue the importance of changing the relationship.

In the 1950s, for example, when the Liberals under Prime Minister Louis St Laurent were seen to be climbing far too deeply into bed with the United States, the Progressive Conservatives under the leadership of John Diefenbaker were encouraged to make the Canadian–American relationship an election issue and to formulate an alternative vision. But when Diefenbaker's relationship with the US deteriorated, the Liberals under Lester Pearson were able to make the improvement of the relationship an important element of their 1963 election campaign.

Likewise, in the early 1980s, when relations between the government of Pierre Elliott Trudeau and the Reagan administration deteriorated, Brian Mulroney was able to make refurbishing the relationship with the US a priority. Mulroney enjoyed an exceptional relationship with both Reagan and his successor, George H. Bush. And it was the very exceptional nature of that relationship that provided considerable fodder for Jean Chrétien to attack Mulroney's record on Canada–US relations during the 1993 election campaign.

We can see this dynamic unfold at present. No sooner had the Canadian–American relationship sunk to the low point in March 2003 than the pendulum began to swing yet again. The forces of reaction gathered steam with considerable alacrity, forcing the prime minister to muzzle the more anti-American voices in his government and prompting Paul Martin, the leading contender for the Liberal leadership, to speak out about the need to repair the relationship.

However, while the new Liberal leader may be able to repair the relationship sufficiently to forestall some of the more damaging economic effects, it is likely to be more difficult to recover Canada from its faded diplomatic status and to ensure that Canadian views are considered by the American administration. The United States has embarked on a new course in global politics; Canadians have a deep interest in being able to influence that course as much as possible. Unfortunately, to recover our voice in Washington will likely require more political capital than any contender for the Liberal leadership possesses.

Chapter 26

The Governance of North America: NAFTA's Stunted Institutions

STEPHEN CLARKSON, SARAH DAVIDSON LADLY,*
MEGAN MERWART, AND CARLTON THORNE

*Stephen Clarkson is a Professor of Political Science at the University of Toronto.
Sarah Davidson Ladly practises law at Blake, Cassels & Graydon LLP in Toronto.

Europe's astonishing development of a unique form of regional political authority, in which transnational governance combined member-state governments with players from the market place and the citizenry, presents those trying to understand other regions with a conceptual conundrum. Does the European Union's evolution towards some kind of constitutionalized federation of states with its strong Commission, its ambitious parliament, its asymmetry-reducing voting, and its effective judiciary provide the heuristic model for understanding other regions, albeit those at a more embryonic stage?

This Europe-is-our-model view has been implicit in much of the past decade's analysis of the western hemisphere's evolution. With Mercosur bringing Brazil, Argentina, Uruguay, and Paraguay into a common market and with the Canada-United States Free Trade Agreement (FTA, 1989) pulling Mexico into a North America[n] Free Trade Agreement (NAFTA, 1994), many saw the New World following in the footsteps of the Old, albeit with a few decades' delay.

While agreeing that North America in the past ten years has developed new forms of transnational decision-making and while accepting that NAFTA coordinates significant political-economy functions among its three members, in our view this putatively "free trade" agreement masks the enhancement of the United States' dominance over its periphery. In other words, while NAFTA opened up a more integrated economic space and while it constitutes a codified legal system that formally reconstituted political authority for its three members, it did this with a very different valence for each. By causing Canada and then Mexico to accept some of its norms, the U.S. extended its sovereignty beyond its borders. By ingesting in their own legal orders rules designed to further U.S. interests, the two peripheral states curtailed their own sovereignty.

In order to address the general complexities involved in assessing the significance of the United States' evolving relationship with Mexico and Canada, we will develop the case that, behind its façade of equality, NAFTA's reconstitution of political authority in North America undermines its peripheral states while strengthening the centre. Let us start by looking at the continental system created by NAFTA as if it were a traditional government, analyzing it in the way that the European Union (EU) often is, that is, in terms of:

1. its *constitution*, which defines the system's norms and establishes its institutions;

2. an *executive* that makes decisions and policies to sustain its operation;

3. a *legislature* whose prime electoral function is to represent the public in the policy-making process;

4. a *judiciary* which resolves conflicts among constituents by interpreting the constitution's norms;

5. a *bureaucracy*, which makes the whole system actually function;

6. an ability to *enforce* public law, administrative regulations, and judicial rulings.

Examining North America's government under the same six rubrics should allow us to determine whether this region is undergoing a transformation analogous to the European case. Because the two continents' regimes are so startlingly similar in their capitalist economic system and demographic size and because their dominant cultures share common Judeo-Christian roots, looking at one in terms of the qualities of the other has an inherent fascination.[1] But we must note at the outset that there are important differences complicating any effort at comparison. Ethnically, North America has an indigenous population whose political salience ranges from high in Mexico to medium in Canada to low in the United States. Developmentally, the discrepancy between the wealth and technological capacity of the American and Canadian societies, on the one hand, and Mexico on the other as well as the crushing power asymmetry between the central state and its two neighbours stands in sharp contrast to the greater homogeneity among EU members, which are nevertheless more divided linguistically and historically than their North American counterparts.

CONSTITUTION

If a polity's constitution is the rulebook that defines its institutions and establishes the norms by which they are run, then the complex transnational jigsaw in North America has various constitutionalizing elements. For instance, 60 years of binational defence cooperation between the United States and Canada have generated an elaborate structure of reciprocal defence obligations that were in effect constitutionalized by over 80 treaty-level agreements such as the North American Air Defence Command (NORAD), 250 memoranda of understanding, and 145 bilateral defence discussion forums. FTA created a more general constitutional framework for the United States-Canada relationship with strong rules but weak administration. Though much more conflictual, even antagonistic, the United States-Mexico relationship also developed constitutionalizing elements, particularly in the form of agreements defining modalities for managing flows of all kinds across the common border.

NAFTA was the first North American accord with trinational scope. But, compared to the elaborate system created by the European community's various treaties, it contains a thin, even unidimensional set of economic norms—national treatment being of prime importance—which have supralegislative weight in the sense that they can trump acts of the member-states' legislatures. The agreement also contains hundreds of pages of rules directing member-states' legislative and regulatory actions, whether negative, "thou shalt not" injunctions (Canada was forbidden to set different prices for exported and domestically consumed petroleum products) or positive, "thou shalt" commandments (Mexico had to create a new trade-law system). These measures applied to a wide range of policy fields

---

[1] Stephen Clarkson, "Fearful Asymmetries: The Challenge of Analysis Continental Systems in a Globalizing World," *Canadian-American Public Policy* 35 (1998): 1–66.

such as telecommunications and agriculture, government procurement and energy, cultural development and industrial promotion.

Beyond these norms and rules, the constitution that NAFTA created for North America comprises a weak executive, a non-existent legislature, an uneven set of adjudicatory mechanisms, an ineffectual bureaucracy, and almost no coercive capacity—institutions to whose analysis we now turn.

LEGISLATURE

Constitutions cannot be the only source of a polity's norms, as no single document can anticipate future problems, which require existing rules to be adapted or new ones to be created. In obvious contrast to the World Trade Organization, whose Doha Round negotiations will create still more global trade rules, NAFTA has no institution through which its rule book can be adapted to changing circumstances.

NAFTA's legislative incapacity leaves the evolution of new, continentally applicable economic rules to other negotiating forums. For instance, the rule stipulating that, when tariffs on a good have fallen to zero, its cross-border commerce may not be subjected to anti-dumping or countervailing duties emerged from the bilateral negotiations between Canada and Chile. New trade norms were expected to emerge in the western hemisphere through the negotiation of a Free Trade Area of the Americas (FTAA) which, had it not been blocked in 2003 by Brazil's opposition, would presumably have trumped those of NAFTA.

EXECUTIVE

According to the NAFTA treaty, the North American Free Trade Commission supervises the implementation of NAFTA, oversees its further elaboration, resolves disputes that arise from interpretations of the Agreement, and observes the work of the committees and working groups it established.[2]

This substantial mandate notwithstanding, the North American Free Trade Commission turned out not to be an institution at all. It has no quarters, still less an address, a staff, or secretariat to call its own. "Trade Commission" is just a label for three NAFTA trade ministers' periodic meetings, which, according to the United States Trade Representative, are "intended to assess the implementation of the agreement, resolve any new disputes, and oversee the work of numerous committees established to address specific issues described in each chapter in the agreement."[3] It convenes quite infrequently: "only as required, or for annual meetings."[4]

JUDICIARY

No constitution is effective unless it has some means by which to resolve disputes that inevitably surface when opposed interests take differing positions on the meanings of its norms. Although NAFTA was not established with an actual court and judges, it does have

---

[2]   NAFTA, Article 2001, 2.a–e.

[3]   Robert Pastor, *Toward a North American Community: Lessons from the Old World for the New* (Washington, DC: Institute for International Economics, 2003), 73–4.

[4]   See: http://www.dfait-maeci.gc.ca/nafta-alena/inst-en.asp. Accessed 12 October 2005.

provisions for mitigating disputes over trade harassment (Chapter 19), for empowering aggrieved companies to sue member governments (Chapter 11), for addressing certain environmental and labour-law issues, for settling conflicts concerning financial institutions and energy, and for resolving general disputes about the Agreement's implementation (Chapter 20).

Chapter 19: Trade Remedy Disputes

Had NAFTA created a true free-trade area, its members would have abandoned their right to impose anti-dumping (AD) or countervailing duties (CVD) on imports coming from their partners' economies. Refusing to give up its sovereignty over trade remedy actions and so allow a real levelling of national trade barriers that would have created a single continental market, the United States simply agreed to cede appeals of its protectionist rulings to ad hoc binational panels which were restricted to investigating whether the defendant's AD or CVD determinations properly applied its own *domestic* trade law.

NAFTA's Chapter 19's putatively binding judicial expedient turned out to be less binding than originally billed. When the United States' CVD against Canadian softwood lumber exports was remanded for incorrectly applying the notion of subsidy as defined in U.S. law, Congress simply changed its definition of subsidy to apply to the Canadian situation. Beyond softwood lumber's long-lasting evidence—the U.S. is still pursuing Canada on the grounds of its exports being subsidized—Canada has not had a satisfactory experience in using Chapter 19 to appeal other American trade determinations. In 1993, for instance, there were multiple remands in five cases, which led the panels to surpass their deadlines significantly. Further problems have arisen over the inconsistency among Chapter 19 panel decisions, which have shown significantly different degrees of deference to agency determinations.

Although AD and CVD jurisprudence may have been ineffective in helping the peripheral states constrain their hegemon, the opposite is not true. Canadian trade agencies have had to adjust the standards they apply in AD or CVD determinations to American interpretations out of a concern for what the binational panels, which necessarily include American jurists, may later decide on appeal.

In striking contrast to the minor modification of its trade remedy interpretations that Chapter 19 panels imposed on Canada's protective administrative procedures, NAFTA caused Mexico to import holus bolus into its legal system a complete trade remedy system. All the more extraordinary because of its civil law tradition, Mexico had to create from scratch judicial procedures to satisfy its interlocutors that their companies would be treated the same way in challenging protectionist rulings as they would in the U.S. or Canada's common law systems.[5]

The experience of Chapter 19 has also been replicated in Chapter 20 disputes: NAFTA's judicial function is asymmetrical in its impact. It does not constrain the behavior of the hegemon on politically sensitive issues, but this does not stop the hegemon from using it to enforce NAFTA rules to its advantage in the periphery. And when these processes don't satisfy Washington, it can still exercise its raw power to achieve its objectives. But

---

[5]   Stephen Clarkson, "Reform from Without versus Reform from Within: NAFTA and the WTO's Role in Transforming Mexico's Economic System," in *Mexico's Political and Society in Transition*, eds. Joseph S. Tulchin and Andrew D. Selée (Boulder, CO: Lynne Rienner, 2002), 215–53.

if Chapters 19 and 20 have proven to be surprisingly weak as institutions of continental governance, Chapter 11 is surprisingly strong.

Chapter 11: Investor-State Disputes

NAFTA's Article 1110 stipulates that no government may "directly or indirectly expropriate or nationalize," or take "a measure tantamount to expropriation or nationalization" except for a "public purpose," on a "non-discriminatory basis," in accordance with "due process of law and minimum standards of treatment" *and* on "payment of compensation." What is remarkable about this article is not the wording, which is identical to that found in FTA, but rather its empowerment by a judicial process that gives corporations from other NAFTA parties the power to overturn democratically generated legislative, executive, or bureaucratic decisions deemed necessary to secure the health and safety of the citizenry. Under these investor-state tribunals, for instance, an American or Mexican corporation with interests in Canada can initiate arbitration proceedings against a municipal, provincial, or federal "measure" that harms their interests on the grounds that it has been the victim of expropriation. These disputes are taken for arbitration before an international panel operating by rules established under the aegis of the World Bank's International Convention on the Settlement of Investment Disputes between States and Nationals of other States (ICSID) or the United Nations Commission on International Trade Law (UNCITRAL) for settling international disputes between corporations.[6] Since these forums operate according to the norms of international corporate law, Chapter 11 disputes actually transfer the adjudication of disputes over member-state policies from the realm of public law to private law and from the domestic to the global level.

Article 1110 gives transnational corporations important rights without balancing them with obligations. There are no continental institutions with the clout to regulate, tax, or monitor the newly created continental market that has proceeded to emerge.[7] In other words, NAFTA supported a regime of continental governance less by creating a new institutional structure for it than by reducing member-states' capacities to exercise sovereignty over their own political space. Corporations with continental scope were given both greater freedom from state regulation and a privatized, transnational legal device to discipline those governments that stood in their way.

Although NAFTA has no legislative competence, its Chapter 11 tribunals have proven their ability to create new norms. More accurately, the cases launched by Ethyl, S.D. Myers, and Metalclad Corps. resulted in the repeal of legislation that had already been passed.

In the first instance, when Ethyl Corp. of Virginia initiated an investor-state dispute process, Ottawa settled privately by withdrawing the law that forbade the trade of the octane enhancer and alleged neurotoxin MMT.

In the second Chapter 11 affair, the tribunal ruled that Ottawa's banning the export of PCBs both expropriated the waste disposal company's property and denied it national treatment, even though only a phantom company operated in Canada to generate business

---

[6] Gary Horlick and DeBusk, "Dispute Resolution under NAFTA: Building on the U.S.-Canada FTA, GATT and ICSID," *Journal of World Trade* 27, no. 1 (1993): 52.

[7] Stephen Blank, Stephen Krajewski, and Henry S. Yu, "US Firms in North America: Redefining Structure and Strategy," *North American Outlook* 5 (February 1995): 9–72.

for its processing plant in the United States. In validating the notion that S.D. Myers had suffered action "tantamount to expropriation," the tribunal was both unmaking a federal law and amending the notion of expropriation previously employed in Canadian law.

In the third example, the Chapter 11 tribunal deemed illegal the action taken by a Mexican municipality to close a groundwater-polluting industrial waste site bought by Metalclad.

The Chapter 11 investor-state dispute settlement mechanism is powerful in good part because UNCITRAL and ICSID arbitrations have direct effect in domestic courts. This means that the coercive power of the defendant member-states themselves ensures their compliance with this part of NAFTA's de-territorialized adjudicatory system.

BUREAUCRACY

Just as constitutions establish a judicial system to interpret them, they also set up administrative institutions which need civil servants to staff them. The NAFTA text established a "NAFTA Secretariat [which] administers the NAFTA dispute resolution processes under Chapters 14, 19 and 20 of the NAFTA, and has certain responsibilities related to Chapter 11 dispute settlement provisions."[8] In their anti-institutional wisdom, the signatories never created this secretariat, contenting themselves with opening their own national NAFTA secretariats, each of which has turned out to be a small office within its trade department with only minor record-keeping responsibilities such as maintaining a court-like registry relating to panel, committee, and tribunal proceedings.

NAFTA established some twenty committees and working groups (CWGs) to monitor and direct each chapter's implementation. Since these groups had the potential to become instruments for a genuine, coordinated and transnational decision-making authority within the new continental structure created by NAFTA, it is worth comparing their official purposes with their actual performance.

Official Purposes

The CWGs were officially set up not to be supranational, but rather intergovernmental and explicitly *professional*. They were to be forums in which civil servants from the three countries could exchange information, resolve minor disputes, and discuss further liberalization. Their structure and composition were intended to favour objective analysis and the pre-emptive resolution of conflicts through the formation of small networks of experts.[9] It was hoped that the resulting epistemic communities would be inclined to treat issues impartially and focus on long-term benefits of increased economic activity that would be mutually rewarding, rather than on the short-term costs of immediate dislocations that might be politically contentious.[10]

---

[8]   See: http://www.pict-pcti.org/courts/NAFTA.html. Accessed 12 October 2005.

[9]   Joseph McKinney, "NAFTA-Related Institutions in the Context of Theory," in *Created from NAFTA: The Structure, Function, and Significance of the Treaty's Related Institutions*, ed. Joseph McKinney (Armonk, NY: M.E. Sharp, 2000), 17.

[10]   Ibid., 22.

Indeed, the implicit connotation of professional was *apolitical*. Although "political direction for the NAFTA work program [was to be] provided by ministers through the Free Trade Commission,"[11] the groups were to be insulated from direct political pressures in their day-to-day activities. The basis for having specialized groups staffed by civil servants who were drawn from various agencies and ministries and were selected for their detailed knowledge of the issue at hand—be it pesticides, trucking standards, or customs issues[12]—was the belief that NAFTA was more likely to operate by its rules if their operation was at least partly removed from the sphere of domestic politics and placed in new, problem-solving transnational institutions.[13]

In the spirit of the new continentalism, they were created with a view to *trilateralize* relations by evaluating and even helping direct trade-related public policy within all three member-states. The groups were mandated to meet from one to four times yearly, or as issues arose, and to produce reports for the Free Trade Commission. Meetings were to take place in Canada, the U.S., and Mexico in rotation.[14] Trilateral forums were expected to be more likely to defuse bilateral conflicts and so provide a means to transcend the double bilateralism of pre-NAFTA trade politics in North America.

Trilateralism had its own implicit corollary—symmetry—a step in the direction of a new continental relationship founded on the legal equality of its constituents. There was to be approximately equal representation of the three countries [i]n each group, which was to be co-chaired by an official from each member-state. The mere existence of such trilateral institutions could be expected to offset the asymmetry in power that existed between the United States and its neighbours, ensuring that all three states were given a "voice" with which to make their views known and possibly give them effect.[15]

The CWGs' trilateral, professional, and symmetrical nature marked a significant innovation for North American relations. Whether this novelty had any substance was another matter entirely.

Activities and Processes of the Committees and Working Groups

Just as the CWGs' mandates vary, so do their actual processes and functions. Most groups are engaged in a combination of activities which fall into five categories: 1) implementing or overseeing the implementation of the agreement; 2) exchange of information; 3) resolution of conflicts; 4) harmonization of regulations; and 5) forums for the relay of information between the governments and interested parties.

To give an example of a committee's functions, the Telecommunications Standards Sub-Committee's (TSSC) key responsibility is the coordination of efforts and exchange of information with the Consultative Committee for Telecommunications (CCT), an organization that represents the interests of the telecommunications industry in North America. The TSSC's membership consists of two or three government officials from each of the

---

[11] Claude Carrière, interview with author, 10 April 2002.
[12] Ibid.
[13] McKinney, "NAFTA-Related Institutions in the Context of Theory," 22.
[14] Carrière, interview.
[15] McKinney, "NAFTA-Related Institutions in the Context of Theory," 14.

NAFTA states, but since 1999, the chair and the vice-chairs of the CCT have additionally been invited to all of the committee's meetings with the goal of enhancing the degree of feedback coming from the pertinent business communities of the three countries.[16]

While most CWGs operate as forums for relaying private sector concerns and ideas to government officials charged with interpreting and implementing NAFTA, the degree of private sector participation and consultation varies from group to group.[17] Although the involvement of private-sector interests is appropriate in the context of a free trade agreement, CWGs blur the lines between consultant and consulted in some cases. Despite the fact that the level of consultation is "nothing beyond the usual day-to-day interaction" for an administrative entity such as the U.S. Department of Commerce,[18] the democratic legitimacy of these groups is questionable.

Actual Performance

Rather than become new agents of continental government, the CWGs have proven largely inconsequential as governance. By 2002, approximately 60% of them were inactive. In the case of the Committee on Trade in Goods (CTG), inactivity signified success, as its final round of tariff acceleration, completed ahead of schedule, left it without an agenda. However, the CTG stands out as the only example of a group that has completed, to the satisfaction of all three parties, NAFTA's mission, which specified the items requiring further tariff reduction.[19]

If a CWG's mandate is too politically sensitive to address, it becomes deadlocked and thereby inactive. Some groups, such as the Committee on Trade in Worn Clothing and the Working Group on Emergency Action, were born out of the inability to reach consensus on certain controversial issues during the NAFTA negotiations. To forestall delay in signing the agreement, some unresolved but contentious issues were assigned to working groups as a way to "soften the failure of a lack of resolution."[20] In these cases, establishing working groups was simply a "graceful way of pretending there would be more discussion" about a failed negotiation.[21] These CWGs encountered considerable difficulties operating, as issues that were too contentious prior to 1994 did not become any easier to navigate subsequently.

One particularly instructive case of a contentious bilateral issue that defied resolution through NAFTA's bureaucratic and judicial frameworks is trucking.

The Mexico-U.S. Trucking Dispute

In the NAFTA negotiations, the U.S. agreed to end long-standing restrictions against Mexican trucking companies and gradually allow them to operate in the United States in

---

[16] Response from a Canadian civil servant via questionnaire.

[17] Jeffery Dutton, interview with author, Office of NAFTA and Inter-American Affairs, U.S. Department of Commerce, Washington, DC, 11 April 2002.

[18] Ibid.

[19] Kent Shigetomi, interview with author, Director of Mexico and NAFTA Affairs, Office of the U.S. Trade Representative, Washington, DC, 10 April 2002.

[20] Ibid.

[21] Charles Doran, interview with author, Johns Hopkins University, Washington, DC, 11 April 2002.

a process that was to have been completed by 1 January 2000.[22] However, the restrictions were maintained by the Clinton administration because of strong pressure from interest groups benefiting from the status quo.[23] Financial stakes were substantial: the cross-border trucking industry carried $250 billion in Mexican-U.S. trade. If American truckers were to be transporting fewer goods, the U.S. insurance companies' market share and profits would decrease.[24] For their part, American trucking unions argued that Mexican trucks would not adhere to American safety standards.

In 1995, the Mexican government requested that a dispute resolution process be activated under the aegis of NAFTA's Chapter 20. American manoeuvring managed to drag out the adjudicatory process, but finally, in February 2001, the panel ruled that the U.S. moratorium violated NAFTA and ordered the Department of Transportation to begin processing all Mexican applications.[25]

Beyond confirming the impoverished justice offered by Chapter 20, this long, unhappy episode illustrated the failure of NAFTA's working group system. The Land Transportation [Standards] Subcommittee [LTSS] had been established under NAFTA's Chapter 9 "to address developments of more compatible standards related to truck, bus, and rail operations and the transport of hazardous materials among the United States, Mexico and Canada."[26] Within this general mandate, the [LTSS] established a Cross-Border Operations and Facilitation (TCG #1) Consultative Working Group to deal with the Mexican-U.S. border issue. Since its inception, however, the group's most significant activity has been to arrange for "a meeting of the trilateral ad hoc government-industry insurance group formed by TCG #1."[27] Thus, the [LTSS] has merely functioned to exchange information and study national regulatory systems, despite Annex 913.5.a-1 explicitly directing that:

> *No later than three years after the date of entry into force of the Agreement, [the Subcommittee shall determine] standards-related measures respecting vehicles, including measures relating to weights and dimensions, tires, brakes, parts and accessories, securement of cargo, maintenance and repair, inspections, and emissions and environmental pollution levels.*[28]

This list contained many of the safety concerns expressed by the United States. The task of harmonizing weight standards for bus and truck operations fell within the mandate of the [LTSS], and as such, it was an issue that was meant to be resolved in a trilateral, professional fashion by a group of experts. The bilateral nature of the dispute is one reason why it did not function well in the trilateral framework. Canada remained involved in this issue only to the extent that it desired to be kept informed of developments, and that it wanted to see the dispute resolved. Despite being formally a NAFTA issue, it remained primarily a bilateral dispute.

---

22 Bradly Condon and T. Sinha, "An Analysis of an Alliance: NAFTA Trucking and the U.S. Insurance Industry," *The Estey Centre Journal of International Law and Trade Policy* 2, no. 2 (2001): 238.
23 Ibid., 237.
24 Ibid., 235–236, 240.
25 Ibid., 238.
26 Meeting of the NAFTA Land Transportation Standards Subcommittee (1999).
27 Ibid.
28 NAFTA, Ch. 9. Annex 913.5.a-1, 2 (a) iii.

Politics played a contradictory, but illuminating role both in provoking and resolving this dispute. On the one hand, it was the highly politicized nature of the dispute which prevented the [LTSS] from dealing with the issue in any meaningful way. On the other, the transnationalizing of the United States' southern border gave Mexico more clout than had NAFTA. The increasing importance of Mexican-Americans in U.S. presidential and congressional politics necessitated a politically negotiated solution. The issue was only resolved by high-level negotiations between Presidents Bush and Fox in 2001.

The Land Transportation [Standards] Subcommittee was reinvigorated as a result of the Bush administration's decision to honour the panel's decision. The procedures for implementing the dispute panel's ruling were defined when the U.S. Congress set specific guidelines that the Department of Transportation was to follow. In November 2002, President Bush modified the moratorium on granting operating authority to Mexican motor carriers and enabled the Department of Transportation to review the 130 applications already received from Mexico-domiciled truck and bus companies. Ultimately, the [LTSS] had little to do with the resolution of this dispute. The United States' non-compliance with its obligation was primarily determined by other political considerations such as a continuing obstruction through the U.S. trucking interests' use of the courts.

CWG Resurgence

The CWG story is not all about decline. It is also partly about revival. Certain groups have been revitalized as a result of a particular working group incorporating the continued bilateralism of North American relations. Some of the more active trilateral committees are those that deal with bilateral issues, such as the Committee on Standards Related Measures, the Temporary Entry Working Group, the Committee on Sanitary and Phytosanitary Measures, as well as the technical working groups set up in this area to deal, for example, with pesticides and animal health. That these groups maintain fruitful information exchanges and meet more regularly than some of their more exclusively trilateral counterparts suggests that bilateral realities continue to drive the North American relationship.

A further factor contributing to higher levels of working group activity involves political leaders redirecting activity from related areas of government policy. Since the negotiation and implementation of "smart border" initiatives between the United States and Canada and Mexico following 9/11, the Customs Subgroup of the Working Group on Rules of Origin has been largely concerned with issues of border security.[29] That extraneous political motivations recharged this working group's mandate suggests that the existence of a latent structure may generate an active function.

In sum, due to the incongruity between the working groups' trilateral, professional, and symmetrical nature and the bilateral, political, and asymmetrical reality which continues to characterize the power relations of Canada and Mexico with their common behemoth, the committees and working groups set up under NAFTA have turned out to be largely insignificant. In practice, purportedly continental issues play out bilaterally, being of little interest to the uninvolved government, thus rendering the groups an inappropriate mechanism for the resolution of disputes or the discussion of emerging issues. Further, the stakes

---

[29]   David Decarme, interview with author, U.S. Department of State, Washington DC, 11 April 2002.

in these relations are generally too high for discussions and disputes to be channelled through technocratic institutions built on the principle of formal legal equality. Politically sensitive controversies require a political arena with more appropriate representation of the interests involved and more flexible processes that provide room for compromise. Such bilateral political realities constitute a serious impediment to the formation of active and effective transnational institutions in the shadow of the continental hegemon.

ENFORCEMENT

No executive, no bureaucracy, and no judiciary has clout without some means by which the decisions of those in command, the rulings of the judges, and the determinations of the bureaucrats can be given effect. Not having coercive power at their disposal is generally the Achilles' heel of regimes established by intergovernmental agreements, but many a system operates effectively nonetheless, because its members find it in their interest to play by its rules and participate in its institutions. In these cases, even when they suffer some losses along the way, the members feel they gain in the long run.

In a transnational institution as unbalanced as NAFTA, the problem of compliance is constantly on the agenda. "Trucking" and "softwood lumber" are phrases that evoke the problem of American non-compliance for Mexicans and Canadians. If Washington uses its muscle with threats of direct coercion to enforce rules or rulings that serve its purpose, it may achieve enforcement in the short term, but, in the long term, it does not increase the legitimacy of a system from which it may be the prime beneficiary. Asymmetrical compliance produces asymmetrical justice. With the United States so obviously able and willing to flout both NAFTA's letter and spirit, its peripheral members have ample reason to look elsewhere to defend their interests.

CONCLUSION

This analysis has two main implications for conceptualizing the state in the context of growing transnational connections.

First, the various patterns of global transformation that are occurring have different sovereignty effects in the region where the global hegemon is situated than in regions blessed by more symmetrical power relations. NAFTA not only allowed the United States to resist giving up sovereignty, but extended its sovereignty over its peripheral neighbours by inducing them to accept a legal regime incorporating U.S. norms in sectors such as intellectual property rights.

While the dominant reality for the United States as *rule maker* for the continent was to strengthen its sovereignty, there were limits to this process. Washington was ultimately constrained in some cases by its own values, eventually having to comply with the Chapter 20 ruling on Mexican trucks. While its control of various aspects of the two peripheral political economies increased, it was not able to impose its will on a purely political issue, that of waging war on Iraq.

For the peripheries as *rule takers*, the dominant reality was to have their sovereignty reduced by accepting constraints on their policy-making powers. For Canada, this represented less a loss of its monopoly over decision-making than a change of form and of degree in its relative autonomy. Having never enjoyed a sovereignty defined as freedom from external interference, Canada, as Mexico, found its territory being further denationalized as American-dictated norms prevailed in its political space. It was not so much a question of a separation between its domestic and foreign policies being transcended as it was a case of the peripheral states' porosity being intensified. These cooperative states were not just able and willing: they were forced by pressure from the outside and by their own elites on the inside to intensify their continental integration under U.S. terms.

They nevertheless still enjoyed considerable internal policy autonomy. Continuing pressures to privatize their public services still met strong internal resistance. And American pressure in another domain actually served to increase the peripheries' sovereignty. The demands from Washington that Canada and Mexico strengthen their border security compelled the two states to strengthen their own security apparatus.

Second, in contrast to the highly integrated, relatively symmetrical, and member-controlled European Union, NAFTA has not created a more balanced framework for North American *governance*, let alone continental *government*. But despite its institutional ineffectiveness, NAFTA's legitimacy is precarious. As the 2004 presidential election campaigns showed, the connotation that it had acquired was entirely negative, being associated with outsourcing and the growth of unemployment. In Mexico, where the elites had forced NAFTA down the country's throat, hostility to NAFTA was rife even in the countryside, whose corn economy was devastated by massive imports of subsidized American product. Only in Canada, where the triumphalist discourse has not been effectively challenged, has there been high approval for what is still seen as a trade-generating and economy-boosting deal.

NAFTA's lack of institutional content leaves North American governance without an overarching structure. Nation-states still provide the bulk of the continent's government, and North American politics remains constituted by two separate, asymmetrical, U.S.-dominated relationships—in striking contrast to the far more integrated, symmetrical, and member-controlled arrangement across the Atlantic.

Chapter 27

Sustainability Law: Respecting the Laws of Nature

DAVID R. BOYD*

*__David R. Boyd__ is an environmental lawyer, professor, writer, and activist. He is a Senior Associate with the University of Victoria's POLIS Project on Ecological Governance, an Adjunct Professor with Simon Fraser University's graduate Resource and Environmental Management program, and the former Executive Director of the Sierra Legal Defence Fund.

Current environmental changes are unique in the 3.5 billion years of life on Earth in that they are being caused predominantly by human activity. Anthropogenic greenhouse gas emissions have pushed atmospheric concentrations of carbon dioxide to their highest level in at least 200,000 years, causing climate change.[1] The Earth's protective ozone layer was badly damaged during the 20th century by man-made chemicals.[2] Vast areas of native forests, grasslands, coral reefs, and other ecosystems have been destroyed or damaged, invasive species have spanned the planet, and industrial pollution is ubiquitous.[3] The majority of the world's fisheries are in decline and large marine fish populations have fallen roughly 90% since 1950.[4] As a result of the cumulative impact of these changes, current rates of extinction are estimated to be 100 to 10,000 times the rate during periods of stasis, and are on par with the cataclysmic epoch when dinosaurs disappeared from the planet 65 million years ago.[5]

Every year there are hundreds of thousands of deaths in developing countries due to air pollution.[6] Over a billion people lack access to potable drinking water.[7] Over a billion people still live on less than a dollar per day.[8] The world's human population is projected to

[1] Intergovernmental Panel on Climate Change, *Climate Change 2001: Third Assessment Report of the Intergovernmental Panel on Climate Change* (Cambridge: Cambridge University Press, 2001).

[2] World Meteorological Organization, *Scientific Assessment of Ozone Depletion: 2002* (Geneva: WMO, 2002).

[3] UN Environment Program. *GEO3: Global Environmental Outlook: Past, Present and Future Perspectives* (New York: Oxford University Press, 2002).

[4] D. Pauly, V. Christensen, J. Dalsgaard, et al., "Fishing Down Marine Food Webs," *Science* 279 (1998): 860–3. R. Myers and B. Worm, "Rapid Worldwide Depletion of Predatory Fishes," *Nature* 423 (2003): 280–3.

[5] V. Heywood and R. Watson, eds., *Global Biodiversity Assessment* (Cambridge: Cambridge University Press/UN Environment Program, 1995). E.O. Wilson, *The Diversity of Life* (Cambridge: Harvard University Press, 1992).

[6] World Health Organization, *Air Quality Guidelines* (Geneva: WHO, 1999).

[7] World Health Organization and UN Children's Fund. *Global Water Supply and Sanitation Assessment* (Geneva: WHO, 2000).

[8] World Bank, *World Development Indicators, 2004.* See the World Bank's website: *http://www.worldbank.org/data/wdi2004/*.

surpass nine billion by the year 2050.[9] The richest 20% of the world's population consume over 80% of the resources while the poorest 20% consume only 1.3%.[10] The inexorable rise of both resource consumption and the human population foreshadows a collision between human demands and the carrying capacity of the planet.

THE FAILURE OF ENVIRONMENTAL LAW

The purpose of environmental law, as it has been conceived to date, is primarily to limit or mitigate the ecological damage caused by industrial economic activity and contemporary Western lifestyles. A rapid proliferation of laws, regulations, policies, and programs over the past four decades has contributed to substantial progress on specific environmental issues in industrialized nations. Sulphur dioxide emissions, the use of ozone-depleting chemicals, lead emissions, and emissions of other air pollutants, including nitrogen oxides, volatile organic compounds, and carbon monoxide have decreased significantly. Water pollution from some industrial sources has declined. More people are connected to sewage treatment plants, and the quality of sewage treatment is rising. Quantities of per capita municipal waste have fallen, while recycling rates have risen. The area of land in parks increased by millions of hectares during the 1990s. Some harmful chemicals, including a dozen persistent organic pollutants (e.g. PCBs, chlordane, and dieldrin), have been banned.[11]

Although some battles have been won, the war is being lost. As noted earlier, critical global issues including climate change, biodiversity loss, and toxic contamination continue to worsen. Human populations and per capita environmental impacts (as measured by our 'ecological footprint'—the area of land required to produce the resources and assimilate the waste of a single person) are still increasing.[12] Overall, environmental laws and policies have managed to "reduce and even reverse some environmental damage, but only marginally to moderate the larger national and global forces of population growth, landscape transformation, natural resource use, and waste generation that define modern human history."[13] Environmental law is "based on the assumption that environmental problems can be managed without significant changes in existing production technologies and consumption patterns."[14] The litany of problems listed above proves beyond a reasonable doubt that this assumption is unwarranted. We must come to terms with the fact that existing laws and policies are incapable of addressing the root causes of our problems.

---

[9]   UN Population Fund, *People, Poverty, and Possibilities: Making Development Work for the Poor* (2004).

[10]   UN Development Programme, *Human Development Report* (New York: UNDP, 1998).

[11]   Organization for Economic Cooperation and Development, *Environmental Data Compendium, 2001* (Paris: OECD, 2003).

[12]   J. Venetoulis, D. Chazan, and C. Gaudet, *Ecological Footprint of Nations, 2004* (San Francisco: Redefining Progress, 2004).

[13]   R.N. Andrews, *Managing the Environment, Managing Ourselves: A History of American Environmental Policy* (New Haven: Yale University Press, 1999), 409.

[14]   N. Vig and M. Kraft, *Environmental Policy: New Directions for the Twenty-first Century* (Washington: CQ Press, 2003), 399.

We can either continue with our current approach, or we can choose a different path forward—a revolutionary approach. In light of continuing environmental decline, the former option is no longer tenable. As Professor Benjamin Richardson observes, "the idea of a discrete body of environmental law is perhaps anachronistic because of the need to embed and diffuse ecological considerations throughout social and economic governance structures."[15] Successfully untangling the Gordian knot of today's environmental problems will require dramatic and far-reaching changes to current patterns of production and consumption. Paradigm shifts in law, economics, and ethics are urgently needed.[16]

SUSTAINABILITY LAW

One potentially vital paradigm shift is from environmental law to sustainability law (see Table). Sustainability law would not be about merely *mitigating* the damage inflicted by industrial economies and western lifestyles. Sustainability law would focus on *transforming* the relationship between humans and the natural environment from one based on minimizing harm to one based on maximizing harmony. Instead of asking if we can limit the ecological damage caused by contemporary industrial society, sustainability law asks if we can do things in a completely different way that avoids creating environmental problems in the first place. Sustainability law will challenge the belief that human activities must inevitably damage the natural world. Can't human beings strive to do good, instead of merely aiming to be less bad? In the words of world-renowned green designers William McDonough and Michael Braungart, "to be less bad is to accept things as they are, to believe that poorly designed, dishonourable, destructive systems are the best humans can do. This is the ultimate failure of the "be less bad" approach: a failure of the imagination."[17]

THE CONTRASTING CHARACTERISTICS OF ENVIRONMENTAL LAW AND SUSTAINABILITY LAW	
Environmental Law	Sustainability Law
Mitigates	Transforms
Short-term	Long-term
Reactive, crisis-driven	Proactive, precautionary
Ad hoc	Systemic
Incremental	Radical
Fragmented	Holistic
Unscientific	Ecological
Prescriptive	Results-oriented
Rigid	Adaptive
Confrontational	Cooperative
Narrow	Diverse, pluralistic
Ineffective, inefficient, inequitable	Effective, efficient, equitable

[15]   B.J. Richardson, "Trends in North America and Europe," in *Environmental Law for a Sustainable Society*, eds. K. Bosselmann and D. Grinlinton (Auckland: New Zealand Centre for Environmental Law, 2002), 59.

[16]   For examples of proposed paradigm shifts in economics and ethics, respectively, see H. Daly, *Beyond Growth: The Economics of Sustainable Development* (Boston: Beacon Press, 1996), and Tenzin Gyatso (His Holiness the Dalai Lama), *Ancient Wisdom, Modern World: Ethics for the New Millennium* (London: Abacus, 1999).

[17]   W. McDonough and M. Braungart, *Cradle to Cradle: Remaking the Way We Make Things* (New York: North Point Press, 2002).

Sustainability law would represent an attempt to imagine a system of laws and policies that facilitate processes, products, and patterns of behaviour which are good for the planet.

Environmental law is plagued by a failure to apply contemporary scientific knowledge and understanding, reflected in a reductionist approach that underestimates the complexity, uncertainty, and unpredictability of biological and physical systems.[18] In contrast, sustainability law would be firmly rooted in science and the laws of nature, beginning with a clear understanding of the laws of thermodynamics and explicit recognition of the biophysical limits of the planet Earth. Scientists have observed that "the thermodynamic laws are ideologically neutral but when combined with the concept of sustainability, have far-reaching consequences."[19] The first law of thermodynamics states that energy (and matter) can neither be created nor destroyed. Although energy and resources taken from nature may change form, the total amount remains constant and will eventually return to nature as waste or pollution. The second law is that although the total amount of energy in an isolated system remains constant (pursuant to the first law), the quantity of energy in a useful form decreases. In other words, energy always goes from high quality to low quality, decreasing its ability to do work and increasing entropy. This is why you cannot burn the ashes from a fire.

The key implication of the laws of thermodynamics is that the more energy and resources consumed by society, the more entropy, i.e. disorder in the form of waste and pollution, will be created.[20] The second law is widely misunderstood as meaning that all economic activities cause an *irreversible* process of decay, making fewer resources available in the future.[21] In the words of Nicholas Georgescu-Roegen, the economist who inspired the field of ecological economics, "every Cadillac means fewer ploughshares for some future generations."[22] While entropy is indeed a fundamental fact of life, the Earth is not an isolated system in terms of energy. The planet receives vast amounts of solar energy (equal, annually, to 10,000 times the total use of energy by all of humanity).

In natural systems, the quantity and quality of 'wastes' are such that they can all be recycled into useful resources, resulting in a circular and inherently sustainable process powered by solar energy. The quantity and qualities of humanity's waste and pollution are no longer within nature's assimilative capacity, as climate change, ozone depletion, and the accumulation of persistent organic pollutants in the Arctic demonstrate. By intelligently redesigning

---

[18] D. Ludwig, R. Hilborn, and C. Walters, "Uncertainty, Resource Exploitation, and Conservation: Lessons from History," *Science* 260 (1993): 17, 36.

[19] J. Holmberg, K.-H. Robert, and K.-E. Eriksson, "Socio-ecological Principles for a Sustainable Society," in *Getting Down to Earth: Practical Applications of Ecological Economics*, eds. R. Costanza, O. Segura, and J. Martinez-Alier (Washington: Island Press, 1996), 22.

[20] For a detailed discussion of the implications of the laws of thermodynamics on sustainability, see J. Holmberg, K.-H. Robert, and K.-E. Eriksson, "Socio-ecological Principles for a Sustainable Society," in *Getting Down to Earth: Practical Applications of Ecological Economics*, eds. R. Costanza, O. Segura, and J. Martinez-Alier (Washington: Island Press, 1996).

[21] M. Wackernagel and W. Rees, *Our Ecological Footprint: Reducing Human Impact on Earth* (Gabriola Island, BC: New Society Press, 1996), 43. J. Rifkin and T. Howard, *Entropy: Into the Greenhouse World* (New York: Bantam Books, 1989).

[22] Georgescu-Roegen is quoted in T. Beard and G. Lozada, *Economics, Entropy, and the Environment: The Extraordinary Economics of Nicholas Georgescu-Roegen* (Cheltenham, UK: Edward Elgar, 1999).

our systems of production and consumption, using natural cycles as models, humans can ensure that our 'wastes' are also of a quality and quantity capable of being recycled as useful inputs. We need to design products and processes so that everything we use and make can enter one of two waste streams—the biological stream or the technological stream.[23] Items placed in the biological stream must be capable of safely biodegrading, while items in the technological stream, such as metals, must be capable of being used over and over again in our industrial economy. Emulating nature by creating cyclical patterns of production and consumption and ultimately relying on solar energy to convert 'wastes' into resources will enable humans to mitigate the inescapable effects of the entropy law.

Sustainability law would also recognize that the Earth is finite: there are physical limits to the volume of nonrenewable substances like fossil fuels and minerals, and limits to the productive capacity of ecosystems. Even more importantly, there are the limits to the assimilative capacity of the Earth—limits which humans exceed at our collective peril—such as the tolerance of the ozone layer for ozone-depleting chemicals or the planet's capacity for absorbing greenhouse gases. The explicit recognition of biophysical limits is necessarily followed by acceptance that current patterns of growing resource consumption and population must be fundamentally altered.[24]

It is difficult, if not impossible, to state with any degree of precision what the planet's productive and assimilative limits are, as illustrated by ongoing debates about the "oil peak" and the projected pace of global climate change.[25] A more productive approach is to identify the basic conditions necessary for attaining sustainability. A group of about 50 Swedish scientists working under the auspices of an organization called The Natural Step identified four system conditions representing a simple, clear, and comprehensive elaboration of what must be done to achieve long-term sustainability.[26] These system conditions establish the normative basis for sustainability law:

In the sustainable society, nature is not subject to systematically increasing i) concentrations of substances extracted from the Earth's crust; ii) concentrations of substances produced by society; iii) degradation by physical means; and iv) people are not subject to conditions that systematically undermine their capacity to meet their needs. If the system conditions are being violated then the society is not sustainable, period.

All elements of sustainability law can be traced back to the imperative of fulfilling these conditions. It follows from the system conditions that the environmental imperative in industrialized nations is to reduce our consumption of resources (dematerialization) and substitute clean, natural substances for substances that are known or suspected to be acutely toxic, persistent, bioaccumulative, carcinogenic, mutagenic, endocrine-disrupting, or otherwise harmful to human health and the environment. In order to achieve dematerialization

23 W. McDonough and M. Braungart, *Cradle to Cradle: Remaking the Way We Make Things* (New York: North Point Press, 2002).

24 David R. Boyd, "Root Causes of Environmental Degradation," in *Unnatural Law: Rethinking Canadian Environmental Law and Policy* (Vancouver: UBC Press, 2003).

25 R. Heinberg, *The Party's Over: Oil, War, and the Fate of Industrial Societies* (Gabriola Island, BC: New Society Press, 2003). B. Lomborg, *The Skeptical Environmentalist: Measuring the Real State of the World* (Cambridge: Cambridge University Press, 2001).

26 K.-H. Robert, *The Natural Step Story: Seeding a Quiet Revolution* (Gabriola Island, BC: New Society Press, 2002).

and substitution, two things need to happen: the invention, innovation, diffusion, and use of new technologies; and the modification of individual, business, and government behaviour.

THE DEFINING CHARACTERISTICS OF SUSTAINABILITY LAW

Long-term

Sustainability law would require the identification of ambitious yet pragmatic long-term goals, recognizing the constraints imposed by: the rate of capital stock turnover; lead times for the invention, innovation, and diffusion of new technologies; competing priorities for human resources and ingenuity (such as health care reform); and inertia in social attitudes and behaviour. Long-term targets provide the level of certainty and consistency that enables individuals, businesses, and governments to plan ahead, and make good investment decisions. It should be obvious that achieving the system conditions described earlier is not possible within ordinary political time frames. Sustainability goals "can only be achieved with a much longer time horizon than we are accustomed to in democratic societies."[27] The Aboriginal concept of considering the consequences of today's actions for seven generations and the German idea of *Jahrhundertaufgabe*, or 'the task of the century,' offer more useful time frames.

An immediate need, critical to meeting the challenge of sustainability, is the development of long-term generational strategies. In 2002, an international survey found that two-thirds of the sustainability experts polled believe that the most effective action governments could take would be to declare a time-specific generational objective for sustainability with measurable milestones, similar to President Kennedy's "man on the moon within a decade" objective.[28] Many European nations have national sustainability plans, including global leaders in environmental performance like Sweden and the Netherlands. Sweden's ambitious plan is based on fulfilling the system conditions within a single generation (i.e. 20–25 years), and significant progress has already occurred.[29]

Long-term thinking also increases the probability that radical changes, which might seem implausible in the short term, can be accomplished. The word 'radical' has acquired a pejorative connotation in today's world which is unfortunate in light of its etymological origins. Radical comes from the Latin word for root, and means getting at the root of a problem. Sustainability law will be conducive to 'radical' proposals, such as: substantive constitutional rights to clean air, clean water, and a healthy environment; Tobin taxes on short-term, cross-border foreign exchange transactions; a global tax on luxury goods, with revenue allocated to reducing poverty; and replacing the World Bank, International Monetary Fund, and World Trade Organization with a global sustainability organization.

[27] N. Vig and M. Kraft, *Environmental Policy: New Directions for the Twenty-first Century* (Washington: CQ Press, 2003), 404.

[28] World Bank and Environics International, *The Global Public's Agenda for the World Summit on Sustainable Development: Exclusive Release of Expert Survey Findings*, 31 January 2002.

[29] D.R. Boyd, *Canada vs. Sweden: An Environmental Face-off* (Victoria: Eco-Research Chair in Environmental Law and Policy, 2002).

Systemic, Holistic, Proactive, and Precautionary

Sustainability law would strive to be holistic, proactive, and precautionary. The four system conditions would facilitate a systemic approach. For example, the second system condition requires the elimination of substances that cannot be safely assimilated into nature (unless these substances can be tightly controlled in perpetuity within the industrial system). Sustainability law would use the precautionary principle to reverse the burden of proof in the regulation of pesticides, other chemicals, and genetically modified organisms. Producers or importers of substances that are acutely toxic, persistent, bioaccumulative, carcinogenic, mutagenic, endocrine disrupting, or similar in structure and qualities to chemicals known to exhibit these properties would have the onus of demonstrating an absence of health or environmental impacts.[30] Sustainability law would assume that any given chemical, if released to the environment, will likely have interactive, synergistic and cumulative effects. Producers or importers could overcome this precautionary presumption by providing peer-reviewed scientific evidence. When less harmful alternatives become available, their substitution for more harmful products would be mandatory, as in Sweden.[31]

Diverse

Sustainability law would reject the notion that one tool or set of tools is superior to all others or that one actor bears primary responsibility for taking the steps necessary to fulfill the system conditions and achieve sustainability. There are no silver bullets, no one-size-fits-all solutions, no panaceas, and no knights in shining armour. The path to sustainability will demand all of the ingenuity that we can muster and will require cooperation from every sector of society. Sustainability law would take a pragmatic approach to the selection of policy instruments, as opposed to the existing polarized ideological approach (centralized government control vs. market-based and voluntary). Market-based instruments are opposed by some environmentalists who argue that they provide a "right to pollute", yet this attitude is at odds with the reality of the existing system and the potential benefits of a different approach. On the other hand, industry often has a knee-jerk response to regulation and tax proposals, regardless of the merits or potential benefits. The full range of law and policy options will need to be employed in innovative combinations and sequences in order to fulfill the system conditions. In other words, sustainability law does not rely solely on the design and implementation of a new generation of policy instruments, but on a radically different approach to problem-solving that is holistic, proactive, adaptive and results-oriented.

Adaptive

Unlike the rigidity inherent in environmental law, sustainability law would be intentionally adaptive. As Professor Daniel Farber wrote, "one of the main lessons we should learn from the last three decades is the centrality of learning to the enterprise of environmental

---

[30] P. Sandin, B.-E. Bengtsson, A. Bergman, et al, "Precautionary Defaults: A New Strategy for Chemical Risk Management," *Human and Ecological Risk Assessment* 10 (2004): 1–18.

[31] *Chemical Products Act*, Sweden SFS 1985: 426, s. 5. Consider *http://www.kemi.se*.

protection."[32] Sustainability law would recognize that there is considerable uncertainty about the best laws, regulations, policies, and programs for achieving the system conditions. Under uncertainty, one of the best approaches is experimentation.[33] Policy experiments will enable policy-makers to determine the most effective, efficient, and equitable approaches for subsequent iterations of policy. Therefore adaptive regulation and learning by doing are vital. Laws, regulations, and policies must be assessed on a regular basis in order to determine whether progress is being made toward meeting the system conditions. In the absence of adequate progress, different (and presumably stronger) approaches are warranted. For example, Denmark introduced taxes when voluntary agreements failed to meet specified targets (for collection of nickel-cadmium batteries, reduced use of PVC and phthalates).[34] Even if progress is occurring, there should still be a process of monitoring and evaluation to determine whether there are more effective, cost-efficient, or equitable routes to meeting the system conditions.

Cooperative

Studies indicate that cultivating cultures of cooperation will result in more effective environmental protection, at a lower cost, than a system that is based on conflict.[35] Thus sustainability law will endeavour to build "a partnership in which governments, businesses, modern environmentalists, and scientists cooperate in the restructuring of the capitalist political economy along more environmentally defensible lines."[36] There is a growing role for civil society, responsible businesses, and financial institutions in devising and implementing solutions. The re-emergence of traditional Aboriginal governance offers an opportunity to create innovative approaches to sustainability.[37]

GUIDING PRINCIPLES AND DESIGN CRITERIA FOR SUSTAINABILITY LAW

Sustainability has three aspects: social, economic, and environmental. Accordingly, sustainability law will have three principal design criteria for judging its success: effectiveness, efficiency, and equity. As noted earlier, there is growing recognition that

[32]   D.A. Farber, *Eco-pragmatism: Making Sensible Environmental Decisions in an Uncertain World* (Chicago: University of Chicago Press, 1999), 179.

[33]   D. Fiorino, "Rethinking Environmental Regulation: Perspectives from Law and Governance," *Harvard Environmental Law Review* 23 (1999): 441.

[34]   European Environment Agency, *Environmental Taxes: Recent Developments in Tools for Integration* (Luxembourg: EEA, 2000).

[35]   J. Badaracco, *Loading the Dice: A Five Country Study of Vinyl Chloride Regulation* (Boston: Harvard Business School Press, 1985).

[36]   J.S. Dryzek, *The Politics of the Earth: Environmental Discourses* (New York: Oxford University Press, 1997), 145.

[37]   J. Borrows, *Recovering Canada: The Resurgence of Indigenous Law* (Toronto: University of Toronto Press, 2002).

environmental law is generally ineffective and inefficient.[38] There is also a growing body
of evidence indicating that environmental law fails to prevent inequity, as minority groups
and the poor are exposed to higher levels of environmental risks.[39] Studies show "a strong
likelihood that members of these same groups experience higher levels of environmentally generated disease and death as a result of this elevated risk."[40] The issue of environmental justice is complicated by the presence of temporal and spatial inequities that pose
complex challenges. For example North Americans, because of our high levels of fossil
fuel consumption, cause a disproportionate share of the greenhouse gas emissions that
contribute to climate change. However, the environmental consequences of these emissions will be borne largely by people in other parts of the world and by future generations.
Applying the 'polluter pays' and 'common but differentiated responsibility' principles suggests that wealthy nations should move forcefully to reduce emissions while contributing
more to mitigation and adaptation programs in developing countries.

Sustainability law will strive to be effective in attaining ecological objectives, efficient
in minimizing the economic costs to society, and equitable in the sense that costs and benefits should be justly distributed, both temporally and spatially. Through the consistent
application of these criteria, sustainability law should achieve the kind of integrated policies, plans, and decisions that have been sought but not attained for decades. The effectiveness of sustainability law will be measured by monitoring concrete progress toward
long-term objectives and fulfilling the system conditions.

Sustainability law will also incorporate recognized and emerging legal norms including the precautionary principle, the polluter pays and user pays principles, the concept of
common but differentiated responsibility, intergenerational equity, and intra-generational
equity. Some of these principles are evolving into accepted norms of international environmental law and are being incorporated into domestic law.[41]

CONCLUSION

Human beings are a unique species in that through our fecundity, seemingly insatiable
desire for material wealth, and development of powerful technologies, we are causing significant environmental degradation on a global scale. Fortunately, we are also unique in
two positive ways. First, we are conscious of the destructive consequences of our actions.

[38]   D.R. Boyd, *Unnatural Law: Rethinking Canadian Environmental Law and Policy* (Vancouver: UBC
       Press, 2003). P. Portney and R. Stavins, eds., *Public Policies for Environmental Protection*
       (Washington: Resources for the Future, 2000).

[39]   E.J. Ringquist, "Environmental Justice: Normative Concerns, Empirical Evidence, and Government
       Action," in *Environmental Policy: New Directions for the Twenty-first Century*, eds. N. Vig and M.
       Kraft (Washington: CQ Press, 2003), 249–273. J. Agyeman, R. Bullard, and B. Evans, eds., *Just
       Sustainabilities: Development in an Unequal World* (London: Earthscan, 2003).

[40]   E.J. Ringquist, "Environmental Justice: Normative Concerns, Empirical Evidence, and Government
       Action," in *Environmental Policy: New Directions for the Twenty-first Century*, eds. N. Vig and M.
       Kraft (Washington: CQ Press, 2003), 272.

[41]   P.W. Birnie and A.E. Boyle, *International Law and the Environment* (New York: Oxford University
       Press, 2002). *Rio Declaration on Environment and Development*, 13 June 1992, 31 I.L.M. 874, Principle 7.
       114957 Canada Ltee (Spraytech, Societe d'arrosage) vs. Hudson (Town), [2001] 2 S.C.R. 241.

Second, we have consciences to tell us that since we are damaging the Earth, we have an obligation to mend our ways. In the words of the Dalai Lama, "if we have the capacity to destroy the earth, so, too, do we have the capacity to protect it."[42] It is implausible to suggest that by relying on environmental law to smooth the rough edges of our industrial economy we can solve our myriad ecological problems. Sustainability is a revolutionary concept, and humanity will require revolutionary changes in governance, technology, and behaviour to achieve and maintain a decent quality of life for the nine billion humans who will inhabit the Earth by 2050 without causing irreparable harm to the planet.

The challenges seem daunting, yet one need only look back 100 years to understand the magnitude of change that humans are capable of in the geologically insignificant span of a century. In 1900, life expectancy was less than half what it is today, infectious diseases were rampant, infant mortality rates were ten times higher, school enrolment and literacy rates were far lower, neither women nor Aboriginal people could vote, and human rights were rarely respected. Modern inventions, discoveries, and accomplishments—people traveling to outer space, the human genome, Einstein's theory of relativity, the Internet, magnetic resonance imaging machines, the damage and subsequent protection of the Earth's ozone layer, and thousands more—were either in the realm of science fiction or beyond imagination. Sustainability law is an expression of confidence in the human capacity for harnessing compassion, ingenuity, and wisdom in pursuit of a better world and a better future.

SECTION 5 TERMINOLOGY

Arms control

Ba'athist

Chapter 19 (NAFTA)

Coalition Provisional Authority (CPA)

Committees and Working Groups (CWG)

Consultative Committee for Telecommunications (CCT)

Dayton Peace Accord

Democracy

Disarmament

Environmental law

European Union (EU)

Foreign Direct Investment (FDI)

Free Trade Agreement (FTA)

General Agreement on Tariffs and Trade (GATT)

Globalization

Greenhouse gas

Gross Domestic Product (GDP)

Group of 8 (G-8)

Guerilla warfare

Human security

Humanitarian intervention

Implementation Force (IFOR)

Interdependence

Intergovernmental Panel on Climate Change (IPCC)

International Convention on the Settlement of Investment Disputes (ICSID)

International Criminal Court (ICC)

International Criminal Tribunal for the former Yugoslavia (ICTY)

International law

International organizations

Internationalism

Iraqi Governing Council (IGC)

---

[42] Tenzin Gyatso (His Holiness the Dalai Lama), *Ancient Wisdom, Modern World: Ethics for the New Millennium.*

Land Transportation Standards Subcommittee (LTSS)

Middle power

Mutual assured destruction

National security

Non-governmental organization (NGO)

North American Aerospace Defence Command (NORAD)

North American Free Trade Agreement (NAFTA)

North American Free Trade Commission

North Atlantic Treaty Organization (NATO)

Office of Reconstruction and Humanitarian Assistance (ORHA)

Organization for Economic Co-operation and Development (OECD)

Organization for Security and Co-operation in Europe (OSCE)

Ottawa Process

Ottawa Treaty

Overseas Development Assistance

Paradigm

Polychlorinated biphenyls (PCB)

Quad

RAND Corporation

Security Council

Sovereignty

Stabilization Force (SFOR)

Sustainability law

Terrorism

Transitional National Assembly (TNA)

United Nations (UN)

United Nations Commission on International Trade Law (UNCITRAL)

United Nations Protection Force (UNPROFOR)

SECTION 5 DISCUSSION QUESTIONS

1. What is terrorism a response to? How might terrorism be linked to democracy?

2. How is globalization causing both "connection" and "division"? What are the implications for growing nationalism?

3. Can law, international or otherwise, enforce our environmental targets?

4. Does the NAFTA enhance, or decrease, Canada's economic position? Are there alternatives?

5. Can we reconcile humanitarian intervention with the principle of national sovereignty?

Section 6

Issues in Politics

SECTION SUMMARY

Creating categories for our studies is a useful way to organize our thoughts and our ideas. But sometimes our categories can't be cleanly divided, or some topics don't fit neatly into our groupings. This final section of the book contains five readings that could be placed in several different sections, but that do not wholly belong in any of them. The readings cover selected issues in politics that deserve our attention, and cause us to think about other themes that other readings in the book have addressed.

Politics is an inevitable part of our lives, and therefore the innumerable activities that take place in society have political characteristics. In this section of the book we have assembled readings that apply some of the concepts, issues, and approaches that we have dealt with earlier in the reader.

To begin this section, Maurice Strong tackles the potential effects of continued environmental degradation in "Report to the Shareholders." Written as though from the future, Strong imagines the domino effect of related problems that could be connected back to the way we treat our environment today. While his picture of impending events may be implausible, Strong challenges us to consider the interrelationship of politics, economics, resources, environmental damage, and spirituality. He suggests that the world as we know it is already experiencing a shifting balance and that inaction could bring about the kind of doomsday setting he describes. In "The Civilization of Difference," the Right Honourable Beverley McLachlin (currently Chief Justice of the Canadian Supreme Court) addresses identity and conflict in the world. She suggests that despite the seemingly insurmountable obstacles placed before us, there is more that binds humans together than that separates them. Canada, she feels, offers a good example of how nations might better achieve peace among communities through what she terms "accommodation."

Next, Warren Allmand examines the slow process of recognizing indigenous rights here in Canada and abroad. Charting the small steps that have been made for the rights of indigenous peoples, Allmand concludes that governments often exaggerate the implications of self-determination as leading to secession. Important declarations on the rights of indigenous peoples, he suggests, have been misinterpreted by governments as legally binding, which often leads to no progress at all. Health care in Canada is arguably the most significant issue on the minds of citizens, and Gerard W. Boychuk takes on some of the myths associated with it. Contrary to the common and popular view that Canada's health care is in crisis, Boychuk shows in his article that health care expenditure is more at risk from flawed federal–provincial relations than from a lack of money or services.

Finally, Walter Russell Mead analyzes another conventional wisdom in contemporary politics: that religion (particularly in the United States) has overtaken the political process. The United States, like many other nations, has always been strongly influenced by matters of faith. But this has changed in recent years, and these changes have broad implications for policy at home and abroad. Mead provides a useful historical overview of the role of religion in American politics and documents how strains of religious influence are tied to political theories (reinforcing again the importance of political thought!). Religion, like other influences in politics, has not run its course in America, and there are simply too many diverse interests in play to suggest that any one calls all the shots. The lessons provided by the American case apply to a number of countries, including Canada.

Chapter 28

Report to the Shareholders

MAURICE STRONG*

*Maurice Strong was Senior Advisor to former United Nations' Secretary General Kofi Annan and former Secretary-General of the United Nations Conference on the Human Environment and Executive Director of the United Nations Environment Programme.

This is how it might go, unless we're very, very lucky, or very, very wise:

1 JANUARY 2031
REPORT TO THE SHAREHOLDERS, EARTH INC.

The best that can be said of the past year—and the past tumultuous decade, the most devastating in human experience—is that it's behind us. If this were a business, the board of directors would have recommended shutting the doors and padlocking the gates, turning the workforce loose to pick up scraps where they might. But of course this is not a business; it is the Prison of Life, and there is nothing beyond the gates of Planet Earth but the formless void. Since we cannot escape, we must endure, and since we cannot give up, we must continue the struggle. We must also grasp at what straws there are. Perhaps the past decade has been so awful that it must get better. Perhaps in the chaos and degradation we have experienced, the seeds of a new order have finally been planted, and deep in the muck strong new wood is growing.

Perhaps not. But life without hope is a living death.

The year began with another grotesque failure, that of world leaders at the Global Summit held in The Hague to agree on how to reverse the accelerating breakdown in relations between states, to agree even on co-operating to discuss the lack of international co-operation. The summit was supposed to bring nations together on key issues affecting the security and future of the world community. It was also supposed to revive the United Nations as the only available forum for doing this, to attempt to bring that once august body back to a semblance of the prestige and authority it had briefly enjoyed at the end of the Cold War between the former Communist empires and the former American one—a prestige dealt a fatal blow by its contemptuous dismissal by an America confident still of its own manifest destiny.

On both these issues the summit failed dismally, with the predictable consequences we have all seen: the chaos that has engulfed the world in the past decade shows no sign of abating. Central authority has now broken down in thirty-two more nations, from which sixty-nine (or is it seventy? seventy-one?) new nations emerged, declaring themselves sovereign and independent. The greatest of these was of course China, whose central government finally had to succumb to the centrifugal forces that had already resulted in the breakup of Indonesia and smaller states like Sri Lanka. A severely weakened government in Beijing has had to acquiesce in conceding virtually full autonomy to Guangdong, Tibet, Manchuria, Hunan and the former commercial enclaves of Shanghai and Hong Kong, which insisted on fully independent status and resisted inclusion in what Beijing is forlornly describing as a "new Chinese Federal Union."

India has long since disintegrated. It's hard to remember what really set the process off—the Sikh separatists in the northwest, or the squabble between Tamil Nadu and Karnataka over the water of the Cauvery River. In a way it no longer matters: frontier posts have gone up all over the formerly united subcontinent, and minor conflicts flare every few months.

The other formerly great power in Asia, Japan, has thus far been able to contain these tendencies. But it has, nevertheless, had to concede a much greater degree of autonomy to its principal regions, while at the same time resorting to an increasingly authoritarian style of government.

Korea split apart again at the beginning of the decade and this year continued to fragment.

Attempts to revive the moribund European Union collapsed—again. The European Parliament, which hadn't met for five years, was called into special session, but it failed even to achieve a quorum—no one could agree on how to assess the credentials of many of the delegates who bothered to show up. Was Scotland an independent country, as its delegates declared? Was Alsace? Brittany? The new Basque state carved from parts of Spain and France at least seemed viable. The big news from Eastern Europe was the further breakdown of what had been called Russia. The small "states," governed mostly by warlords, that had sprung up along the banks of the Volga met briefly in the Tatar city of Kazan, but failed to agree not only on a constitution but even on a style of government, and after the convenor was assassinated, the delegates fled. A whole series of new "countries" sprang up around the Black and Caspian seas, and some of the Siberian tribes declared that their allegiance to Moscow had ended, following the lead of the Asian republics, some of whom had joined with Iran earlier in the decade, only to split again in a disastrous civil war as the mullahs came into conflict with the oil oligarchy.

Almost everywhere in the region law and order have disintegrated, and local governments are run by strong autocratic leaders who ignore or are no longer bound by normal principles of accountability. Some are closely allied with and strongly influenced by criminal elements, which wield much of the economic power. In other cases there is no distinction at all between the local "mafias" and government, and governance has become a protection racket. Gang warfare, too, is common: the region is rife with local conflicts that claimed the lives and property of many thousands of citizens while terrorizing and exploiting the remainder.

In other places there is precarious order. The tiny nation of Chechnya has exploited the breakdown of government and order in its neighbours and has assumed de facto control of the region. Although it has imposed its rule and the constitutional measures purported to legitimize it, it has nevertheless received the passive support of the people concerned for the discipline, order and stability that the regime has restored. Much of the economy of the region has been paralyzed by shortages and disruption of energy supplies.

Of the seventy-three nuclear power plants in Russia, only three are now functioning, and attempts to refurbish others have foundered for lack of capital and components. As we have learned to our cost, there is a flourishing criminal trade in the deadly components of nuclear weapons, many looted from power stations or the former Russian arsenals. The sabotage of transmission lines and relay stations has deprived large segments of the population and industry of power supplies. Gas pipelines also have been sabotaged, which has severely disrupted supplies to domestic markets and to Ukraine and Western Europe, where it has exacerbated already serious energy shortages. Massive forest fires in Siberia have effectively destroyed a number of key towns, cities and industries there, while the continuing drought in the Trans-Ural regions and torrential rains in the Ukrainian lands mockingly called the "breadbasket" area have devastated crops and produced severe shortage of food.

Nine more countries in Latin America reverted to military dictatorships, but the reversion to authoritarianism has been even more extensive, as the democratic process in many countries that retain a formal commitment to democracy has been effectively subverted by or come under the control of the military, often in collaboration with criminal elements.

In the United States, where the office of the president has been severely weakened since the assassination of President Brady in 2023, President Reynolds has become even more politically impotent with effective power increasingly concentrated among the extremists who now control Congress in concert with the military and the FBI. Their action in pushing through Congress a motion calling for a new constitutional conference constituting a powerful Preparatory Committee under the chairmanship of Senator Torrence McKelvie ostensibly to deal with the decisions taken by the state governments of Texas and Florida to secede from the union, has effectively consolidated the shift of power to this group and left the president with the formal trappings of power but devoid of its substance. Speculation about why they did not use their majority in power to impeach the president centres on their need to resolve rivalries within their own group before acting to claim presidency.

At the same time there is effectively a state of guerrilla warfare in several mountain states, as "citizen militias" become increasingly assertive.

Canada has been luckier. Two decades ago, prodded by Quebec and British Columbia separatist movements, the Canadians opted for an innovative system that divided the country into four separate sovereign states united in the Canadian Union, which helped to keep a functioning democracy. The members of the Canadian Union have suffered the same economic devastation experienced world-wide, and many parts of the union have reverted to locally managed subsistence-level economies. Overall, Canadians have thus far done a better job of managing their crisis than most. They have been able, with the help of volunteer brigades, to maintain security, so violent conflicts have been avoided or contained. A notable exception was the outbreak of violent clashes in Vancouver's Chinatown in July, when it was invaded by a large mob bent on seizing the hoards of food and medicine they believed had been stockpiled there. The rioting was eventually brought under control, but not before much of the area had been looted and destroyed.

THE STATE OF THE ENVIRONMENT

The short period of benign weather experienced in many parts of the world as the year began inspired hopes that there would be a return to more stable and reliable weather. Unfortunately, it was not to be: 2030 gave us hitherto unprecedented extremes of weather. Hurricanes, tornadoes, and record rainfall took more lives and caused more damage than both world wars of the twentieth century. Much of Florida is now under water, and the lowlands of the Carolinas are lagoons. The devastation of much of the California coast has accelerated the exodus of people from what was once one of the most attractive places in the world to live. Its economy has been shattered by the almost complete devastation of its infrastructure, particularly the road system, much of which was earlier destroyed or weakened by the Great Earthquake of 2026. Many other coastal areas around the world were similarly devastated. An estimated 6 million people died as a result of the flooding of the low-lying plains of Bangladesh, and many more are now dying of starvation and disease. Widespread flooding has also occurred in the Netherlands, despite reinforcements of its unique system of dikes, and much of its productive farmland has been lost. The rise of several centimetres in the sea level has exacerbated the effects of storms and required the evacuation of many coastal areas and several South Pacific Islands as well as the Maldives in the Indian Ocean.

Another consequence of the turbulence and destructiveness of the weather in the past year has been the disruption of water supplies. Shortages and the progressive contamination of existing supplies have deprived many cities and towns of potable and even nonpotable water. In Central Asia, cities like Bukhara and Tashkent have faced the forced evacuation of most of their residents and the closing-down of industries. Twenty years ago more than a billion people were without safe water. The number has more than doubled and is still increasing.

Oil supplies are increasingly erratic. Seizure by remnants of the military of some of the principal oil and gas fields and related facilities have been tolerated because they have restored production, despite the fact that they control the output in order to sell it to the highest bidders in a world market starved for energy.

The heavy blanket of grey smoke that hung over Siberia during the summer affected the people of this once pristine region with air pollution, while, paradoxically, their compatriots in most of the cities of the region who had long suffered from air pollution experienced some relief because of the closing of the industrial plants that had caused it. Unemployment became so bad that people were actually clamouring for pollution—at least that would have meant the reopening of the factories and plants that provided their jobs. Later in the year the pollution indeed resumed. But it was useless, unproductive pollution, the result of the coal and wood fires that warmed houses when gas and oil supplies dried up.

In the Middle East the precarious peace persisted. Iran and Iraq consolidated their control of the oil-producing states of the region, which now produce some 70 percent of the world's oil. Their reconciliation in 2021, for the purpose of freeing the region of foreign control, led to a joint guardianship of Gulf States that has proven remarkably effective, particularly now that both Kuwait and Saudi Arabia are ruled by regimes installed with the support and agreement of both Iran and Iraq.

During the year there were renewed but increasingly futile calls in the United States in particular for military action to assert Western control of the region on which its economic lifeblood depends. Cooler heads knew it was too late. It might have been feasible immediately following the rapprochement of Iran and Iraq, but was then judged unnecessary. No one expected the alliance to survive, and there were fears even then that an invasion would seriously disrupt oil supplies. A year or two afterwards was already too late. By then Iran and Iraq (the United Islamic Republic) had demonstrated their power and their joint control of OPEC by raising oil prices again to $50 a barrel. All the West could do was bluster futilely: the UIR had by then made elaborate and sophisticated arrangements for the demolition of all oil fields and facilities in the region in the case of an attack. America made noises but took no action. The price would have been too high—much higher than just paying up.

In point of fact most sober observers now admit that the new Middle Eastern power has conducted itself responsibly vis-à-vis the rest of the world and has ensured security and a certain stability of supply in an otherwise uncertain international political climate.

Although the stability of the oil situation in the region was reinforced during the year, there has been no end to the conflicts over water—which is now, barrel for barrel, more expensive than oil in many arid regions of the world. Concerted attacks by Arab guerrillas supported by Iraq have failed to dislodge Israel's control of the Jordan River, but they have demonstrated Israeli vulnerability to future attacks, particularly as the weakened economy makes it extremely difficult for the Israelis to maintain, let alone strengthen, their occupation of the basin. After an incursion of Iraqi troops deep into Turkey the two countries have reached a truce of sorts in their conflict over the Tigris, but the fundamental problems of sharing the depleted water flows of the river have not been resolved. Even more complicated is the struggle over the Euphrates. Iraq's control of Syria has strengthened its hand in the conflict with Turkey, but its preemption of a major portion of Syria's historical share of Euphrates water is creating immense human and economic problems for Syria and strong resentment against its new overlord.

Elsewhere, the Great Plains area of the midwest United States and Canada suffered the seventh consecutive year of drought, and the dried-out soil of what was once the world's most productive farming region has been swirling away on great clouds of dust, which have darkened the Prairie skies and buried whole farms and towns. Grain and animal production now barely meet local needs, and no one foresees the time when surpluses will again be available for export to those who had long relied on this source of supply. Elsewhere, too, the granaries of the world have been ravaged by either continuing drought or debilitating floods—Ukraine, Australia, the grain belt of Argentina, all have suffered. And even where grain has been produced in export quantities, the deteriorating infrastructure has meant it can't get to markets. As a consequence the price of wheat rose above $50 a bushel, but with the disruption of commodity markets, much of what was traded was sold in the black market at even higher prices.

The Ogallala aquifer, which had been the main source of groundwater for eight of the states of the Great Plains, has been sucked dry and is not being replenished. Which means the whole area—comprising farms and cities—is entirely dependent on rainfall. Consequently, the plains are among the areas hardest his by the drought.

The Colorado River was long since stolen from the Mexicans by California, but now only a trickle is reaching California itself, and farmers in the Imperial Valley have either reverted to subsistence farming or have fled. For the first time water vendors with armed guards roam the streets of Los Angeles, providing the only source of water for the few people left in those parts of the city where the water system is no longer functioning.

Last summer's record heat wave added to the toll of deaths and suffering in many parts of the world. Washington, D.C., came to a standstill as the failure of electric power left the city without air conditioning. The deaths from heat-related causes exceeded a hundred thousand, many of whom could undoubtedly have been saved if the district's remaining hospitals and medical services had not been overwhelmed.

The year has been catastrophic for humans, but insects and rodents have thrived, and the explosion in their populations has contributed immensely to the death and suffering. The outbreak of plague, which took so many lives in Russia and Central Asia, is attributed to the proliferation of the rat population; a new strain of killer bee played havoc in the southern and western United States; great swarms of locusts devoured what little there was of crops in North Africa; and mosquitoes and flies have multiplied to the point that they have made many places in the tropics as well as in northern regions virtually uninhabitable for humans. For example, a new and virulent strain of mosquito-borne malaria has emptied the bayous of Louisiana and turned New Orleans into a shrinking fortress held only with poisonous amounts of increasingly lethal pesticides.

The fires that continue to rage in the Amazon region and the forests of West Africa have reduced these to some 20 percent of their original size, and unusually dry weather, in some cases bordering on drought, combined with the relentless cutting of trees, seems to ensure that these regions will be stripped of their original growth within the next five years.

Reliable figures are not available at this point, but one of the world's leading experts at the Smithsonian in Washington has estimated that in this year alone some 25 percent of the world's prime concentrations of biological diversity have been lost, and something like the same proportion of species of animals and bird life have become extinct. There is no sign that this process is being arrested. Not only is it robbing many people who are immediately dependent on these resources for their livelihoods, but it is depriving all people of the resources that will be required to create a sustainable future for those who survive the current tumult.

The human tragedy is on a scale hitherto unimagined. In earlier periods there would have been an outpouring of sympathy and convoys of relief to the stricken areas, but no longer. People preoccupied with their own survival have little alternative but to turn their back on the more distant tragedies of others.

It's not possible to more than hazard a guess at the total number of those who have died as a result of these calamities. But for the decade it certainly must be on the order of 200 million if the victims of disease are included, a large proportion people weakened by hunger and malnutrition. The outbreak of cholera in Brazil in June has claimed at least 1.5 million victims and has still not been brought under control. A combination of famine and pervasive outbreaks of malaria, cholera and other water-borne diseases, as well as a particularly virulent virus for which there is no known cure, has further devastated the populations of much of sub-Saharan Africa, deepening the region's slide into economic chaos and anarchy. The populations of China, India, Pakistan, Bangladesh, Indonesia and other Asian countries have suffered deaths that surely exceed 1000 million. Europe, America, Australia, New Zealand and Japan have not escaped, as some 2 million people in these countries have fallen victim to the virulent nerve-destroying "virus X," originating in Africa, and to resurgent communicable diseases.

One consequence of these multiple disasters is that the troubled peoples of the world are on the move, in numbers previously beyond imagining. In great urban centres such as Cairo, Bangkok, Lagos and São Paulo, the lack of potable water and food and the breakdown of services have forced the exodus of the majority of the population. In the countryside they are almost always met with hostility by the rural population. There is frequent violent conflict. Some people resort to every possible means of entering America, Europe and other countries thought to offer refuge, waves of desperate refugees crashing against every border. Even the brutal measures that these countries have adopted to keep them out have not been sufficient, and the number of illegal immigrants to the United States, Canada and Western Europe has increased by at least 50 percent in the past year. Armoured vehicles patrolling the full length of the border between the United States and Mexico with "shoot on sight" instructions have failed to stem the flow. It has proven impossible to monitor the thousands of kilometres of coastline, and tens of thousands more come by boat. Refugees are even entering North America from the north, stumbling over the polar icecaps, perishing in their hundreds.

The Europeans have set up huge "confinement camps" to contain the flow, but they have proven unmanageable. Even basic services are lacking, and in the past few months alone, rioting inmates have broken out of at least a third of the camps in Europe and are to be seen everywhere along the roads and in the streets and cities and towns. Feelings against immigrants run high, and they are often shot on sight. The authorities are helpless to intervene.

Some take comfort from the fact that no new official war was declared last year, but it is scant comfort indeed. By year's end there was scarcely a region in the world free of conflict and few places where life and property were secure. If there are no new wars in the formal sense, it is because the limited capacity of most governments to mobilize and deploy conventional military forces is needed to try to keep order at home. Most conflicts involved armed gangs, criminal syndicates or local warlords. In many places police and former military forces have become the main predators, and those who do still provide security do so at a steep price. The wealthy retreated into gated and armed enclaves long ago, but even their guards are now turning on them, and the number of incidents of the wealthy becoming the hostages of their hired security are increasing.

Some of the most dramatic conflicts of the past year have taken place at sea. The shrinking of land-based food supplies drove many more to turn to the sea for sustenance. A number of the main species have been depleted to the point of extinction, and the lesser species are following as the oceans are sucked clean of life. There has been a resurgence of piracy on the seas. Much of the conflict is between individual boats and groups of boats, or between those who resort to piracy when their fishing is unsuccessful. A hysterical mob recently hacked to pieces a whale that had been beached on the coast of Maine, and when they had finished with the whale they turned on each other. One of the most dramatic fights at sea occurred in August, when private gunboats sank a fleet of twenty-seven Spanish fishing boats in international waters on the Grand Banks.

What about the good news, if any?

There is, of course, good news—much of it from people who had faced up to their difficulties—but even some of the good news is in fact bad. For example, the best estimates of emissions of carbon dioxide and other greenhouse gases from human sources indicate that they have now stabilized and should be in the process of receding somewhat. But this is not because we have become more prudent or disciplined. Our use of fossil fuels has been drastically reduced because of the breakdown of the world economy. Scientists can only speculate about the degree to which this may be offset by the large-scale desecration of the forests and grasslands, which provide sinks for the absorption of carbon dioxide.

And there is still one island of relative calm. The strongest and most resourceful political leader of the years is undoubtedly Germany's new chancellor, Rolf Schmidt. Elected in a landslide on a platform of restoring stability and discipline in Germany, he has set out to make it an island of strength, security and survival in a troubled world. He's no Adolf Hitler, but he nevertheless borrowed from Hitler the tactic of winning his office democratically and then granting himself emergency powers, giving him virtually total authority. Unlike Hitler, however, he has in his few months in office demonstrated a remarkable combination of benevolence, fairness and toughness. In instituting reform and marshalling the resources of German society he has sought to ensure that all Germans work together for the common good and share equitably in both the sacrifices and the benefits achieved through a total mobilization of citizens to deal with their problems. Schmidt's initiatives have ignited a new spirit of determination and optimism among his people, and at this point he enjoys their virtually unanimous support. Already the tough new regimen of national mobilization he has imposed is producing results in establishing personal security throughout the country, increasing food production and ensuring that food and other essential supplies are made available to all on an equal basis.

But benevolent dictators are increasingly rare. The majority of other authoritarian regimes that have emerged around the world are neither so benevolent nor so effective.

Still, other scattered islands of sanity and order are to be found in many regions, beacons of civility and hope, playing the same role in our modern chaos as the medieval monasteries did in the European Dark Ages, keeping alive the flickering embers of learning and wisdom. In Crestone, Colorado, for example, a community created as a spiritual retreat in recent materialistic times has proven to be a haven for the virtues of sustainability, harmony and "ethical husbandry."

Similar havens have appeared in the Altai in Russia and in the remote fastnesses of Tibet, a traditional refuge for asceticism and spirituality. A farmer in Manitoba has synthesized the best attributes of the Hutterite self-help communities and the Amish farmers and has set up a refuge around a large groundwater reservoir. Its ready success has prompted him to expand it to include others, as the capacity to absorb them permits, giving priority to displaced children and young families. Everywhere, indigenous peoples are rediscovering their traditional way of life. The Inuit in the Chesterfield Inlet of northern Canada have once again established a community like that of their ancestors; tribes in the Brazilian Amazon have abandoned their new-found reliance on chainsaws and tobacco and are once again dwelling in harmony with the forest—albeit with an "educational facility" set up for foreigners who wish to learn how it is done. In the war-ravaged cities of Mozambique, a demobilized soldier named João has helped to restore order and basic amenities through an innovative system of volunteer cadres supported and paid for by the grateful community. A similar system was set up in Texas by an enterprising former colonel of the U.S. Army, Mike Ryan, who put together a volunteer security service for schools, hospitals and other institutions serving the needs of people, particularly young people. This "volunteer security corps" has spread rapidly to other parts of America and Canada, and counterparts are now springing up throughout the world.

THE STATE OF THE SOUL

In the face of these multiple disasters, massive numbers of people turned away from science, which was blamed for the chaos, and toward religion. There was a resurgence of religions and spiritual movements of all sorts. Some have been promulgating messages of hope and calling to their followers to help relieve the distress and suffering of others, while an increasing number have been pointing to the current travails as a sign that the end of the world is near. The prudent habits and communal practices of the Mormons have enabled them to maintain a reasonable degree of security, order and subsistence in communities they dominate. But their commitment has been challenged by the growing migration of others to these communities, and their hostility toward these newcomers has in some cases turned violent.

Old ethnic and religious conflicts, such as the continuing open warfare between Catholics and Protestants in Ireland, have flared up again. The return of "the church militant" has also given rise to new conflicts as religious groups band together to stake competing claims to living space and livelihoods.

One of the more dramatic events of the past year was the emergence of a new movement for spiritual unity under the charismatic leadership of the man who calls himself Tadi.

As almost everyone by now knows, his message is deceptively simple, little more than an exhortation to people to return to the roots of their own religions, while tolerating and respecting all others as differing expressions of a universal spirituality that unites all people. Simple, perhaps, but exceptionally sophisticated. Tadi has persuasively isolated the basic spiritual, ethical and moral values underpinning all the world's religions, from the imperial legions of Christianity and Islam to Judaism, the many variants of the Tao, Buddhism and even the smaller, more isolated philosophies like those of Nummo, the great god of the Dogon in North Africa. Ecumenism or unitarianism is not, of course, a new notion. What is new and remarkable is that people of all faiths have embraced Tadi's formulations. This is due as much to the timeliness of the message as it is to the exceptional qualities of the messenger.

Tadi is of mixed Welsh, Armenian and Moroccan origin. After being educated in the United States and spending some ten years as a Christian missionary in Guyana, he came to reject his own narrow fundamentalist vision of the world, concluding that in this Time of Troubles God must call all to a new and transcendent unity. By now he has come under intense media and security service scrutiny, but nothing has been found that would cast doubt on his integrity. His modest style of living sets an example for all to whom it has become a necessity as well as a virtue, and he works tirelessly not only to promulgate his message but to give effect to it in practical ways. Tadi disclaims formal leadership of the movement, yet he is clearly the inspiration for the proliferation of Spiritual Unity groups and communities throughout the world.

The movement has also evoked vigorous and often hostile responses from fundamentalists of various religions. Tadi has been condemned by the Christian Alliance in the United States as the voice of the devil who seeks to undermine the commitment to Christ as the only saviour and the exclusive route to heaven. In the Sudan fundamentalist Muslims have rallied to the call of a new Mahdi, personally leading attacks on Christian churches and communities and threatening death to anyone who joins the Spiritual Unity movement. A few of the more militant Orthodox rabbis in Jerusalem have labelled Tadi a blasphemer.

PROGNOSIS

Most people can't afford the luxury of looking to the long-term. But at year-end we must have faith that there will be a future for the human family. Those who survive and the generations that will follow them will eventually benefit from the traumatic chastisement that nature has visited on our generation. Soothsaying is always risky, but surely it is revealing (as well as ironic) that some of the concerns commonly expressed at the beginning of this century have proven unfounded, and that certain worrying trends have even reversed—as a result not of good sense but of cataclysm.

Population growth, for instance. At the end of the twentieth century the exponentially expanding human population was perceived as the greatest problem facing humankind, the "ur-problem" underpinning all others. Yet now population growth has ceased; population levels are declining precipitously almost everywhere, and some areas of our planet have been almost entirely depopulated. More people are dying, and dying younger—birth rates have dropped sharply while infant mortality increases. At the end of the decade, the best guesstimates of total world population is some 4.5 billion, fewer than at the beginning of this century. And experts have predicted that the reduction of the human population may well continue to the point that those who survive may not number more than the 1.61 billion people who inhabited the Earth at the beginning of the twentieth century. A consequence, yes, of death and destruction—but in the end a glimmer of hope for the future of our species and its potential for regeneration.

Tadi teaches us what we should already know: that we must inculcate in those of our children who survive the bitterest lesson of all, which is that the human suffering and cataclysms we are now experiencing need never have happened, that they occurred not through chance or the will of malevolent gods, and that the revenge of nature and the devastation of our civilization are direct results of the uncaring arrogance of our forebears and of our own self-indulgence, greed and neglect. What we have suffered is our own fault, and only through our own efforts can it be reversed and a hopeful and sustainable future secured.

Chapter 29

The Civilization of Difference

THE RIGHT HONOURABLE BEVERLEY MCLACHLIN, P.C.*

*__Beverley McLachlin__ is Chief Justice of the Supreme Court of Canada.

One problem, more than any other, dominates human history—the problem of how we deal with those who are different than us. Human beings share a vast catalogue of commonalities. Our genetic differences are negligible; women and men are equally creative and capable; those we label as ill or old or disabled are no less virtuous, deserving, or capable of contribution than others; and people from all cultures and societies share similar aspirations to be safe, to be loved, and to feel fulfilled. In sum, the similarities that unite human beings by far overshadow their differences.

Why is it then that our differences dominate discourse on every level—political, legal, social and domestic? Our headlines tell the story. East against west in the cold war. Serb against Croat in the Balkans. Hutus against Tutsis in Rwanda–Burundi. Barely do these crises subside than a new schism seizes the front pages—fundamentalist Islam versus the western world. On the legal, social and domestic front we debate our differences with passion—the right of women to equal pay, the legitimacy of same-sex families, the place of religion in public life.

Tonight I propose to explore with you this issue. Why does difference dominate? How can we better manage difference? Canada, like other countries, has struggled with these questions. Sometimes we have answered them with exclusion and violence. Yet even in our beginnings we find another response—the response of respect, inclusion, and accommodation. Accommodation, in this context, means more than grudging concessions. Accommodation, in the strong sense in which I wish to use it, means ending exclusion, encouraging and nourishing the identity of the other, and celebrating the gifts of difference. It is this response that has come to characterize the modern Canada, shaping our thinking and our policy on women, First Nations people and the profusion of races and cultures that constitute Canada in the 21st century.

I will return to the Canadian experience. But first, let me take a few moments to explore the underlying dynamic of difference.

THE DYNAMIC OF DIFFERENCE

Why, despite our manifest commonality, do our differences, real and perceived, tend to define our world and dominate our discourse and our conduct? Philosophers have long debated the phenomenon. Jean-Paul Sartre wrote of the "other" as the concept by which we define ourselves. In his book on identity and language, *Oneself as Another*, Paul Ricoeur wrote of the "work of otherness at the heart of selfhood".[1] Michael Ignatieff has written

---

[1]   P. Ricoeur, *Oneself as Another*, trans. K. Blamey (Chicago: University of Chicago Press, 1992) at 318.

movingly of "The Stranger in our Midst" in his book *The Needs of Strangers*, tracing the dialectic of difference and need in history and literature. Despite their varying contexts and perspectives, all agree on the essential role of difference in human experience.

An answer to the question of why we place so much emphasis on our differences lies in the inescapable human need to construct one's identity within a social context. For all the celebrated individualism of recent decades, human beings are social beings. "A person only becomes a person through other people," proclaims the African aphorism. To be human is to communicate, speak, and relate to other human beings. As Charles Taylor reminds us, group living is a prerequisite to full human agency. Yet in this intercourse with others, we are confronted by difference; and in the face of this difference we are impelled to a sense of what distinguishes us as physically, historically, and culturally unique. Indeed, we need this sense of identity to make sense of our worlds. Yet identity does not remain purely personal; identity itself becomes social. As we discover our distinguishing attributes—those elements in ourselves, our history, and our culture that we value—we bind ourselves to others who share these attributes and values. In the process, each person becomes a constellation of group identities—race, ethnicity, language, gender, religion and a host of other affiliations.

Group identity is a good thing. It binds us to a horizon formed by a common history and shared memory in which we can orient ourselves and give meaning to our lives. It tells us who we are and reassures us that we are worthy. And it grounds our cultures—the aggregations of norms, achievements, and institutions that are peculiar to a people. So long as group identity focuses on shared values, it is enriching and constructive.

But group identity can also be a bad thing. The obverse of commonality is difference. To say I am part of a group is also to say that I am *not* part of a *different* group. From here it is but a short step to seeing the different group as less worthy than the group to which we belong. What we see in the other but not in ourselves may seem strange and abject. The celebration of the attributes of one group quickly slips into the denial of the attributes of others; the affirmation of one group's identity into the undermining of another group's identity. The positive "We are good", becomes the superlative "We are best", with its implication that those different from us are less worthy and less entitled to the full measure of human dignity and respect. Differences are magnified, even imagined, to serve the end of vaunting the merits of the dominant group. In its ultimate manifestation, this distortion of the group ethic results in the dehumanization of those perceived as different. They are no longer perceived as human beings, but as some lesser species whose rights may be denied with impunity.

The negative aspects of group identity tend to be self-reinforcing. Treating others as less worthy or able makes us feel stronger, more righteous, more powerful. We are doubly affirmed, first by our kinship with other members of our "superior" group, second by the presumed deficiencies of those outside the group. Treating those whom we perceive as different or whom we do not understand with dignity and respect is much more difficult.

The force of this dynamic of difference should not be denied, but faced full on in its historical reality. As John Ralston Saul stated in his 2000 Lafontaine-Baldwin Lecture, "the past is not the past. It is the context. The past—memory—is one of the most powerful, practical tools available to a civilized democracy".[2] The history of human beings is the

---

2   J.R. Saul, A. Dubuc, G. Erasmus, *The Lafontaine-Baldwin Lectures: A Dialogue on Democracy in Canada*, vol. 1, ed. by R. Griffiths (Toronto: Penguin, 2002) at 3.

history of oppression based on real and imagined difference. The Athenians invented democracy, but women and slaves were not recognized as part of the polis. The Romans treated the peoples they conquered as slaves. Medieval Christians crusaded against the Infidel. Societies from Russia to India relegated ordinary folk to the sub-human rank of serf or "untouchable", denying them the most basic rights and opportunities. And in an atrocious distortion of group identity, the twentieth century witnessed the calculated dehumanization and destruction of Jews, gypsies and the mentally and physically disabled. We ignore this history at our peril.

This past is not our past; it is ever-present. Modern society condemns slavery, yet still women and children suffer its ravages. The world community decries discrimination, yet people are still treated as less worthy because of their race, ethnicity, gender, religion or disability. In Canada, we vaunt our multi-cultural society, yet still racism, anti-Semitism and religious intolerance lurk in our dark corners. The modern world holds out the promise of inclusion, but delivers the reality of exclusion; the exclusion of refugees driven from their homes; the exclusion of women and minorities from mainstream institutions; even the more mundane exclusion of the schoolyard bully. We proclaim the right of every human being to life, yet so long as the memory of the events of September 11, 2001 remains we cannot deny that the stark goal of eliminating those seen as different dominates the agendas of many.

The imperative seems clear. President Wilson's observation that "nothing . . . is more likely to disturb the peace of the world than the treatment which might . . . be meted out to minorities" is as true today as it was in 1920.[3] If we are not to perpetuate the tragedies of the past we must tame the dark side of difference. But how? Two solutions emerge.

The first solution looks at world history, deduces that human beings cannot be relied upon to treat those different from them with decency and dignity, and concludes that the only solution is to separate groups within autonomous nation states. Michael Ignatieff, in *The Needs of Strangers*, argues that ethnic groups "cannot depend on the uncertain and fitful protection of a world conscience defending them as examples of the universal abstraction Man",[4] and therefore must be secured "their own place to be". The reorganization of Europe along ethnic lines and the creation of Israel reflect this thinking. And it is not without its virtues. As Georges Erasmus explained in his 2002 Lafontaine-Baldwin Lecture, self-rule confers a measure of respect and cultivates self-reliance and dignity. The sense of security gained from community self-determination is particularly important in cases where the countries of the world have been historically unable or unwilling to tend to the needs of given minority groups.

Yet for all of its attractions, the solution of finding an ethnic home for each of the peoples of the world does not offer the complete answer. First, in a world where most nation-states contain ethnic minorities and global movement of peoples is the norm, the ethnically defined nation state is difficult to maintain. Second, even if one could achieve and maintain the ethnically defined nation-state, this would not prevent the confrontations between groups of states and ethnic blocks that dominate recent history. Third, the ethnic

---

[3]   Plenary Session, 31 May 1920: HWV Temperley, *A History of the Peace Conference of Paris*, vol 5 (London/New York: Oxford University Press, 1969).

[4]   M. Ignatieff, *The Needs of Strangers* (London: Penguin, 1984) at 53.

nation state solution only addresses part of the problem—the political part. It leaves untouched and even threatens to conceal other forms of discrimination and exclusion within the nation-state because it says nothing about respect or the essential value of human beings. Finally, as Alain Dubuc warned in his 2001 Lafontaine-Baldwin Lecture, nationalism, "if it is exalted, can easily become a tool of exclusion rather than a window on the world".[5] We should not abandon the idea of the nation-state as one means of attending to the struggles of a pluralistic democracy; to quote John Ralston Saul in his 2000 Lecture, "[d]emocracy was and is entirely constructed inside the structure of the Western nation state".[6] Yet if the goal is to address the negative potential of group identity, the nation-state solution simply cannot go the whole distance.

This brings us to the second way of addressing the negative aspects of difference—promoting mutual respect and accommodation within the nation state. This approach rests on a single proposition—the intrinsic worth of every human being. In historical perspective, the idea is revolutionary. Throughout human history, the powerful and privileged have always treated those they view as different as less worthy. When historians look back on the last half of the 20th century and the beginning of the 21st, they will describe the idea that all people are equally worthy as one of the seminal ideas of our time.

Yet the ethic of respect and accommodation possesses venerable roots. One hears its echo in the declarations of western religion that all humans are created "in the image and likeness of God". The European Enlightenment contributed to the secular conception of fundamental human worth by celebrating the universality of reason, and Immanuel Kant urged that we treat humans as ends and never only as means. The Romantic movement furnished a robust notion of authenticity, premised on the idea that each person held a unique and intrinsically valuable potential that would be unlocked through genuine expression in life. These and other streams of thought converged and were filtered through the horrors of the first half of the 20th century.

The result was a coalesced notion of the intrinsic worth of all humans and a palpable sense that social and political recognition of this idea was critical. John P. Humphrey, one of Canada's great contributors to the project of recognizing human rights, reflected this historical truth when he stated that, although human rights did not figure on the international stage prior in time, "[b]y 1945 . . . the historical context had changed, and references to human rights run through the United Nations Charter like a golden thread".[7] We can now look back to the ultimate product of the work of Humphrey and others, the *Universal Declaration of Human Rights*, and find the clarion assertion that "recognition of the inherent dignity and of the equal and inalienable rights of all members of the human family is the foundation of freedom, justice and peace in the world."

The new idea of the equal worth of every person finds expression in the legal language of rights—human rights. If all people are equal, it follows that all people are equally entitled to freedom, fair treatment, and respect. The rights are easily stated. The more difficult problem is to move them off the sterile page and into the reality of people's lives.

---

[5]   *Lafontaine-Baldwin Lectures, supra*, at 59.

[6]   *Ibid.*, at 24.

[7]   J.T.P. Humphrey, *Human Rights & The United Nations: A Great Adventure* (Dobbs Ferry, NY: Transnational Publishers, 1984) at 12.

Formal declarations of equality are not enough to remove discrimination and exclusion. Indeed, they may perpetuate them. Formal equality is the equality of "separate but equal". The group is hived off, labeled "different", and told that they are equal with one important qualification—equal within their designated sphere. Cloaked by the façade of formal equality, group difference perpetuates denial. Examples are not hard to find. Formal equality allowed African Americans to live in forced segregation for decades. In the eyes of many, it still justifies treating women as different. You are equally worthy, these groups are told. It is just that you are different. Understanding and accommodating difference is essential to true equality. But when differences are manufactured, exaggerated or irrelevant, the result is to perpetuate inequality. True equality requires an honest appraisal of actual similarities and differences—an understanding of the context in which human devaluation occurs. To make equal worth a reality we need more than what Michael Ignatieff calls "rights talk". We need to look beyond the words to the reality, or context of the individual and group, to understand the other in his or her full humanity. This requires an open and honest mind, a willingness to bridge the gap between groups with empathy. Only when we look at the member of a different group in this way are we able to give effect to the promise of equal worth and dignity.

Understood in this way, rights, like the nation-state, create a protected space for difference within society; a space within which communities of cultural belonging can form and flourish under the broad canopy of civil society. This applies to the traditional "individual" rights which enable individuals to form and maintain the groups that constitute civil society, to adapt these groups to changing circumstances, and to promote their views and interests to the wider population. Will Kymlicka states: "It is impossible to overstate the importance of freedom of association, religion, speech, mobility, and political organization for protecting group difference."[8] But a second kind of rights—group rights—are also important. These are rights that inhere in an individual not qua individual, but by reason of the groups to which he belongs, like protections for minority language and religion. "[W]ere it not for these group-differentiated rights, the members of minority cultures would not have the same ability to live and work in their own language and culture that the members of majority cultures take for granted".[9] Together, individual and group rights contribute to an ethic of respect for difference and meaningful inclusion of multiple "others" in a diverse society.

Rights that acknowledge people as members of groups do not lead to a fragmented state. True, they are important to the communities they protect. But they also help us reach across the borders between groups and to establish a civic community embracing sometimes profoundly different groups. The language of rights can serve as a common language of understanding. As Harvard Law Professor Martha Minow puts it, "[r]ights provide a language that depends upon and expresses human interconnection at the very moment when individuals ask others to recognize their separate interests".[10]

We must confront the dark side of human difference. We must recognize the price the marginalization of the other in our midst exacts—a price we pay in the coin of war, suffering

---

[8]   W. Kymlicka, *Multicultural Citizenship* (Oxford: Oxford University Press, 1995) at 26.

[9]   *Ibid.*, at 126.

[10]   M. Minow, *Making All the Difference* (Ithaca: Cornell University Press, 1990) at 296.

and unrealized human potential. We must provide refuges for our minorities—the physical refuge of the protective nation state and the conceptual refuge of respect and accommodation embodied in the principle that all people, regardless of the group to which they are born or assigned, are equally worthy and equally deserving of respect. Only thus can we combat the discrimination and exclusion that have marred so much of human history.

THE CANADIAN EXPERIENCE

With this backdrop in mind, I now wish to turn to Canada's experience with the dynamic of difference and what it means for us as Canadians as we enter the 21st century. Formed as it was from powerful groups with different linguistic, religious and cultural attributes, Canada, from its earliest days, recognized the need to practice the habits of respect and tolerance and to enshrine them in the law through the language of rights. In order to form a nation, Canadians had to come to terms with difference by learning to respect other cultural and linguistic groups and by expressing a commitment to this respect through the provision of rights. Yet Canada was born in an era of ethno-nationalism, religious and linguistic intolerance, racism and gender inequality. These aspects of our past manifested as exclusionary, assimilationist, and discriminatory practices at various periods of our country's life. We must also look at these dark points in our past and be humbled by their existence. So a close examination of Canada's past can disclose both a strong foundation in the ethic of tolerance and inclusion, as well as the dark side of group belonging in the form of intolerant treatment. I want to explore both of these aspects of our heritage, in the hopes of ultimately demonstrating that, as Canada has matured and grown as a nation, we have embraced and cultivated the first of these traditions in order to do a better job of confronting the second— we have learned to value and institutionalize the ethic of respect for difference as a means of combating exclusionary thinking.

Canada is one of the few countries in the world which has from its beginning dealt with the issue of minorities and sub-groups by the two-pronged mechanism of the nation-state and respect and tolerance of minorities within the nation-state. Most of the world's countries grew up around and continue to adhere to the model of the ethnic nation-state, often in the face of diverse ethnic groups within their borders. European nations like Germany and France still cling—with increasing difficulty to be sure—to the ideal of ethnic nationalism.

Canada's history is quite different. Other countries are only now awaking to the critical issue of dealing with the other in their midst. Canada, by contrast, was forced to come to terms with this reality from its very inception. The peace accords that ended the century-long wars between England and France in the late 18th century, left England in possession of France's former colonies in America. Two of the most important—Quebec and the Maritimes—lay within the territory of the future Canada. People in these lands spoke a different language and adhered to a different religion than their new rulers. England dealt with these two distinctive colonies in different ways.

The first epitomized the ethnic-exclusionary approach to dealing with minorities. England required the Maritime Francophones, the Acadians, to conform, at least to the extent of swearing oaths of allegiance to the British Crown. The failure to conform, perceived or real, led to the deportation of the Acadians to what is now the United States and to far-flung points of Europe. Many eventually found their way back, but only after the separations and sufferings that inevitably follow such dispersion. The treatment of the Acadians remains a paradigmatic illustration of an exclusionary nation-state policy.

The Lower Canadian French population, on the other hand, was too large and too firmly implanted to be uprooted and disposed of in this way. England had little appetite for a conflict with its colonists in Quebec. And so, in the end, to truncate a long and complex story full of historical intricacies, it acceded to the demands of Governor Carleton (who camped three years in London insisting on his position) that the French-speaking people of Quebec be allowed to retain their language, religion and civil law tradition. Although motivated largely by pragmatic considerations, the product was a commitment to accommodation, embodied in the Quebec Act of 1774—respect and tolerance, implemented through the mechanism of rights. Half a century later, discontent with colonial strictures led to democratic movements and rebellion in both Upper and Lower Canada. Lord Durham was sent out from England to find solutions. Lord Durham's Report of 1840 turned its back on Canada's history of accommodation and tolerance and recommended return to an assimilationist policy that gave prime place to England and English traditions. But, under the leadership of Lafontaine and Baldwin, the colonials rejected Lord Durham's vision of the assimilated unitary nation-state. The former colonies of Upper and Lower Canada, Nova Scotia and New Brunswick that met in 1866 and 1867 to create the country of Canada had learned a critical lesson: the only way the new country could succeed was on the basis of a constitution that guaranteed mutual respect and tolerance. And so Canada was born, not of nationalism, but of the pragmatic necessity to accept difference.

This beginning created the space in which the colonies, soon to be joined by the colonies of British Columbia and Vancouver Island, Prince Edward Island, the prairie territories, and later Newfoundland and Labrador, could come together and grow. Confederation and the constitutional guarantee of rights provided a mechanism through which the dialogue of accommodation could be pursued—a dialogue that is still being pursued today on all manner of subjects, from government provision of medical care and federal-provincial views on the environment to the rights of sexual minorities and Aboriginal land claims.

One of the most discussed issues regarding group difference in Canada has been the provision of guarantees for minority language rights. Language, as much as any other feature, marks the minority as different than the majority since language forms the basis of communication. Human beings seem instinctively to view those who do not speak their own language as outside their cultural group. It is thus no surprise that despite the reality that many countries are multi-lingual, a single common language continues to be seen by many as the essential glue without which a nation will fall apart. Thus the distinguished American historian Arthur Schlesinger Jr. in *The Disuniting of America* argues that it would be folly for the United States to permit Spanish to achieve any sort of official status. Schlesinger argues that "[i]nstitutionalized bilingualism shuts doors. It nourishes self-ghettoization, and ghettoization nourishes racial antagonism . . . Using some language other than English dooms people to second-class citizenship in American society".[11]

In fact, however, the Canadian experience with bilingualism can be argued to support the opposite conclusion—that in states facing the reality of widely entrenched linguistic difference, recognition of the right to use minority languages furthers national unity.

---

[11]   A. Schlesinger, *The Disuniting of America: Reflections on a Multicultural Society* (New York and London: W.W. Norton & Co., 1998) at 113.

Canada's minority language and religion guarantees continue to serve their intended purpose—the purpose of providing security to minority citizens that the majority will respect their identities. Minority linguistic rights serve as a bulwark against fear of marginalization, allowing them to participate as equal citizens secure in the knowledge that they will not be excluded because of their linguistic identity. The economic cost of bilingual services is far outweighed by the benefits of inclusion. As Chief Justice Dickson stated for the Supreme Court of Canada in 1990, "any broad guarantee of language rights . . . cannot be separated from a concern for the culture associated with the language. Language is more than a mere means of communication, it is part and parcel of the identity and culture of the people speaking it. It is the means by which individuals understand themselves and the world around them".[12] To draw linguistic interests into the protective embrace of the state is, therefore, a means of expressing society's commitment to the integrity of cultures and respect for the dignity of individuals.

Canada's foundation in the ethic of respect and tolerance provided space for citizens of two diverse cultures to work out their political, linguistic and religious differences in a climate of mutual accommodation. It did not, however, mean that the old exclusionary way of thinking did not persist. Sadly, against the backdrop of our remarkable history of accommodation and respect, Canada's first century was marred by the ethic of the assimilation and exclusion of peoples it slotted into special groups—its first inhabitants, the Aboriginal Peoples; immigrants of so-called "different" races—that is, neither French nor English; and the 52% or so of the population who were women.

Our country's policy toward the ancestral inhabitants of Canada's lands, the Aboriginal Peoples, has throughout its history veered between exclusion and assimilation on the one hand and respectful acceptance on the other. Prior to Confederation, Aboriginal groups were more often than not treated as autonomous nations. Indeed, the Huron and Mohawk nations played important opposing roles in the Franco–British wars on what was to become Canadian Territory. But in the 19th Century, as settlement progressed, exclusion, confinement and assimilation came to dominate Canadian policy. The results, most now agree, were at best a failure, at worst tragic. Only in recent decades have First Nations people begun to reclaim their group identity and their rightful place in our country.

The 1996 report of the Royal Commission on Aboriginal Peoples laid bare for Canadians a history which can without exaggeration be characterized as institutionalized discrimination. The Royal Proclamation of 1763 recognized the entitlement of Aboriginal Peoples to their lands and stipulated that these must not be taken from them unless they consented by agreement with the Crown. Translated into the Realpolitik of the 19th Century, this meant the Treaty system, whereby the Indians, as they were called, gave up right to their larger territories in return for a small parcel of reserved land—the reservation—and minor gifts. In British Columbia, treaties were not entered into; First Nations people were simply allotted parcels upon which to live.

The second-class status of Aboriginal Peoples was clear. In 1857 Upper Canada passed the *Act to Encourage the Gradual Civilization of the Indian Tribes in this Province*, which provided for the enfranchisement of Indians of "good character" who would, thereafter, be declared to be "non-Indian." The theory was clear. Aboriginal Peoples were regarded as

---

[12]   *Mahe v. Alberta*, [1990] 1 S.C.R. 342, at para. 32.

"uncivilized savages". The only solution was to change them to "non-Indians", or in words of Prime Minister John A. Macdonald to "do away with the tribal system, and assimilate the Indian people in all respects with the inhabitants of the Dominion." Following passage of the first *Indian Act* in 1876, native cultural institutions and spiritual practices came under attack. On the west coast, the potlatch ceremony was prohibited. On the plains, the police were called in to break up the sun dance, a ceremony thick with cultural significance for the Aboriginal Peoples of the prairies.

In illogical locked step, assimilationist policies were paired with exclusionary practices in the pervasive reserve system. The very peoples the leaders were proclaiming should be assimilated found themselves virtual prisoners on their reservations with the Department of Indian Affairs' adoption of the pass system in 1885. The residential school system, established first in 1849 in Alderville, Ontario, and subsequently expanded, likewise combined exclusionary and assimilationist impulses, with the often tragic consequences that are only now coming fully to light. Policies were no better in the early part of the 20th century. The assimilation-exclusion model persisted. On the exclusionary side, Canadian Aboriginals were not permitted to vote until the 1950s and 60s, unless they renounced their aboriginal status. On the assimilation side, Duncan Campbell Scott, Deputy Superintendent of Indian Affairs, stated in 1920 that government policy was "to continue until there is not a single Indian in Canada that has not been absorbed into the body politic and there is no Indian question and no Indian department."

The simultaneous pursuit of exclusion and assimilation produced cultural displacement, marginalization, and tragic loss of identity and self-esteem. The policy of exclusion cut Aboriginal Peoples off from opportunities available to the rest of the country. At the same time, the policy of assimilation undermined their identity as members of a group—their shared history, language and culture. The good aspects of the group dynamic—a solid identity rooted in one's history and culture—were weakened; the negative aspects—isolation, alienation and lack of opportunity—enhanced. Despite the often good intentions of well-meaning men, it is difficult to conceive in retrospect of a more problematic approach to the other.

Aboriginal Peoples responded to the policy of assimilation-exclusion with "consistent resistance", as Georges Erasmus explained in his 2002 Lecture.[13] Recent years have witnessed community renaissance. Aboriginal Peoples have begun a process of rediscovering their traditions and values, rebuilding communities, and exploring and sharing their cultures. Constitutional protections have been extended to the Aboriginal community, providing a legal safe-haven in which Aboriginal group interests can flourish. On the non-Aboriginal side, paternalism and exclusion are increasingly being replaced by respect and accommodation. To quote Georges Erasmus once more: "[g]aining recognition of Aboriginal rights in the courts and entrenchment in the Constitution have been critical to restoring Aboriginal peoples as active agents in directing our collective lives".[14]

Canada's history of minority exclusion and marginalization of those belonging to groups labeled "different" is not confined to the Aboriginal community. Chinese-Canadians came to Canada to help build our railroads. Their task completed, they found

[13] *Lafontaine-Baldwin Lectures, supra,* at 118.
[14] *Ibid.,* at 104–105.

themselves burdened with oppressive and discriminatory laws. Head taxes were imposed on entry. Impediments to the immigration of women were adopted. The lack of Chinese women in turn gave rise to irrational fears that Chinese men would prey on white women, and led to prohibitions on the employment of white women by Chinese men.

Black Canadians too felt the cold touch of exclusion and racism. Between 1782 and 1785 about 3,500 blacks, most former slaves who had fought for Britain in return for freedom, fled to what is now Nova Scotia and New Brunswick at the close of the American Revolution. Once in the Maritimes, they were cheated of land, forced to work on public projects like road building and denied equal status with whites. Disappointed, 1,190 men, women and children left Halifax on 15 ships for Sierra Leone. Sixty-five died on route. In 1796 six hundred Maroons—people with a long tradition of resistance to European rule—arrived in the Maritimes to face the same miserable conditions as the freed Black Loyalists. They too left for Sierra Leone. In 1814–15, 3,000 or so American black refugees from the war of 1812 settled in the Maritimes, and in the 1920s hundreds of Caribbean immigrants, called "later arrivals", came to Cape Breton to work in the mines and steel mills. Quebec and Ontario saw similar migrations, and black colonies were established in the west of Canada. Black people came to Canada expecting respect and accommodation. They found little of either. Despite the abolition of slavery in 1833, black Canadians found themselves excluded from schools, churches, restaurants, hospitals and public transportation, and denied equal housing and employment opportunities.

The list of racial groups that have suffered exclusion and discrimination goes on and on. Ukrainian Canadians were interned in World War I. Japanese Canadians, as well as men of German and Italian origin, were sent to camps during World War II. Well into the 20th century anti–Semitism forbade Jewish Canadians from holding property in designated areas. And in a dramatic expression of intolerance and lack of respect for the "other" who is labeled as different, legislation in the mid-twentieth century permitted the eugenic policy of sterilizing people deemed mentally deficient.

Perhaps the most far-reaching example of exclusionary-thinking is the history of our treatment of women. Women make up 52% of the Canadian population. Yet for much of Canadian history, women have been relegated to an inferior status in society. Why? Again the familiar premise—women are different. The obvious biological difference between men and women was extrapolated to apply to all forms of feminine functioning. Women had smaller and less clever brains. Women were congenitally weaker. Women functioned emotionally; only men could think. From here it was but a short logical leap to conclude that women should not be permitted to vote or practice medicine or law and should be barred from public office. The effect of these illogical leaps into stereotype was to deny women first-class status. Their identity as thinking, responsible human beings was challenged, their humanity denied. People perhaps, full persons, certainly not.

Women in Canada, as elsewhere in the western world, began to challenge these assumptions at the end of the 19th century. They fought for legal rights and they won them. It took a long time. Canadian women did not win the right to vote in federal elections until 1920. And it was only in 1929, with the now-famous "Persons Case", that the law recognized that women were "persons" entitled to hold public office.

However, as with the struggle of Aboriginal Peoples, legal equality for women did not translate into actual equality. Old ideas die hard. In the minds of many, women remained a fundamentally different kind of human being, with corresponding fundamental limitations. Women were fit for domestic roles, fit to serve as secretaries and nurses and other kinds of assistants. They clearly were not, however, up to the big jobs. This exclusionist thinking was buttressed by ingrained attitudes that the primary place of women was in the home with the children. Women who wanted to serve in law, medicine or politics could attempt to do so, but they faced an up-hill struggle against the prevailing attitudes of the day and seldom got to the top. The difficulties they faced led to statements like that of French journalist Françoise Giroud, "Women's problems will be solved when a mediocre woman holds a major job".[15]

It is now widely accepted that there is no justification for sweeping negative generalizations about the ability and temperament of women. It is accepted that women can and do play with equal effectiveness in all walks of life. And it is accepted—by many if not all—that cooking and childcare is not an exclusively feminine gift; men too can enjoy and excel in these activities. Why then did we persist so long in our belief that women were fundamentally unsuited for anything but working in the home and assisting men in grander pursuits? The answer brings us back to the dynamic of difference. Instead of evaluating the differences between men and women honestly and with an open mind, people magnified those differences and extrapolated them into conclusions which bore no relation to the actual abilities of women and paid no respect to their right to choose their path in life. In a word, stereotype transmuted into popular, hence unassailable, wisdom. Myth supplanting reality shut women out.

Why did the myth of female inadequacy persist so long? Why indeed does it still exert a tenacious power over our deepest attitudes and actions? Why can we not simply acknowledge, as we increasingly do with ethnic minorities, that the biological differences between men and women should not limit their place in society? Why, in short, can we not, where women are concerned, move from an exclusionary mentality to and inclusionary mentality? The answers are complex. Social and religious institutions may buttress an exclusionary mentality, as may the very structures of our institutions.

For example, many Canadian offices and workplaces continue to be organized on the Edwardian model of a century past. The family breadwinner (presumptively Papa) is expected to be available for work and travel at any time. This is made possible because the family homemaker (presumptively Mama) devotes her exclusive efforts to the home and family. This model no longer fits the reality of Canadian families, where increasingly both parents must work outside the home to earn the necessary income and both parents are involved with domestic and child-rearing tasks. We are beginning to explore ways to bring our workplace organization into synch with the reality of our lives—day care centres on the jobsite, childcare programs, flex time and working from home are among the options being explored. So long as we organize our workplaces on Edwardian lines, women will find themselves at best stressed and at worst falling back into the default role of sole domestic care-giver, reinforcing the old attitudes.

If Canada has not won the war against the exclusion of women, we have fought the first important battles. We have rejected the exclusionary politics that once denied women access to the levers of influence, power and full societal participation. We lead other nations in the opportunities we open to women. We have more senior female judges, more female university professors, more practicing physicians than many western countries. Personally, I believe that in my own profession, the law, it is easier for a woman to succeed in Canada

---

[15]   From Lysiane Gagnon column in *The Globe & Mail*, weekend of Jan 27–28.

than almost anywhere else. Yet despite these achievements—and they are not inconsiderable—we still have terrain to take. Women's equality issues remain very much alive. Few women occupy the highest seats of political office and commerce. Statistics Canada tells us we have not achieved pay equity.[16] And violence against women is a persistent problem.

Canada's record on the treatment of Aboriginal Peoples, racial minorities and women—not to mention gays and lesbians—teaches us that notwithstanding our nation's foundation in the ethic of tolerance and accommodation, we are not immune from the evils of exclusionary thinking. The natural inclination of the majority and the powerful to see the minority and less powerful as less worthy and less entitled to share in all aspects of the country's life, has repeatedly surfaced on Canadian territory. We devalued Aboriginal Peoples, ethnic minorities, disabled people, and women, much as others elsewhere devalued the same groups. This must not be minimized. Yet from this complex and troubling history, we are slowly progressing towards a society where all people are fully valued, whatever their race, religion or gender. Since the Second World War and the international acknowledgment of the equal worth of all and the concomitant right to equal treatment, Canada has moved more quickly than many other countries to a more inclusionary, respectful model of society.

The law, while not the entire answer, has played a pivotal role in this progression. Canadian legislators reacted swiftly in the wake of World War II and the horrors of the Holocaust to protect minority rights. In 1944 Ontario passed the *Racial Discrimination Act* which prohibited the publication or dissemination of materials that expressed racial or religious discrimination. In 1947, the *Saskatchewan Bill of Rights Act* began a revolution in legislation that sought to be broadly protective of rights and civil liberties. These legislative innovations dove-tailed with the momentum building at the international level around the adoption of the Universal Declaration of Human Rights. In 1962, the first *Ontario Human Rights Code* proclaimed "the inherent dignity and the equal and inalienable rights of all members of the human family . . . in accord with the Universal Declaration of Human Rights as proclaimed by the United Nations." Nova Scotia's *Human Rights Act* came in the next year, followed by Alberta, New Brunswick, and P.E.I. By 1973, all provinces had enacted human rights laws and in 1976, the federal government followed suit.

The adoption of the *Charter of Rights and Freedoms* in 1982 elevated the basic human rights, aboriginal rights and equality to the status of supreme law, against which all government actions and legislation must be assessed. The *Charter* stands as Canada's ultimate expression of our commitment to freedom and human dignity.

The *Charter* has had a monumental impact on Canadian law and, indeed, in what Kent Roach has called a "heavy export trade in the *Charter*",[17] the law of other countries. Yet the *Charter* is more than a litigation tool or a lawyer's text. A glance at our newspapers shows the extent to which the *Charter*, and the values and principles it embodies, have been internalized by Canadians. Alain Dubuc has argued that the speed and readiness with which the rights enshrined in the *Charter of Rights and Freedoms* were taken up by Canadians was the product of an abiding national insecurity about our identity.[18] I prefer to think that the *Charter* manifests an ethic of respect and inclusion that has been part of Canada's fabric

---

[16]   Statistics Canada, *Average Earnings by Sex and Work Pattern*, based on CANSIM II, Table 202–0102.
[17]   K. Roach, *The Supreme Court on Trial: Judicial Activism or Democratic Dialogue* (Toronto: Irwin Law, 2001) at 60.
[18]   *Lafontaine-Baldwin Lectures, supra*, at 72.

from its beginnings, and the way in which Canadians have embraced the *Charter* demonstrates its tremendous resonance with our country's identity. As I have tried to show, in Canada a unique political and cultural history is intertwined with a universalized ethic of respect and accommodation. The former constitutes our roots and shows us the path we have traveled as a nation. The second expands our sense of ourselves by including a commitment to respect for all kinds of difference in an unknowable future. Both are now immutable aspects of our country's identity, and both are reflected in the *Charter*.

In this way, the *Charter*, more than any other document, expresses the Canadian ethic, the country's sense of itself. The *Charter* also provides all of us, regardless of race, religion, or gender, with a secure space in which to realize our aspirations. Finally, the language of the *Charter* provides a common vocabulary in which we can cast our various perspectives, giving all Canadians access to the public space in which some of our country's most difficult and contentious issues are debated. The *Charter* has not created consensus. But by expressing our most fundamental values—above all the respect we hold for others, regardless of their differences—it has strengthened us and given each of us a place to stand. And by giving us the common vocabulary of rights it has provided a forum for understanding one another's circumstances and working out the accommodations so essential in a diverse, multi-cultural society.

The *Charter* protects difference. But, independent of any particularized rights, respect for minorities has become an inseverable component of our constitutional fabric. On August 20, 1998, the Supreme Court of Canada rendered its judgment in the *Reference re: the Secession of Quebec*.[19] Noting our long tradition of protecting minority rights, the Court recognized the protection of minorities, along with federalism, democracy, constitutionalism and the rule of law, as one of the foundational principles subtending our constitutional architecture.

Canada, as a nation grounded in difference and respect, has erected an impressive legal structure to protect difference. But this structure is not merely law. This is no alien, imposed legal order. It is a structure that expresses our history of respecting minorities and our ever-strengthening commitment to the policies of inclusion and accommodation and to the belief in the fundamental dignity and worth of each human being. Inclusion and equality cannot be achieved by mere rights. But when the rights reflect a nation's values and are accepted as a means of brokering our differences and finding accommodation, they take on profound importance. And when we add to the mix attitudes of tolerance, respect and generosity—attitudes which Canadians possess in good measure—the prospects become bright for the inclusive society of which we dream. Michael Ignatieff writes in *The Needs of Strangers* that "Love . . . is perhaps the most desperate and insistent of all human needs. Yet we cannot force someone to love us. We cannot claim love as a human right."[20]

My hope is this. If we cannot claim love, we must strive for respect and accommodation. And as national ambitions go, that's not bad.

"The Civilization of Difference" was presented by the Right Honourable Chief Justice of Canada, Beverley McLachlin, P.C., as part of the Dominion Institute's March 2003 LaFontaine-Baldwin Symposium (www.lafontaine-baldwin.com).

---

[19]   [1998] 2 S.C.R. 217.
[20]   *The Needs of Strangers, supra*, at 18-19.

Chapter 30

The International Recognition of Indigenous Rights

WARREN ALLMAND*

*The **Honourable Warren Allmand**, P.C., O.C., Q.C., was Minister of Indian Affairs and Northern Development and Minister of Consumer and Corporate Affairs under Prime Minister Pierre Trudeau. From 1997 to 2002 he was President of Rights and Democracy (The International Centre for Human Rights and Democratic Development). He is now a Montreal city councillor.

Throughout the world, it is widely recognized that indigenous peoples are among the most disadvantaged and vulnerable. It is estimated that there are 300–500 million indigenous people in more than 70 countries around the world, representing over 5,000 languages and cultures on every continent. Today, many indigenous peoples are engaged in a struggle to assert their self-determination, to reclaim their lands and natural resources, to control their own development and to employ their traditional languages, cultures and institutions. This struggle has led them to the United Nations, the Specialized Agencies, the Organization of American States (OAS) and other international bodies.

While certain indigenous representatives pursued their grievances in European capitals as early as the eighteenth century, the first formal approach by indigenous peoples to have their collective rights recognized by the international community was in 1923, when Cayuga Chief Deskaheh went to the League of Nations as the representative of the Six Nations of the Iroquois in Ontario. He spent a year in Geneva working to garner support for his cause, but in the end, the League denied him access. This attempt was followed in 1924 and 1925 by T.W. Ratana, a Maori leader from New Zealand, who travelled to London and Geneva to protest the breaking of the 1840 Treaty of Waitangi, which guaranteed the Maori ownership of their lands. Like Chief Deskaheh, he too was cast aside. These and other approaches to international bodies by indigenous peoples were made because they were denied justice at home; their only hope was to appeal to international bodies which they believed stood for fair treatment and human rights. While the creation of the United Nations in 1945 seemed to offer more hope, the doors of the UN were virtually closed to indigenous peoples until the 1970s. Finally in 1971, the United Nations Commission on Human Rights (UNCHR) Sub-Commission on the Prevention of Discrimination and Protection of Minorities made a significant decision to appoint a Special Rapporteur to conduct a comprehensive study of the status of the world's indigenous peoples. This mandate was assigned to Jose Martinez Cobo, one of the 26 with the "Sub-Commission." Cobo worked for ten years, producing interim reports in the years following 1971 and a five-volume final report between 1981 and 1984. These reports made a strong appeal for action on indigenous rights and encouraged the opening of the UN to indigenous peoples.

VITAL STEPS

In the 1980s and '90s, many steps were taken to advance the recognition of the rights of indigenous peoples:

1982   The Working Group on Indigenous Populations (WGIP) was established by the UNCHR Sub-Commission on the Promotion and Protection of Human Rights.

1989   ILO Convention 169 was adopted by the International Labour Organization and is a revision of ILO's earlier Convention 107 of 1957.

1992   The Nobel Peace Prize was awarded to Rigoberta Menchu Tum, an Indigenous Mayan woman from Guatemala who led the struggle for indigenous rights in that country.

1993   The Vienna Declaration, adopted by the UN World Conference on Human Rights, repeated and re-emphasized that all peoples have the right to self-determination, and in Article 20 urged action on the rights of indigenous people.

1993   The International Year of the Indigenous People was proposed by the WGIP in 1987 and approved by the UN General Assembly in 1990 which proclaimed 1993 as the first such year. The International Year was based on the theme "A New Partnership."

1994   The Draft Declaration on the Rights of Indigenous Peoples (DDIP) was completed by the WGIP on 26 August 1994 and reported to the "Sub-Commission." The "Sub-Commission" in turn adopted the text and reported it to the UNCHR.

1994   The International Decade of the World's Indigenous People was recommended in the 1993 Vienna Declaration and proclaimed by the UN General Assembly on 21 December 1993. It started on 10 December 1994 and was to last until December 2004.

1995   The open-ended Inter-Sessional Working Group on the Draft Declaration (WGDD) was established in 1995 in accordance with UNCHR resolution 1995/32 and ECOSOC resolution 1995/32. The purpose of the WGDD was to elaborate a Draft Declaration on the Rights of Indigenous Peoples, considering the draft prepared by the WGIP dated 26 August 1994.

INTERNATIONAL DECADE OF THE WORLD'S INDIGENOUS PEOPLE

In late 1993, following a recommendation by the Vienna World Conference on Human Rights, the General Assembly proclaimed the International Decade of the World's Indigenous People (1994–2004). Later, the General Assembly decided that the theme of the decade would be "Indigenous People; Partnership in Action." The goal of the decade was to foster international cooperation to help solve problems faced by indigenous peoples in such areas as human rights, culture, the environment, development, education, and health. In 1995, the General Assembly adopted the program of activities for the Decade and identified a number of specific objectives. Among these objectives were the proposals to establish a UN Permanent Forum for Indigenous Issues (PFII) and the adoption of the UN Draft Declaration on the Rights of Indigenous Peoples (DDIP). The most important accomplishments of the decade are the following:

1. Study on Treaties

An important contribution was the final report by Miguel Alfonso Martinez, Special Rapporteur, on 22 June 1999, respecting his study on treaties, agreements, and other constructive arrangements between states and indigenous populations. This final report was preceded by three progress reports in 1992, 1994 and 1996.

In 1989, the Economic and Social Council (ECOSOC) authorized the "Sub-Commission" to appoint Miguel Alfonso Martinez, a member of the Working Group on Indigenous Populations (WGIP), as Special Rapporteur, with the task of preparing a study on the potential utility of treaties, agreements and other constructive arrangements between states and indigenous populations. The Special Rapporteur was mandated to give particular attention to universal human rights standards and to suggest ways of achieving the maximum possible promotion and protection of indigenous peoples' treaty rights in domestic as well as international law. This report provides us with some useful information and recommendations which are particularly relevant for indigenous peoples in North America and the South Pacific where many treaties had been concluded between indigenous nations and European states through their settlers. Among the numerous Martinez conclusions, his principal ones are:

In establishing formal legal relationships with peoples overseas, the European parties were clearly aware that they were negotiating and entering into contractual relations with sovereign nations, with all the international legal implications of that term during the period under consideration (par. 100).

In the case of indigenous peoples who concluded treaties with the European settlers, the Special Rapporteur has not found any sound legal argument to sustain the case that they have lost their international juridical status as nations/peoples (par. 265).

This leads to the issue of whether or not treaties concluded by the European settlers with indigenous nations currently continue to be instruments with international status in the light of international law. The Special Rapporteur is of the opinion that these instruments indeed maintain their original status and continue fully in effect, and consequently, are sources of rights and obligations for all the original parties to them (or their successors), who shall implement their provisions in good faith (pars. 270, 271).

These were treaties of peace and friendship, destined to organize coexistence in, not indigenous peoples' exclusion from, the same territory and not to regulate restrictively their lives under the overall jurisdiction of non-indigenous authorities (par. 117).

The Special Rapporteur reaffirms the right of indigenous peoples to self-determination (par. 256), their right to their lands and resources (par. 252), and that the treaty-making process is the most suitable way to secure their rights and resources (pars. 260 and 263). Overall, solutions cannot be achieved exclusively on a legal basis; considerable political will is required (par. 254).

In the application of treaties, they must be interpreted according to their original spirit and intent (par. 278), with the understanding that indigenous treaty-making was totally oral in nature, and not in European languages and legal systems (par. 281).

2. Special Rapporteur

In 2001, the UNCHR appointed Rodolfo Stavenhagen as a Special Rapporteur on the situation of the human rights and fundamental freedoms of indigenous peoples (SRIP). This was done in response to the growing international concern regarding the marginalization and discrimination against indigenous peoples worldwide. The mandate, created by UNCHR resolution 2001/57, represents a significant moment for the on-going pursuit of indigenous peoples to safeguard their human rights. The Rapporteur's mandate is complementary to those of the WGIP and the PFII and aims at strengthening the mechanisms of protection of the human rights of indigenous peoples. The Special Rapporteur made an unofficial visit to Canada in 2003 when he met with Indigenous First Nations in British Columbia, Saskatchewan, Manitoba and Nova Scotia, and an official visit in 2004, when he met with First Nations in Manitoba, Ontario, Quebec and the Maritimes. He has tabled special and annual reports with the UNCHR in 2002, 2003 and 2004.

3. Other Special Rapporteurs

In recent years, indigenous peoples have also lodged grievances with other UNCHR Special Rapporteurs, such as: the Special Rapporteurs on Contemporary Forms of Racism; Religious Intolerance; Summary or Arbitrary Executions; Violence Against Women; and the Right to Development. These mechanisms provide additional avenues to raise indigenous issues and bring them to international attention—always with the goal of achieving justice at home.

4. The Permanent Forum

The PFII was first recommended in the Vienna Declaration on Human Rights in 1993. It was then proposed as one of the main objectives of the International Decade by a resolution of the General Assembly. In consequence, the Permanent Forum was created by ECOSOC (res. 2000/22) to: a) discuss indigenous issues within the Council's mandate, including economic and social development, culture, environment, education, health and human rights; b) provide expert advice and recommendations to the council and to the programs, funds, and agencies of the United Nations; and c) raise awareness about indigenous issues and help to integrate and coordinate activities in the UN system.

The Forum is made up of 16 independent experts, functioning in their personal capacities, with eight of the members nominated by indigenous peoples and eight nominated by governments. The 16 members are appointed for three years with the possibility of reappointment. The Forum meets for ten days each year in New York or Geneva or a location chosen by the Forum. The first Forum took place in 2002, and each year since that time. The general theme for the 2003 Forum was indigenous children, and for the 2004 Forum, indigenous women. With the establishment of the Forum, indigenous peoples, for the first time, have become members of a UN body, and as such, help set the Forum's agenda and determine its outcome. This is unprecedented within the UN system.

Organizations of indigenous peoples may participate as observers in the meetings of the Permanent Forum in accordance with the procedures that are applied in the WGIP where meetings are open to all indigenous peoples' organizations, regardless of their consultative status with ECOSOC. States, UN bodies and organs, intergovernmental organizations and NGOs that have consultative status with ECOSOC may also participate as observers. As a result, at the first three meetings, there were not only a large number of indigenous organizations but also UN agencies such as the UNDP, ILO, FAO, WHO, WIPO, UNCHR, UNICEF, UNEP and many others which have general or special programs available to indigenous peoples.

The agenda provides time for all of these agencies to report on their programs for indigenous peoples and to answer questions or complaints, which are put to them by members of the Forum or by the observers. At the end of the 10 days, the 16-member Forum draws up a report which includes recommendations. Since the Forum is relatively new and still unknown to many indigenous nations, it may take some time before it is used to its full potential.

5. The UNCHR, the OHCHR, and the Sub-Commission

In recent years indigenous peoples have been making greater use of the UNCHR (replaced in 2006 by the UN Human Rights Council), its 'Sub-Commission,' and the Office of the High Commission for Human Rights (OHCHR). The UNCHR met annually in Geneva for a six-week session and since 1996, two or three days were usually set aside for indigenous issues—including reports from the Special Rapporteur, the Working Group on the Draft Declaration (WGDD), the Permanent Forum and the Decade. It provided an opportunity for indigenous organizations and their NGO allies to lobby, make comments and to raise grievances.

The OHCHR, situated in Geneva, also has a special unit dealing with indigenous rights. While not large, it is made up of dedicated individuals who support and coordinate the various indigenous programs. It has also been helpful to indigenous organizations in providing them with information and direction and has carried on constructive relations with the Indigenous Caucus.

6. Treaty Bodies

The UN treaty-based human rights system includes legal procedures through which indigenous peoples can and have sought protection for their human rights. In this respect, there are six major international human rights treaties within the UN human rights system that deal with civil and political rights, economic and social rights, racial discrimination, torture, gender discrimination, and children's rights respectively.

There is a supervisory committee (also known as a treaty body) for each of these treaties that monitors the way in which the States Parties are fulfilling their human rights obligations as stated in the relevant treaty. Indigenous peoples can only make use of those treaties and treaty bodies which have been ratified by those countries in which they are situated. Canadian indigenous peoples have used the Treaty Bodies in several important cases: the Lubicon Lake case before the Human Rights Committee in 1984 and the Lovelace Case before the same committee in 1977.

7. Specialized Agencies

As a result of the WGIP, the Vienna Declaration, the International Decade, and the increased participation of indigenous peoples in UN Charter- and Treaty-based bodies, all agencies of the UN have become more sensitive to indigenous concerns and have attempted to mainstream indigenous input into their various programs. The UN special agencies, which have a considerable degree of independence, address specific issues such as health, food, education, labour, and development, and include such organizations as WHO, FAO, UNESCO, ILO, and UNDP, each of which has an interest in the situation of indigenous peoples and which now reports annually to the Permanent Forum.

8. Participation by Indigenous Peoples

One of the greatest accomplishments of the International Decade has been the increased participation and effectiveness of indigenous peoples in the UN system. Not only is there an increasing number of indigenous organizations with ECOSOC status, which is necessary for participation in the UNCHR and the Sub-Commission, but a great many more take part in the WGIP, the WGDD, and the Permanent Forum without ECOSOC status as a result of a less formal registration system to accommodate indigenous peoples and their allies. The indigenous representatives at these meetings are able to raise their concerns, lobby government and UN officials, and network with other indigenous organizations and NGOs from all over the world. Furthermore, there are NGOs based in Geneva whose principal objective is to help indigenous participants operate more effectively. The Documentation Centre for Indigenous Peoples (DOCIP) and the International Service for Human Rights (ISHR) provide assistance with secretarial services and translation. Indigenous organizations have also become adept at preparing and submitting formal communications or grievances, making speeches, and in contacting the OHCHR, the Special Rapporteurs and the Working Groups.

THE DRAFT DECLARATION ON THE RIGHTS OF INDIGENOUS PEOPLES

The most significant item of unfinished business resulting from the International Decade was the Draft Declaration. As part of its mandate to develop international standards concerning the rights of indigenous peoples, the WGIP—a group of five experts—developed and wrote the Draft Declaration on the Rights of Indigenous Peoples (DDIP) between 1985 and 1994. In carrying out this task the Working Group consulted closely with indigenous groups, governments, academics and NGOs.

When the WGIP had completed its work on the DDIP in 1994, it was reported to the Sub-Commission on the Promotion and Protection of Human Rights which, in return, reported it to the UNCHR. At this point, the indigenous caucus which had been intimately involved in its development in Geneva, declared that, as set out in Article 42 of the Draft Declaration, the rights recognized therein were acceptable as a minimum set of international standards for the survival, dignity and well-being of indigenous peoples throughout the world and that they should not be changed or weakened.

The Draft Declaration consisted of 18 preambular paragraphs and 45 operative paragraphs dealing with the rights to self-determination, nationality, equality, survival, indigenous cultures, traditions, education, languages, media, health and medical care, economic and social systems, the control of their lands, waters and resources and self-government. One of the specific goals of the International Decade was the completion and adoption of the Draft Declaration before the end of the Decade in 2004.

In 1995, by UNCHR Resolution 1995/32 and ECOSOC Resolution 1995/32, the Draft Declaration was referred to a new open-ended Working Group on the Draft Declaration (WGDD) with the purpose of elaborating a Draft Declaration on the Rights of Indigenous Peoples and considering the 1994 draft prepared by the WGIP. It should be noted that this new working group, the WGDD, was made up of governments with their different political agendas while the WGIP, which prepared the original DDIP, was made up of experts not associated with their governments.

The WGDD did, however, continue the tradition of the WGIP and allowed indigenous representatives and NGOs to intervene and actively participate. The practice developed whereby final decisions were made by governments in the formal sessions of the WGDD, but for the most part, discussion and debate was carried on in informal sessions where indigenous peoples and NGOs participated fully with governments.

Unfortunately, several governments opposed articles in the DDIP and suggested amendments. Generally, these were rejected by the Indigenous Caucus and thus progress in the WGDD was extremely slow. As of 15 December 2004, following nine years of work, only two articles (Article 5, Right to a Nationality and Article 43, Gender Equality) out of 45 had been adopted.

A major difficulty for some governments were Articles 25–30 in Part 6 of the Draft Declaration relating to lands, waters and resources and the right of indigenous peoples to own, develop, control their traditional lands, and the right to restitution of lands and resources which have been taken, confiscated, occupied, used or damaged without their free and informed consent.

In the great land-grab, which occurred in all parts of the "newly discovered world" beginning in the sixteenth century, land, minerals, and timber were plundered from the indigenous populations who were often left impoverished or enslaved. Today, many governments and their citizens are fearful of Part 6 in that it could leave them with less wealth and power than they presently possess. On the other hand, some states already have policies and institutions to deal with indigenous land claims and some settlements have taken place. On the whole, however, progress has been deplorable.

This, of course, was one of the arguments by human rights activists for the adoption of such provisions in an international human rights instrument. The issue of land rights is central to the question of survival of indigenous peoples and their cultures. The indigenous concept of land as collective property was alien to the new settlers in much of the world; their relationship to the land was deeply spiritual and the destruction of that link was often equally damaging to their identity. Consequently, the articles on lands and resources were critical to any international instrument on the rights of indigenous peoples.

The most serious obstacle for the acceptance of the DDIP by governments was Article 3 on self-determination. Although the Article is an exact reproduction of Article 1 in both the Covenant of Civil and Political Rights and the Covenant on Economic, Social and Cultural Rights ratified by 150 and 147 states respectfully (including Canada, the U.S., and most of the countries involved in the Draft Declaration debate), many of these same states opposed its application to indigenous peoples.

Article 1 in both of the covenants states that "all peoples have the right to self-determination." Article 3 in the DDIP states that "Indigenous peoples have the right to self-determination." Indigenous peoples argue that they were logically covered by Article 1 of the two covenants since they are in fact "peoples" and that Article 3 of the DDIP is simply a confirmation of that fact. Governments, on the other hand, fearing threats of secession by indigenous peoples, vehemently tried to deny them this right. There was also a fear that indigenous peoples would use this article to enact laws contrary to those in force in the surrounding federal or provincial jurisdiction and thereby create disorder and disunity. In opposing Article 3, states first used the so-called "Blue Water Thesis," according to which only colonies separated from the colonizer by water—seas or oceans—had the right to self-determination. This theory was rejected by the International Court of Justice in its 1975 Western Sahara decision and has been discarded by the United Nations on several occasions.

Secondly, some governments tried to remove Article 3 from the DDIP on the grounds that "indigenous peoples" did not exist. They may be described as "indigenous people" or "indigenous populations" but they were not "peoples" and therefore not beneficiaries of Article 1 of the two covenants. This nonsense led to strong opposition from the indigenous caucus in Geneva and others around the world. While this proposal was dropped at the WGDD, the UN still used the alternative terms for other matters, i.e., the Working Group on Indigenous Populations and the International Decade of the World's Indigenous People. With Article 3 intact at the WGDD and the "s" still attached to "peoples," governments then tried to restrict the meaning of self-determination as it applies to indigenous peoples. Several attempts were made to add a clause to Article 3 or to other parts of the draft declaration which would read "The use of the term 'peoples' in this convention shall not be construed as having any implications as regards the rights which may attach to the term under international law."

Similar words were used in the final declaration of the World Conference Against Racism. These schemes were also rejected by indigenous peoples who insisted that they have always had an inherent right to self-determination and that this right was never surrendered. They went on to ridicule the World Conference Against Racism for formally practicing prejudice against indigenous peoples in its final declaration.

Since Article 3 was a key provision of the DDIP which is essential to the practice and implementation of the other rights of the instrument, the opposition of governments to this article resulted in a stalemate and as of 15 December 2004, only two of 45 articles had been adopted after nine years of discussion.

On 30 March 2004, anticipating the end of the International Decade and the possible demise of the DDIP, the Grand Council of the Crees (Canada), supported by other indigenous groups and NGOs, made a Joint Submission to the OHCHR assessing the

International Decade and urging a renewed mandate for the WGDD and improvements in the standard-setting process.

They said that the adoption by the UN General Assembly of a Declaration on the Rights of Indigenous Peoples was a major objective of the Decade and that it was a grave and widespread concern among indigenous peoples that this essential goal could be facing impending failure. Rather than penalizing over 300 million indigenous peoples worldwide by terminating the standard-setting process relating to their human rights, they said that the UN should examine ways to ensure that all participating states fulfill their responsibilities and respect their obligations under international law.

Fortunately, as a result of this and other efforts, some limited progress was made at the WGDD on September 13 to 24, 2004. As a result of more open, flexible, and frequent meetings between the Indigenous Caucus and several governments—in particular, those of Canada, Mexico, Peru, Ecuador and Guatemala—a new proposal concerning the right to self-determination was put forward by the Indigenous Caucus. This initiative, supported by Canada and others, constituted an important breakthrough in developing consensus on this provision. Nevertheless, neither Article 3 (self-determination) nor the Draft Declaration was approved as the International Decade ended on 31 December 2004.

However, at the beginning of 2005 the UNCHR agreed to extend the WGDD for another year, which resulted in critical negotiations. As a result, at the last session of the WGDD on 16 December 2005, agreement was reached on a large number of articles and there was a growing consensus on others.

In these circumstances, the WGDD instructed the Chair to draw up a report on what he believed to be a consensus on the entire Declaration and to submit it to the UNCHR for approval.

This was done on 24 February 2006. However, because the UN early in 2006 decided to replace the UNCHR with the new Human Rights Council, the approval process was postponed until 29 June 2006. On that date, the Human Rights Council adopted the Declaration by 30 votes to 2. The only countries voting against were Canada and Russia. It should be noted that until 2006, Canada was a strong supporter of the Declaration, but with an election and a new government in early 2006, Canada changed its position and voted against it.

Following its adoption by the Human Rights Council, the Declaration was sent to the UN General Assembly for final approval. However, when it was taken up for consideration by the General Assembly's Third Committee in the fall of 2006, certain concerns were raised by African countries and approval was postponed until 2007. During this period the new Canadian government, together with the United States and Australia, continued to oppose and lobby against the Declaration. Finally some minor amendments were made to meet the African concerns and on 13 September 2007, the General Assembly adopted the Declaration by a vote of 143 to 4 (11 abstentions). The four opposing countries were Canada, the USA, Australia, and New Zealand. A majority of countries from all continents except North America supported the Declaration. Canada's recent contention that the Declaration conflicts with the Canadian Charter of Rights is unfounded. Article 46 of the Declaration states, "In the exercise of the rights enunciated in the present Declaration, human rights and fundamental freedoms of all shall be respected." Furthermore, the Declaration is an aspirational instrument and not a legally binding treaty. It does, however, provide universal benchmarks for indigenous peoples in all countries including those which voted against it. Indigenous peoples and human rights organizations will continue to campaign throughout the world for the Declaration's universal acceptance and implementation.

CONCLUSIONS

The continuing opposition of some governments to the Declaration in general, and to Article 3 (self-determination) in particular, is based on scenarios which are grossly exaggerated and unreasonable. According to most international legal experts, the right to self-determination is now a peremptory norm of international law (*jus cogens*) from which there can be no derogation. This is supported by Article 53 of the Vienna Convention of the Law of the Treaties. The codification of the right to self-determination has been set out in the following international instruments and judicial decisions:

The UN Charter, Article 1 (2), Article 55, Chapters XI and XII, 1945; Declaration on the Granting of Independence to Colonial Countries and Peoples, 1960; Declaration on Friendly Relations, 1970; International Covenant on Civil and Political Rights, 1966 (76); International Covenant on Economic, Social and Cultural Rights, 1966 (76); The Helsinki Declaration, 1975; The International Court of Justice, Western Sahara Case, 1975; and the Human Rights Committee, Canada's Report 1999, Concluding Observations.

It appears to this author that the fears of governments with respect to secession and territorial integrity are exaggerated, not only because of the limitations to self-determination set out in the above-mentioned international instruments, but also because Article 3 in the UN Declaration on the Rights of Indigenous Peoples (UNDIP) is balanced by Article 4 (which deals with a local self-government as an exercise of self-determination), and by Article 46 (which provides compliance with international human rights standards and which provides that nothing in the declaration would permit activities contrary to the UN Charter).

While most experts agree that the right to self-determination includes secession, it does not automatically trigger secession, and in fact, most international instruments would only permit secession as a remedy of last resort. Consequently, if a state conducted itself in compliance with the principal of equal rights and possessed a government which respected the rights of indigenous peoples within its state boundaries to determine their unique political status and to pursue their own economic, social and cultural development, then such a state would respect the right to self-determination and have no fear of secession.

Finally, the Declaration is a "declaration" and not a "treaty." As a result, it is an aspirational instrument with moral and political value but it is not legally binding. Regretfully, governments have dissected and opposed it as if it were a legally binding treaty.

The growing importance of international instruments to indigenous peoples and their recourse to international tribunals is demonstrated in a number of cases. In 1977 Sandra Lovelace, a Maliseet woman from Tobique, New Brunswick, appealed to the UN Human Rights Committee (HRC) under several sections of the International Covenant on Civil and Political Rights to contest Sect. 12 (1) (b) of the Canadian Indian Act and to claim her rights to gender equality which had been denied to her by the Canadian courts. In 1981 the HRC ruled in her favour and the Canadian Parliament amended the law to conform with the ruling. In a similar way, Chief Bernard Ominayak of the Lubicon Lake Band appealed to the HRC in 1990 on a land issue. While the Band did not succeed under Article 1 of the International Covenant, it did win its case under Article 27. There were also significant successes before the Inter-American Commission on Human Rights by Mary and Carrie Dann of the Western Shoshone of Nevada (2002) and by the Mayagna (Sumo) Awas Tigni

Community vs. Nicaragua in 2001. These monumental cases show the importance of the international recognition of indigenous rights. Success can be won in the international realm when battles appear fruitless at home.

Ted Moses, former chief of the Grand Council of the Crees of Northern Quebec, has been a long-time advocate of indigenous rights at the United Nations, having first attended at Geneva in 1981. On several occasions, he has explained why international law, international institutions and the UNDIP are essential to indigenous peoples. In 1998 he said:

> *The Crees brought their issues to the international community as a last resort . . . it was easier to gain a hearing in Canada by stepping outside of Canada and speaking to the rest of the world, [and] when domestic laws fail to provide adequate protection against racism, the antidote is recourse to international human rights law.*

Earlier in 1994, he wrote:

> *. . . indigenous peoples must have recourse to a neutral jurisdiction and the possibility of the Draft Declaration which recognizes the dignity of indigenous peoples, their rights to self-determination, their right to land, to control resources, to practice their own religions, to manifest their own cultures, and their right to their own identity . . . the declaration, in its present form, would be non-binding but it would establish an appropriately high standard, set a principle and place the administration of justice for indigenous peoples on a level with other principles of international law and the aspirations of the indigenous peoples themselves.*

Chapter 31

The Illusion of Financial Unsustainability of Canadian Heath Care

GERARD W. BOYCHUK*

*Gerard W. Boychuk *is Associate Professor of Political Science at the University of Waterloo. This article is based on the author's paper, "The Changing Political and Economic Environment of Health Care in Canada," prepared for the Royal Commission on the Future of Health Care, 2002.*

Public health care in Canada is portrayed with increasing frequency and urgency as being financially unsustainable. However, current patterns of public health expenditures in Canada provide little evidence for this claim. The real crisis of the Canadian health-care system lies in the paradoxical situation by which its institutional underpinnings—especially the nature and dynamics of federal–provincial relations—undermine rather than bolster public support for the system.

The political weakness of the health-care system is the result of powerful dynamics generated out of nearly a decade of federal–provincial wrangling over funding in a context of fiscal restraint. The incentives built into federal–provincial arrangements and the resulting patterns of federal–provincial interaction have led to increasingly widespread perceptions that the public health-care system in Canada is of rapidly declining quality, is wracked by a funding crisis, is unable to control costs, and is ultimately unsustainable. Because these perceptions are rooted in its institutional framework, pressures on the health-care system have not eased—and should not be expected to ease—as fiscal pressures abate or as mechanisms to control future cost pressures are implemented. Reorienting the health-care system to a more politically sustainable basis requires a serious rethinking of the relative roles and responsibilities of the federal and provincial governments in the funding and delivery of public health care.

The Canadian Institute for Health Information (CIHI) data on provincial health expenditures are unequivocal. Total provincial public health expenditures comprised *exactly* the same proportion of gross domestic product in 2001 (6.2 percent) as they did in 1990 and were actually down slightly from their peak level of 6.9 percent in 1992 (see Figure 1). Where, then, do the claims that health care is now financially unsustainable come from?

Two approaches generally underpin arguments regarding the financial unsustainability of health care. The first is to extrapolate future health-care costs from current spending patterns (primarily since 1996); the second is to focus on expenditures expressed as a proportion of total provincial program expenditure. But there are serious problems with both approaches.

Extrapolations of health-care costs based on the late 1990s tend to ignore the fact that expenditure restraint in the middle of the decade created pent-up demand that was reflected in higher annual spending levels later in the decade. Annual provincial health expenditures did increase significantly after 1996. However, from 1993 to 1996, actual expenditures were

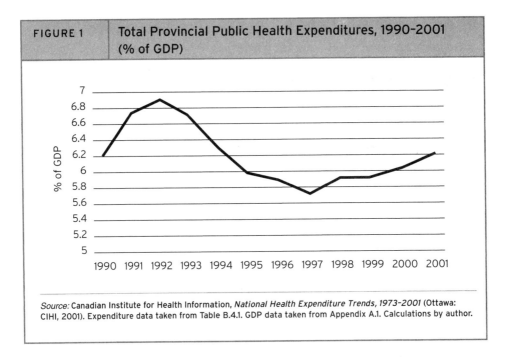

FIGURE 1 — Total Provincial Public Health Expenditures, 1990–2001 (% of GDP)

Source: Canadian Institute for Health Information, *National Health Expenditure Trends, 1973–2001* (Ottawa: CIHI, 2001). Expenditure data taken from Table B.4.1. GDP data taken from Appendix A.1. Calculations by author.

lower than if they had simply been maintained at 1992 per capita levels. While provinces began to reinvest in health care after 1996, actual cumulative expenditures by 2001 did not—but almost—reached the amount that provinces would have spent in the 1992–2001 period if 1992 levels of per capita expenditure had simply been maintained. As the provincial and territorial ministers report on health care costs notes, the "severe restraint directed toward health care in the early-to-mid 1990s produced a very low annual average growth rate" and [s]ince 1996, provinces and territories have been reinvesting, partly to make up for the restraint applied in the early years of the decade."

Cost expansion driven by pent-up demand resulting from earlier (and sometimes ill-considered) programs of expenditure restraint is not evidence of the inevitability of future cost increases. One only has to think of the costs incurred by Ontario in first laying off and then recruiting and rehiring thousands of nurses. Extrapolating from current expenditure patterns without clearly demarcating the various underlying drivers of cost escalation and identifying their different implications for future expenditure patterns is not an appropriate methodology for forecasting future expenditure patterns.

The second explanation for the perceptions of financial unsustainability is that numerous reports and public debates have increasingly focused on health-care expenditures expressed as a proportion of total provincial program expenditures. While provincial public health expenditures are no higher relative to GDP than they were a decade ago, they have increased relative to total provincial program expenditure. There are two dynamics and each provides a partial explanation for this apparent discrepancy.

First, *total* provincial program expenditures remained static from 1991 to 2000 in real dollar terms and have dropped to 78 percent of their 1991 levels relative to GDP. Thus, provincial health expenditures rose as a proportion of total provincial program expenditures even while remaining static relative to GDP.

Second, the overall contribution the federal government makes to provincial total revenues has declined. (All major federal transfers to the provinces including those under the
Canada Health and Social Transfer (CHST) for health go directly into the consolidated revenue fund, so to identify particular transfers for health, as is often attempted, is simply not
relevant to the question of the overall fiscal sustainability of provincial health-care expenditures. At the same time, the issue of federal contributions to health is an extremely
important issue in discussing the legitimacy of the conditional nature of specific transfers.)

Restraint in federal transfers has meant that an increasing proportion of the growth in
provincial revenues is going to health care rather than other provincial programs or
provincial deficit reduction or debt retirement. To this extent, health care is crowding out
the provision of other public goods and, clearly, this is a serious problem from the provincial perspective. The financial sustainability of health-care expenditures is a very real
problem *from the provincial perspective.* It is not, however, indicative of the unsustainability of the overall financial burden of health care relative to the overall ability of
Canadian governments to bear this burden.

In the longer term, the financial sustainability of public health care in Canada becomes
a serious issue under two scenarios; provincial governments become increasingly unable
(or unwilling) to maintain current taxation levels (for which there is currently no evidence); alternatively, there is a future escalation of health-care costs. However, according
to the provincial and territorial ministers of health report, *Understanding Canada's Health
Care Costs,* which presents a detailed forecast of health-care costs to 2026–2027, cost
drivers such as aging and population growth are *not* expected to increase the burden of
public health expenditures relative to GDP in the foreseeable future. Including the effects
of population growth, aging, inflation and a 1 percent per year increase to reflect "other"
health-care service needs, the report concludes that *health expenditures will remain fairly
constant as a share of GDP over the next 25 years.*

Questions of fiscal sustainability emerge only under a scenario of *accelerating* costs
and, indeed, there are compelling reasons to expect considerable future cost pressures. The
fact that current patterns of expenditure are not demonstrably unsustainable does not mean
that questions of affordability pose no future threat or that there is no need for fiscal
restraint in health management. The main question is whether the acceleration of costs to
unsustainable levels is inevitable. The claim that inevitable cost acceleration will make
public health expenditures unsustainable in the future is a much different claim than the
one that current levels of health expenditure are unsustainable.

Despite the fact that provincial health expenditures relative to GDP are the same as they
were at the beginning of the 1990s, there is now an increasingly widespread perception of
a financial crisis in public health care. The roots of this perception lie, to some significant
degree, in the institutional underpinnings of health care—especially federal–provincial fiscal arrangements.

The preponderance of jurisdictional responsibility for the provision of health services
lies with provincial governments, while the federal role lies primarily in sharing the costs
of provincially provided health services under terms governed by the federal Canada
Health Act (CHA). Given this division of responsibility, the dynamics of federal–provincial
relations regarding health are relatively straightforward. The federal government strives to
minimize its fiscal commitment to the degree possible while ensuring both its visibility in
health and its ability to claim credit for enforcing the CHA. Provincial governments, for
their part, strive to maximize federal fiscal commitment while also preserving their room

to manoeuvre vis-à-vis constraints imposed directly or indirectly through public pressure as a result of the CHA. Pressures on these arrangements began to build as the federal government restrained transfers first under the Established Programs Financing (EPF) arrangements and then, more drastically, under the CHST. Three crucial effects were thus generated.

The first is the illusion of health care as a rapidly growing fiscal burden relative to the ability of governments as a whole to bear this burden. Public health-care expenditures do not constitute a higher proportion of GDP than they did a decade ago. Yet, as a result of federal transfer restraint, provincial governments now make a compelling case that public health care as it currently exists is no longer affordable. From the provincial perspective, this concern is real.

Second, partly as a result of federal transfer retrenchment, the federal government's fiscal position is disproportionately brighter relative to the provinces. The situation in which surpluses are held at the federal level (which has limited direct involvement in the delivery of health-care services) and deficits or near deficits are held at the provincial level of government (whose most important single program responsibility is health care) contributes to the political construction of a strong linkage between health care and the issue debts and deficits. The goals of providing public health care and debt/deficit reduction are cast into sharp political competition as a result of the fiscal imbalance between levels of government that has been exacerbated by the capricious federal manipulation of health-care transfers.

Finally, these fiscal arrangements have generated perverse incentives for provincial governments. Provinces face limited incentives to forcefully combat public perceptions regarding the declining quality of health care and the sensationalist media coverage that strongly reinforces such perceptions. There are incentives for provincial governments to leverage their demands for greater federal funding by allowing such perceptions to flourish (if not actually encouraging them) so long as some measure of the blame can be successfully shifted to the federal government.

Provinces have a similar incentive to focus disproportionately on the funding aspect of the health-care issue, emphasizing the perception that a central explanation for problems with the health-care system is a lack of financial resources. Also as part of the blame-shifting strategy, provinces have an incentive to claim that the CHA is a straitjacket that does not allow for serious innovation in the health-care system and limits their ability to respond to the problems of health care themselves. Not surprisingly, the *National Post* recently called for the CHA " . . . to be scrapped, given the intolerable constraints it imposes on provinces' freedom to innovate", as noted by Andrew Coyne on January 11, 2002.

This provincial approach has culminated, somewhat predictably, in claims that the current public health-care system is unsustainable. In concluding a recent meeting of premiers in Victoria, Premier Gordon Campbell of British Columbia noted, "We all agree as premiers that health care under the current situation is not sustainable", as reported in the *Globe and Mail* on January 25, 2002. The *National Post* reported the following comments by Don Mazankowski: "Public health care in Canada will soon collapse unless bold reforms are introduced" (January 5, 2002). A final illustration is the Ontario government advertisements which, in a banner headline, claim: "Unless Ottawa pays its fair share for health care, the prognosis isn't good." These responses simply represent the provincial calculation of a rational response to the incentives structured into existing federal–provincial arrangements.

Public perceptions regarding health care, which otherwise might seem puzzling, are more clearly explicable in light of these political dynamics which help explain three relatively stable and well-documented trends in public opinion.

1) *A belief that the system is in crisis and that the quality of health care is declining despite personal experiences to the contrary.*

The growing perception among Canadians that health care is the highest priority facing the country is nothing short of astounding. Over the course of the 1990s, health care has shifted from being a non-issue to being far and away the highest priority among Canadians. While concern for other more perennial issues such as the economy has waxed and waned, health care emerged out of nowhere to become the top issue of concern in less than five years. In part, health care has become such an important issue because of growing perceptions that the system is in crisis—a belief now held by nearly four out of five survey respondents.

This increase in the salience of health care as an issue is related to the staggering decline in public perceptions of the quality of the Canadian health-care system. This shift did not take place gradually; rather, it first emerged only in the early 1990s, accelerated rapidly in the mid-1990s, and has remained relatively stable since 1997 despite the fact that provinces have begun to reinvest in health care.

The most obvious explanation for such a pattern would be that the system is in crisis. However, to the degree that Canadians' perceptions of their own personal interaction with the health-care system have been overwhelmingly positive, the image of crisis must lie elsewhere.

There is evidence of a decline in the positive nature of personal experiences with the health-care system but it is limited and has emerged only relatively recently. For the most part, individual perceptions regarding the quality of care in Canada have been strikingly high and any decline in perceptions of personal experiences have followed—rather than led—declining perceptions of the quality of the overall system. Similarly, Canadians have been much more sanguine about the system's ability to meet their own personal health needs and those of their families than to meet the needs of the population as a whole. This discrepancy is most plausibly explained by media reports of many stories depicting the stresses and strains in the health-care system. While these problems are certainly not imaginary, neither are they are representative of the norm in health-care provision. Key in this process is the apparent willingness of provincial governments to allow and sometimes even encourage such perceptions.

2) *A belief that we are now in a major funding crisis and that the system needs more resources.*

There is a widespread belief that the system is either currently facing a funding crisis or that a funding crisis is imminent. These public perceptions are not surprising given ongoing provincial government efforts to publicly demonstrate the existence of a health-care funding crisis. In this context, it is also not surprising that four out of five Canadians believe that too little is being spent on health care. Certainly, while most citizens do not believe that increased funding alone is the answer, most Canadians are skeptical that the system can be improved without increased funding.

3) *A striking decline in public approval ratings for how both the federal and provincial governments are handling the issue of health care and a belief that governments are losing ground in solving the issues facing health care.*

Public satisfaction with both the federal and provincial governments' handling of health care reached a peak in the early 1990s. After 1992, public approval ratings for both governments' performance on this issue began a precipitous yet enduring decline and have not recovered much beyond their lowest points in the late 1990s. This trend has certainly been exacerbated by intergovernmental strategies in which each level of government, in an effort to avoid accepting public blame for problems with the health-care system, attempts to shift responsibility to the other.

Despite the fact that the sustainability of the health-care system has been overwhelmingly portrayed in current debates as a financial issue, political sustainability must also be considered. Political sustainability requires ensuring the ongoing ability of the health-care system to maintain widespread popular support sufficient to guarantee that there are incentives for governments to adequately fund and effectively provide public health-care services. The trends in public opinion outlined above are suggestive of how seriously this ability is coming to be challenged. Fiscal sustainability is a moot issue if the health-care system is politically unsustainable and *vice versa*. Reforms that address only one of these components of sustainability—without consideration for the other—are likely to founder.

The most simplistic solution to the problems of political sustainability, yet one we are likely to repeatedly hear echoed from various quarters this autumn [2002], is to suggest that the federal and provincial governments simply "get their act together and fix health care." Certainly, the public is unlikely to disagree with this motherhood prescription. The failure of both orders of government to collaborate effectively has significantly contributed to fuelling public cynicism regarding governments' ability to deal with health-care issues.

Naively suggesting that the two orders simply work together, without fundamentally rethinking the incentives faced by each order of government under the current set of institutional arrangements, will merely raise public expectations for such cooperation without significantly increasing the likelihood that governments will deliver. It is a facile prescription that avoids the toughest issues and entails greater risk than promise. In the absence of institutional change that addresses the incentives generated by existing federal–provincial arrangements, a continuing and not easily reversible decline in public perceptions of both the quality and the sustainability of the public health-care system in Canada seems likely. It is here that the real potential for crisis lies.

Chapter 32

God's Country?

WALTER RUSSELL MEAD*

*Walter Russell Mead is Henry A. Kissinger Senior Fellow for U.S. Foreign Policy at the Council on Foreign Relations.

Summary: Religion has always been a major force in U.S. politics, but the recent surge in the number and the power of evangelicals is recasting the country's political scene—with dramatic implications for foreign policy. This should not be cause for panic: evangelicals are passionately devoted to justice and improving the world, and eager to reach out across sectarian lines.

EVANGELICALS AND FOREIGN POLICY

Religion has always been a major force in U.S. politics, policy, identity, and culture. Religion shapes the nation's character, helps form Americans' ideas about the world, and influences the ways Americans respond to events beyond their borders. Religion explains both Americans' sense of themselves as a chosen people and their belief that they have a duty to spread their values throughout the world. Of course, not all Americans believe such things—and those who do often bitterly disagree over exactly what they mean. But enough believe them that the ideas exercise profound influence over the country's behavior abroad and at home.

In one sense, religion is so important to life in the United States that it disappears into the mix. Partisans on all sides of important questions regularly appeal to religious principles to support their views, and the country is so religiously diverse that support for almost any conceivable foreign policy can be found somewhere.

Yet the balance of power among the different religious strands shifts over time; in the last generation, this balance has shifted significantly, and with dramatic consequences. The more conservative strains within American Protestantism have gained adherents, and the liberal Protestantism that dominated the country during the middle years of the twentieth century has weakened. This shift has already changed U.S. foreign policy in profound ways.

These changes have yet to be widely understood, however, in part because most students of foreign policy in the United States and abroad are relatively unfamiliar with conservative U.S. Protestantism. That the views of the evangelical Reverend Billy Graham lead to quite different approaches to foreign relations than, say, those popular at the fundamentalist Bob Jones University is not generally appreciated. But subtle theological and cultural differences can and do have important political consequences. Interpreting the impact of religious changes in the United States on U.S. foreign policy therefore requires a closer look into the big revival tent of American Protestantism.

Why focus exclusively on Protestantism? The answer is, in part, that Protestantism has shaped much of the country's identity and remains today the majority faith in the United States (although only just). Moreover, the changes in Catholicism (the second-largest faith and the largest single religious denomination in the country) present a more mixed picture with fewer foreign policy implications. And finally, the remaining religious groups in the United States are significantly less influential when it comes to the country's politics.

A QUESTION OF FUNDAMENTALS

To make sense of how contemporary changes in Protestantism are starting to affect U.S. foreign policy, it helps to understand the role that religion has historically played in the country's public life. The U.S. religious tradition, which grew out of the sixteenth-century Reformations of England and Scotland, has included many divergent ideologies and world-views over time. Three strains, however, have been most influential: a strict tradition that can be called fundamentalist, a progressive and ethical tradition known as liberal Christianity, and a broader evangelical tradition. (Pentecostals have theological differences with non-Pentecostal evangelicals and fundamentalists, but Pentecostalism is an offshoot of evangelical theology, and thus the majority of American Pentecostals can be counted with evangelicals here.)

It would be wrong to read too much precision into these labels. Most American Christians mix and match theological and social ideas from these and other strands of Protestant and Christian thought with little concern for consistency. Yet describing the chief features of each strand and their implications for the United States' role in the world will nevertheless make it easier to appreciate the way changes in the religious balance are shaping the country's behavior.

Fundamentalists, liberal Christians, and evangelicals are all part of the historical mainstream of American Protestantism, and as such all were profoundly affected by the fundamentalist-modernist controversy of the early twentieth century. For much of the 1800s, most Protestants believed that science confirmed biblical teaching. When Darwinian biology and scholarly "higher criticism" began to cast increasing doubt on traditional views of the Bible's authorship and veracity, however, the American Protestant movement broke apart. Modernists argued that the best way to defend Christianity in an enlightened age was to incorporate the new scholarship into theology, and mainline Protestant denominations followed this logic. The fundamentalists believed that churches should remain loyal to the "fundamentals" of Protestant faith, such as the literal truth of the Bible.

The fundamentalists themselves were divided into two strands, originally distinguished as much by culture and temperament as by theology. The "separatists" argued that true believers should abandon churches that compromised with or tolerated modernism in any form. As U.S. society and culture became more secular and pluralistic, the separatists increasingly withdrew from both politics and culture. The other strand of the original fundamentalist movement sought continual engagement with the rest of the world. This strand was originally called neo-evangelical. Today, the separatists proudly retain the label of fundamentalist, while the neo-evangelicals have dropped the prefix and are now simply known as evangelicals.

The three contemporary streams of American Protestantism (fundamentalist, liberal, and evangelical) lead to very different ideas about what the country's role in the world should be. In this context, the most important differences have to do with the degree to which each promotes optimism about the possibilities for a stable, peaceful, and enlightened international order and the importance each places on the difference between believers and nonbelievers. In a nutshell, fundamentalists are deeply pessimistic about the prospects for world order and see an unbridgeable divide between believers and nonbelievers. Liberals are optimistic about the prospects for world order and see little difference between Christians and nonbelievers. And evangelicals stand somewhere in between these extremes.

Self-described fundamentalists are a diverse group, partly because there are many competing definitions of the term "fundamentalist" and, in keeping with the decentralized and sectarian character of American Protestantism, there is no generally accepted authoritative body to define what fundamentalists are or believe. As used here, the term "fundamentalist" involves three characteristics: a high view of biblical authority and inspiration; a strong determination to defend the historical Protestant faith against Roman Catholic and modernist, secular, and non-Christian influence; and the conviction that believers should separate themselves from the non-Christian world. Fundamentalists can be found throughout conservative Protestant Christianity, and some denominations more properly considered evangelical (such as the Southern Baptists and the Missouri Synod Lutherans) have vocal minorities that could legitimately be called fundamentalist. Fundamentalist denominations, such as the ultra-Calvinist Orthodox Presbyterian Church, tend to be smaller than liberal and evangelical ones. This is partly because fundamentalists prefer small, pure, and doctrinally rigorous organizations to larger, more diverse ones. It is also because many fundamentalist congregations prefer to remain independent of any denominational structure.

Many outsiders think of fundamentalism as an anti-intellectual and emotional movement. And it is true that most conservative American Protestants attach great importance to emotional and personal spiritual experience. But the difference between fundamentalists and evangelicals is not that fundamentalists are more emotional in their beliefs; it is that fundamentalists insist more fully on following their ideas to their logical conclusion. Fundamentalists are more interested than evangelicals in developing a consistent and all-embracing "Christian worldview" and then in systematically applying it to the world. It is one thing to reject (as many evangelicals do) Darwinian evolution because personal experience leads one to consider the Bible an infallible guide. It is something else entirely to develop (as some fundamentalists do) an alternative paradigm of "scientific creationism," write textbooks about it, and seek to force schools to teach it or withdraw one's children from those schools that will not. Fundamentalist-dominated institutions, such as the Independent Baptist movement and Bob Jones University, are not hotbeds of snake-handling revivalist Holy Rollers but host intense, if often unconventional, scholarship.

Devastated by a string of intellectual and political defeats in the 1920s and 1930s, fundamentalists retreated into an isolation and a pessimism that were foreign to the optimistic orientation of nineteenth-century American Protestantism. The effect of this retreat was to give fundamentalists a defensive and alienated outlook that bore a marked resemblance to the Puritan Calvinism of early New England. Like the Puritans, many fundamentalists hold the bleak view that there is an absolute gap between those few souls God has chosen to redeem and the many he has predestined to end up in hell. Calvinists once labored to establish theocratic commonwealths—in Scotland by the Covenanters and the Kirk Party, in England during Oliver Cromwell's ascendancy, and in New England, all during the seventeenth century. But in the last three centuries, theocratic state building has become both less attractive to and less feasible for hard-line fundamentalists. It is not only that demographic changes have made it difficult to imagine circumstances in which fundamentalists would constitute a majority. The experience of past commonwealths also shows that successor generations usually lack the founders' fervor. Sadder and wiser from these experiences, contemporary American fundamentalists generally believe that human efforts to build a better world can have only very limited success. They agree with the nineteenth-century American preacher Dwight Moody, who, when urged to focus on political action, replied, "I look upon this world as a wrecked vessel. God has given me a lifeboat and said, 'Moody, save all you can.'"

If fundamentalists tend to be pessimistic about the prospects for social reform inside the United States, they are downright hostile to the idea of a world order based on secular morality and on global institutions such as the United Nations. More familiar than many Americans with the stories of persecuted Christians abroad, fundamentalists see nothing moral about cooperating with governments that oppress churches, forbid Christian proselytizing, or punish conversions to Christianity under Islamic law. To institutions such as the UN that treat these governments as legitimate, they apply the words of the prophet Isaiah: "We have made a covenant with death, and with hell we are at agreement." It is no coincidence that the popular *Left Behind* novels, which depict the end of the world from a fundamentalist perspective, show the Antichrist rising to power as the secretary-general of the UN.

Fundamentalists, finally, are committed to an apocalyptic vision of the end of the world and the Last Judgment. As biblical literalists, they believe that the dark prophecies in both the Hebrew and the Greek Scriptures, notably those of the book of Revelation, foretell the great and terrible events that will ring down the curtain on human history. Satan and his human allies will stage a final revolt against God and the elect; believers will undergo terrible persecution, but Christ will put down his enemies and reign over a new heaven and a new earth. This vision is not particularly hospitable to the idea of gradual progress toward a secular utopia driven by technological advances and the cooperation of intelligent people of all religious traditions.

LIBERAL THINKING

Liberal Christianity finds the core of Christianity in its ethical teachings rather than in its classic doctrines. As far back as the seventeenth century, this current of Christian thinking has worked to demythologize the religion: to separate the kernel of moral inspiration from the shell of legend that has, presumably, accreted around it. Liberal Christians are skeptical about the complex doctrines concerning the nature of Jesus and the Trinity that were developed in the early centuries of the church's history. They are reluctant to accept various biblical episodes—such as the creation of the world in seven days, the Garden of Eden, and Noah's flood—as literal narrative. And their skepticism often also extends to the physical resurrection of Jesus and the various miracles attributed to him. Rather than believing that Jesus was a supernatural being, liberal Christians see him as a sublime moral teacher whose example they seek to follow through a lifetime of service—often directed primarily at the poor. The Unitarian Church, introduced to the United States in 1794 by the English scientist and theologian Joseph Priestly, is a denomination organized around these core ideas. Priestly was a friend of Benjamin Franklin and a significant theological influence on Thomas Jefferson, although both Franklin and Jefferson attended Episcopalian services when they went to church. As Darwinism and biblical criticism led others to question the literal accuracy of many biblical stories, liberalism spread widely through the mainline Protestant denominations—including the Methodist, Presbyterian, American Baptist, Congregational, Episcopal, and Lutheran churches—to which the United States' social, intellectual, and economic elites have generally belonged.

Although more doctrinally conservative Christians often consider progressives to be out-side the Christian mainstream, liberal Christians claim to represent the essence of Protestantism. The Reformation, in their view, was the first stage of reclaiming the valuable core of Christianity. The original reformers purged the church of the sale of indulgences and ideas such as purgatory, papal infallibility, and transubstantiation. In attacking such established Christian doctrines as the Trinity, original sin, and the existence of hell, liberal Christians today believe they are simply following the "Protestant principle."

Liberal Christianity has a much lower estimate of the difference between Christians and non-Christians than do the other major forms of American Protestantism. Liberal Christians believe that ethics are the same all over the world. Buddhists, Christians, Hindus, Jews, Muslims, and even nonreligious people can agree on what is right and what is wrong; every religion has a kernel of ethical truth. The idea of the church as a supernatural society whose members enjoy special grace plays very little role in liberal Christianity.

Because most liberal Christians (with the important exception of "Christian realists" such as the theologian Reinhold Niebuhr) discard the doctrine of original sin, liberal Christianity leads to optimism both about the prospects for a peaceful world order and about international organizations such as the UN. Indeed, liberal Christians have often seen the fight to establish the kingdom of God as a call to support progressive political causes at home and abroad. They argue that the dark prophecies of Revelation point to the difficulty of establishing a just social order on earth—but that this order will nonetheless come to pass if everyone works together to build it.

Liberal Protestantism dominated the worldview of the U.S. political class during World War II and the Cold War. Leaders such as Franklin Roosevelt, Harry Truman, Dean Acheson, Dwight Eisenhower, and John Foster Dulles were, like most American elites at the time, steeped in this tradition. The liberal Christian approach also opened the door to cooperation with Roman Catholics and Jews, who were then becoming much more influential in the United States. Some of the optimism with which many liberal Christians today approach the problems of world order and cooperation across ethnic and religious lines reflects their earlier success at forming a domestic consensus.

In recent years, however, liberal Christianity has been confronted with several challenges. First, liberal Protestantism tends to evanesce into secularism: members follow the "Protestant principle" right out the door of the church. As a result, liberal, mainline denominations are now shrinking—quickly. Second, liberal Christians are often only tepidly engaged with "religious" issues and causes. Liberal Christians may be environmentalists involved with the Sierra Club or human rights activists involved with Amnesty International, but those activities take place in the secular world. Third, alienated from the Catholic hierarchy by their position on issues such as abortion and gay rights, and from Jews by their decreasing support for Israel, liberal Christians are losing their traditional role as the conveners of an interfaith community. Finally, the mainline denominations themselves are increasingly polarized over issues such as gay rights. Consumed by internal battles, they are less able to influence U.S. society as a whole.

EVANGELICALS AND THE MIDDLE PATH

Evangelicals, the third of the leading strands in American Protestantism, straddle the divide between fundamentalists and liberals. Their core beliefs share common roots with fundamentalism, but their ideas about the world have been heavily influenced by the optimism endemic to U.S. society. Although there is considerable theological diversity within this group, in general it is informed by the "soft Calvinism" of the sixteenth-century Dutch theologian Jacobus Arminius, the thinking of English evangelists such as John Wesley (who carried on the tradition of German Pietism), and, in the United States, the experience of the eighteenth-century Great Awakening and subsequent religious revivals.

The leading evangelical denomination in the United States is the Southern Baptist Convention, which, with more than 16.3 million members, is the largest Protestant denomination in the country. The next-largest evangelical denominations are the African American churches, including the National Baptist Convention, U.S.A., and the National Baptist Convention of America (each of which reports having about 5 million members). The predominately African American Church of God in Christ, with 5.5 million members, is the largest Pentecostal denomination in the country, and the rapidly growing Assemblies of God, which has 2.7 million members, is the largest Pentecostal denomination that is not predominately black. The Lutheran Church-Missouri Synod, which has 2.5 million members, is the second-largest predominately white evangelical denomination. Like fundamentalists, white evangelicals are often found in independent congregations and small denominations. So-called parachurch organizations, such as the Campus Crusade for Christ, the Promise Keepers, and the Wycliffe Bible Translators, often replace or supplement traditional denominational structures among evangelicals.

Evangelicals resemble fundamentalists in several respects. Like fundamentalists, evangelicals attach a great deal of importance to the doctrinal tenets of Christianity, not just to its ethical teachings. For evangelicals and fundamentalists, liberals' emphasis on ethics translates into a belief that good works and the fulfillment of moral law are the road to God—a betrayal of Christ's message, in their view. Because of original sin, they argue, humanity is utterly incapable of fulfilling any moral law whatever. The fundamental message of Christianity is that human efforts to please God by observing high ethical standards must fail; only Christ's crucifixion and resurrection can redeem man. Admitting one's sinful nature and accepting Christ's sacrifice are what both evangelicals and fundamentalists mean by being "born again." When liberal Christians put ethics at the heart of their theology, fundamentalists and evangelicals question whether these liberals know what Christianity really means.

Evangelicals also attach great importance to the difference between those who are "saved" and those who are not. Like fundamentalists, they believe that human beings who die without accepting Christ are doomed to everlasting separation from God. They also agree with fundamentalists that "natural" people—those who have not been "saved"—are unable to do any good works on their own.

Finally, most (although not all) evangelicals share the fundamentalist approach to the end of the world. Virtually all evangelicals believe that the biblical prophecies will be fulfilled, and a majority agree with fundamentalists on the position known as premillennialism: the belief that Christ's return will precede the establishment of the prophesied thousand-year reign of peace. Ultimately, all human efforts to build a peaceful world will fail.

Given these similarities, it is not surprising that many observers tend to confuse evangelicals and fundamentalists, thinking that the former are simply a watered down version of the latter. Yet there are important differences between the fundamentalist and the evangelical worldviews. Although the theological positions on these issues can be very technical and nuanced, evangelicals tend to act under the influence of a cheerier form of Calvinism. The strict position is that Christ's sacrifice on the cross was only intended for the small number of souls God intended to save; the others have no chance for salvation. Psychologically and doctrinally, American evangelicals generally have a less bleak outlook. They believe that the benefits of salvation are potentially available to everyone, and that God gives everyone just enough grace to be able to choose salvation if he wishes. Strict Calvinist doctrine divides humanity into two camps with little in common. In the predominant evangelical view, God loves each soul, is unutterably grieved when any are lost, and urgently seeks to save them all.

All Christians, whether fundamentalist, liberal, or evangelical, acknowledge at least formally the responsibility to show love and compassion to everyone, Christian or not. For evangelicals, this demand has extra urgency. Billions of perishing souls can still be saved for Christ, they believe. The example Christians set in their daily lives, the help they give the needy, and the effectiveness of their proclamation of the gospel—these can bring lost souls to Christ and help fulfill the divine plan. Evangelicals constantly reinforce the message of Christian responsibility to the world. Partly as a result, evangelicals are often open to, and even eager for, social action and cooperation with nonbelievers in projects to improve human welfare, even though they continue to believe that those who reject Christ cannot be united with God after death.

Evangelicals can be hard to predict. Shocked by recent polls showing that a substantial majority of Americans reject the theory of evolution, intellectuals and journalists in the United States and abroad have braced themselves for an all-out assault on Darwinian science. But no such onslaught has been forthcoming. U.S. public opinion has long rejected Darwinism, yet even in states such as Alabama, Mississippi, and South Carolina, which have large actively Christian populations, state universities go on teaching astronomy, genetics, geology, and paleontology with no concern for religious cosmology, and the United States continues to support the world's most successful scientific community. Most evangelicals find nothing odd about this seeming contradiction. Nor do they wish to change it—unlike the fundamentalists. The pragmatism of U.S. culture combines with the somewhat anti-intellectual cast of evangelical religion to create a very broad public tolerance for what, to some, might seem an intolerable level of cognitive dissonance. In the seventeenth century, Puritan Harvard opposed Copernican cosmology, but today evangelical America is largely content to let discrepancies between biblical chronology and the fossil record stand unresolved. What evangelicals do not like is what some call "scientism": the attempt to teach evolution or any other subject in such a way as to rule out the possibility of the existence and activity of God.

Evangelicals are more optimistic than fundamentalists about the prospects for moral progress. The postmillennial minority among them (which holds that Christ will return after a thousand years of world peace, not before) believes that this process can continue until human society reaches a state of holiness: that the religious progress of individuals and societies can culminate in the establishment of a peaceable kingdom through a process of gradual improvement. This is a view of history very compatible with the optimism of liberal Christians, and evangelicals and liberal Christians have in fact joined in many common efforts at both domestic and international moral improvement throughout U.S. history. Although the premillennial majority is less optimistic about the ultimate success of such efforts, American evangelicals are often optimistic about the short-term prospects for human betterment.

In his 2005 book *Imagine! A God-Blessed America: How It Could Happen and What It Would Look Like*, the conservative evangelical Richard Land describes and justifies this evangelical optimism: "I believe that there could be yet another Great Awakening in our country, a nationwide revival . . . . Scripture tells us that none of us can know with certainty the day or hour of the Lord's return. Thus, we have no right to abandon the world to its own misery. Nowhere in Scripture are we called to huddle pessimistically in Christian ghettoes, snatching converts out of the world."

THE BALANCE OF POWER

Recent decades have witnessed momentous changes in the balance of religious power in the United States. The membership of the liberal, historically dominant mainline Protestant churches mostly peaked in the 1960s. Since then, while the number of American Christians has grown, membership in the mainline denominations has sharply dropped. According to *Christianity Today*, between 1960 and 2003, membership in mainline denominations fell by more than 24 percent, from 29 million to 22 million. The drop in market share was even more dramatic. In 1960, more than 25 percent of all members of religious groups in the United States belonged to the seven leading mainline Protestant denominations; by 2003, this figure had dropped to 15 percent. The Pew Research Center reports that 59 percent of American Protestants identified themselves as mainline Protestants in 1988; by 2002–3, that percentage had fallen to 46 percent. In the same period, the percentage of Protestants who identified themselves as evangelical rose from 41 percent to 54 percent.

In 1965, there were 3.6 million Episcopalians in the United States — 1.9 percent of the total population. By 2005, there were only 2.3 million Episcopalians — 0.8 percent of the population. Membership in the United Methodist Church fell from 11 million in 1965 to 8.2 million in 2005. In the same period, that in the Presbyterian Church (U.S.A.) fell from 3.2 million to 2.4 million, and the United Church of Christ saw its membership decline by almost 50 percent.

Meanwhile, despite some signs of slowing growth after 2001, the Southern Baptist Convention gained more than 7 million members to become the nation's largest Protestant denomination. Between 1960 and 2003, the Southern Baptists gained more members than the Methodists, Presbyterians, Episcopalians, and the United Church of Christ together lost. In 1960, there were almost 2 million more Methodists than Southern Baptists in the United States; by 2003, there were more Southern Baptists than Methodists, Presbyterians, Episcopalians, and members of the United Church of Christ combined.

The impact of these trends on national politics has not been hard to find. Self-identified evangelicals provided roughly 40 percent of George W. Bush's total vote in 2004. Among white evangelicals, Bush received 68 percent of the national vote in 2000 and 78 percent in 2004. (The majority of African American evangelicals continue to vote Democratic. Among Hispanics, Bush ran much stronger among the growing Protestant minority than among Catholics; however, both Hispanic Protestants and Hispanic Catholics were more likely to support Bush if they were religiously observant.) Evangelicals have been playing a major role in congressional and Senate elections as well, and the number of self-identified evangelicals in Congress has increased from around 10 percent of the membership in both houses in 1970 to more than 25 percent in 2004.

Fundamentalists, despite some increase in their numbers and political visibility, remain less influential. This is partly because the pervasive optimism of the United States continues to limit the appeal of ultra-Calvinist theology. Moreover, religious politics in the United States remains a coalition sport—one that a fundamentalist theology, which continues to view Catholicism as an evil cult, is ill equipped to play. To make matters more complicated, fundamentalists themselves are torn between two incompatible political positions: a sullen withdrawal from a damned world and an ambitious attempt to build a new Puritan commonwealth.

Finally, many evangelicals remain resistant to fundamentalist attitudes. "I believe the Word of God, I'm just not mad about it," explained the Reverend Frank Page, the new president of the Southern Baptist Convention, after his election in June 2006.

OUT IN THE WORLD

The growing influence of evangelicals has affected U.S. foreign policy in several ways; two issues in particular illustrate the resultant changes. On the question of humanitarian and human rights policies, evangelical leadership is altering priorities and methods while increasing overall support for both foreign aid and the defense of human rights. And on the question of Israel, rising evangelical power has deepened U.S. support for the Jewish state, even as the liberal Christian establishment has distanced itself from Jerusalem.

In these cases as in others, evangelical political power today is not leading the United States in a completely new direction. We have seen at least parts of this film before: evangelicals were the dominant force in U.S. culture during much of the nineteenth century and the early years of the twentieth. But the country's change in orientation in recent years has nonetheless been pronounced.

Evangelicals in the Anglo-American world have long supported humanitarian and human rights policies on a global basis. The British antislavery movement, for example, was led by an evangelical, William Wilberforce. Evangelicals were consistent supporters of nineteenth-century national liberation movements—often Christian minorities seeking to break from Ottoman rule. And evangelicals led a number of reform campaigns, often with feminist overtones: against suttee (the immolation of widows) in India, against foot binding in China, in support of female education throughout the developing world, and against human sexual trafficking (the "white slave trade") everywhere. Evangelicals have also long been concerned with issues relating to Africa.

As evangelicals have recently returned to a position of power in U.S. politics, they have supported similar causes and given new energy and support to U.S. humanitarian efforts. Under President Bush, with the strong support of Michael Gerson (an evangelical who was Bush's senior policy adviser and speechwriter), U.S. aid to Africa has risen by 67 percent, including $15 billion in new spending for programs to combat HIV and AIDS. African politicians, such as Nigeria's Olusegun Obasanjo and Uganda's Yoweri Museveni, have stressed their own evangelical credentials to build support in Washington, much as China's Sun Yat-sen and Madame Chiang Kai-shek once did. Thanks to evangelical pressure, efforts to suppress human trafficking and the sexual enslavement of women and children have become a much higher priority in U.S. policy, and the country has led the fight to end Sudan's wars. Rick Warren, pastor of an evangelical megachurch in Southern California and the author of *The Purpose Driven Life* (the single best-selling volume in the history of U.S. publishing), has mobilized his 22,000 congregants to help combat AIDS worldwide (by hosting a conference on the subject and training volunteers) and to form relationships with churches in Rwanda.

Evangelicals have not, however, simply followed the human rights and humanitarian agendas crafted by liberal and secular leaders. They have made religious freedom—including the freedom to proselytize and to convert—a central focus of their efforts. Thanks largely to evangelical support (although some Catholics and Jews also played a role), Congress passed the International Religious Freedom Act in 1998, establishing an Office of International Religious Freedom in a somewhat skeptical State Department.

Despite these government initiatives, evangelicals, for cultural as well as theological reasons, are often suspicious of state-to-state aid and multilateral institutions. They prefer grass-roots and faith-based organizations. Generally speaking, evangelicals are quick to support efforts to address specific problems, but they are skeptical about grand designs and large-scale development efforts. Evangelicals will often react strongly to particular instances of human suffering or injustice, but they are more interested in problem solving than in institution building. (Liberal Christians often bewail this trait as evidence of the anti-intellectualism of evangelical culture.)

U.S. policy toward Israel is another area where the increased influence of evangelicals has been evident. This relationship has also had a long history. In fact, American Protestant Zionism is significantly older than the modern Jewish version; in the nineteenth century, evangelicals repeatedly petitioned U.S. officials to establish a refuge in the Holy Land for persecuted Jews from Europe and the Ottoman Empire.

U.S. evangelical theology takes a unique view of the role of the Jewish people in the modern world. On the one hand, evangelicals share the widespread Christian view that Christians represent the new and true children of Israel, inheritors of God's promises to the ancient Hebrews. Yet unlike many other Christians, evangelicals also believe that the Jewish people have a continuing role in God's plan. In the seventeenth and eighteenth centuries, close study of biblical prophecies convinced evangelical scholars and believers that the Jews would return to the Holy Land before the triumphant return of Christ. Moreover, while the tumultuous years before Jesus' return are expected to bring many Jews to Christ, many evangelicals believe that until that time, most Jews will continue to reject him. This belief significantly reduces potential tensions between evangelicals and Jews, since evangelicals do not, as Martin Luther did, expect that once exposed to the true faith, Jews will convert in large numbers. Luther's fury when his expectation was not met led to a more anti-Semitic approach on his part; that is unlikely to happen with contemporary evangelicals.

Evangelicals also find the continued existence of the Jewish people to be a strong argument both for the existence of God and for his power in history. The book of Genesis relates that God told Abraham, "And I will make of thee a great nation, and I will bless thee.... And I will bless them that bless thee, and curse him that curseth thee: and in thee all families of the earth be blessed." For evangelicals, the fact that the Jewish people have survived through the millennia and that they have returned to their ancient home is proof that God is real, that the Bible is inspired, and that the Christian religion is true. Many believe that the promise of Genesis still stands and that the God of Abraham will literally bless the United States if the United States blesses Israel. They see in the weakness, defeats, and poverty of the Arab world ample evidence that God curses those who curse Israel.

Criticism of Israel and of the United States for supporting it leaves evangelicals unmoved. If anything, it only strengthens their conviction that the world hates Israel because "fallen man" naturally hates God and his "chosen people." In standing by Israel, evangelicals feel that they are standing by God—something they are ready to do against the whole world. Thus John Hagee—senior pastor of an 18,000-member evangelical megachurch in San Antonio, Texas, and author of several New York Times bestsellers— writes that if Iran moves to attack Israel, Americans must be prepared "to stop this evil enemy in its tracks." "God's policy toward the Jewish people," Hagee writes, "is found in Genesis 12:3," and he goes on to quote the passage about blessings and curses. "America is at the crossroads!" Hagee warns. "Will we believe and obey the Word of God concerning Israel, or will we continue to equivocate and sympathize with Israel's enemies?"

The return of the Jews to the Holy Land, their extraordinary victories over larger Arab armies, and even the rising tide of hatred that threatens Jews in Israel and abroad strengthen not only the evangelical commitment to Israel but also the position of evangelical religion in American life. The story of modern Jewry reads like a book in the Bible. The Holocaust is reminiscent of the genocidal efforts of Pharaoh in the book of Exodus and of Haman in the book of Esther; the subsequent establishment of a Jewish state reminds one of many similar victories and deliverances of the Jews in the Hebrew Scriptures. The extraordinary events of modern Jewish history are held up by evangelicals as proof that God exists and acts in history. Add to this the psychological consequences of nuclear weapons, and many evangelicals begin to feel that they are living in a world like the world of the Bible. That U.S. foreign policy now centers on defending the country against the threat of mass terrorism involving, potentially, weapons of apocalyptic horror wielded by anti-Christian fanatics waging a religious war motivated by hatred of Israel only reinforces the claims of evangelical religion.

Liberal Christians in the United States (like liberal secularists) have also traditionally supported Zionism, but from a different perspective. For liberal Christians, the Jews are a people like any other, and so liberal Christians have supported Zionism in the same way that they have supported the national movements of other oppressed groups. In recent decades, however, liberal Christians have increasingly come to sympathize with the Palestinian national movement on the same basis. In 2004, the Presbyterian Church passed a resolution calling for limited divestment from companies doing business with Israel (the resolution was essentially rescinded in 2006 after a bitter battle). One study found that 37 percent of the statements made by mainline Protestant churches on human rights abuses between 2000 and 2004 focused on Israel. No other country came in for such frequent criticism.

Conspiracy theorists and secular scholars and journalists in the United States and abroad have looked to a Jewish conspiracy or, more euphemistically, to a "Jewish lobby" to explain how U.S. support for Israel can grow while sympathy for Israel wanes among what was once the religious and intellectual establishment. A better answer lies in the dynamics of U.S. religion. Evangelicals have been gaining social and political power, while liberal Christians and secular intellectuals have been losing it. This should not be blamed on the Jews.

THE NEW GREAT AWAKENING

The current evangelical moment in the United States has not yet run its course. For secularists and liberals in the United States and abroad, this is a disquieting prospect. Measured optimism, however, would be a better response than horror and panic. Religion in the United States is too pluralistic for any single current to dominate. The growing presence and influence of non-Christian communities in the country—of Jews, Muslims, Buddhists, Hindus, and, above all, secularists—will continue to limit the ability of any religious group to impose its values across the board.

Liberals, whether religious or not, may want to oppose the evangelical agenda in domestic politics. For the most part, however, these quarrels can cease at the water's edge.

As the rising evangelical establishment gains experience in foreign policy, it is likely to prove a valuable—if not always easy—partner for the mostly secular or liberal Christian establishment. Some fears about the evangelical influence in foreign policy are simply overblown. After the attacks of September 11, for example, fears that evangelical Christians would demand a holy war against Islam were widespread. A few prominent religious leaders (generally fundamentalists, not evangelicals) made intemperate remarks; Jerry Falwell, for one, referred to the Prophet Muhammad as "a terrorist." But he was widely rebuked by his colleagues.

U.S. evangelicals generally seek to hold on to their strong personal faith and Protestant Christian identity while engaging with people across confessional lines. Evangelicals have worked with Catholics against abortion and with both religious and secular Jews to support Israel; they could now reach out to Muslims as well. After all, missionary hospitals and schools were the primary contact that most Middle Easterners had with the United States up until the end of World War II; evangelicals managed more than a century of close and generally cooperative relations with Muslims throughout the Arab world. Muslims and evangelicals are both concerned about global poverty and Africa. Both groups oppose the domination of public and international discourse by secular ideas. Both believe that religious figures and values should be treated with respect in the media; neither like the glorification of casual sex in popular entertainment. Both Islam and evangelicalism are democratic religions without a priesthood or hierarchy. Muslims and evangelicals will never agree about everything, and secular people may not like some of the agreements they reach. But fostering Muslim–evangelical dialogue may be one of the best ways to forestall the threat of civilizational warfare.

Nervous observers, moreover, should remember that evangelical theology does not automatically produce Jacksonian or populist foreign policy. A process of discussion and mutual accommodation can in many cases narrow the gap between evangelicals and others on a wide range of issues. Worrying that evangelical politics will help lock the United States into inflexible and extreme positions is a waste of time; working with thoughtful evangelical leaders to develop a theologically grounded approach to Palestinian rights, for example, will broaden the base for thoughtful—though never anti-Israel—U.S. policies.

Similarly, engaging evangelicals in broader foreign policy discussions can lead to surprising and (for some) heartening developments. A group of leading conservative evangelicals recently signed a statement on climate change that stated that the problem is real, that human activity is an important contributing cause, that the costs of inaction will be high and disproportionately affect the poor, and that Christians have a moral duty to help deal with it. Meanwhile, evangelicals who began by opposing Sudanese violence and slave raids against Christians in southern Sudan have gone on to broaden the coalition working to protect Muslims in Darfur.

Evangelicals are likely to focus more on U.S. exceptionalism than liberals would like, and they are likely to care more about the morality of U.S. foreign policy than most realists prefer. But evangelical power is here to stay for the foreseeable future, and those concerned about U.S. foreign policy would do well to reach out. As more evangelical leaders acquire firsthand experience in foreign policy, they are likely to provide something now sadly lacking in the world of U.S. foreign policy: a trusted group of experts, well versed in the nuances and dilemmas of the international situation, who are able to persuade large numbers of Americans to support the complex and counterintuitive policies that are sometimes necessary in this wicked and frustrating—or, dare one say it, fallen—world.

SECTION 6 TERMINOLOGY

Anti-Semitism

Canadian Health and
   Social Transfer (CHST)

Canadian Health
   Association (CHA)

Catholicism

Christian Realism

Christian worldview

Civil liberties

Civic nationalism

Cold War

Darwinian

Draft Declaration on the
   Rights of Indigenous
   Peoples (DDIP)

Economic and Social
   Council (ECOSOC)

Evangelical

Food and Agricultural
   Organization (FAO)

Fundamentalism

Great Awakening

Gross Domestic Product
   (GDP)

Indigenous peoples

International Labour
   Organization (ILO)

Non-governmental organi-
   zation (NGO)

Office of the High
   Commission for Human
   Rights (OHCHR)

Pentecostal

Protestantism

Racism

Refugees

Rights

Scientific creationism

Terrorism

United Nations
   Commission on Human
   Rights (UNCHR)

United Nations
   Educational, Scientific
   and Cultural
   Organization
   (UNESCO)

Working Group on the
   Draft Declaration
   (WGDD)

Working Group on
   Indigenous Populations
   (WGIP)

World Health Organization
   (WHO)

SECTION 6 DISCUSSION QUESTIONS

1. Is there any hope of extending the Canadian tradition of "accommodation" to the rest of the world?

2. Health care is commonly ranked as the number one public policy issue in Canada. Is this justifiable? Are there other issues that demand more attention?

3. Does religion have a positive or negative influence on American foreign policy? Explain how you came to your conclusion.

4. In what ways has the fear of terrorist attacks changed the world? Are Canadians at risk?

5. Do indigenous rights threaten national identity in Canada or elsewhere?

GLOSSARY OF TERMINOLOGY

Accountability: requirement that a person or group accept responsibility for an action or outcome.

Activist: a person who takes direct and sometimes militant action to bring about political or social change.

Analytical approach: perspective that views politics as an empirical discipline, rather than a science. The basis of this approach is that politics cannot be broken down into parts, and must be viewed as a whole.

Anarchy: in political philosophy, a theoretical society without formal law or system of government. In more general use, a state of disorder and lawlessness caused by absence of government (from the Greek, "without rule").

Anti-Semitism: racial prejudice in theory, action, or practice that is directed against Semites (Arabs and Jews). In practice, it is used almost exclusively to refer to prejudice against Jews.

Arms control: cooperative agreements among two or more states/blocs to regulate arms levels by restricting their growth or use.

Auditor-General: person authorized by the Canadian Parliament to audit federal government operations to provide independent information on the use of public funds.

Autarky: condition of complete self-sufficiency and isolation from the rest of the system; used to describe states that seek to be economically self-sufficient.

Authoritarianism: political system requiring absolute obedience to a constituted authority.

Autocratic: describes a system of absolute rule by one person.

Ba'athist: principles of the Ba'ath political party in Iraq and Syria, typified by pan-Arab socialism and radical Arab nationalism.

Bretton Woods agreements: post–World War II system of fixed exchange rates and heavy controls on private banks and other financial institutions so that their role in international finance could be controlled. Named after the conference that took place at Bretton Woods, New Hampshire, in 1944.

Brokerage party: in any given political situation, a party whose actions are dictated by the desire to maintain harmony between various social divisions in society.

Bureaucracy: branch of government responsible for carrying out public policy and staffed by public employees (public or civil servants).

Cabinet ministers: see ministers of the Crown.

Canadian Charter of Rights and Freedoms: constitutional amendment adopted in 1982, setting out Canadian individual and collective rights and freedoms.

Canadian Health and Social Transfer (CHST): means through which the Canadian federal government transfers funding for health and social funding to provincial and territorial governments for their specific social programs.

Capitalism: economic system in which production and distribution of goods relies on private capital and investment.

Casework: activities of legislative members (for example, Members of Parliament) to deal with concerns and problems of their constituents.

Catholicism: practices, customs, and beliefs of the Catholic Church.

CCT: Consultative Committee for Telecommunications.

CEE: Central and Eastern European states

CHA: Canada Health Act; also Canadian Health Association.

Chapter 19: Part of the North American Free Trade Agreement (NAFTA) that permits parties to have trade legislation determined by a binational review by the affected countries instead of domestic judicial review.

Charlottetown Accord (1992): agreement on major constitutional changes between the Canadian federal and provincial governments and Native groups, which was defeated in a nationwide referendum.

Checks and balances: system of mutual oversight and countervailing powers between different levels and branches of government, with the aim of preventing centralization of power in any one branch or level.

Christian Realism: the philosophy that God is alive in humans but that, due to their corrupt inclinations, the kingdom of heaven on Earth may not be realized.

Christian worldview: religious and philosophical beliefs that form a distinctive set of elements predominant among Christians.

Citizen: status of an individual, whether claimed by right (of birthplace or parentage) or granted by law, that confers certain rights and freedoms and establishes certain duties vis-à-vis the state.

Civic literacy: level of political knowledge and ability that allows citizens to effectively engage in the political system.

Civic nationalism: form of nationalism where the state gains political legitimacy from active participation of its citizenry, or the "will of the people."

Civil liberties: individual freedoms that are protected by law from government interference.

Civic responsibility: responsibilities of citizens to be engaged in the activities of their political community, including social participation, voting, and civic interest.

Civil servants: employees of government departments.

Civil society: body or community of citizens.

Civil Society Organizations (CSOs): associations that are neither of the state nor of the family, often characterized by voluntary organizations.

Clash of civilizations: view that religious, cultural, and nationalistic identities will be the main cause of conflict in post-Cold War international politics.

Cold War: a period of rhetorical hostility not marked by violence; most often used in reference to the period of 1945–91 and the relationship that existed between the alliance systems centred around the United States and the Union of Soviet Socialist Republics (USSR).

Command economy: a planned economy where economic decisions are made on behalf of the public by government.

Common law: legal system characterized by unwritten law generally developed through decisions of the court rather than by statute.

Communism: political theory based on the writings of Karl Marx (1818–83) and Friedrich Engels (1820–95) that espouses class conflict as a means to form a system where all property is publicly owned, and each citizen works to his or her own best ability with equitable compensation.

Comparative advantage: classical economic theory that suggests that every individual in a system ought to work toward his or her personal maximum potential to serve the interests of the larger society.

Compulsory voting: practice of some countries (for example, Australia) *requiring* citizens to vote in elections.

Concepts: abstractions employed to describe phenomena according to their characteristics, e.g. political alienation, social class.

Concurrent majority (double majority): procedure requiring majority support of at least two subunits within a unit for approval.

Congress: legislative chamber of government in the United States, made up of the House of Representatives and the Senate.

Conservative: person who adheres to conservatism, or a perspective related to it.

Conservatism: political perspective that seeks to conserve the best of what has come before for future generations and is concerned with maintaining political and social traditions and customs.

Constituency: territorial or geographical locality (riding) represented by a politician chosen through the electoral process. Or, a group whose interests are repre-

sented by a politician or party, whether or not they live in a certain locality.

Constitution: the fundamental laws and principles upon which a political system is governed.

Constitutionalism: form of rule based on the belief that government power should be limited by the rules and principles enshrined in the constitution.

Convention: meeting of party members to discuss and determine policy and/or to select a party leader.

CPA: Coalition Provisional Authority.

CPSU: Communist Party of the Soviet Union.

Culture: way of life, language, art, customs, and institutions of a community, whether that community is defined ethnically, historically, or politically.

CWG: Committees and Working Groups.

Darwinian: evolution by natural selection (survival based on environmental adaptation).

Dayton Peace Accord: agreement that ended the war in the former Yugoslavia, negotiated at Dayton, Ohio, in November 1995.

DDIP: Draft Declaration on the Rights of Indigenous Peoples.

Decision making: mechanism or pattern of relations involving different levels of government where determinations and judgments regarding the governance of political systems are made.

Democracy: political system based on the principle that governance requires the assent of all citizens through participation in the electoral process, articulation of views, and direct or indirect representation in governing institutions.

Democratization: the process of transition to a democracy.

Despotism: government rule of absolute and arbitrary authority.

Developed world (First World): industrialized nations that are part of a structurally integrated system of global capitalism; they are primarily located in Western Europe, North America, Japan, Australia, and New Zealand. (The term "Second World" used to refer to the former communist countries of the Soviet Union and China, and their satellites.)

Developing world (Third World): largely non-industrialized or industrializing countries that are economically and technologically deprived; they are primarily located in Africa, South America, and Asia. (The term "Second World" used to refer to the former communist countries of the Soviet Union and China, and their satellites.)

Digital divide: gap between those who have access to information and communications technologies, and those who do not.

Direct democracy: political system where citizens are directly involved in the decision-making process.

Disarmament: reduction of military forces and destruction of equipment by negotiated agreement between countries or groups of countries.

Econometrics: application of mathematics to economic data or theories.

ECOSOC: Economic and Social Council.

E-democracy: use of computer networks or digital processes to enhance the process of democratic participation.

E-government: government activities conducted over computer networks or using digital processes.

Elected assembly: see Legislature (House).

Elections: procedure normally employing a vote to select the winner of a political office or position.

Electoral system: the complete set of legal rules governing the selection of political representatives.

Electoralism: belief that the holding of elections is a sufficient condition for the existence of democracy.

Electorate: body of those who have the right to vote in an election to a given representative chamber.

Enumeration: process of determining the number of individuals eligible to vote in a constituency; in Canada, this consists of door-to-door contact by enumerators.

Environmental law: legal ordinance regulation relating to the protection of the environment.

Environmentalism: political ideology based on the notion that modern economic systems are the main source of damage for the natural world; it also views modern industrialism as a hierarchical system that restricts human freedom.

Ethnicity: identification with a group having common ancestors, history, sense of identity, geography, or cultural roots.

EU: European Union.

Evangelical: interpretation of the Christian Bible, especially as it is presented in the four Gospels.

Executive: branch of government that initiates and enacts policy, according to the preoccupations of the dominant political party. The head of the executive branch is usually considered a country's head of government (such as the prime minister, in Canada), and

may also be that country's head of state (such as the president, in the United States).

Factions: groups of people holding similar beliefs and opinions within a larger group.

FAO: Food and Agricultural Organization.

Fascism: ideology that holds that the nation should be organized by the state, under the unquestioned authority of a national leader; in practical terms this means a combination of ethnic nationalism and extreme authoritarianism, and the will to use force to ensure order and compliance.

FDI: Foreign Direct Investment.

Federalism: form of governance that divides powers between the central government and regional governments, with particular roles and capacities being given to the different levels of government.

Feminism: an ideology based on the demand for the complete legal, political, economic, and social equality of women with men.

First World: see developed world.

First-past-the-post: see single-member plurality system.

Free market: economic system governed by supply and demand and not restrained by government intervention, regulation, or subsidy.

Free trade: international trade among political systems unimpeded by restrictions or tariffs on imports or exports.

Free vote: voting according to one's belief or personal opinion, as opposed to voting along party lines.

FSU: Former Soviet Union.

FTA: Free Trade Agreement (Canada–United States).

Fundamentalism: the literal interpretation of the doctrine of a religion or holy canon.

G-8: Group of Eight (formerly G-7 [Group of Seven], without Russia); refers to major industrialized nations: United States of America, United Kingdom, France, Germany, Canada, Italy, Japan, and Russia.

Game theory: research method that analyzes interactions and predicts actual behaviour by using formalized "games"—situations where "players" try to maximize their effectiveness by anticipating responses to their actions.

GATT: General Agreement on Tariffs and Trade.

GDP: Gross Domestic Product—total value of goods and services produced in a country in one year.

Glass ceiling: an unofficial obstacle to occupational advancement, especially for women or ethnic minorities.

Globalization: the intensification of economic, political, social, and cultural relations across borders.

GNP: Gross National Product; total value of goods and services produced in a country in one year plus total of net income earned abroad.

Gold standard: monetary system in which currencies are linked to a standard unit of gold, which has a value of a fixed weight.

Governance: functions and arrangements by which a political system is administered.

Governing party: political party with political authority to exercise public affairs and hold sovereign power.

Government: the institutions and people responsible for carrying out the affairs and administration of a political system.

Great awakening: early eighteenth century movements in the American colonies in which adherents "awakened" to

Christianity through experiential knowledge and personal conversion to Jesus Christ.

Greenhouse gas: any gas that absorbs infra-red radiation in the atmosphere.

GSS: General Social Survey.

Guerrilla warfare: irregular—usually politically motivated—armed forces fighting regular forces; from the Spanish for "little war."

Hegemony: dominance of one set of beliefs, practices, and groups over all others.

Hierarchy: a classification of successive ranks (e.g. grades, authority, or classes), one above another.

Human security: security that places primary emphasis on the individual rather than the nation-state.

Humanitarian intervention: intrusion in another state, often without the agreement of that state's government, to deal with a humanitarian disaster, usually the contravention of human rights.

ICAO: International Civil Aviation Organization.

ICC: International Criminal Court.

ICJ: International Court of Justice; body of the United Nations responsible for settling international legal disputes, and for giving advisory opinions on legal questions referred to it by duly authorized international organs and agencies.

ICSID: International Convention on the Settlement of Investment Disputes.

ICT: information communication technology.

ICTY: International Criminal Tribunal for the former Yugoslavia.

Ideology: set or system of ideas that form the basis of a political or economic system and provide guidance and direction for political leadership.

IFOR: Implementation Force (former Yugoslavia).

IGC: Iraqi Governing Council.

ILO: International Labour Organization.

IMF: International Monetary Fund.

Indigenous peoples: original inhabitants who have a historical connection with a geographic region before colonization.

Industrialization: process whereby countries improve and strengthen their industrial capability and production.

Interdependence: mutual dependence; a method of measuring dependent relationships among countries, based on the level of sensitivity and vulnerability one country has to the actions of another.

Interest group: organization in a political system that seeks to either alter or maintain the policy of government without taking a formal role in elections or an official capacity in government (also called public interest group).

International anarchy: condition where there is no "world government"; the sovereign nation-state is the highest authority in the international system.

International law: law based on treaties between states.

International organizations: international alliance involving many different countries; may be governmental or non-governmental.

International politics: relations of a political nature that exist at the international level.

Internationalism: political movement urging greater interaction between states in a spirit of peaceful cooperation.

Invisible Hand: Adam Smith's notion that economic forces, if left to themselves, would automatically maximize efficiency and economic growth over time as the actors in an economy engage in competition with each other; benefits to society as a whole would arise from this competition without political interference.

IPCC: Intergovernmental Panel on Climate Change.

IPE: international political economy; political and economic activity on an international stage that demonstrates the intimate connection between national and international processes.

Judiciary: the branch of government responsible for the interpretation and application of the law and for the administration of the court system.

Keynesian system (Keynesianism): economic system based on the writings of John Maynard Keynes, who proposed that governments should stimulate business and employment through monetary and fiscal programs.

Laissez-faire: "to let be"—economic theory that suggests that a reduction in political control will benefit the economic system.

Legislature (House): also known as legislative assembly, elected assembly; legislative branch of a political system, with the responsibility to make laws. In Canada, the legislative assembly is Parliament, made up of the House of Commons (or simply, the House) and the Senate.

Legitimacy: government's or individual politician's legal and moral quality of having the right to exercise power, based on a mandate (usually an election) from the people; by extension, also a quality possessed by their actions.

Liberal: person who adheres to liberalism, or a perspective related to it.

Liberal democracy: political system based on freedom and individual liberty, and on the principle that governance requires the assent of all citizens through participation in the electoral process, articulation of views, and direct or indirect representation in governing institutions.

Liberalism: view of politics that favours liberty, free trade, and moderate social and political change.

Liberty: freedom from despotic control.

Lobbying: actions designed to influence government decision makers to favour or oppose any legislation.

LTSS: Land Transportation Standards Subcommittee.

Macroeconomic policy: monetary and fiscal policies that affect the economy as a whole.

Majority government: government by the party that received a majority of seats in an election to a legislative assembly.

Majority rule: principle that the numerical majority (50 percent + 1) of an organized group can make decisions binding on the whole group.

Mandate: command or authorization given by a political electorate to its representatives.

Market: economic and legal environment—domestic or international—within which the exchange of goods and services takes place.

Market economy: economy that is subject to and determined by free competition.

Marxism: the study of society as the conflict or struggle of social classes, derived from the writings of Karl Marx.

Marxism-Leninism: Marxism interpreted by Vladimir Lenin, stressing imperialism as the "final stage" of capitalism.

Melting pot: term employed in U.S. cultural history to describe the assimilation of immigrant groups with disparate ethnic origins into the dominant culture.

Middle power: state that is not considered a superpower or great power, but still has influence in the international system, often due to relational power and reputation.

Ministers of the Crown (or cabinet ministers): members of cabinet in a parliamentary system, who collectively form the government of the day.

MNC: multinational corporation; business organizations that operate in more than one country.

Morality: good conduct and behaviour, in conformity with customary conduct and duty.

MPs: Members of Parliament; representatives of constituencies elected to the House of Commons.

Multicultural society: society that emphasizes and encourages the retention of unique cultures, particularly immigrant-receiving nations such as Canada.

Multilateralism: integration or coordination of policies or decision making by three or more nation-states.

Mutual assured destruction: doctrine prevalent in the Cold War period (1945–91) among countries possessing nuclear weapons, recognizing that the use of those weapons would result in the destruction of both the attacker and the defender.

NAFTA: North American Free Trade Agreement, involving Canada, the United States, and Mexico.

Nation: group of persons who share an identity that is based on, but not limited to, shared ethnic, religious, cultural, or linguistic qualities.

National security: the safety of a nation and its people from threats.

National Socialism: Political ideology most closely related to the fascist Nazi party led by Adolf Hitler in Germany from 1933 to 1945. Based on a "citizen-nation relationship," referring to the common duties of German citizens in service of the government.

Nationalism: political movement, based on national identity, to create a political state; may also be interpreted as a strong feeling of patriotism.

Nation-state: state formed on the basis of national identity.

NATO: North Atlantic Treaty Organization.

New public management: management philosophy for public sector modernization.

NGO: non-governmental organization; term popularized with creation of United Nations (1945) to describe international private groups. Often development, social, or cultural bodies, they are independent from government control, are non-profit, and are non-criminal.

NORAD: North American Aerospace Defence Command.

Norms: pattern of standard or expected behaviour in a political community.

North American Free Trade Commission: NAFTA body made up of cabinet-level representatives of the Parties or their designees who supervise and oversee the implementation the Agreement.

Notwithstanding clause: section 33 of the Canadian Charter of Rights and Freedoms that allows legislatures to pass legislation that violates or limits the rights and

freedoms outlined in sections 2, and 7 through 15 of the Charter, under certain conditions.

OECD: Organization for Economic Co-operation and Development.

OHCHR: Office of the High Commission for Human Rights.

Oligarchy: government by the few.

Order-in-council: an order issued by the cabinet, either on the basis of authority delegated by legislation or by virtue of the prerogative powers of the Crown.

ORHA: Office of Reconstruction and Humanitarian Assistance.

OSCE: Organization for Security and Co-operation in Europe.

Ottawa Process: partnership of civil society and governmental groups, with leadership from middle powers such as Canada that led to the Ottawa Treaty (1997), which banned the production, sale, or use of anti-personnel landmines.

Ottawa Treaty: 1997 Anti-Mine Treaty (Convention on the Prohibition of the Use, Stockpiling, Production and Transfer of Anti-Personnel Mines and on Their Destruction).

Overseas Development Assistance: foreign aid given to developing countries either bilaterally, or through multilateral institutions such as the Development Assistance Committee of the Organization for Economic Co-operation and Development (OECD).

Paradigm: general theory, model, or "worldview" influential in determining a discipline or subdiscipline.

Parliament: legislature in Westminster form of government.

Parliamentary sovereignty: the principle in parliamentary systems that there is no higher authority than Parliament and no external limits on what a Parliament can do.

Party: group of individuals engaged in the attempt to control government through the election of their members.

Party discipline: the practice of elected party members' voting in the legislative assembly as a collective, according to the policy of their leadership.

Patronage: the appointment of individuals to positions or the granting of government business on the basis of rewards for past service rather than merit.

Pentecostal: Christian denomination with a focus on direct spiritual and emotional links with God.

Permanent voters list: permanent list of eligible voters employed in Canada derived from, among other things, income tax returns and provincial driver's licence data.

Pinball capital: rapid global movement of short-term speculative capital (money invested for speculative purposes, often with volatile results).

Pluralism: society where several disparate groups (minority and majority) maintain their interests, and a number of concerns and traditions persist.

Plurality: requirement that the winning candidate or option receive more votes than any other, but not necessarily a majority of votes cast.

Plurality system: a type of electoral system in which candidates are required to earn a plurality rather than a majority of votes in order to win seats. The main alternative systems are proportional representation and mixed systems.

Policy: aims, based on political principles, that a governing party attempts to put into practice through legislation or executive order.

Polis: Greek city-state.

Political culture: set of political attitudes, beliefs, and values that underpin any political system.

Political cynicism: belief that politicians, political institutions, and/or the political system are inherently corrupt.

Political efficacy: degree to which people feel they have an impact or can exert some influence on public affairs.

Political participation: action by individuals or groups on public issues that affect their lives.

Political philosophy: branch of political science that tries to understand both what we do and what we ought to do, normally flowing from assumptions about human nature.

Political system: conglomerate of numerous political structures that work together to drive the political aspects of a country's social interaction.

Political theory: body of work within political science devoted to the critical and systematic development of models, concepts and prescriptions related to power in both its public and private forms.

Politics: the governance of social units, allocation of power and responsibility, and relationship among political actors in society.

Pollster: someone who conducts public-opinion surveys or compiles data obtained by political polling.

Polychlorinated biphenyls (PCB): once used for industrial and electrical purposes, now banned for their cancer-causing properties.

Populism: support for the preferences of ordinary people, as opposed to those of political or business elites.

Post–Cold War: period following the end of the Cold War, generally accepted to have begun in 1992, following the formal dissolution of the Soviet Union on December 31, 1991.

Post-modern values: emerging set of post-war values identified by Ronald Inglehart as giving priority to self-expression and quality of life rather than to economic and physical security.

Power: ability to achieve goals in a political system and to have others do as you wish them to.

Prescription: rule or direction to be followed based on sustained customs.

Presidentialism: political regime in which executive power is independent and separate from the legislative power; normally contrasted with the parliamentary system.

Primary: an election held within a party to select candidates for election to public office.

Privy Council Office (PCO): central agency that works for the Canadian Prime Minister, and which is responsible for coordinating the work of cabinet, and cabinet committees.

Programmatic party: political party that prioritizes adherence to an ideologically consistent set of policies over pragmatic strategies for winning elections.

Proportional representation (PR): electoral system in which seats in the legislature are won more or less in proportion to the parties' popular vote. The main alternative systems are plurality and mixed systems.

Proportionality: the principle that the share of seats in a legislature won by a party should reflect the share of electoral votes obtained in an election.

Protestantism: Christian movement that broke off from the Roman Catholic Church during the Reformation.

Prudence: discretion regarding the most appropriate course of action.

Public administration: management of public affairs and government by politicians and public servants.

Public interest: common comfort and security; well-being.

Public policy: laws or principles of performance that are adopted by a government and that affect a political system.

Public realm: arena in which government activity legitimately occurs.

Public service: also known as civil service, the administrative personnel of government.

Quad: United States of America, the EU, Japan, and Canada, the world's largest market economies.

Qualified majority: requirement that a proposal (or bill) achieve greater than simple majority support (50 percent + 1) in order to pass.

Quebec Referendum (1995): second referendum in Quebec (the first took place in 1980) on the question of whether Quebec should pursue a path toward independent statehood ("sovereignty"); in both cases, the majority voted against the proposal.

Question Period: specific time period in a sitting of the legislative assembly in parliamentary systems where the Prime Minister and cabinet must respond to written and oral questions posed by the Members of Parliament.

Racism: discrimination against people based on their perceived or ascribed race; theory that human characteristics and abilities are determined by race.

RAND Corporation: (RAND = Research and Development) research institute created to offer research and analysis to the American armed forces.

Reference question: in Canadian law, a submission by either the federal or a provincial government to the courts asking for an opinion on a legal issue.

Referenda (referendums): mechanisms that allow citizens to vote directly on pieces of legislation or constitutional amendments.

Refugees: those who avoid political persecution by seeking refuge in a foreign country.

Regime: the set of rules, individual personalities, institutions, and process comprising a system of government.

Regionalism: economic or political integration in a defined territorial area.

Regionalization: process of forming regional associations.

Representative democracy: political system in which voters elect political representatives to govern in their interests.

Representatives: individuals elected or appointed to act in the political interests of a constituency.

Responsible government: convention of the Canadian parliamentary system that the executive must retain the confidence of the elected assembly in order to remain in power.

Riding: see constituency.

Rights: privilege, immunity, or authority to act, to which members of a political community are entitled. They range in importance from the most fundamental, which are claimed by humans simply by virtue of being human (human rights), and citizens of a state (civil rights), to the less crucial, which can be characterized as privileges granted by legislation.

Rule of law: principle that law rather than arbitrary authority

should govern actions by all actors in a society, and that the law should be known by and applied equally to all in society.

Scientific creationism: perspective that scientific methods can prove that life and the universe were specially created by God.

Security Council: body of the United Nations primarily responsible for the maintenance of international peace and security.

Self-determination: people's act of deciding their own form of government, free from outside influence.

SFOR: Stabilization Force (UN troops deployed in the former Yugoslavia).

Single-member plurality system: electoral system (also known as first-past-the-post) in which the winner is the person or party receiving the greatest number (but not necessarily a majority) of votes.

Social capital: the collective value of the norms of trust, reciprocity, and relationships developed within societies that can be argued to be crucial to building and maintaining democracy.

Social movement: broad and fluid political associations attentive to a particular political issue; e.g. feminist and environmental movements.

Socialism: economic and political theory of society that holds that citizens as a whole should own the means of production, exchange, and allocation.

Socialist: person who adheres to socialism, or a perspective related to it.

Society: persons living collectively in an ordered community.

Sovereignty: political community's independence and self-determination.

Spin doctors: skilled practitioners of "spin"—the art of portraying an event or group in the best possible light, often in a heavily biased, even deceptive, manner.

State: a recognized political unit with a defined territory and citizens, and a central government responsible for administration and considered to be sovereign.

Suffrage: the right to vote.

Sustainability law: transforming the relationship between humans and the natural environment to avoid creating environmental problems in the first place.

Terrorism: use of violence and fear by individuals and organized groups to achieve political goals.

Third World: see developing world.

TNA: Transitional National Assembly.

Totalitarian: person who adheres to totalitarianism, or perspectives related to it.

Totalitarianism: authoritarian political system that controls not only the economy and most social interaction, but that is also marked by the government's desire to force its citizens to accept its objectives and values in an unlimited manner.

Trilateral democracies: democractic industrialized nations of the Trilateral Commission (Japan, European Union, and North America), which was created in 1973 to increase co-operation among its members and share global leadership responsibilities.

Turnout rate: proportion of the registered electorate (or population) that turns out to vote in an election.

Tyranny: corrupt form of political power in which rulers rule only in their own interest.

UN: United Nations.

UNCHR: United Nations Commission on Human Rights.

UNCITRAL: United Nations Commission on International Trade Law.

UNESCO: United Nations Educational, Scientific and Cultural Organization.

UNPROFOR: United Nations Protection Force (deployed in the former Yugoslavia).

USSR: Union of Soviet Socialist Republics.

Utopia: ideal social, legal, and political system, as imagined by philosophers and writers.

Western civilization: the culture and societies of Europe and their genealogical, colonial, and philosophical descendants (such as North America, Australia, and New Zealand), characterized by political systems enshrining personal liberties, the rule of law, and free market economies.

WGDD: Working Group on the Draft Declaration.

WGIP: Working Group on Indigenous Populations.

Whip: an officer of a political party whose task is to ensure that members of the party attend and vote with the party leadership.

WHO: World Health Organization.

World Bank: development bank (formally known as the International Bank for Reconstruction and Development, or IBRD), which provides assistance to low- and middle-income countries.

WTO: World Trade Organization, created in 1995 as a forum for promoting and regulating free trade between nations in goods and services, and for resolving trade disputes between member countries.